Posting of Workers in EU Law

Bulletin of Comparative Labour Relations

VOLUME 108

Founding Editor

The series started in 1970 under the dynamic editorship of Professor Roger Blanpain (Belgium), former President of the International Industrial Relations Association. Professor Blanpain, Professor Emeritus of Labour Law, Universities of Leuven and Tilburg, was also General Editor of the International Encyclopedia of Laws (with more than 1,600 collaborators worldwide) and President of the Association of Educative and Scientific Authors Authors. He passed away in October 2016.

General Editor

In 2015 Frank Hendrickx, Professor of labour law at the Faculty of Law of the University of Leuven (Belgium) joined as a co-Editor. Frank Hendrickx has published numerous articles and books and regularly advises governments, international institutions and private organisations in the area of labour law as well as in sports law. He is the Editor-in-Chief of the European Labour Law Journal and General Editor of the International Encyclopaedia of Laws.

Introduction

The Bulletins constitute a unique source of information and thought-provoking discussion, laying the groundwork for studies of employment relations in the 21st century, involving among much else the effects of globalization, new technologies, migration, and the greying of the population.

Contents/Subjects

Amongst other subjects the Bulletins frequently include the proceedings of international or regional conferences; reports from comparative projects devoted to salient issues in industrial relations, human resources management, and/or labour law; and specific issues underlying the multicultural aspects of our industrial societies.

Objective

The Bulletins offer a platform of expression and discussion on labour relations to scholars and practitioners worldwide, often featuring special guest editors.

The titles published in this series are listed at the end of this volume.

BULLETIN OF COMPARATIVE LABOUR RELATIONS – 108

Posting of Workers in EU Law

Challenges of Equality, Solidarity and Fair Competition

Matteo Bottero

Wolters Kluwer

Published by:
Kluwer Law International B.V.
PO Box 316
2400 AH Alphen aan den Rijn
The Netherlands
E-mail: international-sales@wolterskluwer.com
Website: lrus.wolterskluwer.com

Sold and distributed by:
Wolters Kluwer Legal & Regulatory U.S.
7201 McKinney Circle
Frederick, MD 21704
United States of America
Email: customer.service@wolterskluwer.com

ISBN 978-94-035-2860-1

e-Book: ISBN 978-94-035-2864-9
web-PDF: ISBN 978-94-035-2872-4

About the Author

Matteo Bottero is a Postdoctoral fellow at the Faculty of Law, University of Copenhagen (Denmark). His main research fields are EU law, EU constitutional law, EU labour law, and European integration. He obtained his PhD in Law from the University of Copenhagen, Faculty of Law, in September 2020, with a PhD thesis entitled *Posting of Workers in EU Law: Challenges of Equality, Solidarity and Fair Competition*, under the supervision of Professor Ulla Neergaard. In Autumn 2018, he spent a period at the Institute for Labour Law at the Faculty of Law, University of Leuven (Belgium), as a visiting researcher under the supervision of Professor Frank Hendrickx. Besides conducting his research activity, he was also a Lecturer in Advanced EU Constitutional Law at the Faculty of Law, University of Copenhagen. He holds a Master in Law from the University of Turin (Italy).

Table of Contents

Foreword

In Europe, the prevailing COVID-19 crisis has challenged us all on many levels. Perhaps most essentially, the way many of us used to perceive the world and what we could take for granted is under change. For instance, especially in the start of the outburst of the crisis, the increase in the preservation of self-interests at both the individual and Member State level appeared as rather shocking, despite the fact that solidarity has for a long time served both as a profound value or principle of and a dominant aim to be pursued by the EU and its constituent members. However, how to transform the general visions of solidarity and other claimed values into concrete action has always been the Achilles heel of the EU, and therefore it is easily exposing itself to criticism. In the example, perhaps so much that it urged EU President, Ms Ursula von der Leyen, early on in relation to solidarity to emphasise that – despite of all – Europe is 'the world's beating heart' thereof.

By now, EU Law builds on many narratives; stories which are being told again and again, thereby creating ideas or truths, which often are hardly ever being challenged. Solidarity is the glue binding the EU, one of its finest virtues, something which apparently is viewed as positively distinguishing it from other continents is just one of such stories. Equality and fair competition constitute other such important values or principles upon which prevailing narratives are being constructed. In this book, the author Matteo Bottero not only intends to analyse the state of EU Law in relation to the phenomenon of posting of workers, an area which has proved deeply divisive, but also somehow courageously and almost stubbornly to test and contest the common narratives told in that context and to point to some of the inherent self-contradictions. In particular, he takes his point of departure in exactly these three central concepts: 'equality', 'solidarity' and 'fair competition', concepts which are seen as permeating the European Union, which at the same time provides an impression of a value-laden and extraordinarily sympathetic union, but also dangerously may make it rather vulnerable if not living up to its own, nearly biblical standards. Ironically, perhaps, this was a task he thus decided to take up long before the outburst of the COVID-19 crisis, which so deeply – with reference to the fairy-tale by the Danish author, Hans Christian Andersen – may by some be seen as having undressed 'the emperor'.

In other words, Matteo Bottero intends to challenge the possible self-deception in relation to the new legal framework provided for by Directive (EU) 957/2018 amending the Posting of Workers Directive 96/71/EC and, more broadly, the narratives underpinning the reform. He argues that it to him worryingly falls out of alignment with the EU values or principles of 'equality', 'solidarity' and 'fair competition'.

Thus, for any reader genuinely interested in understanding the newly adopted Directive (EU) 957/2018 amending the Posting of Workers Directive 96/71/EC in detail, as well as understanding its troubled birth process, its disputable content, the larger context of which it is a part of and influenced by, and its expected effects and shortcomings, the present book is inescapable to consult. It lays on an ambition of striving for a dual nature, being at the same time descriptive and normative. It is based upon research activities undertaken mainly at the Faculty of Law at the University of Copenhagen, but also on an influential research stay at the University of Leuven. It has naturally been inspired by these institutions' academic cultures, but it is first and foremost genuine academic dedication to thorough research, which has driven Matteo Bottero to reach the results in this book.

Ulla Neergaard*

* Ulla Neergaard is Professor of EU Law at the University of Copenhagen, Faculty of Law.

Preface

Posting of workers is a hybrid type of intra-EU labour mobility based on the free movement of services, which has experienced a seamless expansion during the last years. Although this phenomenon concerns only a rather limited fraction of the EU labour market, its regulation at EU level has proved deeply divisive. This book explores the evolving EU regulatory framework for posting, focusing on both the relevant internal market law and the EU labour and social security provisions. This legal analysis is complemented by an investigation of the actual quantitative dimension of the phenomenon under consideration, as well as of its multifaceted impact on the European labour market. Against this backdrop, the newly adopted Directive (EU) 957/2018 amending the Posting of Workers Directive 96/71/EC is carefully examined, looking at its troubled birth process, its disputable content and its expected effects and shortcomings.

This book challenges the new legal framework provided for by Directive (EU) 957/2018 and, more broadly, the whole narrative underpinning the reform, by arguing that it worryingly falls out of alignment with the EU values and principles of 'equality', 'solidarity' and 'fair competition'. On the basis of the expected impact of the new rules on the current state of play, the analysis intends to discern the model of European integration actually advanced by the EU legislator. It concludes with a reflection on the need to pursue an idea of 'Social Europe' which, rather than merely preserving the integrity of the most advanced national social systems, promotes upward socio-economic convergence and cohesion at EU level.

This book is based on the author's PhD thesis, defended at the Faculty of Law, University of Copenhagen (Denmark) on 11 September 2020. It is the result of three years of independent research carried out at the Faculty of Law, University of Copenhagen (Denmark), at the Faculty of Law, University of Leuven (Belgium), and involving the participation in several conferences, congresses, seminars and courses all over Europe.

List of Abbreviations

3F	*Fagligt Fælles Forbund* (United Federation of Danish Workers)
CEC	*Confédération Européenne des Cadres* (European Confederation of Managers)
CEECs	Central and Eastern European Countries
CEEMET	Council of European Employers of the Metal, Engineering and Technology-Based Industries
CFREU	Charter of Fundamental Rights of the European Union
CJEU	Court of Justice of the European Union
CLA	Collective Labour Agreement
COREPER	Committee of Permanent Representatives in the European Union
EBC	European Builders Confederation
ECJ	European Court of Justice
EEA	European Economic Area
EEC	European Economic Community
EESSI	Electronic Exchange of Social Security Information
EFBWW	European Federation of Building and Woodworkers
EFTA	European Free Trade Association
ELA	European Labour Authority
EMPL	Employment and Social Affairs Committee of the European Parliament
EPP	European People's Party
EPSCO	Employment, Social Policy, Health and Consumer Affairs configuration of the Council of the European Union
ESF	European Social Fund
ESSN	European Social Security Number
ETF	European Transport Workers' Federation
ETUC	European Trade Union Confederation

EU	European Union
Eurociett	European Confederation of Private Employment Services
FIEC	European Construction Industry Federation
FNV	*Federatie Nederlandse Vakbeweging* (Dutch Trade Union Confederation)
FTE	Full-Time Equivalent
GDP	Gross domestic product
IMI	Internal Market Information System
LIMOSA	*Landenoverschrijdend Informatiesysteem ten behoeve van Migratie Onderzoek bij de Sociale Administratie* (Belgian Cross-border Information system for the benefit of Migration Examination at the Social Administration)
OECD	Organisation for Economic Co-operation and Development
OJ	Official Journal of the European Union / Official Journal of the European Communities
PD A1	Portable Document A1
PIL	Private International Law
PWD	Posting of Workers Directive
RUT	*Registret for udenlandske tjenesteydere* (Danish Register of Foreign Service Providers)
SMEs	Small and medium-sized enterprises
S&D	Socialists & Democrats
TAWD	Temporary Agency Work Directive
TCN	Third-country national
TEC	Treaty establishing the European Community
TEU	Treaty on European Union
TFEU	Treaty on the Functioning of the European Union
TRAN	Committee on Transport and Tourism of the European Parliament
UEAPME	European Association of Craft, Small and Medium-Sized Enterprises
UK	United Kingdom
WAGA	*Wet Arbeidsvoorwaarden Grensoverschrijdende Arbeid* (Dutch Terms of Employment of Posted Workers Act)

Acknowledgements

This book is based on my PhD thesis, defended at the Faculty of Law, University of Copenhagen (Denmark) on 11 September 2020. Therefore, I am profoundly grateful to the institution for the exceptional opportunity of pursuing a three-year PhD research programme and for providing me with all the resources to conduct independent and in-depth legal research at an international level.

Foremost, I would like to express my deepest gratitude to my supervisor, Professor *Ulla Neergaard*, for the extremely valuable guidance, encouragement and support throughout the PhD programme. A heartfelt thank you for all the inspiring conversations we had, for the precious suggestions and for sharing with me her vast research experience and knowledge.

I am grateful to Professor *Dagmar Schiek* for the insightful comments and constructive feedback delivered when she acted as external evaluator and discussant for the evaluation seminar of my PhD thesis in December 2019.

My sincere thanks to Professors *Hanne Petersen*, *Frank Hendrickx* and *Vassilis Hatzopoulos* for serving as members of the assessment committee of my PhD thesis.

Besides, I would like to thank all the members of the Centre for European and Comparative Legal Studies (CECS) for their countless suggestions in an always friendly and professional atmosphere. My gratitude is extended to the vibrant research community and staff at the Faculty of Law, University of Copenhagen. Their great enthusiasm and expertise constantly supported my research work in many different ways.

I also wish to express my appreciation to the LERU Law PhD Exchange Scheme for offering me the opportunity to be a visiting researcher at the Institute for Labour Law at the Faculty of Law, University of Leuven (Belgium). This highly stimulating and challenging academic environment warmly received me and definitely contributed to the quality of my research.

Equally important, I am grateful to the publishers of this book: Kluwer Law International, the Bulletin of Comparative Labour Relations with its professional and experienced publication team and, in particular, Professor *Frank Hendrickx* for making this publication possible.

Last but not least, a special debt of gratitude is devoted to my parents, my brother and my sister, for their endless encouragement and support in pursuing my goals. And to *Theodora Kostoula (Dora)*, who has always been by my side with her moral strength, positive spirit and professional competence.

Matteo Bottero
Copenhagen
15 September 2020

CHAPTER 1
Introduction

1.1 A HOTLY DEBATED CONTEXT

On 28 June 2018, the new Directive (EU) 2018/957[1] was adopted with a view to introducing significant changes to the European Union (EU) legal framework for posting of workers, towards the achievement of 'a level playing field for businesses' and 'greater protection for workers'.[2] This legislative innovation is the product of a long and arduous process characterised by heated debates between, on the one hand, the Western EU Member States which for years pushed for a targeted revision of the Posting of Workers Directive 96/71/EC[3] and, on the other hand, the Central and Eastern EU Member States which were utterly opposed to it.[4] The motivations behind the emergence of such diametrically divergent positions have to be sought in the

1. Directive (EU) 2018/957 of the European Parliament and of the Council of 28 June 2018 amending Directive 96/71/EC concerning the posting of workers in the framework of the provision of services 2018 (OJ L 173/16).
2. *Ibid.* Preamble Recitals 1 and 10.
3. Directive 96/71/EC of the European Parliament and of the Council of 16 December 1996 concerning the posting of workers in the framework of the provision of services 1997 (OJ L 18/1) (hereinafter also referred to as the 'Posting of Workers Directive' or with its acronym 'PWD'.)
4. The existence of such a conflict between the Central and Eastern and the Western Member States is testified, *inter alia*, by the diametrically opposed positions respectively expressed by, on the one hand, Austria, Belgium, France, Germany, Luxembourg, the Netherlands, and Sweden and, on the other hand, Bulgaria, the Czech Republic, Estonia, Hungary, Lithuania, Latvia, Poland, Romania and Slovakia, in the form of two letters addressed to Ms Marianne Thyssen, Commissioner for Employment, Social Affairs, Skills and Labour Mobility. Austrian, Belgian, French, German, Luxembourg, Dutch and Swedish Ministers of Labour, 'Letter to Ms Marianne Thyssen Commissioner for Employment, Social Affairs, Skills and Labour Mobility' (18 June 2015); Bulgarian, Czech, Estonian, Hungarian, Latvian, Lithuanian, Polish, Romanian and Slovakian Ministers of Labour, 'Letter to Ms Marianne Thyssen Commissioner for Employment, Social Affairs, Skills and Labour Mobility' (31 August 2015). On this point, *see* Diane Fromage and Valentin Kreilinger, 'National Parliaments' Third Yellow Card and the Struggle over the Revision of the Posted Workers Directive' (2017) 10 European Journal of Legal Studies 125, 147.

progressive expansion of the phenomenon of posting of workers and its anomalous form of regulation at European level.

The practice whereby a worker is sent ('posted')[5] for a limited period of time to another Member State in order to provide a service has developed as a peculiar type of short-term transnational labour mobility since the dawn of the Common Market.[6] The great deal of political and scholarly attention constantly given to it is largely due to its conceptual position at the crossroads of conflicting interests of, on the one hand, the European project towards the creation of a fully integrated internal market economy through more effective and profitable resource allocation and, on the other hand, the Member States' aims to protect domestic social standards and preserve their sovereignty in regulating their national labour markets.[7] A proper definition pursuant to Union law of the notions of 'posted worker' and 'posting' activity is, therefore, made extremely complicated by the concurrent application of different EU and national legal regimes, including labour law, social security law and tax law.[8]

In light of the peculiar nature of the type of cross-border mobility under consideration, the question about which national legal regime should apply to the employment relationship, namely whether the workers involved should be subject to the same rules as national workers in the host state or they should be treated differently, has been a controversial issue for decades, albeit with highs and lows.[9] The first solution in this sense was offered by Regulation (EEC) 1408/71 on social security,[10] which provided for a specific derogation from the generally applicable principle of *lex loci laboris*, in case of posting assignments lasting less than twelve months (with possible extension to further twelve months). Accordingly, unlike persons migrating in the framework of the freedom of movement for workers, posted

5. One cannot avoid noting that the inelegant English term 'posted workers' has in itself a negative connotation, implying a sort of commodification of the workers involved. Conversely, such a trait is not present, for instance, in the Danish *udstationerede arbejdstagere*, in the Dutch *Gedetacheerde werknemers*, in the French *travailleurs détachés*, in the German *entsandte Arbeitnehmer*, in the Greek *αποσπασμένοι εργαζόμενοι*, in the Italian *lavoratori distaccati*, nor in the Spanish *trabajadores desplazados*.
6. The practice of posting employees was already under discussion in early cases of the Court of Justice, namely in *Bestuur der Sociale Verzekeringsbank v J H van der Vecht* [1967] ECJ Case C-19/67, ECR 345; *Manpower v Caisse primaire d'assurance maladie de Strasbourg* [1970] ECJ Case C-35/70, ECLI:EU:C:1970:120. *See* Aukje A.H. van Hoek and Mijke Houwerzijl, '"Posting" and "Posted Workers": The Need for Clear Definitions of Two Key Concepts of the Posting of Workers Directive' (2012) 14 Cambridge Yearbook of European Legal Studies 419, 419.
7. Jens Arnholtz and Søren Kaj Andersen, 'Extra-Institutional Changes under Pressure from Posting: Extra-Institutional Changes' (2018) 56 British Journal of Industrial Relations 1, 1–2. Interestingly, such a conflict of interests may also be framed in terms of clash between, on the one hand, the cross-border service providers and their posted employees and, on the other hand, the employers and workers in the host states. Aukje A.H. van Hoek and Mijke Houwerzijl, 'Where Do EU Mobile Workers Belong, According to Rome I and the (E)PWD?' in Herwig Verschueren (ed.), *Residence, Employment and Social Rights of Mobile Persons: On How EU Law Defines Where They Belong*, vol. 36 (Intersentia 2016) 236; Herwig Verschueren, 'The European Internal Market and the Competition between Workers' (2015) 6 European Labour Law Journal 128, 145.
8. Verschueren (n 7) 145.
9. Catherine Barnard, 'Posting Matters' (2014) 11 Arbeidsrett 1, 1–2.
10. Regulation (EEC) No 1408/71 of the Council of 14 June 1971 on the application of social security schemes to employed persons and their families moving within the Community 1971 (OJ L 149/2).

workers were allowed to remain affiliated to their country of origin's social security system.[11] Such a principle still remains valid today in accordance with the most recent Regulation (EC) 883/2004 on the coordination of social security systems,[12] as implemented by Regulation (EC) No 987/2009,[13] with the maximum duration of transnational service provision raised to twenty-four months.

Conversely, the posted workers' legal treatment with regard to pay and working conditions has traditionally been less straightforward. The 1990 ruling of the Court of Justice of the European Union[14] (CJEU) in *Rush Portuguesa*, while firmly placing the practice at stake under the Treaty rules governing the free provision of services and consequently giving effect to the workers' home state law, still allowed the host Member State to apply all its labour legislation and collective labour agreements (CLAs) to foreign workers who were posted in its territory.[15] A few years later, the EU legislator, with the adoption on 16 December 1996 of the Posting of Workers Directive 96/71/EC, circumscribed the host country's wide discretion in relation to the part of domestic regulation it can impose on posted employees. The latter's legal position was therefore shaped in a way that they would in principle remain covered by the labour law of their country of origin (i.e., of the country where their employers are established) while, at the same time, being subject to a set of rules on minimum protection (including 'minimum rates of pay') determined by the Member State where they are temporarily employed. In essence, then, neither under EU labour law nor under EU social security law, posted workers traditionally enjoyed full equal treatment with local workers in the host state.[16]

11. For the record, such a particular social insurance treatment for posted workers is still currently into force, albeit with a few changes introduced by subsequent interventions of the EU legislator and of the Court of Justice. Jan Cremers, 'Economic Freedoms and Labour Standards in the European Union' (2016) 22(2) Transfer: European Review of Labour and Research 149, 152–153.
12. Regulation (EC) No 883/2004 of the European Parliament and of the Council of 29 April 2004 on the coordination of social security systems 2004 (OJ L 166/1) (hereinafter also referred to as the 'Basic Regulation').
13. Regulation (EC) No 987/2009 of the European Parliament and of the Council of 16 September 2009 laying down the procedure for implementing Regulation (EC) No 883/2004 on the coordination of social security systems 2009 (OJ L 284/1).
14. Court of Justice of the European Union (hereinafter referred as the 'Court of Justice', the 'Court' or with its acronym 'CJEU').
15. *Rush Portuguesa Lda v Office national d'immigration* [1990] ECJ Case C-113/89, ECLI: EU:C:1990:142 [18]. Jan Cremers, 'Free Provision of Services and Cross-Border Labour Recruitment' (2013) 34 Policy Studies 201, 210; Verschueren (n 7) 138.
16. Paul Davies, 'Posted Workers: Single Market or Protection of National Labour Law Systems?' (1997) 34 Common Market Law Review 571, 571–572; Jan Cremers, 'In Search of Cheap Labour in Europe - Working and Living Conditions of Posted Workers' (2011) CLR News 6, 6; Catherine Barnard, 'EU Employment Law and the European Social Model: The Past, the Present and the Future' (2014) 67 Current Legal Problems 199, 219; Kristina Maslauskaite, 'Posted Workers in the EU: State of Play and Regulatory Evolution' (2014) Policy Paper, Notre Europe Jaques Delors Institute 20, 8; Barnard, 'Posting Matters' (n 9) 1–2; Verschueren (n 7) 140; Dagmar Schiek et al., 'EU Social and Labour Rights and EU Internal Market Law' (European Parliament, EMPL Committee 2015) IP/A/EMPL/ST/2014-02, 40; Catherine Jacqueson and Frans Pennings, 'Equal Treatment of Mobile Persons in the Context of a Social Market Economy' (2019) 15 Utrecht Law Review 64, 74–75.

Partly also by reason of such a peculiar legal framework for cross-border posting activities, the phenomenon at issue has recently experienced a seamless quantitative expansion, which went hand-in-hand with the opening of the public procurement markets for works, supply and service contracts[17] and with the overall enhancement of transnational labour mobility resulting from the EU's Southern and Eastern enlargements. In particular, after the accession of Spain and Portugal in 1986, and especially after the 2004 and 2007 European enlargements towards the East,[18] the share of migrating workforce driven by the intention of profiting from the economic opportunities offered by the internal market dramatically increased.[19] All this, despite the imposition of 'transitional arrangements' intended to limit the inflow of workers from the 'new' to the 'old' Member States, as part of the respective accession treaties.[20]

---

17. Directive 2004/18/EC of the European Parliament and of the Council of 31 March 2004 on the coordination of procedures for the award of public works contracts, public supply contracts and public service contracts 2004 (OJ L 134/114); Directive 2004/17/EC of the European Parliament and of the Council of 31 March 2004 coordinating the procurement procedures of entities operating in the water, energy, transport and postal services sectors 2004 (OJ L 134/1). *See* Philippa Watson, *EU Social and Employment Law* (Second Edition, Oxford University Press 2014) 280.
18. It is recalled that ten new countries, namely Cyprus, Czech Republic, Estonia, Hungary, Latvia, Lithuania, Malta, Poland, Slovakia and Slovenia, joined the EU in the 2004, followed by Bulgaria and Romania in 2007.
19. Stein Evju and Tonia Novitz, 'The Evolving Regulation: Dynamics and Consequences' (2012) 33 FORMULA Working Paper, University of Oslo, Department of Private Law 7–8; Magdalena Bernaciak, 'Social Dumping: Political Catchphrase or Threat to Labour Standards?' (2012) ETUI European Trade Union Institute – Working Paper 2012.06, 10 and ff.; Rebecca Zahn, 'Revision of the Posted Workers' Directive: A Europeanisation Perspective' (2017) 19 Cambridge Yearbook of European Legal Studies 187, 193–194.
20. After the accession of new Member States to the EU, the introduction of a transitional regime delayed the full implementation of the free movement rights of the workers coming from the acceding countries, for a period of up to seven years ('2 + 3 + 2' formula). The adoption of such arrangements was due to the fear of an 'invasion' of new migrant workers as a result of substantial wage differences between the 'old' and the 'new' EU countries. Restrictions varied significantly according to different accession treaties, depending also on the date the new Member States joined the EU. For the countries involved in the 2004 enlargement, the transitional period expired on 30 April 2011. For Bulgaria and Romania – which joined the EU in 2007 – it ended on 31 December 2013. For Croatia, it expired on 30 June 2020. On this point, *see* Paul Craig and Gráinne de Búrca, *EU Law: Text, Cases, and Materials* (Sixth Edition, Oxford University Press 2015) 758. For a detailed analysis of different types of transitional regimes and their impact in concrete terms, *see* IDEA Consult and ECORYS Netherlands, 'Study on the Economic and Social Effects Associated with the Phenomenon of Posting of Workers in the EU' (European Commission, Directorate-General Employment, Social Affairs and Equal Opportunities 2011) 57 and ff.; Aukje A.H. van Hoek and Mijke Houwerzijl, 'Comparative Study on the Legal Aspects of the Posting of Workers in the Framework of the Provision of Services in the European Union' (2011) 51–53; Torben Krings, 'A Race to the Bottom? Trade Unions, EU Enlargement and the Free Movement of Labour' (2009) 15 European Journal of Industrial Relations 49, 52 and ff.; Craig and de Búrca 758; Frederic De Wispelaere and Jozef Pacolet, 'Posting of Workers as Stabilising Mechanism: An Enlarged Notion of Labour Mobility as a Prerequisite for an Optimal Currency Area' (KU Leuven Research Institute for Work and Society (HIVA) 2015) 6. Interestingly, it is worth pointing out that the transition period contained in the 1986 Accession Treaty to the European Economic Community of Portugal and Spain, while restricting the free movement of workers, did not concern the provision of services and, therefore, the posting of workers. The famous ECJ judgment in *Rush Portuguesa* was, indeed, the direct outcome of this first partial liberalisation. Schiek et al. (n 16) 40; Aukje A.H. van Hoek, 'Re-Embedding the Transnational Employment Relationship: A Tale about the Limitations of

In light of the competitive advantage of posting enterprises coming from the 'new' low-wage Member States over their local competitors in the 'old' high-wage Member States, resulting from the (at times very considerable) existing differences in wages, social security contributions and tax rates,[21] the common public, political and academic debate at EU level started putting into question the European model of integration by means of liberalisation of the internal market for services.[22] The latter was for that reason accused of acting as a Trojan horse, eroding the highest welfare standards in the 'old' Member States.[23] Notably, the approach taken by the Court of Justice in the (in)famous series of decisions released between 2007 and 2008, known as the *Laval quartet*,[24] was highly criticised for sensibly narrowing down the scope for national measures and industrial action aimed at imposing additional elements of domestic law on cross-border service providers.[25] Hence, it was considered as one of the main factors leading to the general absence of a level playing field between local and foreign service providers.

What is more, the reputation of posting has been strongly affected by the proliferation of a number of unlawful and fraudulent practices. In this sense, there have been recorded various cases of abuses of the posted workers' vulnerable conditions

(EU) Law?' (2018) 55 Common Market Law Review 449, 463–464; Jens Arnholtz and Nathan Lillie, 'European Integration and the Reconfiguration of National Industrial Relations: Posted Work as a Driver of Institutional Change' in Jens Arnholtz and Nathan Lillie (eds), *Posted Work in the European Union: The Political Economy of Free Movement* (Routledge 2019) 6.

21. Herwig Verschueren, 'Cross-Border Workers in the European Internal Market: Trojan Horses for Member States' Labour and Social Security Law?' (2008) 24/2 International Journal of Comparative Labour Law and Industrial Relations 167, 198; Verschueren (n 7) 129; Frans Pennings, 'Principles of EU Coordination of Social Security' in Frans Pennings and Gijsbert Vonk (eds), *Research Handbook on European Social Security Law* (Edward Elgar Publishing 2015) 333; Arnholtz and Lillie (n 20) 8.
22. The risks stemming from this radical stance, have been distinctly highlighted by the so-called 'Monti Report' where it is stated that: 'The revival of this divide [between advocates of greater market integration and those who feel that the call for economic freedoms and for breaking up regulatory barriers is code for dismantling social rights protected at national level] has the potential to alienate from the Single Market and the EU a segment of public opinion, workers' movements and trade unions, which has been over time a key supporter of economic integration.' Mario Monti, 'A New Strategy for the Single Market: At the Service of Europe's Economy and Society. Report to the President of the European Commission José Manuel Barroso' (European Commission Bureau of European Policy Advisers (BEPA) 2010) 68.
23. Marc De Vos, 'Free Movement of Workers, Free Movement of Services and the Posted Workers Directive: A Bermuda Triangle for National Labour Standards?' (2006) 7 ERA Forum - Springer 356, 370; Verschueren (n 21) 198.
24. The so-called 'Laval quartet' refers to the four rulings of the Court in *International Transport Workers' Federation and Finnish Seamen's Union v Viking Line ABP and OÜ Viking Line Eesti* [2007] ECJ Case C-438/05, ECLI:EU:C:2007:772; *Laval un Partneri Ltd v Svenska Byggnadsarbetareförbundet, Svenska Byggnadsarbetareförbundets avdelning 1, Byggettan and Svenska Elektrikerförbundet* [2007] ECJ Case C-341/05, ECLI:EU:C:2007:809; *Dirk Rüffert v Land Niedersachsen* [2008] CJEU Case C-346/06, ECLI:EU:C:2008:189; *Commission of the European Communities v Grand Duchy of Luxemburg* [2008] ECJ Case C-319/06, ECLI:EU:C:2008:350.
25. Jon Erik Dølvik and Jelle Visser, 'Free Movement, Equal Treatment and Workers' Rights: Can the European Union Solve Its Trilemma of Fundamental Principles?: Free Movement, Equal Treatment and Workers' Rights' (2009) 40 Industrial Relations Journal 491, 503; Yves Jorens, Saskia Peters and Mijke Houwerzijl, 'Study on the Protection of Workers' Rights in Subcontracting Processes in the European Union (Final Study)' (Ghent University, Department of Social Law (in consortium with University of Amsterdam) 2012) DG EMPL/B2-VC/2011/0015, 6.

and development of artificial company structures and malpractices, such as 'letterbox companies', bogus self-employment and false declarations of social security certificates, aimed at circumventing the applicable EU rules and the relatively higher employment standards in the countries of destination.[26] On top of that, the exploitation of existing regulatory loopholes by foreign service providers led, in certain circumstances, to cases of 'regime shopping'[27] which are, eventually, supposed to result in a 'race to the bottom' in terms of social standards between the Member States.[28] Evidently, the proper individuation of a posting arrangement within the legal limits, besides the huge problems in the definition of the activity at stake, is made even more complicated by the spread of extra-legal situations. In such a context dominated by extreme uncertainty when it comes to distinguishing between illegal recruitment of 'cheap' labour within the EU and negative repercussions intrinsically related to the legal secondment of workforce, the phenomenon of posting has been labelled *tout court* as a source of 'unfair competition' and 'social dumping'.[29]

The first concrete reaction, put in place by the European legislator with a view to strengthening the practical application of the regulatory framework set by the Posting of Workers Directive, was the adoption in 2014 of the Enforcement Directive 2014/67/EU.[30] That normative intervention sought to curb the spread of frauds and abuses by bringing more legal clarity with regard to the recognition of genuine posting activities, improving administrative coordination and cooperation between national

26. Jan Cremers, Jon Erik Dølvik and Gerhard Bosch, 'Posting of Workers in the Single Market: Attempts to Prevent Social Dumping and Regime Competition in the EU' (2007) 38 Industrial Relations Journal 524, 526.
27. Eckhard Voss et al., 'Posting of Workers Directive: Current Situation and Challenges' (European Parliament, EMPL Committee 2016) IP/A/EMPL/2016-07, 30.
28. Dorothee Bohle, 'Race to the Bottom? Comparative Institutional Advantages? Competition of Capitalisms in the Enlarged EU' in Jan Drahokoupil and Laura Horn (eds), *Contradictions and Limits of Neoliberal European Governance: From Lisbon to Lisbon*, vol. 8 (Palgrave Macmillan 2008); Kristina Maslauskaite, 'Social Competition in the EU: Myths and Realities' (2013) Policy Paper, Notre Europe Jaques Delors Institute 62, 10 and 12; Magdalena Bernaciak, 'Conclusion' in Magdalena Bernaciak (ed.), *Market Expansion and Social Dumping in Europe* (Routledge 2015) 14; Cremers, 'Economic Freedoms and Labour Standards in the European Union' (n 11) 157; Jean-Philippe Lhernould and Barbara Palli, 'Posted Workers Remuneration: Comparative Study in Nine EU Countries and Four Sectors' (2017) 24 Maastricht Journal of European and Comparative Law 108, 109.
29. *See*, in this sense, Toulon speech on 1 December 2011 of the former President of France Sarkozy, as reported by The Economist, 'The Euro Crisis – One Problem, Two Visions (Part II): Two Speeches by Nicolas Sarkozy and Angela Merkel about the Euro Zone's Crisis Reveal Their Differences Ahead of a Key Summit' (2 December 2011) <https://www.economist.com/blogs/charlemagne/2011/12/euro-crisis-0> (accessed 15 May 2018). As far as the academic literature is concerned, *see* Bohle (n 28); Verschueren (n 21) 198; Maslauskaite (n 16) 3; Jan Cremers, 'EU Economic Freedoms and Social Dumping' in Magdalena Bernaciak (ed.), *Market Expansion and Social Dumping in Europe* (Routledge 2015) 186–187; Magdalena Bernaciak, 'Market Expansion and Social Dumping in Europe, Conclusion', *Market Expansion and Social Dumping in Europe* (Routledge, Magdalena Bernaciak 2015) 200; Cremers, 'Economic Freedoms and Labour Standards in the European Union' (n 11) 10; Lhernould and Palli (n 28) 109.
30. Directive 2014/67/EU of the European Parliament and of the Council of 15 May 2014 on the enforcement of Directive 96/71/EC concerning the posting of workers in the framework of the provision of services and amending Regulation (EU) No 1024/2012 on administrative cooperation through the Internal Market Information System ('the IMI Regulation') 2014 (OJ L 159/11) (hereinafter also referred to as the 'Enforcement Directive').

authorities in the sending and receiving Member States and assuring cross-border implementation of financial penalties. It also introduced a number of technical measures of worker protection, such as vicarious liability of the main employer in case of subcontracting.[31] Importantly, though, the limited scope of the above-mentioned act of secondary EU legislation left substantially untouched the legal framework designed by the 1996 Directive.

Even before the expiring, on 18 June 2016, of the Enforcement Directive's term of implementation into national laws, ministers from high-wage Member States called for an update of the existing rules in order to better adjust to the different economic effects of the Posting of Workers Directive resulting from the European enlargements towards the East and the consequent enhanced division between low-wage and high-wage national economies.[32] More specifically, the key to guaranteeing undistorted competition and effective worker protection was identified in the establishment of the principle of 'equal pay for equal work in the same place'.[33] Despite the concern expressed by the Central and Eastern European Countries (CEECs) about the incompatibility of such a principle with the internal market structure, considering pay rate differences as one legitimate element of competitive advantage for service providers, the request of reform was acknowledged positively by the Commission which, on 8 March 2016, proposed a targeted review of the 1996 Posting of Workers Directive.[34]

Just two years later, after sailing right through a 'yellow-card' procedure triggered by fourteen national parliamentary chambers from eleven Member States,[35] the reform was completed with the adoption of the new Directive (EU) 2018/957. The new rules on posting of workers are now fully effective as Directive (EU) 2018/957 had to

31. European Commission – Employment, Social Affairs & Inclusion, 'Posted Workers' <https://ec.europa.eu/social/main.jsp?catId=471> (accessed 3 April 2019).
32. European Commission, Impact Assessment, Accompanying the document Proposal for a Directive of the European Parliament and the Council amending Directive 96/71/EC concerning the posting of workers in the framework of the provision of services 2016 [SWD(2016) 52 final] 50; Federica Mustilli and Jacques Pelkmans, 'Access Barriers to Services Markets' (2013) 77 CEPS Centre for European Policy Studies 84, 51.
33. Austrian, Belgian, French, German, Luxembourg, Dutch and Swedish Ministers of labour (n 4). *See also* European Commission, 'Speech of President Jean-Claude Juncker, State of the Union Address' (13 September 2017) <http://europa.eu/rapid/press-release_SPEECH-17-3165_en.htm> (accessed 15 October 2018). On this point, *see* Elena Vaccarino and Zsolt Darvas, '"Social Dumping" and Posted Workers: A New Clash within the EU' (*Bruegel*, 7 March 2016) <http://bruegel.org/2016/03/social-dumping-and-posted-workers-a-new-clash-within-the-eu/> (accessed 13 May 2018); Rebecca Zahn, 'Revision of the Posted Workers' Directive: Equality at Last?' (2016) 5 European (Legal) Studies on-line papers, Queen's University Belfast – School of Law – Centre of European and Transnational Legal Studies 13.
34. European Commission, Proposal for a Directive of the European Parliament and of the Council amending Directive 96/71/EC of the European Parliament and of the Council of 16 December 1996 concerning the posting of workers in the framework of the provision of services 2016 [COM(2016) 128 final].
35. Not surprisingly, ten out of the eleven national parliaments that submitted (negative) reasoned opinions on the revision of the PWD (namely Bulgaria, Croatia, Czech Republic, Denmark, Estonia, Hungary, Latvia, Lithuania, Poland, Romania and Slovakia) are from Central and Eastern Europe. Zahn (n 33) 14–15; Valentin Kreilinger, 'National Parliaments' 3rd Yellow Card: A Preliminary Assessment' (*euractiv.com*, 12 May 2016) <https://www.euractiv.com/section/social-europe-jobs/opinion/national-parliaments-3rd-yellow-card-a-preliminary-assessment/> (accessed 23 April 2019); Fromage and Kreilinger (n 4) 133.

be implemented in national regulation by 30 July 2020 at the latest. A number of novelties have been introduced with the intention to curtail the competitive advantage of cross-border service providers, which make recourse to posting of workers, vis-à-vis their local counterparts, especially by increasing the workers' salaries and setting a limit of duration to this form of labour mobility.[36] In essence, since the entry into force of the new rules, the seconded employees are entitled to the same 'remuneration' as local employees – instead of equal 'minimum rates of pay' as provided for under the original version of the Posting of Workers Directive – and also to reimbursements for accommodation, travel, board and lodging expenses.[37] The applicability of collective agreements is then extended to all economic sectors and even to situations previously excluded.[38] Furthermore, the maximum period of a posting assignment is determined at twelve months, with possible extension to eighteen months, following prior motivated notification to the competent authority in the receiving country.[39] This means that, whenever the transnational service provision lasts longer, posted workers are nearly entitled to equal treatment with local employees in the host state as regards wages and working conditions, i.e., they are treated almost in the same way as workers migrating in the framework of the freedom of movement for workers. Interestingly, the maximum limit of twelve months refers to the cumulative duration of the posting, taking into account all possible replacement of workforce for the same tasks at the same place.[40]

Dwelling for a while on the reasons underpinning the above-mentioned normative reform, it is worth noting that a decisive contribution was made by a political campaign fuelled by exaggeration of negative and abusive repercussions deriving from the temporary secondment of workforce from low-wage to high-wage Member States. The benefit resulting from the former rules for service providers coming from the Member States with relatively low employment standards – and thus mainly from the

36. Marco Rocca, 'Not Dead yet: Legal Strategies at National Level and the Reform of the EU Posting of Workers Directive' (2018) 5.
37. In addition, the new Directive requires the Member States to publish on a single official national website all information about the constituent elements of remuneration (and further mandatory employment conditions) applicable to workers posted to their territory. Marek Benio, 'New Rules of the Posting of Workers in 2020. The Countdown.' (*Labour Mobility Initiative*, 30 July 2018) <https://www.mobilelabour.eu/12521/new-rules-of-the-posting-of-workers-in-2020-the-final-countdown/> (accessed 30 August 2018); Jean-Philippe Lhernould, 'Directive (EU) 2018/957 of 28 June 2018 Amending Directive 96/71/EC Concerning the Posting of Workers in the Framework of the Provision of Services: What Will Change in 2020?' (2019) ERA Forum – Springer 9 <http://link.springer.com/10.1007/s12027-019-00573-x> (accessed 16 September 2019).
38. This is the case of collective agreements concluded by the most representative organisations, which are made applicable also 'in the absence of, or in addition to' universally applicable ones. Article 1(2)(d) of Directive (EU) 2018/957 of the European Parliament and of the Council of 28 June 2018 amending Directive 96/71/EC concerning the posting of workers in the framework of the provision of services (n 1). On this point, *see* Rocca (n 36) 6.
39. Lhernould (n 37) 5.
40. Stefan Schwarz, Marcin Kiełbasa and Marek Benio, 'Limited Cumulative Period of Posting in the Revised Posting of Workers Directive – In Search of a Legal Justification' (2018) *Labour Mobility Initiative Association* 4–5 <https://www.mobilelabour.eu/wp-content/uploads/2018/10/paper-Limited-cumulative-period-of-posting-in-the-revised-PWD-%E2%80%93-in-search-of-a-legal-justification-by-LMIA.pdf> (accessed 19 October 2018).

Central and Eastern EU Countries – and especially those operating in labour-intensive economic sectors, such as construction, industry and transport, is undeniable.[41] However, the actual relatively limited dimension of the phenomenon at issue, along with its multifaceted impact on economic actors in both the sending and receiving countries and on the EU labour market as a whole, has basically been overlooked. Rather than building on the various opportunities provided by the development of genuine posting arrangements in terms of, *inter alia*, upward socio-economic convergence and welfare redistribution at EU level,[42] the ordinary legal and political discourse mainly focused on solving issues of inclusion and relative equal treatment.[43] The resulting narrative constantly points out the existence of a dichotomic juxtaposition between the economic and social dimensions of the Union, disguising the ongoing clash between Eastern and Western European countries.[44]

1.2 AIMS AND RESEARCH QUESTIONS

The absence in European legal scholarship of reference to the concept of social justice has been denounced by various distinguished legal scholars.[45] In such a context, the emerging legal, social and economic issues related to the functioning of the internal market are, instead, commonly framed in terms of (im)balance between economic and social aims of the Union.[46] The EU legislative process, in turn, appears to be primarily

41. Cremers, 'Free Provision of Services and Cross-Border Labour Recruitment' (n 15) 220; Uglješa Grušić, *The European Private International Law of Employment* (Cambridge University Press 2015) 256–257; European Commission, *Employment and Social Developments in Europe 2014* (European Commission, Directorate Général for Employment, Social Affairs and Inclusion 2015) 156; Frederic De Wispelaere and Jozef Pacolet, 'An Ad Hoc Statistical Analysis on Short Term Mobility – Economic Value of Posting of Workers: The Impact of Intra-EU Cross-Border Services, with Special Attention to the Construction Sector' (KU Leuven Research Institute for Work and Society (HIVA) 2016) Research commissioned by DG EMPL within the framework of Contract VT/2015/096, 11.
42. Frederic De Wispelaere and Jozef Pacolet, 'The Benefits of Posting: Facts and Figures on the Use and Impact of Intra-EU Posting' in Jens Arnholtz and Nathan Lillie (eds), *Posted Work in the European Union: The Political Economy of Free Movement* (Routledge 2019) 38.
43. Alexander Somek, 'From Workers to Migrants, from Distributive Justice to Inclusion: Exploring the Changing Social Democratic Imagination: Exploring the Changing Social Democratic Imagination' (2012) 18 European Law Journal 711, 12 and ff.
44. Notably, the conflict between Eastern and Western European countries has been also effectively portrayed by Damjan Kukovec as a conflict between the EU 'centre' and 'periphery'. Damjan Kukovec, 'A Critique of the Rhetoric of Common Interest in the European Union Legal Discourse' (2012) SSRN Electronic Journal 11; Damjan Kukovec, 'Hierarchies as Law' (2014) 21 Columbia Journal of European Law 131; Damjan Kukovec, 'Law and the Periphery' (2015) 21 European Law Journal 406.
45. Joseph H.H. Weiler expressed his concern in this sense with an intervention during the launch of the book *The Transformation of Europe: Twenty-Five Years On*, held at the University of Copenhagen on 7 May 2018. Miguel Poiares Maduro and Marlene Wind (eds), *The Transformation of Europe: Twenty-Five Years On* (Cambridge University Press 2017). In this sense, *see also* Somek (n 43); Andrea Sangiovanni, 'Solidarity in the European Union' (2013) 33 Oxford Journal of Legal Studies 213; Andrea Sangiovanni, 'Solidarity as Joint Action: Solidarity as Joint Action' (2015) 32 Journal of Applied Philosophy 340.
46. As shown further in this book, this is the case, indeed, of much of the academic literature on posting of workers.

driven by the need of finding a political compromise between the multitude of actors and interests involved, often leaving aside any consideration to European fundamental values and principles. This book embraces the challenge by trying to offer a perspective on the evolution of the EU legal framework for posting of workers, until the most recent adoption of Directive (EU) 2018/957, which takes into account the wider picture of social justice issues deriving from the European integration process.

More concretely, this book aims, first and foremost, at providing an in-depth analysis *sine ira et studio* of the intensely debated phenomenon under consideration, looking at both its relevant regulation at EU level, its actual quantitative dimension, and its impact on the EU labour market, with a special focus on the novelties introduced by the adoption of Directive (EU) 2018/957. Against this background, a critical assessment based on the previous findings intends to ascertain in which way the entry into effect of the latter legislative reform will alter the current state of play. Such an analysis is not limited, however, to a mere technical appraisal of the impact of the new rules and of their practical suitability to solve the issues emerged. The main purpose of this book entails a theoretical reflection on the way in which that act of secondary EU law is supposed to operate, without losing sight of the rhetoric underpinning it. In particular, with a view to discerning the future legal position of posting of workers under EU law, the innovative legal framework laid down in Directive (EU) 2018/957 is carefully evaluated in light of the EU values and principles of 'equality', 'solidarity' and 'fair competition'. This primary aim is reflected, therefore, in the following main research question:

> *To what extent is the new legal framework provided for by Directive (EU) 2018/957 in line with the EU values and principles of equality, solidarity and fair competition?*

The choice of assessing the new legal framework from the perspective of the EU values and principles coming into play in the context of posting of workers is justified by the intention to take seriously the Union's commitment to the development of a 'European social model', which cannot avoid taking into account the relevant matters of equality, solidarity and fair competition. Accordingly, the answer to this question does not merely concern the approach taken by the EU legislator in regulating the type of labour mobility at stake. It assumes, indeed, an extremely symbolic relevance when looking at the model of EU integration actually pursued. In this sense, given the increasing prominence of the free movement of services in shaping a European labour market characterised by an ever-growing degree of mobility,[47] the analysis of the phenomenon of posting of workers may serve as a litmus test of the political and legislative action at EU level.

47. Ninke Mussche, Vincent Corluy and Ive Marx, 'The Rise of the Free Movements: How Posting Shapes a Hybrid Single European Labour Market' (2017) European Journal of Industrial Relations 3; Ninke Mussche and Dries Lens, 'The EU Free Movement of Services and the Growing Mobility of Third-Country Nationals as Posted Workers' (2018) CSB Working Paper No. 18.13 University of Antwerp – Herman Deleeck Centre for Social Policy 1.

The more normative part of the research dealing with the above-mentioned main question is preceded, physically and functionally, by a more strictly analytical part, which is guided by five research sub-questions:

(1) *How is the 'posting of workers' defined under EU law?*
(2) *How is the 'posting of workers' regulated under EU law?*
(3) *What is the actual dimension of the posting phenomenon?*
(4) *What sort of impact does the posting phenomenon have on the EU labour market, and which kind of issues have emerged in the sector?*
(5) *How was the new Directive (EU) 2018/957 conceived, and in which way does it alter the former legal framework and the overall state of play?*

These five sub-questions have a mainly descriptive - and yet critical - purpose and the provision of adequate corresponding answers is considered an essential condition for the purpose of this book. In fact, a consistent and comprehensive examination of Directive (EU) 2018/957 necessarily presupposes a precise legal delimitation of the posting phenomenon. The latter, in turn, requires an investigation of the relevant EU regulatory framework, focusing on the legal position of the actor involved under internal market law in the context of the cross-border service provision, as well as on the relevant EU labour and social security provisions. Besides, the analysis of the sector needs to be complemented by accurate figures on the actual quantitative dimension of posting practices and on their concrete impact in terms of costs and benefits at both EU and national levels. In fact, the punctual scrutiny of the several issues emerged in the context under consideration is deemed crucial for assessing the measure and scope of the various normative interventions in the field of posting. The different analytical sections, aimed at addressing specifically the aforementioned five research sub-questions, are located in the early core chapters (more precisely, the first research sub-question is addressed in Chapter 2; the second one in Chapters 3, 4 and 5; the third one in Chapter 6; the fourth one in Chapter 7; and the fifth one in Chapter 8). Subsequently, this book takes a more normative turn in Chapter 9 when dealing with the main research question.[48]

The investigation of the radical changes that the EU regulatory framework for posting of workers is currently facing is expected to bring a valuable contribution to knowledge in this field of research. Notably, the first note of originality is given by the comprehensive analysis of the regulation of posting of workers under EU law, taking into account both the relevant EU labour and social security provisions. Yet, the main innovative character of this book lies in the angle from which the new Directive (EU) 2018/957, and especially its underlying purpose of removing almost all elements of differentiation between the treatment reserved to local and posted workers as regards remuneration and working conditions, is examined. On the one hand, it is confronted with the actual quantitative dimension of the posting phenomenon and with the latter's

48. For a detailed description of the book structure and the respective content of the chapters, *see infra* section 1.5.

multifaceted impact on the EU labour market. On the other hand, taking into consideration its expected negative impact on the worse-off posted workers moving from low-wage to high-wage Member States, the 2018 legislative reform is evaluated in light of the EU values and principles of equality, solidarity and fair competition. The latter values and principles are mainly considered in their European dimension, which is regarded as a major source of inspiration for the progressive development of a European social model that reflects the EU's commitment to social justice and cohesion. Importantly, such a critical analysis is not an end in itself. It is rather intended to represent a starting point for future discussions and developments in the area of intra-EU labour mobility.

1.3 METHODOLOGY AND MATERIALS

The choice of the methodological approach adopted is inevitably intertwined with the aforementioned very purpose of this book entailing, on the one hand, an in-depth analysis of the posting phenomenon which takes into account both its regulation under EU law and its material dimension and, on the other hand, a weighing up of the newly established legal framework against the EU values and principles of equality, solidarity and fair competition. Accordingly, a dual methodological approach, given by the combination of legal doctrinal analysis with an 'EU law in context' approach, is followed.

More specifically, this book relies on a 'legal doctrinal method' as a starting point for the analysis of the existing EU legal framework for posting of workers. The exegesis of the whole spectrum of relevant legal sources, involving an analysis of positive law, key rulings and literature, is indeed regarded as crucial for accurately identifying 'what the law is'.[49] In this respect, the prominent role of the Court of Justice in shaping the EU legal framework by means of interpretation of primary and secondary Union provisions and developing general principles is carefully observed.[50] Nonetheless, a pure 'black letter' approach, by its very nature, is not deemed sufficiently appropriate to deal with the myriad of implications arising from the multidimensional context of intra-EU temporary secondment of workforce under the freedom to provide services. Both the

49. Karen J. Alter, Renaud Dehousse and Georg Vanberg, 'Law, Political Science and EU Legal Studies: An Interdisciplinary Project?' (2002) 3 European Union Politics 113, 114–117; Terry Hutchinson and Nigel Duncan, 'Defining and Describing What We Do: Doctrinal Legal Research' (2012) 17 Deakin Law Review 83, 112; Jan M. Smits, 'What Is Legal Doctrine?: On the Aims and Methods of Legal-Dogmatic Research' in Rob van Gestel, Hans-W Micklitz and Edward L Rubin (eds), *Rethinking Legal Scholarship* (Cambridge University Press 2017) 227.
50. Takis Tridimas, *The General Principles of EU Law* (Second Edition, Oxford University Press 2007) 29; Mia Rönnmar, 'Labour Law in the Courts. The Role of European Case Law on Fundamental Trade Union Rights in an Evolving EU Industrial Relations System' in Ulla Neergaard, Ruth Nielsen and Lynn M. Roseberry (eds), *The Role of Courts in Developing a European Social Model – Theoretical and Methodological Perspectives* (Djøf Publishing 2010) 178; Vassilis Hatzopoulos, *Regulating Services in the European Union* (Oxford University Press 2012) 179–180; Vassilis Hatzopoulos, 'The Court's Approach to Services (2006-2012): From Case Law to Case Load?' (2013) 50 Common Market Law Review 459, 500; Rob Van Gestel, Hans-W Micklitz and Edward Rubin, 'Introduction' in Rob van Gestel, Hans-W Micklitz and Edward L Rubin (eds), *Rethinking Legal Scholarship* (Cambridge University Press 2017) 265.

main research question and the research sub-questions 3-5 necessarily require, indeed, a wider view on the concrete impact of the rules as well as on the material dimension of the posting phenomenon.

In this regard, an 'EU law in context' approach[51] is adopted, thus enabling to discern 'what the law ought to be' by grasping all the different facets of one of the most complex challenges that the European integration process is currently facing.[52] The practical functioning of the existing EU regulatory framework and the preconceptions underlying the 2018 legislative reform are, in this way, questioned by moving the focus away from only the strict 'letter of the law' towards the broader economic, social and political context at issue.[53] Notably, in countercurrent against the alleged general absence of an empirical basis for EU law scholarship,[54] empirical data collection and analysis constitute the ground for investigation of the actual quantitative dimension of the posting phenomenon and of its multifaceted impact on the EU labour market. Importantly, though, given the strictly theoretical nature of this book, no direct empirical research is thereby conducted. Reliance is placed, to that extent, on relevant empirical information already available in published research results. In addition, empirical evidence is collected for the delimitation and examination of the several issues emerged in the sector, involving both economic and sociological aspects, also

51. Robert Cryer et al., *Research Methodologies in EU and International Law* (First Edition, Hart Publishing 2011) 86–88; Jan M Smits, 'Law and Interdisciplinarity: On the Inevitable Normativity of Legal Studies' (2014) Critical Analysis of Law 1:1 (2014), 75–86, 12, 76; Mark Van Hoecke, 'Methodology of Comparative Legal Research' (2015) Law and Method <https://www.bjutijdschriften.nl/tijdschrift/lawandmethod/2015/12/RENM-D-14-00001> (accessed 30 April 2019); Laura Cahillane and Jennifer Schweppe (eds), *Legal Research Methods: Principles and Practicalities* (Clarus Press 2016) 27.
52. In this sense, Weiler's warning about the risks of adopting a pure dogmatic legal approach to EU law, and his invitation to take into due consideration the economic, social and political context in which the legal system is embedded, are fully endorsed. In particular, reference is made to Weiler's opinion that '[a pure dogmatic legal approach to EU law] might, however, lead to flawed analysis. It might be read (and has been read) as suggesting that the cardinal material locus of change has been the realm of law and that the principal actor has been the European Court. But this would be deceptive. Legal and constitutional structural change have been crucial, but only in their interaction with the Community political process.' And again that 'The plea for a "Law and ..." approach is of course de rigueur, be it Law and Economics, Law and Culture, Law and Society–Law in Context.' Joseph H.H. Weiler, 'The Transformation of Europe' (1991) 100 The Yale Law Journal 2403, 2407 and 2409.
53. On the necessity for EU legal scholarship to take into account the practical functioning of the rules in a wider context, *see* Ulla Neergaard and Marlene Wind, 'Studying the EU in Legal and Political Sciences Scholarship' in Ulla Neergaard and Ruth Nielsen (eds), *European Legal Method – In a Multi-Level EU Legal Order* (Djøf Publishing 2012) 278–279; Hutchinson and Duncan (n 49) 114; Frank Hendrickx, 'Completing Economic and Social Integration: Towards Labour Law for the United States of Europe' in Nicola Countouris and Mark Freedland (eds), *Resocialising Europe in a Time of Crisis* (Cambridge University Press 2013) 64; Gestel, Micklitz and Rubin (n 50) 2.
54. Rob Van Gestel and Hans-W Micklitz, 'Revitalizing Doctrinal Legal Research in Europe: What About Methodology?' in Ulla Neergaard, Ruth Nielsen and Lynn M Roseberry (eds), *European Legal Method – Paradox and Revitalisation* (Djøf Publishing 2011) 23–26; Catherine Barnard, 'The Calm after the Storm: Time to Reflect on EU (Labour) Law Scholarship Following the Decisions in Viking and Laval' (2015) University of Cambridge Faculty of Law Research Paper No. 55/2015, later published in Alan Bogg, Cathryn Costello and ACL Davies (eds), *Research Handbook on EU Labour Law* (Edward Elgar Publishing) 337, 18–20.

touching upon the sphere of industrial relations. When it comes to determining the opportunity and the measure of a legislative intervention at EU level within the intrinsically highly divisive sector of cross-border labour mobility, the use of empirical data is indeed considered indispensable in order to express an opinion as much as possible supported by scientific evidence.[55]

On top of that, the chosen method of analysis cannot refrain from referring to the intrinsic interaction between EU law and politics,[56] looking at the variety of interests at play, let alone the political motivations and consequences of certain normative interventions. In this way, the orientation of political influence during the drafting process of relevant EU legislation, especially in relation to the most recent reform of the Posting of Workers Directive, is taken into due account. This book draws some inspiration from arguments of political economy as well, for their ability to provide valuable insight and, consequently, an enrichment of the discussion on the actual impact of posting on the EU labour market and on the economic effects of the newly adopted Directive (EU) 2018/957. Political economy considerations are also taken into account at the points where the newly established legal framework for posting of workers is confronted with the EU value of solidarity and recommendations for future improvements are put forward. Finally, arguments of political philosophy are considered in the analysis of the EU values and principles of equality, solidarity and fair competition.

The methodological approach undertaken aims to be, therefore, both descriptive and normative at the same time. This book assumes a mostly descriptive character in the legal positivist analysis of the relevant EU legal framework for posting of workers, as well as in the investigation of the material dimension of the empirical phenomenon under consideration. In turn, it becomes progressively more normative when the new form of regulation established by Directive (EU) 2018/957 is tested against empirical findings and, eventually, evaluated in light of the EU values and principles of equality, solidarity and fair competition. Accordingly, the present research is evaluative in so far as is intended to test the practical functioning of the newly established legal framework, as well as the latter's alignment with desirable moral, political and economic aims.[57]

The chosen approach is reflected in the wide variety of sources used, including both legal and non-legal, written and non-written materials. The point of departure is the investigation of the conceptual framework of EU law, with particular reference to the provisions concerning the free movement of workers and services in the internal market. While constantly maintaining an EU law perspective, the following theoretical analysis is proposed to look closely at relevant EU labour law and social security law, with some reference to elements of private international law (PIL) and tax law. More specifically, the spectrum of legal sources examined consists of both normative and

55. Incidentally, the overall opportunity of the reform cannot be assessed on the basis of empirical evidence only, but necessarily involves considerations of a political kind.
56. Alter, Dehousse and Vanberg (n 49) 114, 117 and 120; Neergaard and Wind (n 53) 274–277 and 287.
57. Mark van Hoecke (ed.), *Methodologies of Legal Research: Which Kind of Method for What Kind of Discipline?* (Hart 2011) Preface v.

authoritative ones,[58] namely primary and secondary EU law, international conventions and national legislation, as well as Court of Justice case law, Advocate Generals' opinions and academic literature. Literature review, *inter alia*, holds a privileged position, encompassing a critical analysis of textbooks, articles, periodicals and papers. Further non-binding legal materials include preparatory documents produced during the various stages of the EU legislative process, such as Commission legislative proposals, Commission impact assessments, Council common positions and European Economic and Social Committee opinions.[59]

As mentioned earlier, besides traditional legal materials, this book relies also on further source categories typical of other social sciences, such as political science, industrial relations, political philosophy, economics and political economy. In this sense, documents and reports from EU Institutions and social partners, policy papers, policy letters, specialised journal articles, blog posts and media reports are taken into consideration, together with academic presentations at conferences, seminars, public events and public political speeches. In addition, in accordance with the great emphasis placed on the empirically proven actual dimension and impact of the intra-EU posting phenomenon, data collection and analysis in this sense are deemed crucial. Accordingly, the useful information provided by *Eurostat*[60] is included in the range of sources of statistical data. Given the absence of an EU-wide database with information about the number of posted workers across the European labour market, a method of data triangulation between different sources is adopted. Reference is made to the research work carried out by academic scholars and other independent researchers in the form of quantitative estimations or qualitative case studies, often reported in official studies drafted on behalf of the European Commission.

1.4 DELIMITATIONS

In line with the main purpose of this book to capture the wider picture stemming from the constantly evolving EU legal framework for posting of workers in light of the European integration process, the scope of the research has been narrowed down accordingly. In this sense, the Court of Justice case law is considered as one of the most valuable legal sources for determining the applicable legal regime for posting activities within the internal market. Nevertheless, albeit thorough research of the latter has been necessarily performed, no Court of Justice's case-by-case analysis *stricto sensu* –

58. As explained by van Hoecke, normative legal sources include 'statutory texts, treaties, general principles of law, customary law, binding precedents, and the like'. In turn, 'case law, if they are not binding precedents, and scholarly legal writings' are classified as authoritative sources. Mark van Hoecke, 'Legal Doctrine: Which Method(s) for What Kind of Discipline?' in Mark van Hoecke (ed.), *Methodologies of Legal Research: Which Kind of Method for What Kind of Discipline?* (Hart 2011) 11.
59. 'Preparatory Documents – EUR-Lex' (*EUR-Lex, Access to European Union Law*) <https://eur-lex.europa.eu/collection/eu-law/pre-acts.html> (accessed 8 May 2019).
60. Eurostat is a Directorate-General of the European Commission located in Luxembourg, responsible for providing high quality statistics for Europe.

i.e., involving an extensive presentation of the facts and circumstances of the proceedings under consideration – is provided. Such a kind of investigation would result, indeed, in an excessively long and dispersive analysis, likely to lose sight eventually of the book's primary goal. In the same vein, this book does not include any comprehensive analysis of national measures implementing acts of secondary EU legislation. However, such a delimitation does not exclude the possibility to refer, from time to time, to specific regulatory interventions adopted by certain Member States in the context at issue.

As noted above, the following analysis encompasses different areas of law. Nonetheless, given the choice made of restricting the number of legal sectors explored to EU law, EU labour law and EU social security law, the area of tax policy in the European Union remains excluded from the scope of this book. Reference is made only to the taxation regime generally applicable to posting situations, without looking into the different 'double taxation conventions' agreed between the Member States.

When dealing with the issue of social dumping, the emphasis is placed on the major role played by the phenomenon of undeclared work to that extent. The number of repercussions deriving from shadow economy is, by the way, presented as something apart from the legal practice of posting and only indirectly related to it. For this reason, undeclared economic activities are not investigated in detail.

Finally, the legal implications arising from Brexit remain out of the scope of this analysis. This is notwithstanding the relative importance of the United Kingdom (UK) in terms of share of both sent and received posted workers,[61] as well as in terms of comparatively lower tax rates and labour costs in comparison to the majority of the other EU Member States. In effect, Brexit may have a quite significant indirect impact on companies formally incorporated under UK law with the aim of delocalising their production facilities in the more convenient, when it comes to infrastructure and workforce costs, Central and Eastern European Countries. Nevertheless, data referring to the UK are still included in this book, as they had all been collected and analysed before the UK's exit from the European Union.

The implications of the Coronavirus (COVID-19) pandemic are, in turn, taken into consideration only to a limited extent. The quantitative dimension of the posting phenomenon has clearly been affected by a number of national measures exceptionally adopted in this respect with a view to limiting the movement of persons across borders. However, a proper analysis of this issue would be, for the time being, too premature as precise data are not available yet.

For the sake of consistency, a limitation to relevant sources in English has been made, also due to the fact that English has de facto become the leading language in the area of research under consideration. Cases, legal materials, data information, publications, etc. dated after 15 August 2020 are not included in this book.

61. Incidentally, it is worth mentioning that in the UK the issue of cheaper foreign workforce 'stealing local jobs' has been at the heart of both the 'Leave' and 'Remain' campaigns during the vote on Brexit in June 2016. Piet Van Nuffel and Sofia Afanasjeva, 'The Posting of Workers Directive Revised: Enhancing the Protection of Workers in the Cross-Border Provision of Services' (2018) 3 European Papers 1401, 1402.

1.5 OUTLINE

The dual nature of this book, being at the same time descriptive and normative, is reflected in its dynamic structure. While the first chapters (Chapters 2-8) are mostly descriptive of the phenomenon of posting of workers, focusing on both its EU legal framework and its material dimension, the later ones (partially Chapter 8, and Chapters 9 and 10) are intended to offer a more normative reflection on the direction taken by the European legislator with the most recent revision of the Posting of Workers Directive. This book is composed of ten chapters, including the present introductory chapter. With the exception of the introductory Chapter 1 and the concluding Chapter 10, all chapters follow the same structure consisting of an introduction, a number of substantive sections (often composed in their turn of subsections, which sometimes are divided into sub-subsections) and a concluding section presenting a recapitulation of and reflection on the main findings.

Following this Introduction, Chapter 2 contextualises the phenomenon of posting of workers under EU law. It introduces and properly defines the concepts of 'posting' and 'posted worker', bringing to light the inconsistencies between the Posting of Workers Directive and Regulation (EC) 883/2004 on the coordination of social security systems. At the same time, by emphasising the peculiar position of the phenomenon under consideration at the crossroads between conflicting economic interests of the parties concerned, it explores the rationale for the special treatment reserved to posted workers vis-à-vis migrant workers.

The following trio of chapters seeks to outline the EU regulatory framework governing the phenomenon of posting of workers before the entry into force of Directive (EU) 2018/957. The analysis starts, in Chapter 3, with the regulation of posting from the point of view of labour law. *In primis*, the law applicable to the employment relationship is individuated by making reference to the relevant EU rules in the area of private international law, whose peculiar interface with the Posting of Workers Directive is clearly emphasised. The original Posting of Workers Directive itself is then thoroughly examined, starting with its extremely interesting drafting history and carrying on with the exceptional terms and conditions of employment reserved to workers temporarily employed in the territory of another Member State.

The analysis of the regulation of posting under EU law goes on with Chapter 4, which mainly focuses on the interpretation and enforcement of the rules set out in the Posting of Workers Directive. In this sense, the considerable amount of Court of Justice case law related to the specification of the Member States' margin of appreciation in determining the elements of national law applicable to posting situations is accurately scrutinised. Afterwards, the chapter looks into the 2014 Enforcement Directive, presenting the whole spectrum of technical solutions introduced in order to enhance the degree of compliance with the Posting of Workers Directive. Lastly, the analysis takes a look at the most recent steps taken by the EU legislator towards the adoption of Directive (EU) 2020/1057 on posting drivers in the road transport sector.

The first area of regulation of the posting phenomenon at European level, namely that of coordination of national social security systems, is eventually dealt with in

Chapter 5. At that stage, the possibility for posted workers of remaining affiliated to their home country's social security scheme is examined by paying special attention to the number of conditions posed by the EU legislator, as interpreted by the Court of Justice over the years. Furthermore, the suggestions proposed on the occasion of the recent negotiations to revise the coordination rules are carefully assessed.

After concluding the analysis of the EU regulation of posting prior to the 2018 reform, the actual quantitative dimension of this peculiar form of intra-EU labour mobility is explored in Chapter 6. Based on empirical evidence, the seamless expansion of the phenomenon over the last few years is confronted with its relatively limited size and economic relevance in absolute terms. Moreover, this section reflects on the interesting dynamics of posting within the internal market, looking at the distribution of seconded workers by economic sector and the major trends of workforce mobility across the Member States. In this way, the popular stereotype that portrays the transnational posting as merely concerning low-skilled workers directed from the 'poorer' Central and Eastern to the 'richer' Western Member States is definitively debunked.

Subsequently, in Chapter 7, this book turns towards the investigation of the concrete impact of posting on the EU labour market. With the support of empirical evidence, a series of positive effects is demonstrated along with an overview of the several contentious issues encountered. The latter's effective incidence on the supposed absence of a level playing field for businesses and sufficient worker protection is ascertained by making a clear distinction between negative repercussions intrinsically related to the practice of posting and unlawful situations resulting from the misuse of this practice. In that regard, the direct correlation between posting of workers and 'social dumping' is critically questioned.

With a look to the future, the following couple of chapters are dedicated to an assessment of the direction undertaken by the EU legislator, in response to the increasingly mobile European labour market, with the adoption of the new Directive (EU) 2018/957. An in-depth analysis of such a controversial revision of the former labour rules is thereby conducted in Chapter 8, which encompasses its troubled birth process, its substantive content and the related expected outcomes. With a view to discerning the actual impact of the reform on the current state of play and, at the same time, identifying possible shortcomings, the range of novelties envisaged is tested against the findings emerged from the previous chapters.

A further normative perspective on the 2018 regulatory intervention is then developed in Chapter 9, where the resulting altered EU legal framework for posting of workers and, more broadly, the whole narrative underpinning the reform are evaluated in light of the EU values and principles of equality, solidarity and fair competition. After dealing with the main research question of this book, the normative arguments developed in the course of the analysis are eventually reconsidered in order to put forward some recommendations for future improvements in the field of posting of workers.

This book rounds off with the concluding Chapter 10, which recapitulates and puts together the main findings of all the previous chapters. Eventually, it concludes with a reflection on the need to pursue an idea of 'Social Europe' which, rather than merely preserving the integrity of the most advanced national social systems, promotes upward socio-economic convergence and cohesion at EU level.

1.6 CONCEPTS AND TERMINOLOGY

The analysis of the phenomenon of posting of workers necessarily entails the use of specific concepts and terms which allow to immediately refer to particular conditions and situations. Most importantly, this is the case of the so-called 'home Member State', 'country of origin' and 'sending country' which, for the purpose of this book, refer to the Member State whose law is objectively applicable to the employment relationship in light of Article 8 of the Rome I Regulation (EC) No 593/2008 on the law applicable to contractual obligations.[62] In a normal posting scenario, rather than to the country where the employer is established, it corresponds to the country of the worker's habitual place of work.[63] On the other hand, the 'host Member State', 'country of destination' and 'receiving country' refer to the Member State where the cross-border worker is directed in order to perform a working activity in the framework of the EU freedom of movement.

The above-mentioned differentiation makes it possible to understand the so-called 'country of origin' principle, also known as 'home state control', that implies the application of the law of the country of origin when a worker is employed in another Member State. Because of the resulting exportation of the law of the 'country of origin' to a different country, this circumstance is also referred to as 'regime portability'. In turn, the principle of *lex loci laboris*, also known as 'host state law' or territorial application of the law, means that the regulations of the host country fully apply to an employment relationship involving out-of-state migrant workers which, as a consequence, enjoy full equal treatment as local workers.

Another important terminological remark relates to the classification of the Member States into two macro-blocks reflecting the composition of the European Union prior to and after the 2004 and 2007 enlargements towards the East. Accordingly, the group of the 'old' EU Member States, also referred to as 'EU-15', includes Belgium, Greece, Luxembourg, Denmark, Spain, Netherlands, Germany, France, Portugal, Ireland, Italy, United Kingdom, Austria, Finland and Sweden; while the group of the 'new' EU Member States, or 'EU-13', includes Croatia, Romania, Bulgaria, Poland, Czech Republic, Latvia, Lithuania, Slovenia, Estonia, Slovakia, Hungary, Cyprus and Malta.

62. Regulation (EC) No 593/2008 of the European Parliament and of the Council of 17 June 2008 on the law applicable to contractual obligations (Rome I) 2008 (OJ L 177/6) (hereinafter also referred to as the 'Rome I Regulation').
63. Such a rule may help, indeed, to overcome the possible confusion created in case of discrepancy between the employer's state of establishment and the Member State where the employee habitually performs his work, or where he is recruited, or where he is a national citizen. van Hoek and Houwerzijl, 'Where Do EU Mobile Workers Belong, According to Rome I and the (E)PWD?' (n 7) 223–224.

Finally, it is clarified that the use of the generic 'he' is by no means used with sexist intentions, but rather as a mere grammatical practice aimed at favouring the fluency of the text. Accordingly, any reference to a person of a specific gender must be deemed also to constitute a reference to a person of any other gender.

CHAPTER 2

Defining 'Posting of Workers' in EU Law

2.1 INTRODUCTION

Posting of workers constitutes a relatively new form of intra-EU labour mobility, which has developed in the last years in order to serve the increasing need of work flexibility (both of workers and employers) within the internal market.[1] In essence, it allows companies to fully reap the opportunities offered by the EU freedom of movement and exploit their competitive advantage resulting from the special legal treatment reserved to their workers when temporarily posted across borders.[2] The latter workers, in their turn, may also benefit from new employment possibilities offered by the secondment across borders. In light of the intrinsically controversial nature of this cross-border phenomenon, a clear definition of the relevant EU legal framework is deemed to be a fundamental step towards the proper comprehension of the legal, social and economic implications involved, as well as the recognition of the future perspectives and challenges taking shape in the sector at issue. Accordingly, the purpose of the present

1. As punctually pointed out by Mussche et al.: 'Posting seems to be an adaptation to the realities of a culturally and linguistically very heterogeneous market. It is a response to the desire of EU citizens to remain permanently in their home country for cultural, linguistic and family reasons, while at the same time seizing economic opportunities posed by the EU free movements.' Ninke Mussche, Vincent Corluy and Ive Marx, 'The Rise of the Free Movements: How Posting Shapes a Hybrid Single European Labour Market' (2017) European Journal of Industrial Relations 16.
2. European Commission, *Employment and Social Developments in Europe 2014* (European Commission, Directorate Général for Employment, Social Affairs and Inclusion 2015) 156. In this sense, *see also* Herwig Verschueren, 'Cross-Border Workers in the European Internal Market: Trojan Horses for Member States' Labour and Social Security Law?' (2008) 24/2 International Journal of Comparative Labour Law and Industrial Relations 167, 198; Kristina Maslauskaite, 'Posted Workers in the EU: State of Play and Regulatory Evolution' (2014) Policy Paper, Notre Europe Jaques Delors Institute 20, 4; Herwig Verschueren, 'The European Internal Market and the Competition between Workers' (2015) 6 European Labour Law Journal 128, 129; Jens Arnholtz and Nathan Lillie, 'European Integration and the Reconfiguration of National Industrial Relations: Posted Work as a Driver of Institutional Change' in Jens Arnholtz and Nathan Lillie (eds), *Posted Work in the European Union: The Political Economy of Free Movement* (Routledge 2019) 8.

chapter is to provide a comprehensive overview of the different legal concepts underlying the type of labour mobility under consideration, with the aim of answering the research sub-question: *How is the 'posting of workers' defined under EU law?*

The starting point entails an identification of the peculiar legal position of posting of workers among different forms of intra-EU labour mobility. Thus, in section 2.2, the relevant primary EU law governing the phenomenon at stake is thoroughly examined. The distinguishing features among the freedom of movement for workers (Article 45 of the Treaty on the Functioning of the European Union (TFEU)),[3] the freedom of establishment (Article 49 TFEU) and the free provision of services (Article 56 TFEU) are addressed by taking into account the different forms of transnational labour migration within the European internal market. The measure of the influence of posting on, at the same time, the labour market of two (or more) Member States – namely the home state by temporary emigration of workforce and the host state(s) with temporary competition posed by incoming foreign workers – is then clearly emphasised. Importantly, the relevant novelty introduced by Directive (EU) 2018/957[4] with regard to the substantive shift in the posted workers' legal treatment is carefully explained.

An analytical definition of the concepts of 'posting' and 'posted worker' follows in section 2.3, underlying the several discrepancies existing between substantially different notions provided for by the relevant EU regulatory instruments. In particular, the red thread running through this section is a comparison between the relevant EU labour law – namely the Posting of Workers Directive 96/71/EC[5] in combination with the Enforcement Directive 2014/67/EU[6] – and EU social security law – namely Regulation (EC) 883/2004 on social security coordination[7] – with a specific focus on the changes brought about by the 2018 revision of the Posting of Workers Directive. Finally, towards the end of the same section, special attention is dedicated to the notion of 'temporary' nature of posting. The controversial character of this concept contributes indubitably to the gloomy atmosphere surrounding the sector at stake, resulting in an insurmountable obstacle to the achievement of a univocal definition of the posting activity at EU level. This chapter rounds off with the concluding section 2.4 whereby all different aspects leading to the determination of the concept of posting of workers are recapitulated. At the same time, the limits of the current regulatory framework are straightforwardly exposed.

3. Consolidated version of the Treaty on the Functioning of the European Union 2012 (OJ C 326/47) (hereinafter also referred to with its acronym 'TFEU').
4. Directive (EU) 2018/957 of the European Parliament and of the Council of 28 June 2018 amending Directive 96/71/EC concerning the posting of workers in the framework of the provision of services 2018 (OJ L 173/16).
5. Directive 96/71/EC of the European Parliament and of the Council of 16 December 1996 concerning the posting of workers in the framework of the provision of services 1997 (OJ L 18/1).
6. Directive 2014/67/EU of the European Parliament and of the Council of 15 May 2014 on the enforcement of Directive 96/71/EC concerning the posting of workers in the framework of the provision of services and amending Regulation (EU) No 1024/2012 on administrative cooperation through the Internal Market Information System ('the IMI Regulation') 2014 (OJ L 159/11).
7. Regulation (EC) No 883/2004 of the European Parliament and of the Council of 29 April 2004 on the coordination of social security systems 2004 (OJ L 166/1).

2.2 DIFFERENT FORMS OF INTRA-EU LABOUR MOBILITY

Within the common public discourse, there is a general feeling that identifies any foreign worker coming from a low-wage Member State, who performs a working activity (especially in the construction sector) in a high-wage Member State, as a posted worker.[8] Such a widespread misperception clearly testifies the current existence of a significant degree of uncertainty around the differences between labour mobility in the form of posting (in the framework of the freedom to provide services) and in the broader form of worker migration (under the freedom of movement for workers).[9] It goes without saying that a proper distinction in this sense is deemed to be essential in order to better understand and delineate the scope of the present analysis. Interestingly, the EU legislator seems to be of the same opinion when, in the Preamble of the Enforcement Directive 2014/67/EU, it states that: '[i]t is necessary for the purpose of the posting of workers to distinguish [the freedom to provide services] from the free movement of workers'.[10]

Over the years, three forms of labour mobility have emerged within the European Union: migration to another Member State under the provisions of the Treaty concerning the freedom of movement for workers and the freedom of establishment (Articles 45 and 49 TFEU), daily or weekly cross-border commuting covered by the freedom of movement for workers (Article 45 TFEU) and temporary mobility through posting of workers in the framework of the freedom to provide services (Article 56 TFEU).[11] In view of the complexity of the following analysis, a schematic representation of the legislation applying to each of the three forms of intra-EU labour mobility is provided in Table 2.1. To that extent, the elements of wage and labour conditions, social security contributions and personal income taxation are taken into consideration.

8. Stefan Schwarz and Marcin Kiełbasa, 'Posted or Sent in the Context of the Revision of Social Security Coordination Regulations' (2018) *Labour Mobility Initiative Association* 5, 4.
9. Roberto Pedersini and Massimo Pallini, 'Posted Workers in the European Union' (Eurofound 2010) 2.
10. Preamble Recital 2 of Directive 2014/67/EU of the European Parliament and of the Council of 15 May 2014 on the enforcement of Directive 96/71/EC concerning the posting of workers in the framework of the provision of services and amending Regulation (EU) No 1024/2012 on administrative cooperation through the Internal Market Information System ('the IMI Regulation') (n 6).
11. Catherine Barnard, *EU Employment Law* (Fourth Edition, Oxford European Union Law Library 2012) 143 and ff.; Frederic De Wispelaere and Jozef Pacolet, 'Posting of Workers as Stabilising Mechanism: An Enlarged Notion of Labour Mobility as a Prerequisite for an Optimal Currency Area' (KU Leuven Research Institute for Work and Society (HIVA) 2015) 5; Frederic De Wispelaere and Jozef Pacolet, 'An Ad Hoc Statistical Analysis on Short Term Mobility – Economic Value of Posting of Workers: The Impact of Intra-EU Cross-Border Services, with Special Attention to the Construction Sector' (KU Leuven Research Institute for Work and Society (HIVA) 2016) Research commissioned by DG EMPL within the framework of Contract VT/2015/096, 9; Harriet Bradley et al., '2017 Annual Report on Intra-EU Labour Mobility, Final Report' (European Commission 2018) KE-BQ-18-001-EN-N 21.

Table 2.1 Legislation That Applies to Intra-EU Labour Mobility[12]

	Migrant Workers (Articles 45 and 49 TFEU)	*Frontier Workers (Article 45 TFEU)*	*Posted Workers (Article 56 TFEU)*
	Migrating to a different Member State where they also work	*Working in a different Member State than the one of residence*	*Temporarily working in a different Member State than the one in which their employer is based*
Wage and labour conditions	**Host country** (Full equal treatment)	**Host country** (Full equal treatment)	**Minimum 'hard core' set of terms and conditions of the host country + same remuneration as local workers + allowances** and, after 12 (+6) months of posting, almost full equal treatment
Social security contributions	**Host country** (Full equal treatment)	**Host country** (Full equal treatment)	**Less than 24 months:** country of origin **More than 24 months:** host country
Personal income taxes	**Host country** (Full equal treatment)	**Less than 183 days per year:** country of residence **More than 183 days per year:** host country	**Less than 183 days per year:** country of origin **More than 183 days per year:** host country

2.2.1 Labour Mobility under Articles 45 and 49 TFEU

Labour migration of both dependent and independent (self-employed) workers under the freedom of movement for workers (Article 45 TFEU) and the freedom of establishment (Article 49 TFEU) has been traditionally considered by both European founders, policymakers and academia as the normal way of exercising free movement within the EU internal market.[13] By virtue of Article 45 TFEU, EU nationals are granted the right to work in a relationship of subordination with their employer – i.e., in an

12. *Source*: Author's own work, taking inspiration from Frederic De Wispelaere, 'Intra-EU Posting and the Threat of Social Dumping: A Comprehensive Assessment' (Industrial Relations in Europe Conference (IREC), Leuven, Belgium, 10 September 2018) 2.
13. Catherine Barnard and Jukka Snell, 'Free Movement of Legal Persons and the Provision of Services' in Catherine Barnard and Steve Peers (eds), *European Union Law* (Second Edition, Oxford University Press 2017) 377–378; Dries Lens, Ninke Mussche and Ive Marx, 'Europe's Ever Expanding Mobility Patterns – Posting, Third-Country Nationals and the Single European Labour Market' (2019) CSB Working Paper No. 19.08 University of Antwerp – Herman Deleeck Centre for Social Policy 3.

employed/dependent status – in another Member State. The nature of the employment relationship as dependent labour performed for a certain period of time, under the direction of an employer and in return of retribution, has been clarified by the Court of Justice in *Lawrie-Blum*.[14]

The freedom of movement for workers entails the abolition of any discrimination – direct or indirect – based on nationality between workers coming from different Member States as regards employment, remuneration and other working conditions. More specifically, it ensures the right for every EU citizen to move to another Member State in order to accept employment offers or to seek for a job, to reside there with their family for the purpose of employment and to remain in the new host country after having been employed.[15] Moreover, workers who move across the EU labour market under Article 45 TFEU are also subject to the general rule that the host country's social security legislation applies.[16] The framework of rights guaranteed to migrant workers is, therefore, guided by the so-called principle of *lex loci laboris*, which means that the regulations of the host country fully apply and migrant workers enjoy full equal treatment as local workers.[17] The application of this principle is justified by the fact that a person moving under Article 45 TFEU (dependent worker) fully accedes to the labour

14. *Deborah Lawrie-Blum v Land Baden-Württemberg* [1986] ECJ Case C-66/85, ECLI: EU:C:1986:284 [17]. On this point, *see* Siofra O'Leary, 'Free Movement of Persons and Services' in Paul Craig and Gráinne de Búrca (eds), *The Evolution of EU Law* (Second Edition, Oxford University Press 2011) 526–527; Barnard and Snell (n 13) 377.
15. Barnard, *EU Employment Law* (n 11) 156 and ff.; ACL Davies, *EU Labour Law* (Edward Elgar Publishing Ltd 2014) 72–73; Paul Craig and Gráinne de Búrca, *EU Law: Text, Cases, and Materials* (Sixth Edition, Oxford University Press 2015) 744 and ff.; Catherine Barnard, *The Substantive Law of the EU: The Four Freedoms* (Fifth Edition, Oxford University Press 2016) 243 and ff. *See also* Preamble Recital 2 of Directive 2014/67/EU of the European Parliament and of the Council of 15 May 2014 on the enforcement of Directive 96/71/EC concerning the posting of workers in the framework of the provision of services and amending Regulation (EU) No 1024/2012 on administrative cooperation through the Internal Market Information System ('the IMI Regulation') (n 6).
16. Article 11(3)(a) of Regulation (EC) No 883/2004 of the European Parliament and of the Council of 29 April 2004 on the coordination of social security systems (n 7). Frans Pennings, 'Principles of EU Coordination of Social Security' in Frans Pennings and Gijsbert Vonk (eds), *Research Handbook on European Social Security Law* (Edward Elgar Publishing 2015) 331; Rob Cornelissen and Guido Van Limberghen, 'Social Security for Mobile Workers and Labour Law', in *Research Handbook on European Social Security Law* (Edward Elgar Publishing 2015) 356; Jaan Paju, *The European Union and Social Security Law* (First Edition, Hart Publishing 2017) 31.
17. In other words, the same rights and duties of local workers are guaranteed also to workers moving across borders under Article 45 TFEU. IDEA Consult and ECORYS Netherlands, 'Study on the Economic and Social Effects Associated with the Phenomenon of Posting of Workers in the EU' (European Commission, Directorate-General Employment, Social Affairs and Equal Opportunities 2011) 49; Dagmar Schiek, *Economic and Social Integration: The Challenge for EU Constitutional Law* (Edward Elgar 2012) 149; Jan Cremers, 'EU Economic Freedoms and Social Dumping' in Magdalena Bernaciak (ed.), *Market Expansion and Social Dumping in Europe* (Routledge 2015) 174; Verschueren, 'The European Internal Market and the Competition between Workers' (n 2) 135; Catherine Barnard, 'The Commission's Proposal Deletes the Treaty Distinction between Migrant Workers and Posted Workers' (IV European Labour Mobility Congress (ELMC), Krakow (Poland), 7 November 2016) <https://www.elmc.eu/2016/the-commissions-proposal-deletes-the-treaty-distinction-between-migrant-workers-and-posted-workers-prof-catherine-barnards-speech-at-the-iv-european-labour-mobility-cong/> (accessed 13 May 2018).

market of the host state, where he is also willing to take part actively in the social environment.[18]

What is more, host state law finds application even in the situation of a self-employed worker – who is outside of a relationship of subordination – migrating within the European internal market as independent professional, in the exercise of his freedom of establishment.[19] Such a treatment is justified by the fact that, as specified by the Court in *Gebhard*,[20] a self-employed person establishing himself in a Member State other than his state of origin under Article 49 TFEU participates 'on a stable and continuous basis' in the economic life, hence in the labour market, of the host state.[21] Accordingly, he is entitled to pursue an economic activity by means of a permanent or settled place of business in the Member State of destination for an indefinite period of time, enjoying the same conditions as the nationals of the latter state. The same right is granted to companies, branches and agencies as well.[22] A self-employed person is also subject to the social security rules defined by the country where he carries out his work.[23]

Finally, the principle of *lex loci laboris* regulates also the case of the second form of intra-EU labour mobility, that of 'frontier workers' (also called 'cross-border commuters') and seasonal workers. These are individuals who live and reside in one Member State while working in another, where they are subject to the same wages and working conditions as local workers of the host state.[24] These workers move across

18. As stressed by the Court of Justice, the reason for equal treatment for migrant workers lies in the existence of a 'sufficient link of integration' with the host state's society, which follows, *inter alia*, from their financial contribution made to the social policies of the host state through the payment of taxes. *European Commission v Kingdom of the Netherlands* [2012] CJEU Case C-542/09, ECLI:EU:C:2012:346 [65–66]; *Elodie Giersch and Others v État du Grand-Duché de Luxembourg* [2013] CJEU Case C-20/12, ECLI:EU:C:2013:411 [63]. In this sense, *see* Charlotte O'Brien, *Unity in Adversity: EU Citizenship, Social Justice and the Cautionary Tale of the UK* (First Edition, Hart Publishing Ltd 2017) 35.
19. A definition of 'self-employed' worker may be found in the decision of the Court in *Jany*, where a series of requisites have been identified, namely the exclusion of any a relationship of subordination, the work under the own personal responsibility of the worker and in return of direct full payment. *Aldona Malgorzata Jany and Others v Staatssecretaris van Justitie* [2001] ECJ Case C-268/99, ECLI:EU:C:2001:616 [34 and 70–71]. Importantly, the 'self-employed' worker is protected by Article 49 TFEU against any restriction on his freedom of establishment in another Member State. Barnard, *The Substantive Law of the EU: The Four Freedoms* (n 15) 242.
20. *Reinhard Gebhard v Consiglio dell'Ordine degli Avvocati e Procuratori di Milano* [1995] ECJ Case C-55/94, ECLI:EU:C:1995:411.
21. *Ibid.* 25.
22. *The Queen v Secretary of State for Transport, ex parte Factortame Ltd and others* [1991] ECJ Case C-221/89, ECLI:EU:C:1991:320 [20]. On this point, *see* O'Leary (n 14) 528–529; Craig and de Búrca (n 15) 794–797; Barnard, *The Substantive Law of the EU: The Four Freedoms* (n 15) 382; Barnard and Snell (n 13) 378.
23. Article 11(3)(a) of Regulation (EC) No 883/2004 of the European Parliament and of the Council of 29 April 2004 on the coordination of social security systems (n 7). Paju (n 16) 31.
24. Frederic De Wispelaere and Jozef Pacolet, 'The Size and Impact of Intra-EU Posting on the Belgian Economy: With a Special Focus on the Construction Sector – Summary' (KU Leuven Research Institute for Work and Society (HIVA) 2017) 5.

borders regularly, and they are supposed to return to their country of residence 'as a rule daily or at least once a week'.[25]

2.2.2 Labour Mobility under Article 56 TFEU

Besides the aforementioned types of intra-EU labour mobility in the framework of the freedom of movement for workers and the freedom of establishment, the European labour market is currently facing high levels of workforce mobility finding its legal basis in the Treaty provisions concerning the freedom to provide services (Article 56 TFEU). In concrete terms, this third form of intra-EU labour mobility, called 'posting of workers', concerns the activity of a company sending ('posting') manpower for a limited period of time from one Member State (the sending or home state) to another Member State (the receiving or host state) in order to fulfil a contract of service supply.[26] Interestingly, from the perspective of the posted workers, their temporary cross-border mobility is construed as an expression of their employer's freedom to provide services. In other words, the posted workers are not providers of services themselves, as they move to another Member State under their employer's freedom to provide services.[27] *Inter alia*, it is worth noting that a further posting scenario can even take the shape of a self-employed person who temporarily posts himself to a different Member State with the purpose of rendering a particular service.[28]

Article 56 TFEU regulates the posting activity to the extent it entails the freedom of an employer, established in one Member State, to deliver a service in another

25. Article 1(f) of Regulation (EC) No 883/2004 of the European Parliament and of the Council of 29 April 2004 on the coordination of social security systems (n 7). Bradley et al. (n 11) 84.
26. Paul Davies, 'Posted Workers: Single Market or Protection of National Labour Law Systems?' (1997) 34 Common Market Law Review 571, 571–572; Craig and de Búrca (n 15) 835; Mia Rönnmar, 'Labour and Equality Law' in Catherine Barnard and Steve Peers (eds), *European Union Law* (Second Edition, Oxford University Press 2017) 608; Piet Van Nuffel and Sofia Afanasjeva, 'The Posting of Workers Directive Revised: Enhancing the Protection of Workers in the Cross-Border Provision of Services' (2018) 3 European Papers 1401, 1403.
27. Philippa Watson, *EU Social and Employment Law* (Second Edition, Oxford University Press 2014) 280; Dagmar Schiek, 'Perspectives on Social Citizenship in the EU – From Status Positivus to Status Socialis Activus via Two Forms of Transnational Solidarity' (2015) 4 Queen's University Belfast School of Law: Research Paper 2015 – 10, 12; Dagmar Schiek et al., 'EU Social and Labour Rights and EU Internal Market Law' (European Parliament, EMPL Committee 2015) IP/A/EMPL/ST/2014-02, 39; Claire Dhéret and Andreia Ghimis, 'The Revision of the Posted Workers Directive: Towards a Sufficient Policy Adjustment?' (2016) *European Policy Center (EPC) Discussion Paper* 5 <http://www.epc.eu/pub_details.php?cat_id=17&pub_id=6475> (accessed 23 October 2016); Dagmar Schiek, 'A Constitution of Social Governance for the European Union' in Nuno Ferreira and Dora Kostakopoulou (eds), *The Human Face of the European Union* (Cambridge University Press 2016) 39; Robert Schütze, *European Union Law* (Second Edition, Cambridge University Press 2018) 670.
28. It is noticeable, though, that the eventuality of a self-employed person who posts himself to another Member State is envisaged exclusively by the rules on social security, while any application of the PWD remains excluded. For a more detailed investigation on this point, *see infra* section 2.3. Wispelaere and Pacolet, 'The Size and Impact of Intra-EU Posting on the Belgian Economy: With a Special Focus on the Construction Sector – Summary' (n 24) 5; Bradley et al. (n 11) 21.

Member State.[29] More specifically, 'the freedom to provide services includes the right of undertakings to provide services in another Member State, to which they may post their own workers temporarily in order to provide those services there'.[30] In line with the clarification made by the Court of Justice in its landmark ruling in *Rush Portuguesa*,[31] the performance of a service by an EU-based employer may also be carried out by bringing all its own 'staff' from its country of origin to the country of destination.[32] In particular, the specific case at issue, by considering third-country national ('TCN', i.e., non-EU) workers also as employer's staff, denotes the loom of a further sub-form of labour mobility. According to that ruling, third-country nationals are free to enjoy all the gamma of EU free movement rights, as long as they are entitled to a work permit in an EU Member State.[33] Recent figures show, indeed, a constant growth of the number of TCNs entering the EU labour market by means of posting arrangements, in comparison to those following the regular path of requiring work permit and visa to national authorities of the host state. As a result, concerns have been expressed about

29. *Johannes Henricus Maria van Binsbergen v Bestuur van de Bedrijfsvereniging voor de Metaalnijverheid* [1974] ECJ Case 33-74, ECLI:EU:C:1974:131, 14 [11]. Barnard, *The Substantive Law of the EU: The Four Freedoms* (n 15) 290 and ff.; Eckhard Voss et al., 'Posting of Workers Directive: Current Situation and Challenges' (European Parliament, EMPL Committee 2016) IP/A/EMPL/2016-07, 14; Barnard and Snell (n 13) 415.
30. Preamble Recital 2 of Directive 2014/67/EU of the European Parliament and of the Council of 15 May 2014 on the enforcement of Directive 96/71/EC concerning the posting of workers in the framework of the provision of services and amending Regulation (EU) No 1024/2012 on administrative cooperation through the Internal Market Information System ('the IMI Regulation') (n 6).
31. *Rush Portuguesa Lda v Office national d'immigration* [1990] ECJ Case C-113/89, ECLI:EU:C:1990:142.
32. *Ibid.* 12; *Raymond Vander Elst v Office des Migrations Internationales* [1994] ECJ Case C-43/93, ECLI:EU:C:1994:310. On this point, *see* Werner Eichhorst, 'European Social Policy between National and Supranational Regulation: Posted Workers in the Framework of Liberalized Services Provision' (1998) MPIfG discussion paper, No. 98/6 *Max Planck Institute for the Study of Societies (MPIfG), Cologne* 14–15 <https://www.econstor.eu/bitstream/10419/43182/1/248171305.pdf> (accessed 17 January 2019); Barnard, *EU Employment Law* (n 11) 213; Mijke Houwerzijl, 'Regime Shopping across (Blurring) Boundaries' in Stein Evju (ed.), *Regulating Transnational Labour in Europe: The Quandaries of Multilevel Governance* (Department of Private Law 2014) 8; Nicola Countouris and Samuel Engblom, '"Protection or Protectionism?": A Legal Deconstruction of the Emerging False Dilemma in European Integration' (2015) UCL Labour Rights Institute On-Line Working Papers – LRI WP 14; Schütze (n 27) 670.
33. Hence, the fact that third-country nationals can be posted within the entire European labour market allows, in practice, the circumvention of the work permit procedures required in certain countries. Mussche, Corluy and Marx (n 1) 3. The possibility of employing TCNs for the transnational provision of services, and the consequent prohibition of any sort of discrimination and limitation to that extent, has been confirmed in a number of subsequent decisions. *Inter alia, see Raymond Vander Elst v Office des Migrations Internationales* (n 32); *Commission of the European Communities v Grand Duchy of Luxemburg* [2004] ECJ Case C-445/03, ECLI:EU:C:2004:655. Interestingly, on February 1999, a draft Directive specifically concerning the posting of workers of third-country nationals was proposed by the Commission, although without success. European Commission, Communication on the posting of workers who are third-country nationals for the provision of cross-border services 1999 [COM(1999) 3 final]. On this point, *see* Vassilis Hatzopoulos, *Regulating Services in the European Union* (Oxford University Press 2012) 199–201.

the possible undermining of the Member States' sovereignty in the field of migration policy and regulation.[34]

In light of the foregoing, labour mobility in the form of posting of workers is evidently employer-driven, unlike the worker-driven type of labour mobility represented by worker migration under the freedom of movement for workers and the freedom of establishment.[35] In effect, in case of mobility under Article 56 TFEU, the initiative, responsibility and costs of the posting fall entirely on the employer, who exercises its freedom to provide services in another Member State from the one it is established in. From this standpoint, it is clear that the posted workers' chances to benefit from the economic opportunities offered by the secondment across borders are directly dependent on their employer's competitiveness. Conversely, migrant workers move actively to another Member State in order to work there or to look for a job, by bearing all the costs connected with the setting up in a new country (included travel and accommodation). Hence, unlike posted workers, they are economically autonomous. In other words, the mobility of workers posted under Article 56 TFEU can be considered as 'passive', in contrast to the 'active' character of the mobility exercised by workers migrating under Article 45 or 49 TFEU.[36]

The placement of the phenomenon of posting of workers in the framework of the Treaty rules governing the free provision of services is the result of the interpretation of the Court of Justice in the above-mentioned famous ruling in *Rush Portuguesa* as well. On that occasion, the judges in Luxembourg, by making use of their wide discretionary power, established de facto a new legal basis for the peculiar intra-EU movement of workforce at issue.[37] As further specified in subsequent decisions, such an approach was justified by the distinguishing feature, characterising the type of mobility under consideration, of the performance of an economic activity on a 'temporary' basis.[38] Looking closely at this definition, the existence of the first requirement – i.e., the economic nature of the activity carried out – is deemed to constitute a 'decisive factor' in order to consider the activity within the scope of the Treaty provisions, and it is presumed whenever the working performance is being rewarded with remuneration, as in the case of posting.[39]

34. Ninke Mussche and Dries Lens, 'The EU Free Movement of Services and the Growing Mobility of Third-Country Nationals as Posted Workers' (2018) CSB Working Paper No. 18.13 University of Antwerp – Herman Deleeck Centre for Social Policy; Lens, Mussche and Marx (n 13).
35. Wispelaere and Pacolet, 'An Ad Hoc Statistical Analysis on Short Term Mobility – Economic Value of Posting of Workers: The Impact of Intra-EU Cross-Border Services, with Special Attention to the Construction Sector' (n 11) 13.
36. Aukje A.H. van Hoek and Mijke Houwerzijl, '"Posting" and "Posted Workers": The Need for Clear Definitions of Two Key Concepts of the Posting of Workers Directive' (2012) 14 Cambridge Yearbook of European Legal Studies 419, 422, 445–446; Houwerzijl (n 32) 21; Wispelaere and Pacolet, 'Posting of Workers as Stabilising Mechanism: An Enlarged Notion of Labour Mobility as a Prerequisite for an Optimal Currency Area' (n 11) 11.
37. *Rush Portuguesa Lda v Office national d'immigration* (n 31) paras 10–11. For more detailed analysis of the case at issue, *see infra* Chapter 3.
38. *Ibid.* 15.
39. *Hans-Dieter Jundt and Hedwig Jundt v Finanzamt Offenburg* [2007] CJEU Case C-281/06, ECLI:EU:C:2007:590 [32]. Catherine Barnard, 'Free Movement of Natural Persons and Citizenship of the Union' in Catherine Barnard and Steve Peers (eds), *European Union Law* (Second Edition, Oxford University Press 2017) 375–376.

With regard to the temporary character, as specified by the Court in *Trojani*,[40] the eventuality of a service supply lasting for an indefinite period, or having permanent duration, would fall outside the scope of the rules concerning the free provision of services.[41] Unfortunately, though, a univocal definition of the concept of 'temporary' nature of the work supply is not provided for by the Treaty. Nevertheless, looking at the interpretation of the judges in Luxembourg, it is possible to discern the essence of such a relevant factor by individuating differentiation traits - besides the several overlapping aspects involved - between the freedom of movement for workers under Articles 45 and 49 TFEU and the mobility under Article 56 TFEU. In this sense, in the *Gebhard*[42] case, the Court of Justice, on the one hand, pointed out the 'stable and continuous basis' of the performance of the economic activity as a decisive feature characterising the situation of establishment, attested by the presence of an economic base in the host country. On the other hand, it acknowledged that, despite the presence of some form of infrastructure necessary for the actual exercise of a service supply in the host state, the temporary nature of the activity is to be determined 'in the light, not only of the duration of the provision of the service, but also of its regularity, periodicity or continuity'.[43] Interestingly, however, this determination appears in sharp contrast to the decision taken in *Insurance Services*,[44] where the Court prevented an undertaking, which maintained a permanent office in the host Member State (Germany), from the possibility of enjoying the freedom to provide services in that country. In the case at issue, it considered that, because of the permanent character of the economic infrastructure in the host country, the activity carried out by the undertaking would fall within the scope of the rules concerning the freedom of establishment.[45]

Another obstacle, particularly relevant in the context of posting of workers, towards the identification of the temporary or permanent nature of the economic activity performed is the extended duration of certain service provisions, such as the restructuring or construction of a large building. Nevertheless, even in such eventualities where the service supply might last a long time, even several years, and hence a distinction between situations covered by Article 56 and others falling under Article

40. *Michel Trojani v Centre public d'aide sociale de Bruxelles (CPAS)* [2004] ECJ Case C-456/02, ECLI:EU:C:2004:488.
41. *Ibid.* 28. On this point, *see* Houwerzijl (n 32) 19; Barnard, *The Substantive Law of the EU: The Four Freedoms* (n 15) 302.
42. *Reinhard Gebhard v Consiglio dell'Ordine degli Avvocati e Procuratori di Milano* (n 20).
43. *Ibid.* 25–27. In the same direction, *see also Commission of the European Communities v Italian Republic* [2003] ECJ Case C-131/01, ECLI:EU:C:2003:96 [22]; *Bruno Schnitzer* [2003] ECJ Case C-215/01, ECLI:EU:C:2003:662 [28]. The possibility for a service provider to set up agencies, branches or subsidiaries has been acknowledged as well by the Court of Justice in *Michel Trojani v Centre public d'aide sociale de Bruxelles (CPAS)* (n 40) para. 27. Houwerzijl (n 32) 18–19; Craig and de Búrca (n 15) 798–799; Barnard, 'Free Movement of Natural Persons and Citizenship of the Union' (n 39) 378–379.
44. *Commission of the European Communities v Federal Republic of Germany (Insurance Services)* [1986] ECJ Case C-205/84, ECLI:EU:C:1986:463.
45. Besides, the Court recognised also that the activity of service provision entirely or principally directed towards the state where the undertaking has its permanent office, but where it had chosen not to establish itself, constitutes an abuse of Article 56 TFEU (at that time Article 59 of the EEC Treaty). *Ibid.* 21–22. Craig and de Búrca (n 15) 820; Barnard, *The Substantive Law of the EU: The Four Freedoms* (n 15) 426–427.

49 results complicated, the Court has generally considered it included within the scope of the freedom to provide services.[46] Conversely, the only borderline situation in which the Court of Justice recognised the cross-border service provision as governed by the rules concerning the freedom of establishment, instead of the freedom to provide services, is the one in which it ascertained an abuse of Article 56 TFEU. The rare case at issue involved individuals who deliberately set their place of establishment in another Member State, from which they provided the most of their services directed to their country of origin, with the sole purpose of evading the more restrictive professional rules of the latter country. The judges in Luxembourg came to this conclusion on two occasions, namely in *Veronica*[47] and *TV10*,[48] both involving the compatibility with Article 56 TFEU of a Dutch law prohibiting a provider of broadcasting services to invest in companies in the same economic sector in other Member States, as long as they directed the major part of their services towards the Netherlands. The Dutch regulation was, indeed, conceived for the purpose of stemming the phenomenon of national companies setting up broadcasting branches in Luxembourg with the exclusive aim of circumventing national rules by taking advantage of the freedom to provide services across borders.[49] In such situations, the burden of proving the actual existence of abuse remained on the state, which was required to demonstrate the supplier's intention to evade legitimate impositions, rather than effectively benefitting from the Treaty provisions on free movement. For the record, however, the cases in which the Court adopted such an approach remain very limited, and the subsequent rulings seemed to be more focused on fostering the exercise of free movement rights within the European single market.[50]

Finally, getting back to the reasoning developed by the Court in *Rush Portuguesa*, the further criterion for distinction between labour mobility under Article 45 TFEU and under Article 56 TFEU was that of 'labour market access'. The argument offered by the Court on that occasion was that, in case of mobility in the framework of Article 56 TFEU, the posted worker never seeks access to the host country labour market. This is because of the temporary nature of the service provision across borders, whereby the worker normally returns to his home state after the completion of his assignment

46. Notably, in *Commission v Portugal*, the Court declared incompatible with Article 56 TFEU the imposition, by Portugal, of authorisation rules for construction activities requiring the same duties on both temporary and established service providers. *European Commission v Portuguese Republic* [2010] CJEU Case C-458/08, ECLI:EU:C:2010:692. *See also Bruno Schnitzer* (n 43) para. 30. Vassilis Hatzopoulos and Thien Uyen Do, 'The Case Law of the ECJ Concerning the Free Provision of Services: 2000 - 2005' (2006) 43 Common Market Law Review 923, 927–928; O'Leary (n 14) 533; Houwerzijl (n 32) 18–19; Craig and de Búrca (n 15) 820–821; Schiek et al. (n 27) 35; Alexis Lubow and Susanne K Schmidt, 'A Hidden Champion? The European Court of Justice as an Agenda-Setter in the Case of Posted Workers' (2020) Public Administration (John Wiley & Sons Ltd.) 1, 7.
47. *Vereniging Veronica Omroep Organisatie v Commissariaat voor de Media* [1993] ECJ Case C-148/91, ECLI:EU:C:1993:45.
48. *TV10 SA v Commissariaat voor de Media* [1994] ECJ Case C-23/93, ECLI:EU:C:1994:362.
49. Craig and de Búrca (n 15) 821; Barnard, *The Substantive Law of the EU: The Four Freedoms* (n 15) 427.
50. In this sense, *see VT4 Ltd v Vlaamse Gemeenschap* [1997] ECJ Case C-56/96, ECLI:EU:C:1997:284 [22]; *Centros Ltd v Erhvervs- og Selskabsstyrelsen* [1999] ECJ Case C-212/97, ECLI:EU:C:1999:126 [27].

abroad.[51] In turn, a person who migrates under Article 45 or 49 TFEU to another Member State, where he concludes an employment contract with an employer established there or simply seeks for a job, undoubtedly accedes to the employment market of the host state.

Very interestingly, though, on one occasion the line between the free movement of services and the free movement of workers appeared to be not so well marked. In the decision in *Vicoplus*,[52] the category of posted agency workers[53] (unlike those of workers posted intra-group or through subcontracting) was considered as acceding de facto to the labour market of the host state, given that those workers are 'typically assigned [...] to a post within the user undertaking which would otherwise have been occupied by a person employed by that undertaking'.[54] It would seem, therefore, that the activity of hiring-out posted agency workers, in light of its impact on the labour market of the host Member State, could be governed not only by Article 56 TFEU but also by certain elements of equal treatment typical of Article 45 TFEU.[55] Nevertheless,

51. *Rush Portuguesa Lda v Office national d'immigration* (n 31) para. 15. It is worth noting that, in the two subsequent decisions in *Vander Elst* and *Finalarte*, the posted workers' return to their country of origin after the completion of their assignment abroad was de facto indicated as a condition for benefitting from the rules on free movement of services. *Raymond Vander Elst v Office des Migrations Internationales* (n 32) para. 21; *Finalarte Sociedade de Construção Civil v Urlaubs- und Lohnausgleichskasse der Bauwirtschaft* [2001] ECJ Joined Cases C-49/98, C-50/98, C-52/98 to C-54/98 and C-68/98 to C-71/98, ECLI:EU:C:2001:564, 22. On this point, *see* Paul Davies, 'The Posted Workers Directive and the EC Treaty' (2002) 31 Industrial Law Journal 298, 300; Verschueren, 'Cross-Border Workers in the European Internal Market: Trojan Horses for Member States' Labour and Social Security Law?' (n 2) 174–175; Stein Evju, 'Posting Past and Present: The Posting of Workers Directive – Genesis and Current Contrasts' (2009) 8 FORMULA Working Paper, University of Oslo, Department of Private Law 13; van Hoek and Houwerzijl, '"Posting" and "Posted Workers": The Need for Clear Definitions of Two Key Concepts of the Posting of Workers Directive' (n 36) 445–446; Stein Evju and Tonia Novitz, 'The Evolving Regulation: Dynamics and Consequences' (2012) 33 FORMULA Working Paper, University of Oslo, Department of Private Law 14; Barnard, *The Substantive Law of the EU: The Four Freedoms* (n 15) 422–423; Mijke Houwerzijl and Lisa Berntsen, 'Posting of Workers: From a Blurred Notion Associated with "Cheap Labour" to a Tool for "Fair Labour Mobility"?' in Jens Arnholtz and Nathan Lillie (eds), *Posted Work in the European Union: The Political Economy of Free Movement* (Routledge 2019) 148.
52. *Vicoplus SC PUH, BAM Vermeer Contracting sp zoo and Olbek Industrial Services sp zoo v Minister van Sociale Zaken en Werkgelegenheid* [2011] CJEU Joined cases C-307/09, C-308/09 and C-309/09, ECLI:EU:C:2011:64.
53. For a definition of this particular form of posting envisaged by Article 1(3)(c) of the PWD, *see infra* sub-subsection 2.3.1.1.
54. *Vicoplus SC PUH, BAM Vermeer Contracting sp. zoo and Olbek Industrial Services sp. zoo v Minister van Sociale Zaken en Werkgelegenheid* (n 52) paras 30–31. *See* Monika Schlachter, 'Equal Treatment for Transnational Temporary Agency Workers?' in Stein Evju (ed.), *Regulating Transnational Labour in Europe: The Quandaries of Multilevel Governance* (Universitetet i Oslo, Det Juridiske Facultet 2014) 268; Marco Rocca, *Posting of Workers and Collective Labour Law: There and Back Again* (Intersentia 2015) 205–208, 210–211.
55. *Alfred John Webb* [1981] ECJ Case C-279/80, ECLI:EU:C:1981:314 [10]; *Vicoplus SC PUH, BAM Vermeer Contracting sp. zoo and Olbek Industrial Services sp. zoo v Minister van Sociale Zaken en Werkgelegenheid* (n 52) para. 28. Aukje A.H. van Hoek and Mijke Houwerzijl, 'Comparative Study on the Legal Aspects of the Posting of Workers in the Framework of the Provision of Services in the European Union' (2011) 185–186; Rocca (n 54) 207; Verschueren, 'The European Internal Market and the Competition between Workers' (n 2) 146; Schiek et al. (n 27) 43–44. On the special treatment reserved to temporary agency posted employees, *see infra* Chapter 3.

the actual measure of such a partial inclusion of these particular channels of mobility under the rules on the free movement of workers still remains rather unclear.[56]

2.2.3 Posted Workers' Special Legal Treatment

The absolute importance of the aforementioned differentiation between labour mobility under Articles 45 and 49 TFEU or under Article 56 TFEU lies in the fact that it permits to identify the law governing the employment relationship between the employer and the worker (at least until the entry into effect of the new Directive (EU) 2018/957). While in the first case the principle of *lex loci laboris* (host state law) applies, in the second case, the posted workers' overall terms and conditions of employment have traditionally been set by their country of origin (home state law), thus not by the state of destination (host state) where the work is actually performed.[57] The peculiarity of the posted workers' legal position is thus evident, given the relevance of more than one legal system. In fact, while the employment contract is concluded in their country of origin, the actual performance of the service is carried out in another Member State (host state).[58]

The adoption of the so-called 'country of origin' principle, also known as 'home state control', fundamentally resolved the potential conflict between overlapping regulations of two different Member States.[59] The case of posting represents, therefore, an exception to the general principle of territorial application of the labour and social security law of the Member States, designed to ensure equal treatment to all workers moving within the EU internal market.[60] In effect, while the posted workers perform a service supply in another Member State, the law of their home country – i.e., normally that of the country where the posting company is established – is usually designated as the one applicable to the employment relationship. Nevertheless, by virtue of the Posting of Workers Directive, besides the general application of the home state law, employees who were temporarily posted to another Member State are also guaranteed a minimum core of terms and conditions of employment as nationals of the host state, determined by the host Member State.[61] Crucially, therefore, the posted workers do not

56. Houwerzijl (n 32) 22–27; Rocca (n 54) 205–208, 210–211; Verschueren, 'The European Internal Market and the Competition between Workers' (n 2) 146.
57. Barnard, *EU Employment Law* (n 11) 215; Barnard, 'Free Movement of Natural Persons and Citizenship of the Union' (n 39) 378–379; Barnard, 'The Commission's Proposal Deletes the Treaty Distinction between Migrant Workers and Posted Workers' (n 17).
58. Houwerzijl (n 32) 10.
59. Barnard, *The Substantive Law of the EU: The Four Freedoms* (n 15) 424; Evju (n 51) 21; Evju and Novitz (n 51) 4.
60. Verschueren, 'Cross-Border Workers in the European Internal Market: Trojan Horses for Member States' Labour and Social Security Law?' (n 2) 196; Verschueren, 'The European Internal Market and the Competition between Workers' (n 2) 148; Jan Cremers, 'Market Integration, Cross-Border Recruitment, and Enforcement of Labour Standards – A Dutch Case' in Jens Arnholtz and Nathan Lillie (eds), *Posted Work in the European Union: The Political Economy of Free Movement* (Routledge 2019) 128. On this point, *see infra* Chapters 3 and 5.
61. Article 3(1) of Directive 96/71/EC of the European Parliament and of the Council of 16 December 1996 concerning the posting of workers in the framework of the provision of services (n 5). For a detailed analysis of the content of Article 3(1) *see infra* Chapter 3.

traditionally enjoy full equal treatment as local workers, as their employment relationship remains subject to a sort of mitigated principle of *lex loci laboris*.[62]

The peculiar type of intra-EU labour mobility under consideration represents an exception also with regard to the principle applicable in the field of social security. Even in this case, in derogation from the general rule requiring an employed or self-employed person to be affiliated to the social security system of the country where he is working, the peculiar position of the posted workers allows them to remain under their home state regime.[63] Yet, such a condition finds a limit in Regulation (EC) 883/2004 on the coordination of social security systems, which sets the roof of twenty-four months as the maximum period for application of the social security legislation of the sending Member State.[64] This means that, for example, Belgian social security rules do not apply to a worker posted to Belgium from another Member State in an ordinary posting situation. He remains subject to the legislation of his home state, where he pays his social security contributions – and of course, this amount may differ from those applied in Belgium – unless the duration of the cross-border temporary secondment exceeds the maximum limit of twenty-four months.[65]

As far as the taxation regime for posting of workers is concerned, on that front too, a difference between posted workers and migrant workers is respected. Unlike persons migrating under Article 45 TFEU towards another Member State, the posted workers are exempted from paying personal income taxes in the Member State of temporary employment for a certain period of time.[66] Notably, in the absence of EU coordinating tax rules determining which Member State is entitled to levy tax income during short-term periods of mobility abroad, the 'double taxation conventions',

62. Evju and Novitz (n 51) 37–38; Catherine Barnard, 'EU Employment Law and the European Social Model: The Past, the Present and the Future' (2014) 67 Current Legal Problems 199, 219; Watson (n 27) 286; Uglješa Grušić, *The European Private International Law of Employment* (Cambridge University Press 2015) 278; Schiek, 'Perspectives on Social Citizenship in the EU' (n 27) 12; Schiek et al. (n 27) 39–40; Cornelissen and Van Limberghen (n 16) 344; Barnard, 'The Commission's Proposal Deletes the Treaty Distinction between Migrant Workers and Posted Workers' (n 17).
63. Article 12 of Regulation (EC) No 883/2004 of the European Parliament and of the Council of 29 April 2004 on the coordination of social security systems (n 7). Watson (n 27) 289; Jan Cremers, 'Economic Freedoms and Labour Standards in the European Union' (2016) 22(2) Transfer: European Review of Labour and Research 149, 175.
64. Article 12 of Regulation (EC) No 883/2004 of the European Parliament and of the Council of 29 April 2004 on the coordination of social security systems (n 7). It remains possible, according to Article 16 of Regulation 883/2004, for two or more Member States, by common agreement, to provide for exceptions to this rule, therefore to consent a posted worker to exceed the period of 24 months and continuing to remain integrated in the social security regime of his home country. Watson (n 27) 290; Wispelaere and Pacolet, 'The Size and Impact of Intra-EU Posting on the Belgian Economy: With a Special Focus on the Construction Sector – Summary' (n 24) 5. It is worth noting that the EU social security rules currently in force impose also a further series of conditions for benefitting of the special treatment reserved to posted workers. The latter are extensively analysed *infra* in Chapter 5.
65. In such an eventuality, the posted worker falls under the social security regime of the host state for the entire duration of the labour mobility. For a detailed analysis of the social security rules for posted workers, *see infra* Chapter 5.
66. Wispelaere and Pacolet, 'An Ad Hoc Statistical Analysis on Short Term Mobility – Economic Value of Posting of Workers: The Impact of Intra-EU Cross-Border Services, with Special Attention to the Construction Sector' (n 11) 11.

agreed between the Member States along the lines of the OECD Model Convention on Income and on Capital,[67] allow the posted workers to remain under the taxation regime of their home state for a maximum (aggregate) period of 183 days within a period of twelve months starting or ending in the fiscal year concerned.[68]

The derogation to the principle of equal treatment between local and posted workers was traditionally justified in light of the intrinsic nature of posting. Already in *Manpower*,[69] an early case of 1970 concerning the payment of social security contributions by temporary agency workers, the Court of Justice motivated such an approach with the need to protect both the employers and the workers from obstacles likely to restrict their freedom of movement. In particular, with a view to encouraging economic interpenetration within the European internal market, it ruled in favour of the avoidance of costly administrative complications for workers, employers and social security organisations.[70] Furthermore, as mentioned above, an important peculiarity of the workers involved is that they do not seek access to the labour market of the host State, considering that they return to their home country after the completion of their work.[71] Consequently, the substantial differentiation of the rules applying to posting activities is motivated by the particular situation at issue. In principle, given the temporariness of their service provision, limited to the strict duration of their work, the

67. OECD (Organisation for Economic Co-operation and Development), *Model Tax Convention on Income and on Capital: Condensed Version, 21 November 2017* (OECD Publishing 2017).
68. *Ibid.* Article 15 (2). Evidently, the purpose of this exception is, rather than to benefit the employee, to protect the employer against double fiscal burdens and loss of tax deductions. Furthermore, the cross-border employment may, in certain case, qualify the employer for special tax reductions, granted by the sending or receiving countries in order to compensate for the extra costs deriving from posting workers abroad. Kristina Maslauskaite, 'Social Competition in the EU: Myths and Realities' (2013) Policy Paper, Notre Europe Jaques Delors Institute 62, 28–30; Wispelaere and Pacolet, 'Posting of Workers as Stabilising Mechanism: An Enlarged Notion of Labour Mobility as a Prerequisite for an Optimal Currency Area' (n 11) 8 and 12–14; Voss et al. (n 29) 26–27; Frans Pennings, 'Mismatches between Tax and Social Security in Cross Border Situations' (Workshop on 'Tax and Social Security – EU Perspective', University of Copenhagen, Faculty of Law, 20 September 2017); Aukje A.H. van Hoek, 'Re-Embedding the Transnational Employment Relationship: A Tale about the Limitations of (EU) Law?' (2018) 55 Common Market Law Review 449, 460 and 472.
69. *Manpower v Caisse primaire d'assurance maladie de Strasbourg* [1970] ECJ Case C-35/70, ECLI:EU:C:1970:120.
70. Interestingly, in *Manpower* the posting of temporary agency workers was conceived under the freedom of movement of workers while, thirty years later, in *FTS* and *Plum* it was considered by the same Court as (mainly) covered by the rules concerning the freedom to provide services, albeit maintaining a link to the free movement of workers. *Ibid.* 10; *Fitzwilliam Executive Search Ltd v Bestuur van het Landelijk instituut sociale verzekeringen* [2000] CJEU Case C-202/97, ECLI:EU:C:2000:75 [28]; *Josef Plum v Allgemeine Ortskrankenkasse Rheinland, Regionaldirektion Köln* [2000] ECJ Case C-404/98, ECLI:EU:C:2000:607 [19]; *Altun* [2018] CJEU Case C-359/16, ECLI:EU:C:2018:63 [32]. Houwerzijl (n 32) 28. On this point, *see infra* Chapter 3.
71. *Rush Portuguesa Lda v Office national d'immigration* (n 31) para. 15; *Raymond Vander Elst v Office des Migrations Internationales* (n 32) para. 21; *Finalarte Sociedade de Construção Civil v Urlaubs- und Lohnausgleichskasse der Bauwirtschaft* (n 51) para. 22. Craig and de Búrca (n 15) 796. On the particular relevance of the decision in *Finalarte*, notably on the difference with the previous judgments in *Rush Portuguesa* and *Vander Elst*, *see* Verschueren, 'Cross-Border Workers in the European Internal Market: Trojan Horses for Member States' Labour and Social Security Law?' (n 2) 174–177.

posted workers do not integrate within the labour market of the Member State of destination.[72]

The existing normative balance, entailing only a partial application of the *lex loci laboris*, has, nonetheless, recently been altered by the adoption of the famous Directive (EU) 2018/957. This act of secondary EU legislation, besides acknowledging the temporary nature of the type of labour mobility at issue, recognising that 'posted workers usually return to the Member State from which they were posted after completion of the work for which they were posted',[73] sensibly extends the spectrum of terms and conditions of employment that the host Member State is entitled to apply to incoming posted workers. While leaving the in-depth technical analysis of the latter EU legislative act to Chapter 8, it is worth pointing out here that this Directive essentially brings about a progressive shift from the application of the rules governing the free provision of services according to Article 56 TFEU (i.e., home state law) to the application of those typical of the free movement of workers under Article 45 TFEU (i.e., host state law). Notably, this shift effectively materialises in cases of long-term posting, whereby the posted workers are treated almost as fully-fledged migrant workers. In fact, in accordance with the new provisions, in such an event, the host Member State is entitled to apply 'all the applicable terms and conditions of employment'[74] to the posted workers, thus nearly replacing de facto the principle of the 'country of origin' with that of *lex loci laboris*.

2.3 THE CONCEPTS OF 'POSTING' AND 'POSTED WORKER'

A proper definition of 'posting' and 'posted worker' is considered to be essential in the perspective of reaching an effective implementation of the rules. This first step represents, on the one hand, the indispensable prerequisite for a substantial detection of genuine posting situations and, on the other hand, the key to the enhancement of effective monitoring of the sector and, consequently, to the prevention of law abuses and circumventions. A definition of both the concepts of 'posting of workers' and of 'posted worker' may be found in two EU regulatory instruments, namely the Posting of Workers Directive (hereby considered after the amendments introduced by the new Directive (EU) 2018/957) and Regulation (EC) 883/2004 on social security coordination (*see* Table 2.2). Interestingly, though, when looking more closely at those acts of secondary EU legislation, the first thing that becomes clear is the existence of a substantial mismatch between the two different notions of 'posted worker' and 'posted person' respectively provided therein.[75]

72. European Commission – Employment, Social Affairs & Inclusion, 'Posted Workers' < https://ec.europa.eu/social/main.jsp?catId = 471 > (accessed 3 April 2019).
73. Preamble Recital 9 of Directive (EU) 2018/957 of the European Parliament and of the Council of 28 June 2018 amending Directive 96/71/EC concerning the posting of workers in the framework of the provision of services (n 4).
74. *Ibid.* Article 1(2)(b).
75. For an in-depth comparative analysis of the notions of 'posted worker' and of 'posted person' referred to in the PWD and in the Basic Regulation on social security respectively, *see* Schwarz and Kiełbasa (n 8) 6. *See also* Cornelissen and Van Limberghen (n 16) 370; Frederic De

Table 2.2 Notions of 'Posted Worker/Person' under the Posting of Workers Directive (As Amended by Directive (EU) 2018/957) and the Basic Regulation on Social Security Coordination[76]

Posting of Workers Directive 96/71/EC (as Amended by Directive (EU) 2018/957)	*Regulation (EC) 883/2004 on Social Security Coordination*
Article 2 (1) – Posted worker: 'a worker who, for a limited period, carries out his work in the territory of a Member State other than the State in which he normally works [when his employer **Article 1(3)**]: (a) posts him to the territory of a Member State on his account and under his direction, under a contract concluded between the undertaking making the posting and the party for whom the services are intended, operating in that Member State, provided there is an employment relationship between the undertaking making the posting and the worker during the period of posting; [or] (b) posts him to an establishment or to an undertaking owned by the group in the territory of a Member State, provided there is an employment relationship between the undertaking making the posting and the worker during the period of posting; [or] (c) being a temporary employment undertaking or placement agency, hire out a worker to a user undertaking established or operating in the territory of a Member State, provided there is an employment relationship between the temporary employment undertaking or placement agency and the worker during the period of posting.'	**Article 12 (1) – Posted person:** 'a person who pursues an activity as an employed person in a Member State on behalf of an employer which normally carries out its activities there and who is posted by that employer to another Member State to perform work on that employer's behalf shall continue to be subject to the legislation of the first Member State, provided that the anticipated duration of such work does not exceed 24 months and that he/she is not sent to replace another posted person.' (or) **Article 12(2) – Posted self-employed person:** 'a person who normally pursues an activity as a self-employed person in a Member State who goes to pursue a similar activity in another Member State shall continue to be subject to the legislation of the first Member State, provided that the anticipated duration of such activity does not exceed 24 months.'

The prospect above clearly shows all the relevant differences between the definitions provided for by the EU legislator in the two referring documents. In

Wispelaere and Jozef Pacolet, 'Posting of Workers: Report on A1 Portable Documents Issued in 2017' (KU Leuven Research Institute for Work and Society (HIVA) 2018) European Commission, Directorate-General for Employment, Social Affairs and Inclusion 8; Frederic De Wispelaere, Lynn De Smedt and Jozef Pacolet, 'Coordination of Social Security Systems at a Glance: 2018 Statistical Report' (KU Leuven Research Institute for Work and Society (HIVA) 2018) European Commission, Directorate-General for Employment, Social Affairs and Inclusion Unit D/2 12.

76. *Source*: Author's own work, taking inspiration from Schwarz and Kiełbasa (n 8) 2.

particular, the use of the same notion of 'posted' worker or person to describe different situations is evident.[77] The following analysis intends to clarify the problematic context at issue by individuating a definition of 'posting' and of 'posted worker' within such diverse EU regulatory instruments.

2.3.1 Posting under the Posting of Workers Directive

In the first paragraph of Article 1 of the Posting of Workers Directive, it is possible to identify three elements characterising the posting activity.[78] In accordance with the legal basis of the Directive itself in the Treaty provisions establishing the freedom to provide services, it entails situations involving (a) a cross-border service supply, (b) provided by an undertaking established in a Member State (sending country), (c) which sends ('posts') its own workers to another Member State (receiving country).[79] From the wording of the European legislator, the existence of a genuine employment relationship between the posted worker and his employer in the country of origin – i.e., the company established in the home state – appears, therefore, essential. In other words, it is not disputed that the activity carried out by an employee posted to a different EU country has to be regulated by a direct employment contract signed by the employee himself with his employer in the home country.[80] Naturally, it follows that workers moving independently towards another Member State for the purpose of reaching an employment agreement with an undertaking established in that country – namely migrant or self-employed workers – remain excluded from this scenario.[81]

77. Such a conceptual inconsistency has been noticed by the Commission, which proposed the introduction of an additional notion of 'sent person' in its 2016 proposal for the revision of Regulation (EC) 883/2004. The notion of 'sent persons' was intended as a broader concept, including both workers posted in accordance with the PWD, self-employed persons and other persons who are covered by the Basic Regulation only. European Commission, Proposal for a Regulation of the European Parliament and of the Council amending Regulation (EC) No 883/2004 on the coordination of social security systems and regulation (EC) No 987/2009 laying down the procedure for implementing Regulation (EC) No 883/2004, 2016 [COM(2016) 815 final]. In this sense, *see* Schwarz and Kiełbasa (n 8) 2 and 4. For an in-depth investigation of the 2016 Commission's proposal to amend Regulation (EC) 883/2004, *see infra* Chapter 5.
78. 'This Directive shall apply to undertakings established in a Member State which, in the framework of the transnational provision of services, post workers, in accordance with paragraph 3, to the territory of a Member State.' Article 1(1) of Directive 96/71/EC of the European Parliament and of the Council of 16 December 1996 concerning the posting of workers in the framework of the provision of services (n 5).
79. van Hoek and Houwerzijl, 'Comparative Study on the Legal Aspects of the Posting of Workers in the Framework of the Provision of Services in the European Union' (n 55) 30.
80. Jan Cremers, 'In Search of Cheap Labour in Europe – Working and Living Conditions of Posted Workers' (2011) CLR News 6, 7–8; Barnard, *EU Employment Law* (n 11) 219.
81. Davies, 'Posted Workers: Single Market or Protection of National Labour Law Systems?' (n 26) 575–576; Rocca (n 54) 2–3; Voss et al. (n 29) 14; Frederic De Wispelaere and Jozef Pacolet, 'Measuring the Size of Intra-EU Posting on the Basis of Data Collected at European and National Level' (Conference Intra-EU posting: costs and benefits, Leuven, Belgium, 28 April 2017); Frederic De Wispelaere and Jozef Pacolet, 'Coordination of Social Security Systems at a Glance: 2017 Statistical Report' (KU Leuven Research Institute for Work and Society (HIVA) 2017) European Commission, Directorate-General for Employment, Social Affairs and Inclusion Directorate D – Labour Mobility Unit D/2 – Social security coordination 16; Wispelaere and Pacolet, 'Posting of Workers: Report on A1 Portable Documents Issued in 2017' (n 75) 8;

Nonetheless, it is worth stressing that, by virtue of Article 2(2) of the Posting of Workers Directive, the individuation of the elements constituting the notion of a 'worker' is still reserved to the host Member State.[82]

With regard to the material elements constituting a posting undertaking, as specified by the Enforcement Directive 2014/67/EU, it has to be a genuine company, properly established in the country from which the posting takes place (the sending state), from which it 'genuinely performs substantial activities, other than purely internal management and/or administrative activities'.[83] The criteria for determining whether an employer actually carries out substantial activities in its state of origin are indicated by the EU legislator and relate to all the specific features of each employer, as well as to the real nature of the business carried out.[84] Importantly, then, the reason of the posting must reside in a commercial contract for the temporary provision of services, stipulated between the company settled in the sending country and another one - user/client undertaking - established in a receiving country, towards which the service supply has to be performed.

2.3.1.1 *Three Posting Patterns*

The Posting of Workers Directive, in the third paragraph of Article 1, clearly specifies three possible configurations of a posting arrangement and, hence, three different posting patterns. The first and most obvious pattern envisages the stipulation of a contract for the transnational provision of the services in question, concluded between the undertaking making the posting and the party for whom the services are intended, according to which the workers are sent to the territory of another Member State on the account and under the direction of their employer.[85] Besides the case of a company

Wispelaere, Smedt and Pacolet (n 75) 12. By the way, it is worth noting that a distinction between a self-employed person posting himself to another Member State in order to provide a service and a posted worker is, in practice, sometimes very complicated to make. Relevant consequences in terms of legal treatment obviously follow, given that the first one only is a full-fledged service provider exempted from the application of the host state's minimum set of labour standards. Marc De Vos, 'Free Movement of Workers, Free Movement of Services and the Posted Workers Directive: A Bermuda Triangle for National Labour Standards?' (2006) 7 ERA Forum - Springer 356, 358.

82. Interestingly, therefore, the possible conflict of laws arising in the case of a posted self-employed person who performs activities which are considered as wage-earner activities by the host state, has to be resolved in light of Article 2(2) of the PWD, whereby 'the definition of a worker is that which applies in the law of the Member State to whose territory the worker is posted'. Accordingly, in such an event, the person would be considered, for all intents and purposes, as a posted worker subject to the nucleus of terms and conditions of employment set by the host state.
83. Article 4(2) of Directive 2014/67/EU of the European Parliament and of the Council of 15 May 2014 on the enforcement of Directive 96/71/EC concerning the posting of workers in the framework of the provision of services and amending Regulation (EU) No 1024/2012 on administrative cooperation through the Internal Market Information System ('the IMI Regulation') (n 6).
84. On the specific content of the Enforcement Directive 2014/67/EU, *see infra* Chapter 4.
85. Article 1(3)(a) of Directive 96/71/EC of the European Parliament and of the Council of 16 December 1996 concerning the posting of workers in the framework of the provision of services (n 5).

sending abroad its own employees to provide services directly to a recipient in the receiving country, the scenario at issue entails most often the situation of subcontracting, whereby the workers are seconded to another EU country to execute a contract stipulated between their home undertaking and another undertaking in the host state (user undertaking).[86] Through this arrangement, the main contractor in the host state outsources single specialities or tasks to out-of-state subcontractors.[87] Furthermore, a borderline practice, yet developed within the limits of this regulatory context, foresees the creation of 'subcontracting chains'.[88]

The second form of posting envisaged by the Posting of Workers Directive is the so-called 'intra-group' posting. It concerns the situation of an employee sent to another Member State to work to an establishment or an undertaking owned by the same group of the original employer, in respect of whom he still remains in a relationship of subordinate employment.[89] In concrete terms, this situation reflects an administrative arrangement within a company or group of companies, according to which a person employed in a certain place of business in his home country is seconded to a branch or subsidiary located in another Member State.[90]

The third and last scenario concerns the labour supply provided by a temporary work agency or a placement agency established in the home state, in favour of a user undertaking located or operating in the territory of a different Member State.[91] More

86. In such an occurrence, large construction companies (in terms of turnover), established in the Member State of destination of the service, often operate as principal contractors acting as site managers on large construction projects, while small and medium-sized companies function as subcontractors, providing the majority of workforce. Wispelaere and Pacolet, 'An Ad Hoc Statistical Analysis on Short Term Mobility – Economic Value of Posting of Workers: The Impact of Intra-EU Cross-Border Services, with Special Attention to the Construction Sector' (n 11) 16–17. *See also* Davies, 'Posted Workers: Single Market or Protection of National Labour Law Systems?' (n 26) 576; van Hoek and Houwerzijl, 'Comparative Study on the Legal Aspects of the Posting of Workers in the Framework of the Provision of Services in the European Union' (n 55) 5; IDEA Consult and ECORYS Netherlands (n 17) 285; Evju and Novitz (n 51) 31; van Hoek and Houwerzijl, '"Posting" and "Posted Workers": The Need for Clear Definitions of Two Key Concepts of the Posting of Workers Directive' (n 36) 433–434; Maslauskaite (n 2) 8.
87. Incidentally, subcontracting has become extremely popular in the building and construction sector, as well as in other industries and service sectors, such as shipbuilding, transport, tourism and cleaning industry. Yves Jorens, Saskia Peters and Mijke Houwerzijl, 'Study on the Protection of Workers' Rights in Subcontracting Processes in the European Union (Final Study)' (Ghent University, Department of Social Law (in consortium with University of Amsterdam) 2012) DG EMPL/B2-VC/2011/0015; European Commission, Impact Assessment, Accompanying the document Proposal for a Directive of the European Parliament and the Council amending Directive 96/71/EC concerning the posting of workers in the framework of the provision of services 2016 [SWD(2016) 52 final] 14–15.
88. For a definition of such 'subcontracting chains' and an overview of the several risks connected with their use, *see infra* Chapter 7.
89. Article 1(3)(b) of Directive 96/71/EC of the European Parliament and of the Council of 16 December 1996 concerning the posting of workers in the framework of the provision of services (n 5).
90. The recourse to intra-company posting is primarily made by multinational companies, and to a limited extent also by specialised small and medium-sized enterprises (SMEs) with international activities. IDEA Consult and ECORYS Netherlands (n 17) 151.
91. Davies, 'Posted Workers: Single Market or Protection of National Labour Law Systems?' (n 26) 576; van Hoek and Houwerzijl, 'Comparative Study on the Legal Aspects of the Posting of Workers in the Framework of the Provision of Services in the European Union' (n 55) 30;

specifically, while a 'temporary work agency' (TWA) directly hires its own employees which are, only in a second stage, hired out to a third undertaking, a 'placement agency' (or 'employment agency') acts as an agent between prospective employees and employers.[92] The posting activity through temporary agency work is characterised by a triangular relationship between three parties: a worker is employed by an agency and is then hired out to perform work assignments at a user undertaking in the state of destination, on the basis of a commercial contract between the temporary work agency and the latter company.[93] In this case, the employment relationship between the temporary employment agency and the worker must be preserved during the whole period of posting, but temporary agency workers perform their job under the control and direction of the user company in the host state.[94] Unlike the typical posting situation where the workers' mobility is driven by the performance of a service contract, here the movement of temporary agency workers to different Member States constitutes 'the very purpose' of the provision of services.[95]

In light of the foregoing classification, it is worth noting that the category of workers sent to another Member State, but still providing services in favour of their employer situated in their home country, remains excluded from the notion of posting under the Posting of Workers Directive. In such an eventuality, indeed, the cross-border element required by the EU free movement rules is missing, since no service is provided to any recipient located in another Member State. This is the case, in

Schlachter (n 54) 264. Importantly, it should be noted that cross-border activities of temporary work agencies are regulated by the PWD in combination with Directive 2008/104/EC of the European Parliament and of the Council of 19 November 2008 on temporary agency work 2008 (OJ L 327/9) (hereinafter also referred to as the 'Temporary Agency Work Directive' or with its acronym 'TAWD'). On the interplay between the PWD and the TAWD, *see infra* Chapter 3.

92. Schiek et al. (n 27) 42.
93. Eurofound (European Foundation for the Improvement of Living and Working Conditions), 'Temporary Agency Work in Europe' (27 January 1999) <https://www.eurofound.europa.eu/observatories/eurwork/comparative-information/temporary-agency-work-in-europe> (accessed 18 May 2018); IDEA Consult and ECORYS Netherlands (n 17) 50–51.
94. Article 1(3)(c) of Directive 96/71/EC of the European Parliament and of the Council of 16 December 1996 concerning the posting of workers in the framework of the provision of services (n 5). *See also Vicoplus SC PUH, BAM Vermeer Contracting sp. zoo and Olbek Industrial Services sp. zoo v Minister van Sociale Zaken en Werkgelegenheid* (n 52). More specifically, the agency remains the only employer responsible for payment of the worker's salary and social security contributions, as well as for compliance with labour standards, health and safety legislation. Davies, 'Posted Workers: Single Market or Protection of National Labour Law Systems?' (n 26) 576; Schiek et al. (n 27) 42.
95. This concept was specified by the Court of Justice in *Vicoplus SC PUH, BAM Vermeer Contracting sp. zoo and Olbek Industrial Services sp. zoo v Minister van Sociale Zaken en Werkgelegenheid* (n 52) para. 46. *See also Alfred John Webb* (n 55) para. 9; *Essent Energie Productie BV v Minister van Sociale Zaken en Werkgelegenheid* [2014] CJEU Case C-91/13, ECLI:EU:C:2014:2206 [33]; *Martin Meat kft v Géza Simonfay and Ulrich Salburg* [2015] CJEU Case C-586/13, ECLI:EU:C:2015:405 [33]. On this point, *see* European Commission, Impact Assessment, Initiative to partially revise Regulation (EC) No 883/2004 of the European Parliament and of the Council on the coordination of social security systems and its implementing Regulation (EC) No 987/2009, Accompanying the document Proposal for a regulation of the European Parliament and of the Council amending Regulation (EC) No 883/2004 on the coordination of social security systems and regulation (EC) No 987/2009 laying down the procedure for implementing Regulation (EC) No 883/2004, 2016 [SWD(2015) 460 final] 15–16. *See also* Barnard, *EU Employment Law* (n 11) 219.

particular, not only of tour operators, film crews, commercial travellers and other representatives but also of workers on business trips, attending conferences, meetings or fairs.[96] A further contentious situation concerns the trainees who are sent abroad as part of their training programme, but who do not properly offer a cross-border service supply in favour of a service recipient in another Member State.[97] This category is generally excluded from the scope of the Posting of Workers Directive as well, even if those people might be considered, to some extent, as service recipients themselves. In turn, employees active in two or more Member States[98] are normally covered by the range of terms and conditions laid down in the Posting of Workers Directive, and thus subsumed under its broader notion of 'posted workers'.[99] This is usually the case of workers in the road transport sector (i.e., truck drivers) which, unlike the seagoing personnel of merchant navy undertakings,[100] fall undoubtedly within the personal scope of the Directive.[101] Nonetheless, the new rules on posting will be applicable to cabotage and non-bilateral international transport activities only, and not to transit,

96. Davies, 'Posted Workers: Single Market or Protection of National Labour Law Systems?' (n 26) 576; Aukje A.H. van Hoek and Mijke Houwerzijl, 'Complementary Study on the Legal Aspects of the Posting of Workers in the Framework of the Provision of Services in the European Union' (2011) 286–287; European Commission, 'Practical Guide on Posting' (2019) 7.
97. van Hoek and Houwerzijl, 'Complementary Study on the Legal Aspects of the Posting of Workers in the Framework of the Provision of Services in the European Union' (n 96) 286.
98. Notably, an employed person active in two or more Member States is defined as a person who: '(a) while maintaining an activity in one Member State, simultaneously exercises a separate activity in one or more other Member States, irrespective of the duration or nature of that separate activity; [or] (b) continuously pursues alternating activities, with the exception of marginal activities, in two or more Member States, irrespective of the frequency or regularity of the alternation.' In turn, a self-employed person working simultaneously in two or more Member States is defined as a person who 'simultaneously or in alternation pursues one or more separate self-employed activities, irrespective of the nature of those activities, in two or more Member States'. These definitions are provided by Article 14(5) and (6) of Regulation (EC) No 987/2009 of the European Parliament and of the Council of 16 September 2009 laying down the procedure for implementing Regulation (EC) No 883/2004 on the coordination of social security systems 2009 (OJ L 284/1). Importantly, as already pointed out *supra*, self-employed persons who are active in two or more Member States remain excluded from the personal scope of the PWD due to the lack of an employment relationship with any employer in their home country.
99. European Commission, 'Practical Guide on the Applicable Legislation in the European Union (EU), the European Economic Area (EEA) and in Switzerland' (Social Europe, European Commission, Employment, Social Affairs and Equal Opportunities 2013) 24; Frederic De Wispelaere and Jozef Pacolet, 'Posting of Workers: Report on A1 Portable Documents Issued in 2015' (KU Leuven Research Institute for Work and Society (HIVA) 2016) European Commission, Directorate-General for Employment, Social Affairs and Inclusion Unit D/2 12; Wispelaere and Pacolet, 'Measuring the Size of Intra-EU Posting on the Basis of Data Collected at European and National Level' (n 81); Wispelaere, Smedt and Pacolet (n 75) 12.
100. This category of workers is expressly excluded by the PWD's scope, pursuant to Article 1(2) of Directive 96/71/EC of the European Parliament and of the Council of 16 December 1996 concerning the posting of workers in the framework of the provision of services (n 5).
101. The application of the PWD to cabotage activities is expressly confirmed by Preamble Recital 17 of Regulation (EC) No 1072/2009 of the European Parliament and of the Council of 21 October 2009 on common rules for access to the international road haulage market 2009 (OJ L 300/72). Nevertheless, as punctually emphasised by van Hoek and Houwerzijl, the borderline condition of road transport workers results evident in the fact that they 'do not work in a specific country but rather from a specific country'. van Hoek and Houwerzijl, 'Comparative Study on the Legal Aspects of the Posting of Workers in the Framework of the Provision of Services in the European Union' (n 55) 36 and 187.

bilateral transport operations and the road leg of combined transport anymore, as soon as the newly adopted Directive (EU) 2020/1057 on posting drivers in the road transport sector[102] will enter into effect at the end of its implementation period on 2 February 2022.[103]

2.3.1.2 'Posted Worker' under the Posting of Workers Directive

As far as the employee involved in the posting activity is concerned, in line with Article 2(1) of the Posting of Workers Directive – which has remained untouched by the 2018 legislative reform – the posted worker is defined as 'a worker who, for a limited period, carries out his work in the territory of a Member State other than the State in which he normally works'. Three elements can be hereby identified.[104] At first, the existence of a working relationship is necessary and, to this extent, the status of a worker is determined by the law of the Member State where a person is posted.[105] Accordingly, it is possible that a person who is not considered as a 'worker' in his home country could be classified as such in the host Member State where he temporarily delivers a service.[106]

As clearly stated by the Directive, a second requirement consists of the temporary nature of the posting. In this respect, the original text of the Posting of Workers Directive did not provide any specification about the actual duration of the limited period of time.[107] The only clarification in this sense was provided by the Court of

102. Directive (EU) 2020/1057 of the European Parliament and of the Council of 15 July 2020 laying down specific rules with respect to Directive 96/71/EC and Directive 2014/67/EU for posting drivers in the road transport sector and amending Directive 2006/22/EC as regards enforcement requirements and Regulation (EU) No 1024/2012, 2020 (OJ L 249/49). For an analysis of the aforementioned new piece of EU legislation, *see infra* Chapter 4.
103. Article 3(3) of Directive (EU) 2018/957 of the European Parliament and of the Council of 28 June 2018 amending Directive 96/71/EC concerning the posting of workers in the framework of the provision of services (n 4). On this point, *see* European Commission Impact Assessment, Accompanying the document Proposal for a Directive of the European Parliament and the Council amending Directive 96/71/EC concerning the posting of workers in the framework of the provision of services (n 87) 50; European Commission – Employment, Social Affairs & Inclusion (n 72).
104. van Hoek and Houwerzijl, 'Comparative Study on the Legal Aspects of the Posting of Workers in the Framework of the Provision of Services in the European Union' (n 55) 30; Cremers, 'In Search of Cheap Labour in Europe – Working and Living Conditions of Posted Workers' (n 80) 7-8; van Hoek and Houwerzijl, '"Posting" and "Posted Workers": The Need for Clear Definitions of Two Key Concepts of the Posting of Workers Directive' (n 36) 424; Jan Cremers, 'Posting of Workers in Practice' (2018) INT-AR Paper 8 Tilburg Law School.
105. Article 2(2) of Directive 96/71/EC of the European Parliament and of the Council of 16 December 1996 concerning the posting of workers in the framework of the provision of services (n 5).
106. Watson (n 27) 285.
107. van Hoek and Houwerzijl, 'Comparative Study on the Legal Aspects of the Posting of Workers in the Framework of the Provision of Services in the European Union' (n 55) 187. Strikingly, the concept of 'limited period' was not even discussed during the whole drafting process of the PWD, and neither by the Court of Justice in occasion of its landmark decision in *Rush Portuguesa Lda v Office national d'immigration* (n 31). On this point, *see* Evju and Novitz (n 51) 30. For the record, the only form of temporal limit (consisting in eight days or one month) for the exemption from the respect of minimum rates of pay and/or minimum annual paid

Justice, which recognised the incompatibility of an indefinite or endless duration of this form of cross-border secondment.[108] Nevertheless, the new Directive (EU) 2018/957 introduced a remarkable innovation in this regard with the setting of a twelve-month limit (with a possible extension to eighteen months) after which postings lasting for a longer period of time must abide the whole more stringent rules of the host Member State.[109]

The third and last element formulated by the Posting of Workers Directive requires the posted worker to carry out his cross-border activity in a country different from the one 'in which he normally works'.[110] In this regard, as specified by the Court in its recent decision in *Dobersberger*,[111] in order to consider a worker as effectively 'posted', the performance of the working activity must have a sufficient connection with the territory of the receiving Member State.[112] Besides, in line with a strict reading of the aforementioned provision, the existence of a habitual place of work plays a key role in the identification of a posting situation, with the consequent exclusion of all cases where the worker has not been previously employed in his home country. A more precise and literal analysis of Article 2(1) of the Posting of Workers Directive indicates, however, the non-necessary identity between the employer in favour of which the work is normally performed in the country of origin and the employer that is responsible for the posting. This second reading of the requirement prescribed by the Directive seems also more consistent with the provisions set out in the social security Regulation (EC) 883/2004. In fact, the requirement for a posted worker to be already covered by the social security scheme in his home country in order to benefit from the faculty to remain subject to the latter's regime does not specifically imply the existence of any previous engagement of the posted worker with the posting undertaking.[113]

---

holidays, concerns only few specific cases in which an ad hoc authorisation is granted by the receiving Member State. Article 3(2)(3)(4)(5)(6) of Directive 96/71/EC of the European Parliament and of the Council of 16 December 1996 concerning the posting of workers in the framework of the provision of services (n 5). Watson (n 27) 285 and 288. On this point, *see infra* Chapter 3.

108. The indefinite or permanent duration of posting has been, indeed, excluded by the Court of Justice from the ambit of application of the rules concerning the free provision of services. *Michel Trojani v Centre public d'aide sociale de Bruxelles (CPAS)* (n 40) para. 28.
109. Preamble Recital 9 and Article 1(2)(b) of Directive (EU) 2018/957 of the European Parliament and of the Council of 28 June 2018 amending Directive 96/71/EC concerning the posting of workers in the framework of the provision of services (n 4). Given the contentious nature of the temporary condition of posting, a more detailed analysis is provided in subsection 2.3.3 below.
110. Article 2(1) of Directive 96/71/EC of the European Parliament and of the Council of 16 December 1996 concerning the posting of workers in the framework of the provision of services (n 5).
111. *Michael Dobersberger v Magistrat der Stadt Wien* [2019] CJEU Case C-16/18, ECLI: EU:C:2019:1110.
112. *Ibid.* 31–35. In the case at issue, due to the lack of sufficient connection with the territory of the receiving country, the Court excluded from the personal scope of the PWD those workers providing on-board services, such as cleaning, food and drink services for railway passengers on international trains. Notably, the above-mentioned activity was excluded from the scope of Article 1 of the PWD, given that a significant part of the work was still carried out in the workers' home country.
113. Article 12 of Regulation (EC) No 883/2004 of the European Parliament and of the Council of 29 April 2004 on the coordination of social security systems (n 7). van Hoek and Houwerzijl, 'Comparative Study on the Legal Aspects of the Posting of Workers in the Framework of the

Finally, in order to determine whether a person is to be considered as a posted worker under Article 2(2) of the Posting of Workers Directive, another act of secondary EU legislation can be helpful. The 2014 Enforcement Directive, indeed, expressly indicates a list of elements to be taken into account for the assessment, namely the limited duration of the working activity, the actual existence of the cross-border element, the fact that the posted worker returns to or is expected to resume working in his home country after completion of the service supply, as well as the coverage of all mobility costs by the employer.[114]

2.3.2. Mismatch with Regulation (EC) 883/2004

As outlined *supra*, the definition of posting is not identical in the Posting of Workers Directive (and the Enforcement Directive 2014/67/EU) and in the Basic Regulation on social security coordination, even though a few similarities may be found as well.[115] By virtue of Article 12 of the latter regulatory instrument, a posted worker is defined as 'a person who pursues an activity as an employed person in a Member State on behalf of an employer which normally carries out its activities there and who is posted by that employer to another Member State to perform work on that employer's behalf [...] provided that the anticipated duration of such work does not exceed twenty-four months and that he is not sent to replace another person'.[116] In the comparison with the notion of posted worker given by the Posting of Workers Directive, a first common trait can be found in the requirement of the existence of a direct employment relationship between the sending employer and the posted employee during the whole duration of the assignment abroad.[117] Furthermore, also the requirement of the posting company's genuine establishment in the sending Member State, as specified by the Enforcement Directive 2014/67/EU, finds a correspondent provision in Regulation (EC) 883/2004. The latter, indeed, imposes the posting undertaking to 'normally carry out its activities' in the territory of that Member State of origin.[118]

Provision of Services in the European Union' (n 55) 44; Aukje A.H. van Hoek and Mijke Houwerzijl, 'Where Do EU Mobile Workers Belong, According to Rome I and the (E)PWD?' in Herwig Verschueren (ed.), *Residence, Employment and Social Rights of Mobile Persons: On How EU Law Defines Where They Belong*, vol. 36 (Intersentia 2016) 242.

114. Article 4(3)(5) of Directive 2014/67/EU of the European Parliament and of the Council of 15 May 2014 on the enforcement of Directive 96/71/EC concerning the posting of workers in the framework of the provision of services and amending Regulation (EU) No 1024/2012 on administrative cooperation through the Internal Market Information System ('the IMI Regulation') (n 6). Cornelissen and Van Limberghen (n 16) 369–370.
115. Maslauskaite (n 2) 5 and 10; Pennings (n 68); Schwarz and Kiełbasa (n 8); Frederic De Wispelaere, 'Intra-EU Posting Costs and Benefits' (25th International Conference of Europeanists, Chicago, 28 March 2018); Wispelaere, Smedt and Pacolet (n 75) 12.
116. Article 12(1) of Regulation (EC) No 883/2004 of the European Parliament and of the Council of 29 April 2004 on the coordination of social security systems (n 7).
117. Paul Schoukens and Danny Pieters, 'The Rules within Regulation 883/2004 for Determining the Applicable Legislation' (2009) 11 European Journal of Social Security 81, 82; Watson (n 27) 290.
118. Importantly, though, a discrepancy arises in respect of Article 2(1) of the PWD. In fact, on the one hand, the latter provision requires the worker to normally carry out a working activity in his home state, while, on the other, the prescription of the Basic Regulation requires the worker

Besides the above-mentioned similarities, two main distinguishing features can be easily individuated vis-à-vis the original version of the Posting of Workers Directive. First, the anticipated duration of the mobility is not expected to last more than twenty-four months and, second, according to the non-replacement condition, a worker cannot be posted in order to replace another worker who already ran out of his limited period of mobility.[119] With specific reference to the first condition, it should be noted that, under Regulation (EC) 883/2004, the activity of posting workers is defined as an exception to the EU coordination rules for social security. In fact, as stressed in the previous part of the current analysis, the typical principle applying in cases of intra-EU labour mobility across borders is that of *lex loci laboris*. When a temporary transnational secondment is performed in the form of posting, instead, the worker remains affiliated to the social security system of his home country, but only for a maximum period of twenty-four months.[120] After the expiration of the two-year term, the posted worker results compulsorily integrated into the social security regime of the host Member State for the entire period of the posting. He is thus compelled by the same rules applying to migrant and frontier workers, hence losing all prerogatives related to his previous peculiar status.

The conceptual contrast with the 1996 version of the Posting of Workers Directive is, therefore, more than evident. Indeed, according to the latter regulatory instrument, a posted worker was still retaining his status after twenty-four months of mobility abroad. It follows that, whenever a worker was seconded to another Member State for a period longer than twenty-four months, his employment relationship remained governed by his home country law, except for the nucleus of terms and conditions of minimum protection determined by the host state. In turn, at the same time, he had to be covered by the social security regime of the host state for the entire period of mobility.[121]

The most recent intervention of the European legislator with the targeted revision of the Posting of Workers Directive has helped to reach a sort of alignment between EU labour and social security provisions. More specifically, the amended version of the Posting of Workers Directive, which is explored in detail further in Chapter 8, determines the time limit of twelve months after which almost full host state labour law applies. Moreover, when calculating this term, it requires to take into consideration the cumulative duration of the posting, including also the cases of replacement of a posted

to be attached to an employer which normally operates in the country where is established. Cornelissen and Van Limberghen (n 16) 357. For a proper analysis of all the conditions for the application of social security rules on posting activities, *see infra* Chapter 5.

119. For a thorough analysis of the conditions posed by Regulation (EC) 883/2004 in order to benefit from the special treatment for transnational posting, *see infra* Chapter 5.

120. For the record, Article 16 of Regulation (EC) 883/2004 allows two or more countries to agree on exceptions to the twenty-four months rule, thereby authorising the posted workers to retain their home country social security affiliation for a longer period. Watson (n 27) 289–290; Cremers, 'Posting of Workers in Practice' (n 104).

121. European Commission Impact Assessment, Accompanying the document Proposal for a Directive of the European Parliament and the Council amending Directive 96/71/EC concerning the posting of workers in the framework of the provision of services (n 87) 16–17.

worker by another one performing the same type of work at the same place.[122] In other words, the *lex loci laboris* now regulates (almost entirely) both the employment relationship and the social security regime of all posting assignments exceeding (cumulatively) twenty-four months. A new misalignment, however, unavoidably emerges in relation to postings lasting for a period comprised between twelve and twenty-four months, which are supposed to fall under the social security regime of the sending state, while following the *lex loci laboris* with regard to the employment conditions.

The number of mismatches between the two acts of secondary EU legislation under consideration concerns also the treatment reserved to self-employed persons, persons finding themselves in borderline transnational situations and persons who normally pursue a working activity in two or more Member States. In a regular posting scenario, like the one envisaged by the Posting of Workers Directive, an employer-based in state A sends its employees to state B to work there for a certain period of time. Yet, Regulation (EC) 883/2004 contemplates also the possibility for self-employed persons to post themselves temporarily to a different Member State in order to render a particular service.[123] More specifically, it guarantees the possibility to remain under the social security scheme of the country of origin for 'a person who normally pursues an activity as a self-employed person in a Member State who goes to pursue a similar activity in another Member State [...] provided that the anticipated duration of such activity does not exceed twenty-four months'.[124] In addition, unlike the Posting of Workers Directive, the Basic Regulation also covers further borderline situations where the activity is carried out by a worker in the territory of a Member State other than the state in which he normally works, but there is no service directed abroad, or the service is not provided for a recipient established in the host country.[125] Finally, the last case of discrepancy arising vis-à-vis the Posting of Workers Directive regards the legal position of employed persons who normally work simultaneously or in alternation in

122. Article 1(2)(b) of Directive (EU) 2018/957 of the European Parliament and of the Council of 28 June 2018 amending Directive 96/71/EC concerning the posting of workers in the framework of the provision of services (n 4). Stefan Schwarz, Marcin Kiełbasa and Marek Benio, 'Limited Cumulative Period of Posting in the Revised Posting of Workers Directive – In Search of a Legal Justification' (2018) *Labour Mobility Initiative Association* 4–5 <https://www.mobilelabour.eu/wp-content/uploads/2018/10/paper-Limited-cumulative-period-of-posting-in-the-revised-PWD-%E2%80%93-in-search-of-a-legal-justification-by-LMIA.pdf> (accessed 19 October 2018).
123. Wispelaere and Pacolet, 'The Size and Impact of Intra-EU Posting on the Belgian Economy: With a Special Focus on the Construction Sector – Summary' (n 24) 5.
124. Article 12(2) of Regulation (EC) No 883/2004 of the European Parliament and of the Council of 29 April 2004 on the coordination of social security systems (n 7).
125. Practical cases in which a cross-border worker is considered as a posted worker only by the Basic Regulation and not by the PWD might be, for example, that of a German employee sent by his home employer to an international trade fair in France in order to oversee an exhibition stand of the employer; that of a scholar employed at a Danish university spending on a one-year research stay in Italy; or that of a Slovakian ski instructor hired by a Slovakian tourist company in order to provide skiing lessons in the Italian Alps to Slovakian tourists, clients of that tourist company. Schwarz and Kiełbasa (n 8) 2–3.

several Member States other than their country of origin.[126] As previously explained, those workers are normally covered by the host state's set of terms and conditions laid down in the Posting of Workers Directive. In turn, Regulation (EC) 883/2004 envisages, at Article 13, an ad hoc treatment for this category of workers, thus excluding the latter from the notion of 'posted persons'.[127]

To sum up, what becomes clear is that the situation of an employment relationship subject to the labour law of one Member State, while the worker is affiliated to the social security system of another Member State, is not so uncommon.[128] This is because, under the EU normative framework on social security coordination, the wording 'posted worker' assumes a much wider connotation in comparison to the one intended by the Posting of Workers Directive (even after the 2018 reform). In effect, the notion of posted worker provided for by Regulation (EC) 883/2004 includes both posted workers, posted self-employed persons, persons performing cross-border activity without providing any service abroad, as well as those who operate transnationally, but without providing services for a recipient established in the host country. In turn, the personal scope of the Posting of Workers Directive is limited to posted employees, including those who are working on behalf of their employer, at the same time, in two or more Member States. Notably, without forgetting the exclusive competence of the Member State to the territory of which the person is posted to qualify the latter as a 'worker'.[129] On top of that, a time limit for posting is posed by EU social security law at twenty-four months and by the new Directive (EU) 2018/957 at twelve months (extendable to eighteen months), while no maximum duration was envisaged under the Posting of Workers Directive. As accurately explained *infra* in Chapter 6, the obvious result of the highly complex picture given by the combination of EU labour and social security provisions on posting activities leads to an unavoidable misrepresentation of the phenomenon.[130] Table 2.3 below may offer a schematic summary of all different cases of posting situations and the correspondence with their respective regulatory framework.

126. As showed *infra* in Chapter 6, this category of cross-border labour mobility is present the highest share of workers in the transport sector.
127. For an overview of the treatment reserved by social security legislation to this category of cross-border workers, *see infra* Chapter 5.
128. This is often, indeed, the situation involving workers who are posted for a period longer than two years or those who are sent to work, at the same time, in two or more Member States. Cornelissen and Van Limberghen (n 16) 345 and 372.
129. Because of this exclusive competence, certain persons considered as 'posted' under the Regulation may not even be considered as 'workers' by the Member State of destination, consequently remaining excluded from the concept of 'posted worker' pursuant to the PWD. Schwarz and Kiełbasa (n 8) 4.
130. Wispelaere and Pacolet, 'Posting of Workers: Report on A1 Portable Documents Issued in 2015' (n 99) 11–12; Wispelaere and Pacolet, 'Measuring the Size of Intra-EU Posting on the Basis of Data Collected at European and National Level' (n 81).

Table 2.3 Different Cases of Posting[131]

	'Posted Worker' under the Posting of Workers Directive (Original Version)	*'Posted Worker' under the Posting of Workers Directive (as Amended by Directive (EU) 2018/957)*	*'Posted Person' under Regulation (EC) 883/2004 on Social Security Coordination*
Employed person sent by his employer to work in another Member State for a certain period of time	✓	✓	✓
Self-employed person who carries out work in the territory of a Member State other than the State in which he normally works	x	x	✓
Person performing cross-border activity without providing any service abroad	x	x	✓
Person performing cross-border activity, but the service is not provided for a recipient established in the host country	x	x	✓
Employed person sent to work, at the same time, in two or more Member States	✓	✓	x
Person performing cross-border activity for a (cumulative) period comprised between twelve and twenty-four months	✓	x	✓
Person performing cross-border activity for a (cumulative) period exceeding twenty-four months	✓	x	x

2.3.3 The 'Temporary' Issue

'Posting is temporary in nature.' This is the incipit of Preamble Recital 9 of Directive (EU) 2018/957, where the intrinsically limited duration of the secondment of workers across borders for the provision of services is set out in black and white. The temporary

131. *Source*: Author's own work, taking inspiration from Schwarz and Kiełbasa (n 8) 2.

nature of posting represents, indeed, one of the main distinguishing elements characterising this particular type of intra-EU labour mobility. Oddly enough, until the adoption of the above-mentioned act of secondary legislation, and apart from the relevant EU social security law framework, a precise and unequivocal definition of 'temporary' could not be traced to either legislation based on Article 56 TFEU or case law of the Court of Justice. Nevertheless, considering also the emerging shortcomings of the new Directive in that respect, the latter concept still remains one of the most controversial issues, which comes into play especially at national enforcement level. An investigation of a whole series of attempts to reach a definition to that extent, up to the eventually adopted Directive (EU) 2018/957, is proposed below.

Following the previously conducted analysis, the mismatch between the undefined concept of 'limited period of time' a worker is treated as a posted worker in accordance with the original text of the Posting of Workers Directive, and the twenty-four-month period after which the same worker is supposed to automatically fall under the social security regime of the host Member State, set out by Regulation (EC) 883/2004, appears evident. In the former scenario, even after a long period of posting (lasting more than twenty-four months) the same rules concerning the terms and conditions of employment laid down in the Posting of Workers Directive continued to apply.[132] In order to identify a more coherent definition of the maximum period after which a person employed abroad would lose his status of a posted worker, it has been suggested to refer by analogy to the relevant EU rules on social security. In particular, as a posted worker is covered, pursuant to Regulation (EC) 883/2004, by his home state social security system for a posting timeframe not exceeding twenty-four months, he would, accordingly, have retained the status of posted under the Posting of Workers Directive for a maximum time period of the same duration.[133]

The determination of the notion of 'temporary' posting activity could also be achieved through the use of further legal instruments. In this sense, it is interesting to dwell on the intense debate that arose at the time the 1980 Rome Convention on the law applicable to contractual obligations[134] was converted into the Rome I Regulation.[135] More specifically, despite the impossibility to reach an agreement on a definition of temporary posting included in the final text of the Regulation,[136] some useful elements have been included in the Preamble. Recital 36 of the Rome I Regulation offers indeed some indications, although no specific duration limit.[137] On the one hand, the first

132. European Commission Impact Assessment, Accompanying the document Proposal for a Directive of the European Parliament and the Council amending Directive 96/71/EC concerning the posting of workers in the framework of the provision of services (n 87) 16–17; Voss et al. (n 29) 29.
133. Watson (n 27) 285–286.
134. Convention 80/934/EEC of 19 June 1980 on the law applicable to contractual obligations (the Rome Convention) 1980 (OJ L 266/1).
135. Regulation (EC) No 593/2008 of the European Parliament and of the Council of 17 June 2008 on the law applicable to contractual obligations (Rome I) 2008 (OJ L 177/6).
136. In this sense, *see* Commission of the European Communities, Green paper on the conversion of the Rome Convention of 1980 on the law applicable to contractual obligations into a Community instrument and its modernisation 2003 [COM(2002) 654 final] 35–37.
137. van Hoek (n 68) 455–456.

paragraph, by considering as 'temporary' only the working activity carried out in another country 'if the employee is expected to resume working in the country of origin after carrying out his tasks abroad', provides a narrow formulation of the notion of posting. The second paragraph, on the other hand, expands the concept, considering as 'temporary' also the work carried out under a new employment contract with the original employer or an employer belonging to the same group of companies as the original one.[138] Accordingly, the way indicated by the Rome I Regulation for deducing the temporary nature of the working activity performed abroad entails a case-by-case investigation of the employee's *animus revetendi* – i.e., the worker's intention to return to his home country once his assignment abroad has ended – if not also of the employer's *animus retrahendi* – hence the latter's intention to retrieve the employee.[139] Interestingly, following the reasoning expressed by Advocate General Wahl in *Schlecker*,[140] the assessment of the temporary nature of posting under the Rome I Regulation cannot avoid considering the actual duration of the assignment abroad.[141] When deciding the case, however, the Court preferred to give prominence to the law of the country to which 'the contract is more closely connected', thereby disregarding that of the country where the work was habitually carried out.[142]

138. Pursuant to the Rome I Regulation: 'As regards individual employment contracts, work carried out in another country should be regarded as temporary if the employee is expected to resume working in the country of origin after carrying out his tasks abroad. The conclusion of a new contract of employment with the original employer or an employer belonging to the same group of companies as the original employer should not preclude the employee from being regarded as carrying out his work in another country temporarily.' Preamble Recital 36 of Regulation (EC) No 593/2008 of the European Parliament and of the Council of 17 June 2008 on the law applicable to contractual obligations (Rome I) (n 135). On this point, *see* van Hoek and Houwerzijl, 'Comparative Study on the Legal Aspects of the Posting of Workers in the Framework of the Provision of Services in the European Union' (n 55) 17–18 and 187–188; van Hoek and Houwerzijl, 'Where Do EU Mobile Workers Belong, According to Rome I and the (E)PWD?' (n 113) 242–243.
139. Notably, in order to ascertain the parties' intentions, reference should be made to the terms of the contract as well as to the specific circumstances of the case at issue. Grušić (n 62) 158–159; Marcin Cerwiński, 'The Law Applicable to Employment Contracts Under the Rome I-Regulation' (2015) Adam Mickiewicz University Law Review 147, 156–157.
140. *Anton Schlecker v Melitta Josefa Boedeker* [2013] CJEU Case C-64/12, ECLI:EU:C:2013:551.
141. In particular, according to the Swedish amicus curiae, in the event of a very long posting (over ten years in the case at issue), the host country would have been correctly considered as the habitual place of work under Article 8(2) of the Rome I Regulation, with consequent application of the *lex loci laboris*. This, even though the worker actually returned to her country of origin after the period of mobility abroad. *Anton Schlecker v Melitta Josefa Boedeker, Opinion of Advocate General Nils Wahl delivered on 16 April 2013* [2013] CJEU Case C-64/12, ECLI:EU:C:2013:241 [43].
142. As a consequence, even though the posted employee had habitually carried out her activity abroad without interruption for more than eleven years, the Court considered the law of her country of origin as the *lex contractus*. This is because it found the employment contract to be more closely connected with the country of origin, on the basis of several circumstances: the employer was a legal person governed by home state law; the employment contract referred to the law of the country of origin; the remuneration was paid in home state currency; the employee had pension arrangements with her home country, where she continued to keep her residence and from which she received reimbursements for travel costs. *Anton Schlecker v Melitta Josefa Boedeker* (n 140).

One additional instrument of secondary EU legislation able to clarify the concept of temporary provision of services in the framework of a posting arrangement is the 2014 Enforcement Directive. In particular, Article 4(3) requires, likewise the Posting of Workers Directive, that the service provision is conducted towards another Member State for a 'limited period of time'. Furthermore, similar to the Rome I Regulation, it ascertains the temporariness of the working activity whenever the posted worker returns to his home state or is expected to resume his work there, after completion of the activity for which he had been posted.[143]

As already mentioned, with reference to the contribution of the Court of Justice to that extent, the surprising absence of any appreciable discussion must be recorded. Only a few allusions were made to the supposed return of the workers to their home state after the completion of the service supply[144] and to the necessity to take into account the regular, periodical or continuous nature of the transnational activity.[145] Importantly, though, the judges in Luxembourg clarified the incompatibility of an indefinite or endless duration of the posting with the concept of provision of services.[146]

Several notions of the temporary nature of posting may be traced, in turn, in different interpretations given by the Member States. On some occasions, the temporariness has been referred to postings of short duration,[147] while in other national contexts, the temporary nature of the secondment is assumed whenever a predetermined duration and/or a predetermined, objective cause of termination of the cross-border activity has been already established.[148] The eventuality of determining a maximum time limit for posting, in line with the maximum of twenty-four months granted by the EU Regulation on social security, was proposed, though at the end without success, in Luxembourg.[149] In Germany, a duration limit of twelve months for posting activities to be classified as temporary is set out by law. However, in order for such a rule to find application, specific requirements impose the establishment of the

143. Article 4(3)(a) and (d) of Directive 2014/67/EU of the European Parliament and of the Council of 15 May 2014 on the enforcement of Directive 96/71/EC concerning the posting of workers in the framework of the provision of services and amending Regulation (EU) No 1024/2012 on administrative cooperation through the Internal Market Information System ('the IMI Regulation') (n 6). Cornelissen and Van Limberghen (n 16) 369–370.

144. *Rush Portuguesa Lda v Office national d'immigration* (n 31) para. 15. On this point, *see* Evju and Novitz (n 51) 30.

145. *Reinhard Gebhard v Consiglio dell'Ordine degli Avvocati e Procuratori di Milano* (n 20) para. 27; *Bruno Schnitzer* (n 43) para. 28. *See* Voss et al. (n 29) 29.

146. *Udo Steymann v Staatssecretaris van Justitie* [1988] ECJ Case C-196/87, ECLI:EU:C:1988:475 [16]; *Bruno Schnitzer* (n 43) para. 29; *Michel Trojani v Centre public d'aide sociale de Bruxelles (CPAS)* (n 40) para. 28. In this sense, *see* Watson (n 27) 285; Houwerzijl (n 32) 19; van Hoek and Houwerzijl, 'Where Do EU Mobile Workers Belong, According to Rome I and the (E)PWD?' (n 113) 243–244.

147. The element of short duration is present in the Danish definition of 'temporary' period of posting. Martin Gräs Lind, 'The Danish Law on the Posting of Workers' (2010) 24 FORMULA Working Paper, University of Oslo, Department of Private Law 5.

148. Such an approach is adopted by France and Luxembourg. van Hoek and Houwerzijl, 'Comparative Study on the Legal Aspects of the Posting of Workers in the Framework of the Provision of Services in the European Union' (n 55) 47.

149. The current regulatory framework in Luxembourg does not foresee any specific limit of duration for posting activities. *Ibid.* 48.

centre of the worker's economic activity in another country, as well as the guarantee for the posted employee to return to his home state at the end of the period of mobility. In case of deviation from such prescriptions, German law is deemed to apply according to the Rome I Regulation.[150] Conversely, no maximum duration is contemplated by Italian law, which requires an upfront predetermined or pre-determinable duration of posting in order to recognise its temporariness.[151]

Finally, it is noticeable that, with the definitive adoption on 28 June 2018 of the new Directive (EU) 2018/957 amending the 1996 Posting of Workers Directive, a time limit for the application of the nucleus of terms and conditions of employment of the host state has been eventually determined. Since 30 July 2020, the almost full application of the host country's mandatory labour law is enforceable after a twelve-month period of posting (extendable to eighteen months on the condition of prior motivated notification).[152] Hence, in case of cross-border temporary assignments lasting longer than twelve months, the posted workers are expected to be treated almost as local workers.[153] Of absolute importance is, however, the nature of such a time limit. In fact, given its cumulative application, all previous individual postings to the same workplace have to be taken into consideration for the calculation of the posting period. As a consequence, this legislative *novella* is supposed to eventually result in a higher degree of uncertainty with regard to the determination of the concrete timeframe a posted worker shall be treated according to the rules concerning the free provision of services, rather than almost like a full-fledged migrant worker moving under Article 45 TFEU. More specifically, the paradoxical outcome of the 2018 reform implies that the duration of the period a posted workers' employment relationship remains regulated by the labour law of his country of origin will depend on how many workers performing 'the same task at the same place' have already enjoyed such a freedom. Strikingly, by virtue of the new rules, in the event a worker is posted to an assignment abroad where other colleagues have been previously employed for a cumulative period of twelve months (or eighteen months), he would be immediately treated almost as a migrant worker (even in the event his tasks are expected to last just a few days).[154]

150. *Ibid.*
151. More specifically, Italian law prescribes the termination of the posting activity to be objectively identifiable (e.g., by expressly specifying the end of a construction project). *Ibid.*
152. Article 1(2)(b) of Directive (EU) 2018/957 of the European Parliament and of the Council of 28 June 2018 amending Directive 96/71/EC concerning the posting of workers in the framework of the provision of services (n 4).
153. Preamble Recital 8 and Article 1(1) of the European Commission, Proposal for a Directive of the European Parliament and of the Council amending Directive 96/71/EC of the European Parliament and of the Council of 16 December 1996 concerning the posting of workers in the framework of the provision of services 2016 [COM(2016) 128 final]; Cécile Barbière, 'Posted Workers: Macron's First Victory in Reforming the EU' (*EURACTIV*, 24 October 2017) <https://www.euractiv.com/section/economy-jobs/news/posted-workers-macrons-first-victory-in-reforming-the-eu/> (accessed 26 September 2018); Eric Maurice, 'EU Takes Step Closer to "Posted Workers" Deal' (*euobserver*, 1 March 2018) <https://euobserver.com/social/141166> (accessed 26 September 2018). For a thorough analysis of this rule setting a limited period of posting, *see infra* Chapter 8.
154. Schwarz, Kiełbasa and Benio (n 122) 4.

2.4 CONCLUDING REMARKS

On the basis of the analysis above, the peculiar character of posting of workers as a hybrid type of labour mobility appears evident. Unlike the other, more conventional, forms of intra-EU labour mobility covered by the Treaty provisions concerning the freedom of movement for workers (Article 45 TFEU) and the freedom of establishment (Article 49 TFEU), posting has been traditionally regulated by the EU internal market rules concerning the freedom to provide services (Article 56 TFEU). In particular, the posted workers are temporarily seconded abroad by their employer, in the framework of the freedom to provide services, in order to provide a service in the receiving state. Consequently, unlike the worker-driven type of labour mobility represented by worker migration, labour mobility in the form of posting of workers is evidently employer-driven. This means that, since both the initiative, responsibility and costs of the mobility fall entirely on the employer, the posted workers' chances to benefit from the economic opportunities offered by the secondment across borders are directly dependent on their employers' competitiveness.

The aforementioned choice of legal basis has been conceived by taking into consideration the distinguishing features of the kind of activity involved, which does not require an integration of the posted workers within the labour market of the Member State of destination. Given the temporariness of the service provision, those workers remain, indeed, in the host state only for a limited period of time, while maintaining a direct employment relationship with their employer in the sending state, as well as the social security coverage from their home state.

Crucially, the placement of posting under the freedom to provide services traditionally entailed a fundamentally different legal treatment than in the case of workers' movement under Articles 45 and 49 TFEU. Instead of following the principle of *lex loci laboris* (host state law), the activity of posting remains basically governed by the law of the country of origin (home state law). Such a principle has been enshrined in both the Posting of Workers Directive, Regulation (EC) 883/2004 on the coordination of social security systems and the relevant 'double taxation conventions', albeit with some specific exceptions and limitations. Regardless, with the adoption of the new Directive (EU) 2018/957, the currently applicable 'country of origin' approach will progressively give way to the *lex loci laboris* principle.

The activity of posting of workers, however, cannot be identified as a unique pattern of transnational service supply. It may indeed assume several different shapes. In line with the Posting of Workers Directive, three different posting scenarios may come into play, encompassing: (a) the direct provision of services with workers posted under a service contract between two undertakings established in two different Member States; (b) intra-group posting, i.e., cross-border secondment of workers within the same company; and (c) workers hired out by a temporary work agency or a placement agency and operating under the control of the user undertaking in the host state. Besides, even the activity of those persons who are sent by their employer to work, at the same time, in two or more Member States often results regulated by the host state's labour provisions on posting. Regulation (EC) 883/2004, in turn, includes under the notion of 'posted person' also posted self-employed persons, persons performing cross-border activity without providing any service abroad, as well as those who operate transnationally, but without providing services to any recipient established in the host country.

In such a context, the co-existence of two separate regulatory systems, entailing a variety of rules applying to different posting patterns, gives origin to a highly fragmented picture. Substantial discrepancies between the different notions of 'posting' and 'posted worker' respectively provided by the Posting of Workers Directive (even after the 2018 revision) and Regulation (EC) 883/2004 have been clearly recognised. Strikingly, a coincidence of the personal scope of both these regulatory instruments is present only in the case of a regular posting scenario, whereby an employer sends its employees to work in another Member State for a certain period of time. Yet, prior to the entry into effect of Directive (EU) 2018/957, this alignment referred only to secondments lasting less than two years. In fact, in the event the employees were posted for a period exceeding twenty-four months, they were not anymore considered as posted under Regulation (EC) 883/2004, while preserving the safeguards ensured by the Posting of Workers Directive. Evidently, this condition inevitably resulted in negative repercussions in terms of determination and enforcement of the applicable rules and, at the end, of substantive protection of the workers concerned. A significant novelty has been introduced to that extent by the new Directive (EU) 2018/957, which foresees that the exceptional regime reserved to posted workers by the Posting of Workers Directive no longer covers posting assignments lasting longer than a (cumulative) period of twelve months. However, a new misalignment with the relevant EU social security rules necessarily arises in relation to postings of duration comprised between twelve and twenty-four months.

As clearly pointed out in the investigation conducted in the last subsection 2.3.3, the uncertainty surrounding the concept of 'temporary' nature of posting has been a controversial issue for years. In effect, the different positions identified are not able to reach a univocal position on the matter. A temporal limit was initially set out by the applicable EU rules on social security coordination only, while the Enforcement Directive 2014/67/EU and the Rome I Regulation provide a few indications solely with regard to the intention of the posted worker to return home at the end of his assignment abroad. Moreover, different approaches have been adopted at national level. In turn, the interventions of the Court of Justice were just limited to suggesting to take into account the regular, periodical or continuous nature of the cross-border activity and excluding postings of indefinite or endless duration. Finally, the analysis shows how the EU legislator sadly missed the opportunity to bring clarity once and for all with the 2018 revision of the Posting of Workers Directive. In fact, the introduction of a twelve-month time limit (extendable to eighteen months) for posting has to be read in the light of its cumulative nature, which entails the inclusion of all previous secondments of other workers to the same workplace. Such a novelty is, therefore, expected to result in an absolute uncertainty about the determination of the actual period a posted worker is treated according to the rules concerning the free provision of services rather than almost like a fully-fledged migrant worker. Accordingly, the doubt remains that this sort of intervention was mainly driven by political motive, rather than by a genuine intention to clarify the temporary nature of the posting activity for the benefit of the workers involved.

In conclusion, the proven absence of a univocal legal definition of posting at EU level is stressed once again with particular reference to the unavoidable repercussions in terms of implementation and enforcement of the rules at national level. Indeed, the overall uncertainty that national authorities, as well as the cross-border operators themselves, are constantly facing when trying to discern the applicable regulatory regime to certain posting arrangements cannot be overlooked. All things considered, a possible improvement in this regard could envisage the adoption of an integrated approach at EU level to labour mobility, involving both labour law, social security law and tax policies.[155]

155. Kerstin Ahlberg, 'The Age of Innocence – And Beyond' (2010) 21 FORMULA Working Paper, University of Oslo, Department of Private Law 28–29; van Hoek (n 68) 486.

CHAPTER 3

EU Labour Law Framework

3.1 INTRODUCTION

Since the foundation of the European Economic Community (EEC),[1] European citizens are entitled to move freely across the internal borders of the Common Market in order to search for employment and to work in all the Member States.[2] The transnational movement of workers was – and to a major extent still is – ordinarily governed by the so-called principle of *lex loci laboris*, entailing the full application of the host country rules and the prohibition of any form of discrimination on grounds of nationality.[3] However, as a result of the development of practices of posting of workers, several Member States, in exercising their exclusive competence in the field of labour law,[4]

1. Treaty of Rome (EEC) – Treaty establishing the European Economic Community 1957.
2. Paul Craig and Gráinne de Búrca, *EU Law: Text, Cases, and Materials* (Sixth Edition, Oxford University Press 2015) 4–5.
3. The principle of non-discrimination of workers on grounds of nationality is enshrined in Article 45 TFEU and in Article 7 of Regulation (EU) No 492/2011 of the European Parliament and of the Council of 5 April 2011 on freedom of movement for workers within the Union 2011 (OJ L 141/1). Herwig Verschueren, 'The European Internal Market and the Competition between Workers' (2015) 6 European Labour Law Journal 128, 135–137; Catherine Barnard, *The Substantive Law of the EU: The Four Freedoms* (Fifth Edition, Oxford University Press 2016) 243–269; Jan Cremers, 'Economic Freedoms and Labour Standards in the European Union' (2016) 22(2) Transfer: European Review of Labour and Research 149, 150–151; Catherine Barnard, 'The Commission's Proposal Deletes the Treaty Distinction between Migrant Workers and Posted Workers' (IV European Labour Mobility Congress (ELMC), Krakow (Poland), 7 November 2016) <https://www.elmc.eu/2016/the-commissions-proposal-deletes-the-treaty-distinction-between-migrant-workers-and-posted-workers-prof-catherine-barnards-speech-at-the-iv-european-labour-mobilit y-cong/> (accessed 13 May 2018).
4. It should be noted, indeed, that the Treaty of Rome establishing the European Economic Community (EEC) was primarily directed at the general promotion of a fully integrated European market economy, through more effective and profitable resource allocation. However, the choice of placing the main emphasis on the establishment of a 'Common Market', underpinned by the four freedoms (goods, persons, services and capitals) and competition policy, entailed, at the same time, the exclusion of labour and social security law from the European scope and their

started deviating from the general rule by allowing the application of the workers' home state law. Such a special treatment was motivated by the intrinsic temporary nature of the form of labour mobility under consideration, whereby the cross-border workers are not supposed to permanently accede to the host country's labour market.[5]

The demand for specific coordination rules applicable to transnational employment relationships has been addressed, first and foremost, by the adoption on 19 June 1980 of the Convention on the law applicable to contractual obligations (Rome Convention),[6] which was replaced at the end of 2009 by the Rome I Regulation.[7] Alongside those rules of private international law, the practice of posting of workers was then specifically regulated by the adoption on 16 December 1996, after several years of complex negotiations, of the famous Posting of Workers Directive.[8]

Against this background, this chapter aims to provide an analysis of the labour regulation at EU level of the posting phenomenon prior to the entry into force of Directive (EU) 2018/957, under the guidance of the relevant research sub-question: *How is the 'posting of workers' regulated under EU labour law?* In light of the particular relevance of certain Union rules in the area of private international law, a due reference to the above-mentioned provisions cannot be avoided. Accordingly, in the following section 3.2, the Rome I Regulation is investigated with a view to determining the law actually applicable to the employment relationship in the event of short-term secondment of workforce across borders. In this way, the interface between the Posting of Workers Directive and the relevant EU rules in the sphere of private international law is made explicit, thus shedding light on the particular position in which the Directive is placed.

The analysis of the labour law dimension of the regulatory framework for posting of workers then moves forward, in section 3.3, with an in-depth examination of the Posting of Workers Directive (prior to the entry into effect of the 2018 legislative reform). More specifically, the section at issue is divided into two major parts. With a view to shedding light on the rationale and purpose of the 1996 Posting of Workers Directive, the first part is intended to offer a summary of the extremely interesting drafting phase of this piece of legislation, starting from its conceptual genesis and covering all subsequent steps in the adoption process. Besides providing an outlook on the overall context and on the different interests at stake, this part is intended to help

consequent permanence under national competence. Herwig Verschueren, 'Cross-Border Workers in the European Internal Market: Trojan Horses for Member States' Labour and Social Security Law?' (2008) 24/2 International Journal of Comparative Labour Law and Industrial Relations 167, 167–168; Catherine Barnard, '"British Jobs for British Workers": The Lindsey Oil Refinery Dispute and the Future of Local Labour Clauses in an Integrated EU Market' (2009) 38 Industrial Law Journal 245, 276; Verschueren (n 3) 129–130.

5. Cremers, 'Economic Freedoms and Labour Standards in the European Union' (n 3) 152–153.
6. Convention 80/934/EEC of 19 June 1980 on the law applicable to contractual obligations (the Rome Convention) 1980 (OJ L 266/1).
7. Regulation (EC) No 593/2008 of the European Parliament and of the Council of 17 June 2008 on the law applicable to contractual obligations (Rome I) 2008 (OJ L 177/6). This Regulation applies to employment contracts concluded after 17 December 2009.
8. Directive 96/71/EC of the European Parliament and of the Council of 16 December 1996 concerning the posting of workers in the framework of the provision of services 1997 (OJ L 18/1).

understand the correct interpretation of the rules laid down in the Directive in accordance with the will of the EU legislator.

The second part, in turn, focuses on the substantial content of the Directive, thereby closely looking at the particular kind of balance achieved by the European legislator between, on the one hand, the promotion of the transnational provision of services and, on the other hand, the respect of the Member States' interest to preserve their labour market integrity and the social protection of the cross-border workers concerned. After an investigation of the 'hard core' of employment conditions of the host state extendable to posted workers, the analysis touches on the rather problematic definition of minimum rates of pay. The particular solution envisaged by the Posting of Workers Directive with regard to the means of regulation is then presented. Subsequently, the intersection of the Temporary Agency Work Directive 2008/104/EC[9] with the Posting of Workers Directive is explored in order to discern the exceptional treatment of posted agency workers. Finally, the section concludes with an examination of the special provisions which guarantee the host Member State to extend labour protection beyond the limits set by the nucleus of terms and conditions of employment explicitly indicated in the Directive. At that stage, by taking into consideration the relevant case law of the Court of Justice, it thoroughly reflects on the meaning and scope of the highly debated favourability clause. This chapter closes with section 3.4, which collects all the previous main findings and offers some concluding remarks.

3.2 LAW APPLICABLE TO THE EMPLOYMENT RELATIONSHIP

As extensively explained *supra* in Chapter 2, the cross-border service provision through posting entails, in a nutshell, that a worker departs from a certain Member State to perform, for a temporary period, a working activity in another Member State. Evidently, a conflict of laws issue necessarily emerges when it comes to determining the law applicable in practice to the employment relationship, namely whether that worker shall be covered by his home country law, or by the law of the Member State in which he is temporarily working, or even if both legal regimes shall apply in combination.[10] A solution to such a prominent conflict of laws has been provided by the Convention on the law applicable to contractual obligations, signed in Rome on 19 June 1980,[11] and can now be traced in the Rome I Regulation,[12] which lays down the currently applicable EU rules in the area of private international law.

9. Directive 2008/104/EC of the European Parliament and of the Council of 19 November 2008 on temporary agency work 2008 (OJ L 327/9).
10. Stein Evju and Tonia Novitz, 'The Evolving Regulation: Dynamics and Consequences' (2012) 33 FORMULA Working Paper, University of Oslo, Department of Private Law 4-5; Marzena Madrak, *The Favourability Principle under the Posting of Workers Directive: Minimum Rates of Pay* (Francesco Buffa ed., Key Editore 2019) 27.
11. Rome Convention of 19 June 1980 on the law applicable to contractual obligations, OJ L 1980/266, 1.
12. Regulation (EC) No 593/2008 of the European Parliament and of the Council of 17 June 2008 on the law applicable to contractual obligations (Rome I) (n 7).

Pursuant to Article 3 of the Rome I Regulation, the general principle governing the choice of the law applicable to an individual employment contract is that of freedom of the parties.[13] With a view to protect the weaker contracting party – namely the employee – the autonomy of the parties in designating the *lex causae* is, nevertheless, circumscribed by the requirement, laid down in Article 8(1), of guaranteeing the employee a minimum level of protection, corresponding at least to the standard of protection imposed by the 'objectively applicable law', i.e., by the mandatory provisions of the law applicable in absence of that choice.[14] In this way, the employer remains de facto precluded from abusing his superior bargaining position vis-à-vis the employees, which, in turn, remain covered by the most protective provisions.

For cases of temporary performance of working activity in another country[15] – the typical case of posting – in the event the parties of the contract have not expressly designated the law applicable to the individual working relationship, Article 8(2) of the Rome I Regulation provides for the application of the objectively applicable law of the country of habitual employment.[16] Crucially, under private international law, the

13. 'A contract shall be governed by the law chosen by the parties.' *Ibid.* Article 3(1). On this point, *see* Marek Benio, 'New Rules of the Posting of Workers in 2020. The Countdown.' (*Labour Mobility Initiative*, 30 July 2018) <https://www.mobilelabour.eu/12521/new-rules-of-the-posting-of-workers-in-2020-the-final-countdown/> (accessed 30 August 2018). Previously Article 3 of the Convention 80/934/EEC of 19 June 1980 on the law applicable to contractual obligations (the Rome Convention) (n 6).
14. Article 8(1) of Regulation (EC) No 593/2008 of the European Parliament and of the Council of 17 June 2008 on the law applicable to contractual obligations (Rome I) (n 7). Aukje A.H. van Hoek and Mijke Houwerzijl, '"Posting" and "Posted Workers": The Need for Clear Definitions of Two Key Concepts of the Posting of Workers Directive' (2012) 14 Cambridge Yearbook of European Legal Studies 419, 439; Mijke Houwerzijl, 'Regime Shopping across (Blurring) Boundaries' in Stein Evju (ed.), *Regulating Transnational Labour in Europe: The Quandaries of Multilevel Governance* (Department of Private Law 2014) 13–14; Verschueren (n 3) 137 and 147–148; Rob Cornelissen and Guido Van Limberghen, 'Social Security for Mobile Workers and Labour Law', in *Research Handbook on European Social Security Law* (Edward Elgar Publishing 2015) 360–361; Aukje A.H. van Hoek and Mijke Houwerzijl, 'Where Do EU Mobile Workers Belong, According to Rome I and the (E)PWD?' in Herwig Verschueren (ed.), *Residence, Employment and Social Rights of Mobile Persons: On How EU Law Defines Where They Belong*, vol. 36 (Intersentia 2016) 220. In practice, Article 8(1) entails that the national court carries out a case-by-case comparison between the substantive content of the law chosen by the parties and the 'objectively applicable' law in order to discern the rules which are more favourable to the worker. Cornelissen and Van Limberghen 361.
15. In the wording of the Rome I Regulation, 'work carried out in another country should be regarded as temporary if the employee is expected to resume working in the country of origin after carrying out his tasks abroad. The conclusion of a new contract of employment with the original employer or an employer belonging to the same group of companies as the original employer should not preclude the employee from being regarded as carrying out his work in another country temporarily.' Preamble Recital 36 of Regulation (EC) No 593/2008 of the European Parliament and of the Council of 17 June 2008 on the law applicable to contractual obligations (Rome I) (n 7).
16. According to the Regulation: 'To the extent that the law applicable to the individual employment contract has not been chosen by the parties, the contract shall be governed by the law of the country in which or, failing that, from which the employee habitually carries out his work in performance of the contract. The country where the work is habitually carried out shall not be deemed to have changed if he is temporarily employed in another country.' *Ibid.* Article 8(2). Evju and Novitz (n 10) 5; Verschueren (n 3) 147; Uglješa Grušić, *The European Private International Law of Employment* (Cambridge University Press 2015) 255; van Hoek and Houwerzijl, 'Where Do EU Mobile Workers Belong, According to Rome I and the (E)PWD?' (n

workers who are working abroad only on a temporary basis on behalf of their employer are not deemed to 'habitually' work in the territory of the country in which they are temporarily posted, provided that they are expected to resume working in their country of origin after carrying out their tasks abroad.[17] It follows that, for them, the 'objectively applicable' law is that of the sending state.[18] Oddly enough, therefore, in the regular posting scenario the substantial coincidence of the workers' habitual place of work[19] and their country of origin results, in practice, in the prevention of the mechanism provided for in Article 8(1) from operating.[20] As is evident, the reference made by the Rome I Regulation to the habitual place of work, rather than the actual place of work, inevitably implies the application of the home state legal regime in case of posting arrangements.[21]

Nonetheless, an exception to that rule turns out apparently whenever the employment relationship begins and ends with a temporary posting abroad.[22] In such an event, the element required by the Preamble Recital 36 of the Rome I Regulation for qualifying a working activity in another country as temporary – namely the expectation

14) 226. Notably, the singular national courts remain entitled to determine, in concrete terms, the place where the work is habitually carried out. van Hoek and Houwerzijl, '"Posting" and "Posted Workers": The Need for Clear Definitions of Two Key Concepts of the Posting of Workers Directive' (n 14) 440.

17. Preamble Recital 36 of Regulation (EC) No 593/2008 of the European Parliament and of the Council of 17 June 2008 on the law applicable to contractual obligations (Rome I) (n 7).
18. Cornelissen and Van Limberghen (n 14) 365 and 370.
19. In that respect, it is settled case law of the Court of Justice that the concept of 'habitual place of work' has to be broadly construed. *Heiko Koelzsch v État du Grand Duchy of Luxemburg* [2011] CJEU Case C-29/10, ECLI:EU:C:2011:151 [43]; *Jan Voogsgeerd v Navimer SA* [2011] CJEU Case C-384/10, ECLI:EU:C:2011:842 [35]; *Anton Schlecker v Melitta Josefa Boedeker* [2013] CJEU Case C-64/12, ECLI:EU:C:2013:551 [31].
20. The mechanism of better protection provided for in Article 8(1) of the Rome I Regulation finds application, indeed, only in the event that the parties choose a different law from the objectively applicable law. Grušić (n 16) 154. Besides, it is worth noting that, in certain cases, the notion of 'country of habitual employment' within the meaning of the Rome I Regulation may not correspond to the 'country of origin' of the employer under EU internal market law. van Hoek and Houwerzijl, 'Where Do EU Mobile Workers Belong, According to Rome I and the (E)PWD?' (n 14) 223–224.
21. Simon Deakin, 'Regulatory Competition after Laval' (2007) 10 Cambridge Yearbook of European Legal Studies 581, 594; Evju and Novitz (n 10) 11; Catherine Barnard, *EU Employment Law* (Fourth Edition, Oxford European Union Law Library 2012) 229–230; Stein Evju, *Cross-Border Services: Posting of Workers, and Multilevel Governance* (University of Oslo, Faculty of Law 2013) 12; ACL Davies, *EU Labour Law* (Edward Elgar Publishing Ltd 2014) 93–94; Houwerzijl (n 14) 14; Monika Schlachter, 'Equal Treatment for Transnational Temporary Agency Workers?' in Stein Evju (ed.), *Regulating Transnational Labour in Europe: The Quandaries of Multilevel Governance* (Universitetet i Oslo, Det Juridiske Facultet 2014) 266; Verschueren (n 3) 137–138; Cornelissen and Van Limberghen (n 14) 365; van Hoek and Houwerzijl, 'Where Do EU Mobile Workers Belong, According to Rome I and the (E)PWD?' (n 14) 221; Uglješa Grušić, 'European Labour Market Posted Workers Directive and the Social Implications of the Movement of Labour' in Horatia Muir Watt et al. (eds), *Global Private International Law: Adjudication Without Frontiers* (Edward Elgar Publishing 2018) 478; Aukje A.H. van Hoek, 'Re-Embedding the Transnational Employment Relationship: A Tale about the Limitations of (EU) Law?' (2018) 55 Common Market Law Review 449, 455.
22. This is the case of, e.g., an agency providing workers for temporary cross-border services only, thereby not carrying out any substantial activity (other than administration) in its country of establishment. Schlachter (n 21) 266–267.

of the employee to resume working in his home country after the period of mobility abroad[23] - would inevitably be missing. Consequently, in this particular case of non-genuine posting, the employee's habitual workplace necessarily coincides with the host state, and host state law finds full application.[24]

Despite not being, in typical cases of posting, *lex causae stricto sensu* of the contract, the host country law may, however, still regulate some aspects of the transnational employment relationship.[25] In fact, by virtue of Article 9 of the Rome I Regulation,[26] the *lex loci laboris* may come into play to the extent it has the connotation of 'overriding mandatory provisions'. In particular, the host country is entitled to designate certain provisions which are considered as crucial for safeguarding its public interests, and which find application even when a different national law is governing the employment contract.[27] The flexible margin of appreciation conferred by private international law to the receiving Member States in the designation of such kind of provisions has been, nevertheless, sensibly narrowed down by the case law of the Court of Justice.[28] In this sense, national measures merely founded on pure administrative considerations or exclusive economic motivations, such as the protection of local businesses or the contrast to unemployment, have been excluded from the range of possible justifications for restriction to the free movement of services.[29] On the other hand, the protection of the workers (both posted and local ones) has been recognised

23. On this point, *see supra* Chapter 2.
24. This interpretation seems also consistent with the Court's approach of individuating the employee's habitual place of work in 'the place where he spends most of his working time engaged on his employer's business'. *Herbert Weber v Universal Ogden Services Ltd* [2002] ECJ Case C-37/00, ECLI:EU:C:2002:122 [50]. Schlachter (n 21) 266–267; Grušić (n 16) 160; Marcin Cerwiński, 'The Law Applicable to Employment Contracts Under the Rome I-Regulation' (2015) Adam Mickiewicz University Law Review 147, 157; van Hoek (n 21) 479.
25. van Hoek (n 21) 455.
26. Whose predecessor, although with some differences, was Article 7 of the Convention 80/934/EEC of 19 June 1980 on the law applicable to contractual obligations (the Rome Convention) (n 6).
27. Pursuant to Article 9(1) of the Rome I Regulation: 'Overriding mandatory provisions are provisions the respect for which is regarded as crucial by a country for safeguarding its public interests, such as its political, social or economic organisation, to such an extent that they are applicable to any situation falling within their scope, irrespective of the law otherwise applicable to the contract under this Regulation.' Interestingly, this definition of 'overriding mandatory provisions' derives from the Court's decision in *Arblade & Fils SARL v Sofrage SARL* [1999] ECJ Joined Cases C-369/96 and C-376/96, ECLI:EU:C:1999:575. Grušić (n 16) 210; Cornelissen and Van Limberghen (n 14) 361; van Hoek (n 21) 465. The difference between the 'overriding mandatory provisions' provided for by Article 9(1) and the more favourable provisions regulated in Article 8(1) lies in the peculiar character of the former ones, which have prevalence on both the law chosen by the parties and the law objectively applicable to the contract. Grušić (n 16) 207; Cerwiński (n 24) 158; van Hoek and Houwerzijl, 'Where Do EU Mobile Workers Belong, According to Rome I and the (E)PWD?' (n 14) 221.
28. Verschueren (n 3) 137–138 and 147–148; van Hoek (n 21) 465.
29. *Arblade & Fils SARL v Sofrage SARL* (n 27) para. 37; *Finalarte Sociedade de Construção Civil v Urlaubs- und Lohnausgleichskasse der Bauwirtschaft* [2001] ECJ Joined Cases C-49/98, C-50/98, C-52/98 to C-54/98 and C-68/98 to C-71/98, ECLI:EU:C:2001:564 [39]; *Portugaia Construções Lda* [2002] ECJ Case C-164/99, ECLI:EU:C:2002:40 [26]. Marc De Vos, 'Free Movement of Workers, Free Movement of Services and the Posted Workers Directive: A Bermuda Triangle for National Labour Standards?' (2006) 7 ERA Forum – Springer 356, 365.

as a legitimate 'overriding reason of public interest',[30] albeit on the condition that the employees concerned do not already enjoy an 'essentially similar protection' under their home country law[31] and that they would actually benefit from a better degree of social protection.[32] In addition, the application to out-of-state service providers of certain overriding mandatory provisions of the receiving state is permitted only to the extent it is necessary and proportionate for the protection of the workers concerned.[33]

Importantly, then, in accordance with Preamble Recitals 7–11 of the Posting of Workers Directive, the optional character of the above-mentioned exception provided for by Article 9 of the Rome I Regulation (former Article 7 of the Rome I Convention) is made de facto obligatory by the Directive itself.[34] In fact, the latter instrument specifically designates, at Article 3(1), the host country's elements of employment law applicable to posted workers, regardless of the otherwise applicable law, as 'overriding mandatory provisions'.[35] Besides, by means of Article 3(10), it still leaves the door open to the application of host country's provisions justified by 'public policy' motivations, thus basically replicating the open-ended opportunity guaranteed by private international law to the receiving Member States.[36] In summary, the interplay

30. *Alfred John Webb* [1981] ECJ Case C-279/80, ECLI:EU:C:1981:314 [19]; *Arblade & Fils SARL v Sofrage SARL* (n 27) para. 36; *Mazzoleni v Inter Surveillance Assistance* [2001] ECJ Case C-165/98, ECLI:EU:C:2001:162 [27]; *Portugaia Construções Lda* (n 29) para. 20; *International Transport Workers' Federation and Finnish Seamen's Union v Viking Line ABP and OÜ Viking Line Eesti* [2007] ECJ Case C-438/05, ECLI:EU:C:2007:772 [75]; *Laval un Partneri Ltd v Svenska Byggnadsarbetareförbundet, Svenska Byggnadsarbetareförbundets avdelning 1, Byggettan and Svenska Elektrikerförbundet* [2007] ECJ Case C-341/05, ECLI:EU:C:2007:809 [103].
31. *Guiot v Climatec SA* [1996] ECJ Case C-272/94, ECLI:EU:C:1996:147, 16–17; *Arblade & Fils SARL v Sofrage SARL* (n 27) para. 51; *Portugaia Construções Lda* (n 29) para. 19. On this point, *see* Mijke Houwerzijl and Frans Pennings, 'Double Charges in Case of Posting of Employees: The *Guiot* Judgment and Its Effects on the Construction Sector' (1999) 1 European Journal of Social Security 91, 98–99; Paul Davies, 'The Posted Workers Directive and the EC Treaty' (2002) 31 Industrial Law Journal 298, 303–304.
32. *Finalarte Sociedade de Construção Civil v Urlaubs- und Lohnausgleichskasse der Bauwirtschaft* (n 29) para. 42; *Portugaia Construções Lda* (n 29) para. 29; *Wolff & Müller GmbH & Co KG v José Filipe Pereira Félix* [2004] ECJ Case C-60/03, ECLI:EU:C:2004:610 [38]. On this point, *see* De Vos (n 29) 365–366.
33. *Alfred John Webb* (n 30) para. 17; *Arblade & Fils SARL v Sofrage SARL* (n 27) para. 60; *Finalarte Sociedade de Construção Civil v Urlaubs- und Lohnausgleichskasse der Bauwirtschaft* (n 29) para. 72; *Laval un Partneri Ltd v Svenska Byggnadsarbetareförbundet, Svenska Byggnadsarbetareförbundets avdelning 1, Byggettan and Svenska Elektrikerförbundet* (n 30) para. 101. De Vos (n 29) 367.
34. Noticeably, this condition has not been altered by the entry into effect of Directive (EU) 2018/957.
35. Paul Davies, 'Posted Workers: Single Market or Protection of National Labour Law Systems?' (1997) 34 Common Market Law Review 571, 578–579; van Hoek and Houwerzijl, '"Posting" and "Posted Workers": The Need for Clear Definitions of Two Key Concepts of the Posting of Workers Directive' (n 14) 420 and 437; Houwerzijl (n 14) 14–15; Cerwiński (n 24) 159; Cornelissen and Van Limberghen (n 14) 367; van Hoek and Houwerzijl, 'Where Do EU Mobile Workers Belong, According to Rome I and the (E)PWD?' (n 14) 222; Barnard, 'The Commission's Proposal Deletes the Treaty Distinction between Migrant Workers and Posted Workers' (n 3). As thoroughly explained *infra* in section 3.3, the PWD's scope is limited to the individuation of the list of host state's mandatory requirements applicable to the posted workers, while leaving the definition of the actual content to the single Member States.
36. The test required by Article 3(10) of the PWD for qualifying a public policy provisions is, indeed, substantially identical to the one prescribed by Article 9(1) of the Rome I Regulation for

between the Posting of Workers Directive (even after the entry into effect of Directive (EU) 2018/957) and private international law means that, in case of posting, a number of host country provisions apply to the employment relationship as overriding mandatory rules under Article 9 of the Rome I Regulation, and the Posting of Workers Directive basically regulates their (minimum and maximum) degree of application.[37]

3.3 THE POSTING OF WORKERS DIRECTIVE

On 16 December 1996, the exceptional treatment already reserved to posted workers by the Union rules in the sphere of private international law and autonomously by certain Member States, allowing the application of the workers' home state law, was codified by the European legislator with the adoption of the Posting of Workers Directive. On that occasion, the long-lasting dispute over the law applicable to posting of workers was finally resolved by including the phenomenon at issue under the framework of the free provision of services (Article 56 TFEU, at that time Article 49of the Treaty establishing the European Community (TEC)). The choice of legal basis, perfectly in line with the Court of Justice case law,[38] clearly indicates the Directive's inclination to the promotion of the cross-border provision of services. But yet, it does not reflect its entire purpose. In effect, this piece of legislation was conceived as an instrument of reconciliation of the economic purposes stemming from the creation of the EU internal market with the social rights of the workers involved (in both the sending and receiving countries).[39] The Posting of Workers Directive's ultimate scope of ensuring a level playing field between foreign and local competitors was pursued through measures aimed at preventing social dumping and unfair competition.[40] To that extent, the

regarding a host state's provision as overridingly mandatory. Louise Merrett, 'Posted Workers in Europe from a Private International Law Perspective' (2011) 13 Cambridge Yearbook of European Legal Studies 219, 244; Barnard, *EU Employment Law* (n 21) 231; Grušić (n 16) 209–210.

37. Evju and Novitz (n 10) 37; van Hoek and Houwerzijl, '"Posting" and "Posted Workers": The Need for Clear Definitions of Two Key Concepts of the Posting of Workers Directive' (n 14) 442–443; Barnard, *EU Employment Law* (n 21) 232; van Hoek and Houwerzijl, 'Where Do EU Mobile Workers Belong, According to Rome I and the (E)PWD?' (n 14) 222.
38. *Alfred John Webb* (n 30); *Société anonyme de droit français Seco et Société anonyme de droit français Desquenne & Giral v Etablissement d'assurance contre la vieillesse et l'invalidité* [1982] ECJ Joined Cases C-62/81 and C-63/81, ECLI:EU:C:1982:34; *Rush Portuguesa Lda v Office national d'immigration* [1990] ECJ Case C-113/89, ECLI:EU:C:1990:142; *Raymond Vander Elst v Office des Migrations Internationales* [1994] ECJ Case C-43/93, ECLI:EU:C:1994:310. On this point, *see* Marco Rocca, *Posting of Workers and Collective Labour Law: There and Back Again* (Intersentia 2015) 177.
39. Davies, 'Posted Workers: Single Market or Protection of National Labour Law Systems?' (n 35) 572–573, 591–592 and 598–599; Cornelissen and Van Limberghen (n 14) 345 and 367; Dagmar Schiek et al., 'EU Social and Labour Rights and EU Internal Market Law' (European Parliament, EMPL Committee 2015) IP/A/EMPL/ST/2014-02, 41; Rebecca Zahn, 'Revision of the Posted Workers' Directive: Equality at Last?' (2016) 5 European (Legal) Studies on-line papers, Queen's University Belfast – School of Law – Centre of European and Transnational Legal Studies 1; Rebecca Zahn, 'Revision of the Posted Workers' Directive: A Europeanisation Perspective' (2017) 19 Cambridge Yearbook of European Legal Studies 187, 208–209.
40. Preamble Recitals 1–2 and 5 of Directive 96/71/EC of the European Parliament and of the Council of 16 December 1996 concerning the posting of workers in the framework of the

protectionist approach in favour of domestic labour regulations was combined with a regulatory differentiation between posted and local workers with regard to their terms and conditions of employment, and especially, to their wages.

The firm determination of the law applicable in case of working activity performed for a limited period of time in another Member State definitively resolved the conflict of laws arising in such a peculiar context of transnational labour mobility. In particular, the Directive (even after the 2018 legislative reform) represents an instrument of coordination of the different national labour laws, directed at the definition of a 'hard core' of mandatory rules on minimum protection determined by the receiving Member States and extendable to posted workers.[41] In this sense, as well stated in Preamble Recitals 7-11, it falls perfectly within the private international law framework laid down in the 1980 Rome Convention on the law applicable to contractual obligations,[42] subsequently transposed into the 2008 Rome I Regulation.[43] As far as the specific content of the Posting of Workers Directive is concerned, a detailed examination of the latter is provided in the following analysis, preceded by a reconstruction, in the next section, of its turbulent birth process.

provision of services (n 8). The twofold scope of the PWD has been explicitly recognised by the Court of Justice in *Wolff & Müller GmbH & Co. KG v José Filipe Pereira Félix* (n 32) para. 42; *Commission of the European Communities v Federal Republic of Germany* [2006] ECJ Case C-244/04, ECLI:EU:C:2006:49 [61]; *Laval un Partneri Ltd v Svenska Byggnadsarbetareförbundet, Svenska Byggnadsarbetareförbundets avdelning 1, Byggettan and Svenska Elektrikerförbundet* (n 30) paras 74-75. On this point, *see* Stein Evju, 'Posting Past and Present: The Posting of Workers Directive - Genesis and Current Contrasts' (2009) 8 FORMULA Working Paper, University of Oslo, Department of Private Law 10; Aukje A.H. van Hoek and Mijke Houwerzijl, 'Comparative Study on the Legal Aspects of the Posting of Workers in the Framework of the Provision of Services in the European Union' (2011) 2; Barnard, *EU Employment Law* (n 21) 218; Kristina Maslauskaite, 'Posted Workers in the EU: State of Play and Regulatory Evolution' (2014) Policy Paper, Notre Europe Jaques Delors Institute 20, 1; Verschueren (n 3) 140-141; Mia Rönnmar, 'Labour and Equality Law' in Catherine Barnard and Steve Peers (eds), *European Union Law* (Second Edition, Oxford University Press 2017) 609.

41. Preamble Recital 13 of Directive 96/71/EC of the European Parliament and of the Council of 16 December 1996 concerning the posting of workers in the framework of the provision of services (n 8). The role of the PWD as coordinator of different national labour regulations has been also recognised by the Court in *Commission of the European Communities v Federal Republic of Germany* (n 40) paras 17-19; *Laval un Partneri Ltd v Svenska Byggnadsarbetareförbundet, Svenska Byggnadsarbetareförbundets avdelning 1, Byggettan and Svenska Elektrikerförbundet* (n 30) paras 60, 68 and 108; *Tevfik Isbir v DB Services* [2013] CJEU Case C-522/12, ECLI: EU:C:2013:711 [35]. ACL Davies, 'One Step Forward, Two Steps Back? The Viking and Laval Cases in the ECJ' (2008) 37 Industrial Law Journal 126, 128; Philippa Watson, *EU Social and Employment Law* (Second Edition, Oxford University Press 2014) 284-285; Verschueren (n 3) 139; Grušić (n 16) 278; Robert Schütze, *European Union Law* (Second Edition, Cambridge University Press 2018) 674.
42. Convention 80/934/EEC of 19 June 1980 on the law applicable to contractual obligations (the Rome Convention) (n 6).
43. Regulation (EC) No 593/2008 of the European Parliament and of the Council of 17 June 2008 on the law applicable to contractual obligations (Rome I) (n 7). *See* van Hoek and Houwerzijl, '"Posting" and "Posted Workers": The Need for Clear Definitions of Two Key Concepts of the Posting of Workers Directive' (n 14) 420; Verschueren (n 3) 139. On the relationship between the PWD and the relevant provisions of PIL, *see supra* section 3.2.

3.3.1 Origin

The journey leading to the adoption of the Posting of Workers Directive was long and arduous, lasting almost six years of negotiations, which resulted in the drafting of three different proposals.[44] In order to properly comprehend the reasons underpinning the choices made by the European legislator in this sense, it is worth briefly narrating, first of all, the normative context which gave rise to the above-mentioned legislative process.

3.3.1.1 Conceptual Genesis

From the investigation of several academic sources, four different types of influences can be identified as background for the adoption of the Posting of Workers Directive, which are hereby presented in chronological order. *In primis*, it should be noted that the Directive certainly emerged from the inherent conflict of laws arising in the context of intra-EU labour mobility whereby, given the intrinsic cross-border dimension of posting, the dilemma whether the home or host state legal regime, or a combination of the two, should apply is necessarily at stake.[45] The free movement of workers was originally regulated by two acts of secondary legislation adopting diametrically opposed approaches. On the one hand, Regulation (EEC) 1612/68[46] on freedom of movement for workers envisaged the application from 'day one' of the principle of *lex loci laboris* while, on the other hand, the 'country of origin' principle was foreseen in the field of social security by Regulation 1408/71/EC for all postings lasting less than twelve months.[47]

The first attempt to resolve such a conflict was made by the Commission in 1972 with a proposal for a regulation on conflict of laws pertaining to employment

44. For an in-depth analysis of the troubled genesis of the PWD, *see* Werner Eichhorst, 'European Social Policy between National and Supranational Regulation: Posted Workers in the Framework of Liberalized Services Provision' (1998) MPIfG discussion paper, No. 98/6 *Max Planck Institute for the Study of Societies (MPIfG), Cologne* 17 and ff. <https://www.econstor.eu/bitstream/10419/43182/1/248171305.pdf> (accessed 17 January 2019); Evju, 'Posting Past and Present: The Posting of Workers Directive – Genesis and Current Contrasts' (n 40) 6 and ff.; Stein Evju, 'Revisiting the Posted Workers Directive: Conflict of Laws and Laws in Contrast' (2009) 12 Cambridge Yearbook of European Legal Studies 151, 154 and ff.; Evju and Novitz (n 10) 22 and ff.; Rocca (n 38) 113 and ff.
45. Evju and Novitz (n 10) 4.
46. Article 7 of Regulation (EEC) No 1612/68 of the Council of 15 October 1968 on freedom of movement for workers within the Community 1968 (OJ L 257/2).
47. Article 14(1) of Regulation (EEC) No 1408/71 of the Council of 14 June 1971 on the application of social security schemes to employed persons and their families moving within the Community 1971 (OJ L 149/2). It is noted that, according to Regulation 1408/71/EC, posting lasting more than twelve months were falling under the *lex loci laboris* principle. Evju, 'Revisiting the Posted Workers Directive: Conflict of Laws and Laws in Contrast' (n 44) 155; Evju and Novitz (n 10) 5-6 and 9-10.

relations,[48] which was substantially amended four years later,[49] and eventually withdrawn in 1981, after the adoption of the 1980 Rome Convention.[50] Despite that proposal found its legal basis in the Treaty rules governing the free movement of workers - and thus, not in the free provision of services - it should be considered, nonetheless, as the authentic forerunner of the Posting of Workers Directive. Transnational labour activities in the form of intra-company postings were, indeed, already covered by the 1972 version, whereas the 1976 amended draft included all temporary posting activities.[51] Furthermore, while the first proposal left the decision of the applicable law (of the home state or of the host state) to the parties of the contract themselves, the updated version resolutely moved towards the adoption of the 'country of origin' principle.[52] In addition, just as in Article 3(1) of the Posting of Workers Directive, in both the versions of the proposal, a number of exceptions to the general rule were collected in a list of provisions (*lois de police*) to be set by the host country.[53]

The idea of applying the home state law in combination with a series of terms and conditions of employment established at the place of work was taken up again in 1986 in a project of the European Federation of Building and Woodworkers (EFBWW). The intention was to include a sort of 'social clause' into the Directive on liberalisation of public procurement,[54] along the lines of Article 2 of the ILO Convention No. 94.[55]

48. Commission des Communautes Europeennes, Proposition de reglement (CEE) du Conseil relatif aux dispositions concernant les conflits de lois en matière de relations de travail à l'intérieur de la Communauté 1972 [COM(72) 170 final]. On this point, *see* Evju, 'Revisiting the Posted Workers Directive: Conflict of Laws and Laws in Contrast' (n 44) 156.
49. Commission of the European Communities, Amended proposal for a Regulation of the Council on the provisions of conflict of laws on employment relationships within the Community 1976 [COM(75) 653 final].
50. Convention 80/934/EEC of 19 June 1980 on the law applicable to contractual obligations (the Rome Convention) (n 6). *See supra* section 3.2.
51. In particular, the similarity with the PWD is evident in Article 4 of the 1976 amended proposal concerning all 'workers who are sent by their undertaking to other Member States to carry out temporary activities'.
52. Article 4 of Commission of the European Communities Amended proposal for a Regulation of the Council on the provisions of conflict of laws on employment relationships within the Community (n 49).
53. Article 4(2) of Commission des Communautes Europeennes Proposition de reglement (CEE) du Conseil relatif aux dispositions concernant les conflits de lois en matière de relations de travail à l'intérieur de la Communauté (n 48). Article 8(1) of Commission of the European Communities Amended proposal for a Regulation of the Council on the provisions of conflict of laws on employment relationships within the Community (n 49). On this point, *see* Evju, 'Revisiting the Posted Workers Directive: Conflict of Laws and Laws in Contrast' (n 44) 157-158; Rocca (n 38) 115-118.
54. Directive 89/440/EEC of 18 July 1989 amending Directive 71/305/EEC concerning coordination of procedures for the award of public works contracts 1989 (OJ L 210/1).
55. International Labour Organization (ILO), Labour Clauses (Public Contracts) Convention, 1949 (No. 94): Convention concerning Labour Clauses in Public Contracts (Entry into force: 20 Sep 1952) 1949. Notably, by analogy with the upcoming PWD, Article 2(1) of the ILO Convention provides that: 'Contracts to which this Convention applies shall include clauses ensuring to the workers concerned wages (including allowances), hours of work and other conditions of labour which are not less favourable than those established for work of the same character in the trade or industry concerned in the district where the work is carried on: (a) by collective agreement or other recognised machinery of negotiation between organisations of employers and workers representative respectively of substantial proportions of the employers and workers in the trade or industry concerned; or (b) by arbitration award; or (c) by national laws or regulations.'

However, due to the lack of full *consensus* in the Council of Ministers, the 'social clause' approved was merely optional, conditional on the willingness of the public contractor, and thus without real effectiveness.[56] In spite of the defeat, the EFBWW did not give up and, eventually, managed to influence the content of the 1989 Commission's Action Programme[57] by promoting the inclusion, among its priorities, of the need to reform not only the practice of seconding workers in the building industry but the activity of posting of workers as a whole.[58]

The above-mentioned 1989 Action Programme is deemed to have had a considerable influence on the drafting of the Posting of Workers Directive as well. Such an instrument came to light in order to promote the implementation of the Charter of the Fundamental Social Rights of Workers, adopted on 8 December 1989.[59] Notably, the so-called 'Social Charter', consisting of a combination of these two interlinking documents, was the result of the Jaques Delors' impulse towards the development of social policies in the European internal market.[60] The impact of the Action Programme is mainly reflected in the (at that time) innovative conception of the phenomenon of posting under the EU rules concerning the free provision of services. This is evident in the Commission's proposal for a European legal instrument regarding the working conditions of short-term cross-border workers.[61]

Finally, just a few months after the Action Programme was launched, the regulation of posting of workers was drastically shaped by the decision of the Court of Justice in *Rush Portuguesa*,[62] delivered on 27 March 1990. Evidently, this judgment played a prominent role in the genesis process of the Posting of Workers Directive.[63] In

56. On this point, *see* Eichhorst (n 44) 17–18; Evju, 'Posting Past and Present: The Posting of Workers Directive – Genesis and Current Contrasts' (n 40) 9.
57. Communication from the Commission concerning its Action Programme relating to the implementation of the Community Charter of Basic Social Rights for Workers 1989 [COM(89) 568 final] (hereinafter also referred to as the 'Action Programme').
58. More specifically, the reform envisaged by the EFBWW encouraged the application of host state law from 'day one' of the posting, except in the case of more favourable employment conditions guaranteed to seconded workers in their country of origin. On this point, *see* Evju, 'Posting Past and Present: The Posting of Workers Directive – Genesis and Current Contrasts' (n 40) 9–10.
59. Community Charter of the Fundamental Social Rights of Workers 1989 (Declaration by President Delors on 8 December 1989 at the European Council of Strasbourg).
60. Evju, 'Posting Past and Present: The Posting of Workers Directive – Genesis and Current Contrasts' (n 40) 10; Evju, 'Revisiting the Posted Workers Directive: Conflict of Laws and Laws in Contrast' (n 44) 160.
61. This proposal was listed among the 'New Initiatives' in the context of the 'Freedom of movement' and provided for the elaboration of a 'Community instrument on working conditions applicable to workers from another State performing work in the host country in the framework of the freedom to provide services, especially on behalf of a sub-contracting undertaking.' Communication from the Commission concerning its Action Programme relating to the implementation of the Community Charter of Basic Social Rights for Workers (n 57). The absolute absence in the Action Programme of indication of the legal basis for an eventual legislative proposal is, however, worth noting, as well as the contrast with the Preamble to the Charter of the Fundamental Social Rights of Workers, which exclusively refers to the free movement of workers and the right of establishment. Evju, 'Revisiting the Posted Workers Directive: Conflict of Laws and Laws in Contrast' (n 44) 160–161; Rocca (n 38) 118–119.
62. *Rush Portuguesa Lda v Office national d'immigration* (n 38).
63. Houwerzijl and Pennings (n 31) 102; De Vos (n 29) 361–362; Evju, 'Posting Past and Present: The Posting of Workers Directive – Genesis and Current Contrasts' (n 40) 11; Jon Erik Dølvik and

particular, the case concerned the legitimacy under EU law of the requirement, imposed by the French Immigration Office (*Office national d'immigration*) on a cross-border service provider (namely, the Portuguese company *Rush Portuguesa*), to obtain work permits for all the third-country employees posted in France for the construction of a railway (*TGV*).[64]

The judges in Luxembourg, after placing – firmly for the first time – the posting activity within the EU legal framework concerning the free provision of services,[65] declared the French work permit requirements to be an obstacle to the exercise of such a European fundamental freedom. In the dispute at issue, the Portuguese workers were considered as staff of the service supplier and, for that reason, indirectly covered by their employer's right to provide services under Articles 59 and 60 of the EEC Treaty (now Articles 56 and 57 TFEU).[66] The choice of the legal basis was motivated by taking into account the temporary nature of the cross-border service provision, whereby the posted workers are supposed to return to their country of origin after the completion of their assignment. For that reason, in the view of the Court, the latter workers never gain access to the labour market of the host Member State.[67] In addition, the decision in

Jelle Visser, 'Free Movement, Equal Treatment and Workers' Rights: Can the European Union Solve Its Trilemma of Fundamental Principles?: Free Movement, Equal Treatment and Workers' Rights' (2009) 40 Industrial Relations Journal 491, 496; Claire Kilpatrick, 'Internal Market Architecture and the Accommodation of Labour Rights: As Good as It Gets?' (2011) Law 2011/04 EUI Working Paper 4; Vassilis Hatzopoulos, *Regulating Services in the European Union* (Oxford University Press 2012) 354; Evju and Novitz (n 10) 23; Dorte Sindbjerg Martinsen, 'The European Social Union and EU Legislative Politics' in Frank Vandenbroucke, Catherine Barnard and Geert De Baere (eds), *A European Social Union after the Crisis* (Cambridge University Press 2017) 468.

64. It is recalled that, at that time, Portuguese posted workers were not entitled of full free movement rights, due to the application of specific 'transitional arrangements' consequent to the 1986 accession of Portugal to what was then the European Community. Interestingly, though, no boundary was posed by those 'transitional arrangements' to the free provision of services. Evju and Novitz (n 10) 14.
65. It is noticeable that, in two other occasions, the Court had already considered – even though in a more nuanced way – the cross-border provision of manpower as covered by the EU rules governing the freedom to provide services. In this sense, *see* the judgments in *Alfred John Webb* (n 30); *Société anonyme de droit français Seco et Société anonyme de droit français Desquenne & Giral v Etablissement d'assurance contre la vieillesse et l'invalidité* (n 38). On this point, *see* Houwerzijl and Pennings (n 31) 92–93 and 104; Evju, 'Posting Past and Present: The Posting of Workers Directive – Genesis and Current Contrasts' (n 40) 12–13. Besides, the position taken by Advocate General Van Gerven in the same case is worth noting, as he proposed to limit the exception only to the 'personnel in a position of responsibility and trusted personnel' and to the 'workers who have a specialization or special qualifications which are essential for the provision of the service and who could not be obtained on the labour market', while leaving the other employees under the rules and the protection reserved by the Treaty rules governing the free movement of workers. Opinion of Advocate General Walter Van Gerven in *Rush Portuguesa Lda v Office national d'immigration, Opinion of Advocate General Walter Van Gerven delivered on 7 March 1990* [1990] ECJ Case C-113/89, ECLI:EU:C:1990:107 [17]. *See* Evju and Novitz (n 10) 15.
66. Verschueren (n 4) 172–173. As already noted *supra* in Chapter 2, the freedom to provide services empowers an employer to move freely across borders in order to supply services, with the possibility to bring all his employees.
67. *Rush Portuguesa Lda v Office national d'immigration* (n 38) para. 15. This argument was subsequently confirmed in *Raymond Vander Elst v Office des Migrations Internationales* (n 38) para. 21; *Finalarte Sociedade de Construção Civil v Urlaubs- und Lohnausgleichskasse der Bauwirtschaft* (n 29) para. 22. On this point, *see* Houwerzijl and Pennings (n 31) 93–94;

Rush Portuguesa recognised, in a well-known obiter dictum, the existence of an effective boundary to the free provision of services consisting in the possibility for the host Member State to extend potentially the whole set of domestic labour law to posted workers, thus curbing any potential risk of erosion of the highest standard of social protection applied in the 'old' Member States.[68]

It is worth noting, though, that the landmark judgment at stake diverged from its precursor in *Seco*[69] by expanding the host country's discretion regarding the imposition of virtually all its labour regulation to foreign workers on temporary cross-border service assignments.[70] The latter ruling, in turn, considerably limited such a capacity to

---

Verschueren (n 4) 174–175; Evju, 'Posting Past and Present: The Posting of Workers Directive – Genesis and Current Contrasts' (n 40) 13; van Hoek and Houwerzijl, '"Posting" and "Posted Workers": The Need for Clear Definitions of Two Key Concepts of the Posting of Workers Directive' (n 14) 445–446; Evju and Novitz (n 10) 14; Barnard, *The Substantive Law of the EU: The Four Freedoms* (n 3) 422–423.

68. In the words of the Court: 'Community law does not preclude Member States from extending their legislation, or collective labour agreements entered into by both sides of industry, to any person who is employed, even temporarily, within their territory, no matter in which country the employer is established; nor does Community law prohibit Member States from enforcing those rules by appropriate means.' *Rush Portuguesa Lda v Office national d'immigration* (n 38) para. 18. As interestingly noted by Davies, the principle enunciated by the European Court on that occasion basically entailed the application of the same treatment to both posted and migrant workers. In subsequent rulings in the context of services, the Court took, instead, a different approach whereby, following a reasoning analogous to the one used in case of free movement of goods, it required the abolition of any restriction 'which is liable to prohibit, impede or render less advantageous the activities of a provider of services established in another Member State where he lawfully provides similar services'. This so-called 'market access' test, which focuses on removing restrictions on free movement rather than on the discriminatory character of a certain measure, was used in *Manfred Säger v Dennemeyer & Co Ltd* [1991] ECJ Case C-76/90, ECLI:EU:C:1991:331 [12]; *Raymond Vander Elst v Office des Migrations Internationales* (n 38) para. 14; *Her Majesty's Customs and Excise v Gerhart Schindler and Jörg Schindler* [1994] ECJ Case C-275/92, ECLI:EU:C:1994:119 [43]; *Alpine Investments BV v Minister van Financiën* [1995] ECJ Case C-384/93, ECLI:EU:C:1995:126 [35–38]; *Guiot v Climatee SA* (n 31) para. 10; *Reisebüro Broede v Gerd Sandker* [1996] ECJ Case C-3/95, ECLI:EU:C:1996:487 [25]; *Société civile immobilière Parodi v Banque H Albert de Bary et Cie* [1997] ECJ Case C-222/95, ECLI:EU:C:1997:345 [18]; *Arblade & Fils SARL v Sofrage SARL* (n 27) para. 33. On this point, *see* Davies, 'Posted Workers: Single Market or Protection of National Labour Law Systems?' (n 35) 586, 589–590; Catherine Barnard, 'Social Dumping or Dumping Socialism?' (2008) 67 The Cambridge Law Journal 264; Evju, 'Revisiting the Posted Workers Directive: Conflict of Laws and Laws in Contrast' (n 44) 161; Gareth Davies, 'Discrimination and beyond in European Economic and Social Law' (2011) 18 Maastricht Journal of European and Comparative Law 7, 20; Jan Cremers, 'Free Provision of Services and Cross-Border Labour Recruitment' (2013) 34 Policy Studies 201, 210; Catherine Barnard, 'Free Movement and Labour Rights: Squaring the Circle?' (2013) 23/2013 University of Cambridge Faculty of Law Legal Studies Research Paper 4; Nicola Countouris and Samuel Engblom, '"Protection or Protectionism?": A Legal Deconstruction of the Emerging False Dilemma in European Integration' (2015) UCL Labour Rights Institute On-Line Working Papers – LRI WP 26; Verschueren (n 3) 138; Catherine Barnard, 'The Calm after the Storm: Time to Reflect on EU (Labour) Law Scholarship Following the Decisions in Viking and Laval' (2015) University of Cambridge Faculty of Law Research Paper No. 55/2015, later published in Alan Bogg, Cathryn Costello and ACL Davies (eds), *Research Handbook on EU Labour Law* (Edward Elgar Publishing) 337, 4; Barnard, *The Substantive Law of the EU: The Four Freedoms* (n 3) 423.

69. *Société anonyme de droit français Seco et Société anonyme de droit français Desquenne & Giral v Etablissement d'assurance contre la vieillesse et l'invalidité* (n 38).

70. As a direct consequence of the decision in *Rush Portuguesa*, several Member States, including France and Germany – which were the biggest importers of posted workers – immediately

the 'minimum wages'.[71] The Court of Justice adopted an approach more similar to *Seco* also in its subsequent decision in *Vander Elst*[72] where, after confirming the principles recognised in *Rush Portuguesa*, restricted the host Member State's room for manoeuvre with regard to the employment law applicable to incoming short-term transnational workforce to the 'national rules of public policy'.[73] What is striking in the line of argumentation of the Court in *Rush Portuguesa* was the main concern to the preservation of the Member States' advanced systems of social protection. In fact, the centre of the discourse was, not surprisingly, completely detached from the interests and prerogatives of the posted workers, leaving aside any consideration regarding the labour treatment of posted and local employees.[74]

3.3.1.2 The Drafting Process

The market integrationist approach taken by the EU judiciary, in combination with the political input of the President of the Commission Jaques Delors with the project 'Europe 1992' towards the perfection of the EU single market,[75] paved the way for the drafting of a piece of EU legislation aimed at specifying the Member States' regulatory

started to amend their domestic employment law in a way to include the activity of transnational service providers. For a punctual analysis of the legislative measures undertaken, *see* Davies, 'Posted Workers: Single Market or Protection of National Labour Law Systems?' (n 35) 590–591; Evju and Novitz (n 10) 16–22.

71. *Société anonyme de droit français Seco et Société anonyme de droit français Desquenne & Giral v Etablissement d'assurance contre la vieillesse et l'invalidité* (n 38) para. 14. Notably, on that occasion the Court overruled the Advocate General Van Themaat's opinion, whereby the possibility for foreign service providers to fully benefit from their competitive advantage was mainly emphasised. *Société anonyme de droit français Seco et Société anonyme de droit français Desquenne & Giral v Etablissement d'assurance contre la vieillesse et l'invalidité, Opinion of Advocate General Verloren Van Themaat delivered on 16 December 1981* [1981] ECJ Joined Cases C-62/81 and C-63/81, ECLI:EU:C:1981:305 [4]. *See* Verschueren (n 4) 172–173; Evju and Novitz (n 10) 14; Watson (n 41) 284; Piet Van Nuffel and Sofia Afanasjeva, 'The Posting of Workers Directive Revised: Enhancing the Protection of Workers in the Cross-Border Provision of Services' (2018) 3 European Papers 1401, 1406.
72. *Raymond Vander Elst v Office des Migrations Internationales* (n 38).
73. *Ibid.* 23 and 25. Verschueren (n 4) 173; Verschueren (n 3) 138.
74. Davies, 'Posted Workers: Single Market or Protection of National Labour Law Systems?' (n 35) 590; Evju, 'Posting Past and Present: The Posting of Workers Directive - Genesis and Current Contrasts' (n 40) 14. For a wider perspective on the narrative proposed by the Court of Justice, the European institutions and, more generally, the vast majority of the political discourse at EU level, which was - and still seems to be - mainly oriented to the protection of the interests of the 'centre', rather than of those of the 'periphery' of the Union, *see* Damjan Kukovec, 'A Critique of the Rhetoric of Common Interest in the European Union Legal Discourse' (2012) SSRN Electronic Journal 11; Damjan Kukovec, 'Hierarchies as Law' (2014) 21 Columbia Journal of European Law 131; Damjan Kukovec, 'Law and the Periphery' (2015) 21 European Law Journal 406.
75. Claus-Dieter Ehlermann, 'The "1992 Project": Stages, Structures, Results and Prospects' (1990) 11 Michigan Journal of International Law 23; European Commission, 'Press Release - Presentation by President Jaques Delors of the Commission Programme for 1992 and the Delors II Package at the European Parliament' (*European Commission Press Releases Database*, 12 February 1992) <http://europa.eu/rapid/press-release_SPEECH-92-12_en.htm> (accessed 28 January 2019); van Hoek and Houwerzijl, 'Comparative Study on the Legal Aspects of the Posting of Workers in the Framework of the Provision of Services in the European Union' (n 40) 1.

powers in the context of posting of workers.[76] After extensive consultations with both Member States and European and national social partners already started in September 1990, the first official proposal for a new directive was eventually tabled by the Commission on 28 June 1991.[77] This first text already showed a number of similarities with the final version of the Posting of Workers Directive. More specifically, it unequivocally placed the phenomenon of posting under the framework of the transnational provision of services[78] and identified the three different configurations of the cross-border activity at issue.[79] Along the lines of the 1976 amended version of the proposal for a regulation on conflict of laws with regard to employment relations, it envisaged also a list of 'hard core' terms and conditions of employment of host country law applicable to seconded workers.[80] However, this draft was not fortunate enough to reach a final consensus, mainly due to the controversial three-month threshold for extension of the host state's minimum wages and holidays. A further cause of friction concerned the source of those 'hard core' provisions. In fact, by solely including law and universally applicable collective agreements, it had the effect of excluding all collective agreements devoid of *erga omnes* effect, as well as the wage levels and working conditions de facto applied in certain national realities.[81]

The above-mentioned issues had been subsequently addressed in a second proposal of the Commission, adopted on 16 June 1993.[82] On that occasion, as a result of the pressure from the European Parliament and the Economic and Social Committee, the three-month threshold for the application of host country's rules was reduced to one month.[83] Furthermore, also those collective agreements which are generally applicable in the host state were included among the means to lay down specific terms and conditions of employment to posted workers.[84] Showing stronger sensibility to social concerns, a new 'favourability clause' was incorporated as well, thus leaving the

76. The drafting of the Posting of Workers Directive was not merely aimed at codifying the ECJ's case law in *Seco, Rush Portuguesa* and *Vander Elst*, but also at containing its potential deregulatory effects. Hatzopoulos, *Regulating Services in the European Union* (n 63) 354; Evju and Novitz (n 10) 16–17.
77. Commission of the European Communities, Proposal for a Council Directive concerning the posting of workers in the framework of the provision of services 1991 [COM(91) 230 final]. On this point, *see* Eichhorst (n 44) 17; Evju, 'Revisiting the Posted Workers Directive: Conflict of Laws and Laws in Contrast' (n 44) 165; Evju and Novitz (n 10) 24.
78. Preamble and Article 1 of the Commission of the European Communities Proposal for a Council Directive concerning the posting of workers in the framework of the provision of services (n 77).
79. *Ibid.* Article 2.
80. *Ibid.* Article 3. Interestingly, though, that list was shorter than the one of 1976. Evju and Novitz (n 10) 25; Rocca (n 38) 120.
81. Jan Cremers, 'The Posting Directive: Origins and Assessment' (1995) 1(2) Transfer: European Review of Labour and Research 309, 313; Evju, 'Posting Past and Present: The Posting of Workers Directive – Genesis and Current Contrasts' (n 40) 15–16; Evju and Novitz (n 10) 25–26; Rocca (n 38) 121.
82. Commission of the European Communities, Amended proposal for a Council Directive concerning the posting of workers in the framework of the provision of services 1993 [COM(93) 225 final].
83. *Ibid.* Article 3(2). *See* Martinsen (n 63) 468.
84. Commission of the European Communities Amended proposal for a Council Directive concerning the posting of workers in the framework of the provision of services (n 82) Article 3(4). Besides, the list of 'hard core' provisions was slightly enlarged.

door open for the enforcement of better employment standards.[85] In spite of the efforts made, this second draft directive was no more fortunate than the first one. The threshold period still remained an open issue;[86] there was no agreement on the sources of the host state's 'hard core' provisions and neither on the actual content of the latter list.[87] In the meanwhile, in response to the sharp slowdown of the drafting process at Union level, those Member States opposing to the introduction of a grace period for the application of host state law to posted workers - namely France, Belgium, the Netherlands, Luxembourg, Germany, Denmark, Austria and Sweden - started introducing more restrictive rules for incoming foreign service providers.[88]

A new text was then proposed by France during its presidency in the first half of 1995,[89] foreseeing a number of novelties. The threshold period was reduced to one month with applicability optional to the individual will of the Member States and, a few months later, was reduced to an indefinite number of days. The 'hard core' list was left 'open', thus allowing the introduction of more stringent national requirements and, following the German suggestion, the provisions laid down by collective agreements were made mandatory only for the building sector.[90] Unfortunately, once again, the draft found disagreement at the political level and ran aground during the second half of 1995, under the Spanish Presidency in the Council. However, with the new year and the new Italian presidency, the proposal was revived, and this time for good. In particular, the Italian Minister of Labour, Treu, constantly assisted by the brilliant professor Biagi (at that time consultant to the European Commission's Directorate-General for Employment and Social Affairs), after several consultations with his counterparts, managed to table a consolidated proposal on 16 February 1996.

The so-called 'Italian compromise' was characterised by a series of solutions intended to accommodate, at the same time, the requests of all different actors taking part in the drafting process. With regard to the highly contentious regulation of a threshold period, the general rule of a 'zero threshold' was introduced, although

85. Commission of the European Communities Amended proposal for a Council Directive concerning the posting of workers in the framework of the provision of services (n 82). Article 3(3). On this point, *see* Evju, 'Posting Past and Present: The Posting of Workers Directive - Genesis and Current Contrasts' (n 40) 16–17; Evju and Novitz (n 10) 26; Rocca (n 38) 122.
86. The Council was very much divided on that issue, with six states (*inter alia* France, the Netherlands, Belgium and Denmark) in favour of a 'zero threshold' and the other six torn between a one-, three- or four-month threshold (with especially Portugal and UK more in favour of a solution preserving the competitive economic advantage of transnational service providers). On the other hand, the Commission, with a view to shaping a more efficient internal market, was pushing for a threshold of minimum one month. *See* Evju and Novitz (n 10) 27; Rocca (n 38) 123.
87. Denmark and Italy, in particular, were particularly concerned of the collective agreements issue. The Italian solution envisaged the inclusion of those agreements concluded by 'the most representative' organisations. Germany, on the other hand, proposed to confine the source of collective agreement to the building sector only. *See* Evju and Novitz (n 10) 26–27.
88. As noted *supra*, such reforms were backed by the 1990 decision of the ECJ in *Rush Portuguesa*. Eichhorst (n 44) 20; Rocca (n 38) 124.
89. This revised draft was proposed on 7 February 1995 to the Working Party meetings and COREPER (*Comité des représentants permanents*, i.e., Committee of permanent representatives). Evju, 'Posting Past and Present: The Posting of Workers Directive - Genesis and Current Contrasts' (n 40) 17–18.
90. Evju and Novitz (n 10) 27–28.

mitigated by a number of exceptions. More specifically, the application of minimum wages and minimum annual paid holidays of the host country was excluded for specialised employees posted for a maximum period of eight days for the assembly and initial installation of the infrastructure to be used in the service provision.[91] Furthermore, the Member States were given the possibility, after consulting the social partners, to set a threshold up to one month for the application of minimum wages.[92] The same type of solution could also be envisaged by specific collective agreements in certain sectors of activity.[93] Lastly, the Member States were allowed to exempt an employer from the payment of minimum wages and minimum annual holidays to its seconded workers in case the activity performed was 'not significant'.[94] As for the host country's terms and conditions of employment which should be extended to posted workers, the list provided for by Article 3(1) was considered closed. However, a 'favourability clause' on the model of the one foreseen by the 1993 proposal was introduced, along with the possibility for the Member States to extend the application of domestic law for public policy reasons.[95] Finally, the issue about the means of prescription of the 'hard core' provisions listed by Article 3(1) was resolved by taking into account also the peculiar situations of Denmark and Italy, where the absence of universally applicable collective agreement often implies that the terms and conditions of employment are agreed on a case-by-case basis or fixed by generally applicable collective agreements.[96] Thanks to the larger share of consensus attracted by the higher

91. The mandatory nature of this so-called 'assembly clause' is worth noting, as codified in Article 3(2) of Directive 96/71/EC of the European Parliament and of the Council of 16 December 1996 concerning the posting of workers in the framework of the provision of services (n 8). In addition, a further exception to the exemption of such an 'assembly clause' concerns the building industry, where this possibility is prevented. On this point, *see* Davies, 'Posted Workers: Single Market or Protection of National Labour Law Systems?' (n 35) 583; Evju, 'Posting Past and Present: The Posting of Workers Directive – Genesis and Current Contrasts' (n 40) 19; Watson (n 41) 288; Rocca (n 38) 125–126; European Commission, 'Practical Guide on Posting' (2019) 6.
92. Article 3(3) of Directive 96/71/EC of the European Parliament and of the Council of 16 December 1996 concerning the posting of workers in the framework of the provision of services (n 8).
93. *Ibid.* Article 3(4).
94. *Ibid.* Article 3(5). For the record, the possibility of granting all types of exemptions envisaged by Article 3(3)(4)(5) is excluded in case of workers posted through agencies providing temporary staff.
95. *Ibid.* Article 3(7) and (10). Despite the apparently pacific nature of the 'favourability clause' as referring to the more favourable conditions for posted workers in accordance with their home country regulations, the concept at issue has been a source of debate for years. In this sense, *see infra* sub-subsection 3.3.2.5.
96. Notably, in the event of absence of a system for declaring collective agreements applicable *erga omnes*, the Member States have the possibility to refer to: 'collective agreements or arbitration awards which are generally applicable to all similar undertakings in the geographical area and in the profession or industry concerned, and/or collective agreements which have been concluded by the most representative employers' and labour organizations at national level and which are applied throughout national territory'. *Ibid.* Article 3(8). While the first indent represents the alternative conceived for Denmark, the second provision is known as the 'Italian' clause, since it was specifically designed to address the unique Italian system of industrial relations where no collective bargaining agreement can be considered as universally applicable. Rocca (n 38) 128; Michele Faioli, 'Posted Workers. The Italian Viewpoint' (2016) Economia & Lavoro 47, 50–51. Interestingly enough, pursuant to the following paragraphs of the same article, the extension of the above-mentioned collective agreements to out-of-state service

degree of flexibility of the Italian proposal, and despite the UK voted against and Portugal abstained, the Posting of Workers Directive was eventually adopted by the Council on 24 September 1996. It was then duly signed on 16 December 1996, with a three-year implementation deadline.[97]

3.3.2 Substantive Scope

Consistently with its legal basis, the scope of application of the Posting of Workers Directive is limited to situations involving a transnational provision of services. More specifically, the related regulatory framework solely covers the activity of an undertaking, established in a certain Member State, which posts its own employees to the territory of another Member State in order to carry out a specific service supply.[98] Crucially, then, in line with the nature of the provision of services, the cross-border supply has necessarily to be temporary.[99] Leaving aside the definition of the personal scope of the Directive, envisaging the three possible configurations of posting activities enumerated by Article 1(3) of the Posting of Workers Directive, as well as the notion of 'posted worker' given by Article 2 of the same Directive, both already extensively investigated *supra* in Chapter 2, the present step of analysis focuses on the treatment reserved to posted workers during their mobility abroad. The following investigation refers to the original version of the Posting of Workers Directive, thus prior to the entry into effect of the novelties introduced by the new Directive (EU) 2018/957.

3.3.2.1 'Hard Core' of Terms and Conditions of Employment

By virtue of the Posting of Workers Directive (even after the 2018 legislative reform), whenever a worker is sent by his employer for a limited period of time to another Member State in order to provide a service, he is guaranteed equal treatment as local workers only with regard to a number of terms and conditions of employment. In other words, the host country is not allowed to automatically extend all its labour regulation to incoming posted workers. Pursuant to Article 3(1), the receiving Member State is held to ensure that workers posted to its territory are guaranteed a 'nucleus of

---

providers remains possible only on condition that the equality of treatment vis-à-vis national undertakings which are in a similar position is respected. This means that, in such an event, the host state shall be able to prove that all local undertakings operating in the sector and in the territory concerned are bounded by the same obligations having the same effects.

97. For the record, the formal adoption and signature took place under the Irish presidency of the Council. Evju, 'Posting Past and Present: The Posting of Workers Directive – Genesis and Current Contrasts' (n 40) 20; Evju and Novitz (n 10) 28.
98. Article 1(1) of Directive 96/71/EC of the European Parliament and of the Council of 16 December 1996 concerning the posting of workers in the framework of the provision of services (n 8). Davies, 'Posted Workers: Single Market or Protection of National Labour Law Systems?' (n 35) 575–576; Watson (n 41) 285.
99. On the problematic concept of 'temporary' nature of posting, *see supra* Chapter 2.

mandatory rules for minimum protection'[100] only, which may be complemented, under certain conditions, by further specific provisions. And this, even though the home country does not require the respect of such standards.[101] Technically, however, the Posting of Workers Directive does not confer rights directly upon the posted workers as such. It rather imposes the extension of specific elements of employment protection in force in the host state to the workers posted in the territory of the latter.[102] The establishment of this 'hard core' of terms and conditions of employment has been conceived with a twofold purpose, namely the social protection of cross-border workers and the safeguard of the host state labour market against unfair competition and social dumping.[103]

More in detail, the list laid down by Article 3(1) of the original Posting of Workers Directive included: (a) duration of the work, and thus maximum work periods and minimum rest periods; (b) minimum paid annual holidays; (c) minimum rates of pay, including overtime rates; (d) conditions of hiring-out of workers, especially in respect of temporary employment agencies; (e) rules on health, safety and hygiene at the workplace; (f) protective measures for special groups of employees, namely pregnant women, women who recently gave birth, young people and children; and (g) provisions aimed at ensuring equal treatment between men and women and non-discrimination. As underlined during the analysis of the Directive's drafting history, in the absence of any threshold period for the application of host country rules, all those provisions are enforceable since the very first day of the posting.[104] It should be

100. Preamble Recital 13 of Directive 96/71/EC of the European Parliament and of the Council of 16 December 1996 concerning the posting of workers in the framework of the provision of services (n 8).

101. Davies, 'Posted Workers: Single Market or Protection of National Labour Law Systems?' (n 35) 571–572; Jan Cremers, 'In Search of Cheap Labour in Europe – Working and Living Conditions of Posted Workers' (2011) CLR News 6, 6; Catherine Barnard, 'EU Employment Law and the European Social Model: The Past, the Present and the Future' (2014) 67 Current Legal Problems 199, 219; Catherine Barnard, 'Posting Matters' (2014) 11 Arbeidsrett 1, 1–2; Verschueren (n 3) 140.

102. Zahn, 'Revision of the Posted Workers Directive' (n 39) 7.

103. Preamble Recital 5 of Directive 96/71/EC of the European Parliament and of the Council of 16 December 1996 concerning the posting of workers in the framework of the provision of services (n 8). *Wolff & Müller GmbH & Co. KG v José Filipe Pereira Félix* (n 32) para. 42; *Laval un Partneri Ltd v Svenska Byggnadsarbetareförbundet, Svenska Byggnadsarbetareförbundets avdelning 1, Byggettan and Svenska Elektrikerförbundet* (n 30) paras 74–75; *Sähköalojen ammattiliitto ry v Elektrobudowa Spolka Akcyjna* [2015] CJEU Case C-396/13, ECLI:EU:C:2015:86 [30]. Davies, 'The Posted Workers Directive and the EC Treaty' (n 31) 300; Catherine Barnard and Geert De Baere, 'Towards a European Social Union: Achievements and Possibilities under the Current EU Constitutional Framework' (2014) Euroforum Policy Paper (KU Leuven) 22; Frank Hendrickx, 'A Post-Laval Case: ESA and Minimum Wages for Posted Workers' (2015) 6,1 European Labour Law Journal 2, 3; Verschueren (n 3) 141–142. For a contrasting opinion, considering those two purposes as conflicting with each other and, thus, the PWD as a piece of legislation mainly focusing on the protection of the posted workers and the promotion of the transnational provision of services, *see* Mia Rönnmar, 'Free Movement of Services Versus National Labour Law and Industrial Relations Systems: Understanding the Laval Case from a Swedish and Nordic Perspective' (2007) 10 Cambridge Yearbook of European Legal Studies 493, 505; Rönnmar, 'Labour and Equality Law' (n 40) 609.

104. As it is easy to imagine, particular problems may emerge in cases of very short postings as, for instance, those involving artists or musicians moving to a different Member State simply for a tour date, which entail the application of the provisions laid down in Article 3(1). Frederic De

recalled, likewise, that the legislator envisaged a number of exceptional cases in which the receiving Member States may grant a temporary exemption to cross-border employers from guaranteeing the minimum rates of pay and/or the minimum annual paid holiday period to their posted workers.[105]

Interestingly, the fact that those rules shall apply 'whatever the law applicable to the employment relationship' testifies the limited autonomy of the parties in choosing the law applicable to the employment relationship.[106] At the same time, it reflects the role of the Posting of Workers Directive as a tool for determining the extent of the 'overriding mandatory provisions' applicable by the host state by virtue of private international law.[107] Furthermore, the mere indication of the host state's scope of intervention clearly confirms the coordinating - rather than harmonising - nature of the Directive, which leaves full autonomy to the Member States in individuating the concrete substance of the aforementioned provisions.[108] The other side of the coin of the lack of proper harmonising effect is the consequent development of an extreme variety of legal regimes at EU level.[109] In fact, the host Member States remain entitled to relevant discretion in terms of labour regulation.[110]

Wispelaere and Marco Rocca, 'The Dark Side of the Tour. Labour and Social Security Challenges of Highly Mobile Workers in the Live Performance Sector' (2020) ERA Forum 6.

105. Article 3(3) and (5) of Directive 96/71/EC of the European Parliament and of the Council of 16 December 1996 concerning the posting of workers in the framework of the provision of services (n 8). On this point, *see supra* sub-subsection 3.3.1.2.

106. Evju and Novitz (n 10) 37. As seen *supra* in section 3.2, when it comes to determine the law applicable in practice to the employment relationship, reference has to be made to the relevant EU rules applicable in the area of PIL, namely Regulation (EC) No 593/2008 of the European Parliament and of the Council of 17 June 2008 on the law applicable to contractual obligations (Rome I) (n 7).

107. Article 9 of Regulation (EC) No 593/2008 of the European Parliament and of the Council of 17 June 2008 on the law applicable to contractual obligations (Rome I) (n 7).

108. *Tevfik Isbir v DB Services* (n 41) 36; *Sähköalojen ammattiliitto ry v Elektrobudowa Spolka Akcyjna* (n 103) paras 31–32. Paul Davies, 'Case C-346/06, Rüffert v Land Niedersachsen [2008] IRLR 467 (ECJ)' (2008) 37 Industrial Law Journal 293, 294; Christian Joerges, 'Rechtsstaat and Social Europe: How a Classical Tension Resurfaces in the European Integration Process' (2010) 9 Comparative Sociology 65, 80. Besides, it is worth noting that this way to identify the applicable rules, despite lacking of actual harmonisation effect, has the merit of enabling home state employers to know where they stand by simply checking the minimum labour standards applied in the state of destination of their service supply. Davies, 'Posted Workers: Single Market or Protection of National Labour Law Systems?' (n 35) 592–593; Claire Kilpatrick, 'Laval's Regulatory Conundrum: Collective Standard-Setting and the Court's New Approach to Posted Workers' (2009) 34 European Law Review 844, 4; Houwerzijl (n 14) 13; Grušić (n 16) 278; Schütze (n 41) 672.

109. As punctually predicted by Davies already in 1997 in relation to the element of minimum wage: 'there will still be as many minimum wage levels to be identified and observed as there are States in the Community with minimum wage laws'. Davies, 'Posted Workers: Single Market or Protection of National Labour Law Systems?' (n 35) 593.

110. The only limitation to national discretion in that sense is the respect of the Treaty rules requiring national law to be always non-discriminatory, justified and proportionate. Grušić (n 16) 278. On this point, *see infra* Chapter 4.

3.3.2.2 *Minimum Rates of Pay*

The most relevant element of host state law which could be imposed (until the entry into effect, on 30 July 2020, of Directive (EU) 2018/957) on the incoming posted workers was, evidently, that of local minimum rates of pay. Besides protecting the cross-border employees during their temporary assignment abroad, it constituted also a shield for the host countries' labour markets against wage competition. In this sense, it represented an important step towards promoting competition on the quality of the job performed, rather than on the mere price of it.[111] However, since the entry into force of the Posting of Workers Directive, the concept of minimum rates of pay turned out to be rather ambiguous and its practical definition highly problematic.[112] First of all, while the concrete definition of such an element was delegated directly to the Member States, it remained unclear whether the latter were supposed to come up with a single minimum wage or if the minimum rates of pay could be determined on an individual basis, taking into account a whole set of applicable heterogeneous rules.[113] Besides, the sole indication provided by the European legislator was the inclusion under the concept of minimum rates of pay of overtime rates and all the allowances directly connected with the posting, with the exclusion of contributions to supplementary occupational retirement pensions schemes and reimbursements for travel, board and lodging expenses.[114]

More clarity, in this regard, was brought by the intervention of the Court of Justice. The practice of extension of minimum wages to posted workers was acknowledged since the pre-Directive case law,[115] albeit potentially without boundaries. The first specification was then introduced in 1999 with the decision in *Arblade*,[116] where a condition was imposed to the competent national authorities in the receiving state,

---

111. Federica Mustilli and Jacques Pelkmans, 'Access Barriers to Services Markets' (2013) 77 CEPS Centre for European Policy Studies 84, 50–51.
112. Eckhard Voss et al., 'Posting of Workers Directive: Current Situation and Challenges' (European Parliament, EMPL Committee 2016) IP/A/EMPL/2016-07, 32; Jean-Philippe Lhernould and Barbara Palli, 'Posted Workers Remuneration: Comparative Study in Nine EU Countries and Four Sectors' (2017) 24 Maastricht Journal of European and Comparative Law 108, 109–110.
113. van Hoek and Houwerzijl, 'Comparative Study on the Legal Aspects of the Posting of Workers in the Framework of the Provision of Services in the European Union' (n 40) 191.
114. Article 3(1)(c) and (7) second indent of Directive 96/71/EC of the European Parliament and of the Council of 16 December 1996 concerning the posting of workers in the framework of the provision of services (n 8). Notably, as further specified by the 2014 Enforcement Directive, the deduction from wages of allowances specific to posting is permitted only when expressly provided for by national law, collective agreements and/or practice of the host Member State. Recital 35 of Directive 2014/67/EU of the European Parliament and of the Council of 15 May 2014 on the enforcement of Directive 96/71/EC concerning the posting of workers in the framework of the provision of services and amending Regulation (EU) No 1024/2012 on administrative cooperation through the Internal Market Information System ('the IMI Regulation') 2014 (OJ L 159/11).
115. *Société anonyme de droit français Seco et Société anonyme de droit français Desquenne & Giral v Etablissement d'assurance contre la vieillesse et l'invalidité* (n 38) para. 14; *Rush Portuguesa Lda v Office national d'immigration* (n 38) para. 18; *Raymond Vander Elst v Office des Migrations Internationales* (n 38) para. 23.
116. *Arblade & Fils SARL v Sofrage SARL* (n 27).

consisting of indicating the applicable minimum wages in a 'sufficiently precise and accessible' way, in order to avoid excessive burden to the cross-border service providers in determining their precise obligations.[117] Subsequently, in *Portugaia Construções*,[118] the definition of the minimum wage was specified in a way of solely encompassing the level of retribution de jure applicable *erga omnes*. This approach was taken in order to guarantee effective equal treatment between local and foreign undertakings, thus preventing a national employer to derogate from the generally applicable rules.[119] The decision in *Commission v Germany*,[120] in turn, excluded from the notion of minimum wage all those allowances or supplements which were not encompassed by host state law or practice and which had the effect of altering the symmetry between the work carried out and the consideration paid.[121] On the same occasion, it also clarified that the calculation of the minimum rates of pay should not take into account all different component elements, but rather consider the gross amount of wages.[122] Moreover, it was also settled case law that 'capital formation contribution' had to remain excluded from the gamma of the constituent elements of the minimum rates of pay.[123]

It was, however, the more recent CJEU case law that significantly improved clarity on the matter. With the *Sähköalojen ammattiliitto*[124] ruling, delivered in February 2015, the notion of the minimum wage was considerably extended to a broad range of elements. According to the Court, the concept of minimum rates of pay, besides the minimum wage *stricto sensu*, had to include also the minimum hourly (or piece) rate applicable to specific categories of employees, daily allowances at the same conditions as local workers when they are posted abroad, as well as travel costs to and from the place of work.[125] In turn, compensations for living expenses actually incurred by the workers during their assignments abroad, such as accommodation costs and meal vouchers, remained left out.[126] In practice, by following the same rationale adopted in *Commission v Germany* and *Isbir*,[127] the Court excluded from the concept of

117. *Ibid.* 43. On this point, *see* Rocca (n 38) 178–179.
118. *Portugaia Construções Lda* (n 29).
119. In the case at issue, a local employer was allowed to conclude an ad hoc collective agreement foreseeing the application of wages lower than the minimum level imposed by the generally applicable collective agreement to foreign service providers. *Ibid.* 35. On this point, *see* Rocca (n 38) 179.
120. *Commission of the European Communities v Federal Republic of Germany* [2005] ECJ Case C-341/02, ECLI:EU:C:2005:220.
121. On that occasion, the regularly paid thirteenth and fourteenth months' supplements, such as Christmas and holiday bonuses, were considered as part of the notion of minimum wage, while 'quality bonuses and bonuses for dirty, heavy or dangerous work' were excluded. *Ibid.* 31–39. On this point, *see* Lhernould and Palli (n 112) 115; Van Nuffel and Afanasjeva (n 71) 1408; Marta Głowacka, 'Posting of Workers Directive Reloaded' (2019) 26 Studia z Zakresu Prawa Pracy i Polityki Społecznej (Studies on Labour Law and Social Policy) 29, 35.
122. *Commission of the European Communities v Federal Republic of Germany* (n 120) para. 29.
123. *Tevfik Isbir v DB Services* (n 41) para. 44. *See* Lhernould and Palli (n 112) 111.
124. *Sähköalojen ammattiliitto ry v Elektrobudowa Spolka Akcyjna* (n 103).
125. *Ibid.* 45, 52 and 56.
126. *Ibid.* 60 and 63.
127. *Commission of the European Communities v Federal Republic of Germany* (n 120) para. 39; *Tevfik Isbir v DB Services* (n 41) para. 38.

minimum rates of pay all reimbursement of the costs effectively incurred on account of the posting, whereas it included those elements which do not have the effect of altering the relationship between the service provided and the consideration received in return by the worker.[128]

Interestingly, though, in light of the national competence to define the minimum wages applicable to posted workers,[129] substantial differences inevitably resulted among the Member States in that respect.[130] In fact, when establishing the actual content of the minimum rates of pay, the only imperative condition that had to be always guaranteed by national authorities was the full respect of the cross-border employers' freedom of service provision.[131] The resulting picture showed the existence of a serious lack of precise and transparent individuation of the minimum rates of pay applied within the context of posting of workers, which has been reflected in a profound uncertainty about the determination of the actual wages the service providers had to pay their posted employees. It goes without saying that such a worrying structural condition has affected the practical enforcement of the rules at national level as well.[132]

---

128. *Sähköalojen ammattiliitto ry v Elektrobudowa Spolka Akcyjna* (n 103) para. 36. *See* Schiek et al. (n 39) 41; van Hoek and Houwerzijl, 'Where Do EU Mobile Workers Belong, According to Rome I and the (E)PWD?' (n 14) 238–239; Claire Dhéret and Andreia Ghimis, 'The Revision of the Posted Workers Directive: Towards a Sufficient Policy Adjustment?' (2016) *European Policy Center (EPC) Discussion Paper* 9 <http://www.epc.eu/pub_details.php?cat_id=17&pub_id=6475> (accessed 23 October 2016); Zahn, 'Revision of the Posted Workers' Directive: Equality at Last?' (n 39) 6–7; Lhernould and Palli (n 112) 111 and 115; Zahn, 'Revision of the Posted Workers Directive' (n 39) 10–11; Robert van der Vlies, 'Posting of Workers within the Construction Sector: A Comparative Study within Belgium and The Netherlands on the Protection of Posted Workers' (Tilburg University 2018) 22; Van Nuffel and Afanasjeva (n 71) 1408. Interestingly, as is duly noted *infra* in Chapter 8 as well, the new concept of 'remuneration' introduced by the new Directive (EU) 2018/957 as a replacement of 'minimum rates of pay' envisaged by the original PWD, substantially builds on the enlarged definition of minimum wage provided by the CJEU in *Sähköalojen ammattiliitto*. Zahn, 'Revision of the Posted Workers' Directive: Equality at Last?' (n 39) 13; Marco Rocca, 'Not Dead yet: Legal Strategies at National Level and the Reform of the EU Posting of Workers Directive' (2018) 9.
129. It is worth stressing the express exclusion of pay from the EU's competence by virtue of Article 153(5) TFEU.
130. The same kind of problem concerns annual paid holidays as well. Zahn, 'Revision of the Posted Workers' Directive: Equality at Last?' (n 39) 9; Lhernould and Palli (n 112) 115–117; van Hoek (n 21) 468 and 482. As noted by Advocate General Wahl in *Sähköalojen Ammattiliitto*, differences may occur even within the same national context, in case of 'competing minima' (e.g., one set by legislation and the other by universally applicable collective agreement). Such an occurrence should be resolved by giving prevalence to the lowest of those 'minima'. *Sähköalojen ammattiliitto ry v Elektrobudowa Spolka Akcyjna, Opinion of Advocate General Nils Wahl delivered on 18 September 2014* [2014] CJEU Case C-396/13, ECLI:EU:C:2014:2236 [87]. On this specific caveat, *see* Clemens Kaupa, 'Public Procurement, Social Policy and Minimum Wage Regulation for Posted Workers: Towards a More Balanced Socio-Economic Integration Process?' (2016) 1 European Papers 127, 137.
131. *Tevfik Isbir v DB Services* (n 41) para. 37. In this sense, *see* Rocca (n 128) 5–6.
132. European Commission, Impact Assessment, Accompanying the document Proposal for a Directive of the European Parliament and the Council amending Directive 96/71/EC concerning the posting of workers in the framework of the provision of services 2016 [SWD(2016) 52 final] 11; Voss et al. (n 112) 34; Zahn, 'Revision of the Posted Workers' Directive: Equality at Last?' (n 39) 9; Lhernould and Palli (n 112) 126; Zahn, 'Revision of the Posted Workers Directive' (n 39) 12–13.

3.3.2.3 Temporary Agency Workers

Particular mention deserves also the special treatment reserved by Article 3(1)(d) of the Posting of Workers Directive, in combination with the Temporary Agency Work Directive 2008/104/EC,[133] to temporary agency posted employees. According to the latter legal instrument, a temporary work agency posting workers abroad is indeed bound to guarantee a higher level of labour protection than the one conferred by Article 3(1) of the Posting of Workers Directive to other posting situations.[134] More specifically, the Directive adopted in 2008 provides for the application of the principle of equal treatment between agency workers and workers at the user undertaking with regard to 'basic working and employment conditions', i.e., working time, overtime, breaks, rest periods, night work, holidays and public holidays, and pay.[135]

In practice, before the entry into effect of Directive (EU) 2018/957, once the Temporary Agency Work Directive was transposed in the country of destination in the form of legislation, regulations, administrative provisions, collective agreements and/or other binding general provisions,[136] it applied by virtue of the Posting of Workers Directive also to out-of-state agencies posting their workers to that country.[137] As a matter of fact, pursuant to Article 3(1)(d) and (9) of the Posting of Workers Directive, the host state was granted the faculty to extend the same terms and conditions of hiring-out of workers applicable to national employment relations also to foreign undertakings which posted temporary agency employees across borders.

133. Directive 2008/104/EC of the European Parliament and of the Council of 19 November 2008 on temporary agency work (n 9).

134. Monika Schlachter, 'Transnational Temporary Agency Work: How Much Equality Does the Equal Treatment Principle Provide?' (2011) 25 FORMULA Working Paper, University of Oslo, Department of Private Law 13; Evju and Novitz (n 10) 64; Schlachter (n 21) 269; Dhéret and Ghimis (n 128) 5.

135. Articles 3(1)(f) and 5(1) of Directive 2008/104/EC of the European Parliament and of the Council of 19 November 2008 on temporary agency work (n 9). On this point, *see* Mark Bell, 'The Principle of Equal Treatment: Widening and Deepening' in Paul Craig and Gráinne de Búrca (eds), *The Evolution of EU Law* (Second Edition, Oxford University Press 2011) 623–624; Barnard, *EU Employment Law* (n 21) 219; Consuelo Chacartegui, 'Resocialising Temporary Agency Work through a Theory of "Reinforced" Employers' Liability' in Nicola Countouris and Mark Freedland (eds), *Resocialising Europe in a Time of Crisis* (Cambridge University Press 2013) 216–217; ACL Davies, 'Regulating Atypical Work: Beyond Equality' in Nicola Countouris and Mark Freedland (eds), *Resocialising Europe in a Time of Crisis* (Cambridge University Press 2013) 242–243; Schlachter (n 21) 269; Lisa Berntsen and Nathan Lillie, 'Breaking the Law? Varieties of Social Dumping in a Pan-European Labour Market' in Magdalena Bernaciak (ed.), *Market Expansion and Social Dumping in Europe* (Routledge 2015) 48.

136. The above-mentioned means of implementations are listed in Article 3(1)(f) of Directive 2008/104/EC of the European Parliament and of the Council of 19 November 2008 on temporary agency work (n 9). Notably, the individual contract of employment is not included among the sources of employment and working conditions. Schlachter (n 21) 269.

137. Even in case the TAWD was not fully transposed into domestic law, it has been suggested to consider it nonetheless applicable to posted agency workers as public policy provision. Schlachter (n 134) 16; Schlachter (n 21) 270. As explained further in Chapter 8, the entry into effect of Directive (EU) 2018/957 introduced equal treatment between local and posted temporary agency workers with regard to 'basic working and employment conditions' applicable *ex* Article 5 TAWD. It thereby removed the need of transposition of the TAWD into host country law.

Interestingly enough, in the context of the posting pattern at issue only, the Posting of Workers Directive acknowledged the possibility to implement the principle of equal treatment typical of Article 45 TFEU.[138] It was precisely at this point that the Temporary Agency Work Directive intersected with the Posting of Workers Directive by determining the local working and employment conditions extendable to incoming agency workers.[139] Nonetheless, in accordance with its limited scope and the boundary expressed in Preamble Recital 22,[140] the Temporary Agency Work Directive was not supposed to alter the integrity of the Posting of Workers Directive.[141]

3.3.2.4 *Means of Regulation*

As previously noted during the investigation of the drafting process of the Posting of Workers Directive, the minimum set of employment conditions had to be laid down by law, regulation or administrative provision of the host Member State.[142] Furthermore, with a view to accommodate the variety of national collective bargaining traditions within the Union, the Directive established additional means of regulation. *In primis*, in order to include the particular systems of collective agreement extension in force in countries such as France and Germany, Article 3(1) encompassed also all those 'collective agreements or arbitration awards which have been declared universally applicable'. Second, in case of national systems of industrial relations not envisaging the possibility of signing universally applicable collective agreements, also those collective agreements or arbitration awards having general validity for all undertakings located in a certain territory and belonging to the occupational group or industry concerned, or those having nation-wide application after being concluded by the most representative employers' and labour organisations at national level, could find application.[143] However, the latter options for applying collective agreements, due to

138. *Alfred John Webb* (n 30) para. 10; *Vicoplus SC PUH, BAM Vermeer Contracting sp zoo and Olbek Industrial Services sp zoo v Minister van Sociale Zaken en Werkgelegenheid* [2011] CJEU Joined cases C-307/09, C-308/09 and C-309/09, ECLI:EU:C:2011:64 [28]. van Hoek and Houwerzijl, 'Comparative Study on the Legal Aspects of the Posting of Workers in the Framework of the Provision of Services in the European Union' (n 40) 185–186; Schlachter (n 134) 13; Evju and Novitz (n 10) 64–65; Schlachter (n 21) 268–269; Barnard, *EU Employment Law* (n 21) 219; Rocca (n 38) 207; Schiek et al. (n 39) 43–44.
139. Evju and Novitz (n 10) 65.
140. 'This Directive should be implemented in compliance with the provisions of the Treaty regarding the freedom to provide services and the freedom of establishment and without prejudice to Directive 96/71/EC of the European Parliament and of the Council of 16 December 1996 concerning the posting of workers in the framework of the provision of services.' Preamble Recital 22 of Directive 2008/104/EC of the European Parliament and of the Council of 19 November 2008 on temporary agency work (n 9).
141. Schlachter (n 134) 14; Evju and Novitz (n 10) 65–66.
142. Article 3(1) of Directive 96/71/EC of the European Parliament and of the Council of 16 December 1996 concerning the posting of workers in the framework of the provision of services (n 8).
143. *Ibid.* Article 3(8). *Laval un Partneri Ltd v Svenska Byggnadsarbetareförbundet, Svenska Byggnadsarbetareförbundets avdelning 1, Byggettan and Svenska Elektrikerförbundet* (n 30) para. 65. Unlike the 1991 original proposal of the Commission, the final version of the PWD does not include only those collective agreements or arbitration awards 'having erga omnes

their residual character, were required to respect certain procedural conditions. As clarified in 2003 by the Commission, the Member States wishing to impose those exceptional collective agreements on out-of-state service providers were bound to make an explicit choice in this sense at the implementation stage of the Posting of Workers Directive.[144] Another proviso, formalistically observed by the Court of Justice, allowed the recourse to the alternatives offered by Article 3(8) of the Directive only in the absence, in a given national context, of any legal instrument to declare collective agreements to have *erga omnes* effect.[145]

Interestingly, the observance of labour standards determined by universally applicable collective agreements was made compulsory by the Directive itself insofar as they concerned the building industry only.[146] Nevertheless, such a limitation seemed to be merely apparent as, pursuant to the second indent of Article 3(10), the Member States were still granted the possibility of extending the application of all the above-mentioned three types of collective agreements and arbitration awards to posted workers occupied in other economic sectors. This is on the condition that the Treaty rules and the equal treatment between national and foreign undertakings were respected.[147] Last but not least, it should be noted that the range of legitimate legal instruments for laying down employment provisions of the host country applicable to

---

effect and/or being made legally binding in the occupation or industry concerned'. The scope of Article 3(1), as specified at paragraph (8), extends indeed to all collective agreements or arbitration awards 'which must be observed by all undertakings in the geographical area and in the profession or industry concerned'. Davies, 'Posted Workers: Single Market or Protection of National Labour Law Systems?' (n 35) 580–581; Watson (n 41) 286–287; Houwerzijl (n 14) 13; Grušić (n 16) 266–267. Notably, these provisions were especially designed for countries such as Denmark and Sweden whereby no labour standard was set by law, nor any system for extending the application of employment standards collectively agreed was envisaged. *Ibid.* 267. The possibility of including, besides the obligatory universally applicable collective agreements, also those whose authority derives from their de facto application was, undoubtedly, the most debated argument of discussion during the drafting process of the PWD. For an in-depth analysis of the arduous path leading to the approval of these forms of collective agreements as binding means for imposing the terms and conditions laid down by Article 3(1), *see* Evju and Novitz (n 10) 32–35.

144. European Commission, Communication on the Implementation of Directive 96/71/EC in the Member States 2003 [COM(2003) 458 final] 12. On this point, *see also* Catherine Barnard, 'Viking and Laval: An Introduction' (2008) 10 Cambridge Yearbook of European Legal Studies 463, 476; Kilpatrick (n 108) 5.
145. This independently from the fact that an actual use of such a possibility is made or not. *Dirk Rüffert v Land Niedersachsen* [2008] CJEU Case C-346/06, ECLI:EU:C:2008:189 [27]. On this point, *see* Rocca (n 38) 296–297 and 304.
146. Article 3(1) of Directive 96/71/EC of the European Parliament and of the Council of 16 December 1996 concerning the posting of workers in the framework of the provision of services (n 8). The motivation behind the sole reference to the activities described into the Annex of the PWD, namely those carried out in the construction sector, should be sought in the Member States' concern for the non-uniform application in practice of collective agreements. Davies, 'Posted Workers: Single Market or Protection of National Labour Law Systems?' (n 35) 581; Grušić (n 16) 267.
147. Given that the second indent of Article 3(10), unlike the first indent, does not explicitly confer on the host Member States the power to extend terms and conditions of employment beyond the list laid down in Article 3(1), it is believed that a strict interpretation of the provision at issue would be more consistent with the limited freedom of action allowed in the building industry. Davies, 'Posted Workers: Single Market or Protection of National Labour Law Systems?' (n 35) 581–582; Kilpatrick (n 108) 4.

posted workers was non-extendable to any other measure. In fact, as soundly affirmed by the judges in Luxembourg, the minimum wages which did not fulfil the requirements prescribed by Article 3(8) of the Posting of Workers Directive could not be considered as minimum rates of pay according to Article 3(1)(c) and, therefore, could not be imposed on foreign service providers.[148]

3.3.2.5 Extended Protection Beyond the 'Hard Core'

Besides the minimum protection guaranteed to posted workers by the application of the above-mentioned gamma of mandatory provisions of the state in which the service supply was performed, the Posting of Workers Directive encompassed also a principle of favourability.[149] Since this principle has not been touched by the 2018 legislative reform, the original rules still find application nowadays. According to Article 3(7), the protection of the cross-border employees could – and still can – be extended to all 'terms and conditions of employment which are more favourable to workers'. The actual meaning of this last provision represented, however, a major source of debate, especially after the EU enlargement towards the Central and Eastern European Countries. At that time, it was widely considered as a minimum standard clause allowing the host state to improve the level of social protection ensured to workers employed in its territory. More generally, the whole Posting of Workers Directive was regarded as a 'minimum directive' leaving always the door open for 'the implementation of enhanced national protection', and potentially bounded only by the compliance with the Treaty rules on free movement of services.[150]

148. *Laval un Partneri Ltd v Svenska Byggnadsarbetareförbundet, Svenska Byggnadsarbetareförbundets avdelning 1, Byggettan and Svenska Elektrikerförbundet* (n 30) paras 70–71; *Dirk Rüffert v Land Niedersachsen* (n 145) 23–31. More specifically, in the *Laval* case, the Swedish system for setting wage rates in the construction sector was on trial. In that Member State, no collective agreement was declared universally applicable and no other legal instrument among those foreseen by Article 3(8) of the PWD was envisaged. For that reason, the practice of negotiating wage rates at the workplace, on a case-by-case basis, was considered outside of the scope of Article 3(1) and (8). Just a few months later, the decision in *Rüffert* had the same outcome by excluding the legitimacy of a collective agreement imposed by the *Land Niedersachsen* (Lower Saxony) to a Polish firm posting workers within its territory. This is because that collective agreement was not declared universally applicable, and it could not be subsumed under the second subparagraph of Article 3(8) of the PWD, given the applicability of such a possibility only in the absence of a system for declaring universally applicable collective agreements, which was not the case in Germany. Moreover, due to its limited application to public contracts – and not to private contracts – it could not even be regarded as having general validity for all similar undertakings in the sector, located in that same geographical area. Watson (n 41) 286; Verschueren (n 3) 140–141.
149. van Hoek and Houwerzijl, '"Posting" and "Posted Workers": The Need for Clear Definitions of Two Key Concepts of the Posting of Workers Directive' (n 14) 442–443; Evju and Novitz (n 10) 37–38; Verschueren (n 3) 141; Rocca (n 38) 126.
150. This was, indeed, the point of view of Advocate Generals Mengozzi and Bot in, respectively, *Laval un Partneri Ltd v Svenska Byggnadsarbetareförbundet, Svenska Byggnadsarbetareförbundets avdelning 1, Byggettan and Svenska Elektrikerförbundet, Opinion of Advocate General Paolo Mengozzi delivered on 23 May 2007* [2007] ECJ Case C-341/05, ECLI:EU:C:2007:291 [151 and 197–199]; *Dirk Rüffert v Land Niedersachsen, Opinion of Advocate General Yves Bot delivered on 20 September 2007* [2007] ECJ Case C-346/06, ECLI:EU:C:2007:541, 82–84. On this

However, such an interpretation was evidently in conflict with the historical background of Article 3(7) of the Posting of Workers Directive, the origin of which may be traced back to Article 8(3) of the 1976 draft regulation, subsequently specified in the 1991 version of the proposal. In the latter document, the favourability clause was, indeed, explicitly referred to the law applicable to the employment relation – i.e., the posted workers' home state law – and not that of the country where the job was actually performed.[151] The same line of reasoning was then followed by the Court of Justice in its seminal decisions in *Laval*[152] and *Rüffert*,[153] where the capacity for extension of the posted workers' social protection was recognised only to law or collective labour agreements valid in the Member State of origin[154] or, in alternative, to more favourable collective agreements voluntarily signed by the service provider in the country of destination.[155] As a matter of fact, the recipient Member State was prevented from imposing on cross-border service providers the respect of any element of domestic labour law going 'beyond the mandatory rules for minimum protection' laid down in Article 3(1) of the Posting of Workers Directive.[156]

In light of the foregoing, it follows that the list of mandatory provisions constituting the nucleus of minimum protection had to – and still has to – be read as an exhaustive list.[157] According to the Court, the imposition by the host country of

point, *see* Barnard, 'Viking and Laval: An Introduction' (n 144) 475; Kilpatrick (n 108) 3; Evju and Novitz (n 10) 35 and 55–56; Maslauskaite (n 40) 9.

151. Evju, 'Revisiting the Posted Workers Directive: Conflict of Laws and Laws in Contrast' (n 44) 158–159; Evju and Novitz (n 10) 35.
152. *Laval un Partneri Ltd v Svenska Byggnadsarbetareförbundet, Svenska Byggnadsarbetareförbundets avdelning 1, Byggettan and Svenska Elektrikerförbundet* (n 30).
153. *Dirk Rüffert v Land Niedersachsen* (n 145).
154. Interestingly, the Court did not offer any further indication about what it actually meant by 'the law of the Member State of origin', namely if that of the country where the service provider is established, or rather that of the worker's home state. Though, the latter solution appears more consistent with the aim of worker protection. van Hoek and Houwerzijl, '"Posting" and "Posted Workers": The Need for Clear Definitions of Two Key Concepts of the Posting of Workers Directive' (n 14) 442–443.
155. Mia Rönnmar, 'Labour Law in the Courts. The Role of European Case Law on Fundamental Trade Union Rights in an Evolving EU Industrial Relations System' in Ulla Neergaard, Ruth Nielsen and Lynn M Roseberry (eds), *The Role of Courts in Developing a European Social Model – Theoretical and Methodological Perspectives* (Djøf Publishing 2010) 185–186.
156. *Laval un Partneri Ltd v Svenska Byggnadsarbetareförbundet, Svenska Byggnadsarbetareförbundets avdelning 1, Byggettan and Svenska Elektrikerförbundet* (n 30) paras 80–81; *Dirk Rüffert v Land Niedersachsen* (n 145) 32–34. On this point, *see* Rönnmar, 'Free Movement of Services Versus National Labour Law and Industrial Relations Systems: Understanding the Laval Case from a Swedish and Nordic Perspective' (n 103) 512–513; Barnard, 'Viking and Laval: An Introduction' (n 144) 475; Jonas Malmberg and Tore Sigeman, 'Industrial Actions and EU Economic Freedoms: The Autonomous Collective Bargaining Model Curtailed by the European Court of Justice' (2008) 45 Common Market Law Review 1115, 1138; Christian Joerges and Florian Rödl, 'Informal Politics, Formalised Law and the "Social Deficit" of European Integration: Reflections after the Judgments of the ECJ in *Viking* and *Laval*' (2009) 15 European Law Journal 1, 17; Joerges (n 108) 80; Siofra O'Leary, 'Free Movement of Persons and Services' in Paul Craig and Gráinne de Búrca (eds), *The Evolution of EU Law* (Second Edition, Oxford University Press 2011) 525; Verschueren (n 3) 141; Floris de Witte, *Justice in the EU: The Emergence of Transnational Solidarity* (Oxford University Press 2015) 107.
157. *Commission of the European Communities v Grand Duchy of Luxemburg* [2008] ECJ Case C-319/06, ECLI:EU:C:2008:350 [26]. Kilpatrick (n 108) 3; Vassilis Hatzopoulos, 'Labour Immigration in the EU Through the Back Door? The Free Provision of Services as a Facilitator

additional elements of labour protection would place the out-of-state service provider in a position of competitive disadvantage vis-à-vis its local counterparts.[158] In other words, the imposition of whatever kind of obligation to respect employment standards higher than those envisaged by the Posting of Workers Directive would result in an excessive economic burden for transnational operators, liable to 'prohibit, impede or render less attractive the provision of their services in the host Member State'.[159] For that reason, it would be regarded as a violation, not only of the Directive but also of Article 56 TFEU.[160] In effect, the imposition of full equal treatment between posted as local workers in the host state was supposed to inevitably undermine the Treaty rules on free provision of services.[161]

The very strict interpretation given by the Grand Chamber was motivated on account of the construction of the provisions laid down by Article 3(1) as, substantially, a derogation from the Treaty rules on free movement of services providing for the application of the legislation of the Member State of origin.[162] Such an approach was perfectly consistent with the Posting of Workers Directive's objective of fostering the completion of the EU internal market by ensuring the exercise of free movement rights, as well as with the *raison d'être* of Article 3(10), which otherwise would be rendered meaningless.[163] Nevertheless, the decision in *Laval* left still open the possibility of

of Migration Flows' in Georg Menz and Alexander Caviedes (eds), *Labour Migration in Europe* (Palgrave MacMillan 2010) 157; Evju and Novitz (n 10) 54; Barnard, *EU Employment Law* (n 21) 226; Schütze (n 41) 674; Van Nuffel and Afanasjeva (n 71) 1406.

158. Watson (n 41) 299.
159. *Dirk Rüffert v Land Niedersachsen* (n 145) para. 37. *See also Manfred Säger v Dennemeyer & Co. Ltd.* (n 68) 12; *Laval un Partneri Ltd v Svenska Byggnadsarbetareförbundet, Svenska Byggnadsarbetareförbundets avdelning 1, Byggettan and Svenska Elektrikerförbundet* (n 30) para. 99; *Bundesdruckerei GmbH v Stadt Dortmund* [2014] CJEU Case C-549/13, ECLI:EU:C:2014:2235 [30]. On that occasion, the Court adopted the so-called '*Säger* approach', which has been criticised for being a mere 'market access' test whereby, in the absence of justification and proportionality of the action, the violation of the EU rules on free movement is basically presumed. According to this viewpoint, such an approach is, therefore, deemed to be more inclined to promote the exercise of the EU economic freedom, rather than the safeguard of the social rights in the host Member States. In this sense, *see* Barnard, 'Viking and Laval: An Introduction' (n 144) 486; Barnard, 'Free Movement and Labour Rights: Squaring the Circle?' (n 68) 6; Catherine Barnard, 'A Proportionate Response to Proportionality in the Field of Collective Action' (2015) European Law Review 117.
160. *Dirk Rüffert v Land Niedersachsen* (n 145) para. 36. As interestingly noted by Deakin, the strict interconnection between the PWD and Article 56 TFEU, whereby the violation of first one implicates also the violation of the second and *vice versa*, testifies that they are in practice 'mutually reinforcing'. Deakin (n 21) 595–596. On this point, *see also* Catherine Barnard, 'EU "Social" Policy: From Employment Law to Labour Market Reform' in Paul Craig and Gráinne de Búrca (eds), *The Evolution of EU Law* (Second Edition, Oxford University Press 2011) 670; Verschueren (n 3) 141–142; Barnard, *The Substantive Law of the EU: The Four Freedoms* (n 3) 424; Kaupa (n 130) 137–138.
161. Barnard, *The Substantive Law of the EU: The Four Freedoms* (n 3) 424.
162. *Laval un Partneri Ltd v Svenska Byggnadsarbetareförbundet, Svenska Byggnadsarbetareförbundets avdelning 1, Byggettan and Svenska Elektrikerförbundet, Opinion of Advocate General Paolo Mengozzi delivered on 23 May 2007* (n 150) para. 132. On this point, *see also* Barnard, 'EU "Social" Policy: From Employment Law to Labour Market Reform' (n 160) 670; Barnard, *The Substantive Law of the EU: The Four Freedoms* (n 3) 424.
163. Recitals (1) and (3) of Directive 96/71/EC of the European Parliament and of the Council of 16 December 1996 concerning the posting of workers in the framework of the provision of services (n 8). Evju and Novitz (n 10) 35.

imposing better terms and conditions of employment in the host country, when justified on the grounds of 'overriding reasons of public interest', such as worker protection.[164] This under the proviso that they were applied in a non-discriminatory manner and that the principle of proportionality is respected.[165]

At any rate, it should be noted that the approach taken by the Court of Justice in *Laval* and *Rüffert* has been accused by several authors and, more generally, by a wide public opinion, of altering the character of the Posting of Workers Directive from an instrument of minimum worker protection to a 'maximum directive'. More specifically, after the intervention of the Court, Article 3(1) has been labelled as 'a ceiling, not a floor' for the terms and conditions of employment applicable by local authorities or trade unions to foreign service providers.[166] However, such a perspective appears

164. *Laval un Partneri Ltd v Svenska Byggnadsarbetareförbundet, Svenska Byggnadsarbetareförbundets avdelning 1, Byggettan and Svenska Elektrikerförbundet* (n 30) para. 103. In the case at stake, the Court referred indirectly to the possibility offered by Article 9 of the Rome I Regulation to invoke 'overriding mandatory provisions'. This was due to the fact that the collective agreement for the building sector aiming at the protection of local wages and working conditions, because of its character of negotiation between management and labour (thereby outside the public law framework), could not be subsumed under the exception envisaged by Article 3(10) of the PWD concerning 'public policy provisions'. Rönnmar, 'Labour Law in the Courts. The Role of European Case Law on Fundamental Trade Union Rights in an Evolving EU Industrial Relations System' (n 155) 188; Evju and Novitz (n 10) 54; Ulf Bernitz, 'Horizontal Effects of Private Rights Vested by Union Law on Damages to Be Paid by Another Private Party: The Laval Case as a Model' in Sybe De Vries, Ulf Bernitz and Steve Weatherill (eds), *The Protection of Fundamental Rights in the EU After Lisbon* (Hart Publishing 2013) 144; Verschueren (n 3) 147–148; Barnard, *The Substantive Law of the EU: The Four Freedoms* (n 3) 424; Kaupa (n 130) 138; Vassilis Hatzopoulos, 'Justifications for Restrictions to Free Movement: Towards a Single Normative Framework?' in Mads Andenas, Tarjei Bekkedal and Luca Pantaleo (eds), *The Reach of Free Movement* (Springer Berlin Heidelberg 2017) 143; van Hoek (n 21) 466. Article 3(10) of the PWD is dealt with further in the present section. As for the inclusion of the worker protection under the notion of 'overriding mandatory provisions', *see also Alfred John Webb* (n 30) para. 19; *Arblade & Fils SARL v Sofrage SARL* (n 27) para. 36; *Mazzoleni v Inter Surveillance Assistance* (n 30) para. 27; *Portugaia Construções Lda* (n 29) para. 20; *International Transport Workers' Federation and Finnish Seamen's Union v Viking Line ABP and OÜ Viking Line Eesti* (n 30) para. 75.
165. *Laval un Partneri Ltd v Svenska Byggnadsarbetareförbundet, Svenska Byggnadsarbetareförbundets avdelning 1, Byggettan and Svenska Elektrikerförbundet* (n 30) para. 101. In the same direction, *see also Manfred Säger v Dennemeyer & Co. Ltd.* (n 68) para. 15; *Reinhard Gebhard v Consiglio dell'Ordine degli Avvocati e Procuratori di Milano* [1995] ECJ Case C-55/94, ECLI:EU:C:1995:411 [37]; *Guiot v Climatee SA* (n 31) para. 13; *Arblade & Fils SARL v Sofrage SARL* (n 27) para. 35; *Commission of the European Communities v Federal Republic of Germany* (n 40) para. 24. In particular, in the *Laval* case, the collective action taken by the Swedish trade unions did not pass the proportionality test. On this point, *see infra* Chapter 4.
166. Deakin (n 21) 608–609; Barnard, 'Viking and Laval: An Introduction' (n 144) 475; Kilpatrick (n 108) 3; Jonas Malmberg, 'The Impact of the ECJ Judgements on Viking, Laval, Rüffert and Luxembourg on the Practice of Collective Bargaining and the Effectiveness of Social Action' (Directorate-General for Internal Policies, Policy Department A: Economic and Scientific Policy Employment and Social Affairs Brussels: European Parliament 2010) 7; Antonina Bakardjieva Engelbrekt, 'Institutional Theories, EU Law and the Role of the Courts for Developing a European Social Model' in Ulla Neergaard, Ruth Nielsen and Lynn M Roseberry (eds), *The Role of Courts in Developing a European Social Model – Theoretical and Methodological Perspectives* (Djøf Publishing 2010) 334; Hatzopoulos, 'Labour Immigration in the EU Through the Back Door? The Free Provision of Services as a Facilitator of Migration Flows' (n 157) 157; Wiebke Warneck, 'The ECJ Decisions' in Andreas Bücker and Wiebke Warneck (eds), *Viking – Laval – Rüffert: Consequences and policy perspectives* (ETUI (European Trade Union Institute) 2010)

fundamentally incompatible with the intrinsic nature of the Directive itself which, as a direct result of its peculiar drafting process, was conceived as an exception to the application of the 'country of origin' principle.[167] If anything, the Posting of Workers Directive could rather be defined as 'both a floor *and* a ceiling', depending on the point of view.[168] This interpretation would better reflect the Directive's dual purpose of promoting the transnational provision of services and, at the same time, protecting the host state's labour market from the competition coming from cheaper foreign temporary workers and the posted workers themselves.[169]

Rather than in Article 3(7), an interpretative basis for considering the Posting of Workers Directive as a 'minimum directive' could – and still can – be more appropriately traced in Article 3(10) and its drafting history.[170] By virtue of the first indent of the latter provision, indeed, the Member States are allowed to extend their scope of intervention in the regulation of transnational employment relationships beyond the seven areas listed in Article 3(1), thus imposing the observance of domestic law concerning additional labour terms and conditions. This is permitted only on condition that equal treatment between local and foreign undertakings is respected and when an

10; Kilpatrick (n 63) 12; Barnard, 'EU "Social" Policy: From Employment Law to Labour Market Reform' (n 160) 668; Hatzopoulos, *Regulating Services in the European Union* (n 63) 205; O'Leary (n 156) 525; Barnard, *EU Employment Law* (n 21) 224; Stefano Giubboni, 'European Citizenship and Social Rights in Times of Crisis' (2013) Working Paper-LPF n. 2 Centro Einaudi – Laboratorio di Politica Comparata e Filosofia Pubblica 14–15; Countouris and Engblom (n 68) 15–16; Rocca (n 38) 294; de Witte (n 156) 107–108; Nicola Countouris and Samuel Engblom, 'Civilising the European Posted Workers Directive' in R Mark Freedland and Jeremias Prassl (eds), *Viking, Laval and Beyond* (First Edition, Hart Publishing 2016) 279; Rönnmar, 'Labour and Equality Law' (n 40) 609; van Hoek (n 21) 468; Jotte Mulder, '(Re) Conceptualising a Social Market Economy for the EU Internal Market' (2019) 15 Utrecht Law Review 16, 21.

167. Notably, the Court followed the line of reasoning exposed by Advocate General Mengozzi, according to whom: 'the application of the "core" terms and conditions of employment that must be guaranteed by the host Member State to workers temporarily posted to its territory, under Article 3 of Directive 96/71, constitutes a derogation from the principle of application of the legislation of the Member State of origin to the situation of the service provider of that Member State that posts those workers to the territory of the first Member State'. *Laval un Partneri Ltd v Svenska Byggnadsarbetareförbundet, Svenska Byggnadsarbetareförbundets avdelning 1, Byggettan and Svenska Elektrikerförbundet, Opinion of Advocate General Paolo Mengozzi delivered on 23 May 2007* (n 150) para. 132. For the record, an opposite view, considering the implementation by the Member State where the services are performed of enhanced national protection allowed under Article 3(7), has been clearly expressed by Advocate General Bot in *Dirk Rüffert v Land Niedersachsen, Opinion of Advocate General Yves Bot delivered on 20 September 2007* (n 150) 82–83. On this point, *see* Barnard, 'Viking and Laval: An Introduction' (n 144) 475–477.
168. In particular, the PWD undoubtedly offers a 'floor' of protection for posted workers, which can always be improved by the application of more favourable conditions provided for by law or collective labour agreements valid in their home countries or collective agreements voluntarily signed by their employer in the host country. On the contrary, when seen from the point of view of the Member States with the most advanced levels of social protection, besides providing a set of mandatory rules acting as a shield for their labour markets, it surely constitutes a barrier to more protectionist national intervention. In this sense, *see* Rönnmar, 'Free Movement of Services Versus National Labour Law and Industrial Relations Systems: Understanding the Laval Case from a Swedish and Nordic Perspective' (n 103) 523; Malmberg and Sigeman (n 156) 1140.
169. Davies, 'Case C-346/06, Rüffert v Land Niedersachsen [2008] IRLR 467 (ECJ)' (n 108) 294.
170. Evju and Novitz (n 10) 35–37.

imperative requirement of public interest requires national authorities to adopt certain measures qualified as 'public policy provisions'.[171] According to the exceptional nature of those provisions, entailing de facto a 'double' derogation from the freedom to provide services and from the exhaustive list set out by Article 3(1) of the Posting of Workers Directive, once again the interpretation of the Court of Justice was sensibly narrow.[172] In *Commission v Luxembourg*, the Court clarified that, even though the competence for determining the requirements of public policy undoubtedly belongs to the Member States, the latter's margin of discretion should still be subject to a sort of control by the European institutions. More concretely, the Member States are precluded from determining unilaterally the concept of public policy[173] and are not allowed to proclaim all or much of their employment legislation to be of public policy nature.[174] In turn, only a 'genuine and sufficiently serious threat to a fundamental interest of society' may justify the application of public policy provisions aimed at the protection of such a prominent political, social or economic national interest.[175]

171. Interestingly, as reported by Biagi, who played a fundamental role in the drafting process of the PWD, as soon as the Directive was adopted, Article 3(10) seemed to ensure an almost unlimited discretion to the Member States with regard to the determination of the terms and conditions of employment applicable to foreign service providers as 'public policy provisions'. Marco Biagi, 'Fortune Smiles on the Italian EU Presidency: Talking Half-Seriously about the Posted Workers and Parental Leave Directives' (1996) 12 International Journal of Comparative Labour Law and Industrial Relations 97, 104.
172. *Commission of the European Communities v Grand Duchy of Luxemburg* (n 157) paras 30-31. *See* Kilpatrick (n 108) 3–4; Rönnmar, 'Labour Law in the Courts. The Role of European Case Law on Fundamental Trade Union Rights in an Evolving EU Industrial Relations System' (n 155) 186; Rocca (n 38) 202; Cornelissen and Van Limberghen (n 14) 368.
173. *Commission of the European Communities v Grand Duchy of Luxemburg* (n 157) paras 30 and 50.
174. This was, indeed, the case of Luxembourg, which declared all laws, regulations and administrative provisions concerning certain matters (including matters non-listed in Article 3(1) of the PWD) to be 'mandatory provisions falling under national public policy'. European Commission, Communication on the Implementation of Directive 96/71/EC in the Member States (n 144) 13; Grušić (n 16) 208–209, 267–268; Schütze (n 41) 674–675. By the way, it is worth pointing out that the notion of *ordre public* differs among the Member States. Evju, *Cross-Border Services* (n 21) 12.
175. *Commission of the European Communities v Grand Duchy of Luxemburg* (n 157) paras 29 and 50. *See also* the ECJ's decision in *Arblade & Fils SARL v Sofrage SARL* (n 27) para. 30. Davies, 'Posted Workers: Single Market or Protection of National Labour Law Systems?' (n 35) 582–583 and 593; Dølvik and Visser (n 63) 502–503; Kilpatrick (n 108) 3–4; Davies, *EU Labour Law* (n 21) 98; Houwerzijl (n 14) 13; Verschueren (n 3) 141. The similarity of the definition of public policy motivations given by the Court with Article 9(1) of the Rome I Regulation is more than evident. On this point, *see supra* section 3.2. Besides, it is also worth pointing out that, as follows from the decision under discussion, the rules concerning collective actions remain excluded from the notion of public policy provisions in the meaning of Article 3(10) of the PWD. van Hoek (n 21) 470. Finally, as noted by Barnard, the Court's interpretation of Article 3(10) of the PWD was so restrictive that basically foreclosed any labour legislation on areas left out of Article 3(1), such as the right to a written contract, provisions on unfair dismissal, redundancy payments, 'living wages' and family rights. Catherine Barnard, 'The UK and Posted Workers: The Effect of Commission v Luxembourg on the Territorial Application of British Labour Law: Case C-319/06 Commission v Luxembourg, Judgment 19 June 2008' (2009) 38 Industrial Law Journal 122, 126–129. In this sense, *see also* de Witte (n 156) 108–109.

3.4 CONCLUDING REMARKS

The transnational employment relationship between a posted worker and his employer, entailing the conclusion of a contract in one Member State (home state) and the performance of the service in another Member State (host state), is by its very nature traditionally regulated by the private international law of the recipient state - most of the time according to the principle of *lex loci laboris*.[176] In view of the evident conflict of laws issue, a system of coordination of the various national rules has been introduced by the 1980 Rome Convention on the law applicable to contractual obligations, subsequently converted by the European legislator into the 2008 Rome I Regulation. Pursuant to private international law, the *lex causae* of the posting contract is normally that of the sending country,[177] with the exception of the cases where the host state imposes the respect of 'overriding mandatory provisions'. That is where the Posting of Workers Directive (even after the 2018 legislative reform) comes into play by specifically designating, at Article 3(1), a list of host country's elements of employment law applicable to posted workers, while still granting the opportunity for the host state of imposing further public policy provisions.

The intention to resolve the conflict of laws issue, concretised with the 1972 proposal of the Commission for a regulation on conflict of laws pertaining to employment relations,[178] constituted, indeed, the first of four main factors providing a stimulating background for the Posting of Workers Directive's legislative process. Second, a prominent role in this sense was also played by the attempt of the European Federation of Building and Woodworkers (EFBWW) to include a sort of 'social clause' into the Directive on liberalisation of public procurement.[179] Third, an innovative conception of the phenomenon of posting under the EU rules concerning the free provision of services resulted from the 1989 Action Programme as well. Lastly, the same choice of legal basis was then made by the Court of Justice in its landmark ruling in *Rush Portuguesa*.[180] Oddly enough, the result of that decision was, nonetheless, rather surprising due to the extremely wide margin of discretion acknowledged to the host state in extending domestic labour law to posted workers, de facto assimilating the treatment applied to posted workers to the one reserved to migrant workers.[181]

The Posting of Workers Directive, adopted at the end of 1996, was the result of a gruelling drafting process, started in 1990 and encompassing three different proposals. Notably, considerable frictions occurred at the stage of concretely determining both the elements of national labour law applicable to cross-border workforce, the threshold for the application of such rules, and the means of regulation. The solution reached was a

176. Evju and Novitz (n 10) 5; Houwerzijl (n 14) 10; Verschueren (n 3) 147–148.
177. In turn, host state law is deemed to find full application in situations of non-genuine posting.
178. Commission des Communautes Europeennes Proposition de reglement (CEE) du Conseil relatif aux dispositions concernant les conflits de lois en matière de relations de travail à l'intérieur de la Communauté (n 48).
179. Directive 89/440/EEC of 18 July 1989 amending Directive 71/305/EEC concerning coordination of procedures for the award of public works contracts (n 54).
180. *Rush Portuguesa Lda v Office national d'immigration* (n 38).
181. Albeit with the exclusion of the posted workers from any social benefit provided for by the host country.

compromise between, on the one hand, the promotion of the transnational provision of services and, on the other hand, the respect of the Member States' labour market integrity and the social protection of the posted workers concerned. Pursuant to Article 3(1) of the Directive, the receiving countries were allowed to extend merely a limited range of domestic terms and conditions of employment to cross-border posted workers assigned temporarily to their territory. Posted employees were therefore granted a minimum protection only, and not full equal treatment with local workers.[182] The sole exception to this rule concerned the posting of temporary agency workers, provided that the equal treatment with regard to basic working and employment conditions (including equal pay) between posted agency workers and workers at the user firm found application by virtue of the combination of the Posting of Workers Directive with the Temporary Agency Work Directive 2008/104/EC, once the latter was fully transposed into host country law.[183]

In view of the coordinating - rather than harmonising - character of the Posting of Workers Directive, the Member States were entitled to full autonomy in determining the concrete substance of the aforementioned provisions. Yet, only certain means of regulation were permitted. As pointed out in this chapter, the concrete individuation of the minimum rates of pay applicable to posted workers, as well as the measure and means for extending domestic law beyond the 'hard core' list set out in Article 3(1), has been a controversial matter for years. The rather ambiguous concept of minimum rates of pay stemming from the Posting of Workers Directive has been progressively specified by the case law of the Court of Justice. In particular, the recent decisions in *Commission v Germany*,[184] *Isbir*[185] and, most of all, *Sähköalojen ammattiliitto*[186] provided for a rather detailed classification of the elements respectively included and excluded. Nevertheless, in light of the national competence in defining those minimum rates of pay, the lack of an harmonised conception at EU level undoubtedly has given rise to uncertainties for cross-border operators, while hampering the practical enforcement of the rules.

With regard to the possibility for the host Member State to impose on cross-border service providers the respect of labour standards higher than those prescribed by the Directive, the Court of Justice was decisive once again. In *Laval*[187] and *Rüffert*,[188]

182. Evju and Novitz (n 47) 37–38; Catherine Barnard, 'EU Employment Law and the European Social Model: The Past, the Present and the Future' (2014) 67 Current Legal Problems 199, 219; Watson (n 25) 286; Uglješa Grušić, *The European Private International Law of Employment* (Cambridge University Press 2015) 278; Schiek, Oliver and Alberti (n 25) 39–40; Rob Cornelissen and Guido Van Limberghen, 'Social Security for Mobile Workers and Labour Law', *Research Handbook on European Social Security Law* (Edward Elgar Publishing 2015) 344; Barnard, 'The Commission's Proposal Deletes the Treaty Distinction between Migrant Workers and Posted Workers' (n 16).
183. Directive 2008/104/EC of the European Parliament and of the Council of 19 November 2008 on temporary agency work (n 9).
184. *Commission of the European Communities v Federal Republic of Germany* (n 120).
185. *Tevfik Isbir v DB Services* (n 41).
186. *Sähköalojen ammattiliitto ry v Elektrobudowa Spolka Akcyjna* (n 103).
187. *Laval un Partneri Ltd v Svenska Byggnadsarbetareförbundet, Svenska Byggnadsarbetareförbundets avdelning 1, Byggettan and Svenska Elektrikerförbundet* (n 30).
188. *Dirk Rüffert v Land Niedersachsen* (n 145).

the favourability clause laid down in Article 3(7) was firmly interpreted as strictly encompassing only home state law or collective agreements, or collective agreements voluntarily signed in the country of destination. The recipient Member State was, therefore, prevented from imposing protection that went beyond the scope of Article 3(1) of the Posting of Workers Directive. Any of such national measures would, otherwise, be regarded as an infringement of EU internal market law.[189] By virtue of Article 3(10), the only exception to that rule concerns those national provisions classified as public policy, provided that they are non-discriminatory and they are not determined unilaterally by the Member States.

The approach followed by the Court in defining the scope of Article 3(7) and (10) appears, indeed, consistent with the dual purpose, intrinsic derogatory nature and drafting history of the Posting of Workers Directive. It was, however, sharply criticised by most of academia and public opinion for turning the latter act of secondary EU legislation into a 'maximum directive', de facto preventing the attainment of higher standards of worker protection in the country of destination. Nonetheless, it is worth noting that this kind of observations mainly reflected the interests of workers and trade unions in the Member States with the most advanced social systems and well-developed industrial relations traditions, which receive seconded workers from less developed Member States (mostly Central and Eastern European Countries). Conversely, the posted workers find themselves in a less straightforward condition, given that often they can benefit from the host state's higher standards only as long as their employers continue to profit from the competitive advantage which enables them to obtain contracts for the cross-border provision of services.[190] For this reason, the original Posting of Workers Directive protected the labour market of the recipient Member States only to a limited extent, while preserving a certain comparative advantage in favour of out-of-state service providers and, indirectly, also of the posted workers themselves. Still, the ability of this Directive to limit for the most part wage competition, by imposing the application of a nucleus of terms and conditions of employment of the host Member State, was yet undeniable.[191]

In conclusion, it is worth noting that the whole regulatory framework for posting of workers resulting from the combination of the original Posting of Workers Directive and the Rome I Regulation has been questioned for not being able to cope with the developing (mal)practice of 'search of cheap labour' across the EU.[192] This was also related to the fact that the Directive was conceived and drafted at the time when the European Union was composed of twelve Member States only and adopted by fifteen. As a matter of fact, the thirteen new Member States that joined the Union afterwards

189. Verschueren (n 3) 147–148.
190. Davies, 'Posted Workers: Single Market or Protection of National Labour Law Systems?' (n 35) 574.
191. Frederic De Wispelaere and Jozef Pacolet, 'Posting of Workers as Stabilising Mechanism: An Enlarged Notion of Labour Mobility as a Prerequisite for an Optimal Currency Area' (KU Leuven Research Institute for Work and Society (HIVA) 2015) 13.
192. van Hoek and Houwerzijl, 'Where Do EU Mobile Workers Belong, According to Rome I and the (E)PWD?' (n 14) 216 and 229.

were typically characterised by lower wages and labour standards.[193] Bearing in mind that both the above-mentioned legislative acts were not designed to develop and realise social-policy objectives, the arbitrary choice of establishing a company in the country with the lowest labour standards and subsequently posting workers abroad may be contrasted, when resulting in abuse of EU law, by means of better clarification and enforcement of the rules. Significant improvements in this sense have been made with the adoption on 15 May 2014 of the Enforcement Directive 2014/67/EU,[194] which is thoroughly explored in the following Chapter, along with an investigation of the interpretative activity of the EU judiciary over the substantial content of the Posting of Workers Directive.

193. Maslauskaite (n 40) 9.
194. Directive 2014/67/EU of the European Parliament and of the Council of 15 May 2014 on the enforcement of Directive 96/71/EC concerning the posting of workers in the framework of the provision of services and amending Regulation (EU) No 1024/2012 on administrative cooperation through the Internal Market Information System ('the IMI Regulation') (n 114).

CHAPTER 4

Further Developments in the Regulation of Posting

4.1 INTRODUCTION

As a consequence of the seamless expansion of the recourse to posting practices and the simultaneous progressive transformation of labour mobility across the internal market towards more flexible short-terms patterns, the concrete implementation of the rules set out in the Posting of Workers Directive has become increasingly difficult and problematic. In such a context, the Court of Justice has been seised of a number of cases concerning the compatibility with EU law of the variety of national measures made applicable to foreign undertakings providing services across borders.[1] Interestingly, though, due to the particular approach adopted in the so-called 'Laval trio',[2] the interpretative activity of the EU judiciary on those occasions ended up being extremely controversial. In parallel, the general inadequacy of the existing administrative and

1. As a matter of fact, posting of workers is one of the most relevant fields in which the regulatory activity of the Court of Justice has focused during last years. Accordingly, an accurate examination of the relevant case law is deemed indispensable for determining the actual content of the applicable legal rules. Mia Rönnmar, 'Labour Law in the Courts. The Role of European Case Law on Fundamental Trade Union Rights in an Evolving EU Industrial Relations System' in Ulla Neergaard, Ruth Nielsen and Lynn M Roseberry (eds), *The Role of Courts in Developing a European Social Model – Theoretical and Methodological Perspectives* (Djøf Publishing 2010) 178; Vassilis Hatzopoulos, *Regulating Services in the European Union* (Oxford University Press 2012) 179–180; Vassilis Hatzopoulos, 'The Court's Approach to Services (2006-2012): From Case Law to Case Load?' (2013) 50 Common Market Law Review 459, 500.
2. The so-called 'Laval trio' refers to the three rulings of the Court, forming part of the so-called 'Laval quartet', which have been delivered in the context of posting of workers only. Evidently, therefore, the judgment in *Viking* remains excluded since it did not concern posting activities. More specifically, the 'Laval trio' includes the decisions in *Laval un Partneri Ltd v Svenska Byggnadsarbetareförbundet, Svenska Byggnadsarbetareförbundets avdelning 1, Byggettan and Svenska Elektrikerförbundet* [2007] ECJ Case C-341/05, ECLI:EU:C:2007:809; *Dirk Rüffert v Land Niedersachsen* [2008] CJEU Case C-346/06, ECLI:EU:C:2008:189; *Commission of the European Communities v Grand Duchy of Luxemburg* [2008] ECJ Case C-319/06, ECLI:EU:C:2008:350.

legal frameworks to protect the posted workers' rights and combat circumventive and abusive practices developed in the sector, made a new intervention of the EU legislator necessary. This response took the shape of the 2014 Enforcement Directive, which was specifically designed to provide better enforcement of the Posting of Workers Directive. With regard to the implementation of the posting rules in the European road transport industry instead, in light of the specific difficulties intrinsically connected to such a highly mobile sector, a solution was found in the elaboration of an ad hoc set of norms.

The purpose of this chapter is to provide an overview of further sources of regulation of posting under EU law, developed over the years besides the Posting of Workers Directive and prior to the 2018 amendment of the latter. This analysis intends, thereby, to contribute to addressing the following research sub-question: *How is the 'posting of workers' regulated under EU law?* In this regard, this chapter is divided into two parts; one dealing with the Court of Justice case law, and the other investigating the legislative initiatives taken at EU level. More in detail, section 4.2 explores the important contribution of the Court of Justice in shaping the current regulatory framework, by focusing, at first, on the legitimacy under EU law of national measures imposing certain requirements on incoming cross-border service providers. Second, it considers the approach adopted by the European judiciary in scrutinising the different means, developed at Member State level, for determining the terms and conditions of employment applicable to posted workers. To this end, the important rulings in *Laval,*[3] *Rüffert,*[4] *Commission v Luxembourg,*[5] and *RegioPost*[6] are analysed more thoroughly.[7] The biased rationale followed by the Court in the above-mentioned decisions is then put into question, in section 4.3, for basically reproducing the Western European narrative which tends to present the disputes in terms of dichotomic juxtaposition between social rights and economic freedoms. In turn, an approach able to take into consideration also the interests and prerogatives of the cross-border actors, and especially of the posted workers themselves, is proposed.

The second part of this chapter provides, in section 4.4, an investigation of the whole spectrum of technical improvements brought about by the 2014 Enforcement Directive with the aim of enhancing the degree of compliance with the Posting of Workers Directive. Afterwards, it identifies the shortcomings which were still left out of the legal framework resulting from the combination of the original Posting of Workers Directive and its Enforcement Directive and needed to be addressed by further actions. Lastly, in section 4.5, the analysis takes a look at the newly adopted Directive (EU) 2020/1057 on posting drivers in the road transport sector. This chapter rounds off

3. *Laval un Partneri Ltd v Svenska Byggnadsarbetareförbundet, Svenska Byggnadsarbetareförbundets avdelning 1, Byggettan and Svenska Elektrikerförbundet* (n 2).
4. *Dirk Rüffert v Land Niedersachsen* (n 2).
5. *Commission of the European Communities v Grand Duchy of Luxemburg* (n 2).
6. *RegioPost GmbH & Co KG v Stadt Landau in der Pfalz* [2015] CJEU Case C-115/14, ECLI: EU:C:2015:760.
7. As clearly stated *supra* in Chapter 1, the selection of certain decisions of the Court of Justice has to be considered only in light of the purpose of this thesis, which is not to provide a detailed analysis of all the case law concerning posting of workers.

with the concluding section 4.6, which collects all the previous main findings with the aim of providing a critical reflection on the current regulation of posting at EU level.

4.2 INTERPRETATION OF THE POSTING OF WORKERS DIRECTIVE

As becomes clear from the analysis of the Posting of Workers Directive conducted in the previous chapter, the regulation of the particular type of intra-EU labour mobility under consideration has constantly been reshaped by the intervention of the Court of Justice. The wide interpretative power of the European judiciary becomes manifest when it comes to the implementation of the rules and has materialised, over the years, in the specification of the Member States' margin of appreciation with regard to their faculty of extending national regulations to foreign undertakings providing services in their territory. Besides the indications given in *Commission v Germany*,[8] *Isbir*[9] and *Sähköalojen ammattiliitto*[10] about the constituent elements of the concept of minimum rates of pay (already investigated *supra* in Chapter 3), the scrutiny of the Court invested the legitimacy of the national requirements imposed on incoming cross-border service providers, as well as of the different means for determining labour standards at Member State level. In doing so, it came to the elaboration of an ad hoc version of the proportionality test, whose application gave origin to negative repercussions in the Member States with the highest social standards and the most advanced industrial relations systems.[11]

4.2.1 Legitimacy of National Measures

In line with Article 5 of the Posting of Workers Directive (whose content has been further specified by Directive (EU) 2018/957),[12] the implementation and enforcement of the provisions disposed by the Directive itself is directly delegated to the Member States. The latter's scope of action is, however, limited to the use of appropriate means,[13] which have been shaped by the jurisprudence of the Court of Justice with a

8. *Commission of the European Communities v Federal Republic of Germany* [2005] ECJ Case C-341/02, ECLI:EU:C:2005:220.
9. *Tevfik Isbir v DB Services* [2013] CJEU Case C-522/12, ECLI:EU:C:2013:711.
10. *Sähköalojen ammattiliitto ry v Elektrobudowa Spolka Akcyjna* [2015] CJEU Case C-396/13, ECLI:EU:C:2015:86.
11. Rönnmar, 'Labour Law in the Courts. The Role of European Case Law on Fundamental Trade Union Rights in an Evolving EU Industrial Relations System' (n 1) 189–190.
12. On the specific content of the new Article 5 of the Posting of Workers Directive, *see infra* Chapter 8.
13. Article 5 of Directive 96/71/EC of the European Parliament and of the Council of 16 December 1996 concerning the posting of workers in the framework of the provision of services 1997 (OJ L 18/1). In this sense, *see Société anonyme de droit français Seco et Société anonyme de droit français Desquenne & Giral v Etablissement d'assurance contre la vieillesse et l'invalidité* [1982] ECJ Joined Cases C-62/81 and C-63/81, ECLI:EU:C:1982:34 [14]; *Rush Portuguesa Lda v Office national d'immigration* [1990] ECJ Case C-113/89, ECLI:EU:C:1990:142 [18]; *Guiot v Climatee SA* [1996] ECJ Case C-272/94, ECLI:EU:C:1996:147, 12; *Arblade & Fils SARL v Sofrage SARL* [1999] ECJ Joined Cases C-369/96 and C-376/96, ECLI:EU:C:1999:575, 41; *Commission of the European Communities v Federal Republic of Germany* [2006] ECJ Case C-244/04, ECLI:

specific view to promoting the smooth functioning of the European internal market, while contrasting the spread of fraudulent and abusive practices in the sector. In this sense, the extension of the main contractor's liability for the obligations assumed by its subcontractors with regard to the payment of the workers' minimum wages has been considered perfectly compatible with the provision at stake.[14] Furthermore, a series of judgments focused on the legitimacy of an entire gamma of national control measures and procedures. Requirements entailing a prior declaration of the employment of seconded workers[15] and of their identification data,[16] as well as the keeping at the workplace of the relevant documentation translated in the language of the host country,[17] have all held to be compatible with EU law. Even though such impositions constituted de facto a heavier burden on out-of-state service providers than on local undertakings, their legitimacy was acknowledged as long as they aimed at the overriding public interests of worker protection and fight against social security fraud, and satisfied the proportionality test.[18]

The above-mentioned conditions were not met, instead, in the *Arblade*[19] case, where the obligation of keeping specific individual records of the posted workers was

---

EU:C:2006:49 [36]; *Commission of the European Communities v Republic of Austria* [2006] ECJ Case C-168/04, ECLI:EU:C:2006:595 [47].

14. *Wolff & Müller GmbH & Co KG v José Filipe Pereira Félix* [2004] ECJ Case C-60/03, ECLI: EU:C:2004:610. Yves Jorens, Saskia Peters and Mijke Houwerzijl, 'Study on the Protection of Workers' Rights in Subcontracting Processes in the European Union (Final Study)' (Ghent University, Department of Social Law (in consortium with University of Amsterdam) 2012) DG EMPL/B2-VC/2011/0015, 41–42; Dagmar Schiek et al., 'EU Social and Labour Rights and EU Internal Market Law' (European Parliament, EMPL Committee 2015) IP/A/EMPL/ST/2014-02, 39.
15. *Commission of the European Communities v Federal Republic of Germany* (n 13) para. 41; *dos Santos Palhota and Others* [2010] CJEU Case C-515/08, EU:C:2010:589.
16. *De Clercq and Others* [2014] CJEU Case C-315/13, ECLI:EU:C:2014:2408.
17. *Commission of the European Communities v Federal Republic of Germany* [2007] CJEU Case C-490/04, ECLI:EU:C:2007:430 [71–72].
18. *Arblade & Fils SARL v Sofrage SARL* (n 13) para. 36; *Finalarte Sociedade de Construção Civil v Urlaubs- und Lohnausgleichskasse der Bauwirtschaft* [2001] ECJ Joined Cases C-49/98, C-50/98, C-52/98 to C-54/98 and C-68/98 to C-71/98, ECLI:EU:C:2001:564; *Wolff & Müller GmbH & Co. KG v José Filipe Pereira Félix* (n 14) 28–30; *Commission of the European Communities v Grand Duchy of Luxemburg* [2004] ECJ Case C-445/03, ECLI:EU:C:2004:655 [40]; *Commission of the European Communities v Federal Republic of Germany* (n 13) 36; *De Clercq and Others* (n 16) 71–75. On this point, *see* Paul Davies, 'The Posted Workers Directive and the EC Treaty' (2002) 31 Industrial Law Journal 298, 305; European Commission, Communication: Guidance on the posting of workers in the framework of the provision of services 2006 [COM(2006) 159 final] 5–6; Vassilis Hatzopoulos, 'Labour Immigration in the EU Through the Back Door? The Free Provision of Services as a Facilitator of Migration Flows' in Georg Menz and Alexander Caviedes (eds), *Labour Migration in Europe* (Palgrave MacMillan 2010) 154–155; Catherine Barnard, *EU Employment Law* (Fourth Edition, Oxford European Union Law Library 2012) 215–217; Philippa Watson, *EU Social and Employment Law* (Second Edition, Oxford University Press 2014) 293–294; Marco Rocca, *Posting of Workers and Collective Labour Law: There and Back Again* (Intersentia 2015) 162–163; Uglješa Grušić, *The European Private International Law of Employment* (Cambridge University Press 2015) 276; Yves Jorens et al., 'Fraud and Error in the Field of EU Social Security Coordination: Reference Year: 2016' (European Commission, Directorate-General for Employment, Social Affairs and Inclusion, Unit D2 – Social security coordination 2018) 35.
19. *Arblade & Fils SARL v Sofrage SARL* (n 13).

deemed illegitimate, given that the employees concerned already enjoyed an 'essentially similar protection' under their home country law.[20] In the same vein, the Court condemned the obligation to obtain a permission from the authorities in the receiving country for the secondment of third-country nationals,[21] as well as the requirements for posted workers of residence, work visas, and social security cover in their home Member State,[22] or to have already been employed for at least six months or one year in the sending country before their assignment abroad.[23] In addition, a number of conditions imposed by the Belgian online compulsory registration system (*LIMOSA*) on posting undertakings,[24] and the contextual adoption of criminal penalties as means of enforcement, have all been considered as 'disproportionate restrictions' of the freedom to provide services, and thereby not compatible with Article 56 TFEU.[25] A breach of the latter freedom has even been found in national legislation allowing the competent authorities to order a local commissioning party to suspend payments to a foreign service provider or to pay a guarantee of the fine which could have been potentially imposed on that contractor in case of proven violation of the host state' labour law.[26] Lastly, it should be noted that the requirements for transnational operators to have a subsidiary office in the Member State of destination or to obtain a specific administrative authorisation were not even evaluated in light of their proportionality, having the Court recognised an absolute infringement of the Treaty rules on the free provision of services.[27]

---

20. Davies, 'The Posted Workers Directive and the EC Treaty' (n 18) 303–304; European Commission, Communication: Guidance on the posting of workers in the framework of the provision of services (n 18) 6–7; Vassilis Hatzopoulos and Thien Uyen Do, 'The Case Law of the ECJ Concerning the Free Provision of Services: 2000 – 2005' (2006) 43 Common Market Law Review 923, 972; Hatzopoulos, 'Labour Immigration in the EU Through the Back Door? The Free Provision of Services as a Facilitator of Migration Flows' (n 18) 154–155.
21. *Commission of the European Communities v Republic of Austria* (n 13); *Essent Energie Productie BV v Minister van Sociale Zaken en Werkgelegenheid* [2014] CJEU Case C-91/13, ECLI:EU:C:2014:2206.
22. *Commission of the European Communities v Federal Republic of Germany* (n 13) para. 6.
23. *Commission of the European Communities v Grand Duchy of Luxemburg* (n 18); *Commission of the European Communities v Federal Republic of Germany* (n 13). On this point, *see* Hatzopoulos and Do (n 20) 973; Hatzopoulos, 'Labour Immigration in the EU Through the Back Door? The Free Provision of Services as a Facilitator of Migration Flows' (n 18) 155; Herwig Verschueren, 'The European Internal Market and the Competition between Workers' (2015) 6 European Labour Law Journal 128, 143–144.
24. On the specific requirements imposed by the Belgial *LIMOSA*, *see infra* Chapter 6.
25. *Commission v Belgium* [2012] CJEU Case C-577/10, ECLI:EU:C:2012:814 [55–57]; *dos Santos Palhota and Others* (n 15) paras 51, 53–54. *See* Jorens et al. (n 18) 35.
26. *Čepelnik d.o.o v Michael Vavti* [2018] CJEU Case C-33/17, ECLI:EU:C:2018:896. On this point, *see* European Commission, 'Report from the Commission to the European Parliament, the Council and the European Economic and Social Committee on the Application and Implementation of Directive 2014/67/EU of the European Parliament and of the Council of 15 May 2014 on the Enforcement of Directive 96/71/EC Concerning the Posting of Workers in the Framework of the Provision of Services and Amending Regulation (EU) 1024/2012 on Administrative Co-Operation through the Internal Market Information System ("the IMI Regulation")' (2019) COM(2019) 426 final 21.
27. *Commission of the European Communities v Italian Republic* [2002] ECJ Case C-279/00, ECLI:EU:C:2002:89 [17–18]. *See also Raymond Vander Elst v Office des Migrations Internationales* [1994] ECJ Case C-43/93, ECLI:EU:C:1994:310; *Commission v Belgium* (n 25). On this point,

4.2.2 Determination of Labour Standards

The area in which the Member States' room for manoeuvre was most strikingly affected by the broad interpretative power of the Court of Justice was that of the legal means for concretely determining the terms and conditions of employment applicable to employment relationships involving posted workers. In the cases *Mazzoleni*[28] and *Portugaia Construções*,[29] the EU judiciary acknowledged the theoretical legitimacy of the imposition of the host state's minimum wage legislation on foreign service providers but, nonetheless, required national authorities to verify the concrete pursuit of the public interest objective of worker protection through appropriate means. This requirement was put forward in order to avoid a disproportionate administrative and economic burden on cross-border undertakings for complying with national regulations.[30] In particular, in *Mazzoleni*, the Court required to consider, in the assessment of the respect of the principle of proportionality, not only the minimum wage *stricto sensu*, but also taxation and social security contributions to which frontiers workers between Belgium and France were subject.[31]

With regard to the judgment in *Portugaia Construções*, the scrutiny over proportionality concerned the imposition on cross-border service providers of collective agreements having general binding effect by virtue of the German law transposing the Posting of Workers Directive, namely the *Arbeitnehmer-Entsendegesetz* (Law on the Posting of Employees). Whereas the determination of the appropriateness of that legislation in pursuing an objective of public interest was left to the national authorities or courts of the host Member State, the possibility for local employers to pay wages lower than the minimum wage applicable to incoming posted workers was regarded as

---

see European Commission, Communication: Guidance on the posting of workers in the framework of the provision of services (n 18) 4; Watson (n 18) 293.

28. *Mazzoleni v Inter Surveillance Assistance* [2001] ECJ Case C-165/98, ECLI:EU:C:2001:162.
29. *Portugaia Construções Lda* [2002] ECJ Case C-164/99, ECLI:EU:C:2002:40.
30. *Mazzoleni v Inter Surveillance Assistance* (n 28) paras 31–34; *Portugaia Construções Lda* (n 29) paras 21–24. Hatzopoulos, 'Labour Immigration in the EU Through the Back Door? The Free Provision of Services as a Facilitator of Migration Flows' (n 18) 156; Hatzopoulos, *Regulating Services in the European Union* (n 1) 174–175; Vassilis Hatzopoulos, 'Justifications for Restrictions to Free Movement: Towards a Single Normative Framework?' in Mads Andenas, Tarjei Bekkedal and Luca Pantaleo (eds), *The reach of free movement* (Springer Berlin Heidelberg 2017) 143.
31. In the case at issue, an undertaking established in France, close to the Belgian border, used to send its employees 'on a part-time basis and only for brief periods' to Belgium in order to perform a part of their work. The Court of Justice, in order to avoid an overburden to the cross-border service provider in terms of remuneration, taxation and social security contributions, made an exception to the general rule of automatic extension of national labour provisions on minimum wages. In light of the temporary nature of the posting activity, the Court required, therefore, to 'consider whether the application of those rules is necessary and proportionate for the purpose of protecting the workers concerned'. *Mazzoleni v Inter Surveillance Assistance* (n 28) paras 31 and 34–36. *See* Davies, 'The Posted Workers Directive and the EC Treaty' (n 18) 304; Richard Giesen, 'Posting: Social Protection of Workers vs. Fundamental Freedoms?' (2003) 40 Common Market Law Review 143, 154–155; Hatzopoulos and Do (n 20) 974–975; Hatzopoulos, 'Labour Immigration in the EU Through the Back Door? The Free Provision of Services as a Facilitator of Migration Flows' (n 18) 156.

an unjustified restriction of the out-of-state employers' freedom to provide services.[32] It was, however, in the following famous ruling in *Laval*[33] that the Court of Justice's strict application of the proportionality test played the most effective role in circumscribing the national autonomy (and, in particular, that of trade unions) in setting labour standards for incoming posted workers.

4.2.2.1 *Laval*

The case at issue concerned a dispute between the Latvian company *Laval un Partneri*, which posted thirty-five workers from Latvia to its subsidiary *(L&P Baltic Bygg AB)* in Sweden for the construction of a school in the town of Vaxholm, and the Swedish trade unions, which brought a number of collective actions at the construction site with the aim of forcing the *Laval* to enter into negotiations for the conclusion of a collective agreement.[34] Those industrial actions proved to be, indeed, extremely successful from the point of view of the promoters, given that they eventually led the company *Laval* to bankruptcy.[35] Crucially, though, the terms and conditions of employment (including minimum rates of pay) envisaged by the building sector's collective agreement into question were beyond the hard nucleus determined by the Posting of Workers Directive.[36]

32. *Portugaia Construções Lda* (n 29) paras 24 and 35. *See* Rocca, *Posting of Workers and Collective Labour Law: There and Back Again* (n 18) 173–176.
33. *Laval un Partneri Ltd v Svenska Byggnadsarbetareförbundet, Svenska Byggnadsarbetareförbundets avdelning 1, Byggettan and Svenska Elektrikerförbundet* (n 2).
34. In particular, the Latvian posted workers earned about 40% less than comparable Swedish workers. Interestingly, the company *Laval* had, in the meanwhile, concluded a collective agreement with a Latvian trade union, arguably with the intention of pre-empting any negotiation with the Swedish trade unions. Charles Woolfson and Jeff Sommers, 'Labour Mobility in Construction: European Implications of the Laval Un Partneri Dispute with Swedish Labour' (2006) 12 European Journal of Industrial Relations 49, 54; Dagmar Schiek, 'Perspectives on Social Citizenship in the EU – From Status Positivus to Status Socialis Activus via Two Forms of Transnational Solidarity' (2015) 4 Queen's University Belfast School of Law: Research Paper 2015 - 10, 16; Schiek et al. (n 14) 31–32.
35. For a detailed investigation of the relevant facts of the case, *see* Woolfson and Sommers (n 34) 53–57. *See also* Simon Deakin, 'Regulatory Competition after Laval' (2007) 10 Cambridge Yearbook of European Legal Studies 581, 582; Catherine Barnard, 'Viking and Laval: An Introduction' (2008) 10 Cambridge Yearbook of European Legal Studies 463, 465–466; Jonas Malmberg and Tore Sigeman, 'Industrial Actions and EU Economic Freedoms: The Autonomous Collective Bargaining Model Curtailed by the European Court of Justice' (2008) 45 Common Market Law Review 1115, 1122–1123; Jonas Malmberg, 'The Impact of the ECJ Judgements on Viking, Laval, Rüffert and Luxembourg on the Practice of Collective Bargaining and the Effectiveness of Social Action' (Directorate-General for Internal Policies, Policy Department A: Economic and Scientific Policy Employment and Social Affairs Brussels: European Parliament 2010) 5; Rönnmar, 'Labour Law in the Courts. The Role of European Case Law on Fundamental Trade Union Rights in an Evolving EU Industrial Relations System' (n 1) 182; Rocca, *Posting of Workers and Collective Labour Law: There and Back Again* (n 18) 9–13; Grušić (n 18) 270–271; Mia Rönnmar, 'Labour and Equality Law' in Catherine Barnard and Steve Peers (eds), *European Union Law* (Second Edition, Oxford University Press 2017) 610–611.
36. In particular, it envisaged further provisions on temporary unemployment and waiting time, employment protection and training, as well as obligations on the employer to pay a fee to the trade union for pay review and insurance premiums to the employees. Mia Rönnmar, 'Free

In its decision of 18 December 2007, after recognising the nature of the right to take collective action as a fundamental right,[37] the Court (Grand Chamber) acknowledged the EU competence in this matter.[38] This notwithstanding the fact that Article 153(5) TFEU (at that time Article 137(5) TEC) expressly excluded the right to strike from the scope of EU law.[39] Moreover, the application of the Treaty rules on free movement of services, and especially their horizontal direct effect, in respect of trade

Movement of Services Versus National Labour Law and Industrial Relations Systems: Understanding the Laval Case from a Swedish and Nordic Perspective' (2007) 10 Cambridge Yearbook of European Legal Studies 493, 514.

37. In that regard, the Court stressed the recognition of the right to take collective action by a number of international and European instruments, namely 'the European Social Charter, signed at Turin on 18 October 1961 – to which, moreover, express reference is made in Article 136 EC – and Convention No 87 of the International Labour Organisation concerning Freedom of Association and Protection of the Right to Organise of 9 July 1948 – and [...] the Community Charter of the Fundamental Social Rights of Workers adopted at the meeting of the European Council held in Strasbourg on 9 December 1989, which is also referred to in Article 136 EC, and the Charter of Fundamental Rights of the European Union proclaimed in Nice on 7 December 2000.' *Laval un Partneri Ltd v Svenska Byggnadsarbetareförbundet, Svenska Byggnadsarbetareförbundets avdelning 1, Byggettan and Svenska Elektrikerförbundet* (n 2) para. 90.

38. *Ibid.* 91.

39. *Ibid.* 88. The argument of the Court was that, even though the freedom to regulate the right to strike was left to the Member States, the latter were, nevertheless, still bound to respect EU law in exercising such a prerogative. To corroborate this stance, reference was made to two previous decisions in *Schmidberger* and *Omega* where matters concerning fundamental rights, the freedom of expression and the freedom of assembly and the respect for human dignity respectively, had been considered within the scope of the Treaty rules. Importantly, in those cases – as also, subsequently, in *Laval* – the only condition posed for the admittance of justifications on grounds of protection of fundamental rights was the respect of the principle of proportionality. *Ibid.* 94. *See also Eugen Schmidberger, Internationale Transporte und Planzüge v Republik Österreich* [2003] ECJ Case C-112/00, ECLI:EU:C:2003:333 [77]; *Omega Spielhallen- und Automatenaufstellungs-GmbH v Oberbürgermeisterin der Bundesstadt Bonn* [2004] ECJ Case C-36/02, ECLI:EU:C:2004:614 [36]. On the conflict between fundamental rights and EU fundamental freedoms in the *Schmidberger* and *Omega* cases, *see* Vassilios Skouris, 'Fundamental Rights and Fundamental Freedoms: The Challenge of Striking a Delicate Balance' (2006) 17 European Business Law Review 225, 235–238. With regard to the decision in *Laval*, *see* ACL Davies, 'One Step Forward, Two Steps Back? The Viking and Laval Cases in the ECJ' (2008) 37 Industrial Law Journal 126, 130–131; Barnard, 'Viking and Laval: An Introduction' (n 35) 467–468; Malmberg and Sigeman (n 35) 1126; Rönnmar, 'Labour Law in the Courts. The Role of European Case Law on Fundamental Trade Union Rights in an Evolving EU Industrial Relations System' (n 1) 186–187; Lynn M Roseberry, 'International Human Rights Treaties and Fundamental Rights in the Case Law of the European Court of Justice: Pointing Towards a European Social Model?' in Ulla Neergaard, Ruth Nielsen and Lynn M Roseberry (eds), *The Role of Courts in Developing a European Social Model – Theoretical and Methodological Perspectives* (Djøf Publishing 2010) 222–223; Catherine Barnard, 'EU "Social" Policy: From Employment Law to Labour Market Reform' in Paul Craig and Gráinne de Búrca (eds), *The Evolution of EU Law* (Second Edition, Oxford University Press 2011) 665–666; Hatzopoulos, *Regulating Services in the European Union* (n 1) 203; Sybe A De Vries, 'Balancing Fundamental Rights with Economic Freedoms According to the European Court of Justice' (2013) 9 Utrecht Law Review 169, 182; Steve Weatherill, 'From Economic Rights to Fundamental Rights' in Sybe De Vries, Ulf Bernitz and Steve Weatherill (eds), *The Protection of Fundamental Rights in the EU After Lisbon* (Hart Publishing 2013) 27; Rocca, *Posting of Workers and Collective Labour Law: There and Back Again* (n 18) 248; Silvana Sciarra, *Solidarity and Conflict: European Social Law in Crisis* (Cambridge University Press 2018) 109–110.

unions was also confirmed, arguably exposing the latter to damage liability.[40] In doing so the Court took into account the peculiar construction of the Swedish system of industrial relations, which de facto conferred on trade unions, given their possibility to have recourse to collective actions, an actual regulatory power with regard to the provision of services in that country.[41] And in the exercise of such a power, the trade unions' activity normally did not aim at protecting any wider societal interest, let alone the interest of European labour as a whole, but rather at protecting the private interests of their members.[42] Accordingly, even though those organisations did not formally operate as public authorities in the general interest nor had exclusive regulatory powers within entire economic areas, their possible exclusion from the scrutiny under EU law was prevented by the fact that it would have prejudiced, in practice, the effectiveness of the freedom to provide services.[43] At the same time, the Court of Justice

---

40. *Laval un Partneri Ltd v Svenska Byggnadsarbetareförbundet, Svenska Byggnadsarbetareförbundets avdelning 1, Byggettan and Svenska Elektrikerförbundet* (n 2) para. 98. Similar to the decision taken in *Viking*, also in this case the possibility for cross-border undertakings to invoke the Treaty against trade unions was acknowledged. Davies, 'One Step Forward, Two Steps Back?' (n 39) 126–127 and 136; Malmberg and Sigeman (n 35) 1127; Dagmar Schiek, *Economic and Social Integration: The Challenge for EU Constitutional Law* (Edward Elgar 2012) 164–165; Barnard, 'EU "Social" Policy: From Employment Law to Labour Market Reform' (n 39) 666–667; Martin Mörk, 'An End to the Possibilities – on Horizontal Liability in Laval and the Limits of Judicial Rights Protection' in Sybe De Vries, Ulf Bernitz and Steve Weatherill (eds), *The Protection of Fundamental Rights in the EU After Lisbon* (Hart Publishing 2013); Ulf Bernitz, 'Horizontal Effects of Private Rights Vested by Union Law on Damages to Be Paid by Another Private Party: The Laval Case as a Model' in Sybe De Vries, Ulf Bernitz and Steve Weatherill (eds), *The Protection of Fundamental Rights in the EU After Lisbon* (Hart Publishing 2013) 142–147; Stefano Giubboni, 'European Citizenship and Social Rights in Times of Crisis' (2013) Working Paper-LPF n. 2 Centro Einaudi – Laboratorio di Politica Comparata e Filosofia Pubblica 17; Catherine Barnard, 'A Proportionate Response to Proportionality in the Field of Collective Action' (2015) European Law Review 117, 6; Floris de Witte, *Justice in the EU: The Emergence of Transnational Solidarity* (Oxford University Press 2015) 111; Olha O. Cherednychenko, 'Fundamental Freedoms, Fundamental Rights, and the Many Faces of Freedom of Contract in the EU' in Mads Andenas, Tarjei Bekkedal and Luca Pantaleo (eds), *The reach of free movement* (Springer Berlin Heidelberg 2017) 285; Uglješa Grušić, 'European Labour Market Posted Workers Directive and the Social Implications of the Movement of Labour' in Horatia Muir Watt et al. (eds), *Global Private International Law: Adjudication Without Frontiers* (Edward Elgar Publishing 2018) 474. Instead, no issue related to a possible direct effect (both horizontal and vertical) of the PWD ever seemed to be at stake in the *Laval* case. For a more in-depth analysis of the matter, *see* Alan Dashwood, 'Viking and Laval Issues of Horizontal Direct Effect' (2007) 10 Cambridge Yearbook of European Legal Studies 525, 536–539.
41. *Laval un Partneri Ltd v Svenska Byggnadsarbetareförbundet, Svenska Byggnadsarbetareförbundets avdelning 1, Byggettan and Svenska Elektrikerförbundet, Opinion of Advocate General Paolo Mengozzi delivered on 23 May 2007* [2007] ECJ Case C-341/05, ECLI:EU:C:2007:291 [160]; Dashwood (n 40) 535; Rönnmar, 'Free Movement of Services Versus National Labour Law and Industrial Relations Systems: Understanding the Laval Case from a Swedish and Nordic Perspective' (n 36) 499–500; Alexander Somek, 'The Social Question in a Transnational Context' (2011) LEQS Paper No. 39/2011, 36; Frans Pennings, 'How Do Social and Economic Rights Relate to Each Other in the Social Market Economy: An Introduction to This Special Issue' (2019) 15 Utrecht Law Review 1, 7–8.
42. Dorota Leczykiewicz, 'Conceptualising Conflict between the Economic and the Social in EU Law after Viking and Laval' in R. Mark Freedland and Jeremias Prassl (eds), *Viking, Laval and Beyond* (First Edition, Hart Publishing 2016) 316.
43. *Laval un Partneri Ltd v Svenska Byggnadsarbetareförbundet, Svenska Byggnadsarbetareförbundets avdelning 1, Byggettan and Svenska Elektrikerförbundet* (n 2) para. 98. In support of its reasoning, the Court brought the examples of the decisions in *Walrave and Koch, Bosman* and

made also clear that trade unions, in light of their position outside of the public law sphere, were not entitled to justify a collective action on grounds of public policy in accordance with Article 3(10) of the Posting of Workers Directive.[44]

Afterwards, the attention of the Court moved to the recognition of the collective action as a restriction of the *Laval*'s freedom to provide services[45] and to its possible justification for overriding reasons of public interest, identified in the protection of

---

Wouters whereby the conducts of certain private entities with regulatory powers, such as, respectively, the *Union Cycliste Internationale (UCI)* and the Dutch and Spanish cycling federations, the *Union of European Football Associations (UEFA)*, and the Netherlands Bar Council, were subsumed under EU law competence. *BNO Walrave and LJN Koch v Association Union cycliste internationale, Koninklijke Nederlandsche Wielren Unie and Federación Española Ciclismo* [1974] ECJ Case C-36-74, ECLI:EU:C:1974:140 [17–18]; *Union royale belge des sociétés de football association ASBL v Jean-Marc Bosman, Royal club liégeois SA v Jean-Marc Bosman and others and Union des associations européennes de football (UEFA) v Jean-Marc Bosman* [1995] ECJ Case C-415/93, ECLI:EU:C:1995:463 [83–84]; *J C J Wouters, J W Savelbergh and Price Waterhouse Belastingadviseurs BV v Algemene Raad van de Nederlandse Orde van Advocaten, intervener: Raad van de Balies van de Europese Gemeenschap* [2002] ECJ Case C-309/99, ECLI:EU:C:2002:98 [120]. On this point, *see* Koen Lenaerts and Jose A Gutierrez-Fons, 'The Constitutional Allocation of Powers and General Principles of EU Law' (2010) 47 Common Market Law Review 1629, 1665; Sybe A De Vries, 'The Protection of Fundamental Rights within Europe's Internal Market after Lisbon – And Endeavour for More Harmony' in Sybe De Vries, Ulf Bernitz and Steve Weatherill (eds), *The Protection of Fundamental Rights in the EU After Lisbon* (Hart Publishing 2013) 91–92; Rocca, *Posting of Workers and Collective Labour Law: There and Back Again* (n 18) 237–238; Leczykiewicz (n 42) 316.

44. *Laval un Partneri Ltd v Svenska Byggnadsarbetareförbundet, Svenska Byggnadsarbetareförbundets avdelning 1, Byggettan and Svenska Elektrikerförbundet* (n 2) para. 84. As critically observed by Barnard, trade unions were, in practice, 'treated as states for the purposes of liability, but not when it [came] to defences'. Barnard, 'Viking and Laval: An Introduction' (n 35) 475. In this sense, *see also* Davies, 'One Step Forward, Two Steps Back?' (n 39) 136–137; Malmberg and Sigeman (n 35) 1138–1139; Dagmar Schiek, 'Is There a Social Ideal of the European Court of Justice?' in Ulla Neergaard, Ruth Nielsen and Lynn M Roseberry (eds), *The Role of Courts in Developing a European Social Model – Theoretical and Methodological Perspectives* (Djøf Publishing 2010) 86–87; Edoardo Ales and Giovanni Orlandini, 'The Impact of Viking and Laval on Italian Legislation and Regulations Concerning Collective Action' in Andreas Bücker and Wiebke Warneck (eds), *Viking – Laval – Rüffert: Consequences and Policy Perspectives* (ETUI (European Trade Union Institute) 2010) 79; Barnard, 'EU "Social" Policy: From Employment Law to Labour Market Reform' (n 39) 666–668; De Vries (n 43) 91; Barnard, 'A Proportionate Response to Proportionality in the Field of Collective Action' (n 40) 6; Sjoerd Feenstra, 'How Can the Viking/Laval Conundrum Be Resolved? Balancing the Economic and the Social: One Bed for Two Dreams?' in Frank Vandenbroucke, Catherine Barnard and Geert De Baere (eds), *A European Social Union after the Crisis* (Cambridge University Press 2017) 326–327. For a similar critical interpretation of the Court's approach, considering the treatment reserved to trade unions as a paradox materialised in the refusal 'to consider the system of social relations as a "constitutional order" enjoying the capacity of self-determination', *see* Loïc Azoulai, 'The Court of Justice and the Social Market Economy: The Emergence of an Ideal and the Conditions for Its Realization' (2008) 45 Common Market Law Review 1335, 1350–1351.

45. *Laval un Partneri Ltd v Svenska Byggnadsarbetareförbundet, Svenska Byggnadsarbetareförbundets avdelning 1, Byggettan and Svenska Elektrikerförbundet* (n 2) para. 99. As already pointed out in the previous chapter, on that occasion, the Court followed the so-called 'market access' test developed in the *Säger* ruling, which, in order to detect a possible restriction of the freedom guaranteed by the Treaties, limits the investigation to a check of the presence of any obstacle 'liable to prohibit or otherwise impede the activities of a provider of services established in another Member State'. *Manfred Säger v Dennemeyer & Co Ltd* [1991] ECJ Case C-76/90, ECLI:EU:C:1991:331 [12].

workers against the threat of social dumping.[46] In the case at issue, however, the blockading action for attaining certain employment standards, despite it was aimed at protecting local workers, failed to satisfy the proportionality test. The mere exercise of a fundamental right to strike was, indeed, not considered as a sufficient justification for any collective action.[47] By using the Posting of Workers Directive as a yardstick for measuring the proportionality of the trade unions' action, the Court found the unlawfulness under Article 56 TFEU of the imposition of a level of protection higher than the *minima* specified by Article 3(1).[48] Furthermore, the requirement for foreign service providers to enter into pay negotiations with local trade unions was considered as an excessive burden for the first ones, resulting in a too onerous and uncertain determination of their obligations. In other words, the overly complicated *a priori* determination of the posted workers' remuneration according to the host country's practices was deemed to negatively affect the overall convenience of the transnational provision of services. In substance, therefore, the European judiciary required that it

46. *Laval un Partneri Ltd v Svenska Byggnadsarbetareförbundet, Svenska Byggnadsarbetareförbundets avdelning 1, Byggettan and Svenska Elektrikerförbundet* (n 2) para. 103.
47. Davies, 'One Step Forward, Two Steps Back?' (n 39) 142; Rebecca Zahn, 'The Viking and Laval Cases in the Context of European Enlargement' *Web Journal of Current Legal Issues* (2008) 20, 9; Leczykiewicz (n 42) 313. For a critique of the Court's approach in *Viking* and *Laval* for failing to justify the national measures restricting the EU free movement rights of foreign service providers by taking into account the social purpose of the Union, *see* Steve Weatherill, 'Viking and Laval: The EU Internal Market Perspective' in R Mark Freedland and Jeremias Prassl (eds), *Viking, Laval and Beyond* (First Edition, Hart Publishing 2016) 37–39.
48. *Laval un Partneri Ltd v Svenska Byggnadsarbetareförbundet, Svenska Byggnadsarbetareförbundets avdelning 1, Byggettan and Svenska Elektrikerförbundet* (n 2) para. 108. Following the Court's line of reasoning, the standard of protection offered by the PWD was already satisfactory for ensuring the protection of the workers against social dumping. Barnard, 'Viking and Laval: An Introduction' (n 35) 484; Alicia Hinarejos, 'Laval and Viking: The Right to Collective Action Versus EU Fundamental Freedoms' (2008) 8 Human Rights Law Review 714, 717–718; Lenaerts and Gutierrez-Fons (n 43) 1664–1665; Barnard, 'EU "Social" Policy: From Employment Law to Labour Market Reform' (n 39) 667–668; Rocca, *Posting of Workers and Collective Labour Law: There and Back Again* (n 18) 290; Dagmar Schiek, 'Towards More Resilience for a Social EU – The Constitutionally Conditioned Internal Market' (2017) 13 European Constitutional Law Review 611, 632. Interestingly, the Swedish regulatory framework, at that time, was totally devoid of any provision on minimum wages and working conditions provided for by law, regulations or universally applicable collective agreements, and neither by any of the alternatives envisaged by Article 3(8) of Directive 96/71. *Laval un Partneri Ltd v Svenska Byggnadsarbetareförbundet, Svenska Byggnadsarbetareförbundets avdelning 1, Byggettan and Svenska Elektrikerförbundet* (n 2) para. 67. *See* Dashwood (n 40) 537; Rönnmar, 'Free Movement of Services Versus National Labour Law and Industrial Relations Systems: Understanding the Laval Case from a Swedish and Nordic Perspective' (n 36) 500; Malmberg and Sigeman (n 35) 1117; Christian Joerges and Florian Rödl, 'Informal Politics, Formalised Law and the "Social Deficit" of European Integration: Reflections after the Judgments of the ECJ in *Viking* and *Laval*' (2009) 15 European Law Journal 1, 16; Siofra O'Leary, 'Free Movement of Persons and Services' in Paul Craig and Gráinne de Búrca (eds), *The Evolution of EU Law* (Second Edition, Oxford University Press 2011) 524. On the major criticism made to the Court's reading of the PWD as prohibiting the imposition on cross-border service providers of the respect of any element of domestic labour law going beyond the protection already ensured under Article 3(1), *see* the analysis carried out *supra* in Chapter 3.

could always be possible for posting employers to ascertain the concrete entity of the minimum wage they have to pay their workers.[49]

Finally, further clarification of the boundaries to national autonomy was offered by the Court's answer to the second preliminary question, concerning the legitimacy of the Swedish *Lex Britannia*.[50] Due to its failure to recognise the obligations to which the *Laval* was already subject to under collective agreements concluded in Latvia, this piece of national legislation was condemned for substantially imposing a 'double burden' on the posting undertaking. Hence, by treating in the same way national undertakings which had not signed any collective agreement and foreign undertakings already bound by collective agreements concluded in their home countries, the Swedish law was considered to be discriminatory and, consequently, in breach of the freedom to provide services.[51]

As a matter of fact, the decision in *Laval* censored the Swedish method of implementation of the Posting of Workers Directive across the board. First, the above-mentioned *Lex Britannia* was declared discriminatory. Second, the government was censured for its choice of not making use of one of the alternatives offered by the Posting of Workers Directive, namely the adoption of a state regulation or the extension of the employment standards provided for by collective agreements without *erga*

49. *Laval un Partneri Ltd v Svenska Byggnadsarbetareförbundet, Svenska Byggnadsarbetareförbundets avdelning 1, Byggettan and Svenska Elektrikerförbundet* (n 2) paras 71 and 110. Rönnmar, 'Free Movement of Services Versus National Labour Law and Industrial Relations Systems: Understanding the Laval Case from a Swedish and Nordic Perspective' (n 36) 512 and 516; Davies, 'One Step Forward, Two Steps Back?' (n 39) 132–133; Barnard, 'Viking and Laval: An Introduction' (n 35) 484–485; Lenaerts and Gutierrez-Fons (n 43) 1665; Kerstin Ahlberg, 'The Age of Innocence – And Beyond' (2010) 21 FORMULA Working Paper, University of Oslo, Department of Private Law 17–18; Barnard, 'EU "Social" Policy: From Employment Law to Labour Market Reform' (n 39) 673; Frank Vandenbroucke, 'The Case for a European Social Union: From Muddling Through to a Sense of Common Purpose' (2014) Euroforum Policy Paper (KU Leuven) 15; Rocca, *Posting of Workers and Collective Labour Law: There and Back Again* (n 18) 216. The rationale adopted in that regard was severely criticised for basically proving the Court's very poor understanding of the practical functioning of collective bargaining, whereby neither party can be aware of the applicable wage level before entering into a serious negotiation about contractual terms. Schiek, 'Perspectives on Social Citizenship in the EU' (n 34) 17; Schiek et al. (n 14) 31.
50. On the specific content of the *'Lex Britannia'*, *see* Rönnmar, 'Free Movement of Services Versus National Labour Law and Industrial Relations Systems: Understanding the Laval Case from a Swedish and Nordic Perspective' (n 36) 503–504.
51. *Laval un Partneri Ltd v Svenska Byggnadsarbetareförbundet, Svenska Byggnadsarbetareförbundets avdelning 1, Byggettan and Svenska Elektrikerförbundet* (n 2) paras 115–117. Despite its aim at combating social dumping, the discriminatory *'Lex Britannia'* was not considered to be justified by any of the possible grounds of excuse, namely public policy, public security or public health reasons. Rönnmar, 'Free Movement of Services Versus National Labour Law and Industrial Relations Systems: Understanding the Laval Case from a Swedish and Nordic Perspective' (n 36) 517–518; Davies, 'One Step Forward, Two Steps Back?' (n 39) 132–133; Barnard, 'Viking and Laval: An Introduction' (n 35) 485; Joerges and Rödl (n 48) 16–17; Schiek, 'Is There a Social Ideal of the European Court of Justice?' (n 44) 87; Antonina Bakardjieva Engelbrekt, 'Institutional Theories, EU Law and the Role of the Courts for Developing a European Social Model' in Ulla Neergaard, Ruth Nielsen and Lynn M Roseberry (eds), *The Role of Courts in Developing a European Social Model – Theoretical and Methodological Perspectives* (Djøf Publishing 2010) 334; Hatzopoulos, *Regulating Services in the European Union* (n 1) 112 and 204; Rocca, *Posting of Workers and Collective Labour Law: There and Back Again* (n 18) 13; Sciarra (n 39) 110.

omnes effect, such as the one local trade unions wanted to conclude with the Latvian company *Laval*, to all foreign undertakings temporarily supplying services in Sweden.[52] Third, and more importantly, the mere reliance on unregulated collective bargaining for the administration of posting activities exposed the unions' industrial action to the strict assessment of the Court of Justice.[53] On that occasion, the judges in Luxembourg recognised the protectionist motivation underpinning the strike against the foreign company and, as a result, considerably limited the trade unions' room for justification, preventing them from any possibility of invoking the public policy exception envisaged by Article 3(10) of the Posting of Workers Directive.[54] As for the proportionality of the collective action in the attainment of the objective of worker protection,[55] the approach followed in the judgment, instead of entailing a concrete comparison between the social systems of the host state and of the state of origin, simply required the respect of the nucleus of mandatory rules set out in the Posting of Workers Directive.[56]

Evidently, the interventionist *modus operandi* of the Court of Justice, mainly directed to find a balance between economic and social objectives of the Union[57] by means of application of such a strict proportionality test,[58] demonstrated the proactive

---

52. Dashwood (n 40) 537; Barnard, 'Viking and Laval: An Introduction' (n 35) 476–477; Barnard, 'EU "Social" Policy: From Employment Law to Labour Market Reform' (n 39) 674–675; Barnard, *EU Employment Law* (n 18) 225–226; Bernitz (n 40) 148.
53. Davies, 'One Step Forward, Two Steps Back?' (n 39) 137 and 143.
54. More specifically, as clearly explained by Lenaerts, who was a member of the Grand Chamber of the Court of Justice in the *Laval* judgment, even when they pursue their legitimate intention to protect workers from social dumping, trade unions 'are not entitled to shield local labour markets from competition coming from Member States with low average wages'. Lenaerts and Gutierrez-Fons (n 43) 1666–1667. *See also* Tor-Inge Harbo, 'The Criterion of "Consistent and Systematic Manner"' in Mads Andenas, Tarjei Bekkedal and Luca Pantaleo (eds), *The Reach of Free Movement* (Springer Berlin Heidelberg 2017) 208.
55. Notably, it was the trade union's industrial action, and not the right to strike as such, under the scrutiny of the Court of Justice. Davies, 'One Step Forward, Two Steps Back?' (n 39) 141.
56. A concrete comparison between the treatment reserved to posted workers by the law of the host state in respect of that in their country of origin was proposed by Advocate General Mengozzi in *Laval*, who mainly focused on the differences in terms of gross amounts of wages. On that occasion, he suggested that such a comparison should have been carried out by national courts. *Laval un Partneri Ltd v Svenska Byggnadsarbetareförbundet, Svenska Byggnadsarbetareförbundets avdelning 1, Byggettan and Svenska Elektrikerförbundet, Opinion of Advocate General Paolo Mengozzi delivered on 23 May 2007* (n 41) paras 272–273. Azoulai (n 44) 1351–1352.
57. *Laval un Partneri Ltd v Svenska Byggnadsarbetareförbundet, Svenska Byggnadsarbetareförbundets avdelning 1, Byggettan and Svenska Elektrikerförbundet* (n 2) para. 105. *See* De Vries (n 43) 70 and 93–94. Despite the recognition of the protectionist intentions of local trade unions, it cannot be denied that the judges in Luxembourg showed nonetheless an appreciable degree of concern with regard to the guarantee of social protection. Furthermore, it is noticeable that the relevance of the fundamental right to take collective action in 'horizontal' situations (i.e., in disputes involving private parties) was definitely confirmed. Giesen (n 31) 152; Xavier Groussot, Laurent Pech and Thor Petursson, 'The Reach of Fundamental Rights on Member State Action after Lisbon' in Sybe De Vries, Ulf Bernitz and Steve Weatherill (eds), *The Protection of Fundamental Rights in the EU After Lisbon* (Hart Publishing 2013) 117–118.
58. Incidentally, it should be noted that an even more strict proportionality test was applied in *Viking*, where national courts were required to check whether trade unions, before making use of collective actions, had already exhausted all alternative means for attaining the objective of worker protection in a less restrictive way of the EU economic freedoms. Industrial actions were thereby relegated to a sort of *ultima ratio*. The approach followed in *Viking* was strongly

role of the EU judiciary in the process of regulation of the sector.[59] The chosen method was, nevertheless, strongly criticised for granting precedence to the EU fundamental freedom of transnational service provision over the fundamental social right to take collective action.[60] The line of reasoning followed by the Court aimed at assessing, indeed, the restrictive nature of the Swedish trade union's action, rather than recognising possible limitations of the right to collective action.[61] In other terms, it failed to

criticised for proving the Court's lack of awareness of the practical functioning of collective bargaining. Notably, it was deemed to result in the paradox whereby the success of the strike (e.g., by forcing out of business the employer's undertaking) was inversely proportional to the recognition of its proportionality. *International Transport Workers' Federation and Finnish Seamen's Union v Viking Line ABP and OÜ Viking Line Eesti* [2007] ECJ Case C-438/05, ECLI:EU:C:2007:772 [87]. On this point, *see* Davies, 'One Step Forward, Two Steps Back?' (n 39) 129, 135 and 143; Nikolett Hos, 'The Principle of Proportionality in the Viking and Laval Cases: An Appropriate Standard of Judicial Review?' (2009) 06 EUI Working Paper 31–32; Barnard, 'EU "Social" Policy: From Employment Law to Labour Market Reform' (n 39) 674; Stein Evju and Tonia Novitz, 'The Evolving Regulation: Dynamics and Consequences' (2012) 33 FORMULA Working Paper, University of Oslo, Department of Private Law 59; Barnard, 'A Proportionate Response to Proportionality in the Field of Collective Action' (n 40) 4–5; Rocca, *Posting of Workers and Collective Labour Law: There and Back Again* (n 18) 249.

59. In this sense, the substantial shift of power from national legislatures to judges applying EU law, at horizontal level, and from the Member States to the Court of Justice, at vertical level, has been the subject of criticism. Lenaerts and Gutierrez-Fons (n 43) 1668; Hatzopoulos, *Regulating Services in the European Union* (n 1) 175.
60. Herwig Verschueren, 'Cross-Border Workers in the European Internal Market: Trojan Horses for Member States' Labour and Social Security Law?' (2008) 24/2 International Journal of Comparative Labour Law and Industrial Relations 167, 177; Catherine Barnard, 'Social Dumping or Dumping Socialism?' (2008) 67 The Cambridge Law Journal 264; Catherine Barnard, '"British Jobs for British Workers": The Lindsey Oil Refinery Dispute and the Future of Local Labour Clauses in an Integrated EU Market' (2009) 38 Industrial Law Journal 245, 276; Rönnmar, 'Labour Law in the Courts. The Role of European Case Law on Fundamental Trade Union Rights in an Evolving EU Industrial Relations System' (n 1) 189; Barnard, 'EU "Social" Policy: From Employment Law to Labour Market Reform' (n 39) 673–674; Evju and Novitz (n 58) 59; Stein Evju, *Cross-Border Services: Posting of Workers, and Multilevel Governance* (University of Oslo, Faculty of Law 2013) 14; Catherine Barnard, 'EU Employment Law and the European Social Model: The Past, the Present and the Future' (2014) 67 Current Legal Problems 199, 205; Verschueren (n 23) 146; Catherine Barnard, 'The Calm after the Storm: Time to Reflect on EU (Labour) Law Scholarship Following the Decisions in Viking and Laval' (2015) University of Cambridge Faculty of Law Research Paper No. 55/2015, later published in Alan Bogg, Cathryn Costello and ACL Davies (eds), *Research Handbook on EU Labour Law* (Edward Elgar Publishing) 337, 6; Rebecca Zahn, 'Revision of the Posted Workers' Directive: Equality at Last?' (2016) 5 European (Legal) Studies on-line papers, Queen's University Belfast – School of Law – Centre of European and Transnational Legal Studies 5; Harbo (n 54) 208 and 221; Rebecca Zahn, 'Revision of the Posted Workers' Directive: A Europeanisation Perspective' (2017) 19 Cambridge Yearbook of European Legal Studies 187, 195; Schiek, 'Towards More Resilience for a Social EU – the Constitutionally Conditioned Internal Market' (n 48) 630–631; Daniel Carter, 'Equal Pay for Equal Work in the Same Place? Assessing the Revision to the Posted Workers Directive' (2018) 14 Croatian Yearbook of European Law and Policy 31, 45; Catherine Barnard and Sybe De Vries, 'The "Social Market Economy" in a (Heterogeneous) Social Europe: Does It Make a Difference?' (2019) 15 Utrecht Law Review 47, 50; Catherine Jacqueson and Frans Pennings, 'Equal Treatment of Mobile Persons in the Context of a Social Market Economy' (2019) 15 Utrecht Law Review 64, 76.
61. The right to collective action is indeed traditionally recognised as non-absolute per se. In this sense, according to Article 11 of the European Convention on Human Rights, restrictions on the right of association may take place 'for the protection of the rights and freedoms of others'. Convention for the Protection of Human Rights and Fundamental Freedoms 1950 (Treaty No. 005). Similarly, the Charter of Fundamental Rights of the European Union (CFREU) allows for

place social rights and economic freedoms on an equal footing, thus implying a sort of hierarchical relationship between them.[62] Further concerns were also expressed in relation to the fact that the Court's argumentation basically constituted a 'collage' of judicial formulas developed in years of internal market case law and applied to that novel situation.[63]

What is more, the restrictive reading of the prescriptions of the Posting of Workers Directive in order to circumscribe the exercise of collective actions testified the rigidity of the latter Directive, which did not take into account the possibility for the Member States to define labour relations through other means than those expressly listed. In fact, collective actions could be initiated by local trade unions against foreign service providers only for the enforcement of existing nation-wide or generally applicable collective agreements, which did not envisage a standard of labour protection going beyond the mandatory rules for minimum protection laid down in the Posting of Workers Directive.[64] Such a condition was deemed to specifically affect the so-called 'Nordic social model', hence those countries with highly embedded systems of industrial relations, where the biggest role in determining the terms and conditions of employment is reserved to collective bargaining.[65] Moreover, a sort of chilling effect

restrictions to the right of collective bargaining and action enshrined at Article 28 under certain circumstances specified in Article 52, including the respect of the principle of proportionality and the necessity 'to protect the rights and freedoms of others'. Charter of Fundamental Rights of the European Union (CFREU) 2000 (2000/C 364/01). The declaration of the illegitimacy of the Swedish trade union's action in light of such kinds of considerations would have certainly been better understood. Davies, 'One Step Forward, Two Steps Back?' (n 39) 141; Hinarejos (n 48) 727–728.

62. *European Commission v Federal Republic of Germany, Opinion of Advocate General Verica Trstenjak delivered on 14 April 2010* [2010] CJEU Case C-271/08, ECLI:EU:C:2010:183 [183–185]; Barnard, 'EU "Social" Policy: From Employment Law to Labour Market Reform' (n 39) 673–674; De Vries (n 43) 88–89 and 94; Vandenbroucke (n 49) 15–16; Catherine Barnard and Geert De Baere, 'Towards a European Social Union: Achievements and Possibilities under the Current EU Constitutional Framework' (2014) Euroforum Policy Paper (KU Leuven) 12.
63. More specifically, Azoulai individuated 'a resumption of the solution adopted in Bosman (on the applicability of market freedoms outside the field of the Community competence), a reversal of the socially protective assumptions underlying Defrenne (on the direct horizontal effect of Treaty provisions), a rejection of the suggested analogy with the solution adopted in Albany (which lays down the exemption of collective agreements from the framework of the economic freedoms – there, the competition rules), a confirmation of the analysis adopted in Säger (on the notion of restriction) and an extension of the model set out in Schmidberger (for reconciling conflicting demands)'. Azoulai (n 44) 1339–1340. On this point, *see also* Barnard, 'Viking and Laval: An Introduction' (n 35) 492; Hos (n 58) 3.
64. Frank Vandenbroucke, 'The Idea of a European Social Union: A Normative Introduction' in Frank Vandenbroucke, Catherine Barnard and Geert De Baere (eds), *A European Social Union after the Crisis* (Cambridge University Press 2017) 16–17. This implies that, in the case at issue, had Swedish law been in line with the PWD, the trade unions' collective action against the company *Laval* would have been compatible with Article 56 TFEU. Barnard, 'Viking and Laval: An Introduction' (n 35) 477–478.
65. This is the case of Denmark, Sweden and Finland, where the terms and conditions of employment were negotiated at the workplace on a case-by-case basis. Deakin (n 35) 605; Rönnmar, 'Free Movement of Services Versus National Labour Law and Industrial Relations Systems: Understanding the Laval Case from a Swedish and Nordic Perspective' (n 36) 495–497 and 522; Davies, 'One Step Forward, Two Steps Back?' (n 39) 145 and 148; Barnard, 'Social Dumping or Dumping Socialism?' (n 60); Malmberg and Sigeman (n 35) 1117 and 1141–1143; Rönnmar, 'Labour Law in the Courts. The Role of European Case Law on Fundamental Trade

on collective action involved all the Member States without national rules on minimum wages (thus not only Sweden, Finland and Denmark, but also Germany, Italy and the UK).[66] As a consequence, in the absence of positive regulatory action establishing minimum rates of pay, out-of-state undertakings remained free to fully take advantage of their lower labour costs by paying their posted personnel less than the prevailing standard in the host states.[67] Besides its strong deregulatory effect on collective bargaining arrangements, the decision in *Laval* endorsed, therefore, a sort of regime portability, which allowed undertakings to apply their home country labour regime to their workers seconded abroad.[68]

Nonetheless, it is worth noting that a change in the approach as to include the possibility of extending collective agreements negotiated on a case-by-case basis to posted workers, thereby preserving the so-called 'Nordic social model', would have necessarily resulted in the imposition of a further obstacle to the freedom to provide services. For the company *Laval*, the application of the host country's regime would have entailed the loss of the competitive advantage that allowed it to win the Vaxholm

Union Rights in an Evolving EU Industrial Relations System' (n 1) 189–191; Niklas Bruun and Claes-Mikael Jonsson, 'Consequences and Policy Perspectives in the Nordic Countries as a Result of Certain Important Decisions of the European Court of Justice' in Andreas Bücker and Wiebke Warneck (eds), *Viking – Laval – Rüffert: Consequences and Policy Perspectives* (ETUI (European Trade Union Institute) 2010) 25–28; Andreas Bücker and Wiebke Warneck, 'Analysis and Outlook: In Search of a New Relationship between Market Integration and Social Embedding' in Andreas Bücker and Wiebke Warneck (eds), *Viking – Laval – Rüffert: Consequences and Policy Perspectives* (ETUI (European Trade Union Institute) 2010) 131–132; Andrea Sangiovanni, 'Solidarity in the European Union' (2013) 33 Oxford Journal of Legal Studies 213, 225–226; Barnard, 'EU Employment Law and the European Social Model' (n 60) 205–206; Schiek et al. (n 14) 33; Zahn, 'Revision of the Posted Workers' Directive: Equality at Last?' (n 60) 4–5; Zahn, 'Revision of the Posted Workers Directive' (n 60) 8–9; Grušić (n 40) 475; Aukje A.H. van Hoek, 'Re-Embedding the Transnational Employment Relationship: A Tale about the Limitations of (EU) Law?' (2018) 55 Common Market Law Review 449, 471; Christian Joerges, Vladimir Bogoeski and Lukas Nüse, 'Economic Constitutionalism and the European Social Model: Can European Law Cope with the Deepening Tensions between Economic and Social Integration after the Financial Crisis' in Herwig Hofmann, Katerina Pantazatou and Giovanni Zaccaroni, *The Metamorphosis of the European Economic Constitution* (Edward Elgar Publishing 2019) 144. As punctually observed by Rocca, 'the greater the degree of de-centralisation of a system of industrial relations the harder it will be to extend whatever minimum wage to posting employers'. Rocca, *Posting of Workers and Collective Labour Law: There and Back Again* (n 18) 305.

66. Aukje A.H. van Hoek and Mijke Houwerzijl, 'Comparative Study on the Legal Aspects of the Posting of Workers in the Framework of the Provision of Services in the European Union' (2011) 26–27; Barnard, 'A Proportionate Response to Proportionality in the Field of Collective Action' (n 40) 5.
67. Hatzopoulos, 'Labour Immigration in the EU Through the Back Door? The Free Provision of Services as a Facilitator of Migration Flows' (n 18) 156–159. To put it bluntly, employers established in the low-wage Member States were the winners in the decisions in *Viking* and *Laval*, while trade unions and their members in countries with the most advanced systems of industrial relations were the losers. Barnard, 'Viking and Laval: An Introduction' (n 35) 491–492; Barnard, 'EU "Social" Policy: From Employment Law to Labour Market Reform' (n 39) 674.
68. Deakin (n 35) 587, 605 and 609.

contract.[69] In this sense, the imposition of the practice of collective bargaining on a case-by-case basis was considered as substantially incompatible with the internal market's free movement rights, given that it would have been de facto excessively burdensome for out-of-state employers and employees.[70]

4.2.2.2 *Rüffert and Commission v Luxembourg*

The same route towards a more liberal approach was followed by the Court of Justice also in the subsequent *Rüffert*[71] and *Commission v Luxembourg*[72] rulings, delivered on 3 April and 19 June 2008 respectively. Unlike in *Laval*, in the *Rüffert* case, the defendant was a state body and not a trade union, therefore there was no question of direct applicability of Article 56 TFEU.[73] A further difference related also to the fact that the proportionality of the national measure under scrutiny was not in dispute. More in detail, the case concerned the compatibility with EU law of the Public Procurement Act *(Landesvergabegesetz)* of the *Land Niedersachsen* (Lower Saxony) prescribing that public tenders for construction services could be awarded only to tenderers (and subcontractors) which formally agreed to pay their employees at least the minimum wage prescribed by the 'Buildings and public works' collective agreement in force in the place where the service is provided.[74]

In the case at hand, the main contractor subcontracted the job to a Polish undertaking which was, indeed, employing workers on the building site at a wage below the rate set out in the German collective agreement.[75] However, despite its general scope, such an agreement did not have general validity for all undertakings located in a certain territory and belonging to the profession or industry concerned[76] and neither had been declared universally applicable.[77] And this, even though the

69. Norbert Reich, 'Free Movement v. Social Rights in an Enlarged Union – The Laval and Viking Cases before the ECJ' (2008) 9 German Law Journal 125, 135–136; Bakardjieva Engelbrekt (n 51) 336.
70. Bakardjieva Engelbrekt (n 51) 337–338.
71. *Dirk Rüffert v Land Niedersachsen* (n 2).
72. *Commission of the European Communities v Grand Duchy of Luxemburg* (n 2).
73. Paul Davies, 'Case C-346/06, Rüffert v Land Niedersachsen [2008] IRLR 467 (ECJ)' (2008) 37 Industrial Law Journal 293, 293.
74. Rönnmar, 'Free Movement of Services Versus National Labour Law and Industrial Relations Systems: Understanding the Laval Case from a Swedish and Nordic Perspective' (n 36) 513–514; Catherine Barnard, 'Solidarity and the Commission's "Renewed Social Agenda"' in Malcolm Ross and Yuri Borgmann-Prebil (eds), *Promoting Solidarity in the European Union* (Oxford University Press 2010) 99–100; Piet Van Nuffel and Sofia Afanasjeva, 'The Posting of Workers Directive Revised: Enhancing the Protection of Workers in the Cross-Border Provision of Services' (2018) 3 European Papers 1401, 1412; Francesco Costamagna, 'The Revision of the Posted Workers Directive as a Meaningful Way to Curb Regulatory Competition in the Social Domain?' (2019) 2 Sant'Anna Legal Studies 25, 11.
75. *Dirk Rüffert v Land Niedersachsen* (n 2) para. 11. Claire Kilpatrick, 'Internal Market Architecture and the Accommodation of Labour Rights: As Good as It Gets?' (2011) Law 2011/04 EUI Working Paper 13.
76. *Dirk Rüffert v Land Niedersachsen* (n 2) para. 28.
77. *Ibid.* 26 and 29.

German system envisaged the possibility to declare collective agreements as universally applicable, thus preventing the exercise of the option offered by the second subparagraph of Article 3(8) of the Posting of Workers Directive.[78] Against this backdrop, the Court found that the requirements imposed by the law of the Lower Saxony on foreign undertakings temporarily operating in that territory were above the minimum rates of pay laid down by the collective agreement extended by governmental action to the construction sector.[79] For that reason, they were considered unjustified with respect to Article 56 TFEU for going beyond the prescriptions of the Posting of Workers Directive.[80] As affirmed by the Court itself, a different interpretation would have otherwise allowed the imposition on posted workers of stricter conditions than those binding on local undertakings.[81] At last, given that it applied solely to public contracts and not to private contracts, the *Landesvergabegesetz* could not even be justified on the grounds of worker protection nor of the trade unions' independent organisation of working life.[82]

The host country's room for manoeuvre was substantially restricted by the CJEU decision in *Commission v Luxembourg*[83] as well. This case originated in April 2004 by an infringement procedure raised by the Commission against the Grand Duchy for the supposed incorrect transposition into national law of Article 3(1) and (10) of the Posting of Workers Directive. At first, as already mentioned *supra* in Chapter 3, the Court's ruling drastically narrowed down the possibility for the host state to invoke the exception of public policy for extending its own labour law to incoming cross-border service providers. It did so by taking into account the intrinsic nature of the 'public policy provisions' which are to be intended as a 'double' derogation from both the freedom to provide services and the exhaustive list set out in Article 3(1).[84] As a result,

78. *Ibid.* 27.
79. Barnard, *EU Employment Law* (n 18) 225; Watson (n 18) 286; Verschueren (n 23) 140–141.
80. *Dirk Rüffert v Land Niedersachsen* (n 2) para. 35. On this point, *see* Davies, 'Case C-346/06, Rüffert v Land Niedersachsen [2008] IRLR 467 (ECJ)' (n 73) 295; Catherine Barnard, 'Fifty Years of Avoiding Social Dumping? The EU's Economic and Not So Economic Constitution' in Michael Dougan and Samantha Currie (eds), *50 Years of the European Treaties: Looking Back and Thinking Forward* (First Edition, Hart Publishing 2009) 325; Kilpatrick (n 75) 14; Catherine Barnard, 'The Protection of Fundamental Rights in the EU After Lisbon: A Question of Conflicts of Interests' in Sybe De Vries, Ulf Bernitz and Steve Weatherill (eds), *The Protection of Fundamental Rights in the EU After Lisbon* (Hart Publishing 2013) 40; Verschueren (n 23) 141–142; Rocca, *Posting of Workers and Collective Labour Law: There and Back Again* (n 18) 14–15; Tonia Novitz, 'The Scope for Collective Bargaining in Posting and Procurement – –What Might Come From Recent Court of Justice Case Law and the Proposed Reform of the Posting of Workers Directive?' (*University of Bristol Law School Blog*, 6 April 2016) < https://legalresearch.blogs.bris.ac.uk/2016/04/the-scope-for-collective-bargaining-in-posting-and-procurement/ > (accessed 13 May 2018); van Hoek (n 65) 471; Van Nuffel and Afanasjeva (n 74) 1412; Carter (n 60) 39–40.
81. *Dirk Rüffert v Land Niedersachsen* (n 2) para. 37. Incidentally, on that occasion, the Court confirmed the stance of the Advocate General Bot on the matter. *Dirk Rüffert v Land Niedersachsen, Opinion of Advocate General Yves Bot delivered on 20 September 2007* [2007] ECJ Case C-346/06, ECLI:EU:C:2007:541 [103]. *See also* Van Nuffel and Afanasjeva (n 74) 1412.
82. *Dirk Rüffert v Land Niedersachsen* (n 2) paras 38–41. Wiebke Warneck, 'The ECJ Decisions' in Andreas Bücker and Wiebke Warneck (eds), *Viking – Laval – Rüffert: Consequences and policy perspectives* (ETUI (European Trade Union Institute) 2010) 11.
83. *Commission of the European Communities v Grand Duchy of Luxemburg* (n 2).
84. *Ibid.* 30–31.

any unilateral determination at national level of the concept of public policy was expressly precluded,[85] likewise the inclusion of the whole employment legislation under the exception of public policy.

Second, the Court considered any national provision concerning matters not listed in Article 3(1), such as the indexation of wages to the cost of living[86] or further rules on part-time and fixed-term work,[87] to be outside the scope of Article 3(10) even when labelled as overriding mandatory.[88] Third, the imposition on undertakings wishing to post their workers abroad of a general obligation to promptly provide information, prior to the commencement of the activity, upon the request of the labour inspectorate of the host state, was also deemed incompatible with the freedom to provide services, due to its lack of clarity and the consequent prejudice for cross-border undertakings.[89] Finally, the requirement of designating an 'ad hoc agent' residing in the Member State of destination for keeping all the relevant documentation at disposal of the local monitoring authorities was found disproportionate, given that the purpose of controlling cross-border activities could have been achieved by means of less restrictive obligations.[90]

4.2.2.3 *RegioPost*

A few years after *Rüffert*, the Court returned to the delicate interplay between posting of workers and public procurement with its decision of 17 November 2015 in *RegioPost*.[91] Similar to *Rüffert*, the case at issue concerned a Polish company *(RegioPost)* that participated in an EU-wide call for tender for the awarding of a public contract for postal services, issued by the municipality of Landau, Germany. Also on that occasion, the contracting authority required all tenderers to undertake to pay their workers at least the minimum wage of EUR 8.70 per hour, but this time in accordance with the regional law of the *Land* of Rhineland-Palatinate and not with an existing collective agreement.[92] On the basis of that rule, *RegioPost* was eventually rejected for refusing to pay its workers the German minimum wage and, as a consequence, it challenged the legitimacy of that requirement under EU public procurement law.

---

85. *Ibid.* 30 and 50.
86. *Ibid.* 55.
87. *Ibid.* 60.
88. Jon Erik Dølvik and Jelle Visser, 'Free Movement, Equal Treatment and Workers' Rights: Can the European Union Solve Its Trilemma of Fundamental Principles?: Free Movement, Equal Treatment and Workers' Rights' (2009) 40 Industrial Relations Journal 491, 502–503; Rocca, *Posting of Workers and Collective Labour Law: There and Back Again* (n 18) 203–204; Grušić (n 18) 209.
89. *Commission of the European Communities v Grand Duchy of Luxemburg* (n 2) para. 82.
90. *Ibid.* 89–90. *See* Rocca, *Posting of Workers and Collective Labour Law: There and Back Again* (n 18) 204.
91. *RegioPost GmbH & Co. KG v Stadt Landau in der Pfalz* (n 6).
92. In fact, in the wake of the decision in *Rüffert*, several German *Länder* included the minimum wage applicable to public contracts directly in their regulations on public procurement. Schiek et al. (n 14) 44–45; Marco Rocca, 'Not Dead yet: Legal Strategies at National Level and the Reform of the EU Posting of Workers Directive' (2018) 10.

The outcome of the judgment in front of the CJEU was, however, quite different from that in *Rüffert*. The inclusion in a public contract of a minimum wage clause binding on both tenderers and subcontractors was considered compatible with Article 3(1) of the Posting of Workers Directive, insofar as it was set by law[93] and no other minimum wage was applicable.[94] What is more, the Court acknowledged also the compliance of such a requirement, as well as of the subsequent exclusion of *RegioPost* from the procedure for the award of the public contract, with Article 26 of Directive 2004/18/EC[95] on public procurement, which specifically authorises contracting authorities to include, *inter alia*, social clauses in public procurement contracts.[96] In the same vein, the argument that the German legislation was incompatible with Article 56 TFEU in conjunction with Article 3(1) of the Posting of Workers Directive because it applied solely to public contracts, and not to private ones, was also disregarded, given that it conferred a minimum social protection for the whole postal services sector.[97]

After all, the judgment in *RegioPost*, rather than indicating a deviation of the EU judiciary from its traditional interpretation of the Directive, simply testified an adaptation to the change of relevant secondary EU legislation on public procurement.[98] Most of all, it endorsed the regulatory adjustments operated by the Member States in the wake of the previous case law.[99] From this viewpoint, it conferred an even higher degree of authority on the normative outcomes of the *Laval quartet*.

---

93. *RegioPost GmbH & Co. KG v Stadt Landau in der Pfalz* (n 6) para. 75.
94. *Ibid.* 10 and 21. For the record, at that time there was no federal minimum wage in Germany, while the sectoral collective agreement had recently been declared invalid. *See* Novitz (n 80); Rocca, 'Not Dead yet: Legal Strategies at National Level and the Reform of the EU Posting of Workers Directive' (n 92) 11; Van Nuffel and Afanasjeva (n 74) 1412–1413; Costamagna (n 74) 23.
95. Directive 2004/18/EC of the European Parliament and of the Council of 31 March 2004 on the coordination of procedures for the award of public works contracts, public supply contracts and public service contracts 2004 (OJ L 134/114).
96. Interestingly, it is worth noting that the same approach had been previously suggested by the Advocate General Bot in *Rüffert*. *Dirk Rüffert v Land Niedersachsen, Opinion of Advocate General Yves Bot delivered on 20 September 2007* (n 81) para. 133. Nonetheless, the Court probably discarded such an option considering that, at the time of the events which gave rise to the dispute, Directive 2004/18/EC was not applicable yet (its implementation period expired on 31 January 2006). *See* Daniel Carter, 'CJEU (Finally) Takes Stance against Social Dumping' (*leidenlawblog*, 19 February 2016) <https://leidenlawblog.nl/articles/cjeu-finally-takes-stance-against-social-dumping> (accessed 25 September 2019).
97. *RegioPost GmbH & Co. KG v Stadt Landau in der Pfalz* (n 6) para. 76. As stressed by the Advocate General Mengozzi, a different interpretation of Article 26 of Directive 2004/18/EC in such a way as to preclude the Member States from adopting laws, regulations or administrative provisions laying down employment conditions and minimum rates of pay which apply solely to public contracts, would end up denying its 'practical effect'. *RegioPost GmbH & Co KG v Stadt Landau in der Pfalz, Opinion of Advocate General Paolo Mengozzi delivered on 9 September 2015* [2015] CJEU Case C-115/14, ECLI:EU:C:2015:566 [71]. *See* Clemens Kaupa, 'Public Procurement, Social Policy and Minimum Wage Regulation for Posted Workers: Towards a More Balanced Socio-Economic Integration Process?' (2016) 1 European Papers 127, 135–136.
98. van Hoek (n 65) 471.
99. Rocca, 'Not Dead yet: Legal Strategies at National Level and the Reform of the EU Posting of Workers Directive' (n 92) 11; Marco Rocca, 'Stepping Stones Over Troubled Waters. Recent Legal Evolutions and the Reform of the Posting of Workers Directive' in Jens Arnholtz and Nathan Lillie (eds), *Posted Work in the European Union: The Political Economy of Free Movement* (Routledge 2019) 176.

4.3 REVERSING THE PERSPECTIVE

The above-mentioned several interventions of the EU judiciary in order to provide guidelines for the application of the Posting of Workers Directive concerned, in most cases, matters of cheap labour flows from the Central and Eastern to the Western Member States and comparative advantage of cross-border service providers over local competitors. Notwithstanding the evident purpose of ensuring the free exercise of the European economic freedoms,[100] the rationale adopted may, nonetheless, still remain exposed to criticism for not taking into due account the interests of the posted workers.[101] Especially when it came to determining the minimum wage applicable to the posted workers, the argument generally followed by the Court (shared by most of the legal academia as well) was that to a higher level of employment standards applicable in the host states directly corresponds a higher degree of worker protection. However, such a syllogism works only with regard to the safeguard of the workers in the host state. In fact, the imposition of too high employment standards in respect of those applied in the posted workers' home country might rather potentially imply the latter's loss of their jobs, given that the transnational service provision would not be convenient anymore for their employer.[102] After all, it has been noted that even the implementation of the provisions of the Posting of Workers Directive in full respect of the EU free movement rights may have had the effect, under certain circumstances, of pre-empting Central and Eastern European workers from exploiting their legitimate competitive advantage resulting from their lower wages.[103]

The existing situation where the rights and interests of the workers in Central and Eastern European Countries are often neglected mirrors the reasoning proposed by the Western European narrative, adopted by the Court of Justice as well in deciding the

---

100. The approach followed by the Court in the so-called 'Laval quartet' was, indeed, highly criticised for giving precedence to the EU economic freedoms over social policy. Verschueren (n 60) 177; Davies, 'One Step Forward, Two Steps Back?' (n 39) 147; Barnard, 'Social Dumping or Dumping Socialism?' (n 60) 264; Barnard, '"British Jobs for British Workers"' (n 60) 276; Stein Evju, 'Revisiting the Posted Workers Directive: Conflict of Laws and Laws in Contrast' (2009) 12 Cambridge Yearbook of European Legal Studies 151, 169–170; Evju and Novitz (n 58) 59; Evju (n 60) 14; Barnard, 'EU Employment Law and the European Social Model' (n 60) 205; Verschueren (n 23) 146 and 148; Barnard, 'The Calm after the Storm: Time to Reflect on EU (Labour) Law Scholarship Following the Decisions in Viking and Laval' (n 60) 6; Tonia Novitz, 'The EU and the Right to Strike: Regulation through the Back Door and Its Impact on Social Dialogue' (2016) 27 King's Law Journal 46, 47; Zahn, 'Revision of the Posted Workers' Directive: Equality at Last?' (n 60) 5; Zahn, 'Revision of the Posted Workers Directive' (n 60) 8; Schiek, 'Towards More Resilience for a Social EU – The Constitutionally Conditioned Internal Market' (n 48) 630–631; Harbo (n 54) 208 and 221; Carter (n 60) 45; Jacqueson and Pennings (n 60) 76.
101. Bakardjieva Engelbrekt (n 51) 342; Annette Schrauwen, 'From the Board Towards a Social Europe' (2018) 45 Legal Issues of Economic Integration 323, 326.
102. At the end, indeed, the trade unions' successful industrial action in *Laval* eventually resulted in the posted workers' loss of their jobs. On this point, *see* Davies, 'Case C-346/06, Rüffert v Land Niedersachsen [2008] IRLR 467 (ECJ)' (n 73) 294; Damjan Kukovec, 'Whose Social Europe? The Laval/Viking Judgments and the Prosperity Gap' (2011) Harvard Law School Institute for Global Law and Policy, IGLP Working Paper Series 2011/3 3–4.
103. Federica Mustilli and Jacques Pelkmans, 'Access Barriers to Services Markets' (2013) 77 CEPS Centre for European Policy Studies 84, 51.

Viking[104] and *Laval*[105] cases, that tends to present the disputes arising from transnational labour mobility as a clash between social rights and economic freedoms.[106] According to this view, social rights are commonly perceived as referred to the protection of the weakest actors (namely the workers), while free movement rights are usually associated with the economic interests of the strongest ones (namely the businesses).[107]

However, when reversing the perspective on the matter, the Western trade unions' actions in defence of the higher social and employment standards in the wealthier Member States appear directed to the realisation of economic-protectionist aims.[108] In effect, an aspect which was indirectly emphasised by the judges in Luxembourg is that even the concept of 'social rights' itself may disguise, at times, a different connotation than the commonly portrayed protection of the weakest parts. In both *Viking* and *Laval*, social rights were rather turned into instruments of domination at the service of the most powerful actors, namely the local trade unions.[109] Conversely, the full exercise of the freedom to provide services may as well be regarded as enjoyment of the posted workers' fundamental right to work enshrined in the Universal Declaration of Human Rights[110] and recognised in all Member States' constitutional traditions, or of their social rights to escape unemployment in their home country and make their contribution to the latter's economy.[111]

All things considered, the conflicts in those landmark judgments could, therefore, be equally framed both in terms of a clash between economic interests of two powerful factions (i.e., out-of-state service providers, and local businesses and trade unions) and a clash between social interests of two powerless factions (i.e., posted and local

104. *International Transport Workers' Federation and Finnish Seamen's Union v Viking Line ABP and OÜ Viking Line Eesti* (n 58).
105. *Laval un Partneri Ltd v Svenska Byggnadsarbetareförbundet, Svenska Byggnadsarbetareförbundets avdelning 1, Byggettan and Svenska Elektrikerförbundet* (n 2).
106. Alexander Somek, 'From Workers to Migrants, from Distributive Justice to Inclusion: Exploring the Changing Social Democratic Imagination: Exploring the Changing Social Democratic Imagination' (2012) 18 European Law Journal 711, 2–3; Damjan Kukovec, 'Taking Change Seriously – The Discourse of Justice and the Reproduction of the Status Quo' (2012) SSRN Electronic Journal, later published in Dimitry Kochenov, Gráinne de Búrca, and Andrew Williams (eds), Europe's Justice Deficit? (Bloomsbury Publishing Plc) 2015, 319–336, 4 <http://www.ssrn.com/abstract=2302389> (accessed 13 May 2018).
107. Kukovec, 'Whose Social Europe? The Laval/Viking Judgments and the Prosperity Gap' (n 102); Damjan Kukovec, 'A Critique of the Rhetoric of Common Interest in the European Union Legal Discourse' (2012) SSRN Electronic Journal 11, 9.
108. Davies, 'One Step Forward, Two Steps Back?' (n 39) 148.
109. On such an instrumentalisation of the right to take collective action, *see* Leczykiewicz (n 42) 308.
110. 'Everyone has the right to work, to free choice of employment, to just and favourable conditions of work and to protection against unemployment.' Article 23(1) of the United Nations General Assembly (UN), Universal Declaration of Human Rights (UDHR) 1948.
111. As strikingly pointed out by Kukovec, 'like Wittgenstein's duck-rabbit picture [...], what appears as an economic claim is a social claim and what appears social is economic, depending on the angle from which we see the dilemma'. Damjan Kukovec, 'Hierarchies as Law' (2014) 21 Columbia Journal of European Law 131, 142–145. *See also* Jacqueson and Pennings (n 60) 78.

workers).[112] Importantly, therefore, in light of the involvement of relevant social costs on the part of both posted and local workers, great care must be taken when assessing the impact of the posting regulation.[113]

What is more, the overall approach taken by the Court in seeking to balance the economic purposes of the Union against its social objectives[114] still remains exposed to a further critique. This sort of dogmatic separation between the economic and the social aims of the Union fails to take into consideration the social dimension of EU free movement law.[115] As remarkably stressed by Advocate General Maduro in *Viking*, the exercise of the possibilities offered by the internal market does not merely translate into an economic benefit for the actors directly involved, but it is rather 'instrumental to increasing the economic welfare of all the Member States'.[116] After all, as expressly mentioned in Article 3(3) of the Treaty on European Union (TEU),[117] the realisation of a 'highly competitive social market economy, aiming at full employment and social progress' is among the primary objectives of the Union.[118] Interestingly, this EU purpose was emphasised, a few years later, by the Grand Chamber in its important decision in *AGET Iraklis*,[119] which undoubtedly contributed to reconciling the social and the economic dimensions of the European Union.[120]

In conclusion, it is worth noting that, not surprisingly, the above-mentioned questioned rationale was reproduced also in the Commission's legislative proposal of

112. Kukovec, 'Hierarchies as Law' (n 111) 142–145; Damjan Kukovec, 'Law and the Periphery' (2015) 21 European Law Journal 406, 414; Leczykiewicz (n 42) 311–312.
113. Leczykiewicz (n 42) 318.
114. *International Transport Workers' Federation and Finnish Seamen's Union v Viking Line ABP and OÜ Viking Line Eesti* (n 58) para. 79; *Laval un Partneri Ltd v Svenska Byggnadsarbetareförbundet, Svenska Byggnadsarbetareförbundets avdelning 1, Byggettan and Svenska Elektrikerförbundet* (n 2) para. 105.
115. Leczykiewicz (n 42) 317.
116. *International Transport Workers' Federation and Finnish Seamen's Union v Viking Line ABP and OÜ Viking Line Eesti, Opinion of Advocate General Poiares Maduro delivered on 23 May 2007* [2007] ECJ Case C-438/05, ECLI:EU:C:2007:292 [57]. On the social dimension of the EU internal market, *see also* Vassilis Hatzopoulos, 'A (More) Social Europe: A Political Crossroad or a Legal One-Way? Dialogues between Luxembourg and Lisbon' (2005) 42 Common Market Law Review 1599, 1602.
117. Consolidated version of the Treaty on European Union 2012 (OJ C 326/13) (hereinafter also referred to with its acronym 'TEU').
118. Pennings (n 41) 1; Jotte Mulder, '(Re) Conceptualising a Social Market Economy for the EU Internal Market' (2019) 15 Utrecht Law Review 16, 16; Frans Pennings, 'The Relevance of the Concept of the Social Market Economy: Concluding Observations on the Contributions in This Special Issue' (2019) 15 Utrecht Law Review 95, 95.
119. *Anonymi Geniki Etairia Tsimenton Iraklis (AGET Iraklis) v Ypourgos Ergasias, Koinonikis Asfalisis kai Koinonikis Allilengyis* [2016] CJEU Case C-201/15, ECLI:EU:C:2016:972 [76].
120. By the way, it is worth noting that the *AGET Iraklis* case did not concern the cross-border provision of services through posting, but rather the compatibility of the Greek legislation on collective redundancy with Article 49 of the TFEU on freedom of establishment. Interestingly, though, in that judgment the Court directly referred to its previous decision in *Viking* in order to support its argument. Steve Peers, 'EU Law Analysis: Case C-201/15 AGET Iraklis: Can Governments Control Mass Layoffs by Employers? Economic Freedoms vs Labour Rights' (*EU Law Analysis*, 3 January 2017) <http://eulawanalysis.blogspot.com/2017/01/case-c-20115-aget-iraklis-can.html> (accessed 22 October 2019); Schiek, 'Towards More Resilience for a Social EU – The Constitutionally Conditioned Internal Market' (n 48) 635–638; Mulder (n 118) 30; Pennings (n 118) 96.

21 March 2012, known as the 'Monti II' Regulation,[121] aimed at regulating the right to take collective action, including the right to strike, within the context of the freedoms of establishment and of service provision. Instead of recognising the intrinsic interrelation between the economic and social dimensions of the European Union and the need to take into consideration all the different facets of both economic and social rights, that draft was basically designed to reverse the commonly perceived priority of rights. More specifically, when read in light of the Preamble, the sort of mutual respect between the right to take collective action and the economic freedoms of the internal market apparently envisaged by Article 2 was substantially overturned. By emphasising the prominent place reserved to the 'right to take collective action' by a number of international and European Charters and Conventions, Member States' constitutions and case law of the Court of Justice,[122] the proposal de facto implied the subordination of the economic rights to the social rights.[123] Besides, it also suggested introducing a non-judicial dispute resolution mechanism concerning disputes at EU level originating from the cross-border exercise of the right to take collective action,[124] along with an

121. European Commission, Proposal for a Council Regulation on the exercise of the right to take collective action within the context of the freedom of establishment and the freedom to provide services 2012 [COM(2012) 130 final] (hereinafter also referred to as the 'Monti II' Regulation). Interestingly, the conceptual origin of this proposal may be traced back to the Mario Monti, 'A New Strategy for the Single Market: At the Service of Europe's Economy and Society. Report to the President of the European Commission José Manuel Barroso' (European Commission Bureau of European Policy Advisers (BEPA) 2010).
122. 'The right to take collective action, which is the corollary of the right to collective bargaining, is recognised both by various international instruments which the Member States have signed or cooperated in, such as the European Social Charter, signed at Turin on 18 October 1961, Conventions No 87 and No 98 of the International Labour Organisation concerning Freedom of Association and Protection of the Right to Organise and Collective Bargaining, and by instruments developed by those Member States at EU level, such as the Community Charter of the Fundamental Social Rights of Workers adopted at the meeting of the European Council held in Strasbourg on 9 December 1989 and the Charter of Fundamental Rights of the European Union proclaimed in Nice on 7 December 2000, as adopted at Strasbourg on 12 December 2008 which has the same legal value as the Treaties. It also enjoys constitutional protection in a number of Member States. The right to collective bargaining and to negotiate and enter into collective agreements constitutes an inherent element of the right of association, as set out in Article 11 of the Convention for the Protection of Human Rights and Fundamental Freedoms ("the Convention"). The right to take collective action has also been recognised by the Court of Justice as a fundamental right which forms an integral part of the general principles of Union law the observance of which the Court ensures. However, the right to strike is not absolute and the exercise of that right may nonetheless be subject to certain conditions and restrictions, which may also result from national constitutions, law and practices. As reaffirmed by Article 28 of the Charter of Fundamental Rights of the European Union, the right to take collective action is to be protected in accordance with Union law and national law and practices.' Preamble Recitals 1–4 of the European Commission Proposal for a Council Regulation on the exercise of the right to take collective action within the context of the freedom of establishment and the freedom to provide services (n 121).
123. Catherine Barnard, 'Free Movement and Labour Rights: Squaring the Circle?' (2013) 23/2013 University of Cambridge Faculty of Law Legal Studies Research Paper 16.
124. Article 3 of the European Commission Proposal for a Council Regulation on the exercise of the right to take collective action within the context of the freedom of establishment and the freedom to provide services (n 121). *See* Monti (n 121) 71.

alert mechanism for industrial conflicts entailing serious implications.[125] Nevertheless, this first attempt to regulate the right to take collective action at EU level, designed with Article 352 TFEU as its legal basis,[126] was eventually withdrawn by the Commission on 12 September 2012, after acknowledging the lack of necessary political support for its adoption.[127]

125. Article 4 of the European Commission Proposal for a Council Regulation on the exercise of the right to take collective action within the context of the freedom of establishment and the freedom to provide services (n 121). *See* Barnard, 'Free Movement and Labour Rights: Squaring the Circle?' (n 123) 9; Eurofound, 'Posted Workers' (*EurWORK – European Observatory of Working Life*, 29 June 2018) <https://www.eurofound.europa.eu/observatories/eurwork/industrial-relations-dictionary/posted-workers> (accessed 4 July 2019).
126. The choice of Article 352 TFEU as legal basis, concerning the residual competence of the Union in attaining the objectives set out in the Treaties in the absence of expressed conferral of specific powers to that extent, was motivated by the EU's lack of competence in the field. It was, nonetheless, strongly criticised by several national governments for circumventing the limits imposed by Article 153(5) TFEU. Explanatory Memorandum of the European Commission Proposal for a Council Regulation on the exercise of the right to take collective action within the context of the freedom of establishment and the freedom to provide services (n 121) 10; Barnard and De Baere (n 62) 17–18; Geert De Baere and Kathleen Gutman, 'The Basis in EU Constitutional Law for Further Social Integration' in Frank Vandenbroucke, Catherine Barnard and Geert De Baere (eds), *A European Social Union after the Crisis* (Cambridge University Press 2017) 366–367; Gerhard van der Schyff, 'EU Social Competences and Member State Constitutional Controls: A Comparative Perspective of National Approaches' in Frank Vandenbroucke, Catherine Barnard and Geert De Baere (eds), *A European Social Union after the Crisis* (Cambridge University Press 2017) 397–398. Notably, the unanimous voting in the Council required under the procedure envisaged by Article 352 TFEU presumably represented one of the main causes of the Monti II's failure. *See* Marco Rocca, 'The Proposal for a (So-Called) "Monti II" Regulation on the Exercise of the Right to Take Collective Action within the Context of the Freedom of Establishment and the Freedom to Provide Services: Changing without Reversing, Regulating without Affecting' (2012) 3 European Labour Law Journal 19, 21; Barnard, 'Free Movement and Labour Rights: Squaring the Circle?' (n 123) 9; Barnard, 'EU Employment Law and the European Social Model' (n 60) 206–207; Watson (n 18) 300.
127. In particular, twelve out of forty national parliaments or chambers thereof (namely Belgium, Denmark, Finland, France, Latvia, Luxembourg, Malta, the Netherlands, Poland, Portugal, Sweden and United Kingdom; counting 19 out of 54 votes allocated) issued 'reasoned opinions' against the proposal for alleged violation of the principle of subsidiarity, thus triggering for the first time the so-called 'yellow card procedure' (envisaged by Protocol (No 2) on the application of the principles of subsidiarity and proportionality, annexed to the Treaty on European Union and the Treaty on the Functioning of the European Union by the Treaty of Lisbon of 13 December 2007). For the record, having encountered strong opposition at political level, the Commission ultimately withdrew its proposal, although it had not acknowledged the infringement of the subsidiarity principle. *See* Rocca, 'The Proposal for a (So-Called) "Monti II" Regulation on the Exercise of the Right to Take Collective Action within the Context of the Freedom of Establishment and the Freedom to Provide Services' (n 126); Federico Fabbrini and Katarzyna Granat, '"Yellow Card, but No Foul": The Role of the National Parliaments under the Subsidiarity Protocol and the Commission Proposal for an EU Regulation on the Right to Strike' (2013) 50 Common Market Law Review 115, 135–139; Barnard, 'Free Movement and Labour Rights: Squaring the Circle?' (n 123) 9; Rocca, *Posting of Workers and Collective Labour Law: There and Back Again* (n 18) 269–278; Ian Cooper, 'The Story of the First "Yellow Card" Shows That National Parliaments Can Act Together to Influence EU Policy' (*EUROPP (European Politics and Policy)*, 23 April 2015) <https://blogs.lse.ac.uk/europpblog/2015/04/23/the-story-of-the-first-yellow-card-shows-that-national-parliaments-can-act-together-to-influence-eu-policy/> (accessed 4 March 2019); Eckhard Voss et al., 'Posting of Workers Directive: Current Situation and Challenges' (European Parliament, EMPL Committee 2016) IP/A/EMPL/2016-07, 43; Dorte Sindbjerg Martinsen, 'The European Social Union and EU Legislative Politics' in

4.4 THE 2014 ENFORCEMENT DIRECTIVE

Considering the increasing amount of cases brought in front of the Court of Justice, the normative framework laid down in the Posting of Workers Directive has been facing a number of issues directly connected with its concrete implementation and enforcement at national level.[128] In addition to the structural issues resulting from the different interpretation of the Directive's provisions in national labour law systems,[129] a wide variety of abusive and fraudulent practices have developed in the context of intra-EU posting with a view to circumventing national regulatory regimes in the countries of destination. This is the case of the creation of the so-called 'letterbox companies' and the use of practices of subcontracting chains and bogus self-employment, which often involve exploitation of the workers concerned.[130] At the same time, the serious lack of administrative cooperation between Member States and the unsatisfactory accessibility to national databases on cross-border labour mobility were highlighted in two Commission Communications adopted, respectively, in 2006 and 2007.[131]

The same results emerged a few years later as well from further research projects supported by the European Commission, which lamented a general inadequacy of the existing administrative and legal frameworks in protecting cross-border workers' rights and combating cross-border social fraud. In particular, the lack of specific provisions allowing national inspection services to concretely carry out controls and inspections, and cooperating with their foreign counterparts in cross-border situations was clearly proven.[132] This absence was in contrast to the specific obligations on transnational cooperation and access to information, which were already imposed by Article 4 of the Posting of Workers Directive.[133] In fact, Article 4(1) and (2) envisaged the creation of

Frank Vandenbroucke, Catherine Barnard and Geert De Baere (eds), *A European Social Union after the Crisis* (Cambridge University Press 2017) 471–472; Eurofound (n 125); Barnard and De Vries (n 60) 54.

128. Difficulties in the practical implementation of the PWD were brought to the general attention by the Commission itself already in 2003 with a Communication on the implementation of the Directive. European Commission, Communication on the Implementation of Directive 96/71/EC in the Member States 2003 [COM(2003) 458 final]. In this sense, *see also* van Hoek and Houwerzijl (n 66) 3; Jorens, Peters and Houwerzijl (n 14) 154.
129. Zahn, 'Revision of the Posted Workers Directive' (n 60) 6.
130. For an investigation of such abuses and malpractices, *see infra* Chapter 7.
131. European Commission, Communication: Guidance on the posting of workers in the framework of the provision of services (n 18); European Commission, Communication on the Posting of workers in the framework of the provision of services: Maximising its benefits and potential while guaranteeing the protection of workers 2007 [COM(2007) 304 final].
132. van Hoek and Houwerzijl (n 66) 29; Jorens, Peters and Houwerzijl (n 14) 154–155. For the record, in 2009, the Commission set up a specific 'EU Committee of Experts on Posting of Workers', with the aim of providing support and assistance to the Member States in the practical application and enforcement of the rules laid down in the PWD, while also improving transnational administrative cooperation. The Committee was composed of two experts from each Member State representing the competent national authorities and was supported by the social partners at European level representing sectors with a higher incidence of recourse to posted workers, such as construction, temporary agency work, catering, agriculture and transport. European Commission, Commission Decision of 19 December 2008 setting up the Committee of Experts on Posting of Workers (2009/17/EC) 2009 (OJ L 8/26).
133. Directive 96/71/EC of the European Parliament and of the Council of 16 December 1996 concerning the posting of workers in the framework of the provision of services (n 13).

a monitoring authority in each country, responsible for providing information on the actual establishment of a certain company in its territory, on the effective period of mobility through posting and on the respect of all the prescriptions of the Directive, at the request of foreign national authorities. Article 4(3), for its part, set out a general duty on the Member States to make available all information on the terms and conditions of employment applied in their territory to out-of-state service providers and employees.[134]

Following several years of intense discussions, under the strong political pressure of the European Parliament[135] and the ETUC (European Trade Union Confederation),[136] on 21 March 2012, the EU Commission eventually managed to table a proposal for a directive to improve the enforcement and interpretation of the rules set out in the Posting of Workers Directive.[137] The resulting Enforcement Directive 2014/67/EU[138] was then successfully adopted on 15 May 2014, with transposition term expiring on 18 June 2016.[139] This normative innovation, conceived as a means of refinement of the Posting of Workers Directive and enhancement of the degree of compliance with the latter's prescriptions, mainly focuses on improving administrative coordination and cooperation between national authorities in the sending and receiving Member States.[140] In general terms, this is apparent from its effort to promote the use of the Internal Market Information System (IMI),[141] namely the Union's IT-based information network established by Regulation (EU) 1024/2012[142] with a view to facilitating the exchange of information and shortening the time for replies.

134. European Commission, Communication: Guidance on the posting of workers in the framework of the provision of services (n 18) 8–10; Watson (n 18) 292.
135. European Parliament resolution of 22 October 2008 on challenges to collective agreements in the EU 2008 (2008/2085(INI)).
136. ETUC (European Trade Union Confederation), Business Europe, CEEP (European Centre of Employers and Enterprises providing Public services), UEAPME (European Association of Craft, Small and Medium-Sized Enterprises), 'Report on Joint Work of the European Social Partners on the ECJ Rulings in the Viking, Laval, Rüffert and Luxembourg Cases' (2010). *See* Voss et al. (n 127) 29–30; Zahn, 'Revision of the Posted Workers Directive' (n 60) 9.
137. European Commission, Proposal for a Directive of the European Parliament and of the Council on the enforcement of Directive 96/71/EC concerning the posting of workers in the framework of the provision of services 2012 [COM(2012) 131 final]. This proposal was adopted alongside the unfortunate 'Monti II' proposal, mentioned *supra* in section 4.2.
138. Directive 2014/67/EU of the European Parliament and of the Council of 15 May 2014 on the enforcement of Directive 96/71/EC concerning the posting of workers in the framework of the provision of services and amending Regulation (EU) No 1024/2012 on administrative cooperation through the Internal Market Information System ('the IMI Regulation') 2014 (OJ L 159/11).
139. *Ibid.* Article 23(1). For the record, the adoption process of the Enforcement Directive was highly controversial as well, especially in relation to Article 12 on 'subcontracting liability'. Martinsen (n 127) 472–473.
140. Voss et al. (n 127) 44; Eurofound (n 125).
141. Article 21 of Directive 2014/67/EU of the European Parliament and of the Council of 15 May 2014 on the enforcement of Directive 96/71/EC concerning the posting of workers in the framework of the provision of services and amending Regulation (EU) No 1024/2012 on administrative cooperation through the Internal Market Information System ('the IMI Regulation') (n 138).
142. Regulation (EU) No 1024/2012 of the European Parliament and of the Council of 25 October 2012 on administrative cooperation through the Internal Market Information System and repealing Commission Decision 2008/49/EC ('the IMI Regulation') 2012 (OJ L 316/1).

4.4.1 Material Scope

Looking closer, the 2014 legislative intervention first introduced more legal clarity with regard to a common definition of competent authorities and liaison offices and provided for their mandatory indication in a public list drawn up and constantly updated by the Commission.[143] A novelty of major importance is then represented by the elaboration of a proper criterion for the individuation of the cross-border company's genuine establishment in the Member State where the latter is incorporated.[144] The actual service supply from the Member State of establishment constitutes now a precondition for the recognition of the authenticity and legitimacy of a posting activity. In turn, in case a company is only formally established in a certain country from which it conducts merely administrative or managerial activities, the exercise of its freedom to provide services is no more guaranteed.[145] In order to discern the proper establishment of a company in a certain Member State, a series of elements are to be taken into account: from the place of the undertaking's registered office and administration, to the place of recruitment of posted workers, the law applicable to the employment contracts, the place where the undertaking performs its substantial business activity, up to the number of contracts performed and the overall turnover realised.[146]

A further criterion for the recognition of a genuine posting activity is envisaged by Article 4(3), which indicates a list of factual elements concerning the nature of the temporary service supply across borders and of the employment relationship.[147]

143. Articles 2 and 3 of Directive 2014/67/EU of the European Parliament and of the Council of 15 May 2014 on the enforcement of Directive 96/71/EC concerning the posting of workers in the framework of the provision of services and amending Regulation (EU) No 1024/2012 on administrative cooperation through the Internal Market Information System ('the IMI Regulation') (n 138).
144. Notably, such an innovation was specifically designed to combat the development of the so-called 'letterbox companies', which are dealt with more in detail *infra* in Chapter 7. Karsten Engsig Sørensen, 'The Fight Against Letterbox Companies in the Internal Market' (2015) 52 Common Market Law Review 85, 98; Grušić (n 18) 265.
145. In such an event, the host Member State is not bound by the restrictions set out in the PWD. Sørensen (n 144) 98–99; Jan Cremers and Thomas Hastings, 'Developing an Approach for Tackling Letterbox Companies: Background Paper for the European Platform on Tackling Undeclared Work Seminar', *European Platform Undeclared Work* (2017) 2–3; van Hoek (n 65) 479.
146. More specifically, these elements are: '(a) the place where the undertaking has its registered office and administration, uses office space, pays taxes and social security contributions and, where applicable, in accordance with national law has a professional licence or is registered with the chambers of commerce or professional bodies; (b) the place where posted workers are recruited and from which they are posted; (c) the law applicable to the contracts concluded by the undertaking with its workers, on the one hand, and with its clients, on the other; (d) the place where the undertaking performs its substantial business activity and where it employs administrative staff; (e) the number of contracts performed and/or the size of the turnover realised in the Member State of establishment, taking into account the specific situation of, inter alia, newly established undertakings and SMEs.' Article 4(2) of Directive 2014/67/EU of the European Parliament and of the Council of 15 May 2014 on the enforcement of Directive 96/71/EC concerning the posting of workers in the framework of the provision of services and amending Regulation (EU) No 1024/2012 on administrative cooperation through the Internal Market Information System ('the IMI Regulation') (n 138).
147. In particular, the elements included in that (non-exhaustive) list are: '(a) the work is carried out for a limited period of time in another Member State; (b) the date on which the posting starts;

Notably, the explicit reference to the necessary previous performance of a working activity in the 'habitual country of work' individuated in accordance with the Rome I Regulation,[148] definitely rules out any situation of recruitment of workforce solely for the purpose of posting.[149] In contrast to the approach taken by the Court in *Commission v Luxembourg*[150] whereby exclusive competence on the control of all aspects of the employment relationship was reserved to the authorities in the sending country, the Enforcement Directive assigns a general competence to conduct all the above-mentioned necessary assessments to the competent authority in the host country.[151] Whenever the non-genuine establishment of an undertaking is in this way ascertained, the competent national authorities have the duty to identify the legal person responsible for the posting, on whom specific penalties, sanctions or fines shall be imposed.[152]

The Enforcement Directive also clarifies the host Member States' margin of appreciation in relation to the types of administrative requirements and control measures that can be imposed on cross-border service providers, always under the proviso of their justification and proportionality in accordance with EU law. In line with the previously investigated Court of Justice case law on the matter, the list of legitimate impositions includes the prior declaration of posting with all relevant information on the workers employed and the type of assignment, the retention of

(c) the posting takes place to a Member State other than the one in or from which the posted worker habitually carries out his or her work according to Regulation (EC) No 593/2008 (Rome I) and/or the Rome Convention; (d) the posted worker returns to or is expected to resume working in the Member State from which he or she is posted after completion of the work or the provision of services for which he or she was posted; (e) the nature of activities; (f) travel, board and lodging or accommodation is provided or reimbursed by the employer who posts the worker and, if so, how this is provided or the method of reimbursement; (g) any previous periods during which the post was filled by the same or by another (posted) worker.' *Ibid.* Article 4(3). On this point, *see supra* Chapter 2.

148. Regulation (EC) No 593/2008 of the European Parliament and of the Council of 17 June 2008 on the law applicable to contractual obligations (Rome I) 2008 (OJ L 177/6).
149. Aukje A.H. van Hoek and Mijke Houwerzijl, 'Where Do EU Mobile Workers Belong, According to Rome I and the (E)PWD?' in Herwig Verschueren (ed.), *Residence, Employment and Social Rights of Mobile Persons: On How EU Law Defines Where They Belong*, vol. 36 (Intersentia 2016) 242.
150. *Commission of the European Communities v Grand Duchy of Luxemburg* (n 2).
151. Preamble Recitals 8 and 10 and Article 4 of Directive 2014/67/EU of the European Parliament and of the Council of 15 May 2014 on the enforcement of Directive 96/71/EC concerning the posting of workers in the framework of the provision of services and amending Regulation (EU) No 1024/2012 on administrative cooperation through the Internal Market Information System ('the IMI Regulation') (n 138). It should be noted, however, that no specification is provided in case of conflict arising when an authority in the host country recognises the non-genuine establishment of an undertaking that, nevertheless, respects all the formal requirements for its establishment in its Member State of origin. On this point, *see* Jan Cremers, 'Economic Freedoms and Labour Standards in the European Union' (2016) 22(2) Transfer: European Review of Labour and Research 149, 159–160.
152. Notably, the transnational enforcement of the sanctions imposed on service providers for violation of the rules on posting of workers, shall always observe the principles of mutual assistance and mutual recognition. Preamble Recitals 42–44 and Article 13 of Directive 2014/67/EU of the European Parliament and of the Council of 15 May 2014 on the enforcement of Directive 96/71/EC concerning the posting of workers in the framework of the provision of services and amending Regulation (EU) No 1024/2012 on administrative cooperation through the Internal Market Information System ('the IMI Regulation') (n 138).

translated documentation at disposal of the national authorities, as well as the designation of a contact person in the territory of the country of destination.[153] Conversely, the Member States' discretionary power in that regard has been recently circumscribed by the prohibition of high minimum penalties imposed cumulatively for each single violation of formal obligations, of the addition of a disproportionate contribution connected to the costs of the proceeding, and of the conversion of the penalties into custodial sentences in the event of non-payment.[154]

Crucially, then, in light of the transnational character of the activities at issue, the Directive strongly encourages wider collaboration between the Member States on the investigations and the enforcement of the sanctions across borders.[155] *Inter alia*, specific time limits are fixed with regard to transnational requests for information.[156] With a view to improving access to information on the terms and conditions of employment applicable to posted workers (including those prescribed by the applicable collective agreements), by virtue of Article 5, the Member States are also obliged to collect all relevant information in a single official national website, which must be

153. *Ibid.* Article 9(1). In practice, an electronic system for the prior declaration of posting has been set up in most of the Member States. European Commission, 'Practical Guide on Posting' (2019) 5–6. For an overview of the administrative requirements and control measures applied in each Member State, *see* European Commission, 'Commission Staff Working Document Accompanying the Document Report from the Commission to the European Parliament, the Council and the European Economic and Social Committee on the Application and Implemantation of Directive 2014/67/EU of the European Parliament and of the Council of 15 May 2014 on the Enforcement of Directive 96/71/EC Concerning the Posting of Workers in the Framework of the Provision of Services and Amending Regulation (EU) No 1024/2012 on Administrative Cooperation through the Internal Market Information System ("the IMI Regulation")' (2019) SWD(2019) 337 final. Interestingly, when seen from the perspective of the cross-border employers, the imposition of such requirements appears already fairly restrictive. Deloitte Belgium, 'How Will the Revision of the Posted Workers Directive Impact Your Assignments?' (2018) figure 11 <https://www2.deloitte.com/content/dam/Deloitte/be/Documents/tax/PostedWorkersDirective.pdf> (accessed 26 September 2018).

154. All these restrictions had been implemented by the Austrian administration at the time of the transposition of the Enforcement Directive and, subsequently, considered by the Court as incompatible with EU law. *Zoran Maksimovic and Others v Bezirkshauptmannschaft Murtal and Finanzpolizei* [2019] CJEU Joined Cases C-64/18, C-140/18, C-146/18 and C-148/18, ECLI:EU:C:2019:723. On this point, *see* Marcin Kiełbasa, 'Avalanche of Preliminary Questions to the CJEU on Posting of Workers to Austria' (*Labour Mobility Initiative*, 3 September 2019) <https://www.mobilelabour.eu/13085/avalanche-of-preliminary-questions-to-the-cjeu-on-posting-of-workers-to-austria/> (accessed 22 October 2019).

155. Articles 6–8 of Directive 2014/67/EU of the European Parliament and of the Council of 15 May 2014 on the enforcement of Directive 96/71/EC concerning the posting of workers in the framework of the provision of services and amending Regulation (EU) No 1024/2012 on administrative cooperation through the Internal Market Information System ('the IMI Regulation') (n 138). Notably, such a duty derives also from the European principle of sincere cooperation, codified in Article 4(3) TEU. On this point, *see* Sørensen (n 144) 99; Voss et al. (n 127) 44; Cremers and Hastings (n 145) 3.

156. Article 6(6) of Directive 2014/67/EU of the European Parliament and of the Council of 15 May 2014 on the enforcement of Directive 96/71/EC concerning the posting of workers in the framework of the provision of services and amending Regulation (EU) No 1024/2012 on administrative cooperation through the Internal Market Information System ('the IMI Regulation') (n 138). Cremers (n 151) 158.

freely accessible and displayed in the most relevant languages (included that of the host country).[157]

A further relevant innovation is represented by the introduction of a sort of 'subcontracting liability' on the basis of which the main contractor is considered responsible for any subcontractor's lack of payment of remuneration or contributions suffered by the posted workers.[158] The real effectiveness of this disposition is, however, directly dependent on its degree of implementation at national level. In fact, on the one hand, the Directive imposes an obligation on the Member States to provide for specific measures to that extent in the construction sector only. On the other hand, such a vicarious liability is limited to the first direct subcontractor, thus remaining exposed to a practical ineffectiveness in cases of chains of subcontractors.[159] Nevertheless, the Member States are still granted the faculty to extend this form of liability to further troubled situations and also to other economic sectors.[160]

Serious doubts persist, nonetheless, with regard to the practical effectiveness of liability rules in cross-border situations of subcontracting. As demonstrated by countries that had already implemented systems of joint and several liability, in those cases workers employed under the direction of subcontractors often do not enjoy better protection. This is due to the fact that the posted employees concerned, even when they are victims of abuses, discriminations or unlawful dismissals, are in many cases reluctant to start proceedings against their employers or even the subcontractors. Such an action would, indeed, turn against themselves by affecting the 'good relations' with their employer or the client and eventually preventing them from returning to that host country. Moreover, litigation in a foreign country is often expensive and conducted in a language and a context unknown to the workers.[161] In this sense, the last novelty

157. Article 5(2) of Directive 2014/67/EU of the European Parliament and of the Council of 15 May 2014 on the enforcement of Directive 96/71/EC concerning the posting of workers in the framework of the provision of services and amending Regulation (EU) No 1024/2012 on administrative cooperation through the Internal Market Information System ('the IMI Regulation') (n 138). Cremers (n 151) 159.
158. Article 12 of Directive 2014/67/EU of the European Parliament and of the Council of 15 May 2014 on the enforcement of Directive 96/71/EC concerning the posting of workers in the framework of the provision of services and amending Regulation (EU) No 1024/2012 on administrative cooperation through the Internal Market Information System ('the IMI Regulation') (n 138). On this point, *see* Verschueren (n 23) 144–145; Sørensen (n 144) 99–100; Cremers (n 151) 159–160; Voss et al. (n 127) 44. For the record, the introduction of such a mechanism of joint and several liability was strongly recommended already in 2012 by Jorens et al. as a valuable means of worker protection in subcontracting processes. Jorens, Peters and Houwerzijl (n 14) 157.
159. Tonia Novitz and Rutvica Andrijasevic, 'Reform of the Posting of Workers Regime – An Assessment of the Practical Impact on Unfree Labour Relations' (2020) 58 JCMS: Journal of Common Market Studies 1325, 1331. Evidently, this apparent limitation of the scope of subcontracting liability sensibly limits the effectiveness of this provision in the fight against 'letterbox companies' as well. Sørensen (n 144) 99–100; Cremers and Hastings (n 145) 3.
160. The sole limit posed by the Directive to the Member States' discretion is the respect of the principles of proportionality and non-discrimination. Article 12(4) of Directive 2014/67/EU of the European Parliament and of the Council of 15 May 2014 on the enforcement of Directive 96/71/EC concerning the posting of workers in the framework of the provision of services and amending Regulation (EU) No 1024/2012 on administrative cooperation through the Internal Market Information System ('the IMI Regulation') (n 138).
161. Jorens, Peters and Houwerzijl (n 14) 156–157.

introduced by Directive 2014/67/EU provides for a sensible enhancement of the posted workers' faculty to lodge complaints or engage in proceedings for the protection of their rights and interests. Pursuant to Article 11, national complaints mechanisms shall now ensure the seconded employees to effectively propose direct actions against their employers, also in the country of destination, and to be represented, for the same purposes, by trade unions or other associations.[162]

4.4.2 First Results and Shortcomings

The first Commission's report on the progress achieved during the past five years shows that, following the transposition of the Directive by all the Member States, the enforcement of the Posting of Workers Directive has positively improved. This is due, *in primis*, to the establishment of the Internal Market Information System that has promoted cross-border administrative cooperation between national authorities. Second, the Member States' faculty to introduce administrative requirements, control measures and financial penalties has definitely contributed to better compliance with the rules and worker protection.[163]

After presenting the wide variety of new targeted rules and legal instruments introduced by the Enforcement Directive, the persistence of certain shortcomings must be highlighted as well. In effect, the 2014 legislative intervention left untouched a number of controversial issues. This was the case, first and foremost, of the lack of definition of what constitutes 'fair posting', which had direct implications on the specific individuation of the malpractices and abuses related to the phenomenon at stake, as well as on the way such issues have to be addressed.[164] In the same vein, the concepts of minimum rates of pay and temporary character of posting still remained rather ambiguous and vague.[165] In addition, no remedy was provided with regard to further emerging troublesome practices of regulatory arbitrage and bogus self-employment, where a more clarified definition of a 'worker' was needed in order to enable national competent authorities to identify those workers who falsely declared

162. Article 11 of Directive 2014/67/EU of the European Parliament and of the Council of 15 May 2014 on the enforcement of Directive 96/71/EC concerning the posting of workers in the framework of the provision of services and amending Regulation (EU) No 1024/2012 on administrative cooperation through the Internal Market Information System ('the IMI Regulation') (n 138). Cremers (n 151) 161; Cinzia Peraro, 'The Enforcement of Posted Workers' Rights Across the European Union' (2017) 2 *Freedom, Security & Justice: European Legal Studies* 114, 120 and ff.; European Commission, 'Practical Guide on Posting' (n 153) 22.
163. European Commission, 'Report from the Commission to the European Parliament, the Council and the European Economic and Social Committee on the Application and Implementation of Directive 2014/67/EU of the European Parliament and of the Council of 15 May 2014 on the Enforcement of Directive 96/71/EC Concerning the Posting of Workers in the Framework of the Provision of Services and Amending Regulation (EU) 1024/2012 on Administrative Co-Operation through the Internal Market Information System ("the IMI Regulation")' (n 26) 24.
164. Voss et al. (n 127) 65.
165. Zahn, 'Revision of the Posted Workers' Directive: Equality at Last?' (n 60) 6; Zahn, 'Revision of the Posted Workers Directive' (n 60) 10.

themselves as self-employed persons.[166] The new rules on 'subcontracting liability' could be considered inadequate as well for basically resulting ineffective in tackling issues of chains of subcontractors and 'letterbox companies'.[167]

Evidently, there was ample room for improvement with regard to the adoption of further measures dealing with the still existing issues of cross-border exchange of information, registration, enforcement, and monitoring.[168] Besides that, when looking at the Enforcement Directive more generally, it appears that the European legislator missed the opportunity to provide an effective simplification of the regulation of the sector, likewise a better information system for the benefit of both the workers and the employers involved.[169] The obligation of creating different national monitoring authorities instead of a single EU-wide monitoring system has been criticised, indeed, for failing to effectively cope with disparities of treatment across the Member States.[170] Ultimately, all the above-mentioned deficiencies are deemed to have negative repercussions in terms of implementation and enforcement of proper national contrasting measures.

4.5 POSTING IN THE ROAD TRANSPORT SECTOR

In accordance with the analysis carried out *supra* in Chapter 2, workers in the road transport sector (i.e., truck drivers) fall undoubtedly within the personal scope of the original Posting of Workers Directive.[171] However, due to its intrinsic highly mobile nature, the European road haulage industry becomes extremely problematic when it comes to the implementation of the rules laid down in the Posting of Workers Directive and in the Enforcement Directive.[172] As a matter of fact, the workers involved in this

166. Kristina Maslauskaite, 'Posted Workers in the EU: State of Play and Regulatory Evolution' (2014) Policy Paper, Notre Europe Jaques Delors Institute 20, 16; Voss et al. (n 127) 44–45.
167. Sørensen (n 144) 99–100; Cremers and Hastings (n 145) 3; Novitz and Andrijasevic (n 159) 1331.
168. Yves Jorens, 'Intra-EU Posting: Looking for Solutions: A Herculean or a Sisyphean Task?' (60 Years Social Security Coordination from a Workers' Perspective, Leuven, Belgium, 16 May 2019).
169. Voss et al. (n 127) 64.
170. Claire Dhéret and Andreia Ghimis, 'The Revision of the Posted Workers Directive: Towards a Sufficient Policy Adjustment?' (2016) *European Policy Center (EPC) Discussion Paper* 9 <http://www.epc.eu/pub_details.php?cat_id=17&pub_id=6475> (accessed 23 October 2016); Zahn, 'Revision of the Posted Workers' Directive: Equality at Last?' (n 60) 6; Zahn, 'Revision of the Posted Workers Directive' (n 60) 10.
171. The application of the PWD to cabotage activities is expressly confirmed by Preamble Recital 17 of Regulation (EC) No 1072/2009 of the European Parliament and of the Council of 21 October 2009 on common rules for access to the international road haulage market 2009 (OJ L 300/72).
172. Preamble Recitals 9–10 of the European Commission, Proposal for a Directive of the European Parliament and of the Council amending Directive 2006/22/EC as regards enforcement requirements and laying down specific rules with respect to Directive 96/71/EC and Directive 2014/67/EU for posting drivers in the road transport sector 2017 [COM(2017) 278 final]. *See also* Preamble Recital 10 of the European Commission, Proposal for a Directive of the European Parliament and of the Council amending Directive 96/71/EC of the European Parliament and of the Council of 16 December 1996 concerning the posting of workers in the framework of the provision of services 2016 [COM(2016) 128 final].

type of activity find themselves in a borderline condition whereby they carry out their tasks simultaneously in several Member States (typically 5–6 in one month), often spending only a short amount of time in each country they drive through. In such a context, the establishment of the place where a driver 'habitually' works, in order to determine his salary and his rights to annual paid holidays, is tremendously complicated.[173]

As regards the administrative requirements set out in the Enforcement Directive, the obligations of pre-notification of each operation, of keeping all relevant documentation on board the vehicle (including employment contract, payslips, time-sheets, proofs of payment of wages, all translated into the languages of the different host countries) and preserve it for eighteen months after the period of posting, and of designating a contact person in the territory of each host Member State, have been found excessively burdensome and disproportionate.[174] Especially with regard to specific national measures, the uncoordinated application of posting rules to the road transport sector has been accused of creating an excessive administrative burden liable to unduly restrict the freedom to provide cross-border services and lead to fragmentation of the entire EU transport market.[175] This is the case of the introduction by

173. To that extent, even the Court of Justice' s clarification that 'in a situation in which an employee carries out his activities in more than one Contracting State, the country in which the employee habitually carries out his work in performance of the contract, within the meaning of that provision, is that in which or from which, in the light of all the factors which characterise that activity, the employee performs the greater part of his obligations towards his employer' does not help much. Heiko Koelzsch v *État du Grand Duchy of Luxemburg* [2011] CJEU Case C-29/10, ECLI:EU:C:2011:151. On the other hand, it is worth pointing out that there are also a lot of transport undertakings which carry out a substantial part of their activities in one or two Member States, thus perfectly falling under the regular posting scenario. European Commission, Impact Assessment, Accompanying the document Proposal for a Regulation of the European Parliament and of the Council amending Regulation (EC) 561/2006 as regards minimum requirements on maximum daily and weekly driving times, minimum breaks and daily and weekly rest periods and Regulation (EU) 165/2014 as regards positioning by means of tachographs and Proposal for a Directive of the European Parliament and of the Council amending Directive 2006/22/EC as regards enforcement requirements and laying down specific rules with respect to Directive 96/71/EC and Directive 2014/67/EU for posting drivers in the road transport sector – Part 1/2 2017 [SWD(2017) 186 final] 27. *See also* van Hoek and Houwerzijl (n 66) 36 and 187; Jean-Philippe Lhernould, 'Directive (EU) 2018/957 of 28 June 2018 Amending Directive 96/71/EC Concerning the Posting of Workers in the Framework of the Provision of Services: What Will Change in 2020?' (2019) ERA Forum – Springer 7 < http://link.springer.com/10.1007/s12027-019-00573-x > (accessed 16 September 2019).
174. European Commission Impact Assessment, Accompanying the document Proposal for a Regulation of the European Parliament and of the Council amending Regulation (EC) 561/2006 as regards minimum requirements on maximum daily and weekly driving times, minimum breaks and daily and weekly rest periods and Regulation (EU) 165/2014 as regards positioning by means of tachographs and Proposal for a Directive of the European Parliament and of the Council amending Directive 2006/22/EC as regards enforcement requirements and laying down specific rules with respect to Directive 96/71/EC and Directive 2014/67/EU for posting drivers in the road transport sector – Part 1/2 (n 173) 27–28.
175. Preamble Recital 9 of the European Commission Proposal for a Directive of the European Parliament and of the Council amending Directive 2006/22/EC as regards enforcement requirements and laying down specific rules with respect to Directive 96/71/EC and Directive 2014/67/EU for posting drivers in the road transport sector (n 172).

Germany, France, Austria and Italy, in the period between 2015 and 2017, of regulations imposing the application of their national minimum rates of pay, together with a number of administrative and control requirements, to all foreign operators and drivers carrying out any haulage activities on their territories.[176] Self-evidently, such a situation generates worryingly distortions of competition between service providers who operate in those countries and service providers who engage in transport activities in other Member States with lower administrative costs.[177] Importantly, then, distortions of competition occur also as a result of the development of fraudulent and abusive practices in the sector, which too often translate into the exploitation of the workers concerned.[178]

The above-mentioned serious legal and practical issues clearly emphasise the inadequacy of the legal framework laid down in the Posting of Workers Directive, in combination with its Enforcement Directive, to effectively regulate the road transport sector. Against this background, on 31 May 2017, the Commission submitted, in the context of the 'Europe on the Move' package, its proposal to amend Directive 2006/22/EC[179] on social legislation relating to road transport activities.[180] *Inter alia*, it put forward sector-specific rules prevailing over relevant provisions of both the Posting of Workers Directive and its Enforcement Directive.[181] This draft legislation envisaged a threshold of three days during a one-month period for the full application to posted

176. The result is that, in a typical transport operation across six different Member States, six different rates of pay find application and six different sets of documents in six different national languages of the host countries need to be prepared and kept on board the vehicle, while the driver hardly gets any benefit. European Commission Impact Assessment, Accompanying the document Proposal for a Regulation of the European Parliament and of the Council amending Regulation (EC) 561/2006 as regards minimum requirements on maximum daily and weekly driving times, minimum breaks and daily and weekly rest periods and Regulation (EU) 165/2014 as regards positioning by means of tachographs and Proposal for a Directive of the European Parliament and of the Council amending Directive 2006/22/EC as regards enforcement requirements and laying down specific rules with respect to Directive 96/71/EC and Directive 2014/67/EU for posting drivers in the road transport sector – Part 1/2 (n 173) 17, 27–29.
177. *Ibid.* 30.
178. Schiek et al. (n 14) 45–46; European Commission Impact Assessment, Accompanying the document Proposal for a Regulation of the European Parliament and of the Council amending Regulation (EC) 561/2006 as regards minimum requirements on maximum daily and weekly driving times, minimum breaks and daily and weekly rest periods and Regulation (EU) 165/2014 as regards positioning by means of tachographs and Proposal for a Directive of the European Parliament and of the Council amending Directive 2006/22/EC as regards enforcement requirements and laying down specific rules with respect to Directive 96/71/EC and Directive 2014/67/EU for posting drivers in the road transport sector – Part 1/2 (n 173) 13–16. For an investigation of the fraudulent and abusive practices developed in the posting of workers in the road transport sector, *see infra* Chapter 7.
179. Directive 2006/22/EC of the European Parliament and of the Council of 15 March 2006 on minimum conditions for the implementation of Council Regulations (EEC) No 3820/85 and (EEC) No 3821/85 concerning social legislation relating to road transport activities and repealing Council Directive 88/599/EEC 2006 (OJ L 102/35).
180. European Commission Proposal for a Directive of the European Parliament and of the Council amending Directive 2006/22/EC as regards enforcement requirements and laying down specific rules with respect to Directive 96/71/EC and Directive 2014/67/EU for posting drivers in the road transport sector (n 172).
181. *Ibid.* 10, Preamble Recitals 10–11 and Article 2(1).

drivers of the host state's rules on minimum rates of pay and minimum paid annual holidays.[182] With a view to reducing excessive regulatory burdens and preventing distortions of competition, it placed detailed limitations on the administrative requirements and control measures that host Member State's authorities may impose on cross-border operators.[183] Hence, it allowed the Member States to require the issuing of a posting declaration in electronic form prior to the commencement of the transnational activity, the keeping of all relevant documentation on board the vehicle (including a copy of the posting declaration, tachograph records, employment contract, and payslips, all translated into the languages of the different host countries or into English), and the delivery of such documentation at the request of the competent authorities within a reasonable period of time.[184]

In the following step of the legislative process, the file was allocated to the European Parliament's Committee on Transport and Tourism (TRAN), which, after dealing with a staggering number of amendments, contributed to the drafting of the Parliament's position that was adopted on 4 April 2019.[185] Eventually, after two-and-a-half years of negotiations, a provisional agreement was reached on 12 December 2019 between the Finnish Presidency of the Council, the European Parliament, and the Commission, during the third round of 'trilogue' meetings started a couple of months before. Subsequently, the Council adopted its position at first reading on 7 April 2020.[186] Following the green light from the TRAN Committee on 8 June 2020 and the favourable vote in the European Parliament in Plenary, on 8 July 2020, the new

182. In particular, it lays down a whole list of criteria for the determination of the periods of posting, considering a daily working period shorter than six hours as half a day, and a daily working period of six hours or more as a full day, always including breaks and rest periods in the calculation. *Ibid.* Article 2(2) and (3).

183. *Ibid.* 2–3.

184. *Ibid.* Article 2(4). *See* European Commission, Communication from the Commission to the European Parliament, the Council, the European Economic and Social Committee and the Committee of the Regions, Europe on the move – An agenda for a socially fair transition towards clean, competitive and connected mobility for all 2017 [COM(2017) 283 final] 12.

185. European Parliament, Legislative resolution of 4 April 2019 on the proposal for a directive of the European Parliament and of the Council amending Directive 2006/22/EC as regards enforcement requirements and laying down specific rules with respect to Directive 96/71/EC and Directive 2014/67/EU for posting drivers in the road transport sector 2019 (2017/0121(COD)). For the record, the position of the Parliament basically reflected the general approach agreed only a few months earlier at the Council meeting on transport, telecommunications and energy of 3 December 2018. Council of the European Union, Proposal for a Directive of the European Parliament and of the Council amending Directive 2006/22/EC as regards enforcement requirements and laying down specific rules with respect to Directive 96/71/EC and Directive 2014/67/EU for posting drivers in the road transport sector – general approach 2018 (15084/18). On this point, *see* Council of the European Union, 'Transport, Telecommunications and Energy Council (Transport) – Consilium' (*Press Release*, 12 March 2018) <https://www.consilium.europa.eu/en/meetings/tte/2018/12/03/> (accessed 15 October 2019).

186. Council of the European Union, Position (EU) No 4/2020 of the Council at first reading: with a view to the adoption of a Directive of the European Parliament and of the Council laying down specific rules with respect to Directive 96/71/EC and Directive 2014/67/EU for posting drivers in the road transport sector and amending Directive 2006/22/EC as regards enforcement requirements and Regulation (EU) No 1024/2012, 2020 (OJ C 149/1).

Directive (EU) 2020/1057 on posting drivers in the road transport sector[187] was eventually adopted by the Council and the Parliament on 15 July 2020.[188] Unlike cabotage and non-bilateral international transport operations, transit, bilateral transport operations and the road leg of combined transport have been excluded from the rules on posting.[189] This by reason of the fact that 'a sufficient link to the territory of the host Member State' exists in the first cases only.[190] While the three-day threshold for the full application of host state's rules on remuneration and minimum paid annual leave was finally not included, all the measures proposed by the Commission and concerning specific limitations on the administrative requirements and control measures that host Member State's authorities may impose with respect to the posting of drivers have been approved.[191] At the same time, the new Directive introduces further measures aimed at improving the enforcement of the rules and the cross-border exchange of information, with the use of the Internal Market Information System (IMI).[192]

187. Directive (EU) 2020/1057 of the European Parliament and of the Council of 15 July 2020 laying down specific rules with respect to Directive 96/71/EC and Directive 2014/67/EU for posting drivers in the road transport sector and amending Directive 2006/22/EC as regards enforcement requirements and Regulation (EU) No 1024/2012, 2020 (OJ L 249/49).
188. On 31 July 2020, Directive (EU) 2020/1057 was published in the EU Official Journal as part of the 'Mobility Package I on road transport' including also Regulation (EU) 2020/1054 of the European Parliament and of the Council of 15 July 2020 amending Regulation (EC) No 561/2006 as regards minimum requirements on maximum daily and weekly driving times, minimum breaks and daily and weekly rest periods and Regulation (EU) No 165/2014 as regards positioning by means of tachographs 2020 (OJ L 249); Regulation (EU) 2020/1055 of the European Parliament and of the Council of 15 July 2020 amending Regulations (EC) No 1071/2009, (EC) No 1072/2009 and (EU) No 1024/2012 with a view to adapting them to developments in the road transport sector 2020 (OJ L 249); Regulation (EU) 2020/1056 of the European Parliament and of the Council of 15 July 2020 on electronic freight transport information 2020 (OJ L 249). For a detailed report of the overall legislative process concerning Directive (EU) 2020/1057, *see* European Parliament, 'Road Transport: Enforcement Requirements and Specific Rules for Posting Drivers, Legislative Train Schedule' (24 June 2020) <https://www.europarl.europa.eu/legislative-train> (accessed 22 July 2020).
189. Article 1(3), (4), (5), (6) and (7) of Directive (EU) 2020/1057 of the European Parliament and of the Council of 15 July 2020 laying down specific rules with respect to Directive 96/71/EC and Directive 2014/67/EU for posting drivers in the road transport sector and amending Directive 2006/22/EC as regards enforcement requirements and Regulation (EU) No 1024/2012 (n 187). For the record, a cabotage operation involves a vehicle that is registered in country A, which carries out a transport between several venues within country B (e.g., a Polish transport company that carries cargo between Hamburg and Berlin). A bilateral transport operation involves a vehicle that is registered in country A, which carries out a transport between country A and B or vice versa (e.g., a Polish transport company that carries vodka from Poland to Germany). Transit transport implies the mere crossing of a country without loading or unloading goods, while combined transport is a form of intermodal transport involving the use of two or more modes of transport without handling the goods themselves in changing modes. Fieke van Overbeeke, 'Posting Drivers in the EU Road Transport Sector' (2020) ERA Forum 4–5.
190. Directive (EU) 2020/1057 of the European Parliament and of the Council of 15 July 2020 laying down specific rules with respect to Directive 96/71/EC and Directive 2014/67/EU for posting drivers in the road transport sector and amending Directive 2006/22/EC as regards enforcement requirements and Regulation (EU) No 1024/2012 (n 187) Preamble Recital 13.
191. *Ibid.* Article 1(11) and (12).
192. *Ibid.* Article 1(13), (14), (15) and (16). The complexity of the new regulatory framework, as well as the additional amount of administrative burden, is nonetheless expected to generate

As of 2 February 2022, at the end of its implementation period,[193] the new Directive (EU) 2020/1057 will regulate the posting of workers in the road transport sector as a *lex specialis* which derogates from the general regulatory framework established by the Posting of Workers Directive, as amended by the new Directive (EU) 2018/957, and its Enforcement Directive. In fact, in light of the intrinsic highly mobile nature of the road transport service sector, the European legislator made the choice to defer the application of the new Directive (EU) 2018/957 in relation to that kind of business until the sector-specific legislation amending Directive 2006/22/EC – i.e., Directive (EU) 2020/1057 – will enter into force.[194] In other words, until 2 February 2022, transnational activities of transport workers remain covered by the original version of the Posting of Workers Directive.[195] Evidently, therefore, the initiative of revision of Directive 2006/22/EC has been conceived as complementary to the revision of the Posting of Workers Directive.[196]

4.6 CONCLUDING REMARKS

By its very nature, the Posting of Workers Directive (even after the entry into effect of Directive (EU) 2018/957) allows the receiving Member States to extend part of their domestic terms and conditions of employment to posted workers assigned temporarily to their territory in the framework of the provision of services. Nevertheless, this domestic law has been subject, over the years, to a strict review by the Court of Justice as regards its compatibility with EU internal market law, namely about being non-discriminatory, justified and proportionate. In this sense, national requirements imposed on incoming cross-border service providers with a view to implementing the

further enforcement issues. CLECAT (European Association for Forwarding, Transport, Logistics and Customs Services), 'Reaction to the Provisional Agreement on Mobility Package I' (*CLECAT News*, 13 December 2019) <https://www.clecat.org/news/news/provisional-agreement-on-mobility-package-i> (accessed 11 February 2020); Björn Lindahl, 'EU Agreement on Mobility Package' (*Nordic Labour Journal*, 13 December 2019) <http://www.nordiclabourjournal.org/nyheter/news-2019/article.2019-12-12.5078447113> (accessed 11 February 2020).

193. Article 9 of Directive (EU) 2020/1057 of the European Parliament and of the Council of 15 July 2020 laying down specific rules with respect to Directive 96/71/EC and Directive 2014/67/EU for posting drivers in the road transport sector and amending Directive 2006/22/EC as regards enforcement requirements and Regulation (EU) No 1024/2012 (n 187).

194. Article 3(3) of Directive (EU) 2018/957 of the European Parliament and of the Council of 28 June 2018 amending Directive 96/71/EC concerning the posting of workers in the framework of the provision of services 2018 (OJ L 173/16).

195. Preamble Recital 43 of Directive (EU) 2020/1057 of the European Parliament and of the Council of 15 July 2020 laying down specific rules with respect to Directive 96/71/EC and Directive 2014/67/EU for posting drivers in the road transport sector and amending Directive 2006/22/EC as regards enforcement requirements and Regulation (EU) No 1024/2012 (n 187).

196. European Commission Impact Assessment, Accompanying the document Proposal for a Regulation of the European Parliament and of the Council amending Regulation (EC) 561/2006 as regards minimum requirements on maximum daily and weekly driving times, minimum breaks and daily and weekly rest periods and Regulation (EU) 165/2014 as regards positioning by means of tachographs and Proposal for a Directive of the European Parliament and of the Council amending Directive 2006/22/EC as regards enforcement requirements and laying down specific rules with respect to Directive 96/71/EC and Directive 2014/67/EU for posting drivers in the road transport sector – Part 1/2 (n 173) 8.

provisions laid down in the Directive have been considered appropriate even when constituting de facto a heavier burden on foreign undertakings vis-à-vis their local counterparts. But still, only on the condition that they were justified by the overriding public interest of worker protection and satisfied the proportionality test.

The intervention of the EU judiciary was even more relevant when it came to assessing the legitimacy of the different means, developed at Member State level, for determining the terms and conditions of employment applicable to posted workers. In the highly controversial ruling in *Laval*,[197] the choice by Sweden to leave the determination of labour standards applicable to posted workers to collective agreements negotiated on a case-by-case basis and without *erga omnes* effect was censured for not making recourse to one of the alternatives offered by Article 3(8) of the Posting of Workers Directive. Moreover, the application of a strict version of the proportionality test led the Court to consider the exercise, by the Swedish trade unions, of the EU fundamental social right of collective action as a disproportionate restriction of the Latvian company's EU economic freedom of service provision. This view was taken by the Court notwithstanding the fact that the exercise of that right was justified by an overriding reason of public interest, namely the protection of workers against the threat of social dumping. The demanded level of protection was, indeed, beyond the hard core of mandatory rules set out in the Directive, and the determination in advance of the regime applicable to the posted workers according to the host country's practices was found excessively complicated and burdensome. The rationale adopted was strongly criticised for granting precedence to the EU fundamental freedom of transnational service provision over the fundamental social right to take collective action. Nonetheless, the Court made clear that the exercise of the fundamental social right to take collective action in EU law is not absolute, especially when it represents the expression of trade unions' regulatory power for the protection of the private interests of their members.

A similar approach, entailing a restrictive interpretation of the instruments at disposal of the Member States in order to impose their own labour standards upon foreign service providers, was followed by the Court also in its subsequent decisions in *Rüffert*[198] and *Commission v Luxembourg*.[199] In the latter case, the host country's room for manoeuvre in classifying restrictions to the freedom to provide services as 'public policy provisions' was drastically narrowed down. In turn, in *Rüffert*, the German regional law requiring out-of-state employers to pay their workers the minimum wage prescribed by a local collective agreement lacking universal effect was, once again, considered unjustified with respect to Article 56 TFEU for going beyond the prescriptions of the Posting of Workers Directive. Interestingly, the inclination of the EU judiciary towards the definition by positive legislation of the terms and conditions of employment extendable to posted workers was reaffirmed, a few years later, in another

197. *Laval un Partneri Ltd v Svenska Byggnadsarbetareförbundet, Svenska Byggnadsarbetareförbundets avdelning 1, Byggettan and Svenska Elektrikerförbundet* (n 2).
198. *Dirk Rüffert v Land Niedersachsen* (n 2).
199. *Commission of the European Communities v Grand Duchy of Luxemburg* (n 2).

judgment concerning the interplay between posting and public procurement, namely *RegioPost*.[200]

From the analysis carried out *supra*, it is evident that the Court of Justice's rulings in the so-called 'Laval trio' have contributed much to the liberalisation of the internal market for services, with particular reference to the transnational posting of workers.[201] Contextually, they sensibly narrowed down the scope of territorial and national application of labour law on cross-border seconded workers,[202] while severely affecting national systems of industrial relations, especially in the Scandinavian countries. Notably, in the wake of the opening of the EU labour market to foreign service providers established in the low-wage Central and Eastern Member States following from the 2004 and 2007 EU enlargements, and the consequent increasing recourse to posting practices for cost competition, the approach followed by the Court has been strongly criticised for potentially facilitating the erosion of labour standards and the displacement of workers in the wealthier Member States.[203]

Against this background, this chapter proposed to look at the cases brought before the Court of Justice from a different angle from that taken by the Western European narrative, which gives universal value to the syllogism that to a higher level of employment standards applicable in the host states directly corresponds a higher degree of worker protection. Such an argument is liable, indeed, to lose sight of the interests and prerogatives of all the actors involved, notably of those of the posted workers themselves. And the same goes for the rationale of presenting the disputes in terms of dichotomic juxtaposition between social rights and economic freedoms. In fact, when reversing the perspective on the matter, the Western trade unions' actions in defence of the higher social and employment standards in the wealthier Member

200. *RegioPost GmbH & Co. KG v Stadt Landau in der Pfalz* (n 6).
201. Barnard, 'Viking and Laval: An Introduction' (n 35); Barnard, 'Fifty Years of Avoiding Social Dumping? The EU's Economic and Not So Economic Constitution' (n 80) 322; Fritz W. Scharpf, 'The Asymmetry of European Integration, or Why the EU Cannot Be a "Social Market Economy"' (2010) 8 Socio-Economic Review 211, 227; Malmberg (n 35); Stéphane Lalanne, 'Posting of Workers, EU Enlargement and the Globalization of Trade in Services' (2011) 150 International Labour Review 211, 223–226; Jan Cremers, 'Free Provision of Services and Cross-Border Labour Recruitment' (2013) 34 Policy Studies 201.
202. Verschueren (n 60) 196; Catherine Barnard and Simon Deakin, 'European Labour Law after Laval' in Marie-Ange Moreau (ed.), *Before and After the Economic Crisis. What Implications for the 'European Social Model'?* (Edward Elgar Publishing 2011) 260–262; Barnard, 'The Calm after the Storm: Time to Reflect on EU (Labour) Law Scholarship Following the Decisions in Viking and Laval' (n 60) 6–7. It is noteworthy, anyway, that the restrictive approach taken by the Court with regard to the terms and conditions of employment applicable by the host Member State to posted workers was, nevertheless, counterbalanced by the following decisions in *Sähköalojen ammattiliitto* and *RegioPost*, whereby the social protection character of the PWD was, in turn, strongly emphasised. Kaupa (n 97) 135–136; van Hoek (n 65) 471–472; Sciarra (n 39) 83–84; Rocca, 'Not Dead yet: Legal Strategies at National Level and the Reform of the EU Posting of Workers Directive' (n 92) 11 and 13; Sacha Garben, 'The European Pillar of Social Rights as a Revival of Social Europe' in Maurizio Ferrera (ed.), *Towards a European Social Union: The European Pillar of Social Rights and the Roadmap for a Fully-Fledged Social Union* (Centro di Ricerca e Documentazione Luigi Einaudi 2019) 80.
203. Verschueren (n 60) 198; Hatzopoulos, *Regulating Services in the European Union* (n 1) 113; Verschueren (n 23) 131–133; Schiek et al. (n 14) 96; Zahn, 'Revision of the Posted Workers Directive' (n 60) 14–15.

States appear directed to the realisation of economic-protectionist aims, whereas the full exercise of the freedom to provide services may also be regarded as an enjoyment, by the posted workers, of their social rights to work, to escape unemployment, and to make their contribution to their home country's economy. In this sense, one should take into consideration the social dimension of EU free movement law as well. After all, as suggested by Barnard: 'economic and social rights need to be squared, not put in opposition'.[204]

After the failure of the legislative project of the 'Monti II' Regulation concerning the exercise of the right to take collective action in the context of the freedoms of establishment and of service provision, the EU legislator's response to the broad range of issues related to the implementation and enforcement of the Posting of Workers Directive materialised in 2014 with the adoption of the Enforcement Directive 2014/67/EU. First and foremost, such an instrument improved legal clarity by introducing a non-exhaustive list of criteria to help the competent national authorities in the assessment of genuine postings and in the fight against abuses and circumventions. In light of the intrinsic cross-border nature of posting, that legislative intervention enhanced administrative coordination and cooperation between national authorities in the sending and receiving Member States, especially through the promotion of the Internal Market Information System (IMI), which was specifically created for facilitating the exchange of information. Moreover, it introduced a sort of 'subcontracting liability' aimed at dealing with the issues connected to the frequent subcontractors' lack of payments of the remunerations and social security contributions due to posted employees. The latter workers, in their turn, have been provided with more effective instruments for the enforcement of their rights across borders, such as the possibilities of proposing direct actions against their employers and being represented by trade unions or other associations.

Despite the improvements brought about by the Enforcement Directive, the regulatory framework for posting still presented a number of shortcomings. As a matter of fact, the concepts of 'fair posting', minimum rates of pay, and temporary character of posting still remained rather ambiguous and vague, while no remedy was offered to cope with the emerging troublesome practices of regulatory arbitrage, bogus self-employment, and subcontracting chains. More generally, then, the overall complexity of the posting regulation and of the bureaucratic procedures to be followed remained untouched. Finally, even the creation of different national monitoring authorities has been criticised for not being as effective as a single EU-wide monitoring system would be.

At last, this chapter highlighted that the implementation of the posting rules in the European road haulage industry has become extremely problematic, due to the intrinsic highly mobile nature of the sector. In fact, the uncoordinated application of national measures has been accused of creating an excessive administrative burden liable to unduly restrict the freedom to provide cross-border services and lead to fragmentation of the entire EU transport market. As a consequence, the EU legislator

204. Barnard, 'Free Movement and Labour Rights: Squaring the Circle?' (n 123) 8–9.

took action by elaborating a whole set of sector-specific rules codified in the newly adopted Directive (EU) 2020/1057 on posting drivers in the road transport sector. At the end of its implementation period on 2 February 2022, this piece of EU legislation will regulate the posting of workers in the road transport sector as a *lex specialis* which derogates from the general regulatory framework established by the Posting of Workers Directive, as amended by the new Directive (EU) 2018/957, and the Enforcement Directive. Until then, transnational activities of transport workers remain covered by the original version of the Posting of Workers Directive.

CHAPTER 5
Coordination of Social Security

5.1 INTRODUCTION

Whenever a worker is posted in order to provide a service in another Member State, the structural absence of Union law harmonising national labour and social systems means that he most likely finds himself in a more or less advantageous or disadvantageous situation as regards his social protection.[1] With a view to smoothing the inevitably emerging frictions, the regulatory action at European level developed in the form of coordination of different national systems.[2] This chapter is dedicated to the articulated coordination at EU level of national social security systems in relation to the posting phenomenon, therefore engaging with the relevant research sub-question: *How is the 'posting of workers' regulated under EU law?*

As regards the structure, this chapter is divided into three substantive sections dealing respectively with the current state of the art of the EU regulation of the posting phenomenon (section 5.2), the variety of emerging legal issues (section 5.3), and the future perspective of reform (section 5.4). More specifically, the investigation of the EU social security law framework currently into force starts with an explanation, in section 5.2, of the reasons underpinning the special treatment reserved to the posted workers. It then looks at the number of conditions posed by the European legislator in that respect, dealing first with the twenty-four-month time limit. Second, the prohibition of the replacement of cross-border workforce is carefully scrutinised in light of the Court of Justice case law, whose relevant outcomes are constructively criticised. Finally, the multiple facets of the requirement of maintaining a substantial connection with the

1. Rob Cornelissen and Guido Van Limberghen, 'Social Security for Mobile Workers and Labour Law', *Research Handbook on European Social Security Law* (Edward Elgar Publishing 2015) 371.
2. Herwig Verschueren, 'Cross-Border Workers in the European Internal Market: Trojan Horses for Member States' Labour and Social Security Law?' (2008) 24/2 International Journal of Comparative Labour Law and Industrial Relations 167, 185.

sending state are presented, underlining the different types of provisos envisaged respectively for posted employees or self-employed persons.

Moving forward, section 5.3 focuses on the practical legal issues emerging from the existing normative framework. *In primis*, it investigates the frictions arising as regards the mutual recognition between Member States of the documentation attesting the legislation applicable to posted workers (namely the Portable Documents A1). On that occasion, the wide power acknowledged by the recent jurisprudence of the CJEU to host Member State courts of disregarding social security certificates issued by the competent institutions of the sending state is questioned. Besides, the same section deals with the problematic identification of the applicable legal regime for employed persons working simultaneously or in alternation in two or more Member States, as well as with the existing mismatch between the social security law currently into force and the applicable taxation rules. The core of this chapter runs out with an investigation, in section 5.4, of the EU legislative process undertaken at the end of 2016 with a view to amending the EU legislative framework currently into force. In the concluding section 5.5, the main arguments developed in the previous sections are recapitulated and the important challenges arising in the sector are clearly put forward.

5.2 CURRENT EU SOCIAL SECURITY LAW FRAMEWORK

The regulation of the social security position of workers involved in transnational labour mobility has been traditionally addressed by ad hoc legal instruments. As evidence of this, the Posting of Workers Directive itself (even after the entry into effect of Directive (EU) 2018/957) exempts from its material scope all matters concerning social security benefits and contributions, and supplementary occupational retirement pension schemes.[3] More specifically, the coordination of national social security systems has represented one of the first fields of European regulatory activity, with the adoption in 1958 of two regulations on social security for migrant workers, Regulations 3/1958 and 4/1958.[4] The latter were then replaced in 1971 by Regulation (EEC) 1408/71 on the application of social security schemes to employed persons, to

3. *See*, respectively, Preamble Recital 21 and Article 3(c) of Directive 96/71/EC of the European Parliament and of the Council of 16 December 1996 concerning the posting of workers in the framework of the provision of services 1997 (OJ L 18/1).
4. Règlement (CEE) No 3 concernant la sécurité sociale des travailleurs migrants, Journal officiel des Communautés européennes, P 30 (English version not existent) 1958 (OJ P 30); Règlement (CEE) No 4 fixant les modalités d'application et complétant les dispositions du règlement n° 3 concernant la sécurité sociale des travailleurs migrants, Journal officiel des Communautés européennes, P 30 (English version not existent) 1958 (OJ P 30). For a precise reconstruction of the historical background of the social security coordination at European level, *see* Jaan Paju, *The European Union and Social Security Law* (First Edition, Hart Publishing 2017) 15–18; Anne-Pieter van der Mei et al., 'The External Dimension of EU Social Security Coordination' (2018) 20 European Journal of Social Security 81, 82; Emmanuel Comte, 'Promising More to Give Less: International Disputes between Core and Periphery around European Posted Labor, 1955–2018' (2019) Labor History 1, 2–5.

self-employed persons and to members of their families moving within the Community,[5] as implemented by Regulation (EEC) 574/72,[6] which governed the sector for more than thirty years. While leaving unaltered the individual Member States' competence in defining the form and contents of their own social schemes, the European legislator's intervention progressively extended and specified the rules on transnational coordination, especially with regard to cross-border situations.[7] Both Regulations No 1408/71 and No 574/72 were eventually repealed and replaced with effect from 1 May 2010 by Regulation (EC) 883/2004 on the coordination of social security systems,[8] supplemented by the so-called 'modernised coordination package' – namely, the Implementing Regulation (EC) 987/2009[9] and Regulation (EC) No 988/2009[10] – which set out the currently applicable legal framework for social security coordination within the EU.

The guiding principle in the field is that a person moving within the EU should be compulsorily affiliated to the social security system of one Member State only.[11] This is perfectly consistent with the aim of avoiding the imposition of multiple social security

5. Regulation (EEC) No 1408/71 of the Council of 14 June 1971 on the application of social security schemes to employed persons and their families moving within the Community 1971 (OJ L 149/2). For the record, the original version of Regulation (EEC) 1408/71 included the posting of employed workers only. Special rules for self-employed persons have been introduced by the Council Regulation (EEC) No 1390/81 of 12 May 1981 extending to self-employed persons and members of their families Regulation (EEC) No 1408/71 on the application of social security schemes to employed persons and their families moving within the Community 1981 (OJ L 143/1). Regulation (EEC) No 1408/71 was lastly amended by Regulation (EC) No 1386/2001 of the European Parliament and of the Council of 5 June 2001 amending Council Regulations (EEC) No 1408/71 on the application of social security schemes to employed persons, to self-employed persons and to members of their families moving within the Community and (EEC) No 574/72 laying down the procedure for implementing Regulation (EEC) No 1408/71, 2001 (OJ L 187/1).
6. Regulation (EEC) No 574/72 of the Council of 21 March 1972 fixing the procedure for implementing Regulation (EEC) No 1408/71 on the application of social security schemes to employed persons and their families moving within the Community 1972 (OJ L 74).
7. Jan Cremers, 'EU Economic Freedoms and Social Dumping' in Magdalena Bernaciak (ed.), *Market Expansion and Social Dumping in Europe* (Routledge 2015) 175; Jan Cremers, 'Economic Freedoms and Labour Standards in the European Union' (2016) 22(2) Transfer: European Review of Labour and Research 149, 151.
8. Regulation (EC) No 883/2004 of the European Parliament and of the Council of 29 April 2004 on the coordination of social security systems 2004 (OJ L 166/1).
9. Regulation (EC) No 987/2009 of the European Parliament and of the Council of 16 September 2009 laying down the procedure for implementing Regulation (EC) No 883/2004 on the coordination of social security systems 2009 (OJ L 284/1) (hereinafter also referred to as the 'Implementing Regulation').
10. Regulation (EC) No 988/2009 of the European Parliament and of the Council of 16 September 2009 amending Regulation (EC) No 883/2004 on the coordination of social security systems, and determining the content of its Annexes 2009 (OJ L 284/43).
11. Article 13 of Regulation (EEC) No 1408/71 of the Council of 14 June 1971 on the application of social security schemes to employed persons and their families moving within the Community (n 5). Subsequently transposed into Article 11 of Regulation (EC) No 883/2004 of the European Parliament and of the Council of 29 April 2004 on the coordination of social security systems (n 8). *See* European Commission, 'Practical Guide on the Applicable Legislation in the European Union (EU), the European Economic Area (EEA) and in Switzerland' (Social Europe, European Commission, Employment, Social Affairs and Equal Opportunities 2013) 7. Notably, the disposition at stake is, at the same time, exclusive and binding in nature.

obligations for the same worker operating in a different country from his home state.[12] Notably, the EU coordination rules are inspired by the principle of equal treatment, which entails the same obligations and benefits for any person exercising his freedom of movement across Europe as the nationals of that state towards which he goes to work.[13] The regular scenario of employed or self-employed workers migrating under Article 45 or 49 TFEU respectively envisages, therefore, the general application of the *lex loci laboris*.[14] This means that, regardless of their country of residence or citizenship, those workers have to be insured in the Member State where they work.[15]

Nevertheless, a specific exception, already formulated by the 1971 Regulation, concerns the posting of employed and self-employed persons, which remain insured under the social security system of their country of origin.[16] As clearly explained by the

12. Paul Schoukens and Danny Pieters, 'The Rules within Regulation 883/2004 for Determining the Applicable Legislation' (2009) 11 European Journal of Social Security 81, 81–82; Philippa Watson, *EU Social and Employment Law* (Second Edition, Oxford University Press 2014) 289; Cremers, 'Economic Freedoms and Labour Standards in the European Union' (n 7) 151. On this point, *see Fitzwilliam Executive Search Ltd v Bestuur van het Landelijk instituut sociale verzekeringen* [2000] CJEU Case C-202/97, ECLI:EU:C:2000:75 [20]; *Josef Plum v Allgemeine Ortskrankenkasse Rheinland, Regionaldirektion Köln* [2000] ECJ Case C-404/98, ECLI: EU:C:2000:607 [18]; *Altun* [2018] CJEU Case C-359/16, ECLI:EU:C:2018:63 [29–30].
13. Article 3(1) of Regulation (EEC) No 1408/71 of the Council of 14 June 1971 on the application of social security schemes to employed persons and their families moving within the Community (n 5). Subsequently transposed in Article 4 of Regulation (EC) No 883/2004 of the European Parliament and of the Council of 29 April 2004 on the coordination of social security systems (n 8). In this sense, *see Commission of the European Communities v Federal Republic of Germany* [2001] ECJ Case C-68/99, ECLI:EU:C:2001:137 [22–23]; *José Allard v Institut national d'assurances sociales pour travailleurs indépendants (INASTI)* [2005] ECJ Case C-249/04, ECLI:EU:C:2005:329 [31]; *L H Piatkowski v Inspecteur van de Belastingdienst grote ondernemingen Eindhoven* [2006] ECJ Case C-493/04, ECLI:EU:C:2006:167 [19–20]; *Maija T I Nikula* [2006] ECJ Case C-50/05, ECLI:EU:C:2006:493 [20]; *Philippe Derouin v Union pour le recouvrement des cotisations de sécurité sociale et d'allocations familiales de Paris – Région parisienne (Urssaf de Paris – Région parisienne)* [2008] CJEU Case C-103/06, ECLI:EU:C:2008:185 [20]. *See* Cornelissen and Van Limberghen (n 1) 356; Paju (n 4) 29.
14. Article 11(3)(a) of Regulation (EC) No 883/2004 of the European Parliament and of the Council of 29 April 2004 on the coordination of social security systems (n 8).
15. Verschueren (n 2) 186–187; Stein Evju and Tonia Novitz, 'The Evolving Regulation: Dynamics and Consequences' (2012) 33 FORMULA Working Paper, University of Oslo, Department of Private Law 6; Frans Pennings, 'Principles of EU Coordination of Social Security' in Frans Pennings and Gijsbert Vonk (eds), *Research Handbook on European Social Security Law* (Edward Elgar Publishing 2015) 331; Cornelissen and Van Limberghen (n 1) 356; Paju (n 4) 31; Eckhard Voss et al., 'Posting of Workers Directive: Current Situation and Challenges' (European Parliament, EMPL Committee 2016) IP/A/EMPL/2016-07, 25.
16. Article 14(1)(a)(i) of Regulation (EEC) No 1408/71 of the Council of 14 June 1971 on the application of social security schemes to employed persons and their families moving within the Community (n 5). Subsequently transposed in Article 12 of Regulation (EC) No 883/2004 of the European Parliament and of the Council of 29 April 2004 on the coordination of social security systems (n 8). On the exceptional nature of the rule at issue, *see Manpower v Caisse primaire d'assurance maladie de Strasbourg* [1970] ECJ Case C-35/70, ECLI:EU:C:1970:120 [10]; *Fitzwilliam Executive Search Ltd v Bestuur van het Landelijk instituut sociale verzekeringen* (n 12) para. 30; *Josef Plum v Allgemeine Ortskrankenkasse Rheinland, Regionaldirektion Köln* (n 12) para. 14. *See* Vassilis Hatzopoulos and Thien Uyen Do, 'The Case Law of the ECJ Concerning the Free Provision of Services: 2000 - 2005' (2006) 43 Common Market Law Review 923, 976–977; Verschueren (n 2) 187–188; Schoukens and Pieters (n 12) 82; Kristina Maslauskaite, 'Posted Workers in the EU: State of Play and Regulatory Evolution' (2014) Policy Paper, Notre Europe Jaques Delors Institute 20, 10; Dagmar Schiek et al., 'EU Social and Labour Rights and EU

Court of Justice, the motivation behind such a derogation from the general rule lies in the purpose of 'encouraging economic interpenetration' while minimising the administrative burden for the cross-border workers and undertakings resulting from the application of several social security schemes over short time-periods, which would otherwise jeopardize the latter's freedom to provide services.[17]

From the viewpoint of the employers, the possibility of continuing to pay social contributions in their country of establishment is more than attractive, given the avoidance of gaps in their individual insurance records, extra costs and administrative complications deriving from the switch of the applicable national regime. In turn, the benefit for the posted workers of remaining affiliated to their home country's social security system stems from the fact that they can escape the complications of a temporary change of legislation, or even of multiple short-term affiliations to different social security schemes, which would only partially be counterbalanced by the acquisition of a few rights and advantages under the host state's rules. In some instances, they might even incur a loss of entitlements to specific unemployment or contributory benefits.[18] Furthermore, the avoidance of changing social security scheme would prevent the simultaneous application of more than one national regime or the eventuality of a person left without social security cover.[19]

Internal Market Law' (European Parliament, EMPL Committee 2015) IP/A/EMPL/ST/2014-02, 98; Pennings (n 15) 333; Frederic De Wispelaere and Jozef Pacolet, 'Coordination of Social Security Systems at a Glance: 2016 Statistical Report' (KU Leuven Research Institute for Work and Society (HIVA) 2016) European Commission, Directorate-General for Employment, Social Affairs and Inclusion Directorate D – Labour Mobility Unit D/2 – Social security coordination 16; Frederic De Wispelaere and Jozef Pacolet, 'Posting of Workers: Report on A1 Portable Documents Issued in 2016' (KU Leuven Research Institute for Work and Society (HIVA) 2017) European Commission, Directorate-General for Employment, Social Affairs and Inclusion 11; Frederic De Wispelaere, Lynn De Smedt and Jozef Pacolet, 'Coordination of Social Security Systems at a Glance: 2018 Statistical Report' (KU Leuven Research Institute for Work and Society (HIVA) 2018) European Commission, Directorate-General for Employment, Social Affairs and Inclusion Unit D/2 12. Importantly, though, it should be made clear that the country in which a posted person is socially insured does not necessarily correspond to the one where his home is or that of his nationality. Danny Pieters, 'Posting of Workers: Disease or a Symptom?' (Keynote Speech at the V European Labour Mobility Congress (ELMC), Posting of workers: opportunity for the weaker or a threat for the stronger?, Krakow (Poland), 20 November 2017) <https://www.elmc.eu/wp-content/uploads/2018/01/speech-DANNY-PIETERS_VELMC.pdf> (accessed 14 June 2018).

17. *Manpower v Caisse primaire d'assurance maladie de Strasbourg* (n 16) paras 11–12; *Fitzwilliam Executive Search Ltd v Bestuur van het Landelijk instituut sociale verzekeringen* (n 12) paras 28–30; *Josef Plum v Allgemeine Ortskrankenkasse Rheinland, Regionaldirektion Köln* (n 12) para. 19; *'Walltopia' AD v Direktor na Teritorialna direktsia na Natsionalnata agentsia za prihodite – Veliko Tarnovo* [2018] CJEU Case C-451/17, ECLI:EU:C:2018:861 [38–39]; *Altun* (n 12) paras 31–33. On this point *see* Verschueren (n 2) 188; Schoukens and Pieters (n 12) 106–107; European Commission, 'Practical Guide on The Applicable Legislation in the European Union (EU), the European Economic Area (EEA) and in Switzerland' (n 11) 7; Watson (n 12) 289; Mijke Houwerzijl, 'Regime Shopping across (Blurring) Boundaries' in Stein Evju (ed.), *Regulating Transnational Labour in Europe: The Quandaries of Multilevel Governance* (Department of Private Law 2014) 28; Cornelissen and Van Limberghen (n 1) 356–357; Voss et al. (n 15) 26.
18. This is the case, for example, of Sweden and Ireland. Schiek et al. (n 16) 98.
19. *European Commission v United Kingdom of Great Britain and Northern Ireland* [2016] CJEU Case C-308/14, ECLI:EU:C:2016:436 [64]; *Secretary of State for Work and Pensions v Tolley* [2017] CJEU Case C-430/15, ECLI:EU:C:2017:74 [58]; *'Walltopia' AD v Direktor na Teritorialna*

In light of the variety of national welfare systems across the Union, the derogatory treatment reserved to the posted workers appears indeed necessary in order to ensure the continuity and effectiveness of the workers' rights in their home countries.[20] For all of these reasons, such a rationale was resolutely confirmed by the Court's decision in *Seco*, whereby the imposition by the Grand Duchy of Luxembourg of social security contributions on foreign service providers was considered as indirectly discriminatory for not benefitting de facto the workers involved.[21] Nonetheless, the enjoyment of the aforementioned special treatment for posting activities is subordinated to the fulfilment of five conditions, on pain of the application *ex tunc* of the *lex loci laboris*.[22] Those conditions are investigated further in the following three subsections, concerning the twenty-four-month time limit, the non-replacement condition, and the need to preserve a substantial connection with the home state.

5.2.1 Twenty-Four-Month Time Limit

The first condition laid down in Article 12 of Regulation (EC) 883/2004 requires that the anticipated duration of the transnational service provision does not exceed the limited time period of twenty-four months.[23] Accordingly, whenever the anticipated duration is longer, the special posting rule is not applicable. In the event of unforeseeable overrun of the twenty-four-month time limit, the worker falls under the host state's social security legislation only after the expiration of that period.[24] The proviso at issue, which is applied to both employed and self-employed persons, is the result of the extension in 2004 of the one-year maximum posting period previously envisaged by Article 14(1)(a) of Regulation (EEC) 1408/71. The latter piece of secondary EU legislation contemplated also the possibility – which is no more ensured by the Basic

direktsia na Natsionalnata agentsia za prihodite – Veliko Tarnovo (n 17) para. 41; *SF v Inspecteur van de Belastingdienst* [2019] CJEU Case C-631/17, ECLI:EU:C:2019:381 [33].

20. Maslauskaite (n 16) 11.
21. *Société anonyme de droit français Seco et Société anonyme de droit français Desquenne & Giral v Etablissement d'assurance contre la vieillesse et l'invalidité* [1982] ECJ Joined Cases C-62/81 and C-63/81, ECLI:EU:C:1982:34 [12]. Watson (n 12) 281–282; Houwerzijl (n 17) 29.
22. This is in light of the retroactive effect of the social security rules, which follow the 'day one' principle.
23. Schoukens and Pieters (n 12) 95; Evju and Novitz (n 15) 6; Watson (n 12) 289; Cremers, 'Economic Freedoms and Labour Standards in the European Union' (n 7) 151; Frans Pennings, 'Mismatches between Tax and Social Security in Cross Border Situations' (Workshop on 'Tax and Social Security – EU Perspective', University of Copenhagen, Faculty of Law, 20 September 2017); Frederic De Wispelaere and Jozef Pacolet, 'Coordination of Social Security Systems at a Glance: 2017 Statistical Report' (KU Leuven Research Institute for Work and Society (HIVA) 2017) European Commission, Directorate-General for Employment, Social Affairs and Inclusion Directorate D – Labour Mobility Unit D/2 – Social security coordination 16.
24. Cornelissen and Van Limberghen (n 1) 357. However, there certainly remain some doubts as to the applicable legal regime in the event the real duration of the posting is shorter than the anticipated one. More concretely, this is the case of a posting of anticipated duration of thirty months (falling under the *lex loci laboris*) that ends up being of solely eighteen months (whereby, instead, home state law should apply). Bernhard Spiegel, 'A Commentary on the Results of the Revised Rules on Social Security Coordination: Why Did This Project Fail at the First Attempt?' (60 Years Social Security Coordination from a Workers' Perspective, Leuven, Belgium, 16 May 2019).

Regulation – to request the competent authority in the host Member State, in the event of unforeseeable circumstances, to grant a prolongation of the term by up to further twelve months.[25]

The current rule of twenty-four months as the maximum duration of posting is, nonetheless, subject to possible derogations on the grounds of Article 16(1) of the Basic Regulation. This means that, as long as the competent authorities of two or more Member States manage to reach a specific agreement, the posting period may be extended beyond the prescribed two-year term, up to a maximum of five years. The only condition that has to be respected for the conclusion of such kind of exceptions to the legislation governing posting activities requires that, besides their administrative convenience, the agreements are made primarily in the interest of the person(s) concerned.[26]

5.2.2 Non-replacement Condition

The second condition for derogation from *the lex loci laboris*, already introduced in 1971 as a means to prevent the rotation of personnel for the performance of the same activity,[27] is that the posted worker cannot be sent to replace another posted person who has previously completed his term of employment.[28] The practical definition of this non-replacement condition has been recently subject to a broad interpretation by the Court of Justice with the decision of 6 September 2018 in *Alpenrind*.[29] Because of

25. Article 14(1)(a)(i) of Regulation (EEC) No 1408/71 of the Council of 14 June 1971 on the application of social security schemes to employed persons and their families moving within the Community (n 5). Verschueren (n 2) 188; Schoukens and Pieters (n 12) 83.
26. Arrangements according to Article 16(1) of Regulation 883/2004 might also be used for the retroactive correction of unwanted situations or mistakes in the application the appropriate national regime. In this sense, *see Raad van Arbeid v PB Brusse* [1984] ECJ Case C-101/83, ECLI:EU:C:1984:187. Furthermore, specific arrangements are also made in relation to special categories, such as CEOs and musicians, or to particular cross-border situations, such as the ones existing between Sweden and Denmark, between the Czech Republic and Slovakia, between Cyprus and Greece, and even between the Netherlands, Belgium, France, Luxembourg and Germany with regard to shipping on the river Rhine. Schoukens and Pieters (n 12) 87; European Commission, 'Practical Guide on The Applicable Legislation in the European Union (EU), the European Economic Area (EEA) and in Switzerland' (n 11) 16–17; Cornelissen and Van Limberghen (n 1) 359; Voss et al. (n 15) 26; Aukje A.H. van Hoek, 'Re-Embedding the Transnational Employment Relationship: A Tale about the Limitations of (EU) Law?' (2018) 55 Common Market Law Review 449, 458.
27. Article 14(1)(a)(ii) of Regulation (EEC) No 1408/71 of the Council of 14 June 1971 on the application of social security schemes to employed persons and their families moving within the Community (n 5). Verschueren (n 2) 188.
28. Article 12(1) of Regulation (EC) No 883/2004 of the European Parliament and of the Council of 29 April 2004 on the coordination of social security systems (n 8). Verschueren (n 2) 188; Schoukens and Pieters (n 12) 83. Notably, the non-replacement condition only refers to posted employees and not to self-employed persons.
29. *Alpenrind and Others* [2018] CJEU Case C-527/16, ECLI:EU:C:2018:669. For a punctual analysis of the issue, *see* Marcin Kiełbasa, 'Advocate General Øe against a Broad Interpretation of the Non-Replacement Condition' (*Labour Mobility Initiative*, 23 April 2018) <https://www.mobilelabour.eu/12508/advocate-general-oe-against-a-broad-interpretation-of-the-non-replacement-condition-pursuant-to-article-121-of-regulation-883-2004/> (accessed 30 August 2018).

its highly controversial outcome, the above-mentioned ruling deserves further examination. In particular, the case at issue concerned the consecutive posting of workers by two Hungarian companies, *Martin-Meat* and *Martimpex-Meat*, which had been contracted one after another for the provision of services in a slaughterhouse in Salzburg, operated by the Austrian company *Alpenrind*. The Court's decision imposed, *inter alia*, that all employees posted by the second undertaking had to be covered by the Austrian social security scheme, given that they de facto 'replaced' workers posted by the first company.[30] In other terms, in the view of the Court, an employee shall be considered as being sent by his employer in the framework of the transnational provision of services, in order to replace another worker which has performed his same identical work in the host State, even in case the worker he is replacing has been previously posted by another employer, and even if his employer is not even aware of the earlier posting by another employer.[31]

Interestingly, the motivations leading to such a questionable result are paradoxical, to say the least. The Court requires a strict interpretation of Article 12(1) of Regulation 883/2004 which, following the line of reasoning of the judges of the First Chamber, has to be achieved through a broad interpretation of the non-replacement condition. In other words, the restrictive interpretation of Article 12(1) of the Basic Regulation consists in considering as 'sent to replace another person' any posted worker who has been sent by any employer from any Member State, provided that another posted worker has been previously employed for the performance of the same activity.[32] In the eyes of the Court of Justice, such an approach is justified by the nature of the disposition at issue, which has been conceived as a derogation from the general rule implying that employed persons operating in another Member State must pay their social security contribution in the latter country.[33]

Inter alia, it is noteworthy that the aforementioned decision was delivered in direct contrast with the opinion of Advocate General Øe, who suggested instead a teleological interpretation of Article 12(1) of Regulation 883/2004. He proposed to look at the purpose for which that provision was originally conceived, namely the prevention of the abusive practice taken up by the same employer rotating its posted staff with the aim of circumventing the rules relating to the duration of the posting.[34] Hence, the

30. *Alpenrind and Others* (n 29) para. 99.
31. *Ibid.* 100.
32. *Ibid.* 92–95.
33. *Ibid.* 95.
34. *Alpenrind and Others, Opinion of Advocate General Saugmandsgaard Øe delivered on 31 January 2018* [2018] CJEU Case C-527/16, ECLI:EU:C:2018:52 [87–90]. In concrete terms, such an undue advantage may be achieved through the creation, by a certain undertaking, of a site in a different Member State with lower social security costs. The latter undertaking would then operate through a perpetual replacement of posted workers remaining under the legislation of their country of origin, which requires the payment of lower social contributions in comparison to those required in the Member State where the cross-border workers are temporarily employed. In this regard, *see* the opinion of Advocate General de Lamothe in *Manpower*, who emphasises how such kinds of practices have already been identified half a century ago in the building and timber industries in France, and also in the Netherlands and Germany. *Manpower v Caisse primaire d'assurance maladie de Strasbourg, Opinion of Advocate General Dutheillet De Lamothe delivered on 8 December 1970* [1970] ECJ Case C-35/70, EU:C:1970:104, 1259 II(c).

Advocate General interpreted the concept of a posted person 'sent to replace another person' exclusively as an occurrence related to the same employer.[35] It appears indeed more likely that the intention of a second (and of a third) employer is not to replace a worker posted by the first employer. Such a purpose may be found only in cases of abuse.[36] Moreover, successive employers should not even be required to be aware of any previous work carried out by workers posted by other possible employers.[37] As argued by the Danish amicus curiae, 'the non-replacement condition must be considered solely from the viewpoint of the employer that posts the worker'.[38] It follows that persons posted in accordance with Article 12(1) and carrying out the same activity that was previously performed by other workers posted by a different employer, should remain subject to the social security legislation of their country of origin. At the same time, the freedom to stipulate successive and separate contracts with different employers, concerning the provision of the same type of services by posted workers, should still be granted to the recipient of the service in the host Member State.[39]

Conversely, the practical result of the broader interpretation of the 'non-replacement condition' given by the Court of Justice in *Alpenrind* is liable to jeopardize the principle of legal certainty. Successive postings by different employers would not be entitled to the right of remaining covered by the latter's home country legislation on social security, solely because another undertaking had already profited from the same advantage. As strongly emphasised by Advocate General Øe, such an unjustified occurrence would eventually result in the 'first come, first served' principle, which is far from being included in the wording of the Basic Regulation on social security coordination.[40] In this sense, a contrast with the overall purpose of Article 12(1), namely the promotion of the free movement of workers and of economic interpenetration while reducing administrative burdens for foreign service providers, can also be identified in the interpretation of the Court.[41] An additional limitation to the freedom to provide services may be recognised in the uncertainty the second employer may find itself at the time it needs to find out whether or not the same activity has been previously carried out by employees posted by another undertaking, and thus if the posting would come within the scope of Article 12(1) of Regulation 883/2004.[42]

Moving beyond the mere criticism of the approach taken by the judges in Luxembourg, a reading of the 'non-replacement condition' laid down in Article 12(1) in light of the new dispositions introduced by the recently adopted Directive (EU)

35. *Alpenrind and Others, Opinion of Advocate General Saugmandsgaard Øe delivered on 31 January 2018* (n 34) paras 90–93. On this point, *see also* Kiełbasa, 'Advocate General Øe against a Broad Interpretation of the Non-Replacement Condition' (n 29).
36. *Alpenrind and Others, Opinion of Advocate General Saugmandsgaard Øe delivered on 31 January 2018* (n 34) paras 94–95.
37. *Ibid.* 99.
38. *Ibid.* 95.
39. *Ibid.* 96.
40. *Ibid.* 97.
41. *Ibid.* 100.
42. *Ibid.* 101.

2018/957[43] on posting of workers is proposed. In particular, as discussed below in Chapter 8, Directive (EU) 2018/957 promotes a remedy to the issue of replacement of a posted worker by another posted worker 'performing the same task at the same place' only in case such a rotation of personnel is arranged by the same undertaking with the aim of circumventing the applicable rules. It also requires to examine the whole variety of circumstances occurring in the event of replacement, namely the nature of the service provided, the type of work carried out, and its actual location.[44] Accordingly, also taking into account the new labour dispositions on posting introduced by Directive (EU) 2018/957, in *Alpenrind* the CJEU could have interpreted the non-replacement condition in a stricter sense. Thence, it could have limited the assessment of the respect of the social security rules to the check for possible artificial posting constructions aimed at circumventing the non-replacement condition laid down in Article 12(1) of Regulation 883/2004, by focusing on the personal and organizational links between the recipient of the service in Austria and the Hungarian employers.

5.2.3 Substantial Connection with the Home State

Carrying on with the analysis of the conditions for continuing to be insured under the home country social security law, it should be noted that Article 12 of the Basic Regulation explicitly requires both the employed and the self-employed posted persons to be affiliated to the social security scheme of the sending Member State, already before their mobility abroad.[45] The potential wide impact of this third proviso has been, nevertheless, substantially mitigated by the intervention of the Court of Justice which, in a series of judgments, acknowledged the possibility for a company to send abroad a worker who has just been hired for that purpose. It prohibited, therefore, the imposition by national law of any minimum period of worker's affiliation to the social security system of a certain country before the posting to another Member State.[46] A few years later, the case law of the Court was codified in Article 14(1) of Regulation (EC) No 987/2009, which set the aforementioned rule down in black and white.[47] In

43. Directive (EU) 2018/957 of the European Parliament and of the Council of 28 June 2018 amending Directive 96/71/EC concerning the posting of workers in the framework of the provision of services 2018 (OJ L 173/16).
44. *Ibid.* Preamble Recital 11 and Article 1(b).
45. More specifically, in the wording of the Regulation, the posted workers 'shall continue to be subject to the legislation of the first Member State'. Article 12(1) and (2) of Regulation (EC) No 883/2004 of the European Parliament and of the Council of 29 April 2004 on the coordination of social security systems (n 8). 'Social Security Cover Abroad' (*Your Europe – Citizens*) < https://europa.eu/youreurope/citizens/work/unemployment-and-benefits/country-coverage/index_en.htm > (accessed 8 April 2019).
46. *Manpower v Caisse primaire d'assurance maladie de Strasbourg* (n 16); *Fitzwilliam Executive Search Ltd v Bestuur van het Landelijk instituut sociale verzekeringen* (n 12); *Josef Plum v Allgemeine Ortskrankenkasse Rheinland, Regionaldirektion Köln* (n 12). On this point, *see* Schoukens and Pieters (n 12) 83–84.
47. 'For the purposes of the application of Article 12(1) of the basic Regulation, a "person who pursues an activity as an employed person in a Member State on behalf of an employer which normally carries out its activities there and who is posted by that employer to another Member State" shall include a person who is recruited with a view to being posted to another Member

practice, however, as further indicated by the Decision A2 of the Administrative Commission of 12 June 2009, the workers are still required to be already subject for at least one month to the legislation of their employer's home state.[48]

The fourth requirement set out by the European rules on the matter pertains to the direct employment relationship that must continue to persist between the sending employer and the posted employee during the whole duration of the assignment abroad.[49] Following the indications of the Court of Justice, the permanence of such a necessary link has to be ascertained by the competent national authorities and can be deduced by taking into account a number of elements, from the general authority in the employment relationship, to the payment of the salary, the competence for dismissal, the power of imposing disciplinary measures, or the responsibility for any debts incurred.[50] All these specific requirements have been subsequently transposed into the

State, provided that, immediately before the start of his employment, the person concerned is already subject to the legislation of the Member State in which his employer is established.' Article 14(1) of Regulation (EC) No 987/2009 of the European Parliament and of the Council of 16 September 2009 laying down the procedure for implementing Regulation (EC) No 883/2004 on the coordination of social security systems (n 9). Interestingly, as further specified by the CJEU in *Walltopia*, even if the posted employee is not insured in the sending state immediately before the start of his employment, it is sufficient for him to have his residence in the latter country. In the words of the Court: 'an employee recruited with a view to being posted to another Member State must be regarded as having been "just before the start of his employment … already subject to the legislation of the Member State in which his employer is established", within the meaning of Article 14(1) of Regulation No 987/2009, even if that employee was not an insured person under the legislation of that Member State immediately before the start of his employment, if, at that time, that employee had his residence in that Member State, which is for the referring court to ascertain.' *'Walltopia' AD v Direktor na Teritorialna direktsia na Natsionalnata agentsia za prihodite – Veliko Tarnovo* (n 17).

48. After a case-by-case evaluation, a shorter period may nevertheless be granted. Point 1 of the Administrative Commission on Social Security for Migrant Workers (European Commission), Decision No A2 of 12 June 2009 concerning the interpretation of Article 12 of Regulation (EC) No 883/2004 of the European Parliament and of the Council on the legislation applicable to posted workers and self-employed workers temporarily working outside the competent State (Text of relevance to the EEA and to the EC/Switzerland Agreement) 2010 (OJ C 106/5). *See* ILO DWT and Country Office for Central and Eastern Europe, 'Coordination of Social Security Systems in the European Union: An Explanatory Report on EC Regulation No. 883/2004 and Its Implementing Regulation No. 987/2009' (ILO 2010) 11 <http://www.ilo.org/public/libdoc/ilo/2010/461829_engl.pdf> (accessed 18 March 2019); European Commission, 'Practical Guide on Posting' (2019) 14–15.
49. *Fitzwilliam Executive Search Ltd v Bestuur van het Landelijk instituut sociale verzekeringen* (n 12) para. 24; *Altun* (n 12) para. 34. This requirement, originally elaborated by the Court of Justice case law, was subsequently transposed in the Administrative Commission of the European Communities on social security for migrant workers, Decision No 181 (2001/891/EC) of 13 December 2000 concerning the interpretation of Articles 14(1), 14a(1) and 14b(1) and (2) of Council Regulation (EEC) No 1408/71 on the legislation applicable to posted workers and self-employed workers temporarily working outside the competent State 2001 (OJ L 329/73) para. 3(b)(i). Schoukens and Pieters (n 12) 82; Watson (n 12) 290; Cornelissen and Van Limberghen (n 1) 357–358.
50. *Bestuur der Sociale Verzekeringsbank v J H van der Vecht* [1967] ECJ Case C-19/67, ECR 345 [354]; *Manpower v Caisse primaire d'assurance maladie de Strasbourg* (n 16) paras 18–19. European Commission, 'Practical Guide on the Applicable Legislation in the European Union (EU), the European Economic Area (EEA) and in Switzerland' (n 11) 9–11.

aforementioned 2009 Decision A2 of the Administrative Commission.[51] As far as the posting of self-employed persons is concerned, in the absence of any employment relationship, the correspondent requirement implies, instead, the maintenance of an infrastructural bond with their country of origin, testified by the use of offices, the payment of taxes and social security contributions, the retention of a work permit and a VAT number, or of the registration with chambers of commerce and professional organisations.[52]

Finally, the fifth and last condition refers to the requirement for the workers concerned to be attached to a posting undertaking that 'normally carries out its activities' in the Member State from which it sends out personnel.[53] Such an additional requirement was not originally envisaged by the 1971 Regulation, but it was developed by the Court with a view to contrasting the creation of the so-called 'letterbox companies',[54] and it was subsequently codified in Regulation 883/2004. More specifically, an undertaking is considered as normally performing its activity in the Member State of establishment when it 'habitually carries out significant activities' in the

51. According to this Decision, 'In order to establish whether such a direct relationship continues to exist, assuming therefore that the worker continues to be under the authority of the employer which posted him, a number of elements have to be taken into account, including responsibility for recruitment, employment contract, remuneration (without prejudice to possible agreements between the employer in the sending State and the undertaking in the State of employment on the payment to the workers), dismissal, and the authority to determine the nature of the work.' Point 1 of the Administrative Commission on Social Security for Migrant Workers (European Commission) Decision No A2 of 12 June 2009 concerning the interpretation of Article 12 of Regulation (EC) No 883/2004 of the European Parliament and of the Council on the legislation applicable to posted workers and self-employed workers temporarily working outside the competent State (Text of relevance to the EEA and to the EC/Switzerland Agreement) (n 48). ILO DWT and Country Office for Central and Eastern Europe (n 48) 11.
52. *Barry Banks and Others v Theatre royal de la Monnaie* [2000] ECJ Case C-178/97, ECLI: EU:C:2000:169 [25–26]. This list of requirements has been lately codified into Article 14(3) of Regulation (EC) No 987/2009 of the European Parliament and of the Council of 16 September 2009 laying down the procedure for implementing Regulation (EC) No 883/2004 on the coordination of social security systems (n 9). A further specification in this sense, is provided by Point 2 of the Administrative Commission on Social Security for Migrant Workers (European Commission) Decision No A2 of 12 June 2009 concerning the interpretation of Article 12 of Regulation (EC) No 883/2004 of the European Parliament and of the Council on the legislation applicable to posted workers and self-employed workers temporarily working outside the competent State (Text of relevance to the EEA and to the EC/Switzerland Agreement) (n 48). Schoukens and Pieters (n 12) 86–87; European Commission, 'Practical Guide on the Applicable Legislation in the European Union (EU), the European Economic Area (EEA) and in Switzerland' (n 11) 14–15.
53. Article 12(1) of Regulation (EC) No 883/2004 of the European Parliament and of the Council of 29 April 2004 on the coordination of social security systems (n 8). It is worth noting that, unlike EU labour law, EU social security law does not require the worker to habitually carry out a working activity in his home state, but rather that he is attached to an employer which normally operates in its country of establishment. Cornelissen and Van Limberghen (n 1) 357.
54. *Fitzwilliam Executive Search Ltd v Bestuur van het Landelijk instituut sociale verzekeringen* (n 12) para. 40; *Josef Plum v Allgemeine Ortskrankenkasse Rheinland, Regionaldirektion Köln* (n 12) para. 21. On this point, *see* Verschueren (n 2) 189–190; Schoukens and Pieters (n 12) 96–97; Cornelissen and Van Limberghen (n 1) 358. For an investigation of the abusive fictitious constructions known as 'letterbox companies', *see infra* Chapter 7.

territory of that state.[55] In order to determine the effective habitual performance of substantial economic activities, other than mere internal management, in the country of establishment, the European judiciary suggested the competent authorities to take into account all the distinguishing features of the activities carried out by the undertaking under observation.[56] Accordingly, the relevant factors to be considered shall include (non-exhaustively) the place where the undertaking has its seat and administration, the number of administrative staff employed in the home state and in the state of destination, the places where the workers are recruited and where the majority of the contracts with clients are concluded, the law applicable to the employment contracts with, respectively, the employees and the clients, and the turnover with reference to a specific period of posting.[57]

In addition, it should be noted that this last condition takes once more a rather different form in respect of self-employed persons. In this regard, the infrastructure criterion, requiring the maintenance of a genuine business base in the country of origin, whose existence has to be proven under request of the competent national authorities,[58] is combined with the further requirement for the self-employed worker to have already pursued a similar working activity in his home country before his mobility to

55. This definition has been provided by the Administrative Commission of the European Communities on social security for migrant workers Decision No 181 (2001/891/EC) of 13 December 2000 concerning the interpretation of Articles 14(1), 14a(1) and 14b(1) and (2) of Council Regulation (EEC) No 1408/71 on the legislation applicable to posted workers and self-employed workers temporarily working outside the competent State (n 49) para. 3(b)(ii). Furthermore, the requirement for the posting employer to normally carry out its activities in its Member State of origin has been further specified in the sense that: 'The possibility of posting should [...] be confined solely to undertakings normally carrying on their business in the territory of the Member State whose legislation remains applicable to the posted worker; assuming therefore that the above provisions apply only to undertakings which ordinarily perform substantial activities in the territory of the Member State in which they are established.' Preamble Recital 5 of the Administrative Commission on Social Security for Migrant Workers (European Commission) Decision No A2 of 12 June 2009 concerning the interpretation of Article 12 of Regulation (EC) No 883/2004 of the European Parliament and of the Council on the legislation applicable to posted workers and self-employed workers temporarily working outside the competent State (Text of relevance to the EEA and to the EC/Switzerland Agreement) (n 48).
56. Also on this occasion, the criterion elaborated by the Court has been codified in Article 14(2) of Regulation (EC) No 987/2009 of the European Parliament and of the Council of 16 September 2009 laying down the procedure for implementing Regulation (EC) No 883/2004 on the coordination of social security systems (n 9). In particular, 'For the purposes of the application of Article 12(1) of the basic Regulation, the words "which normally carries out its activities there" shall refer to an employer that ordinarily performs substantial activities, other than purely internal management activities, in the territory of the Member State in which it is established, taking account of all criteria characterising the activities carried out by the undertaking in question. The relevant criteria must be suited to the specific characteristics of each employer and the real nature of the activities carried out.'
57. *Fitzwilliam Executive Search Ltd v Bestuur van het Landelijk instituut sociale verzekeringen* (n 12) paras 42–43. Schoukens and Pieters (n 12) 84–85; European Commission, 'Practical Guide on the Applicable Legislation in the European Union (EU), the European Economic Area (EEA) and in Switzerland' (n 11) 8–9; Watson (n 12) 290; Frederic De Wispelaere and Jozef Pacolet, 'Posting of Workers as Stabilising Mechanism: An Enlarged Notion of Labour Mobility as a Prerequisite for an Optimal Currency Area' (KU Leuven Research Institute for Work and Society (HIVA) 2015) 13.
58. *Barry Banks and Others v Theatre royal de la Monnaie* (n 52) para. 25. Schoukens and Pieters (n 12) 87.

another state.[59] In order to determine whether the working activity pursued in another Member State is 'similar' to the activity already performed by the worker in his home state, the real nature of the working activity, and not its formal qualification given in the country of origin, has to be taken into account.[60] To that extent, the burden of the proof is on the self-employed person himself, who can, e.g., produce previous working contracts.[61]

5.3 EMERGING LEGAL ISSUES

The EU social security law framework presented above inevitably gives rise to a variety of practical legal problems. The latter assume an administrative nature when concerning the validity and mutual recognition of the documentation attesting the legislation applicable to posted workers. Further issues often occur when it comes to identifying the proper legal regime for employed persons working simultaneously or in alternation in two or more Member States, or due to the existing mismatch between the social security law currently into force and the applicable taxation rules. A more detailed overview of these issues is outlined below.

5.3.1 Validity of Portable Documents A1

The requirement for both employed and self-employed persons of keeping a substantial connection with their Member State of social security affiliation is evidently intended to prevent situations in which they are insured under the social security system of a country with which they have no authentic relation. This situation would result, indeed, in a loss of rights and benefits for the workers involved, as well as in a possible undue economic advantage for posting undertakings and self-employed persons. As further explained in the following Chapter 6, in case of an inspection by the authorities of the recipient state, evidence of the posted worker's continuous affiliation to his

59. Thus, for example, a self-employed bricklayer cannot post himself to perform activities as an electrician in another EU country. Article 12(1) of Regulation (EC) No 883/2004 of the European Parliament and of the Council of 29 April 2004 on the coordination of social security systems (n 8). Article 14(3) of Regulation (EC) No 987/2009 of the European Parliament and of the Council of 16 September 2009 laying down the procedure for implementing Regulation (EC) No 883/2004 on the coordination of social security systems (n 9). More specifically, the period of at least two months of previous performance of working activity in the country of origin is indicated by Point 2 of the Administrative Commission on Social Security for Migrant Workers (European Commission) Decision No A2 of 12 June 2009 concerning the interpretation of Article 12 of Regulation (EC) No 883/2004 of the European Parliament and of the Council on the legislation applicable to posted workers and self-employed workers temporarily working outside the competent State (Text of relevance to the EEA and to the EC/Switzerland Agreement) (n 48). On this point, *see* Schoukens and Pieters (n 12) 97; ILO DWT and Country Office for Central and Eastern Europe (n 48) 12.
60. Article 14(4) of Regulation (EC) No 987/2009 of the European Parliament and of the Council of 16 September 2009 laying down the procedure for implementing Regulation (EC) No 883/2004 on the coordination of social security systems (n 9). ILO DWT and Country Office for Central and Eastern Europe (n 48) 12.
61. European Commission, 'Practical Guide on the Applicable Legislation in the European Union (EU), the European Economic Area (EEA) and in Switzerland' (n 11) 15–16.

home social security system is given by the exhibition of the Portable Document A1 (former E101 certificate, hereinafter 'PD A1'). However, the acceptance of the validity of this document by the competent institutions in the receiving country, and thus its mutual recognition between Member States, is constantly at the heart of the debate.

Initially, the position of the Court of Justice was firmly anchored to the binding character of the certificates at issue on the host state's administrative and even judicial authorities, as long as they were not withdrawn or declared invalid by the issuing institution.[62] Such an approach was motivated on the basis of the respect of the principle of sincere cooperation between competent national institutions *ex* Article 4(3) TEU.[63] Consequently, whenever the competent institution in the receiving state questioned the validity of a foreign social security certificate, it had to refer its concern to the issuing institution, which had to operate an accurate re-examination of all factual grounds and, where appropriate, withdraw it.[64] As a last resort, in the event a Member State was still not convinced of the validity of a PD A1, it could start a so-called 'dialogue and conciliation procedure', as provided for in Decision A1 of the Administrative Commission for the Coordination of Social Security systems.[65]

Recently, however, the judges in Luxembourg with the decision of 6 February 2018 in *Altun*[66] took a radical change of approach on the matter. The case at issue concerned E101 and A1 certificates issued by the competent institution in Bulgaria for

62. In the wording of the Court, 'a court of the host Member State is not entitled to scrutinise the validity of an E 101 certificate as regards the certification of the matters on the basis of which such a certificate was issued, in particular the existence of a direct relationship between the undertaking which posted the worker and the posted worker himself.' *Rijksdienst voor Sociale Zekerheid v Herbosch Kiere NV* [2006] ECJ Case C-2/05, ECLI:EU:C:2006:69 [32]. Such an approach was subsequently confirmed in *A-Rosa Flussschiff GmbH v Union de recouvrement des cotisations de sécurité sociale et d'allocations familiales d'Alsace (Urssaf), venant aux droits de l'Urssaf du Bas-Rhin and Sozialversicherungsanstalt des Kantons Graubünden* [2017] CJEU Case C-620/15, ECLI:EU:C:2017:309 [43].
63. *Fitzwilliam Executive Search Ltd v Bestuur van het Landelijk instituut sociale verzekeringen* (n 12) paras 52–53; *Rijksdienst voor Sociale Zekerheid v Herbosch Kiere NV* (n 62) paras 23 and 30. Schoukens and Pieters (n 12) 85–86.
64. *Fitzwilliam Executive Search Ltd v Bestuur van het Landelijk instituut sociale verzekeringen* (n 12).
65. Administrative Commission for the Coordination of Social Security systems (European Commission), Decision No A1 of 12 June 2009 concerning the establishment of a dialogue and conciliation procedure concerning the validity of documents, the determination of the applicable legislation and the provision of benefits under Regulation (EC) No 883/2004 of the European Parliament and of the Council 2010 (OJ C 106/1) 4. *See Fitzwilliam Executive Search Ltd v Bestuur van het Landelijk instituut sociale verzekeringen* (n 12) para. 57; *Rijksdienst voor Sociale Zekerheid v Herbosch Kiere NV* (n 62) para. 28; *A-Rosa Flussschiff GmbH v Union de recouvrement des cotisations de sécurité sociale et d'allocations familiales d'Alsace (Urssaf), venant aux droits de l'Urssaf du Bas-Rhin and Sozialversicherungsanstalt des Kantons Graubünden* (n 62) para. 45; *Altun* (n 12) para. 44; *European Commission v Kingdom of Belgium* [2018] CJEU Case C-356/15, ECLI:EU:C:2018:555 [91]. On this point, *see also* Marianne Thyssen – EU Commissioner for Employment, 'Parliamentary Questions: Answer given by Ms Thyssen on Behalf of the Commission (Question Reference: E-004944/2017)' (21 September 2017) <http://www.europarl.europa.eu/doceo/document/E-8-2017-004944-ASW_EN.pdf> (accessed 27 March 2019); Yves Jorens, 'Intra-EU Posting: Looking for Solutions: A Herculean or a Sisyphean Task?' (60 Years Social Security Coordination from a Workers' Perspective, Leuven, Belgium, 16 May 2019).
66. *Altun* (n 12).

workers posted to Belgium by certain Bulgarian undertakings operating as subcontractors of the Belgian company *Absa NV*. Following a Belgian judicial investigation conducted in Bulgaria through letters rogatory, which discovered that no significant activity was actually carried out by those companies in their country of incorporation,[67] the Belgian Social Security Inspectorate sent to its Bulgarian counterpart a reasoned request for review or withdrawal of the E101 and A1 certificates. Notwithstanding that, the issuing institution refrained from taking that evidence into consideration and confirmed still the validity of the certificates. In the meanwhile, the parallel judicial proceeding in front of the Court of Appeal in Antwerp ended with the declaration of the fraudulent nature of those certificates.[68] The Court of Justice ruling, by overcoming the boundaries set by the unconditional respect of the principles of mutual recognition and sincere cooperation, acknowledged the power of a host Member State court to 'disregard' social security certificates issued by competent institutions of the sending state. More specifically, such a faculty was made conditional upon the encountering of a lack of cooperation from the sending state's authorities, and the finding out that those certificates were fraudulently obtained or relied on.[69]

As appears evident, the decision in *Altun*, conceived as a way of censoring unacceptable refusals of administrative cooperation by certain national institutions, could turn out to have potentially disruptive consequences on the established system of mutual recognition of social security certificates throughout the EU. Moreover, the Court's approach inevitably gives rise to serious doubts as to the practical ability and competence – if not even the legitimacy – of a host state court to collect evidence and judge on the supposed fraudulent, or simply materially mistaken, issue of social security certificates in another country.[70]

The principle affirmed in *Altun* was confirmed a few months later with the decision in *Commission v Belgium*,[71] even though not to the point of allowing the Member State in which a worker is posted to adopt legislation that would entitle national institutions to unilaterally declare invalid an A1 certificate issued by the competent authority of another Member State.[72] In its subsequent ruling in *Alpenrind*,[73] the Court made a couple of further partial adjustments as well. On the one hand,

67. According to the Belgian investigations, the Bulgarian undertakings were nothing but labour-only subcontractors – i.e., mere artificial employment arrangements – of the main Belgian contractor *Absa NV*.
68. Interestingly, though, the Belgian authorities had not exhausted the 'dialogue and conciliation procedure' envisaged by the Administrative Commission for the Coordination of Social Security systems (European Commission) Decision No A1 of 12 June 2009 concerning the establishment of a dialogue and conciliation procedure concerning the validity of documents, the determination of the applicable legislation and the provision of benefits under Regulation (EC) No 883/2004 of the European Parliament and of the Council (n 65).
69. *Altun* (n 12) paras 42–46.
70. For a critical analysis of the case, *see* Marcin Kiełbasa, 'Court of Justice of the EU: A Host Member State Court May "disregard" A1 PD Certificates' (*Labour Mobility Initiative*, 27 February 2018) <https://www.mobilelabour.eu/12334/court-justice-eu-host-member-state-court-may-disregard-a1-pd-certificates/> (accessed 30 August 2018).
71. *European Commission v Kingdom of Belgium* (n 65).
72. *Ibid.* 94.
73. *Alpenrind and Others* (n 29).

it explicitly circumscribed the possibility for the courts of the receiving countries to disregard A1 documents in 'cases of fraud or abuse of rights' only.[74] On the other hand, it reiterated the binding nature of the A1 certificates regularly issued on both the institutions and the courts of the host Member States, as long as they are not withdrawn or declared invalid by the issuing authority in the sending country, adding that this holds true even when the Administrative Commission considers those documents as incorrectly issued.[75] Along the same lines, the recent ruling of the Grand Chamber in *CRPNPAC and Vueling Airlines*[76] further limited the powers of the courts of the State of destination to disregard fraudulent certificates. This action can only be taken following the initiation of the reconciliation procedure in front of the Administrative Commission for the Coordination of Social Security systems,[77] a prompt request from the social security institution of the host Member State to its counterpart in the State of origin to review the certificates in the light of concrete evidence of fraud, and in case the latter has failed to do so within a reasonable time.[78]

The criticism of the approach adopted by the EU judiciary in the above-mentioned *Altun* case is not intended, under any circumstances, to disclaim nor underestimate the serious troubles emerging at the stage of implementation and enforcement of social security rules.[79] *Au contraire*, it is stressed that, when it comes to enforcing the provisions at stake, in light of the almost exclusive competence of the sending state's authorities to that extent, the receiving country remains de facto precluded from carrying out any effective control or taking appropriate countermeasures in case of supposed violations of the rules. Additionally, this worrying situation is exacerbated by the persistent lack of an effective sanctioning mechanism against states that violate their duty of loyal cooperation. It is therefore apparent that the current regulatory context, in combination with the structural lack of transnational cooperation between Member States, represents the ideal incubator for the development of shadow economies.[80] In practice, companies that post their workers without any prior registration in the social security system of the country of origin are very rarely discovered in due time by the two administrations concerned. And even in case

74. *Ibid.* 46.
75. *Ibid.* 47 and 64. *See* Francesco Costamagna, 'The Revision of the Posted Workers Directive as a Meaningful Way to Curb Regulatory Competition in the Social Domain?' (2019) 2 Sant'Anna Legal Studies 25, 23.
76. *Caisse de retraite du personnel navigant professionnel de l'aéronautique civile (CRPNPAC) v Vueling Airlines SA v Vueling Airlines SA and Jean-Luc Poignant* [2020] CJEU Joined Cases C-370/17 and C-37/18, ECLI:EU:C:2020:260.
77. Administrative Commission for the Coordination of Social Security Systems (European Commission) Decision No A1 of 12 June 2009 concerning the establishment of a dialogue and conciliation procedure concerning the validity of documents, the determination of the applicable legislation and the provision of benefits under Regulation (EC) No 883/2004 of the European Parliament and of the Council (n 65).
78. Nicolas Rennuy, 'Posting of Workers: Enforcement, Compliance, and Reform' (2020) 22 European Journal of Social Security 212, 216.
79. As a matter of fact, there is an urgent need of reliable databases, as well as of effectively functioning institutions which monitor the regularity of the operations, provide cross-border information and prevent frauds. Cremers, 'Economic Freedoms and Labour Standards in the European Union' (n 7) 151–152.
80. Rennuy (n 78) 216.

the authorities in the host state ascertain the existence of an illegal situation, a further obstacle is posed by the fact that the sending country would have to recognise retroactively the posting arrangement into question.[81]

5.3.2 Provision of Services in Two or More Member States

The issues connected with the social security regulation of posting activities are not limited to the enforcement dimension, considering that specific troubles may arise in relation to the proper individuation of the applicable regime, especially when an employed person is regularly working in different countries. Besides the posting activity, Regulation (EC) 883/2004 on social security coordination envisages also a special treatment for employed persons who simultaneously or in alternation perform professional activities in two or more Member States.[82] More specifically, Article 13 distinguishes between the case in which employed persons active in two or more EU countries carry out a substantial volume of work in their home state or are employed by various undertakings or various employers with a registered office or place of business in different Member States, and the situation where they do not substantially operate in their home country. The applicable social security legislation is, respectively, that of the Member State of residence in the first case,[83] and that of the Member State in which the registered office or place of business of the employer is situated in the second eventuality.[84] In other terms, unlike employed persons active in two or more Member States who pursue a substantial part of their activity in their home country, those employees who do not carry out a substantial part of their work at home are not benefitting from their home state's regime.

Evidently, therefore, the criterion for determining whether a substantial part of the activities is performed in a certain Member State is of crucial importance.

81. Schoukens and Pieters (n 12) 112; Rennuy (n 78) 219.
82. For the record, the case of self-employed persons active in two or more Member States is not taken into consideration as it is excluded from the scope of the Posting of Workers Directive.
83. The Member State of residence is defined as the place where a person habitually resides by Article 1(j) of Regulation (EC) No 883/2004 of the European Parliament and of the Council of 29 April 2004 on the coordination of social security systems (n 8). The elements for determining the worker's place of residence are indicated by Article 11 of Regulation (EC) No 987/2009 of the European Parliament and of the Council of 16 September 2009 laying down the procedure for implementing Regulation (EC) No 883/2004 on the coordination of social security systems (n 9). In particular, they include: '(a) the duration and continuity of presence on the territory of the Member States concerned; (b) the person's situation, including: (i) the nature and the specific characteristics of any activity pursued, in particular the place where such activity is habitually pursued, the stability of the activity, and the duration of any work contract; (ii) his family status and family ties; (iii) the exercise of any non-remunerated activity; [...] (v) his housing situation, in particular how permanent it is; (vi) the Member State in which the person is deemed to reside for taxation purposes.'
84. Article 13 of Regulation (EC) No 883/2004 of the European Parliament and of the Council of 29 April 2004 on the coordination of social security systems (n 8). Schoukens and Pieters (n 12) 99; ILO DWT and Country Office for Central and Eastern Europe (n 48) 12–13; European Commission, 'Practical Guide on the Applicable Legislation in the European Union (EU), the European Economic Area (EEA) and in Switzerland' (n 11) 21–24; Cremers, 'Economic Freedoms and Labour Standards in the European Union' (n 7) 152.

Regulation (EC) No 987/2009 provides the indicative criteria to be taken into account to that end, namely remuneration and working time. In addition, it clarifies that the term 'substantial' does not necessarily imply the major part of activities, considering the attainment of 25% of the above-mentioned requirements sufficient for testifying the performance of certain activity in a certain country.[85]

When looking back at the analysis carried out *supra* in Chapter 2, it is worth noting that, in turn, the Posting of Workers Directive does not make such a distinction, and it regulates in the same way both employed persons active in two or more Member States who perform a substantial part of their job in their country of origin, and those who carry out the major part of their service supply abroad. Notably, they are both included under the notion of 'posted worker' given by the Posting of Workers Directive.[86] Furthermore, unlike the Posting of Workers Directive as amended by Directive (EU) 2018/957, the Basic Regulation does not determine any maximum period for the provision of services in two or more Member States. Hence, the rule of twenty-four months applicable to posting according to Article 12 is not valid for the category of workers falling under Article 13.

As one can well imagine, considerable difficulties are often encountered when trying to discern whether an employee who is sent abroad to different countries by his employer should be considered as properly posted according to Article 12 of the Basic Regulation or, instead, covered by the specific provisions on simultaneous performance of activities in different countries under Article 13.[87] It goes without saying that relevant differences in treatment follow accordingly,[88] let alone the resulting several issues of administrative nature arising at the enforcement level.[89] With a view to bring

85. Article 14(8) of Regulation (EC) No 987/2009 of the European Parliament and of the Council of 16 September 2009 laying down the procedure for implementing Regulation (EC) No 883/2004 on the coordination of social security systems (n 9). On this point, *see* Schoukens and Pieters (n 12) 98; European Commission, 'Practical Guide on the Applicable Legislation in the European Union (EU), the European Economic Area (EEA) and in Switzerland' (n 11) 21; Cornelissen and Van Limberghen (n 1) 358; Wispelaere and Pacolet, 'Posting of Workers: Report on A1 Portable Documents Issued in 2016' (n 16) 11; van Hoek (n 26) 458–459.
86. Importantly, self-employed persons remain excluded from notion of 'posted worker' under the PWD.
87. An interesting practical example of possible troublesome situation sees the case of a posted self-employed person who performs activities abroad, which are considered as wage-earner activities by the host state. If considered as active in two or more Member States, this person would fall under the social security system of the host country. In turn, when considered as a posted worker, he would remain socially insured as a self-employed person in his country of origin. Schoukens and Pieters (n 12) 110.
88. As a matter of fact, only those employees who are active in two or more EU countries while carrying out a substantial part of their work at home, are de facto subject to the same social security treatment as the posted workers.
89. This issue is particularly evident with regard to workers in the international transport sector, which is intrinsically characterised by a high degree of transnational mobility. Schoukens and Pieters (n 12) 110–111; Frederic De Wispelaere and Jozef Pacolet, 'Measuring the Size of Intra-EU Posting on the Basis of Data Collected at European and National Level' (Conference Intra-EU posting: costs and benefits, Leuven, Belgium, 28 April 2017); Rob Cornelissen, 'The Protection of Social Security Rights in a Cross-Border Situation. A Historical Overview' (60 Years Social Security Coordination from a Workers' Perspective, Leuven, Belgium, 16 May 2019). Notably, during 2016 various Member States (*inter alia* Austria, Finland, Hungary, Malta, and Latvia) have reported issues in the determination of the applicable legislation in the case of

more clarity, the Court of Justice, in the *Calle Grenzshop*[90] ruling, firmly excluded from the scope of Article 12 of the Basic Regulation the situation of a person, employed by an undertaking established in another Member State, who partly carried out working activity also in his home state for a period of time exceeding the limit prescribed for posting activities.[91] Conversely, the case of several consecutive postings to different Member States is supposed to be treated as a series of different new corresponding postings within the meaning of Article 12.[92] In turn, in the event of two postings involving the same worker employed by the same company in the same host state, a period of at least two months has to elapse between the two periods of mobility abroad.[93]

5.3.3 Mismatch with Taxation Rules

In conclusion, a further concern is expressed with regard to the evident mismatch existing between social security and taxation rules for posted workers. In fact, as already mentioned in Chapter 2, the time limit envisaged by the bilateral tax agreements between EU countries along the lines of the OECD Model Convention on Income and on Capital for benefitting of an exemption from the receiving state's tax regime, and thus the possibility to remain under their home country legislation, is of 183 days within a period of twelve months starting or ending in the fiscal year.[94]

The picture resulting from the combination with the twenty-four-month limit set by Regulation (EC) 883/2004 is, therefore, extremely complex. Whenever the posting period lasts less than 183 days, the sending Member State remains entitled to levy both income taxes and social security contributions. In turn, for periods of mobility longer

persons working simultaneously or in alternation in different EU countries. Yves Jorens et al., 'Fraud and Error in the Field of EU Social Security Coordination: Reference Year: 2016' (European Commission, Directorate-General for Employment, Social Affairs and Inclusion, Unit D2 – Social security coordination 2018) 54–55.

90. *Calle Grenzshop Andresen GmbH & Co KG v Allgemeine Ortskrankenkasse für den Kreis Schleswig-Flensburg* [1995] ECJ Case C-425/93, ECLI:EU:C:1995:37.
91. Interestingly, though, in the event the activities performed in the home state had not been of substantial nature and had respected the time limit of twenty-four months, the workers' activity would have been subsumed under the posting rules. Schoukens and Pieters (n 12) 111.
92. Point 3(a) of the Administrative Commission on Social Security for Migrant Workers (European Commission) Decision No A2 of 12 June 2009 concerning the interpretation of Article 12 of Regulation (EC) No 883/2004 of the European Parliament and of the Council on the legislation applicable to posted workers and self-employed workers temporarily working outside the competent State (Text of relevance to the EEA and to the EC/Switzerland Agreement) (n 48). European Commission, 'Practical Guide on the Applicable Legislation in the European Union (EU), the European Economic Area (EEA) and in Switzerland' (n 11) 12.
93. Point 3(c) of the Administrative Commission on Social Security for Migrant Workers (European Commission) Decision No A2 of 12 June 2009 concerning the interpretation of Article 12 of Regulation (EC) No 883/2004 of the European Parliament and of the Council on the legislation applicable to posted workers and self-employed workers temporarily working outside the competent State (Text of relevance to the EEA and to the EC/Switzerland Agreement) (n 48). ILO DWT and Country Office for Central and Eastern Europe (n 48) 11–12.
94. Article 15 (2) of the OECD (Organisation for Economic Co-operation and Development), *Model Tax Convention on Income and on Capital: Condensed Version, 21 November 2017* (OECD Publishing 2017).

than two years, the receiving Member State has the competence to levy both taxes and contributions. Finally, when the duration of the posting is comprised between 183 days and twenty-four months, income taxes are levied by the receiving country, while social security contributions are collected by the sending Member State.[95] In addition to the practical inconvenience for both service providers and monitoring national authorities resulting from the application of such mismatched regulations, the discrepancy highlighted above is deemed to represent a serious source of concern to the extent it provokes arbitrary income effects when applied in different Member States.[96]

5.4 NEW EU SOCIAL SECURITY RULES?

On 13 December 2016, the Commission submitted its proposal to amend Regulation (EC) No 883/2004 on the coordination of social security systems and Regulation (EC) No 987/2009 laying down the procedure for implementing Regulation (EC) No 883/2004.[97] As part of the so-called 2016 European Commission's 'Labour Mobility Package', that initiative was intended to adapt the EU legislation on social security coordination to the evolving social and economic reality of the Union.[98] Accordingly, it focused on improving legal clarity, promoting a more equitable distribution of the financial burden among the Member States, and enhancing the enforcement of the rules by simplifying administrative procedures.[99] *Inter alia*, the revision package included also a number of technical amendments to the rules concerning posted workers and persons working in two or more Member States. Those amendments were specially designed to bring clarity with regard to the existing terminological mismatch between EU social security rules and the Posting of Workers Directive[100] and to facilitate the verification of the social security status of posted workers and the exchange of the relevant information between national authorities.[101]

---

95. Wispelaere and Pacolet, 'Posting of Workers as Stabilising Mechanism: An Enlarged Notion of Labour Mobility as a Prerequisite for an Optimal Currency Area' (n 57) 8; Voss et al. (n 15) 26–27; Pennings (n 23).
96. Pennings (n 23).
97. European Commission, Proposal for a Regulation of the European Parliament and of the Council amending Regulation (EC) No 883/2004 on the coordination of social security systems and regulation (EC) No 987/2009 laying down the procedure for implementing Regulation (EC) No 883/2004, 2016 [COM(2016) 815 final].
98. European Commission, 'Press Release – Fairness at the Heart of Commission's Proposal to Update EU Rules on Social Security Coordination' (*European Commission Press Releases Database*, 13 December 2016) <http://europa.eu/rapid/press-release_IP-16-4301_en.htm> (accessed 9 June 2019); Wispelaere and Pacolet, 'Coordination of Social Security Systems at a Glance: 2017 Statistical Report' (n 23) 11.
99. Explanatory Memorandum accompanying the European Commission Proposal for a Regulation of the European Parliament and of the Council amending Regulation (EC) No 883/2004 on the coordination of social security systems and regulation (EC) No 987/2009 laying down the procedure for implementing Regulation (EC) No 883/2004 (n 97) 2.
100. On this point, *see* the extensive analysis carried out *supra* in Chapter 2.
101. Explanatory Memorandum accompanying the European Commission Proposal for a Regulation of the European Parliament and of the Council amending Regulation (EC) No 883/2004 on the coordination of social security systems and regulation (EC) No 987/2009 laying down the procedure for implementing Regulation (EC) No 883/2004 (n 97) 3; European Commission,

5.4.1 The Commission's Proposal

The 2016 Commission's proposal intended to remedy the discrepancy between the Basic Regulation and the Posting of Workers Directive with regard to the concept of 'posted worker' by amending Article 12(1) in such a way that the term 'posting' only referred to transnational secondments within the meaning of the Posting of Workers Directive, while introducing an additional notion of 'sent person'.[102] Allegedly, this broader concept of 'sent person' was supposed to include both posted workers, self-employed persons, as well as further borderline situations covered by the Basic Regulation (EC) 883/2004 only, namely when the activity is carried out by a worker in the territory of a Member State other than the state in which he normally works, but there is no service directed abroad, or the service is not provided for a recipient established in the host country.[103] With the adoption, on 23 October 2017, of a partial general approach, the EPSCO (Employment, Social Policy, Health and Consumer Affairs) Council even suggested using the term 'sent person' only, incorporating under the latter also the concept of posting under the Posting of Workers Directive.[104] This seemed to be, indeed, also the orientation of the EU legislator as resulted from the provisional agreement on the proposal reached between the European Parliament and the Council on 25 March 2019.[105]

Impact Assessment, Initiative to partially revise Regulation (EC) No 883/2004 of the European Parliament and of the Council on the coordination of social security systems and its implementing Regulation (EC) No 987/2009, Accompanying the document Proposal for a regulation of the European Parliament and of the Council amending Regulation (EC) No 883/2004 on the coordination of social security systems and regulation (EC) No 987/2009 laying down the procedure for implementing Regulation (EC) No 883/2004 – Part 5/6 2016 [SWD(2015) 460 final] 309.

102. In the wording of the proposal, Article 12(1) of Regulation (EC) No 883/2004 was supposed to be replaced by the following: 'A person who pursues an activity as an employed person in a Member State on behalf of an employer which normally carries out its activities there and who is posted within the meaning of Directive 96/71/EC of the European Parliament and of the Council of 16 December 1996 concerning the posting of workers in the framework of the provision of services or sent by that employer to another Member State to perform work on that employer's behalf shall continue to be subject to the legislation of the first Member State, provided that the anticipated duration of such work does not exceed 24 months and that the person is not posted or sent to replace another employed or self-employed person previously posted or sent within the meaning of this Article.' Article 1(13) of the European Commission Proposal for a Regulation of the European Parliament and of the Council amending Regulation (EC) No 883/2004 on the coordination of social security systems and regulation (EC) No 987/2009 laying down the procedure for implementing Regulation (EC) No 883/2004 (n 97). *Ibid.* Preamble Recital 7 and Explanatory Memorandum 11.
103. Stefan Schwarz and Marcin Kiełbasa, 'Posted or Sent in the Context of the Revision of Social Security Coordination Regulations' (2018) *Labour Mobility Initiative Association* 5, 4.
104. Employment, Social Policy, Health and Consumer Affairs (EPSCO) Council, Partial general approach on the coordination of social security systems and regulation 2017 (13139/17) 8. On this point, *see* Marcin Kiełbasa, 'Posted or Sent? In the Context of the Revision of Social Security Coordination Regulation – Analysis' (*Labour Mobility Initiative*, 25 January 2018) <https://www.mobilelabour.eu/12203/posted-sent-context-revision-social-security-coordination-regulation-lmias-analysis/> (accessed 30 August 2018).
105. Article 1(13) of the 'Proposal for a Regulation of the European Parliament and of the Council Amending Regulation (EC) No 883/2004 on the Coordination of Social Security Systems and Regulation (EC) No 987/2009 Laying down the Procedure for Implementing Regulation (EC)

Besides the aforementioned terminological clarification, the proposal focused also on the second paragraph of Article 12, extending to self-employed persons the prohibition of replacement with other posted employees or self-employed persons.[106] The character of the non-replacement condition laid down in both paragraphs 1 and 2 of Article 12 was specified with the drafting, in the 2019 provisional agreement, of an additional paragraph 2a which prescribed to consider the overall duration of the cross-border activity, thus setting a cumulative maximum time limit of twenty-four months.[107] A further innovation concerned then Article 14 of the Implementing Regulation (EC) 987/2009, entailing the alignment with the reviewed provisions of the Basic Regulation and, most importantly, the requirement for the posted or sent workers to be previously affiliated to the social security system of their country of origin, rather than to the scheme of the Member State where their employer was established.[108] Interestingly, though, the subsequent provisional agreement went in the opposite direction by imposing that a person recruited with a view to being sent abroad was previously covered by the social security system of his employer's home state for at least three months.[109] The agreement provided for a timeframe of the same duration

No 883/2004 – Analysis of the Final Compromise Text with a View to Agreement' (Council of the European Union 2019) 7698/19 <https://data.consilium.europa.eu/doc/document/ST-7698-2019-ADD-1-REV-1/en/pdf> (accessed 11 June 2019).

106. Article 1(13) of the European Commission Proposal for a Regulation of the European Parliament and of the Council amending Regulation (EC) No 883/2004 on the coordination of social security systems and regulation (EC) No 987/2009 laying down the procedure for implementing Regulation (EC) No 883/2004 (n 97). *Ibid.* Preamble Recital 7 and Explanatory Memorandum 11.

107. Article 1(13) of the 'Proposal for a Regulation of the European Parliament and of the Council Amending Regulation (EC) No 883/2004 on the Coordination of Social Security Systems and Regulation (EC) No 987/2009 Laying down the Procedure for Implementing Regulation (EC) No 883/2004 – Analysis of the Final Compromise Text with a View to Agreement' (n 105).

108. The new Article 14(1) of Regulation (EC) No 987/2009 was therefore supposed to state: 'For the purposes of the application of Article 12(1) of the basic Regulation, a "person who pursues an activity as an employed person in a Member State on behalf of an employer which normally carries out its activities there and who is posted within the meaning of the Directive 96/71/EC of the European Parliament and of the Council of 16 December 1996 concerning the posting of workers in the framework of the provision of service or sent by that employer to another Member State" shall include a person who is recruited with a view to being posted or sent to another Member State, provided that immediately before the start of his employment, the person concerned is already subject to the legislation of the sending Member State in accordance with Title II of the basic Regulation.' Article 2(8)(a) of the European Commission Proposal for a Regulation of the European Parliament and of the Council amending Regulation (EC) No 883/2004 on the coordination of social security systems and regulation (EC) No 987/2009 laying down the procedure for implementing Regulation (EC) No 883/2004 (n 97). *Ibid.* Explanatory Memorandum 14.

109. Article 2(8.a) of the 'Proposal for a Regulation of the European Parliament and of the Council Amending Regulation (EC) No 883/2004 on the Coordination of Social Security Systems and Regulation (EC) No 987/2009 Laying down the Procedure for Implementing Regulation (EC) No 883/2004 – Analysis of the Final Compromise Text with a View to Agreement' (n 105). Incidentally, that measure was welcomed by Houwerzijl and Berntsen for discouraging abusive situations whereby the workers are posted from a different Member State than the one of their social security affiliation (so-called 'triangular posting'). Mijke Houwerzijl and Lisa Berntsen, 'Posting of Workers: From a Blurred Notion Associated with "Cheap Labour" to a Tool for "Fair Labour Mobility"?' in Jens Arnholtz and Nathan Lillie (eds), *Posted Work in the European Union: The Political Economy of Free Movement* (Routledge 2019) 159.

also with regard to the performance by self-employed persons of working activity in their country of origin[110] and required the elapsing of a minimum two-month period between two consecutive assignments abroad.[111]

With a view to making the administrative procedure smoother, the Commission proposed the addition of two more paragraphs to Article 19 of Regulation (EC) 987/2009. In accordance with the duty of sincere cooperation strongly emphasised by the Court of Justice,[112] paragraph 3 required the competent institutions in the sending Member States to materially verify and guarantee the accuracy and completeness of the Portable Documents A1 issued. In turn, paragraph 4 provided for the direct cross-border exchange of relevant information regarding the social security rights and obligations of the persons concerned between social security institutions, labour inspectorates, tax and immigration authorities.[113] The 2019 provisional agreement went even further with the draft of a new Article 19a laying down an extremely detailed cooperation procedure for cases of doubts about the validity of the documents attesting the applicable legislation in case of cross-border situations.[114] Finally, the introduction by the 2016 proposal of a new Article 76a was supposed to confer on the Commission a specific power to adopt implementing acts, in accordance with Article 291 TFEU, aimed at laying down standard procedures for the issuance, contestation and withdrawal of the PDs A1.[115]

110. Article 2(8)(ab)new of the 'Proposal for a Regulation of the European Parliament and of the Council Amending Regulation (EC) No 883/2004 on the Coordination of Social Security Systems and Regulation (EC) No 987/2009 Laying down the Procedure for Implementing Regulation (EC) No 883/2004 – Analysis of the Final Compromise Text with a View to Agreement' (n 105).

111. *Ibid.* Article 2(8)(aa)new.

112. *Fitzwilliam Executive Search Ltd v Bestuur van het Landelijk instituut sociale verzekeringen* (n 12) para. 51; *Rijksdienst voor Sociale Zekerheid v Herbosch Kiere NV* (n 62) para. 22.

113. Article 2(11) of the European Commission Proposal for a Regulation of the European Parliament and of the Council amending Regulation (EC) No 883/2004 on the coordination of social security systems and regulation (EC) No 987/2009 laying down the procedure for implementing Regulation (EC) No 883/2004 (n 97). In particular, *see* point 15 of the related Explanatory Memorandum and the European Commission Impact Assessment, Initiative to partially revise Regulation (EC) No 883/2004 of the European Parliament and of the Council on the coordination of social security systems and its implementing Regulation (EC) No 987/2009, Accompanying the document Proposal for a regulation of the European Parliament and of the Council amending Regulation (EC) No 883/2004 on the coordination of social security systems and regulation (EC) No 987/2009 laying down the procedure for implementing Regulation (EC) No 883/2004 – Part 5/6 (n 101) 309.

114. Article 2(11a.new) of the 'Proposal for a Regulation of the European Parliament and of the Council Amending Regulation (EC) No 883/2004 on the Coordination of Social Security Systems and Regulation (EC) No 987/2009 Laying down the Procedure for Implementing Regulation (EC) No 883/2004 – Analysis of the Final Compromise Text with a View to Agreement' (n 105).

115. In the wording of the proposal, the new Article 76a of Regulation (EC) No 987/2009 was designed as follows: 'The Commission shall be empowered to adopt implementing acts specifying the procedure to be followed in order to ensure uniform conditions for the application of Articles 12 and 13 of this Regulation. Those acts shall establish a standard procedure including time limits for – the issuance, the format and the contents of a portable document certifying the social security legislation which applies to the holder, – the determination of situations in which the document shall be issued, – the elements to verified before the document can be issued, – the withdrawal of the document when its accuracy and validity is

Despite the great effort made to achieve the above-mentioned elaborate and relevant draft for the revision of the EU rules on social security coordination, the process started in 2016 eventually experienced a major setback on 18 April 2019.[116] Also due to divergent positions on the applicable legislation in posting situations, the European Parliament (with 291 votes in favour, 284 against and 6 abstentions) decided to postpone the endorsement of this prominent regulatory review until a new parliamentary composition was in place.[117] Until now, due also to the incumbent issues dealt with by the EU in the first half of 2020 (mainly related to the COVID-19 pandemic), no further legislative initiative has been taken on this matter.

5.4.2 Shortcomings and Recommendations

With regard to the potential impact of the 2016 Commission's proposal, a critical overview of the proposed amendments cannot avoid pointing out the mere terminological innovation of the new Article 12(1), which would have left the substantial discrepancy between the Basic Regulation and the Posting of Workers Directive with

contested by the competent institution of the Member State of employment.' Article 1(25) of the European Commission Proposal for a Regulation of the European Parliament and of the Council amending Regulation (EC) No 883/2004 on the coordination of social security systems and regulation (EC) No 987/2009 laying down the procedure for implementing Regulation (EC) No 883/2004 (n 97). In this sense, *see* points 3 and 13 of the related Explanatory Memorandum and the European Commission Impact Assessment, Initiative to partially revise Regulation (EC) No 883/2004 of the European Parliament and of the Council on the coordination of social security systems and its implementing Regulation (EC) No 987/2009, Accompanying the document Proposal for a regulation of the European Parliament and of the Council amending Regulation (EC) No 883/2004 on the coordination of social security systems and regulation (EC) No 987/2009 laying down the procedure for implementing Regulation (EC) No 883/2004 – Part 5/6 (n 101) 309.

116. European Sources Online (ESO), 'Proposal to Amend Regulation (EC) No 883/2004 on the Coordination of Social Security Systems and Regulation (EC) No 987/2009 Laying down the Procedure for Implementing Regulation (EC) No 883/2004' (21 June 2018) <https://www.europeansources.info/record/proposal-to-amend-regulation-ec-no-883-2004-on-the-coordination-of-social-security-systems-and-regulation-ec-no-987-2009-laying-down-the-procedure-for-implementing-regulation-ec-no-883-2004/> (accessed 12 June 2019); Spiegel (n 24).

117. In particular, the motion of postponement of the vote under Rule 190(4) of the Rules of Procedure of the European Parliament was proposed by the Belgian MEP Helga Stevens, on behalf of the ECR faction (European Conservatives and Reformists). European Parliament, 'Minutes – Coordination of Social Security Systems ***I (Vote) – Thursday, 18 April 2019' (18 April 2019) <http://www.europarl.europa.eu/doceo/document/PV-8-2019-04-18-ITM-010-05_EN.html> (accessed 12 June 2019). On this point, *see* Marcin Kiełbasa, 'Regulations on the Coordination of Social Security – Revision Only after the Elections to the EP' (*Labour Mobility Initiative*, 2 May 2019) <https://www.mobilelabour.eu/13023/regulations-on-the-coordination-of-social-security-in-the-eu-revision-only-after-the-elections-to-the-european-parliament/> (accessed 12 June 2019). Nonetheless, the work done so far is unlikely to be wasted as the file has been picked up by the Commission, which promptly reopened the consultations. In this sense, *see* Marcin Kiełbasa and Kamil Gacek, 'EMPL Committee in Favour of Continuing Work on the Revision of Coordination Regulations' (*Labour Mobility Initiative*, 2 October 2019) <https://www.mobilelabour.eu/13101/empl-committee-in-favour-of-continuing-work-on-the-revision-of-coordination-regulations/> (accessed 22 October 2019).

regard to the material concept of 'posted worker' fundamentally unaltered.[118] Nonetheless, despite its limited scope, that sort of intervention would have helped to overcome the existing legal and public confusion when it comes to identifying the applicable social security regime to persons who are temporarily working in another Member State.[119] Moreover, remarkable initiatives such as the extension of the non-replacement condition to self-employed persons, and the requirement of a minimum three-month period of social affiliation in a certain Member State before a worker posted abroad could be allowed to maintain his home country's social insurance, would have properly dealt with the risk of *à la carte* choice of social security systems.[120]

By contrast, the revision has been accused of not addressing a number of shortcomings arising from the existing legal framework. It failed, indeed, to take into due account the multiple facets of intra-EU posting, thereby remaining exposed to the risks of providing too general adjustments unable to solve specific sectorial issues and even affecting economic sectors which are currently trouble-free.[121] More specifically, the twenty-four-month time limit for remaining insured under the home state's regime may prove too short or too long depending on the type of economic activity performed and the country where this activity is carried out.[122] In the same vein, the untouched requirement for posted workers to be already subject for at least one month to the legislation of the sending Member State, as laid down in the Decision A2 of the Administrative Commission of 12 June 2009,[123] is likely constituting a problem for highly mobile workers.[124] In addition, some doubts certainly remain with regard to the

118. Jorens (n 65); Houwerzijl and Berntsen (n 109) 160. Notably, the lack of intention to address the problematic gap in the personal scope between EU social security and labour legislation has been clearly stated in the Explanatory Memorandum accompanying the European Commission Proposal for a Regulation of the European Parliament and of the Council amending Regulation (EC) No 883/2004 on the coordination of social security systems and regulation (EC) No 987/2009 laying down the procedure for implementing Regulation (EC) No 883/2004 (n 97) 11.
119. Schwarz and Kiełbasa (n 103) 5.
120. In particular, serious concerns about such a risk have been expressed in Schoukens and Pieters (n 12) 107–108; Pieters (n 16) 2.
121. Frederic De Wispelaere, 'The Sustainability of the Coordination of Social Security Systems' (60 Years Social Security Coordination from a Workers' Perspective, Leuven, Belgium, 16 May 2019) figures 8–10.
122. In this respect, it is worth noting the different position taken, during the drafting process, by the European Parliament and the Council, which supported an eighteen and a twenty-four time limit respectively. Spiegel (n 24).
123. Point 1 of the Administrative Commission on Social Security for Migrant Workers (European Commission) Decision No A2 of 12 June 2009 concerning the interpretation of Article 12 of Regulation (EC) No 883/2004 of the European Parliament and of the Council on the legislation applicable to posted workers and self-employed workers temporarily working outside the competent State (Text of relevance to the EEA and to the EC/Switzerland Agreement) (n 48). It is worth recalling the intention of the 2019 provisional agreement to extend such a period to three months. Article 2(8.a) of the 'Proposal for a Regulation of the European Parliament and of the Council Amending Regulation (EC) No 883/2004 on the Coordination of Social Security Systems and Regulation (EC) No 987/2009 Laying down the Procedure for Implementing Regulation (EC) No 883/2004 – Analysis of the Final Compromise Text with a View to Agreement' (n 105).
124. Notably, the category of 'highly mobile workers' includes, *inter alia*, workers carrying out activities in the international road (truck drivers) and railway transportation, flight and cabin crew, seafarers, researchers, artists, musicians, athletes, workers employed intra-group, business people, and sales representatives. For those particular situations, a possible effective

applicable legal regime in the event the real duration of a posting is shorter than twenty-four months (supposed application of home state law), while its anticipated duration was longer (thereby falling under the *lex loci laboris*).[125] The non-replacement condition, in its turn, besides the questionable broad interpretation given by the Court in *Alpenrind*,[126] may be counterproductive when applied in economic sectors that are facing labour shortages, as well as in the live-in care sector whereby a certain continuity of care is usually preferable, if not necessary.

In light of the number of shortcomings deriving from the one-size-fits-all approach envisaged by the current social security rules, as well as by the 2016 Commission's proposal for amendment, it is worth mentioning the suggestion made by De Wispelaere of adopting, instead, a sectoral approach or country-specific provisions on the model of bilateral agreements concluded between EU Member States and extra-EU/EFTA (European Free Trade Association) countries.[127] On the contrary, the definition of a uniform procedure at EU level (possibly an electronic procedure) for the application and granting of Portable Documents A1 is recommended in order to ensure a better understanding and enforcement of the rules, as well as reducing the administrative burden for both national authorities and posting undertakings, while promoting the (electronic) exchange of information between Member States.[128] In practical terms, it could be organised in the framework of the newly introduced Electronic Exchange of Social Security Information (EESSI),[129] namely an IT system specifically designed to smooth the exchange of information between social security institutions across the EU. Besides replacing the cross-border shipment of paper files, the EESSI is intended to improve efficiency, speed, accuracy and safety of the information exchange between national institutions.[130]

solution may be represented by the introduction of a specific exemption to apply for a Portable Document A1. Wispelaere (n 121) figure 11; Frederic De Wispelaere and Marco Rocca, 'The Dark Side of the Tour. Labour and Social Security Challenges of Highly Mobile Workers in the Live Performance Sector' (2020) ERA Forum 3, 6–7, and 9.

125. Spiegel (n 24).
126. *Alpenrind and Others* (n 29). On this point, *see supra* subsection 5.2.2.
127. Wispelaere (n 121) figures 7, 25–26. *See also* Wispelaere and Rocca (n 124) 9. Besides, it is worth pointing out that a different solution was proposed by Pennings with a view to limiting the scope of the state-of-employment principle. His suggestion envisaged that, in case the host country law provides for higher levels of contribution than in the country where the person is insured, after three months of posting abroad the contributions would have to be paid at the level of the country of employment, albeit still in the sending country. Pennings (n 15) 333–334.
128. Jorens (n 65). Further recommendations for improvements in the field of social security coordination of posted workers are put forward *infra* in Chapter 9.
129. European Commission – Employment, Social Affairs & Inclusion, 'Electronic Exchange of Social Security Information (EESSI)' (*Electronic Exchange of Social Security Information (EESSI)*) <https://ec.europa.eu/social/main.jsp?catId=869&langId=en> (accessed 28 January 2020). For the record, the EESSI was made available by the Commission in July 2017, with a two-year deadline for national implementation.
130. *Ibid.*; Vincent Aussilloux et al., 'Making the Best of the European Single Market' (2017) Bruegel – Policy Contribution 12 <https://bruegel.org/2017/02/making-the-best-of-the-european-single-market/> (accessed 28 January 2019).

5.5 CONCLUDING REMARKS

Although social security coordination was one of the first areas of intervention of the European legislator, the concrete determination of the specific rights and obligations arising from social insurance schemes has been traditionally left to the national competence. EU law, in the form of Regulation (EC) 883/2004 and the Implementing Regulation (EC) 987/2009, prescribes that workers moving within the Union must be subject to a single social security regime, which is generally that of the Member State where they go to work *(lex loci laboris)*. With a view to encouraging intra-EU labour mobility while, at the same time, preventing unnecessary and costly administrative burdens for the actors involved, in the case of posting the existing regulation envisages, nonetheless, an exception to such a territorial application of social security law. In fact, posted workers (both employed and self-employed persons) are entitled to remain attached to their home state's social security scheme, albeit only under certain conditions, whose interpretation has been refined over the years by the (sometimes questionable) interventions of the Court of Justice.

Posted workers (and indirectly their employers) can benefit from such a special treatment only when their mobility abroad lasts less than twenty-four months and they are not sent in order to replace another posted person who has previously completed his term of employment. Interestingly, with the decision in *Alpenrind*,[131] the latter proviso has been recently subject to an extremely broad jurisprudential interpretation. Instead of solely considering the case of replacement operated by the same employer, the Court extended the prohibition to any situation whereby a posted worker is employed for the performance of a working activity previously carried out by any other posted worker. The potential undermining of the principle of legal certainty is therefore evident from the fact that successive postings by different employers would not be entitled to the due special treatment, solely because another undertaking had already profited from the same advantage. Cross-border companies would also suffer from an additional limitation to their freedom to provide services to the extent they are de facto required to find out themselves whether or not the same activity has been previously carried out by employees posted by another undertaking. A further mismatch would then arise vis-à-vis the new dispositions introduced by Directive (EU) 2018/957 on posting of workers, which merely prohibit the rotation of personnel arranged in *mala fide* by the same undertaking.

Three additional conditions to benefit from a derogatory treatment are related to the existence of a substantial connection of the transnational actors (posted workers, self-employed persons, and employers) with their country of origin. First of all, before their mobility abroad, the cross-border workers are required to be already affiliated to the social security scheme of their home state. Second, a direct employment relationship with their employer must continue to persist during the whole duration of the assignment in another Member State. The third requirement, originally developed by the case law of the Court in order to combat the creation of the so-called 'letterbox

131. *Alpenrind and Others* (n 29).

companies', is the effective habitual performance of a substantial economic activity by the posting undertaking in the Member State from which it sends out personnel. In turn, posted self-employed persons, besides proving that they had already pursued a similar working activity in their home country, are required to maintain an infrastructural base in their country of origin.

This chapter also focused on the impact of the Court of Justice case law at the level of enforcement of social security legislation, in particular when it comes to the recognition by the competent authorities in the host Member State of the Portable Documents A1 issued by their respective counterpart in the sending state. Through an analysis of the controversial outcome in *Altun*,[132] the power conferred by the CJEU to national courts in the host Member States to disregard social security certificates issued by the competent institutions of the sending states has been presented as an underestimated endangering of the principle of mutual recognition. Such a risk has been nevertheless mitigated by the further limitations of the powers of the courts of the State of destination to disregard fraudulent certificates, introduced by the Court with its more recent rulings in *Commission v Belgium*,[133] *Alpenrind*[134] and *CRPNPAC and Vueling Airlines*.[135] This notwithstanding, there is still a huge margin for improvement for the existing legal framework to the extent it has proved not to be able to provide sufficient remedies available to the host Member States dealing with fraudulent or mistaken documentation attesting the application of foreign legal regimes while, at the same time, facing a lack of cooperation from the sending states' authorities. Further concerns are then expressed with regard to the identification of the proper legal regime for employed persons working simultaneously or in alternation in two or more Member States, especially considering the different legal treatment reserved to them in case they carry out a substantial part of their job in their home country or less. Moreover, the mismatch between the social security law currently into force and the applicable taxation rules is pointed out in so far as it is likely to result in arbitrary income effects depending on the different national legislations involved.

The 2016 Commission's proposal to amend Regulations 883/2004 and 987/2009 represented a laudable attempt to address, at least partially, the shortcomings and inconsistencies arising from the existing regulatory framework for posting of workers. The terminological innovation entailing the reference to 'posting' only for transnational secondments within the meaning of the Posting of Workers Directive and the introduction of an additional notion of 'sent person' would have definitely improved the clarity and practical enforcement of the rules. Conversely, however, the substantial discrepancies between EU labour and social security law in relation to the scope of the concept of 'posted/sent worker' was fundamentally left untouched. On the other hand, the legislative reform was supposed to provide effective remedies for cross-border

132. *Altun* (n 12).
133. *European Commission v Kingdom of Belgium* (n 65).
134. *Alpenrind and Others* (n 29).
135. *Caisse de retraite du personnel navigant professionnel de l'aéronautique civile (CRPNPAC) v Vueling Airlines SA v Vueling Airlines SA and Jean-Luc Poignant* (n 76).

administrative issues, by establishing extremely important requirements for the competent institutions in the sending Member States to monitor the authenticity and accuracy of the documentation provided and to promptly exchange relevant information with other national and foreign authorities. In addition, a few technical suggestions were designed to address the risk of *à la carte* choice of social security systems, namely the extension of the non-replacement condition to self-employed persons and the imposition on both posted employees and self-employed persons to be affiliated to the social security system of the sending state for at least three months prior to their mobility abroad.[136]

In conclusion, despite its potentially relevant impact on the regulation of posting, the revision tabled in 2016 was nonetheless criticised for failing to grasp the fragmented character of the phenomenon at issue, characterised by a high degree of concentration in certain Member States, and especially in specific economic sectors. Possible future reform of the EU social security legal framework, rather than seeking to address the whole posting phenomenon as a *unicum*, may take into consideration the development of a sectoral approach or of a series of ad hoc national provisions. By the way, the combination of the normative improvements envisaged by the draft amendments recently left aside and the effective respect of the prescription for posting undertakings to normally carry out their activities in the country from which they send out personnel would have drastically restricted the opportunities to arbitrary choose the most convenient social security regime. Evidently, the promotion of cross-border administrative cooperation and exchange of information between national institutions is of crucial importance for proper enforcement of the rules. To this end, the recent introduction of the Electronic Exchange of Social Security Information (EESSI)undoubtedly represents a step in the right direction.

136. For the record, the latter requirement of a minimum three-month period of social security affiliation in the sending Member State was determined in the provisional agreement on the proposal reached between the European Parliament and the Council on 25 March 2019.

CHAPTER 6
Quantitative Dimension of Posting

6.1 INTRODUCTION

After having identified, in the previous chapters, all the distinguishing features of the posting activity in legal terms, the present step of analysis is intended to shed light on the actual size of this type of intra-EU labour mobility, thus contributing to answering the following research sub-question: *What is the actual dimension of the posting phenomenon?* In particular, this interrogative is here intended in a wide sense, not limited to the material size of posting, but also aimed at clarifying the actual shapes it takes in different national contexts. The path chosen in order to get to a comprehensive and accurate picture of the measure of this phenomenon is the use of existing sources of empirical data, mainly relying on official reports drafted on behalf of the European Commission. Notably, in accordance with the theoretical nature of this book, neither data nor statistics have been directly collected through a field survey. Importantly, then, the implications of the COVID-19 pandemic are taken into consideration only to a limited extent, as a proper analysis of such issues would be, for the time being, still too premature.

More in detail, this chapter is divided into two parts, one focusing on the material quantitative dimension of posting both at European and national levels, and another investigating its relevance within the EU internal market. While the first substantial section 6.2 is intended to provide the necessary premise on the way empirical data are selected and gathered, the proper data analysis begins in section 6.3 with an investigation of the concrete dimension of posting in the EU. In particular, the latter section points out, on the one hand, the relatively limited size in absolute terms of posting and, on the other hand, the exceptional evolution in terms of numbers that has invested the phenomenon over the last years. The strict correlation of such an expansion with the 2004 and 2007 EU enlargements is clearly underlined. Furthermore, the temporal dimension of this type of short-term workforce mobility is considered as well. A specific focus on the actual distribution at Member State level is provided in section 6.4, by carefully taking into consideration whether a person is moving as a posted worker or as a person active in two or more Member States according, respectively, to Article 12 or Article 13 of the Basic Regulation on social security coordination. In this regard, breakdowns by sending and receiving Member States as well as by economic activity are investigated, and the role played by geographic proximity is presented as an important factor. Lastly, this passage tries to individuate patterns and trends testifying specific flows of labour mobility across the EU internal market, thereby debunking the popular stereotype that portrays the transnational posting as merely concerning low-skilled workers directed from the 'poorer' Central and Eastern to the 'richer' Western Member States.

The second part of this chapter presents, in section 6.5, an estimation of the economic relevance of the posting phenomenon in relation to the total EU employment share and in national labour markets. In the following section, a brief glimpse of the impact of COVID-19 is offered with a view to identify the major effects of the pandemic on posting practices. Finally, in the concluding section 6.7, all the main findings are summarised with a view to providing the broader picture that makes it possible to answer the research sub-question at issue.

6.2 THE IMPORTANCE OF RELIABLE DATA

In order to effectively evaluate the impact of the posting phenomenon on the EU internal market, and hence the incidence of the 2018 EU regulatory reform, the present analysis cannot avoid investigating its quantitative dimension. In the wording of the new Directive (EU) 2018/957, '[s]ufficient and accurate statistical data in the area of posted workers is of utmost importance, in particular with regard to the number of posted workers in specific employment sectors and per Member State.'[1] Notably, the need to precisely quantify the actual volume of labour mobility in the form of posting arrangements is deemed crucial in order to recognise abusive situations and, thereby, enable better enforcement of the rules and design good policies.[2]

One of the main issues involved in the sector under consideration, invoked several times by experts, academics, social partners, EU institutions and Member States, has constantly been the absolute lack of reliable data.[3] The first remedy to this uncertain situation was introduced by the requirement for the competent institutions in

1. Preamble Recital 5 of Directive (EU) 2018/957 of the European Parliament and of the Council of 28 June 2018 amending Directive 96/71/EC concerning the posting of workers in the framework of the provision of services 2018 (OJ L 173/16).
2. Kairit Kall and Nathan Lillie, 'Protection of Posted Workers in the European Union: Findings and Policy Recommendations Based on Existing Research' (2017) PROMO Briefing Paper 43, 6.
3. Already in 2007, the EU Commission stressed in a Communication the absolute absence of 'precise figures or estimates of posted workers in the EU'. European Commission, Communication on the Posting of workers in the framework of the provision of services: Maximising its benefits and potential while guaranteeing the protection of workers 2007 [COM(2007) 304 final] 3. Since then, the situation has not improved much. Eckhard Voss et al., 'Posting of Workers Directive: Current Situation and Challenges' (European Parliament, EMPL Committee 2016) IP/A/EMPL/2016-07, 65.

the Member States to collect statistics on the application of Regulation (EC) 883/2004[4] and Regulation (EC) 987/2009[5] on social security, and the consequent duty on the European Commission to disseminate the relative information.[6] However, an EU-wide register tracking all cases of cross-border labour mobility currently does not exist.[7]

A concrete step towards providing a more transparent and useful picture of the current state of play has been taken by the European Commission, Directorate-General Employment, Social Affairs and Equal Opportunities (now Directorate-General for Employment, Social Affairs and Inclusion), through the commissioning of a series of studies starting from 2011.[8] For the purpose of the present analysis, all these official studies drafted on behalf of the European Commission constitute the major source of reliable empirical data. In this sense, an important source is represented by data

4. Regulation (EC) No 883/2004 of the European Parliament and of the Council of 29 April 2004 on the coordination of social security systems 2004 (OJ L 166/1).
5. Regulation (EC) No 987/2009 of the European Parliament and of the Council of 16 September 2009 laying down the procedure for implementing Regulation (EC) No 883/2004 on the coordination of social security systems 2009 (OJ L 284/1).
6. More specifically, in the wording of the European legislator, 'The competent authorities shall compile statistics on the application of the basic Regulation and the implementing Regulation and forward them to the secretariat of the Administrative Commission. Those data shall be collected and organised according to the plan and method defined by the Administrative Commission. The European Commission shall be responsible for disseminating the information.' *Ibid.* Article 91.
7. Claire Dhéret and Andreia Ghimis, 'The Revision of the Posted Workers Directive: Towards a Sufficient Policy Adjustment?' (2016) *European Policy Center (EPC) Discussion Paper* 4 <http://www.epc.eu/pub_details.php?cat_id=17&pub_id=6475> (accessed 23 October 2016).
8. IDEA Consult and ECORYS Netherlands, 'Study on the Economic and Social Effects Associated with the Phenomenon of Posting of Workers in the EU' (European Commission, Directorate-General Employment, Social Affairs and Equal Opportunities 2011); ISMERI Europa, 'Preparatory Study for an Impact Assessment on the Posting of Workers – Final Report' (European Commission 2012); Frederic De Wispelaere and Jozef Pacolet, 'Posting of Workers: Report on A1 Portable Documents Issued in 2012 and 2013' (KU Leuven Research Institute for Work and Society (HIVA) 2014) European Commission; Frederic De Wispelaere and Jozef Pacolet, 'Posting of Workers: Report on A1 Portable Documents Issued in 2014' (KU Leuven Research Institute for Work and Society (HIVA) 2015) European Commission, Directorate-General for Employment, Social Affairs and Inclusion Unit D/2 – Social Security Coordination; Frederic De Wispelaere and Jozef Pacolet, 'Posting of Workers: Report on A1 Portable Documents Issued in 2015' (KU Leuven Research Institute for Work and Society (HIVA) 2016) European Commission, Directorate-General for Employment, Social Affairs and Inclusion Unit D/2; Voss et al. (n 3); Frederic De Wispelaere and Jozef Pacolet, 'Posting of Workers: Report on A1 Portable Documents Issued in 2016' (KU Leuven Research Institute for Work and Society (HIVA) 2017) European Commission, Directorate-General for Employment, Social Affairs and Inclusion; Frederic De Wispelaere, Lynn De Smedt and Jozef Pacolet, 'Coordination of Social Security Systems at a Glance: 2018 Statistical Report' (KU Leuven Research Institute for Work and Society (HIVA) 2018) European Commission, Directorate-General for Employment, Social Affairs and Inclusion Unit D/2; Frederic De Wispelaere, Lynn De Smedt and Jozef Pacolet, 'Posting of Workers: Report on A1 Portable Documents Issued in 2018' (KU Leuven Research Institute for Work and Society (HIVA) 2019) European Commission, Directorate-General for Employment, Social Affairs and Inclusion Directorate D – Labour Mobility Unit D/2 – Social security coordination; Frederic De Wispelaere, Lynn De Smedt and Jozef Pacolet, 'Coordination of Social Security Systems at a Glance: 2019 Statistical Report' (KU Leuven Research Institute for Work and Society (HIVA) 2019) European Commission, Directorate-General for Employment, Social Affairs and Inclusion Directorate D – Labour Mobility Unit D/2 – Social security coordination.

collection within the framework of the Administrative Commission for the Coordination of Social Security Systems[9] and the analysis and statistic reports performed by the Network Statistics FMSSFE.[10] *Inter alia*, the contribution offered by a large amount of accurate research on the topic conducted in recent years by researchers De Wispelaere and Pacolet (HIVA-KU Leuven) is taken into particular consideration.

Before carrying out the announced analysis of the actual size and distribution of the posting phenomenon, the following premise concerning the sources of relevant empirical data is deemed to be indispensable. The estimation method used by the EU Commission relies on the number of issued portable social security documents, which constitutes the only administrative data source of cross-border labour mobility at European level.[11] More in detail, every employed or self-employed person who goes to work temporarily in another EU country needs to apply to the competent authority of the Member State of social security affiliation for the issuance of a specific certificate, namely the Portable Document A1 (PD A1).[12] This PD A1 is, in practice, a declaration of the applicable social security legislation which proves that a certain posted employee or self-employed person, or a certain person working in two or more Member States, pays his social contributions in his home country.[13] Accordingly, it prevents the

9. The Administrative Commission for the Coordination of Social Security Systems, whose composition, operation and tasks are laid down in Articles 71 and 72 of Regulation (EC) No 883/2004, is formed by representatives of the government of each EU-28 Member States and EFTA countries and representatives of the European Commission.
10. The Network Statistics FMSSFE is an independent research network set up by the European Commission DG Employment, Social Affairs and Inclusion, and composed of expert teams from HIVA-KU Leuven (acting as coordinator), Milieu Ltd, IRIS-UGent, Szeged University and Eftheia bvba.
11. Unfortunately, since no breakdown by receiving Member State is available for this activity, the available data are limited to issuing numbers. As indicated further, the referred analysis conducted by De Wispelaere and Pacolet complements the numbers of PDs A1 issued with the figures provided by sources at national level. Wispelaere and Pacolet, 'Posting of Workers: Report on A1 Portable Documents Issued in 2016' (n 8) 12–13.
12. In order to obtain this PD A1 certificate, the worker (or his employer) has to fulfil and submit the corresponding questionnaire, which requires a declaration of: the individual persons' identity, the Member State's applicable legislation, the type of activity (posting or active in two or more Member States), the worker's status (employed or self-employed), the employer's identity, the sector and type of economic activity, and the duration of the transnational period of mobility (with specific indication of the start and end date of the posting, bearing in mind that the maximum period allowed is twenty-four months). Notably, by virtue of Article 19 of Regulation (EC) 987/2009, the competent national authorities are responsible to provide this certificate at the request of the employer or the person concerned. Regulation (EC) No 987/2009 of the European Parliament and of the Council of 16 September 2009 laying down the procedure for implementing Regulation (EC) No 883/2004 on the coordination of social security systems (n 5). Frederic De Wispelaere and Jozef Pacolet, 'Posting of Workers: Report on A1 Portable Documents Issued in 2017' (KU Leuven Research Institute for Work and Society (HIVA) 2018) European Commission, Directorate-General for Employment, Social Affairs and Inclusion 12. For the record, it is worth noting that the PDs A1 have replaced the E101 forms since 1 May 2010. 'Posting Staff Abroad' (*Your Europe – Business*) <https://europa.eu/youreurope/business/human-resources/posted-workers/posting-staff-abroad/index_en.htm> (accessed 8 April 2019).
13. *Fitzwilliam Executive Search Ltd v Bestuur van het Landelijk instituut sociale verzekeringen* [2000] CJEU Case C-202/97, ECLI:EU:C:2000:75 [53]. *See also* Marianne Thyssen – EU Commissioner for Employment, 'Parliamentary Questions: Answer given by Ms Thyssen on Behalf of the Commission (Question Reference: E-004944/2017)' (21 September 2017) <http://www.europarl.europa.eu/doceo/document/E-8-2017-004944-ASW_EN.pdf> (accessed 27 March 2019).

cross-border worker from losing his social security protection during the period of mobility abroad and, at the same time, it excludes the application of any other obligation to pay social security contributions in the country of temporary employment.[14]

As demonstrated further, the analysis of the PDs A1 issued offers a useful indication of the direction of transnational labour migration across the European Union. Nonetheless, as admitted by the authors of the surveys, it should be noted that, due to its limited scope, such a method is not able to provide a reliable, precise and univocal measure of the actual number of postings taking place.[15] In light of the previously conducted investigation of the discrepancies between the notion of 'posted worker' under the Posting of Workers Directive and the Basic Regulation on social security, it appears evident that the number of postings in accordance with the definition given by the Posting of Workers Directive (both before and after the entry into effect of Directive (EU) 2018/957) may significantly differ from the actual quota of issued PDs A1.[16] In fact, unlike the Posting of Workers Directive, the latter data include posted self-employed persons, while not encompassing secondments lasting longer than twenty-four months. Conversely, the new Directive (EU) 2018/957 sets forth a twelve-month time limit for posting. What is more, it should be considered that the PDs A1 are not issued to posted workers only, but also to other categories of mobile workers, such as persons active in two or more Member States, civil servants, contract staff of the EU, mariners and flight or cabin crew members.[17] A further misrepresentation of the phenomenon might also result in case the employer does not apply for PDs A1 when the worker is posted for a very short period of time.[18] Importantly, then, in light of the non-mandatory character of the PDs A1 (due to the fact that they do not constitute a binding condition for posting) and of their possible retroactive effect,[19] the

14. In order to be always able to demonstrate his own social security position, the posted worker (or his employer) should always keep available the PD A1 to be presented to the institution in the country of temporary secondment. Wispelaere and Pacolet, 'Posting of Workers: Report on A1 Portable Documents Issued in 2016' (n 8) 11; Wispelaere and Pacolet, 'Posting of Workers: Report on A1 Portable Documents Issued in 2017' (n 12) 12.
15. Frederic De Wispelaere and Jozef Pacolet, 'An Ad Hoc Statistical Analysis on Short Term Mobility – Economic Value of Posting of Workers: The Impact of Intra-EU Cross-Border Services, with Special Attention to the Construction Sector' (KU Leuven Research Institute for Work and Society (HIVA) 2016) Research commissioned by DG EMPL within the framework of Contract VT/2015/096, 9; Wispelaere and Pacolet, 'Posting of Workers: Report on A1 Portable Documents Issued in 2015' (n 8) 11.
16. Wispelaere and Pacolet, 'Posting of Workers: Report on A1 Portable Documents Issued in 2015' (n 8) 11–12; Wispelaere and Pacolet, 'Posting of Workers: Report on A1 Portable Documents Issued in 2017' (n 12) 8. For an in-depth analysis of the discrepancies in the definition of posting between the PWD (before and after the 2018 reform) and Regulation (EC) 883/2004 on social security coordination, *see supra* Chapter 2.
17. Wispelaere and Pacolet, 'Posting of Workers: Report on A1 Portable Documents Issued in 2016' (n 8) 11; Wispelaere and Pacolet, 'Posting of Workers: Report on A1 Portable Documents Issued in 2017' (n 12) 12.
18. Kristina Maslauskaite, 'Posted Workers in the EU: State of Play and Regulatory Evolution' (2014) Policy Paper, Notre Europe Jaques Delors Institute 20, 5.
19. *Barry Banks and Others v Theatre royal de la Monnaie* [2000] ECJ Case C-178/97, ECLI: EU:C:2000:169. On the possibility to issue PDs A1 retroactively, and thus after the completion of the workers' period of mobility abroad, *see also* Philippa Watson, *EU Social and Employment*

numbers referring to the administrative documents at issue represent only an estimate of the actual number of posted workers.[20]

Finally, and even more importantly, the picture represented by the amount of A1 documents released is misleading in so far as 'the number of PDs A1 issued is not necessarily equal to the number of persons involved'.[21] Such a discrepancy occurs when more than one Portable Document A1 is granted to the same worker during the reference year (in case the same worker spends more than one period of mobility abroad in the same year). As a matter of fact, rather than the number of posted workers, A1 documents merely reflect the number of postings.[22] Available data show, indeed, a significant share of circular mobility in 2018, with individual posted workers corresponding to roughly two-thirds of the total number of PDs A1 issued. During the observed period, each individual person has been posted under Article 12, on average, almost two times.[23] This sort of discrepancy is less pronounced with regard to individual persons employed in two or more Member States. In fact, on average, each of these workers received 1.2 PDs A1 during the reference year 2018 (ratio of roughly 82 % between the number of PDs A1 issued for these persons and the actual number of individuals involved).[24]

Besides the aforementioned inherent issues, further uncertainty and lack of reliability of the estimation method described above stem from implementation weaknesses as well. In this regard, it is noticeable that some Member States have elaborated, over the years, their own registration systems.[25] This is the case of the

Law (Second Edition, Oxford University Press 2014) 291; Wispelaere and Pacolet, 'Posting of Workers: Report on A1 Portable Documents Issued in 2017' (n 12) 14; Mijke Houwerzijl and Lisa Berntsen, 'Posting of Workers: From a Blurred Notion Associated with "Cheap Labour" to a Tool for "Fair Labour Mobility"?' in Jens Arnholtz and Nathan Lillie (eds), *Posted Work in the European Union: The Political Economy of Free Movement* (Routledge 2019) 151; Frederic De Wispelaere and Jozef Pacolet, 'The Benefits of Posting: Facts and Figures on the Use and Impact of Intra-EU Posting' in Jens Arnholtz and Nathan Lillie (eds), *Posted Work in the European Union: The Political Economy of Free Movement* (Routledge 2019) 33.

20. Wispelaere and Pacolet, 'Posting of Workers: Report on A1 Portable Documents Issued in 2016' (n 8) 12; Wispelaere and Pacolet, 'Posting of Workers: Report on A1 Portable Documents Issued in 2017' (n 12) 14; Wispelaere, Smedt and Pacolet, 'Posting of Workers: Report on A1 Portable Documents Issued in 2018' (n 8) 14.
21. Wispelaere and Pacolet, 'Posting of Workers: Report on A1 Portable Documents Issued in 2015' (n 8) 10 and 26; Wispelaere and Pacolet, 'Posting of Workers: Report on A1 Portable Documents Issued in 2016' (n 8) 13; Wispelaere and Pacolet, 'Posting of Workers: Report on A1 Portable Documents Issued in 2017' (n 12) 14; Wispelaere, Smedt and Pacolet, 'Posting of Workers: Report on A1 Portable Documents Issued in 2018' (n 8) 14.
22. Voss et al. (n 3) 15; Houwerzijl and Berntsen (n 19) 151.
23. It is underlined that noteworthy differences among the reporting Member States with regard to such a relationship between the PDs A1 and the number of actual persons involved have been recorded. Thus, in Luxembourg and Slovenia the number of individual posted workers corresponded to only 30% of the number of PDs A1 issued, in Poland one individual employed/self-employed person was sent abroad 1.7 times, while in Iceland, Czech Republic, Sweden and Norway the quota of certificates basically corresponded to the number of cross-border services providers. Wispelaere, Smedt and Pacolet, 'Posting of Workers: Report on A1 Portable Documents Issued in 2018' (n 8) 30–31.
24. Also in this case some discrepancies among the reporting Member States have been observed. *Ibid.* 41–42.
25. The study conducted at the HIVA-KU Leuven combined, indeed, the results from the number of PDs A1 collected with data gathered from existing national registration tools of cross-border

Belgian online compulsory registration system called *LIMOSA*,[26] the 'Déclaration préalable de détachement' in France, the '*Communication de détachement de salariés*' (CDS) in Luxembourg, the '*Meldinggrensoverschrijdende dienstverlening/Notification of cross-border services*' in the Netherlands, the '*Meldepflicht*' (Notification to the Central Coordination Office 'ZKO3') in Austria, the '*Registret for udenlandske tjenesteydere*' (Register of Foreign Service Providers – RUT) in Denmark,[27] and a notification form in Slovakia and Slovenia.[28] Unfortunately, however, the Member States able to arrange an effective national system of estimation of cross-border flows of services and (posted) labour are only a few[29] and, because of the absence of uniformity between different national tools, the data are not directly comparable.[30] What is more, significant discrepancies may be identified between the figures based on Portable Documents A1 and national results.[31]

---

labour mobility. Wispelaere and Pacolet, 'An Ad Hoc Statistical Analysis on Short Term Mobility – Economic Value of Posting of Workers: The Impact of Intra-EU Cross-Border Services, with Special Attention to the Construction Sector' (n 15) 9.

26. Acronym for *Landenoverschrijdend Informatiesysteem ten behoeve van Migratie Onderzoek bij de Sociale Administratie.* Belgian online registration system of employee sent by their employer to work in Belgium and self-employed persons travelling to Belgium for work in Belgium, https://www.international.socialsecurity.be/working_in_belgium/en/limosa.html (accessed on 11 May 2018). In particular, the Belgian tracking system of labour inflow, introduced in 2007, foresees the collection in the archive *GOTOT-IN* (Acronym for *GrensOverschrijdende Tewerkstelling – Occupation Transfrontalière.* Belgian control instrument for occupation from abroad, https://www.smals.be/fr/content/occupation-transfrontaliere-gotot-un-instrument-de-controle-pour-loccupation-depuis (accessed on 11 May 2018)) of all data referred to both posted and self-employed service providers established in another Member State, travelling to Belgium to supply service there. It involves any sort of transnational service provision, irrespective of the duration of the mobility. Besides, the *LIMOSA* requires to report certain specific information to the Belgian administrative authorities, including a detailed indication of the identity of the posted worker, of his employer and of the Belgian service user, as well as of the period and location of the service delivery in Belgium. As pointed out *supra* in Chapter 4, the amount of information that the Belgian authorities are allowed to ask from the employers has, nonetheless, been resized by the restrictive interpretation of the Court of Justice. Ninke Mussche, Vincent Corluy and Ive Marx, 'The Rise of the Free Movements: How Posting Shapes a Hybrid Single European Labour Market' (2017) European Journal of Industrial Relations 8; Frederic De Wispelaere and Jozef Pacolet, 'The Size and Impact of Intra-EU Posting on the Belgian Economy: With a Special Focus on the Construction Sector – Summary' (KU Leuven Research Institute for Work and Society (HIVA) 2017) 6–7; Kall and Lillie (n 2) 18.
27. Martin Gräs Lind, 'The Danish Law on the Posting of Workers' (2010) 24 FORMULA Working Paper, University of Oslo, Department of Private Law 7; Frederic De Wispelaere and Jozef Pacolet, 'Measuring the Size of Intra-EU Posting on the Basis of Data Collected at European and National Level' (Conference Intra-EU posting: costs and benefits, Leuven, Belgium, 28 April 2017).
28. Wispelaere and Pacolet, 'Posting of Workers: Report on A1 Portable Documents Issued in 2015' (n 8) 11–12; Wispelaere and Pacolet, 'Measuring the Size of Intra-EU Posting on the Basis of Data Collected at European and National Level' (n 27). For a comprehensive and detailed overview of the variety of information systems in different EU Member States, *see* Roberto Pedersini and Massimo Pallini, 'Posted Workers in the European Union' (Eurofound 2010) 7–13.
29. Wispelaere and Pacolet, 'Posting of Workers: Report on A1 Portable Documents Issued in 2016' (n 8) 23.
30. Maslauskaite (n 18) 4.
31. The weaknesses of the available data have been acknowledged also by the European Commission: 'From a receiving perspective, data from national compulsory registration systems show a relevant gap between EU and national figures, with the latter being up to five times higher in the case of Denmark'. European Commission, Impact Assessment, Accompanying the document

6.3 A HIGHLY EXPANDING PHENOMENON

Moving to the concrete dimension of the posting phenomenon, the actual figures show an overall number of almost 3 million PDs A1 issued in 2018 (latest available data),[32] involving approximately 1.9 million of individual workers posted across borders.[33] In particular, the share of postings to one specific Member State amounts to nearly 1.8 million PDs A1 (corresponding to 61% of the total share), while the amount of A1 documents referring to persons active in two or more Member States under Article 13 of the Basic Regulation is of about 1.1 million (roughly 37% of the total share),[34] and the remaining share concerning other categories is of only 55,000 (almost 2%).[35] *Inter alia*, a quite relevant 6.8% of the postings in accordance with Article 12 of Regulation (EC) 883/2004 were referred to self-employed workers,[36] while 9.4% was the share of A1 forms issued to self-employed persons active in two or more Member States under Article 13(2) of the Basic Regulation.[37]

6.3.1 Quantitative Evolution of Posting

The starting point of the present analysis of the quantitative dimension of posting entails a closer observation of the actual booming of the sector during the last years, as clearly depicted in the Figure 6.1.

Proposal for a Directive of the European Parliament and the Council amending Directive 96/71/EC concerning the posting of workers in the framework of the provision of services 2016 [SWD(2016) 52 final] 57. Similar discrepancies of numbers have been recorded also in Belgium and France. Voss et al. (n 3) 15.

32. Wispelaere, Smedt and Pacolet, 'Posting of Workers: Report on A1 Portable Documents Issued in 2018' (n 8) 15.
33. This number includes the approximately 1 million individual persons that received a PD A1 according to Article 12 and the approximately 900,000 individual persons that received a PD A1 according to Article 13 in 2018. *Ibid.* 31 and 41.
34. Data on A1 documents referring to persons active in two or more Member States are also taken into account given that, as clarified *supra* in Chapter 2, those workers are de facto covered by the host state's set of terms and conditions laid down in the PWD, thus resulting included into the notion of 'posted worker' provided for by the PWD.
35. Wispelaere, Smedt and Pacolet, 'Posting of Workers: Report on A1 Portable Documents Issued in 2018' (n 8) 15.
36. *Ibid.* 28–29. It is recalled that, as ascertained *supra* in Chapter 2, self-employed persons do not fall into the scope of the PWD.
37. *Ibid.* 36.

Figure 6.1 Evolution of the Number of PDs A1/E101 Forms Issued over the Period 2007–2018[38]

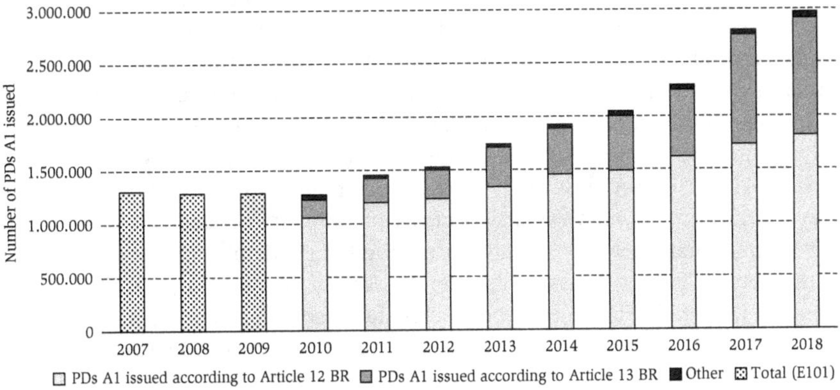

Figure 6.1 *supra* displays the evolution of the number of portable social security documents issued over the period 2007–2018, testifying an overall increase of more than 100% during the reference period.[39] As already mentioned, since data are referred to PDs A1 and E101 forms, they give only an indicative (although quite clear) picture of the actual number of postings.[40] From the bar chart above, it appears evident that, after a period of stagnation between 2007 and 2010,[41] the phenomenon of posting of workers is facing a seamless expansion over the last few years. Noticeably, the numbers suggest a strict correlation of the observed exceptional increase of labour mobility in the form of posting with the expiration of the period of validity of transitional arrangements following the 2004 and 2007 European enlargements towards the East.[42] More specifically, the total number of PDs A1 issued to persons insured in a Member State other than the Member State of (temporary) employment has experienced a remarkable growth corresponding to a 58% increase between 2011

38. *Ibid.* 9.
39. *Ibid.*
40. Wispelaere and Pacolet, 'Posting of Workers: Report on A1 Portable Documents Issued in 2016' (n 8) 12.
41. Maslauskaite (n 18) 4–5; Wispelaere and Pacolet, 'Posting of Workers: Report on A1 Portable Documents Issued in 2016' (n 8) 45; Wispelaere, Smedt and Pacolet, 'Posting of Workers: Report on A1 Portable Documents Issued in 2018' (n 8) 9; Wispelaere, Smedt and Pacolet, 'Coordination of Social Security Systems at a Glance: 2019 Statistical Report' (n 8) 10.
42. As demonstrated in the following section, a consistent share of posted workers comes indeed from the so-called 'new' EU Member States. Dhéret and Ghimis (n 7) 4; Rebecca Zahn, 'Revision of the Posted Workers' Directive: A Europeanisation Perspective' (2017) 19 Cambridge Yearbook of European Legal Studies 187, 194; Houwerzijl and Berntsen (n 19) 149.

and 2016,[43] even a 22% increase between 2016 and 2017,[44] and a roughly 6% of growth rate during the period 2017–2018.[45]

Evidently, in 2018 the growth rate was significantly lower in comparison to previous years, especially with respect to 2017, when the overall 22% increase in the share of PDs A1 issued was almost double than the 12% increase recorded in 2016.[46] The outstanding outcome registered during 2017 was mainly influenced by the remarkable exploit of Germany (+139,677 PDs A1 issued) and, to a lesser extent, by the growing number of postings from Poland (+59,386).[47] In turn, the 2018 growth is mainly due to Germany (+75,959 PDs A1 issued), Spain (+57,384 PDs A1 issued), and Austria (+41,731 PDs A1 issued).[48] Besides, it is noticeable that, while in the phase between 2013 and 2017 the expansion of the phenomenon concerned especially the EU-13 Member States (+106%), rather than the EU-15 Member States (+64%),[49] in 2018 the number of PDs A1 issued by the EU-13 even decreased by 3%.[50]

More in detail, Figure 6.1 above classifies separately the quota referring to postings according to Article 12 of the Basic Regulation on social security coordination from that concerning PDs A1 issued to persons employed in two or more Member States (Article 13 of the Basic Regulation) and from the quota of documents regarding other categories of workers. The most recent figures show that, in comparison to 2017, the number of certificates A1 granted to posted workers to one specific Member State (in line with Article 12 of the Basic Regulation) faced a 4.7% increase.[51] More specifically, while the EU-15 Member States demonstrated a significant growth – led by Germany (+77,249 PDs A1, corresponding to +23%) – the EU-13 Member States showed, in turn, a surprising decrease for the second year in a row. While in 2017 such an effect was directly related to the strong decline of Polish certificates (-24,163 PDs A1,

43. Frederic De Wispelaere and Jozef Pacolet, 'Coordination of Social Security Systems at a Glance: 2016 Statistical Report' (KU Leuven Research Institute for Work and Society (HIVA) 2016) European Commission, Directorate-General for Employment, Social Affairs and Inclusion Directorate D – Labour Mobility Unit D/2 – Social security coordination 17; Wispelaere and Pacolet, 'Posting of Workers: Report on A1 Portable Documents Issued in 2016' (n 8) 45.
44. For the record, the growth rate experienced in the period 2016–2017 is the highest since data on PDs A1 are collected at EU level. Wispelaere and Pacolet, 'Posting of Workers: Report on A1 Portable Documents Issued in 2017' (n 12) 9.
45. Wispelaere, Smedt and Pacolet, 'Posting of Workers: Report on A1 Portable Documents Issued in 2018' (n 8) 20.
46. Wispelaere, Smedt and Pacolet, 'Coordination of Social Security Systems at a Glance: 2018 Statistical Report' (n 8) 12.
47. At the same time, a considerable increase has been observed in Malta (+175%) and Lithuania (+128%), opposed to a decrease in France, Austria, Finland, Sweden, Liechtenstein and Norway. Wispelaere and Pacolet, 'Posting of Workers: Report on A1 Portable Documents Issued in 2017' (n 12) 20–21.
48. Wispelaere, Smedt and Pacolet, 'Posting of Workers: Report on A1 Portable Documents Issued in 2018' (n 8) 20.
49. Wispelaere and Pacolet, 'Posting of Workers: Report on A1 Portable Documents Issued in 2017' (n 12) 20–21.
50. This decrease is mainly related to the decreased number of PDs A1 issued by Slovenia (-63,917). Interestingly, the quota of PDs A1 issued by the four countries belonging to the European Free Trade Association (EFTA), namely Iceland, Liechtenstein, Norway and Switzerland, decreased as well (-7%). Wispelaere, Smedt and Pacolet, 'Posting of Workers: Report on A1 Portable Documents Issued in 2018' (n 8) 9, 20–21.
51. *Ibid.* 9 and 27.

corresponding to -9.3%),[52] in 2018 the decline occurred in Slovenia (-77,877 PDs A1) shall be deemed mainly responsible.[53]

The 4.7% growth rate of transnational postings according to Article 12 of the Basic Regulation registered during 2018 has been accompanied by a solid 7.2% increase of activities in two or more Member States according to Article 13 of the Basic Regulation. In particular, Spain (+44,050 PDs A1), Poland (+26,440 PDs A1) and Slovakia (+19,738) have released much more PDs A1 with respect to 2017. The increasing relevance of PDs A1 issued for activities performed simultaneously or in alternation in different Member States is portrayed even better by the comparison of the number of 168,279 PDs A1 issued in 2010 with the most recent picture of about 1.1 million PDs A1 granted in 2018.[54] This growth is largely due to Poland that passed from 44,018 PDs A1 issued in 2010 to over 351,000 PDs A1 issued in 2018. Notably, an impressive 64% overall growth of such a form of *intra*-EU labour mobility was registered during the timeframe 2010–2017, and it was led by the outstanding performance of Poland (+76,785 PDs A1), followed by Germany (+40,099), Lithuania (+38,361), Romania (+36,042) and Spain (+33,323).[55] From the numbers above, it is therefore evident that a substantial shift from the pattern of cross-border mobility under Article 12 to the one envisaged by Article 13 of Regulation (EC) 883/2004 has progressively taken place between 2016 and 2017.[56] During 2018, however, the balance between those two shares remained basically unchanged.[57]

6.3.2 Duration of Posting

The analysis of the quantitative dimension of posting cannot avoid taking into consideration the actual duration of the transnational posting. This prominent statistic is, in fact, strongly indicative of the concrete use of this type of short-term labour mobility. Empirical numbers indicate an average duration of ninety-one days for each posting to one specific Member State according to Article 12 of Regulation (EC)

52. For the record, a sensible decreasing phase in comparison to 2016 was experienced also in France (-22,844 PDs A1) and Austria (-12,223 PDs A1). Wispelaere and Pacolet, 'Posting of Workers: Report on A1 Portable Documents Issued in 2017' (n 12) 9–10 and 28.
53. In 2018, a significant slowdown phase invested also Portugal (-12,415 PDs A1). Wispelaere, Smedt and Pacolet, 'Posting of Workers: Report on A1 Portable Documents Issued in 2018' (n 8) 27.
54. In other terms, the activities carried out by persons active in two or more Member States have been involved in an impressive over 84% increase during the timeframe 2010–2018. *Ibid.* 37.
55. In particular, the overall growth of such a form of *intra*-EU labour mobility during 2017 was led by the outstanding performance of Poland (+76,785 PDs A1), followed by Germany (+40,099), Lithuania (+38,361), Romania (+36,042) and Spain (+33,323). Wispelaere and Pacolet, 'Posting of Workers: Report on A1 Portable Documents Issued in 2017' (n 12) 39–40.
56. Notably, during that timeframe, the share of PDs A1 issued to persons working, at the same time, in several Member States almost tripled in comparison to the total number of PDs A1 released (from 13% in 2010 to 36% in 2017). Vice versa, a correspondent decrease from 83% in 2010 to 62% in 2017 has involved the share of PDs A1 issued to posted workers. *Ibid.* 21–22.
57. Wispelaere, Smedt and Pacolet, 'Posting of Workers: Report on A1 Portable Documents Issued in 2018' (n 8) 21–22.

883/2004 during 2018.[58] Still, it is worth noting that marked discrepancies of posting duration exist among the sending Member States, from twelve days in Luxembourg, to about one month in France and Belgium, to 122 days in Poland, up to more than 200 days in Estonia, Ireland, Croatia, Latvia and Hungary.[59] Moreover, given that on average a posted worker is sent abroad almost two times per year, the estimated average period an individual person is posted in the territory of another Member State amounts to 165 days.[60]

In turn, with regard to the average timeframe of transnational mobility for persons active in two or more Member States, considering that no maximum period is set by Article 13 of Regulation (EC) 883/2004, the reported quota amounts to almost 300 days (a complete year per individual person).[61] Also in this case, the numbers vary significantly among national realities, from 171 days reported in the Czech Republic to 516 days in Finland.[62]

To sum up, what appears evident from the interesting numbers set out above is that the period of mobility in the latter case lasts significantly more than the average duration of a temporary secondment according to Article 12 of Regulation (EC) 883/2004. Such a relevant discrepancy reflects, indeed, the differences arising from the current rules on social security coordination which, on the one hand, prescribe a maximum time limit of twenty-four months for postings under Article 12 of the Basic Regulation, while, on the other hand, no maximum period is determined by Article 13 for the provision of services in two or more Member States.[63]

58. *Ibid.* 31. Interestingly, the average duration of posting is apparently decreasing, given that it amounted to ninety-three days in 2017. Wispelaere and Pacolet, 'Posting of Workers: Report on A1 Portable Documents Issued in 2017' (n 12) 34.
59. Wispelaere, Smedt and Pacolet, 'Posting of Workers: Report on A1 Portable Documents Issued in 2018' (n 8) 32.
60. The average period a person is posted abroad is obtained by multiplying the average duration per PD A1 by the number of times a person is posted during the year. Nevertheless, it should be noted that, in light of the maximum period of twenty-four months for pursuing an activity covered by Article 12 of the Basic Regulation on social security coordination, the calculated 165 days do not necessarily refer to the same year. *Ibid.* This average duration of mobility over a year appears, indeed, consistent with the '183-days-rule' for taxation of the workers' personal income, established by Article 15 (2) of the OECD (Organisation for Economic Co-operation and Development), *Model Tax Convention on Income and on Capital: Condensed Version, 21 November 2017* (OECD Publishing 2017). More specifically, as mentioned *supra* in Chapter 2, this provision allows a posted worker to be taxed according to his home Member State rules, on condition that he provides services on a temporary basis in another Member State 'for a period or periods not exceeding in the aggregate 183 days in any twelve month period commencing or ending in the fiscal year concerned'.
61. Wispelaere, Smedt and Pacolet, 'Posting of Workers: Report on A1 Portable Documents Issued in 2018' (n 8) 42–43.
62. *Ibid.*
63. Wispelaere and Pacolet, 'Posting of Workers: Report on A1 Portable Documents Issued in 2015' (n 8) 38; Wispelaere and Pacolet, 'Posting of Workers: Report on A1 Portable Documents Issued in 2017' (n 12) 44; Wispelaere, Smedt and Pacolet, 'Posting of Workers: Report on A1 Portable Documents Issued in 2018' (n 8) 43.

6.4 DISTRIBUTION WITHIN THE EU INTERNAL MARKET

A proper understanding of the distribution of the posting phenomenon is considered to be the key to pass an informed and well-balanced judgment on the matter. Moreover, it would allow to better comprehend the decisional dynamics within the European institutions, in light of the varying dimension of the national interests at stake. Indeed, the Member States are not equally affected by this form of transnational labour mobility. As explained further, a decisive role to this extent is played by geographic proximity. Besides, the concentration of posting practices differs greatly within the EU internal market, in line with the different economic sectors involved in different national realities.[64] The respective odds at Member State level represent, therefore, a decisive factor influencing the cross-border mobility of different types of economic activities.

6.4.1 Distribution at Member State Level

With regard to the apportionment in absolute terms among the Member States of the total share of 3 million PDs A1 issued in 2018, Poland is the country that issued the highest quota of A1 documents (605,785 PDs A1 issued, corresponding to 20% of the overall PDs A1), followed by Germany (475,704 PDs A1 issued, corresponding to 16% of the overall PDs A1).[65] As is apparent, the existence of a substantial discrepancy in numbers between those two first sending countries, which released together the 36% of the overall number of PDs A1, and the other Member States is striking. Indeed, Spain (248,532 PDs A1 issued) follows in third place, with roughly half the numbers of Germany, and Italy is the fourth (169,774 PDs A1 issued).[66] Interestingly, all these four countries together counted the majority of the total EU quota of postings during the reference year 2018. Besides, the shares of Belgium, Slovakia, Slovenia, France, Austria and the Netherlands are noticeable as well, with more than 100,000 PDs A1 issued.[67] On the other hand, data analysis in relative terms, i.e., in respect to the percentage of the employed population in 2018, is in many ways revealing when demonstrating the most incidence of posting in Luxembourg (18%) and Slovenia (12%).[68] In contrast with an intuitive, yet misleading perception, in Poland and Germany – by far the two major sending countries in absolute terms – the share of postings corresponded to only a 3.7% and 1.1% respectively of the employed population over the same period.[69]

---

64. Marco Rocca, *Posting of Workers and Collective Labour Law: There and Back Again* (Intersentia 2015) 36.
65. Wispelaere, Smedt and Pacolet, 'Posting of Workers: Report on A1 Portable Documents Issued in 2018' (n 8) 15 and 19.
66. *Ibid.* 15–17.
67. *Ibid.*
68. Notably, the relevance of posting in Slovenia sensibly decreased by 20% in 2017. Wispelaere and Pacolet, 'Posting of Workers: Report on A1 Portable Documents Issued in 2017' (n 12) 20.
69. Wispelaere, Smedt and Pacolet, 'Posting of Workers: Report on A1 Portable Documents Issued in 2018' (n 8) 20.

Looking in detail at the pattern of cross-border labour mobility falling under Article 12 of the Basic Regulation (i.e., postings *stricto sensu*), in the overall 1.8 million PDs A1 released in 2018 the Member States playing the main role as sending countries were Germany (409,340 PDs A1, corresponding to a roughly 20% of the total), Poland (238,525 PDs A1) and, to a lesser extent, Italy (148,863), Spain (123,670) and France (117,739).[70] In turn, from a receiving perspective, this form of labour migration mainly affected Germany (428,935 PDs A1), France (262,162 PDs A1) and Belgium (156,695 PDs A1).[71] An interesting schematic representation, able to clarify the actual incidence of posting at Member State level, is provided by Figure 6.2 below which displays a breakdown by country of the net balance of postings in relative terms between outgoing and incoming postings.[72]

70. Interestingly, approximately 30% of the total quota of PDs A1 issued during 2018 to self-employed persons according to Article 12(2) of Regulation (EC) 883/2004 came from Slovakia. *Ibid.* 19 and 23.
71. In particular, Germany received a remarkable 24% of the total number of postings during 2018. It is worth mentioning that data by receiving Member State are only available for the PDs A1 issued to posted workers according to Article 12 of Regulation (EC) No 883/2004, the remaining PDs A1 issued to persons active in two or more Member States according to Article 13 of Regulation (EC) No 883/2004 are excluded. *Ibid.* 23; Frederic De Wispelaere, Saena Chakkar and Ludo Struyven, 'Incoming and Outgoing Posted Workers in the Belgian Labour Market Statistics: With a Focus on the Brussels-Capital Region, Summary' (KU Leuven Research Institute for Work and Society (HIVA) 2020) 6. On this point, *see also* Bettina Wagner and Anke Hassel, 'Posting, Subcontracting and Low-Wage Employment in the German Meat Industry' (2016) 22 Transfer: European Review of Labour and Research 163, 168.
72. This net balance is calculated by subtracting the number of PDs A1 received from the number of PDs A1 issued according to Article 12 of the Basic Regulation. Wispelaere, Smedt and Pacolet, 'Posting of Workers: Report on A1 Portable Documents Issued in 2018' (n 8) 25.

Figure 6.2 Net Balance Between the Number of PDs A1 Issued and Received According to Article 12 of the Basic Regulation, 2018[73]

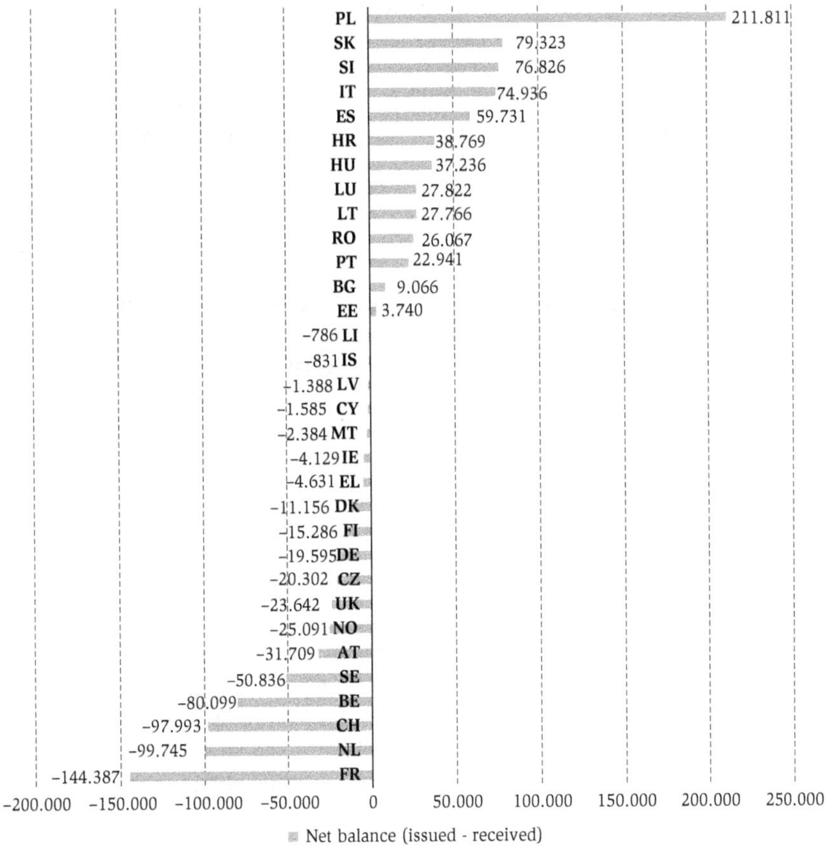

Figure 6.2 indicates thirteen countries as net senders of posted workers (with more PDs A1 issued than received) especially Poland, Slovakia and Slovenia. An opposite trend is recorded in the remaining nineteen net recipients countries (with more PDs A1 received than issued) and, among them, France and the Netherlands are the ones mainly affected in absolute terms.[74] Interestingly, the combination of posting breakdowns by sending and receiving Member States makes it possible to detect the main flows of such a type on intra-EU labour mobility. The largest posting flow in 2018 was the one from Poland to Germany (120,540 PDs A1), corresponding to 7% of the

73. *Ibid.* Figure 6.2 includes, besides the EU Member States, also the EFTA countries.
74. Among the net recipient countries, France and the Netherlands are closely followed by Switzerland, Belgium and Sweden. *Ibid.* 24–25.

total number of PDs A1 issued according to Article 12.[75] Other relevant flows were observed from Germany to Austria (60,753 PDs A1), from Germany to France (54,575 PDs A1), from Germany to Switzerland (52,322 PDs A1), from Germany to the Netherlands (47,502 A1) and from Slovenia to Germany (45,176 PDs A1).

Finally, with respect to the category of persons working at the same time in several Member States, Poland stands distinctly at the top of the ranking with 351,000 certificates released in 2018 out of the total 1.1 million at EU level (thus corresponding to an impressive third of the total EU share). A remarkably high number of PDs A1 was also issued by Spain (121,713 PDs A1).[76]

6.4.2 Mobility Trends

The next step of analysis of the phenomenon under consideration entails the identification of mobility trends across the EU labour market. In this sense, the role of geographic proximity is generally recognised as a decisive factor, the most relevant in determining the distribution of flows of posting across the EU internal market.[77] In fact, in 2018 almost half of the postings took place between neighbouring Member States.[78] Such a trend is particularly evident in Belgium and Luxembourg, whereby more than 80% of posted workers are sent to a neighbouring Member State.[79] Moreover, a significant share of workforce mobility directed to a neighbouring country has been experienced during 2018 in Germany, France and Italy as well.[80]

When looking instead at the wider EU picture, in light of the high tension existing in the current public and political debate between the 'old' and the 'new' EU Member States,[81] the actual measure of posted workers flows among these clusters of Member States is considered of particular interest. The starting point in this sense is represented by the 1.65 million PDs A1 issued by the EU-15 Member States during 2018 (71% of which was issued to persons covered by Article 12) and the 1.28 million PDs A1 released by the EU-13 Member States during the same period (49% of which was issued

75. *Ibid.* 23.
76. *Ibid.* 36–37.
77. ISMERI Europa (n 8) 45.
78. Wispelaere, Smedt and Pacolet, 'Posting of Workers: Report on A1 Portable Documents Issued in 2018' (n 8) 23. This trend is lasting for years. Wispelaere and Pacolet, 'Posting of Workers: Report on A1 Portable Documents Issued in 2017' (n 12) 23. Such a noticeable trend has been recorded in the previous years as well. Wispelaere and Pacolet, 'Posting of Workers: Report on A1 Portable Documents Issued in 2012 and 2013' (n 8) 22–24; Wispelaere and Pacolet, 'Posting of Workers: Report on A1 Portable Documents Issued in 2014' (n 8) 19–20; Wispelaere and Pacolet, 'Posting of Workers: Report on A1 Portable Documents Issued in 2015' (n 8) 20–21.
79. Wispelaere, Smedt and Pacolet, 'Posting of Workers: Report on A1 Portable Documents Issued in 2018' (n 8) 24.
80. *Ibid.*
81. It is recalled that the 'old' EU Member States, also referred to as 'EU-15', are: Belgium, Greece, Luxembourg, Denmark, Spain, Netherlands, Germany, France, Portugal, Ireland, Italy, United Kingdom, Austria, Finland and Sweden; while the 'new' EU Member States, or 'EU-13', are: Croatia, Romania, Bulgaria, Poland, Czech Republic, Latvia, Lithuania, Slovenia, Estonia, Slovakia, Hungary, Cyprus and Malta; and 'EFTA' countries are Switzerland, Liechtenstein, Norway and Iceland.

to persons covered by Article 13).[82] Figure 6.3 may help shed some light on the actual distribution of the 1.8 million postings performed in the framework of Article 12 of Regulation (EC) 883/2004 (i.e., postings *stricto sensu*).

Figure 6.3 PDs A1 for Posted Workers Issued, Breakdown by Classification of Sending and Receiving Countries, 2018[83]

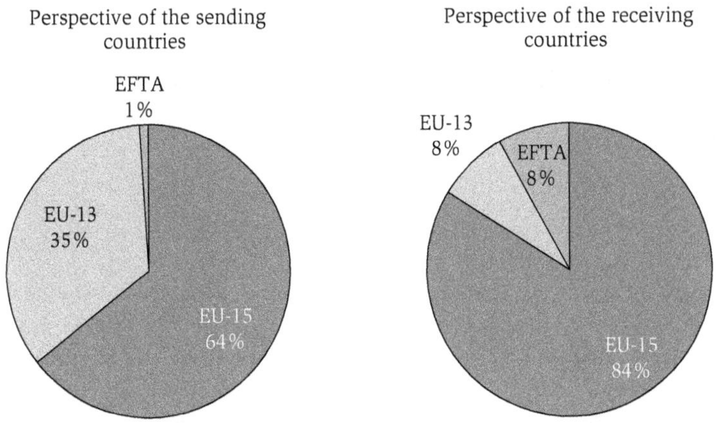

Figure 6.3 clearly depicts the overall posting trends in 2018 from a sending and a receiving perspective. The EU-15 Member States have issued the majority (64%) of the PDs A1 to posted workers according to Article 12 of the Basic Regulation (roughly 1.17 million), while the EU-13 Member States have released the remaining 35% (roughly 625,000).[84] Interestingly, during the last year, the share of EU-15 Member States strongly increased (it was 58% in 2017), mainly due to the growth experienced in Germany and the contextual decline in Slovenia.[85]

The right part of the figure, in turn, shows the 84% rate of postings inflow to the EU-15 Member States, where France (+20,763 PDs A1) and the Netherlands (+14,820 PDs A1) have registered higher numbers of PDs A1 received according to Article 12 than the previous year, while a strong decrease has been recorded in Austria (-21,139) and Belgium (-10,640).[86] What is evident from the available data is that the large majority of postings is carried out on the soil of the EU-15 Member States, but also that this form of labour mobility does not merely concern a movement from the EU-13 to the EU-15 Member States, as it involves a significant percentage (52%) of workers moving

82. Wispelaere, Smedt and Pacolet, 'Posting of Workers: Report on A1 Portable Documents Issued in 2018' (n 8) 9, 15, 17–18.
83. *Ibid.* 26.
84. *Ibid.* 17 and 26.
85. *Ibid.* 26.
86. *Ibid.* 27.

across the EU-15 Member States.[87] In this regard, a detailed picture of the observed flows among EU-15, EU-13 and EFTA countries is provided by Figure 6.4.

Figure 6.4 Flow of Postings According to Article 12 of the Basic Regulation Between EU-15, EU-13 and EFTA Countries, 2018[88]

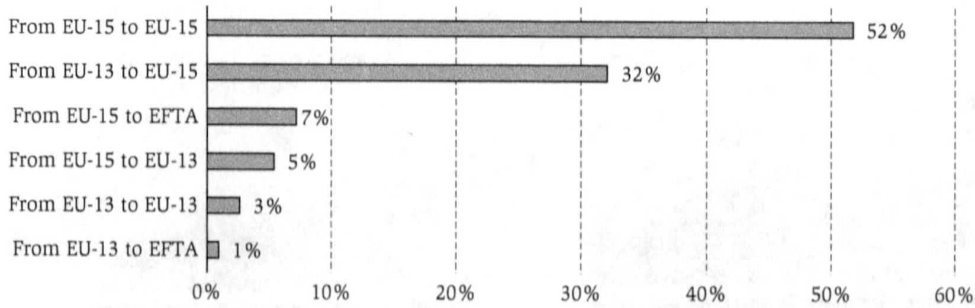

In accordance with the shares displayed above, the highly problematic transnational labour mobility from the 'poorer' Eastern to the 'richer' Western Member States, as generally depicted within the common public discourse in the European Union,[89] is proven to be relatively false. Figure 6.4 clearly demonstrates, indeed, how this type of cross-border service provision concerns mostly *intra*-high-wage Member States movements and, to a lesser extent, low-wage to high-wage Member States movements. In effect, the quota of postings received by EU-15 countries is composed, for the most part, by workers coming from the EU-15 Member States, and only for approximately 38% by workers coming from the EU-13.[90] As a result, the flow from low-wage to high-wage countries corresponds to only a third of the overall number of intra-EU postings.[91]

87. *Ibid.* 26. For the record, in 2017 the EU-13 Member States participated to a higher extent (90%) in cross-border mobility directed to the EU-15 Member States, than the EU-15 Member States themselves (82%). Wispelaere and Pacolet, 'Posting of Workers: Report on A1 Portable Documents Issued in 2017' (n 12) 25–26.
88. Wispelaere, Smedt and Pacolet, 'Posting of Workers: Report on A1 Portable Documents Issued in 2018' (n 8) 26.
89. The viewpoint implicitly expressed by Advocate General Campos Sánchez-Bordona in *Hungary v European Parliament, Council of the European Union* is emblematic is this sense, where he labelled, without question, the 'old' Western Member States as 'exporters' of posted workers and the 'new' Central and Eastern Member States as 'receivers' of such workers. *Hungary v European Parliament, Council of the European Union, Opinion of Advocate General Manuel Campos Sánchez-Bordona delivered on 28 May 2020* [2020] CJEU Case C-620/18, ECLI: EU:C:2020:392 [46].
90. Wispelaere, Smedt and Pacolet, 'Posting of Workers: Report on A1 Portable Documents Issued in 2018' (n 8) 26.
91. In this sense, *see also* Dhéret and Ghimis (n 7) 5–6; Mussche, Corluy and Marx (n 26) 16; Frederic De Wispelaere, 'Intra-EU Posting Costs and Benefits' (25th International Conference of Europeanists, Chicago, 28 March 2018) 3 and 7; Dries Lens, Ninke Mussche and Ive Marx, 'Europe's Ever Expanding Mobility Patterns – Posting, Third-Country Nationals and the Single European Labour Market' (2019) CSB Working Paper No. 19.08 University of Antwerp – Herman Deleeck Centre for Social Policy 10; Wispelaere, Smedt and Pacolet, 'Posting of Workers: Report on A1 Portable Documents Issued in 2018' (n 8) 26.

6.4.3 Distribution by Economic Sector

The last step of the present analysis on the peculiar aspects concerning the distribution of posting of workers within the internal market focuses on the breakdown by economic sector. Public opinion, media and academic literature commonly associate only a few economic activities with posting. Among all, the construction sector is correctly identified as the prevalent type of business where this form of short-term labour mobility is most widespread.[92] However, the context at issue involves a wide variety of other economic activities, including metal industry, maintenance of electric machines, petrochemical industry, ICT (information and communications technology), professional, scientific and technical activities, art, education, health and social work activities, human health and social work activities, transport and storage, food industry, cleaning, agriculture, hunting, and fishing.[93]

The picture of the distribution of postings by economic sector during 2018 is extremely fragmented, with major differences between pattern of cross-border labour mobility under Articles 12 and 13 of the Basic Regulation, respectively. *Inter alia*, empirical evidence clearly proves that posted workers tend to be employed for the provision of labour-intensive services, although a rather relevant share of postings involves medium and high-skilled workers as well, for the provision of administrative, professional and financial services.[94] The two largest sectors in which PDs A1 have been issued in 2018 were the industry sector (i.e., construction and manufacturing) with 775,543 postings and the service sector with 725,345 postings.[95] More specifically, latest available data indicate that on average 40% of the persons posted according to Article 12 of Regulation (EC) 883/2004 worked in the construction sector, thereby testifying a significant decline of 7% from the previous year.[96] This type of activity concerns primarily posted workers *stricto sensu*, rather than person active in two or more Member States. Indeed, 7 out of 10 postings in the construction sector concern persons covered by Article 12 and only 3 out of 10 involve persons covered by Article 13.[97] This is confirmed also by the fact that 'only' 17% of the forms issued to persons

92. Erka Caro et al., 'Posted Migration and Segregation in the European Construction Sector' (2015) 41 Journal of Ethnic and Migration Studies 1600, 1605; Wispelaere and Pacolet, 'Posting of Workers: Report on A1 Portable Documents Issued in 2014' (n 8) 23–27; Wispelaere and Pacolet, 'Posting of Workers: Report on A1 Portable Documents Issued in 2015' (n 8) 24–25; Wispelaere and Pacolet, 'Posting of Workers: Report on A1 Portable Documents Issued in 2016' (n 8) 27; Wispelaere and Pacolet, 'Posting of Workers: Report on A1 Portable Documents Issued in 2017' (n 12) 30–32; Wispelaere, Smedt and Pacolet, 'Posting of Workers: Report on A1 Portable Documents Issued in 2018' (n 8) 29.
93. Mussche, Corluy and Marx (n 26) 14; Wispelaere, Smedt and Pacolet, 'Posting of Workers: Report on A1 Portable Documents Issued in 2018' (n 8) 30.
94. European Commission Impact Assessment, Accompanying the document Proposal for a Directive of the European Parliament and the Council amending Directive 96/71/EC concerning the posting of workers in the framework of the provision of services (n 31) 33; Dhéret and Ghimis (n 7) 6.
95. Wispelaere, Smedt and Pacolet, 'Posting of Workers: Report on A1 Portable Documents Issued in 2018' (n 8) 48–49.
96. *Ibid.* 29–30.
97. *Ibid.* 40.

active in two or more Member States concern the construction sector.[98] The figures at national level show particular popularity of workers posted in this economic area especially in Central and Eastern European Countries, and a correspondent incidence in terms of incoming workforce to Western Member States.[99]

Postings under Article 13 of Regulation (EC) 883/2004 are, in turn, mainly concerning the service sector, including both transport and personal services, such as education, health and social work, and business services, including administrative, professional and financial services. In particular, the provision of road freight transport services is traditionally operated by workers active in two or more Member States. Accordingly, it is not surprising that half of the A1 certificates issued on the basis of Article 13 are referred to persons employed in the road freight transport sector.[100] Notably, workers employed in transport activities mainly came from Poland, which only in 2018 granted almost 180,000 PDs A1 in the sector.[101] The quota of posting in the road freight transport sector has also relative importance in Croatia, Latvia, Lithuania, Luxembourg, Slovakia and Liechtenstein, where it concerned more than 50% of the PDs A1 issued.[102]

In conclusion, an in-depth examination of the previously identified two major labour mobility trends – across high-wage Member States and from low-wage to high-wage Member States – in light of the different economic sectors concerned demonstrates even more interesting connotations of those flows. More specifically, it is possible to detect the presence of substantial differences corresponding to different economic activities respectively involved. A significantly higher concentration of workers posted from low-wage Member States in the construction sector has been detected. In turn, persons coming from high-wage Member States result more frequently employed in more qualified occupations.[103] The two main flows of posted workers within the EU (across high-wage Member States and from low-wage to high-wage Member States) can thereby be further specified. Accordingly, the resulting framework proves the existence of two prevailing flows: one of medium to high-skilled workers posted mainly across high-wage Member States, and another of low to medium-skilled workers providing labour-intensive services from the 'new' to the 'old' Member States.[104]

98. *Ibid.* 30 and 40.

99. Mikkel Barslund, Matthias Busse and Frederic De Wispelaere, 'Posted Workers – For Some It Matters' (2017) CEPS (Centre for European Policy Studies) 4–5; Wispelaere and Pacolet, 'Posting of Workers: Report on A1 Portable Documents Issued in 2017' (n 12) 32; Wispelaere, Smedt and Pacolet, 'Posting of Workers: Report on A1 Portable Documents Issued in 2018' (n 8) 30.

100. Wispelaere, Smedt and Pacolet, 'Posting of Workers: Report on A1 Portable Documents Issued in 2018' (n 8) 40.

101. *Ibid.* 39–40 and 49.

102. *Ibid.* 39–40.

103. Wispelaere and Pacolet, 'Posting of Workers: Report on A1 Portable Documents Issued in 2016' (n 8) 28; Wispelaere, Smedt and Pacolet, 'Posting of Workers: Report on A1 Portable Documents Issued in 2018' (n 8) 30.

104. Wispelaere and Pacolet, 'An Ad Hoc Statistical Analysis on Short Term Mobility – Economic Value of Posting of Workers: The Impact of Intra-EU Cross-Border Services, with Special Attention to the Construction Sector' (n 15) 10; Zahn (n 42) 11.

6.5 ECONOMIC RELEVANCE OF POSTING

The overall 3 million Portable Documents A1 issued in 2018, despite the redundancy of the numbers in absolute terms – having an exceptional echo especially among public opinion and politicians – demonstrate, nevertheless, a rather marginal share when compared to the total 230 million workers in the entire EU labour market (197 million employed and 33 million self-employed persons).[105] In percentage terms, it represents just 1.2% of total EU employment. This includes both posted workers and persons active in two or more Member States which stand, respectively, at 0.8% and 0.4% of total EU employment.[106]

As explained before, however, the quota of PDs A1 released does not constitute the best indicator, due to the lack of necessary correspondence with the actual number of persons involved. In fact, the same individual could be posted multiple times during the same year, implying that more than one PDs A1 may be issued to the same worker during the same referring period. In turn, the numbers of individual persons involved or of workers in full-time equivalents (FTE)[107] are both able to reflect more accurately the actual dimension of this type of labour mobility. In particular, the share of posting within the total EU employment market in terms of unique posted persons and persons in full-time equivalents reduces significantly to 0.8% and 0.6% respectively. Individual workers posted according to Article 12 of the Basic Regulation, in turn, represent 0.4% of total EU employment, corresponding to only 0.2% in terms of full-time equivalents.[108] Curiously, the workload (in FTE) carried out by workers posted under Article 12 during 2018 was almost half the work volume of persons active in two or more countries.[109] A graphical representation of such an interesting point of view is provided by Figure 6.5.

105. Eurostat, 'Self-Employed Persons' (*Eurostat*, 30 April 2019) <https://ec.europa.eu/eurostat/web/products-eurostat-news/-/EDN-20190430-1> (accessed 4 June 2019); Eurostat, 'Employment by Sex, Age and Citizenship (1 000)' (*Eurostat – Data Explorer*, 13 February 2020) <https://appsso.eurostat.ec.europa.eu/nui/submitViewTableAction.do> (accessed 21 February 2020).
106. Wispelaere, Smedt and Pacolet, 'Posting of Workers: Report on A1 Portable Documents Issued in 2018' (n 8) 11.
107. A full-time equivalent (indicated with the acronym 'FTE') is a unit that allows to compare employed persons working for a different number of hours per week. It is obtained by comparing an employee's average number of hours worked with the average number of hours of a full-time worker. Hence, one FTE corresponds to the hours worked by a full-time person, while a part-time worker gets a score in proportion to the hours he actually works. In concrete terms, a part-time worker employed for twenty hours a week where full-time work consists of forty hours, is counted as 0.5 FTE. Eurostat, 'Glossary: Full-Time Equivalent (FTE)' (*Eurostat – Statistics Explained*, 2019) <https://ec.europa.eu/eurostat/statistics-explained/index.php/Glossary:Full-time_equivalent_(FTE)> (accessed 4 June 2019).
108. Wispelaere, Smedt and Pacolet, 'Posting of Workers: Report on A1 Portable Documents Issued in 2018' (n 8) 33–34.
109. This is due to the fact that workers covered by Article 12 stay abroad for a short period of time only, while those moving under Article 13 are usually staying abroad longer. *Ibid.* 34 and 44.

Figure 6.5 Share of PDs A1 in National Employment During 2018[110]

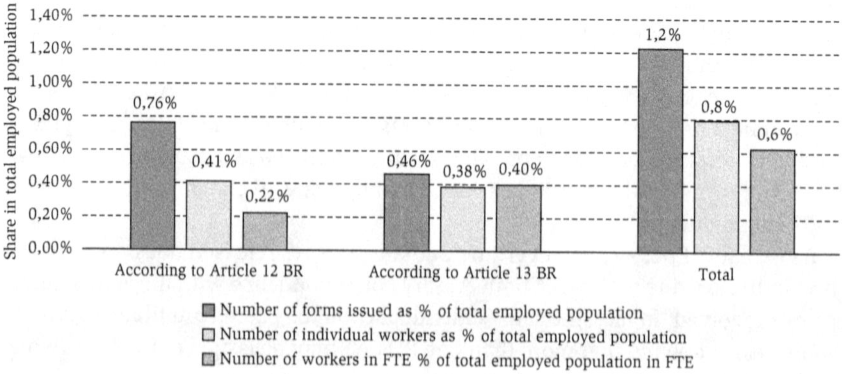

Interestingly, the rather modest dimension of intra-EU labour mobility appears also evident in relation to the higher rates of interstate mobility experienced in the US and Canada, where the share amounts to 3% and 2% respectively.[111] Anyway, when confronted with other forms of transnational labour mobility within the EU internal market, cross-border posting still maintains an important relevance. In that regard, the comparison of the approximately 1.9 million of individual workers posted across borders with the overall 9.7 million of active EU-28 movers (employed or looking for work), which correspond to a rough 4.1% share of the total EU labour force, definitely deserves attention.[112]

Notwithstanding the evidently limited size of posting of workers in absolute numbers, its actual relevance can be better recognised by focusing on its distribution at Member State level. Within the internal market, certain national realities, and especially some specific economic sectors, are indeed confronted with consistent shares of outgoing or incoming temporary workforce mobility in the form of posting. In Luxembourg, 6.6% of the employed population is posted abroad under Article 12 of the Basic Regulation and 4.3% is active in two or more Member States, in Slovenia those shares are both 3.0%, in Slovakia 2.3% and 1.4% respectively. It is apparent, therefore, that posting is extremely relevant in those countries.[113] In particular, the impact on the Slovenian economy was even more significant in 2017, as testified by the estimated EUR 1.25 billion of taxable income (corresponding to almost 1% of annual

110. *Ibid.* 11.
111. Mussche, Corluy and Marx (n 26) 15; Wispelaere and Pacolet, 'An Ad Hoc Statistical Analysis on Short Term Mobility – Economic Value of Posting of Workers: The Impact of Intra-EU Cross-Border Services, with Special Attention to the Construction Sector' (n 15) 9.
112. Elena Fries-Tersch et al., '2019 Annual Report on Intra-EU Labour Mobility: Final Report January 2020' (European Commission, Directorate-General for Employment, Social Affairs and Inclusion Directorate D – Labour Mobility Unit D1 – Free movement of workers, EURES 2020) 17.
113. Wispelaere, Smedt and Pacolet, 'Posting of Workers: Report on A1 Portable Documents Issued in 2018' (n 8) 33 and 44.

gross domestic product (GDP)) and EUR 500 million of social security contributions due on account of posting activities.[114] In parallel, Luxembourg, Belgium and Austria are confronted, in relative terms, with an important amount of incoming posted workers.[115]

As far as the breakdown by sector of economic activity is concerned, a notable share of outgoing posted workers in the construction industry has been observed in Luxembourg and Slovenia, where roughly 41% and 31%, respectively, of employed persons are posted abroad.[116] Interestingly, the numbers of the workers posted in the Slovenian construction sector dramatically decreased during last year, as in 2017 almost 6 out of 10 employed persons were sent abroad in the framework of this form of labour mobility.[117] During 2018, high percentages have also been recorded in Croatia (14%), Slovakia (11%) and Poland (5%).[118] In turn, the Luxembourg, Austrian and Belgian building industries received a huge number of foreign posted workers compared to the total national employment share in the sector.[119] Considering the size of their national markets, relevant shares of incoming posted workers have been recorded also in the construction sectors in Germany and France.[120] Notwithstanding the importance in relative terms of cross-border posting in the construction sector, its limited economic relevance within the overall EU internal market, representing only 0.8% of the total EU-turnover, deserves attention. Looking at the figures at national level, only in Denmark, Slovenia and Estonia this type of labour mobility makes up a significant 5% of total national turnover.[121]

Another sector in which extensive use of posted workers has been observed is that of meat processing in Germany, which involved in 2012 almost 40% of the overall

114. Barslund, Busse and Wispelaere (n 99) 5.
115. Wispelaere and Pacolet, 'An Ad Hoc Statistical Analysis on Short Term Mobility – Economic Value of Posting of Workers: The Impact of Intra-EU Cross-Border Services, with Special Attention to the Construction Sector' (n 15) 10, 26, 29–31; Wispelaere and Pacolet, 'Posting of Workers: Report on A1 Portable Documents Issued in 2016' (n 8) 34–35; Wispelaere (n 91).
116. Wispelaere, Smedt and Pacolet, 'Posting of Workers: Report on A1 Portable Documents Issued in 2018' (n 8) 34.
117. Wispelaere and Pacolet, 'An Ad Hoc Statistical Analysis on Short Term Mobility – Economic Value of Posting of Workers: The Impact of Intra-EU Cross-Border Services, with Special Attention to the Construction Sector' (n 15) 16; Wispelaere and Pacolet, 'Posting of Workers: Report on A1 Portable Documents Issued in 2016' (n 8) 33–34 and 46; Wispelaere and Pacolet, 'Posting of Workers: Report on A1 Portable Documents Issued in 2017' (n 12) 36–37; Wispelaere, Smedt and Pacolet, 'Posting of Workers: Report on A1 Portable Documents Issued in 2018' (n 8) 34.
118. The percentage of Poland has a relative high importance in relation to the high absolute numbers in the sector. Wispelaere, Smedt and Pacolet, 'Posting of Workers: Report on A1 Portable Documents Issued in 2018' (n 8) 34.
119. Wispelaere and Pacolet, 'The Size and Impact of Intra-EU Posting on the Belgian Economy: With a Special Focus on the Construction Sector – Summary' (n 26) 11; Wispelaere and Pacolet, 'Posting of Workers: Report on A1 Portable Documents Issued in 2017' (n 12) 37.
120. Wispelaere (n 91); Wispelaere and Pacolet, 'Posting of Workers: Report on A1 Portable Documents Issued in 2017' (n 12) 37.
121. It should be noted, however, that these data are referring to the whole range of cross-border construction services, being posting of workers just a part of them. On this point, *see* Wispelaere and Pacolet, 'An Ad Hoc Statistical Analysis on Short Term Mobility – Economic Value of Posting of Workers: The Impact of Intra-EU Cross-Border Services, with Special Attention to the Construction Sector' (n 15) 17 and 24.

number of the workers employed in the sector.[122] It is worth noting, nevertheless, that this form of short-term labour mobility is no longer used since the conclusion in 2014 of a sectoral collective agreement introducing a minimum wage for the sector, which was subsequently declared universally binding, and the signing up in 2015 of a Voluntary Agreement by the six largest German meat producers, whereby the phasing out of the use of posted workers was agreed.[123]

Finally, as highlighted in the previous section, the use of posted workers plays also an important economic role in the transport sector, mainly involving persons active in two or more Member States. In fact, in certain countries, a relatively large share of persons employed in the sector of freight transport by road have requested an A1 certificate for the simultaneous performance of the job in different Member States. Notably, the percentage of truck drivers active in two or more Member States amounts to over 60% in Luxembourg, almost 50% in Slovakia, over 40% in Poland and almost 40% in Croatia.[124]

6.6 IMPACT OF COVID-19

As anticipated *supra* in Chapter 1, precise data on the impact of the Coronavirus (COVID-19) pandemic are not available yet. This notwithstanding, the aforementioned tragedy that has involved not only the European Union, but also the entire world has had undoubtedly countless repercussions on the practice of posting of workers. Due to its intrinsic cross-border dimension, the phenomenon at issue has been, indeed, particularly exposed to issues directly connected with the limitation of free movement of persons across borders followed from the action taken at Member State level since March 2020 with a view to circumscribing the effects of the pandemic. As a matter of fact, during the first half of 2020, posting of workers across borders has been extremely complicated, if not sometimes impossible at all. Several contracts for the provision of services have been suspended or terminated.[125]

Against this background, some Member States expressed their concern about not being able to effectively implement the new set of rules laid down in Directive (EU) 2018/957 by the end of the two-year implementation period, namely on 30 July 2020. The level of labour mobility within the internal market has dramatically decreased and a number of companies declared not to be ready for the newly established legal framework. Notably, twelve organisations from Poland, Germany, France, the Netherlands and Spain called on the European Commission to consider the opportunity to

122. In 2012, 47,159 posted workers were employed in German slaughterhouses and 42,449 in meat processing. Wagner and Hassel (n 71) 171.
123. Ines Wagner, 'Changing Regulations, Changing Practices?: The Case of the German Meat Industry' (2017) *Project: 'Protecting Mobility through Improving Labour Rights Enforcement in Europe (PROMO)', VS/2016/0222*, 12, 3 and 6; Marco Rocca, 'Not Dead yet: Legal Strategies at National Level and the Reform of the EU Posting of Workers Directive' (2018) 12–13.
124. Wispelaere, Smedt and Pacolet, 'Posting of Workers: Report on A1 Portable Documents Issued in 2018' (n 8) 45.
125. 'Call on the Postponement of Application of Revised Posting Rules' (*Labour Mobility Initiative*, 29 April 2020) <https://www.mobilelabour.eu/13159/call-on-the-postponement-of-application-of-revised-posting-rules/> (accessed 15 June 2020).

postpone the date of applicability of the legislative *novella* by a year, i.e., until 30 July 2021.[126] However, the Commission considered that such a postponement was not necessary.

6.7 CONCLUDING REMARKS

The practice of posting of workers is one of the channels of intra-EU labour mobility that mostly expanded over the last years, contributing to shaping an EU labour market characterised by an increasingly higher degree of mobility. The analysis carried out in this chapter has demonstrated, nevertheless, that the phase of exceptional quantitative expansion involving the posting phenomenon assumes significant relevance in numerical terms only in some Member States and in certain economic sectors. Despite the absence of an EU-wide register tracking the specific pattern of cross-border labour mobility under consideration, the combination of official studies drafted on behalf of the European Commission with other types of surveys including data collected by national registration tools has proved to be able to provide a sufficiently reliable picture of the material size of posting in the EU.

Latest available data indicate an overall number of 3 million postings in 2018 (including posted workers *stricto sensu* and persons active in two or more Member States), involving approximately 1.9 million of individual workers posted across borders. This numbers directly follow from years of seamless expansion, sealed by an impressive growth rate of more than 100% between 2011 and 2018. A more detailed analysis has shown that this increase has been exceptional in 2017 (+22%), when the number of postings according to Article 13 of Regulation (EC) 883/2004 experienced an outstanding increase. The overall 6% growth rate during the period 2017–2018 concerned both postings under Article 12 and under Article 13 of the Basic Regulation. Noticeably, the numbers suggest a strict correlation of the observed exceptional increase with the 2004 and 2007 European enlargements towards the East. Nonetheless, while in the phase between 2013 and 2017 the expansion of the phenomenon concerned especially the EU-13 Member States (+106%), rather than the EU-15 Member States (+64%), in 2018 the number of PDs A1 issued by the EU-13 even decreased by 3%.

As far as the temporal dimension of this type of short-term workforce mobility is concerned, the average duration of each posting to one specific Member State is estimated at 91 days (165 days per individual posted person), while the period of mobility for persons active in two or more Member States at almost 300 days (one complete year per individual person). Such a relevant discrepancy reflects, indeed, the correspondent differences with regard to the respective normative treatment.

When looking at the distribution at Member State level, Poland and Germany are the undisputed major sending countries in absolute terms (counting in combination

126. Stefan Schwarz and Marek Benio, 'Letter to Mr Nicolas Schmit Commissioner for Jobs and Social Rights' (28 April 2020) <https://www.mobilelabour.eu/wp-content/uploads/2020/04/position-Letter-to-Commission-Revised-posting-of-workers-directive.pdf> (accessed 15 June 2020).

36% of the total EU share), followed by Spain and Italy. In particular, while Germany was the main sender of posted workers in the framework of Article 12 of Regulation (EC) 883/2004, Poland issued almost a third of the overall A1 certificates to persons pursuing activities in two or more Member States. In turn, the perspective is strongly different when focusing on the relative dimension, being Luxembourg and Slovenia the two major sending territories in terms of the percentage of workers involved in relation to their total share of employment. Besides, from a confrontation of outgoing and incoming postings, Poland, Slovakia and Slovenia turn out to be the leading net sender countries, while the main quantitative incidence of this phenomenon has been recorded in France and the Netherlands, which have been identified as the main net receivers. In addition, by means of a combination of breakdowns by sending and receiving Member States, the main posting flow detected during 2018 was from Poland to Germany, and other relevant flows originated from Germany and were directed to Austria, France, Switzerland and the Netherlands.

Accordingly, a first observed trend displays the role of geographic proximity as an important feature of this form of mobility, considering that almost half of the postings take place between neighbouring countries. Although an easy syllogism, generally accepted within the common public discourse in the European Union, may lead to the classification of the overall flow of posted workers as directed from the 'poorer' Central and Eastern to the 'richer' Western Member States, such a rationale has been demonstrated to be relatively false. Indeed, the actual figures depict a preponderance of intra-EU-15 Member States movements (52%) and, to a lesser extent, movements from the EU-13 to the EU-15 Member States (32%). As a result, the flow from low-wage to high-wage countries corresponds only to a third of the overall number of intra-EU postings.

Besides concerning mainly a limited number of countries, the phenomenon at issue is also concentrated in certain sectors. Empirical evidence shows that posted workers tend to be employed for the provision of labour-intensive services, being the industry sector (especially construction) the prevalent type of business where this form of short-term labour mobility is most widespread. Nonetheless, a rather relevant share of postings involves also medium and high-skilled workers who are temporarily seconded abroad for the provision of administrative, professional and financial services. In turn, persons working at the same time in several Member States are employed especially in the road freight transport sector. A combination of this distribution with the actual shares of concentration at Member State level makes it possible to specify the definition of the previously identified two major flow trends of posted workers within the EU internal market. Two major movements of posted workers may thereby be identified: one of medium to high-skilled workers posted mainly across high-wage Member States and another of low to medium-skilled workers providing labour-intensive services from the 'new' to the 'old' Member States.

Even though the size of transnational posting has continued to increase over the last years, its economic relevance on the European labour market has remained rather marginal when compared to the total EU employment. In fact, it represents just a tiny 1.2% of the overall number of workers in the whole EU labour market. More specifically, this quota reduces significantly when observed in terms of individual posted persons and persons in full-time equivalents, to 0.8% and 0.6% respectively. The actual relevance of this phenomenon is better evaluated by looking at its influence within specific national realities and sectors of activity. In fact, in relative terms, countries like Luxembourg and Slovenia are experiencing high shares of outgoing labour force in the construction industry. In turn, the same economic sector in Luxembourg, Austrian and Belgian is confronted with a huge share of incoming workforce, corresponding to over a fifth of the total national employment in the sector. A relevant quota of posted workers is employed in the German and French building industries as well. Besides, an extremely high percentage of truck drivers active in two or more Member States is posted from Luxembourg, Slovakia, Poland and Croatia.

Although precise data are not available yet, the COVID-19 pandemic has had a huge impact on the quantitative dimension of the posting phenomenon and, more generally, the level of labour mobility within the internal market has been dramatically affected. Nonetheless, since it is not clear whether these negative effects will be permanent or only transitory, a proper evaluation of the pandemic's overall impact is, for the time being, still too premature.

In conclusion, this chapter elucidates the actual measure of the phenomenon of posting within the EU internal market, by showing the existence of a high degree of concentration of workers employed, as the case may be, for the provision of labour-intensive services or for highly specialised jobs. Importantly, those coming from the 'new' Member States are not the only ones involved, since this pattern of short-term labour mobility mostly concerns workers posted from the 'old' Member States.

CHAPTER 7

Impact of Posting on the EU Labour Market

7.1 INTRODUCTION

The activity of posting of workers is frequently presented as nothing but a form of erosion of the existing labour and social standards in the wealthier Member States and, consequently, it is usually associated with a series of negative connotations. The aim of this chapter is to provide a clarification of the current situation which may eventually be helpful in the evaluation of the opportunity of the legislative reform introduced by Directive (EU) 2018/957. Naturally, this purpose is reflected in this chapter's leading research sub-question: *What sort of impact does the posting phenomenon have on the EU labour market, and which kind of issues have emerged in the sector?* Accordingly, in the following analysis, the actual measure of the impact of posting on the EU labour market is carefully explored on the basis of official reports drafted on behalf of the European Commission, and of further qualitative and quantitative empirical studies carried out by academic scholars and other independent researchers, entailing both economic and economic policy analyses. The overall poor reputation of posting is basically demystified by recognising the rather limited dimension of negative repercussions when the transnational provision of services is performed within the legal limits.

More specifically, this chapter proceeds as follows. In the next section 7.2, a whole series of positive effects, at individual, national and Union levels, are recognised in light of empirical evidence. The investigation of the benefits is not limited to the perspective of the cross-border actors and the sending countries, but it also considers the favourable impact on the recipient Member States, as well as on the EU labour market as a whole. In turn, the risks and negative consequences intrinsically related to the transnational posting of workers are dealt with in the following section 7.3. At that stage, the actual dimensions of the resulting negative effects, such as regulatory arbitrage by certain posting undertakings, possible downward pressure on national welfare states and limited job displacements effects, are thoroughly examined. In the same section, an analysis of the different regulatory and extra-institutional reactions at both EU and national levels is provided. Section 7.4 addresses, in turn, the whole spectrum of unlawful and fraudulent practices developed in the context of posting, ranging from the exploitation and alienation of the workers involved to the use of subcontracting chains, double postings through temporary work agencies and bogus self-employment, up to the creation of the so-called 'letterbox companies'. The reason for dealing with such major issues separately lies in their nature, which is not directly related to the type of short-term labour mobility at issue, but rather to the evasion of the existing rules.

Finally, in section 7.5, the widespread conception of social dumping as directly related to the inflow of posted workers with lower wages and employment standards from low-wage to high-wage Member States is proven substantially wrong. Moreover, after an investigation of the conceptual meaning of social dumping, the measure of the actual correlation between posting and social dumping is clarified, and the relevance of a number of further (often illegal) practices as major potential sources is strongly stressed. This chapter rounds off with a conclusion in which the findings of the previous sections are collected and the impact of posting of workers on the EU labour market is evaluated in light of the points made. The phenomenon at issue is presented not only as a potential source of problems deriving from fraudulent and abusive circumventions of the rules but also as an opportunity for improvement in the degree of social and economic integration at Union level.

7.2 AN UNDERESTIMATED OPPORTUNITY

Intra-EU posting is having a huge impact on the public and political debate for several years. The 'common narrative', supported by the Member States which are confronted with high numbers of incoming posted workers, tends to emphasise its negative connotations.[1] This phenomenon is often associated with several types of risks and abuses, which are mostly due to deficient enforcement of the rules.[2] Such a condition is exacerbated by the misrepresentation frequently offered by mass media which, by lacking to make the proper distinction between different patterns of labour migration, ends up including all abusive and exploiting situations related to any form of worker

1. A revelatory document supporting that narrative is represented by the Austrian, Belgian, French, German, Luxembourg, Dutch and Swedish Ministers of Labour, 'Letter to Ms Marianne Thyssen Commissioner for Employment, Social Affairs, Skills and Labour Mobility' (18 June 2015).
2. Posting of workers is, indeed, commonly perceived as a source of worker exploitation, business and worker displacement, and social dumping. Kristina Maslauskaite, 'Posted Workers in the EU: State of Play and Regulatory Evolution' (2014) Policy Paper, Notre Europe Jaques Delors Institute 20, 10 and 12; Jean-Philippe Lhernould and Barbara Palli, 'Posted Workers Remuneration: Comparative Study in Nine EU Countries and Four Sectors' (2017) 24 Maastricht Journal of European and Comparative Law 108, 109; Alberto Riesco-Sanz, Jorge García López and María del Mar Maira Vidal, 'The Posting of Workers in the European Road Transport Industry: An Approach Based on the Discourses of Social and Institutional Stakeholders' (2019) European Journal of Industrial Relations 1, 4.

mobility across the European Union under the umbrella of posting.[3] As a consequence, several issues related to situations falling outside the actual posting activity are, in fact, perceived as inherent to the latter.[4]

Furthermore, in the high-wage EU Member States, there is widespread concern about the distortion of competition caused by the inflow of cheap labour coming from the Member States with lower labour costs and employment conditions. In this sense, the regulatory arbitrage of posting companies, moved by the purpose of taking advantage of the most favourable rules in the whole internal market, is supposed to eventually lead to an erosion of labour standards and displacement of workers in the wealthier receiving states.[5] Those kinds of malpractices are then allegedly resulting in a 'race to the bottom' in terms of social standards between the Member States.[6] Such an eventuality has been labelled as 'social dumping' whereby self-interested market participants, with the aim of gaining an advantage over competitors, exploit the lower labour standards in their home countries, thus forcing the host countries to downgrade existing social standards and wages in the hope of preventing unemployment.[7]

The above-mentioned popular (and yet superficial) perception of the posting phenomenon in the public and political discourse appears sadly common to a large part of the academic literature as well.[8] Indeed, an evaluation based on an accurate

3. As a matter of fact, on several occasions, mass media superficially described unlawful working arrangements involving, *inter alia*, excessively long shifts, wages lower than the minimum rate of pay and extremely poor employment conditions, as intrinsically related to the context of posting of workers. Stefan Schwarz and Marcin Kiełbasa, 'Posted or Sent in the Context of the Revision of Social Security Coordination Regulations' (2018) *Labour Mobility Initiative Association* 5, 4.
4. This is the case whereby the cross-border element is absent because the workers habitually work in the host state or because the posting company is not genuinely established in a certain Member State, or when an effective employment relationship between employer and employees is missing. Aukje A.H. van Hoek and Mijke Houwerzijl, 'Where Do EU Mobile Workers Belong, According to Rome I and the (E)PWD?' in Herwig Verschueren (ed.), *Residence, Employment and Social Rights of Mobile Persons: On How EU Law Defines Where They Belong*, vol. 36 (Intersentia 2016) 246.
5. In this vein, Verschueren defined the internal market of service providers as 'a Trojan horse potentially threatening the national welfare state'. Herwig Verschueren, 'Cross-Border Workers in the European Internal Market: Trojan Horses for Member States' Labour and Social Security Law?' (2008) 24/2 International Journal of Comparative Labour Law and Industrial Relations 167, 198. On this point, *see* Kristina Maslauskaite, 'Social Competition in the EU: Myths and Realities' (2013) Policy Paper, Notre Europe Jaques Delors Institute 62, 10–11; Dagmar Schiek et al., 'EU Social and Labour Rights and EU Internal Market Law' (European Parliament, EMPL Committee 2015) IP/A/EMPL/ST/2014-02, 96; Rebecca Zahn, 'Revision of the Posted Workers' Directive: A Europeanisation Perspective' (2017) 19 Cambridge Yearbook of European Legal Studies 187, 202.
6. Maslauskaite (n 5) 10 and 12; Magdalena Bernaciak, 'Conclusion' in Magdalena Bernaciak (ed.), *Market Expansion and Social Dumping in Europe* (Routledge 2015) 14; Lhernould and Palli (n 2) 109.
7. Maslauskaite (n 2) 4; Magdalena Bernaciak, 'Social Dumping and the EU Integration Process' (2014) ETUI European Trade Union Institute – Working Paper 2014.06, 2.
8. Jozef Berghman, 'Social Security in a European Perspective: Present and Future Challenges' in Jozef Pacolet (ed.), *Social Protection and the European Economic and Monetary Union* (Avebury; Aldershot 1996) 44; Catherine Barnard, 'Viking and Laval: An Introduction' (2008) 10 Cambridge Yearbook of European Legal Studies 463, 463; Dorothee Bohle, 'Race to the Bottom? Comparative Institutional Advantages? Competition of Capitalisms in the Enlarged EU' in Jan Drahokoupil and Laura Horn (eds), *Contradictions and Limits of Neoliberal European Governance: From Lisbon to Lisbon*, vole 8 (Palgrave Macmillan 2008); Stéphane Lalanne, 'Posting of Workers, EU Enlargement and the Globalization of Trade in Services' (2011) 150 International Labour Review 211; Jan

collection and analysis of empirical data about the effects of the posting phenomenon on the EU labour market is rarely carried out. Such a different perspective is here proposed by focusing on the outcomes resulting from empirical data collected and analysed by academic scholars and other independent researchers, including studies realised on behalf of the European Commission.

What appears evident from an in-depth factual investigation is that the impact of posting on the EU labour market actually takes different forms, entailing a series of positive as well as negative effects for all the economic actors involved.[9] It affects to different degrees not only the posted workers, the posting undertakings and the national economies (in both the sending and receiving countries), but also the service recipients (both contractors and consumers), the local workers and undertakings and the tax authorities of both the sending and the receiving Member States.[10] The present section is focusing on the benefits resulting from posting, leaving the analysis of the costs to the next section 7.3.

7.2.1 Upward Socio-Economic Convergence

One of the main reasons for the existence of labour mobility lies in the opportunity for the workers involved to get a higher income compared to the salary they would earn in their country of origin. In the case of intra-EU posting, especially workers seconded from the EU-13 to the EU-15 Member States enjoy a significantly higher household income, directly related to the minimum wage gap between the Member States.[11] In

Cremers, 'EU Economic Freedoms and Social Dumping' in Magdalena Bernaciak (ed.), *Market Expansion and Social Dumping in Europe* (Routledge 2015) 186–187; Jan Cremers, 'Economic Freedoms and Labour Standards in the European Union' (2016) 22(2) Transfer: European Review of Labour and Research 149, 157.

9. Frederic De Wispelaere and Jozef Pacolet, 'Posting of Workers as Stabilising Mechanism: An Enlarged Notion of Labour Mobility as a Prerequisite for an Optimal Currency Area' (KU Leuven Research Institute for Work and Society (HIVA) 2015) 10; Frederic De Wispelaere and Jozef Pacolet, 'The Benefits of Posting: Facts and Figures on the Use and Impact of Intra-EU Posting' in Jens Arnholtz and Nathan Lillie (eds), *Posted Work in the European Union: The Political Economy of Free Movement* (Routledge 2019) 37–38.
10. Frederic De Wispelaere, 'Intra-EU Posting Costs and Benefits' (25th International Conference of Europeanists, Chicago, 28 March 2018); Wispelaere and Pacolet, 'The Benefits of Posting: Facts and Figures on the Use and Impact of Intra-EU Posting' (n 9).
11. Such a minimum wage gap has been constantly increasing since 1996, and especially after the EU enlargements, from a ratio of 1:3 to 1:10 between the lowest and the highest minimum wage. For example, in 2015, the national minimum wage in the German meat industry was set at EUR 8.50 per hour whereas in Bulgaria it was EUR 1.04 per hour. In the same year, the minimum wage for unskilled workers in the construction sector in Germany was set at EUR 11.15, corresponding to almost the double of the average hourly gross salary in Poland and the quadruple of the one in Romania and Bulgaria. European Commission, Impact Assessment, Accompanying the document Proposal for a Directive of the European Parliament and the Council amending Directive 96/71/EC concerning the posting of workers in the framework of the provision of services 2016 [SWD(2016) 52 final] 13; Bettina Wagner and Anke Hassel, 'Posting, Subcontracting and Low-Wage Employment in the German Meat Industry' (2016) 22 Transfer: European Review of Labour and Research 163, 168; Wispelaere (n 10) 15. *See also* IDEA Consult and ECORYS Netherlands, 'Study on the Economic and Social Effects Associated with the Phenomenon of Posting of Workers in the EU' (European Commission, Directorate-General Employment, Social Affairs and Equal Opportunities 2011) 155; Frederic De Wispelaere

effect, it is acknowledged that minimum remuneration levels in the high-wage Member States exceed the average income rate in the low-wage Member States. Hence, despite the presence of different pay rates between posted and local workers in the same host state, particularly evident in the receiving high-wage EU countries such as Belgium, Denmark, France, Germany, the Netherlands and Sweden,[12] the seconded workers still receive a higher income than the average remuneration level in their home state.[13] The household income of those cross-border workers is also influenced by other factors, such as differences in social security contributions and price levels. In particular, different price levels among the sending and receiving Member States[14] contribute to the individual perception of a higher purchasing power for posted workers vis-à-vis

and Jozef Pacolet, 'An Ad Hoc Statistical Analysis on Short Term Mobility – Economic Value of Posting of Workers: The Impact of Intra-EU Cross-Border Services, with Special Attention to the Construction Sector' (KU Leuven Research Institute for Work and Society (HIVA) 2016) Research commissioned by DG EMPL within the framework of Contract VT/2015/096, 13; Wispelaere and Pacolet, 'The Benefits of Posting: Facts and Figures on the Use and Impact of Intra-EU Posting' (n 9) 39; Emmanuel Comte, 'Promising More to Give Less: International Disputes between Core and Periphery around European Posted Labor, 1955–2018' (2019) Labor History 1, 10.

12. Different remuneration levels between posted and local workers are the result of differences in productivity and standard of living in the Member States. They are estimated to range from 10–15% in the Danish construction sector, to about 25% and 35% in the construction sectors in the Netherlands and Belgium respectively, and up to 50% in the road transport sector in Belgium. It is evident, therefore, that labour-intensive sectors, such as the construction sector and road transport, present the higher risk of wage differentials. Conversely, high-skilled sectors, such as the care services sector, remain excluded by this sort of issue. European Commission Impact Assessment, Accompanying the document Proposal for a Directive of the European Parliament and the Council amending Directive 96/71/EC concerning the posting of workers in the framework of the provision of services (n 11) 13. On this point, *see also* Rebecca Zahn, 'Revision of the Posted Workers' Directive: Equality at Last?' (2016) 5 European (Legal) Studies on-line papers, Queen's University Belfast – School of Law – Centre of European and Transnational Legal Studies 10–11; Zahn (n 5) 14.
13. A good example is given by the comparison between the statutory minimum wage in 2012 in Belgium (EUR 1,472) and the average wage of a construction worker in Poland (EUR 752) during the same year. It is evident that a Polish worker posted to Belgium would receive as income at least twice the average remuneration level in Poland. Wispelaere and Pacolet, 'An Ad Hoc Statistical Analysis on Short Term Mobility – Economic Value of Posting of Workers: The Impact of Intra-EU Cross-Border Services, with Special Attention to the Construction Sector' (n 11) 14. On the better remuneration of posted workers compared to their local counterparts, *see also* Philippa Watson, *EU Social and Employment Law* (Second Edition, Oxford University Press 2014) 303–304.
14. In 2016, the highest price levels for consumer goods and services among the EU Member States was observed in Denmark (39% above the EU average), while the lowest was observed in Bulgaria (54% below the EU average). Eurostat, 'Price Level Index for Household Final Consumption Expenditure (HFCE), 2016, EU-28 = 100DEC' (*Eurostat – Statistics Explained*, 2016) <http://ec.europa.eu/eurostat/statistics-explained/index.php?title=File:Price_level_index_for_household_final_consumption_expenditure_(HFCE),_2016,_EU-28%3D100DEC.png> (accessed 15 May 2018).

local workers in the sending country, and consequently to higher real wages.[15] In this respect, the redistributive character of posting is more than evident.[16]

An indirect consequence of the increase of household income of posted workers coming from low-wage Member States, when compared to the standard remuneration in their home state, is fostering private consumption in their country of origin.[17] Such an economic impact is considered capable of strengthening upward socio-economic convergence within the EU internal market.[18] A proof of this is given by the remarkably different importance of labour tax revenues received by the sending EU-15 and the EU-13 Member States, standing respectively at 0.3% and 5.7% of their average monthly share in 2017.[19] Besides the individual benefit of increasing household incomes for the seconded workers, posting mobility has therefore also a significant impact on the sending Member States' economies, especially with regard to the collection of a large amount of labour tax revenues.[20] In fact, taxation rules concerning posting activity are construed as an exception from the general principle of paying taxes in the country where the work is performed, since posted workers are still taxed by their home state for a maximum period of 183 days per year.[21] In this sense, a decrease by 77% has been estimated as potential backlash on labour tax revenues collected in the EU-13 Member States in the event workers posted abroad were employed in their country of origin.[22] For the record, the beneficiaries of such a home state taxation rule seem to be, potentially, not only the low-wage but also the high-wage Member States. This means that a high-wage EU country, e.g., France, would benefit more from tax revenues collected from outgoing highly skilled French specialists posted abroad, rather than from generally lower contributions paid by low cost incoming temporary service providers.[23]

15. Wispelaere and Pacolet, 'An Ad Hoc Statistical Analysis on Short Term Mobility – Economic Value of Posting of Workers: The Impact of Intra-EU Cross-Border Services, with Special Attention to the Construction Sector' (n 11) 15; Wispelaere (n 10) 15; Wispelaere and Pacolet, 'The Benefits of Posting: Facts and Figures on the Use and Impact of Intra-EU Posting' (n 9) 39.
16. Wispelaere and Pacolet, 'The Benefits of Posting: Facts and Figures on the Use and Impact of Intra-EU Posting' (n 9) 39.
17. Wispelaere and Pacolet, 'Posting of Workers as Stabilising Mechanism: An Enlarged Notion of Labour Mobility as a Prerequisite for an Optimal Currency Area' (n 9) 13.
18. *Ibid.* 10; Wispelaere and Pacolet, 'An Ad Hoc Statistical Analysis on Short Term Mobility – Economic Value of Posting of Workers: The Impact of Intra-EU Cross-Border Services, with Special Attention to the Construction Sector' (n 11) 16; Comte (n 11) 10–11.
19. Wispelaere (n 10) 16.
20. Wispelaere and Pacolet, 'Posting of Workers as Stabilising Mechanism: An Enlarged Notion of Labour Mobility as a Prerequisite for an Optimal Currency Area' (n 9) 12; Wispelaere and Pacolet, 'The Benefits of Posting: Facts and Figures on the Use and Impact of Intra-EU Posting' (n 9) 40.
21. Article 15(2) of the Organisation for Economic Co-operation and Development, *OECD, Model Tax Convention on Income and on Capital: Condensed Version* (OECD Publishing 2017).
22. Wispelaere (n 10) 16.
23. Maslauskaite (n 2) 11.

7.2.2 Stimulation of Intra-EU Competition

An important feature of the posting phenomenon is that it undoubtedly stimulates intra-EU competition.[24] Its capacity to boost competition among local and foreign service providers derives directly from the undeniable competitive advantage enjoyed by the posting enterprises which, unlike their local competitors in the receiving countries, are allowed to escape some of the most stringent national rules and procedures.[25] As indeed recognised by the European Commission in 2014, '[p]osting workers allows companies to exploit their competitive advantage across borders'.[26] Especially until the entry into effect of Directive (EU) 2018/957, cross-border service providers had the possibility to profit from the (at times very considerable) differentials in wages, social security contributions and income tax rates between the state of origin and the state of destination of the service provision.[27] Accordingly, labour-intensive and price-sensitive activities that are necessarily provided *in loco* (hence without any possibility of delocalisation) were inherently breeding ground for posting companies to exploit their competitive advantage in relation to wage over local companies. Also for these reasons, primarily involved sectors were – and still are – those of construction, manufacturing and personal services.[28]

The nature of the outcome at stake is however ambivalent. On the one hand, it benefits consumers (and, in general, service recipients) to the extent it allows them to minimise the costs of the service supply. On the other hand, particularly within some national realities, it has negative repercussions on wages, labour conditions and rights

24. Wispelaere and Pacolet, 'An Ad Hoc Statistical Analysis on Short Term Mobility – Economic Value of Posting of Workers: The Impact of Intra-EU Cross-Border Services, with Special Attention to the Construction Sector' (n 11) 11–13.
25. Jens Arnholtz and Nathan Lillie, 'European Integration and the Reconfiguration of National Industrial Relations: Posted Work as a Driver of Institutional Change' in Jens Arnholtz and Nathan Lillie (eds), *Posted Work in the European Union: The Political Economy of Free Movement* (Routledge 2019) 8.
26. European Commission, *Employment and Social Developments in Europe 2014* (European Commission, Directorate Général for Employment, Social Affairs and Inclusion 2015) 156. In this sense, *see also* Verschueren (n 5) 198; Maslauskaite (n 2) 4; Herwig Verschueren, 'The European Internal Market and the Competition between Workers' (2015) 6 European Labour Law Journal 128, 129; Arnholtz and Lillie (n 25) 8.
27. Verschueren (n 5) 198; Verschueren (n 26) 129; Frans Pennings, 'Principles of EU Coordination of Social Security' in Frans Pennings and Gijsbert Vonk (eds), *Research Handbook on European Social Security Law* (Edward Elgar Publishing 2015) 333; Wispelaere and Pacolet, 'An Ad Hoc Statistical Analysis on Short Term Mobility – Economic Value of Posting of Workers: The Impact of Intra-EU Cross-Border Services, with Special Attention to the Construction Sector' (n 11) 11; Arnholtz and Lillie (n 25) 8.
28. Eurostat data for 2014 on costs of average hour of work by Member State, clearly show Denmark at the top of the chart with EUR 40, followed by Belgium (EUR 39), while EUR 8.40 is the average cost of work by hour in Poland, and only EUR 4.60 in Romania and EUR 3.80 in Bulgaria. European Commission Impact Assessment, Accompanying the document Proposal for a Directive of the European Parliament and the Council amending Directive 96/71/EC concerning the posting of workers in the framework of the provision of services (n 11) 13. *See also* Zahn (n 12) 10; Diane Fromage and Valentin Kreilinger, 'National Parliaments' Third Yellow Card and the Struggle over the Revision of the Posted Workers Directive' (2017) 10 European Journal of Legal Studies 125, 137–138; Zahn (n 5) 14.

of the workers involved (both local and posted).[29] Nevertheless, empirical evidence resizes the relevance of labour cost differentials as drivers of short-term mobility through posting.[30] In fact, although in several situations posting enterprises used to remunerate their workers with strictly the minimum rate of pay imposed by the receiving Member States, thus making use of their competitive edge, national differentials in social security contributions were – and still are – not directly related to the share of outgoing posted workers in total employment of the sending Member State.[31] This outcome appears also consistent with the not dissimilar average taxation rates between EU-15 and EU-13 Member States. It follows that labour cost differentials are not the sole driver of posting, being labour and skill shortages other important factors as well.[32]

7.2.3 Stabilising Mechanism

Further positive incidence of posting at national level has been observed in terms of overall economic growth in both the sending and receiving countries, through improvement of companies' competitiveness, internationalisation and productivity levels.[33] More specifically, posting firms can enjoy the major flexibility of their workforce to adapt to labour demand fluctuations (especially seasonal)[34] and also new ideas,

29. European Commission (n 26) 156. For a wider perspective on the disparate outcomes of intra-EU competition, *see* Alexander Somek, 'From Workers to Migrants, from Distributive Justice to Inclusion: Exploring the Changing Social Democratic Imagination: Exploring the Changing Social Democratic Imagination' (2012) 18 European Law Journal 711, 5–8.
30. As a matter of fact, since the 2007 EU enlargement towards the East, labour cost differentials between low-wage and high-wage Member States have increased from a factor of 1:3 to 1:10. Marion Schmid-Drüner, 'Briefing: The Revision of the Posting of Workers Directive' (European Parliament, Employment and Social Affairs – Policy Department for Economic, Scientific and Quality of Life Policies 2017) 1 <http://dx.publications.europa.eu/10.2861/308871> (accessed 22 November 2018).
31. The quota of social security contributions represents, indeed, a relevant part of the overall cost of a worker for the employers.
32. Wispelaere and Pacolet, 'An Ad Hoc Statistical Analysis on Short Term Mobility – Economic Value of Posting of Workers: The Impact of Intra-EU Cross-Border Services, with Special Attention to the Construction Sector' (n 11) 13. *See also* IDEA Consult and ECORYS Netherlands (n 11) 134–135; ISMERI Europa, 'Preparatory Study for an Impact Assessment on the Posting of Workers – Final Report' (European Commission 2012) 43–44; Dries Lens, Ninke Mussche and Ive Marx, 'Europe's Ever Expanding Mobility Patterns – Posting, Third-Country Nationals and the Single European Labour Market' (2019) CSB Working Paper No. 19.08 University of Antwerp – Herman Deleeck Centre for Social Policy 19; Agnieszka Wołoszyn, 'The Importance of Posting of Workers for the Member States: Myth and Reality' in Jacek Kubera and Tomasz Morozowski (eds), *A 'Social Turn' in the European Union?: New Trends and Ideas about Social Convergence in Europe* (First Edition, Routledge 2020) 182–183. The importance of labour and skill shortages as drivers of labour mobility in the form of posting is examined further in detail.
33. Richard Giesen, 'Posting: Social Protection of Workers vs. Fundamental Freedoms?' (2003) 40 Common Market Law Review 143, 144; Maslauskaite (n 2) 4; Lucia Dalla Pellegrina and Margherita Saraceno, 'Posting of Workers across the EU: An Empirical Investigation' (2017) 44 European Journal of Law and Economics 423, 447–450.
34. IDEA Consult and ECORYS Netherlands (n 11) 134.

skills and experience acquired abroad by their employees.[35] What is more, the migration of posted persons assigned to work abroad, even if just for a temporary period, likely favours a decrease in unemployment rates in the sending Member States.[36]

Interestingly, the above-mentioned several positive outcomes of posting in the sending Member State are considered to have a beneficial effect in case the country is confronted with an 'asymmetric economic shock',[37] by supporting adjustments in such an occurrence.[38] As a matter of fact, the power of intra-EU labour mobility, irrespective of the form it takes, to work as a tool to keep low the unemployment level in the affected country is generally recognised.[39] In particular, posting of workers can operate as a stabilising mechanism in response to a growing unemployment rate resulting from an asymmetric shock.[40] Such an effect is revealed by an investigation of the positive incidence of posting on national quota of unoccupied persons.[41] In this sense, a decrease in unemployment levels is observed as a direct result of posted worker mobility from regions affected by high rates of unoccupied persons to other regions where this rate is lower.[42] In addition, the sending Member State would benefit from a consequent decrease of public costs related to the contrast of unemployment, along with an increase of revenues in terms of labour taxes, profit of companies providing transnational services and private consumption as a consequence of higher personal income for workers involved.[43] Unlike the case of worker migration under Article 45

35. The advantage for companies may materialise, for example, when sending employees for a short period in another Member State in order to provide training or instal specialised equipment. *Ibid.* 146–149.
36. Wispelaere and Pacolet, 'An Ad Hoc Statistical Analysis on Short Term Mobility – Economic Value of Posting of Workers: The Impact of Intra-EU Cross-Border Services, with Special Attention to the Construction Sector' (n 11) 15–16.
37. An asymmetric economic shock within the EU internal market is defined as an event with economic repercussions affecting just one part of the Union while sparing the remaining part, or having a significantly different impact on the Member States' economies. The concept of asymmetric shock is often mentioned as a problematic issue within the Economic and Monetary Union (EMU), where countries share a common currency. Jennifer Jager and Kurt A Hafner, 'The Optimum Currency Area Theory and the EMU: An Assessment in the Context of the Eurozone Crisis' (2013) 48 Intereconomics 315, 315–316.
38. Wispelaere and Pacolet, 'An Ad Hoc Statistical Analysis on Short Term Mobility – Economic Value of Posting of Workers: The Impact of Intra-EU Cross-Border Services, with Special Attention to the Construction Sector' (n 11) 15–16; Claire Dhéret and Andreia Ghimis, 'The Revision of the Posted Workers Directive: Towards a Sufficient Policy Adjustment?' (2016) *European Policy Center (EPC) Discussion Paper* 6 <http://www.epc.eu/pub_details.php?cat_id=17&pub_id=6475> (accessed 23 October 2016); Wispelaere and Pacolet, 'The Benefits of Posting: Facts and Figures on the Use and Impact of Intra-EU Posting' (n 9) 41.
39. Wispelaere and Pacolet, 'Posting of Workers as Stabilising Mechanism: An Enlarged Notion of Labour Mobility as a Prerequisite for an Optimal Currency Area' (n 9) 9.
40. *Ibid.* 10; Zane Rasnača, 'Identifying the (Dis)Placement of "New" Member State Social Interests in the Posting of Workers: The Case of Latvia' (2018) 14 European Constitutional Law Review 131, 136.
41. Wispelaere and Pacolet, 'Posting of Workers as Stabilising Mechanism: An Enlarged Notion of Labour Mobility as a Prerequisite for an Optimal Currency Area' (n 9) 13–14.
42. Wispelaere (n 10) 17.
43. Interestingly, this stabilisation effect through the practice of posting workers was calculated by De Wispelaere and Pacolet for Greece during 2013. In particular, the collection of approximately EUR 1 billion labour tax revenues was estimated as a result of posting of 10% of the unemployed

TFEU towards other Member States, labour tax revenues collected by the Member State of origin on the basis of the posting activity serve as an effective absorbing instrument of the possible consequences in the event of a negative shock.[44]

Nevertheless, when compared to labour mobility under the freedom of movement for workers, posting of workers has a relatively limited impact as a stabilising mechanism on persistent medium or long run asymmetric shocks. This is due to its temporary nature, which is reflected in the maximum period of twenty-four months to pay workers' social security contributions in their home Member State, as well as in the 183-day rule for application of the country of origin's personal income taxation law.[45]

7.2.4 Better Job Allocation

The available figures show that posting is mainly driven by labour and skill shortages, in the sense that the demand for experienced and specialised workers in a certain Member State determines the measure of posted workers inflow.[46] As is evident, therefore, this form of short-term intra-EU labour mobility has a remarkable ability to address cyclical deficiencies in particular economic sectors in the receiving Member States. Similarly, from a sending perspective, it makes it possible for companies to avoid repeated procedures of firing-and-hiring workers depending on the contingent economic cycle of the Member State of establishment. During a low labour demand period, workers may thereby keep their jobs by being sent to work temporarily in another Member State, while the employers do not have to constantly replace their experienced, trained and qualified employees.[47] Furthermore, it is important to point out that the occupational allocation in the high-wage Member States usually benefits from the inflow of foreign employees who are more inclined to perform activities that local workers are not willing to undertake.[48]

population living in Greece at that time. Wispelaere and Pacolet, 'Posting of Workers as Stabilising Mechanism: An Enlarged Notion of Labour Mobility as a Prerequisite for an Optimal Currency Area' (n 9) 14–16.

44. In effect, all those benefits cannot result from labour migration under Article 45 TFEU, since the latter situation entails the application of the general principle of tax collection in the workers' host state and a consequent erosion of both the tax base and the number of people left to pay for the government debt in the country of origin. *Ibid.* 12.
45. *Ibid.* 11.
46. In particular, posting has been recognised as a reducing factor of qualitative labour shortages in the receiving Member States. Qualitative labour shortages are experienced in specific economic sectors like construction, transport, agriculture and meat processing industry when local workers refuse to do the job because of the poor social image of the job or the difficult working conditions. They may also occur in case of lack of workers specialised in carrying out specific duties. IDEA Consult and ECORYS Netherlands (n 11) 158; Maslauskaite (n 2) 4; Wispelaere and Pacolet, 'An Ad Hoc Statistical Analysis on Short Term Mobility – Economic Value of Posting of Workers: The Impact of Intra-EU Cross-Border Services, with Special Attention to the Construction Sector' (n 11) 15–16; Lens, Mussche and Marx (n 32) 19; Wispelaere and Pacolet, 'The Benefits of Posting: Facts and Figures on the Use and Impact of Intra-EU Posting' (n 9) 42.
47. Maslauskaite (n 2) 4.
48. Magdalena Bernaciak, 'Social Dumping: Political Catchphrase or Threat to Labour Standards?' (2012) ETUI European Trade Union Institute – Working Paper 2012.06, 26.

In conclusion, the demonstrated direct relation of posting flows with labour demand in specific sectors and locations contributes to better job allocation and occupational mobility than other forms of worker migration, while preventing situations of 'welfare tourism'.[49] Accordingly, whenever its nature is demand-driven rather than supply-driven, posting of workers may represent an ideal form of intra-EU occupation mobility.

7.3 THE OTHER SIDE OF THE COIN

As mentioned earlier, the measure of the impact of posting on the EU labour market does not take only a positive shape, entailing negative consequences as well. First of all, the pattern of mobility at issue lends itself to the possibility of regulatory arbitrage by certain cross-border service providers attracted by the economic opportunities offered by the internal market. A further downside of the posting phenomenon might also materialise in the downward pressure on national welfare states, which might eventually result in a detrimental 'regulatory competition' between the Member States. On the other hand, some cases of job displacement effects have been experienced as well. At the same time, in order to adapt to the ever-changing shape of the European labour market, several Member States introduced legislative reforms while national employment relations have been forced to a sort of extra-institutional change. This whole constellation of repercussions related to intra-EU posting is analysed below.

7.3.1 Negative Repercussions

As is well known, the competitive advantage that posting undertakings enjoyed especially prior to the adoption of Directive (EU) 2018/957 – albeit already curtailed by the application, by virtue of the Posting of Workers Directive, of a nucleus of terms and conditions of employment of the host Member State – has had a significant impact on the labour market of the receiving countries. This impact assumed different forms according to the viewpoint taken.

7.3.1.1 Regulatory Arbitrage

A relevant incentive for the cross-border service providers to the practice of intra-EU posting of workers has been traditionally the possibility to maximise their profits by taking advantage of differences in labour costs, social security contributions and tax rates among the Member States. Pursuant to Article 49 TFEU, a company is indeed free to establish itself in any Member State only for the sake of convenience and to employ workers under the terms of labour legislation in force in that country, where the

49. This is proved by the higher unemployment rate of migrants aged 25– 54 when compared to national workers. Wispelaere and Pacolet, 'Posting of Workers as Stabilising Mechanism: An Enlarged Notion of Labour Mobility as a Prerequisite for an Optimal Currency Area' (n 9) 10–11.

workers have their social insurance and where also labour taxes are to be paid.[50] Then, by virtue of Article 56 and within the limits posed by the (now revised) Posting of Workers Directive, that company is free to provide services in any other Member State, including those with higher employment and social standards, by making recourse to posted workers. This means that, especially in case of provision of labour-intensive services from low-wage to high-wage Member States before the entry into effect of Directive (EU) 2018/957, the posted employees were likely to receive a lower level of pay and working conditions in comparison to their local counterparts. In parallel, when the relocation of the company domicile is not followed by the transfer of the economic activity performed, employers are de facto allowed to profit from the higher degree of capitalisation and industrial-technological infrastructure in the host Member States, while not having to bear the economic burden imposed by the respect of higher employment standards.[51]

This arbitrary selection of the most favourable normative regime with a view to exploiting the existing differences between national systems is commonly referred to as 'regulatory arbitrage' or 'regime shopping'.[52] According to several experts, the creation of such a kind of new 'business model' is the result of a more general EU trend towards the liberalisation of the internal market for services.[53] In particular, the Court of

50. Notably, the opportunities for companies to choose their Member State of incorporation have been sensibly strengthened by the Court through a series of famous rulings in *Centros Ltd v Erhvervs- og Selskabsstyrelsen* [1999] ECJ Case C-212/97, ECLI:EU:C:1999:126; *Überseering BV v Nordic Construction Company Baumanagement GmbH (NCC)* [2002] ECJ Case C-208/00, ECLI:EU:C:2002:632; *Kamer van Koophandel en Fabrieken voor Amsterdam v Inspire Art Ltd* [2003] ECJ Case C-167/01, ECLI:EU:C:2003:512. Paul Craig and Gráinne de Búrca, *EU Law: Text, Cases, and Materials* (Sixth Edition, Oxford University Press 2015) 810–815; Schiek et al. (n 5) 35; Catherine Barnard, *The Substantive Law of the EU: The Four Freedoms* (Fifth Edition, Oxford University Press 2016) 382 and ff.
51. Schiek et al. (n 5) 35.
52. Kerstin Ahlberg, 'The Age of Innocence – And Beyond' (2010) 21 FORMULA Working Paper, University of Oslo, Department of Private Law 26; Mijke Houwerzijl, 'Regime Shopping across (Blurring) Boundaries' in Stein Evju (ed.), *Regulating Transnational Labour in Europe: The Quandaries of Multilevel Governance* (Department of Private Law 2014) 30; Lisa Berntsen and Nathan Lillie, 'Breaking the Law? Varieties of Social Dumping in a Pan-European Labour Market' in Magdalena Bernaciak (ed.), *Market Expansion and Social Dumping in Europe* (Routledge 2015) 53–54; Bernaciak, 'Conclusion' (n 6) 230; Cremers, 'EU Economic Freedoms and Social Dumping' (n 8) 187; Cremers, 'Economic Freedoms and Labour Standards in the European Union' (n 8) 152; Eckhard Voss et al., 'Posting of Workers Directive: Current Situation and Challenges' (European Parliament, EMPL Committee 2016) IP/A/EMPL/2016-07, 30; Kairit Kall and Nathan Lillie, 'Protection of Posted Workers in the European Union: Findings and Policy Recommendations Based on Existing Research' (2017) PROMO briefing paper 43, 23; Jan Cremers, 'Posting of Workers in Practice' (2018) INT-AR Paper 8 Tilburg Law School 3; Arnholtz and Lillie (n 25) 4, 10–11; Jan Cremers, 'Market Integration, Cross-Border Recruitment, and Enforcement of Labour Standards – A Dutch Case' in Jens Arnholtz and Nathan Lillie (eds), *Posted Work in the European Union: The Political Economy of Free Movement* (Routledge 2019) 139.
53. Giesen (n 33) 144; Wispelaere (n 10) 12–14.

Justice's rulings in the so-called 'Laval quartet'[54] are deemed to have played a crucial role in the realisation of such a purpose.[55]

In such a context, while certain countries may benefit from the establishment of posting undertakings in terms of tax revenues and social security contributions, in turn, negative repercussions potentially affect both the workers and the overall welfare systems in the receiving Member States. The regulatory arbitrage of undertakings which strategically locate themselves in certain Member States in order to increase their profits from the posting of their employees abroad can materialise in many different ways.[56] The recourse to posted workers may facilitate the delocalisation of the company's production in another Member State, even without the need for the employer to change the place of work. In fact, an undertaking has the faculty to use intra-group transfer of seconded employees from a newly established branch in a country with lower labour costs or to subcontract a part or the totality of its activities to cheaper foreign service providers, or even to hire out workforce through a temporary employment agency established in another Member State with lower wage costs and social security contributions. Further cases may concern a firm that, with a view to maximising profit, hires posted workers for a specific cross-border job only,[57] or of a company that is merely established for a particular assignment.[58] A concrete example in this sense is given by the so-called *'Irish Ferries'* dispute concerning the reflagging in 2005 by the company *Irish Ferries* of its vessels from Ireland to Cyprus with a view to replacing 543 Irish workers with cheaper, predominantly Latvian, temporary agency

54. *International Transport Workers' Federation and Finnish Seamen's Union v Viking Line ABP and OÜ Viking Line Eesti* [2007] ECJ Case C-438/05, ECLI:EU:C:2007:772; *Laval un Partneri Ltd v Svenska Byggnadsarbetareförbundet, Svenska Byggnadsarbetareförbundets avdelning 1, Byggettan and Svenska Elektrikerförbundet, Opinion of Advocate General Paolo Mengozzi delivered on 23 May 2007* [2007] ECJ Case C-341/05, ECLI:EU:C:2007:291; *Dirk Rüffert v Land Niedersachsen, Opinion of Advocate General Yves Bot delivered on 20 September 2007* [2007] ECJ Case C-346/06, ECLI:EU:C:2007:541; *Commission of the European Communities v Grand Duchy of Luxemburg* [2008] ECJ Case C-319/06, ECLI:EU:C:2008:350.
55. Barnard, 'Viking and Laval: An Introduction' (n 8); Jonas Malmberg, 'The Impact of the ECJ Judgements on Viking, Laval, Rüffert and Luxembourg on the Practice of Collective Bargaining and the Effectiveness of Social Action' (Directorate-General for Internal Policies, Policy Department A: Economic and Scientific Policy Employment and Social Affairs Brussels: European Parliament 2010); Jan Cremers, 'Free Provision of Services and Cross-Border Labour Recruitment' (2013) 34 Policy Studies 201. On this point, *see supra* Chapter 4.
56. Berntsen and Lillie (n 52) 53–54; Voss et al. (n 52) 30; Kall and Lillie (n 52) 23; Arnholtz and Lillie (n 25) 4, 10–11; Ines Wagner and Karen Shire, 'Labour Subcontracting in Cross-Border Labour Markets: A Comparison of Rule Evasion in Germany and Japan' in Jens Arnholtz and Nathan Lillie (eds), *Posted Work in the European Union: The Political Economy of Free Movement* (Routledge 2019) 194–195.
57. Erka Caro et al., 'Posted Migration and Segregation in the European Construction Sector' (2015) 41 Journal of Ethnic and Migration Studies 1600, 1606. At any rate, it is worth recalling that Article 4(3) of the Enforcement Directive 2014/67/EU guarantees the genuinity of the posting activity by explicitly requiring the previous performance of a working activity in the 'habitual country of work'. In this sense, *see supra* Chapter 4.
58. Mijke Houwerzijl and Lisa Berntsen, 'Posting of Workers: From a Blurred Notion Associated with "Cheap Labour" to a Tool for "Fair Labour Mobility"?' in Jens Arnholtz and Nathan Lillie (eds), *Posted Work in the European Union: The Political Economy of Free Movement* (Routledge 2019) 152.

seafarers.[59] Oddly enough, all these borderline arrangements, although consisting in fact in the exploitation of administrative unwieldiness or regulatory loopholes, are usually still allowed from a strictly legal point of view, as they frequently fall under a sort of legal 'grey zone'.[60]

Conversely, the exploitation of the aforementioned competitive advantage is liable, at times, to degenerate in circumventive and abusive practices. This is the case of *Bouygues Travaux Publics*, which involved a Cypriot subsidiary of an Irish temporary work agency that made recourse to Polish posted workers for the construction of a nuclear site in Flamanville (France). On that occasion, the seconded workers were not covered by accidents at the workplace and they were getting half the wage of French workers.[61] A further case is that of Irish and British temporary work agencies posting Polish workers to construction sites in Sweden until 2010. In fact, before the introduction of the *Lex Laval*, administrative controls of service providers posting workers in that country were very superficial, mainly relying on the employers' bona fide. In such a context, some unscrupulous service providers exploited the situation by making wide use of false declarations of posting and social security certificates. Before the Swedish authorities managed to exchange information with the correspondent authorities in the sending state, some of the workers concerned had already received new certificates from Cyprus and others had returned back home.[62]

7.3.1.2 *Downward Pressure on National Welfare States*

In light of the existing disparities in terms of remuneration and employment conditions, as well as social security contributions and personal income tax rates, between local and posted workers, the increasing recourse to posting arrangements for cost competition, often involving strategies of 'regulatory arbitrage', evidently raises the risk of generating a downward pressure on national welfare states.[63] Within this framework, a sort of 'regulatory competition' between the Member States, involving a possible detrimental 'race to the bottom' in wages and employment conditions, has been

59. After heated protests and negotiations, a settlement entailing the application of Irish minimum wage standards (EUR 7.65 per hour and EUR 18,615 per annum) to new agency crew was eventually reached at the end of the year. Tony Dobbins, 'Irish Ferries Dispute Finally Resolved after Bitter Stand-Off' (*Eurofound*, 20 December 2005) <https://www.eurofound.europa.eu/publications/article/2005/irish-ferries-dispute-finally-resolved-after-bitter-stand-off> (accessed 11 July 2019); Zahn (n 12) 7–8.
60. Jan Cremers, 'In Search of Cheap Labour in Europe – Working and Living Conditions of Posted Workers' (2011) CLR News 6, 8–9; Berntsen and Lillie (n 52) 57; Aukje A.H. van Hoek, 'Re-Embedding the Transnational Employment Relationship: A Tale about the Limitations of (EU) Law?' (2018) 55 Common Market Law Review 449, 462.
61. ISMERI Europa (n 32) 34.
62. For a detailed description of the circumventive practices used to that extent, *see* Ahlberg (n 52) 26–29.
63. Verschueren (n 5) 198; Nathan Lillie, 'Subcontracting, Posted Migrants and Labour Market Segmentation in Finland: Migrant Workers in Finland' (2012) 50 British Journal of Industrial Relations 148, 162; Vassilis Hatzopoulos, *Regulating Services in the European Union* (Oxford University Press 2012) 113; Verschueren (n 26) 131–133.

frequently indicated as a probable indirect outcome.[64] Markedly, this form of pressure from below is also linked to the fact that the posted workers are generally less covered by collective agreements in comparison to local workers in the Member States with advanced systems of industrial relations, in which wage determination is traditionally negotiated at local level.[65] As pointed out *supra* in Chapter 4, a negative impact on national systems of industrial relations certainly took place as a result of the Court of Justice's rulings in the *Laval quartet*, which entailed a drastic curtailment of the trade unions' and social partners' power to impose labour standards on posted workers.[66]

Notwithstanding the widespread concern and scepticism among academics, European citizens and social partners, the picture offered by some accurate empirical analysis on the matter seems to indicate, however, that the use of posting has not led, in practice, to any substantial downward trend in employment protection in the receiving countries.[67] In this sense, the example provided by data on the amount of social security contributions collected in Belgium in the construction sector shows that

64. A clear example is given by the accusations of Belgium, France and Austria to the German unfair competitive practices in the meat industry, where the employment of posted workers had the effect of dumping wages. European Federation of Food, Agriculture and Tourism Trade Unions (EFFAT), 'Belgian Ministers' Condemnation of Germany's Social Dumping Practices Is Reminder to Act' (European Federation of Food, Agriculture and Tourism Trade Unions (EFFAT) 2013) <https://old.effat.org/en/node/9933> (accessed 17 October 2018). In this sense, *see also* Simon Deakin, 'Regulatory Competition after Laval' (2007) 10 Cambridge Yearbook of European Legal Studies 581, 606; Verschueren (n 5) 198; Catherine Barnard, 'Fifty Years of Avoiding Social Dumping? The EU's Economic and Not So Economic Constitution' in Michael Dougan and Samantha Currie (eds), *50 Years of the European Treaties: Looking Back and Thinking Forward* (First Edition, Hart Publishing 2009) 511–512; Watson (n 13) 281; Verschueren (n 26) 131 and 148; Ines Wagner, 'Changing Regulations, Changing Practices?: The Case of the German Meat Industry' (2017) *Project: 'Protecting Mobility through Improving Labour Rights Enforcement in Europe (PROMO)', VS/2016/0222*, 12, 3–4; Jens Arnholtz and Søren Kaj Andersen, 'Extra-Institutional Changes under Pressure from Posting: Extra-Institutional Changes' (2018) 56 British Journal of Industrial Relations 1, 3.
65. Arnholtz and Andersen (n 64) 17.
66. Due to the highly embedded systems of industrial relations developed in the Scandinavian countries, such an impact specifically affected the so-called 'Nordic social model'. Deakin (n 64) 605; Mia Rönnmar, 'Free Movement of Services Versus National Labour Law and Industrial Relations Systems: Understanding the Laval Case from a Swedish and Nordic Perspective' (2007) 10 Cambridge Yearbook of European Legal Studies 493, 522; ACL Davies, 'One Step Forward, Two Steps Back? The Viking and Laval Cases in the ECJ' (2008) 37 Industrial Law Journal 126, 148; Catherine Barnard, 'Social Dumping or Dumping Socialism?' (2008) 67 The Cambridge Law Journal; Jonas Malmberg and Tore Sigeman, 'Industrial Actions and EU Economic Freedoms: The Autonomous Collective Bargaining Model Curtailed by the European Court of Justice' (2008) 45 Common Market Law Review 1115, 1141–1143; Jon Erik Dølvik and Jelle Visser, 'Free Movement, Equal Treatment and Workers' Rights: Can the European Union Solve Its Trilemma of Fundamental Principles?: Free Movement, Equal Treatment and Workers' Rights' (2009) 40 Industrial Relations Journal 491, 503; Fritz W. Scharpf, 'The Asymmetry of European Integration, or Why the EU Cannot Be a "Social Market Economy"' (2010) 8 Socio-Economic Review 211, 230; Andrea Sangiovanni, 'Solidarity in the European Union' (2013) 33 Oxford Journal of Legal Studies 213, 225–226; Marco Rocca, *Posting of Workers and Collective Labour Law: There and Back Again* (Intersentia 2015) 302; Dagmar Schiek, 'Comparing Labour Laws in the EU Internal Market: A Social Actor Perspective' (2017) 33 International Journal of Comparative Labour Law and Industrial Relations 171, 192; Silvana Sciarra, *Solidarity and Conflict: European Social Law in Crisis* (Cambridge University Press 2018) 105 and ff.; van Hoek (n 60) 476.
67. IDEA Consult and ECORYS Netherlands (n 11) 158–159; Verschueren (n 26) 150.

the increased number of posted workers does not have any considerable negative impact on the Belgian social security funding.[68] Such an outcome is indeed consistent with the actual very limited number, in absolute terms, of the transnational secondments, and especially of the low-skilled workers posted from low-wage to high-wage Member States, which represent only a third of the overall intra-EU postings.[69] Furthermore, before the entry into effect of Directive (EU) 2018/957, while the Posting of Workers Directive already required that posted workers should be paid at least the minimum wage of the host country, the actual salary level awarded by most of them was still above that threshold, even in case of mobility from low-wage to high-wage Member States.[70] In this respect, the impact of the recent decisions in *Sähköalojen ammattiliitto*[71] and *RegioPost*,[72] in combination with the 2004 and 2014 reforms of EU public procurement law,[73] undoubtedly reduced the wage gap between local and posted workers, hence narrowing down the possibilities of regulatory arbitrage by means of posting strategies.[74]

Conversely, the real source of downward pressure on national welfare states is probably represented by the spread of abusive and fraudulent practices, namely bogus self-employment and undeclared work. In addition, one of the main causes of increasing pressure on employment relations in the host Member States can also be traced in the adoption, by the majority of the EU countries, of a series of austerity measures and budget cuts involving, *inter alia*, a consistent reduction of wages, as a

68. Frederic De Wispelaere and Jozef Pacolet, 'The Size and Impact of Intra-EU Posting on the Belgian Economy: With a Special Focus on the Construction Sector – Summary' (KU Leuven Research Institute for Work and Society (HIVA) 2017) 14.
69. On this point, *see* the analysis carried out *supra* in Chapter 6.
70. In this sense, the interesting study conducted by Benio on labour costs in the case of posting of workers from Poland with reference to the period 2013–2015 clearly shows that the average net remuneration of a Polish worker posted abroad amounted at EUR 9.97 per hour, corresponding to 80% more than EUR 5.98 of minimum wage. Marek Benio, 'Labour Costs in Cross-Border Services: The Study on the Labour Cost Structure in the Case of Posting of Workers from Poland' (Department of Public Economy and Administration, University of Economics 2016) 5.
71. *Sähköalojen ammattiliitto ry v Elektrobudowa Spolka Akcyjna* [2015] CJEU Case C-396/13, ECLI: EU:C:2015:86.
72. *RegioPost GmbH & Co KG v Stadt Landau in der Pfalz* [2015] CJEU Case C-115/14, ECLI: EU:C:2015:760.
73. Directive 2004/18/EC of the European Parliament and of the Council of 31 March 2004 on the coordination of procedures for the award of public works contracts, public supply contracts and public service contracts 2004 (OJ L 134/114); Directive 2014/24/EU of the European Parliament and of the Council of 26 February 2014 on public procurement and repealing Directive 2004/18/EC 2014 (OJ L 94/65). More specifically, Article 26 of Directive 2004/18/EC (subsequently repealed by Article 70 of the new Directive 2014/24/EU) specifically authorises contracting authorities to include, *inter alia*, social clauses in public procurement contracts.
74. van Hoek (n 60) 471–472; Marco Rocca, 'Not Dead yet: Legal Strategies at National Level and the Reform of the EU Posting of Workers Directive' (2018) 11 and 13; Arnholtz and Lillie (n 25) 19; Sacha Garben, 'The European Pillar of Social Rights as a Revival of Social Europe' in Maurizio Ferrera (ed.), *Towards a European Social Union: The European Pillar of Social Rights and the Roadmap for a Fully-Fledged Social Union* (Centro di Ricerca e Documentazione Luigi Einaudi 2019) 80; Marco Rocca, 'Stepping Stones Over Troubled Waters. Recent Legal Evolutions and the Reform of the Posting of Workers Directive' in Jens Arnholtz and Nathan Lillie (eds), *Posted Work in the European Union: The Political Economy of Free Movement* (Routledge 2019) 178. For an analysis of the Court's decisions in *Sähköalojen ammattiliitto* and *RegioPost*, *see supra* Chapters 3 and 4.

consequence of the well-known economic and financial crisis.[75] By the way, a consistent evaluation cannot avoid taking into consideration the relatively limited dimension of this negative repercussion of posting on the EU internal market, given that, as evidenced in the previous chapter, the inflow of seconded workers is typically confined to certain economic sectors in a few Member States.[76]

7.3.1.3 Job Displacement

Despite the intrinsic boundary of the overall limited size of intra-EU labour mobility through posting, a further negative consequence of such an activity may be found in some 'job displacement' effects[77] observed in a few Member States, especially in certain economic sectors.[78] A form of substitution effect has indeed been recorded in recent years in the construction sector in France, Belgium, Italy and Austria, with increased employment of foreign posted workers and, concurrently, a decreased number of local workers.[79] Nonetheless, it should be specified that there is no direct correlation between the share of lost working positions in the receiving countries and that of additional posted jobs, and *vice versa*. For example, the number of jobs created via posting in Belgium in the last years is much greater than the number of jobs lost among local employees, with a rate of 5:1 respectively.[80] The resulting environment is defined by De Wispelaere and Pacolet as a 'dual employer market' whereby, on the one hand, SMEs (small and medium-sized enterprises) employing high-cost local workers are struggling for not being driven out of business while, on the other hand, large Belgian contractors are taking advantage of the opportunities presented by the EU internal market.[81] The actual impact of the limited displacement effect is even more downsized by the correspondent growth of local companies in terms of turnover and

75. Sciarra (n 66) 7 and 13.
76. Frederic De Wispelaere, 'Intra-EU Posting and the Threat of Social Dumping: A Comprehensive Assessment' (Industrial Relations in Europe Conference (IREC), Leuven, Belgium, 10 September 2018) figures 13–16.
77. 'Job displacement' effects in a receiving labour market are defined, in this context, as the substitution of local workers by posted ones. Committee of the Regions et al., *Assessment of the Current Legislation and the Possible Impact of Posting of Workers Directive on Local and Regional Authorities* (CoR 2012) 7 <http://dx.publications.europa.eu/10.2863/87753> (accessed 15 May 2018).
78. Wispelaere and Pacolet, 'Posting of Workers as Stabilising Mechanism: An Enlarged Notion of Labour Mobility as a Prerequisite for an Optimal Currency Area' (n 9) 11; Wispelaere and Pacolet, 'The Benefits of Posting: Facts and Figures on the Use and Impact of Intra-EU Posting' (n 9) 42.
79. Particularly with regard to the Belgian case, a substitution of local labour was observed only in certain sub-sectors of the construction industry, namely in the construction of buildings, development of construction projects and plastering. Wispelaere and Pacolet, 'The Size and Impact of Intra-EU Posting on the Belgian Economy: With a Special Focus on the Construction Sector – Summary' (n 68) 13; Wispelaere (n 10) figures 20–21.
80. Wispelaere and Pacolet, 'The Size and Impact of Intra-EU Posting on the Belgian Economy: With a Special Focus on the Construction Sector – Summary' (n 68) 12.
81. Wispelaere (n 10) figure 24.

added value, as well as by the collection of social security contributions in the receiving Member States, favoured by increasing investments in the sector.[82]

Considerable displacement effects have been experienced, in turn, as a result of the external flexibilisation of labour through the employment of foreign posted workers which took place in the slaughter and meat industry between 1999 and 2014 in Germany. In particular, the companies operating in the sector took advantage of the absence, until 2015, of a statutory minimum wage, and the consequent application of the sending countries' rates of pay to incoming posted workers.[83] As a result, notwithstanding the considerable economic growth of the sector, 44,000 workers employed by German companies in the meat industry fell out of job.[84] Apart from the latter cases, there is limited evidence of displacement of local workers within the EU internal market as a consequence of the use of posted workers.[85]

At last, it is worth noting that a further risk has been presented as a potential negative repercussion of transnational posting of workers, namely that of 'brain drain' in the Member State of origin. Nonetheless, the fact that such a repercussion mainly concerns permanent or long-term migration is rather evident. In effect, being the posting activity just of temporary nature, workers sent to another Member State mostly return home after their assignment abroad, thus averting in practice any risk of brain drain.[86]

7.3.2 Legislative Amendments and Extra-Institutional Changes

The seamless expansion of short-term labour mobility in the form of posting experienced in the last years, in combination with the powerful impact of the Court of Justice

82. Wispelaere and Pacolet, 'An Ad Hoc Statistical Analysis on Short Term Mobility – Economic Value of Posting of Workers: The Impact of Intra-EU Cross-Border Services, with Special Attention to the Construction Sector' (n 11) 24.
83. Between 1999 and 2014, posted workers employed in the German slaughter and meat industry were in practice paid as low as EUR 3– 5 per hour. Wagner and Hassel (n 11) 164; Wagner (n 64) 5; Wagner and Shire (n 56) 191. *See also* Federica Mustilli and Jacques Pelkmans, 'Access Barriers to Services Markets' (2013) 77 CEPS Centre for European Policy Studies 84, 52.
84. However, on 21 September 2015, the six largest German meat producers in Germany put a brake on such a relevant job displacement effect by signing a voluntary agreement aimed at improving working and living conditions for employees in the sector, while abandoning the use of posted workers. Wagner (n 64) 6–7.
85. Torben Krings, 'A Race to the Bottom? Trade Unions, EU Enlargement and the Free Movement of Labour' (2009) 15 European Journal of Industrial Relations 49, 64; Wispelaere and Pacolet, 'An Ad Hoc Statistical Analysis on Short Term Mobility – Economic Value of Posting of Workers: The Impact of Intra-EU Cross-Border Services, with Special Attention to the Construction Sector' (n 11) 17–18; Dalla Pellegrina and Saraceno (n 33) 447–450; Rasnača (n 40) 136.
86. IDEA Consult and ECORYS Netherlands (n 11) 154; Martin Guzi and Martin Kahanec, 'Socio-economic Cleavages between Workers from New Member States and Host-Country Labour Forces in the EU during the Great Recession' in Magdalena Bernaciak (ed.), *Market Expansion and Social Dumping in Europe* (First Edition, Routledge 2015) 97 <https://www.taylorfrancis.com/books/9781315766607> (accessed 14 October 2019); Wispelaere and Pacolet, 'Posting of Workers as Stabilising Mechanism: An Enlarged Notion of Labour Mobility as a Prerequisite for an Optimal Currency Area' (n 9) 11.

case law – from the seminal decision in *Rush Portuguesa*,[87] passing through the famous *Laval quartet*, until the more recent *Sähköalojen ammattiliitto*[88] – have necessarily required an adaptation of national regulatory systems, either in the way the minimum wages and working conditions are determined or in the modalities according to which the latter terms are extended to cross-border operators. The variety of responses taken at national level can be grouped into two macro-categories: legislative amendments and extra-institutional changes.

7.3.2.1 Legislative Amendments

In order to adapt to the evolving regulatory framework, several Member States have chosen to implement profound legislative amendments.[89] This is the case of Denmark and Sweden, where a proper re-regulation of national industrial relations systems has been made through, respectively, the Danish *Act on Posting of Workers* approved on 18 December 2008[90] and the Swedish so-called 'Lex Laval', which came into force on 15 April 2010.[91] In both those legislative interventions, Article 3(8) of the Posting of Workers Directive was interpreted in a way as to allow the imposition of a requirement for foreign employers to conclude a collective agreement with local trade unions, that guarantees the same standard of employment assured by collective agreements that are generally applied at national level in the sector.[92] Notably, while in Denmark the social partners could demand solely the application of minimum rates of pay (whose definition has been sensibly extended in order to include holiday bonuses and leave payments), in Sweden all terms and conditions of employment included in the hard nucleus set by the Posting of Workers Directive could be imposed. At the same time, in the latter country, the use of collective actions has been precluded in cases where the

87. *Rush Portuguesa Lda v Office national d'immigration* [1990] ECJ Case C-113/89, ECLI: EU:C:1990:142.
88. *Sähköalojen ammattiliitto ry v Elektrobudowa Spolka Akcyjna* (n 71) para. 70. On this point, *see supra* Chapter 3.
89. Sciarra (n 66) 111–117; Arnholtz and Lillie (n 25) 15–18.
90. For an in-depth analysis of the origin and content of the Danish Law No L 36 of 18 December 2008, *see* Martin Gräs Lind, 'The Danish Law on the Posting of Workers' (2010) 24 FORMULA Working Paper, University of Oslo, Department of Private Law 12–16.
91. Malmberg (n 55) 9; Niklas Bruun and Claes-Mikael Jonsson, 'Consequences and Policy Perspectives in the Nordic Countries as a Result of Certain Important Decisions of the European Court of Justice' in Andreas Bücker and Wiebke Warneck (eds), *Viking – Laval – Rüffert: Consequences and Policy Perspectives* (ETUI (European Trade Union Institute) 2010) 18–22; Marco Rocca, 'Enemy at the (Flood) Gates: EU "Exceptionalism" in Recent Tensions with the International Protection of Social Rights' (2016) 7 European Labour Law Journal 52, 66.
92. That solution represented an adjustment to the rules set in the PWD, according to the clarification made by the Court of Justice in *Laval*: 'It must be noted, in this respect, that since the purpose of Directive 96/71 is not to harmonise systems for establishing terms and conditions of employment in the Member States, the latter are free to choose a system at the national level which is not expressly mentioned among those provided for in that directive.' *Laval un Partneri Ltd v Svenska Byggnadsarbetareförbundet, Svenska Byggnadsarbetareförbundets avdelning 1, Byggettan and Svenska Elektrikerförbundet* [2007] ECJ Case C-341/05, ECLI:EU:C:2007:809, 68.

posted workers are already subject to at least the same employment conditions in their home country.[93]

Another type of legislative adjustment was made in Germany with regard to the public procurement rules of those *Länders* – like the *Land Niedersachsen* (Lower Saxony) – which had been affected by the decision of the Court in *Rüffert*,[94] whereby the obligation for foreign service suppliers to abide by a social clause included in a non-generally binding regional collective agreement was declared illegitimate. In reaction to the judgment, several German *Länders* amended the relevant regulations on public procurement as to include the minimum wage applicable to public contracts.[95] Furthermore, a substantial modification of the regime applicable to workers on posting assignments was realised in Belgium as well. In that country, the Posting of Workers Directive was implemented in such a way as to extend the application of almost the entire national labour law to transnational service providers.[96] The Dutch legislation on posting (*WAGA Act*) was, in turn, already amended in 2005, when the scope of generally applicable collective agreements was broadened outside the mere construction sector.[97]

Lastly, it should be noted that a number of regulatory changes have very recently taken place in certain Member States in connection with the new concept of 'minimum rates of pay' introduced by the Court's ruling in *Sähköalojen ammattiliitto*.[98] In particular, in France, the definition of the minimum wage was reformed so as to include further wage supplements. In Italy, the adaptation of the 'minimum rates of pay' to cover also travel and posting allowances was reached through adjustments at

93. Malmberg (n 55) 8–9; Catherine Barnard and Simon Deakin, 'European Labour Law after Laval' in Marie-Ange Moreau (ed.), *Before and After the Economic Crisis. What Implications for the 'European Social Model'?* (Edward Elgar Publishing 2011) 262–263; Kall and Lillie (n 52) 22–23; Sciarra (n 66) 112–113. For the record, on 1 June 2017, the *Lex Laval* was eventually amended by the 'New posting regulation', which de facto restored the trade unions' faculty to force posting companies to sign agreements in which they undertake to follow the minimum provisions set out in the relevant collective agreements. In this regard, trade unions were given the power to use industrial action as a last resort. Kerstin Ahlberg, 'Lex Laval Revised in Sweden – To What Effect?' (*Nordic Labour Journal*, 1 March 2017) <http://www.nordiclabourjournal.org/nyheter/news-2017/article.2017-03-01.0991266340> (accessed 5 December 2018); Sciarra (n 66) 116–117.
94. *Dirk Rüffert v Land Niedersachsen* [2008] CJEU Case C-346/06, ECLI:EU:C:2008:189.
95. Malmberg (n 55) 8; Torsten Walter, 'The Practical Consequences of the Rüffert Decision' in Andreas Bücker and Wiebke Warneck (eds), *Viking – Laval – Rüffert: Consequences and policy perspectives* (ETUI (European Trade Union Institute) 2010) 43–45; Barnard and Deakin (n 93) 263; van Hoek (n 60) 470–471; Rocca, 'Not Dead yet: Legal Strategies at National Level and the Reform of the EU Posting of Workers Directive' (n 74) 10.
96. Deloitte Belgium, 'How Will the Revision of the Posted Workers Directive Impact Your Assignments?' (2018) figure 7 <https://www2.deloitte.com/content/dam/Deloitte/be/Documents/tax/PostedWorkersDirective.pdf> (accessed 26 September 2018).
97. *Wet Arbeidsvoorwaarden Grensoverschrijdende Arbeid (WAGA)*. Dølvik and Visser (n 66) 500; Mijke Houwerzijl, 'Implementation of the Posting of Workers Directive in the Netherlands' (2010) 16 FORMULA Working Paper, University of Oslo, Department of Private Law 2 <http://www.jus.uio.no/ifp/english/research/projects/freemov/publications/papers/>.
98. *Sähköalojen ammattiliitto ry v Elektrobudowa Spolka Akcyjna* (n 71) para. 70. On this point, *see supra* Chapter 3.

enforcement level, namely by specific instructions from the national labour inspectorate.[99]

7.3.2.2 *Extra-Institutional Changes*

The exceptional development of the recourse to posting arrangements produced, over the years, also a further relevant (although not so evident) effect of altering the functioning of national institutions, which Arnholtz and Andersen labelled as 'extra-institutional change'.[100] On the one hand, the inclination of the relevant EU regulatory framework towards a single, more accessible internal market and, on the other hand, the step into the breach of new economic actors, namely foreign service providers and posted workers, have forced the traditional regimes of employment relations into a (sometimes radical) process of adjustment.[101] Indeed, both companies established abroad and their seconded employees act differently as rule-takers than local undertakings and workers.[102] Cross-border companies are less likely to sign collective agreements in the Member States with higher standards of wages and labour protection which would result in a loss of their economic competitive advantage. The same goes for the posted workers, whose general reluctance in affiliating to trade unions in the host country leaves them out of the decisional process in the regulation of the sector, while making the local systems of collective bargaining increasingly weaker.[103] Moreover, due to their vulnerable and precarious position, often posted workers are not even fully aware of their rights and they face serious obstacles to the enforcement of the latter.[104]

As a result, the advent of the peculiar pattern of intra-EU labour mobility in the form of posting of workers has the effect of creating 'zones of exception', also called 'islands of foreign law', within otherwise well-defined national regulatory frameworks.[105] The problem is exacerbated in those Member States, such as for instance Denmark, Sweden, Italy and Germany until 2015, with no statutory minimum wages and no schemes for the extension of collective agreements in accordance with the Posting of Workers Directive.[106] This because those countries structurally suffer from

99. Rocca, 'Not Dead yet: Legal Strategies at National Level and the Reform of the EU Posting of Workers Directive' (n 74) 12; Rocca, 'Stepping Stones Over Troubled Waters. Recent Legal Evolutions and the Reform of the Posting of Workers Directive' (n 74) 178.
100. The concept of 'extra-institutional change' was recently introduced in Arnholtz and Andersen (n 64).
101. *Ibid.* 2–3.
102. *Ibid.* 10.
103. Watson (n 13) 281; Sciarra (n 66) 11 and 112.
104. Yves Jorens, Saskia Peters and Mijke Houwerzijl, 'Study on the Protection of Workers' Rights in Subcontracting Processes in the European Union (Final Study)' (Ghent University, Department of Social Law (in consortium with University of Amsterdam) 2012) DG EMPL/B2-VC/2011/0015, 156–157; Arnholtz and Andersen (n 64) 8–9.
105. Arnholtz and Andersen (n 64) 4–5; van Hoek (n 60) 463; Arnholtz and Lillie (n 25) 4.
106. More specifically, an autonomous collective bargaining model governs the system of industrial relations in Denmark and Sweden. In Denmark, two-year or three-year sector-specific collective agreements between employers' associations and trade unions play the main role in the regulation of the labour market. In Sweden and Italy (and Germany until 2015), collective

a troubling lack of clarity on whether incoming posted workers should enjoy or not collectively agreed wages.[107] In such contexts, the impact of temporary labour immigration in the form of posting entailed substantial transformations. Notably, in Denmark, given the limited scope of the 2008 legislative reform, in the following years the local trade unions' contribution to the regulation of the employment conditions of posted workers became more and more incisive. The largest trade union in Denmark (3F)[108] managed to introduce specific 'labour clauses' into public procurement tenders by lobbying politicians in municipalities and regional authorities. At the same time, also the national labour court gained increasingly relevance in regulating the field, thus becoming a full-fledged normative actor.[109]

It is therefore apparent that the above-mentioned series of changes, involving a mutation of decision-making forums, different strategies, perception and use of the rules by the several economic actors involved, along with the substantial shift in the normative role from collective bargaining to legislation and labour court case law, have de facto altered the functioning of national institutions. As a consequence, the established systems of industrial relations have been profoundly affected as well. All this, despite no formal institutional reform has taken place.[110] By the way, it is important to stress that the concept of extra-institutional change reflects nothing more than the practical adaptation of national regimes to the evolving EU internal market. The resulting pressure on local employment relations does not necessarily imply an overall negative impact of the posting of workers phenomenon.

7.4 ABUSIVE AND FRAUDULENT PRACTICES

As has been stressed above, the genuine provision of services across borders through posting of workers entails both positive and negative outcomes. Nevertheless, in the context at issue, a whole series of practices going beyond the limit of compliance with the rules unfortunately often occur as well. The undeniable difficulties in monitoring and enforcing the application of national regulations enabled *mala fide* economic actors to come up, over the last years, with a variety of strategies aimed at evading or circumventing employment, tax and social security regulations. The resulting problematic issues, which are investigated in detail below, range from the exploitation and alienation of the posted workers, which are frequently forced into wretched working

bargaining conducted by social partners takes traditionally the place of legislative intervention, being the latter often considered as an undue interference. Conversely, a national minimum wage (set at EUR 8.50 per hour) was introduced in Germany in January 2015. Rönnmar (n 66) 497–500; Ahlberg (n 52) 28; Gerhard Bosch, 'The Making of the German Minimum Wage: A Case Study of Institutional Change: The Making of the German Minimum Wage' (2018) 49 Industrial Relations Journal 19, 19; Sciarra (n 66) 11; Arnholtz and Andersen (n 64) 7.

107. Mustilli and Pelkmans (n 83) 52; Zahn (n 12) 9.
108. *Fagligt Fælles Forbund (3F)* is the United Federation of Danish Workers.
109. Klaus Pedersen, 'New Agreement to Combat Social Dumping' (*Eurofound online*, 10 June 2011) <https://www.eurofound.europa.eu/publications/article/2011/new-agreement-to-combat-social-dumping> (accessed 15 October 2018); Sciarra (n 66) 83; Arnholtz and Andersen (n 64) 13.
110. Arnholtz and Andersen (n 64) 1–4 and 12; Arnholtz and Lillie (n 25) 2 and 12.

and living conditions, to the use of subcontracting chains, double postings through temporary work agencies and bogus self-employment, up to the creation of the so-called 'letterbox companies'. While undoubtedly constituting a source of distortions of competition, all those malpractices may seriously hinder the process of integration of the European market as well. At the same time, they represent a dangerous threat to some fundamental rights of the workers concerned.[111]

7.4.1 Worker Exploitation

Starting with the individual dimension of the unlawful and abusive practices developed within the framework of posting, it is necessary to point out that, sadly, the working and living conditions of the workers involved, and especially of those employed in manual/low-skilled jobs, are in some cases indecent and demeaning.[112] Because of their vulnerable condition, which is directly related to their precarious position in a foreign country, the posted workers are particularly exposed to the risk of exploitation. In effect, all jobs characterised by short-term periods of mobility abroad naturally entail a certain reluctance of the workers to integrate themselves into the host states' social environments. In case of posting for the provision of labour-intensive services, also a considerable degree of tension between local and foreign workers performing exactly the same work on the same site (and frequently working alongside) often results from their different treatment with regard to wages, working conditions, and social security coverage.[113] Notably, the lower pay of posted workers vis-à-vis local workers for the same work follows as a direct consequence of the widespread practice of paying posted workers the rates applicable to the lowest pay group, rather than that corresponding to their job skills, educational level, tasks performed and seniority.[114] What is more, such a condition has been exacerbated by the progressive dismantling of national and sectoral collective bargaining systems resulting from the austerity policies adopted in the aftermath of the 2008 financial crisis.[115]

111. Mario Monti, 'A New Strategy for the Single Market: At the Service of Europe's Economy and Society. Report to the President of the European Commission José Manuel Barroso' (European Commission Bureau of European Policy Advisers (BEPA) 2010) 26; Sciarra (n 66) 84.
112. Undoubtedly, this condition mainly concerns low-skilled workers who are particularly vulnerable by nature, being relatively easy to replace and generally lacking substantial bargaining power. IDEA Consult and ECORYS Netherlands (n 11) 154–155; Zahn (n 12) 11.
113. Lillie (n 63) 150; Schiek et al. (n 5) 62; European Commission Impact Assessment, Accompanying the document Proposal for a Directive of the European Parliament and the Council amending Directive 96/71/EC concerning the posting of workers in the framework of the provision of services (n 11) 13; Wispelaere (n 10) figure 18.
114. European Commission Impact Assessment, Accompanying the document Proposal for a Directive of the European Parliament and the Council amending Directive 96/71/EC concerning the posting of workers in the framework of the provision of services (n 11) 11; Zahn (n 12) 8; Zahn (n 5) 12.
115. Thorsten Schulten and Torsten Müller, 'Wages and Collective Bargaining during the European Economic Crisis: Developments in European Manufacturing Industry' (industriAll (European Trade Union) 2014) Collective Bargaining and Social Policy Conference 98 and ff.; Tonia Novitz, 'The Scope for Collective Bargaining in Posting and Procurement – What Might Come From Recent Court of Justice Case Law and the Proposed Reform of the Posting of Workers

In these circumstances, foreign posted workers often become victims of discrimination and xenophobic attitudes.[116] Furthermore, their frequent segregation from the host state social environment, also due to evident language barriers and spatial isolation (most of the time their workplace is the only space where they reside and socialise and it is often located in remote areas),[117] leads to an employment relationship characterised by an absolute dependence on their employer for accommodation, travel, expenses, medical insurance and any other form of assistance.[118] In addition to that, companies taking advantage of the liberalisation of the internal market for services, besides benefitting from the application of the most favourable rules of their home state, sometimes seek additional increasing of their profits in implementing policies of downgrading employment standards.[119] Consequently, the posted workers are in many cases confronted with excessively long and highly flexible working times, extremely low hourly pay rates, employment insecurity, average poor quality of housing arrangements and general lack of information on their rights.[120] There have been occasions where employers intentionally avoided to pay the minimum wages of the receiving country[121] or the agreed expense compensations, and where they did not pay pension

Directive?' (*University of Bristol Law School Blog*, 6 April 2016) <https://legalresearch.blogs.bris.ac.uk/2016/04/the-scope-for-collective-bargaining-in-posting-and-procurement/> (accessed 13 May 2018).

116. Wispelaere (n 10) figure 18.
117. Caro et al. (n 57) 1603, 1610–1614; Schiek et al. (n 5) 62; Ioana Dodi and Ioana Melenciuc, 'Posted Workers on the Route to a European Labour Market. Case Study: OSH-Related Vulnerabilities of Posted Workers in Spain' (2019) 11 CES Working Papers, Alexandru Ioan Cuza University of Iasi, Centre for European Studies, Iasi 73, 76 and 80.
118. In some cases, the logistic activities aimed at facilitating the access to the foreign labour market are carried out by specialised agencies acting as intermediaries. Posted workers are therefore often depending on such third parties. Houwerzijl (n 52) 5; Caro et al. (n 57) 1603–1604; Lisa Berntsen and Nathan Lillie, 'Hyper-Mobile Migrant Workers and Dutch Trade Union Representation Strategies at the Eemshaven Construction Sites' (2016) 37 Economic and Industrial Democracy 171, 388–389; van Hoek (n 60) 477.
119. Bernaciak, 'Social Dumping: Political Catchphrase or Threat to Labour Standards?' (n 48) 26.
120. Terrible working conditions were reported by several media reports and academic studies with regard to Eastern European workers posted to Germany in the meat industry between 2004 and 2015. On this point, *see* Wagner (n 64) 3–5. For further cases denouncing the extremely poor conditions of posted workers, *see* Roger Blanpain, 'Freedom of Services in the EU: A Social Catastrophe – Are There Lessons to Be Learned from the Belgian Experience?' (2011) 2 European Labour Law Journal 191, 192; Voss et al. (n 52) 41; Vladimir Bogoeski, 'Posting of Workers – Strengthening Labour Rights While Securing Free Movement of Services?' (*migrationonline.cz*, 9 June 2016) <https://migrationonline.cz/en/e-library/posting-of-workers-strengthening-labour-rights-while-securing-free-movement-services> (accessed 21 January 2018); Luisa Veloso, Catarina Sales Oliveira and Joana Soares Marques, 'EU Post Lab: Developing Experiences of Administrative Cooperation and Enhanced Access to Information in the Framework of the Posting of Workers – Assessment Report' (EU Post Lab 2018) <https://repositorio.iscte-iul.pt/bitstream/10071/16878/1/assessment_report_eu_post_lab_0.pdf> (accessed 16 September 2019); Houwerzijl and Berntsen (n 58) 158; Dodi and Melenciuc (n 117) 76.
121. That was, indeed, the case in question in *Sähköalojen ammattiliitto ry v Elektrobudowa Spolka Akcyjna* (n 71). Furthermore, in 2014, three out of ten foreign companies employing posted workers in Belgium were found by the Social Inspection Department in breach of the local collective labour agreement on minimum wages. Wispelaere and Pacolet, 'The Size and Impact of Intra-EU Posting on the Belgian Economy: With a Special Focus on the Construction Sector – Summary' (n 68) 18.

and social security contributions in the sending country.[122] In other cases, the provisions on minimum wages prescribed by the Posting of Workers Directive have been circumvented through the deduction from salaries of taxes and administrative costs, such as accommodation, meals, necessary work equipment and transport to the workplace, or by requiring the seconded workers to refund part of their payments when they returned back home.[123] Further exploitative practices have been realised through the requisition of the workers' passports and the imposition of fines on employees not respecting arbitrary and illegitimate conditions.[124]

The risk of precariousness is even exacerbated with regard to posted agency workers which, due to the need of the user undertaking to cover the fees paid to the temporary work agency, are often paid less than comparable local workers performing the same tasks. On top of that, they are usually excluded from additional benefits granted to regular employees and from the use of social facilities such as canteens, sports facilities or child care services. Such a dramatically precarious condition of agency employees is evident in the frequent lack of their health and safety equipment (such as helmets, work uniforms and protective shoes), which is normally supposed to be provided by the employer.[125] Similarly, the category of workers posted in the road transport sector (i.e., truck drivers) particularly suffers from inadequate working and social conditions as well. Due to the intrinsic highly mobile nature of the sector, combined with the intention of unscrupulous employers to increase productivity and maximise profits at the expenses of their employees, transnational drivers are indeed confronted with long periods away from home, gruelling work shifts, insufficient rest periods in inadequate rest facilities and remuneration below legal standards.[126]

---

122. Verschueren (n 26) 142–143; Magdalena Bernaciak and Zane Rasnača, 'Not as Simple as It Should Be? Why the Judicial Enforcement of Posted Workers' Rights Needs Improvement' (*LSE European Politics and Policy (EUROPP) Blog*, 5 March 2020) 1 <http://eprints.lse.ac.uk/104999/> (accessed 2 August 2020). For an in-depth analysis of the number of litigation processes involving posted workers and posting companies, *see* Zane Rasnača and Magdalena Bernaciak (eds), *Posting of Workers before National Courts* (ETUI (European Trade Union Institute) 2020).
123. Cremers, 'In Search of Cheap Labour in Europe – Working and Living Conditions of Posted Workers' (n 60) 9; Verschueren (n 26) 142–143; Dhéret and Ghimis (n 38) 7; van Hoek and Houwerzijl (n 4) 246; Isabella Biletta and Christine Aumayr-Pintar, 'Pay Inequalities Experienced by Posted Workers: Challenges to the "Equal Treatment" Principle' (Eurofound 2017) 1; Dodi and Melenciuc (n 117) 79.
124. Aukje A.H. van Hoek and Mijke Houwerzijl, 'Comparative Study on the Legal Aspects of the Posting of Workers in the Framework of the Provision of Services in the European Union' (2011) 58–59.
125. Schiek et al. (n 5) 42.
126. *Ibid.* 45; European Commission, Impact Assessment, Accompanying the document Proposal for a Regulation of the European Parliament and of the Council amending Regulation (EC) 561/2006 as regards minimum requirements on maximum daily and weekly driving times, minimum breaks and daily and weekly rest periods and Regulation (EU) 165/2014 as regards positioning by means of tachographs and Proposal for a Directive of the European Parliament and of the Council amending Directive 2006/22/EC as regards enforcement requirements and laying down specific rules with respect to Directive 96/71/EC and Directive 2014/67/EU for posting drivers in the road transport sector –Part 1/2 2017 [SWD(2017) 186 final] 13–14, 19–22; Riesco-Sanz, López and Maira Vidal (n 2) 10–11; Francesco E Iannuzzi and Devi Sacchetto, 'Italian Labour Inspectors Facing Posted Workers Phenomena' in Jens Arnholtz and Nathan Lillie (eds), *Posted Work in the European Union: The Political Economy of Free Movement* (Routledge 2019) 112.

What is more, the difficult situation of the posted workers is made even worse by their distance from home, resulting in further complications in their personal life that is likely more prone to divorces, alienation from family, need of placing children in care homes, and alcoholism.[127] In view of this tragic condition, the need to curb perilous risks of commodification of those people, who are particularly exposed because of the precarious circumstances under which they are forced to work, is apparent and urgent. In this regard, it is worth mentioning the positive novelty introduced by Article 7 of the recently adopted Directive (EU) 2019/1152[128] on transparent and predictable working conditions in the European Union, which imposes on the employer a duty of specifically informing the posted worker, before the secondment abroad, about the destination and duration of the assignment, the modality and entity of the payment of remuneration, including allowances and reimbursements, and the host state's single official national website.[129]

7.4.2 Subcontracting Chains, Double Postings and Bogus Self-Employment

The smooth functioning and reputation of the phenomenon of posting of workers are seriously jeopardised by the development, by some *mala fide* service providers, of particular abusive constructions aimed at evading the rules of the place of work. These abuses basically take different shapes, affecting the genuineness of the contract for the service supply, the nature of the employment relationship or the authenticity of the company's establishment in a certain Member State.

More in detail, the possibility of subcontracting or using temporary work agencies is exposed to a variety of peculiar misuses. On some occasions, the winners of national tenders have subcontracted the service provision to companies established in other Member States with lower labour costs.[130] In other cases, the creation of complicated chains of subcontracting has hindered the detection of the identity of the actual person performing the service, hiding repeated replacements for the same job ('rotational posting').[131] And the same goes for the so-called 'double' or 'chain' postings occurring in the event of a worker posted by a temporary employment

127. IDEA Consult and ECORYS Netherlands (n 11) 154–155.
128. Directive (EU) 2019/1152 of the European Parliament and of the Council of 20 June 2019 on transparent and predictable working conditions in the European Union 2019 (OJ L 186/105).
129. European Commission, 'Practical Guide on Posting' (2019) 15; Houwerzijl and Berntsen (n 58) 160.
130. Mustilli and Pelkmans (n 83) 51–52.
131. van Hoek and Houwerzijl (n 4) 246; Voss et al. (n 52) 29; Yves Jorens, Dirk Gillis and Tiffany De Potter, 'Fraud and Error in the Field of EU Social Security Coordination: Reference Year: 2015' (European Commission, Directorate-General for Employment, Social Affairs and Inclusion, Unit D2 – Social security coordination 2017) 70; Vladimir Bogoeski, 'Chain Liability as a Mechanism for Strengthening the Rights of Posted Workers' (2017) *Project: 'Protecting Mobility through Improving Labour Rights Enforcement in Europe (PROMO)', VS/2016/0222*, 21, 4; Yves Jorens et al., 'Fraud and Error in the Field of EU Social Security Coordination: Reference Year: 2016' (European Commission, Directorate-General for Employment, Social Affairs and Inclusion, Unit D2 – Social security coordination 2018) 75; Cremers, 'Market Integration, Cross-Border Recruitment, and Enforcement of Labour Standards – A Dutch Case' (n 52) 137; Houwerzijl and Berntsen (n 58) 153.

undertaking or placement agency to a user undertaking in a host Member State, which is subsequently posted by that user undertaking to the territory of a third Member State.[132] In such a case, since sometimes not even the first agency is informed of the 'double' secondment, evident difficulties often emerge in the actual determination of the rights and employment treatment to which the workers are entitled.[133] Furthermore, fraudulent use of subcontracting has also been realised by disguising the recruitment of local workers or of foreign workers already present in the host country through the subcontract to temporary work agencies established in another Member State and formally acting as employers, thus bypassing the more stringent local labour rules.[134] In all those kinds of situations, the most common artifice used is that of false declarations of posting through the falsification of the PDs A1 forms.[135] The posted workers involved, in their turn, are de facto treated as commodities and the enforcement of their rights is substantially precluded. Sometimes they face serious problems with regard to the actual payment of their salaries and contributions.[136] On some occasions, they are not even aware of their actual legal position. While they believe to be posted by their employer, they are actually working under a self-employment or a temporary agency contract, or as unregistered workers.[137]

Besides, host countries regulations are often circumvented, especially in economic sectors of construction and road transport, by means of bogus self-employment arrangements. In fact, in certain instances the setting up of postings by self-employed persons is merely motivated by the purpose of circumventing the labour, social and tax rules in the host state.[138] This is due to the fact that self-employed persons who provide their services across borders enjoy a significant competitive advantage vis-à-vis local workers and even compared to posted workers. They remain, indeed, excluded from

132. Jorens et al. (n 131); Piet Van Nuffel and Sofia Afanasjeva, 'The Posting of Workers Directive Revised: Enhancing the Protection of Workers in the Cross-Border Provision of Services' (2018) 3 European Papers 1401, 1424. Due to the frequent absence, in practice, of a continuous employment relationship between the first undertaking making the posting and the posted worker, the second posting is generally considered as not genuine and therefore excluded from the scope of the PWD.
133. Van Nuffel and Afanasjeva (n 132) 1424–1425.
134. Voss et al. (n 52) 30; van Hoek (n 60) 463.
135. This practice is widely used especially in the construction, food and IT industries. Cremers, 'In Search of Cheap Labour in Europe – Working and Living Conditions of Posted Workers' (n 60) 9; Jorens, Gillis and Potter (n 131) 70; Jorens et al. (n 131) 35 and 75; Frederic De Wispelaere, Lynn De Smedt and Jozef Pacolet, 'Coordination of Social Security Systems at a Glance: 2018 Statistical Report' (KU Leuven Research Institute for Work and Society (HIVA) 2018) European Commission, Directorate-General for Employment, Social Affairs and Inclusion Unit D/2 36; Yves Jorens, 'Intra-EU Posting: Looking for Solutions: A Herculean or a Sisyphean Task?' (60 Years Social Security Coordination from a Workers' Perspective, Leuven, Belgium, 16 May 2019). For the definition of Portable Documents A1 / E101 forms, *see supra* Chapter 6.
136. Voss et al. (n 52) 40; Zsolt Darvas, 'Revision of the Posted Workers Directive Misses the Point' (*Bruegel*, 18 October 2017) <https://bruegel.org/2017/10/revision-of-the-posted-workers-directive-misses-the-point/> (accessed 5 October 2018).
137. Houwerzijl and Berntsen (n 58) 155; Tonia Novitz and Rutvica Andrijasevic, 'Reform of the Posting of Workers Regime – An Assessment of the Practical Impact on Unfree Labour Relations' (2020) 58 JCMS: Journal of Common Market Studies 1325, 1327–1329.
138. Caro et al. (n 57) 1606–1607; Dhéret and Ghimis (n 38) 7; Jorens et al. (n 131) 75; Veloso, Sales Oliveira and Marques (n 120) 12–15 and 21.

the scope of the Posting of Workers Directive, and they can even benefit from more flexible social security provisions in comparison to employed workers.[139] In addition, in countries such as Belgium, Bulgaria, Hungary, Estonia, Ireland, Italy, Norway and the UK, the social security contribution rates for self-employed persons are comparatively lower than those of employed persons.[140] In light of this, some employers adapted accordingly by replacing workers regularly employed with (mock) self-employed persons who are, in fact, still in a relationship of subordination.[141] Actually, in some cases, posted workers have been forced by their employers to assume the status of self-employed.[142]

7.4.3 'Letterbox Companies'

A further renowned modality of unfair and abusive profiting of the possibilities offered by the recourse to posting of workers is realised by certain businesses through the creation of the so-called 'letterbox companies'.[143] This stratagem consists of fictitiously establishing the company's domicile, through a simple mailing address, in one Member State with lower rates of labour taxation and social security contributions from which, however, no significant economic activity is carried out. In effect, the purpose is exclusively to benefit from the more favourable home country rules, while operating in other Member States where labour costs are comparatively higher, through the

139. Paul Schoukens and Danny Pieters, 'The Rules within Regulation 883/2004 for Determining the Applicable Legislation' (2009) 11 European Journal of Social Security 81, 86–87; Kall and Lillie (n 52) 24; Wispelaere (n 10) 12–14; Wispelaere and Pacolet, 'The Benefits of Posting: Facts and Figures on the Use and Impact of Intra-EU Posting' (n 9) 37. On this point, *see* the analysis conducted *supra* in Chapters 2 and 5.
140. In this sense, the seamless increase of the share of self-employed persons in the construction sector in Belgium since 2011 is no coincidence. Wispelaere and Pacolet, 'The Size and Impact of Intra-EU Posting on the Belgian Economy: With a Special Focus on the Construction Sector – Summary' (n 68) 11–12 and 18; Wispelaere (n 76).
141. In most cases, these workers are directly brought by their employer to the workplace in the host country and have their accommodation and travel arranged just like posted workers, but they have local employment contracts and social security coverage. Caro et al. (n 57) 1607. *See also* Blanpain (n 120) 192; Christer Thörnqvist and Sebastian Bernhardsson, 'Their Own Stories – How Polish Construction Workers Posted to Sweden Experience Their Job Situation, or Resistance Versus Life Projects' (2015) 21 Transfer: European Review of Labour and Research 23, 29–30.
142. Voss et al. (n 52) 40; Cremers, 'Economic Freedoms and Labour Standards in the European Union' (n 8) 159–160; van Hoek (n 60) 463.
143. 'Letterbox companies' are also commonly referred to as 'mailbox companies', 'paper companies', 'money-box companies', 'brass-plate firms', 'shell companies', 'pro forma-companies' and 'front subsidiaries'. In particular, *see* van Hoek and Houwerzijl (n 124) 14; Dhéret and Ghimis (n 38) 6; Cremers, 'Economic Freedoms and Labour Standards in the European Union' (n 8) 156; Voss et al. (n 52) 39; Jan Cremers and Thomas Hastings, 'Developing an Approach for Tackling Letterbox Companies: Background Paper for the European Platform on Tackling Undeclared Work Seminar', *European Platform Undeclared Work* (2017) 1; van Hoek (n 60) 458–459; Riesco-Sanz, López and Maira Vidal (n 2) 4–5. *See also Cadbury Schweppes plc and Cadbury Schweppes Overseas Ltd v Commissioners of Inland Revenue* [2006] ECJ Case C-196/04, ECLI:EU:C:2006:544 [68]. Incidentally, it is worth noting that several types of letterbox companies may be created for different purposes besides that of posting. For a comprehensive overview, *see* Karsten Engsig Sørensen, 'The Fight Against Letterbox Companies in the Internal Market' (2015) 52 Common Market Law Review 85; Cremers and Hastings.

secondment of workers recruited at the lower cost of the country of formal establishment.[144]

As previously pointed out, the profit-driven setting up of a company in a specific Member State with the intention to obtain an advantage in terms of overall labour costs is still within the possibilities guaranteed by the internal market rules. The famous decision of the Court of Justice in *Centros*[145] confirmed, indeed, the freedom for a company to establish itself in one Member State (and to employ workers under the terms of labour legislation in force in that country) even in case its actual purpose is to set up a branch in another Member State with more restrictive rules, from which it conducts all its commercial activities. Notably, this possibility is granted even if that company does not pursue any economic activity in the state of incorporation.[146] As a matter of fact, subsequent rulings further specified that requiring an undertaking to carry out certain activities in the country of incorporation, or to maintain there its head office or real seat, is beyond the powers of a Member State.[147]

Nevertheless, the risk that the businesses' exercise of their free movement rights spills over into malpractices of regulatory arbitrage may be prevented by the respect of two conditions. First, the company establishing itself in a Member State is always obliged to respect the national requirements in the state of incorporation.[148] Second, as

144. Cremers, 'In Search of Cheap Labour in Europe – Working and Living Conditions of Posted Workers' (n 60) 9; Sørensen (n 143) 85–86; Voss et al. (n 52) 39; Dhéret and Ghimis (n 38) 6–7; Mojca Vah Jevšnik and Sanja Cukut Krilić, 'Posting of Workers: Sharing Experiences, Promoting Best Practices and Improving Access to Information' (European Commission, Republic of Slovenia 2016) Final Expert Report 17; Cremers and Hastings (n 143) 1–2; Darvas (n 136); Jorens et al. (n 131) 75; Wispelaere, Smedt and Pacolet (n 135) 36. The practice at issue is used especially in the road transport sector, whereby posted drivers often operate across several countries. European Commission Impact Assessment, Accompanying the document Proposal for a Regulation of the European Parliament and of the Council amending Regulation (EC) 561/2006 as regards minimum requirements on maximum daily and weekly driving times, minimum breaks and daily and weekly rest periods and Regulation (EU) 165/2014 as regards positioning by means of tachographs and Proposal for a Directive of the European Parliament and of the Council amending Directive 2006/22/EC as regards enforcement requirements and laying down specific rules with respect to Directive 96/71/EC and Directive 2014/67/EU for posting drivers in the road transport sector – Part 1/2 (n 126) 13–14.

145. *Centros Ltd v Erhvervs- og Selskabsstyrelsen* (n 50).

146. *Ibid.* 17, 27 and 29. Incidentally, this principle has been recently confirmed in *Polbud – Wykonawstwo sp z o.o.* [2017] CJEU Case C-106/16, ECLI:EU:C:2017:804. Deakin (n 64) 591; Catherine Barnard and Simon Deakin, 'In Search of Coherence: Social Policy, the Single Market and Fundamental Rights' (2000) 31 Industrial Relations Journal 331, 337–339; Craig and de Búrca (n 50) 811–813; Carsten Gerner-Beuerle et al., 'Study on the Law Applicable to Companies – Final Report' (European Commission, Directorate-General for Justice and Consumers Directorate A – Civil Justice Unit A1 – Civil Justice Policy 2016) 27–32; Barnard, *The Substantive Law of the EU: The Four Freedoms* (n 50) 393–394; Houwerzijl and Berntsen (n 58) 154.

147. *Überseering BV v Nordic Construction Company Baumanagement GmbH (NCC)* (n 50) para. 75; *Kamer van Koophandel en Fabrieken voor Amsterdam v Inspire Art Ltd* (n 50) para. 97. Craig and de Búrca (n 50) 813–814; Catherine Barnard and Jukka Snell, 'Free Movement of Legal Persons and the Provision of Services' in Catherine Barnard and Steve Peers (eds), *European Union Law* (Second Edition, Oxford University Press 2017) 444.

148. *Cartesio Oktató és Szolgáltató bt* [2008] ECJ Case C-210/06, ECLI:EU:C:2008:723, 109–110. Craig and de Búrca (n 50) 810–815; Sørensen (n 143) 90–91; Barnard, *The Substantive Law of the EU: The Four Freedoms* (n 50) 382 and ff.; Cremers and Hastings (n 143) 1. It is worth noting that, nonetheless, the Member States' widespread choice to follow the so-called 'incorporation'

specified by the Court in *Cadbury Schweppes*,[149] companies devoid of any objective element testifying the performance of genuine economic activities in the host Member State are prevented from enjoying the benefits offered by the internal market.[150] This is exactly the case of 'letterbox companies', consisting of mere artificial company structures or employment arrangements intended to fraudulently escape certain national rules.[151]

The illegal nature of the peculiar type of fraudulent posting at issue is not limited to the fictitious establishment in a country with more favourable laws with a view to maximising profits. It often involves a whole series of directly related wrongful practices. In several cases the corporate structure is on purpose complex and obscure, entailing multilevel structures in different Member States, often making use of transnational subcontracting.[152] The form of private limited companies is widespread for obvious reasons of minor costs, limited liability and anonymity of the shareholders.[153] As a result, tax evasion, unlawful social security contribution payments and abuses of workers' rights through undeclared work, use of unregistered workers or under-declared employment covered by false declarations and late pay compensations in the home country, are more likely disguised.[154] Moreover, the (not uncommon) very poor, or even non-existent, registered capital of the service providers exposes the posted workers to the risk of not receiving the salary they are entitled to.[155]

The issues connected to the spread of 'letterbox companies' have been firmly condemned by both the parties directly involved, the academic literature and the European institutions. In particular, the need of intensifying the fight against this kind of fictitious and abusive constructions, together with the exigency of guaranteeing effective legal remedies for posted workers suffering from repeated violations of their fundamental rights at the workplace, has been officially acknowledged in the 2010 Monti Report.[156] Very importantly, as already pointed out *supra* in Chapter 4, the European legislator has shown its sensitivity to the issue by adopting in 2014 the Enforcement Directive 2014/67/EU,[157] which includes a series of practical initiatives specifically designed to provide a concrete response to the matter. In this sense, effective criteria for the recognition of genuine posting activity and the individuation of

doctrine – which considers the jurisdiction in which the legal entity has been incorporated as the applicable one, irrespective of the place where the company has its 'real seat' – undoubtedly favours the proliferation of questionable organisational arrangements. Houwerzijl and Berntsen (n 58) 154.

149. *Cadbury Schweppes plc and Cadbury Schweppes Overseas Ltd v Commissioners of Inland Revenue* (n 143).
150. *Ibid.* 64–68.
151. Jan Cremers, Jon Erik Dølvik and Gerhard Bosch, 'Posting of Workers in the Single Market: Attempts to Prevent Social Dumping and Regime Competition in the EU' (2007) 38 Industrial Relations Journal 524, 526.
152. Voss et al. (n 52) 39; Cremers and Hastings (n 143) 2.
153. Limited liability companies may benefit in several Member States of low or no minimum capital requirements. Sørensen (n 143) 86.
154. Cremers and Hastings (n 143) 1–2; Darvas (n 136); Dodi and Melenciuc (n 117) 76–77.
155. Sørensen (n 143) 97.
156. Monti (n 111) 70.
157. Article 4 of Directive 2014/67/EU of the European Parliament and of the Council of 15 May 2014 on the enforcement of Directive 96/71/EC concerning the posting of workers in the

the actual establishment of a posting company in the sending Member State have been introduced.[158] The fight against 'letterbox companies' has been conducted also with the imposition of specific duties of collaboration between national authorities, especially with regard to the exchange of information aimed at identifying the natural person or legal person who is behind those fictitious constructions, and thus responsible for the posting.[159] In addition, a sort of vicarious liability of the main contractor for any subcontractor's lack of payment has been included in the 2014 legislative *novella*.[160] The latter measure may, indeed, turn out to be very effective whenever employers take advantage of 'letterbox firms' with no share capital. However, as already stressed, unless an extension to subsequent contracting parties is introduced by a regulatory intervention at national level, that form of subcontracting liability, due to its limited scope, leaves its side open to longer chains of subcontractors.[161]

As is apparent, all the aforementioned examples represent just a few of the many different combinations of factors that can be exploited by malicious operators making (ab)use of the internal market's economic freedoms. What immediately sticks out from those cases and, more generally, from the analysis of the several malpractices connected more or less directly with the recourse to posting of workers, is the precariousness of the existing normative framework. The latter is, indeed, characterised by insufficient coordination and cooperation between the Member States and, more concretely, between the national authorities concerned.[162]

---

framework of the provision of services and amending Regulation (EU) No 1024/2012 on administrative cooperation through the Internal Market Information System ('the IMI Regulation') 2014 (OJ L 159/11).

158. *Ibid.* Article 4. Sørensen (n 143) 98–99; Cremers and Hastings (n 143) 2–3.
159. Articles 6–8 of Directive 2014/67/EU of the European Parliament and of the Council of 15 May 2014 on the enforcement of Directive 96/71/EC concerning the posting of workers in the framework of the provision of services and amending Regulation (EU) No 1024/2012 on administrative cooperation through the Internal Market Information System ('the IMI Regulation') (n 157). Sørensen (n 143) 99.
160. Article 12 of Directive 2014/67/EU of the European Parliament and of the Council of 15 May 2014 on the enforcement of Directive 96/71/EC concerning the posting of workers in the framework of the provision of services and amending Regulation (EU) No 1024/2012 on administrative cooperation through the Internal Market Information System ('the IMI Regulation') (n 157).
161. Sørensen (n 143) 99–100; Cremers and Hastings (n 143) 2–3. With regard to the variety of specific measures adopted, in turn, at national level in order to combat fraud and error, *see* Yves Jorens, Dirk Gillis and Joyce De Coninck, 'Fraud and Error in the Field of Social Security Coordination: Reference Year: 2014' (European Commission, Directorate-General for Employment, Social Affairs and Inclusion, Unit D2 – Social security coordination 2015) 40–43; Jorens, Gillis and Potter (n 131) 12–44.
162. As outlined in the preamble to the new Directive (EU) 2018/957, despite the adoption of the Enforcement Directive 2014/67/EU, insufficient transnational cooperation still represents one of the major issues at stake. Preamble Recital 26 of Directive (EU) 2018/957 of the European Parliament and of the Council of 28 June 2018 amending Directive 96/71/EC concerning the posting of workers in the framework of the provision of services 2018 (OJ L 173/16). In this sense, *see* van Hoek and Houwerzijl (n 124) 161–171; Blanpain (n 120) 193; Jorens, Peters and Houwerzijl (n 104) 154–155; Susanne Kraatz, 'European Parliament, Posting of Workers – Fact Sheets on the European Union' (July 2018) <http://www.europarl.europa.eu/factsheets/en/sheet/37/posting-of-workers> (accessed 26 September 2018); Stefan Schwarz, 'Opening Address at the II European Labour Mobility Congress' (VI European Labour Mobility Congress (ELMC), Krakow (Poland), 14 March 2019).

7.4.4 Undeclared Work

Lastly, the presence of a far more important problem in the intra-EU labour mobility context, which is often wrongly confused with the practice of posting, shall be emphasised. The 'elephant in the room' is undeclared work.[163] While this book is not the place for an accurate analysis of such an issue, it should nonetheless be pointed out that, despite its relevant actual dimension, black employment remains inexplicably too often excluded from the common narrative on posting. In effect, undeclared workers employed in high-wage Member States outnumber the posted workers coming from low-wage Member States in a ratio of 100:1.[164] Due to their totally illegal situation, employees involved in the black economy have no labour rights, no social insurance, and are at the complete mercy of their 'employer'. As a result, their remuneration level is often below the minimum wage, and they do not benefit from any sort of labour protection. Apparently, undeclared employees suffer, in the majority of the cases, from even worse working conditions than posted workers.[165]

Against this background, the newly established European Platform to enhance cooperation in tackling undeclared work (the 'Platform'), established by Decision (EU) 2016/344 of the European Parliament and the Council,[166] has been specifically designed to combat frauds in this context, including those borderline situations related to posting of workers.

7.5 WHAT SOCIAL DUMPING?

In the European public discourse, as well as at EU policymaking level, the idioms 'social dumping' and 'unfair competition' are, unfortunately, frequently associated with the phenomenon of posting of workers.[167] The letter sent by Austria, Belgium,

163. Darvas (n 136). In this sense, *see also* Wołoszyn (n 32) 183.
164. Darvas (n 136). For a more detailed survey on the spread of undeclared work at national level, *see* Veloso, Sales Oliveira and Marques (n 120).
165. Maslauskaite (n 5) 46; Zsolt Darvas, 'Could Revising the Posted Workers Directive Improve Social Conditions?' (Conference of think tanks on the revision of the posted workers directive, European Parliament, Brussels, 31 January 2017) 15–16. For an example of the terrible conditions of undeclared workers, *see* Jan Cremers, 'Undeclared Work in the Construction Industry' (2017).
166. Decision (EU) 2016/344 of the European Parliament and of the Council of 9 March 2016 on establishing a European Platform to enhance cooperation in tackling undeclared work 2016 (OJ L 65/12).
167. In this sense, *see* the Toulon speech on 1 December 2011 of the former President of France, Mr Nicolas Sarkozy, who expressed his discontent with 'social and fiscal dumping' and 'disloyal competition' within the EU. The Economist, 'The Euro Crisis – One Problem, Two Visions (Part II): Two Speeches by Nicolas Sarkozy and Angela Merkel about the Euro Zone's Crisis Reveal Their Differences Ahead of a Key Summit' (2 December 2011) <https://www.economist.com/blogs/charlemagne/2011/12/euro-crisis-0> (accessed 15 May 2018). In this sense, *see also* Julie Richert, 'Posted Workers in the EU: Social Dumping vs Competitive Advantage' (*ECIPE*, 18 December 2017) <http://ecipe.org/blog/posted-workers-in-the-eu-social-dumping-vs-competitive-advantage/> (accessed 13 May 2018). As far as the academic literature is concerned, *see* Bohle (n 8); Verschueren (n 5) 198; Barnard, 'Fifty Years of Avoiding Social Dumping? The EU's Economic and Not So Economic Constitution' (n 64) 311–312, 322 and ff.; Krings (n 85) 52–53;

France, Germany, Luxembourg, the Netherlands and Sweden to Marianne Thyssen (at that time Commissioner for Employment, Social Affairs, Skills and Labour Mobility) on 18 June 2015, supporting a revision of the Posting of Workers Directive with a view to 'preventing social dumping and abuse of the free movement of services', is emblematic in this respect.[168]

However, when it comes to defining the concept of 'social dumping', profound uncertainty and vagueness worryingly surround the actual actors and practices involved. In such a context, social partners, politicians, governments, institutions and even academics too often take undue advantage of this lack of definition and relate to the issue at their own convenience.[169] The proof of the influence and political significance of social dumping concerns at European societal level is given by the introduction of transitional periods for the new Member States acceding the European Union during the late 1970s and early 1980s Southern and the 2000s Eastern enlargements, aimed at temporarily restricting the workforce inflow directed to the 'old' EU Member States.[170] Similarly, the failure of the 2005 referenda in France and the Netherlands for the ratification of the Treaty Establishing a Constitution for Europe was the result of widespread preoccupation for a higher degree of European integration, especially with regard to the opening of the EU labour market to Central and Eastern European Countries.[171]

7.5.1 Debunking Misconceptions

In light of the differences in pay level and labour standards between the Member States, the expressions 'social dumping' and 'unfair competition' have been – and frequently still are – used to label any form of employment of posted workers from low-wage to high-wage countries.[172] The argument underpinning great scepticism and massive opposition to the liberalisation of the internal market for services is based on the idea that the inflow of cheap labour from the poorer or less developed Member States through posting arrangements would eventually result in worsening job prospects and

Cremers, 'EU Economic Freedoms and Social Dumping' (n 8) 186–187; Verschueren (n 26) 133–135; Cremers, 'Economic Freedoms and Labour Standards in the European Union' (n 8) 10; Daniel Carter, 'Equal Pay for Equal Work in the Same Place? Assessing the Revision to the Posted Workers Directive' (2018) 14 Croatian Yearbook of European Law and Policy 31, 47–51. Conversely, for a critique of such a stance against posting, *see* Maslauskaite (n 2) 3; Magdalena Bernaciak, 'Introduction: Social Dumping and the EU Integration Process' in Magdalena Bernaciak (ed.), *Market Expansion and Social Dumping in Europe* (Routledge 2015) 2–3; Dhéret and Ghimis (n 38) 6; Lhernould and Palli (n 2) 109; Houwerzijl and Berntsen (n 58) 147.

168. Austrian, Belgian, French, German, Luxembourg, Dutch and Swedish Ministers of labour (n 1).
169. Bernaciak, 'Social Dumping and the EU Integration Process' (n 7) 5.
170. On the content and duration of those 'transitional arrangements', *see supra* Chapter 2.
171. Antonina Bakardjieva Engelbrekt, 'Institutional Theories, EU Law and the Role of the Courts for Developing a European Social Model' in Ulla Neergaard, Ruth Nielsen and Lynn M Roseberry (eds), *The Role of Courts in Developing a European Social Model – Theoretical and Methodological Perspectives* (Djøf Publishing 2010) 335; Bernaciak, 'Social Dumping: Political Catchphrase or Threat to Labour Standards?' (n 48) 5 and 18; Uglješa Grušić, *The European Private International Law of Employment* (Cambridge University Press 2015) 257–258.
172. Bernaciak, 'Social Dumping: Political Catchphrase or Threat to Labour Standards?' (n 48) 16.

downgrading of wage levels and social protection in the wealthier Member States.[173] Public opinion in the Western EU countries fears that the ultimate consequences would be the displacement of local workers by cheaper posted foreign employees and a 'race to the bottom' between nations in terms of social standards.[174]

However, this kind of rough reasoning is based on the misconception that the absolute difference in raw wages and gross domestic product (GDP) per capita directly corresponds to greater competitiveness of cross-border actors and automatically provokes distortion of competition and downward pressure on national welfare states. On the contrary, relative labour costs are strongly influenced by the level of productivity within a certain business environment, and thus by labour skills and techniques, as well as by the company's resources and the national administrative infrastructure.[175] Accordingly, the competitive advantage, given by real differences in labour costs, tax and social security contributions, from which actors established in the poorer countries benefit is counterbalanced, in practice, by the traditionally lower productivity in those systems.[176] Especially with regard to service providers coming from Central and Eastern European Member States, evidence proves that their competitive advantage is progressively decreasing as a result of the progressive upward convergence of wages and labour taxation rates. In fact, the Central and Eastern European workers are experiencing, in the last years, a steady increase in their salary level which is, nonetheless, not yet supported by a correspondent improvement of their productivity.[177] Furthermore, low-earning labour tax rates in the 'new' European countries are substantially in line with those applied in the 'old' continental Member States.[178]

In contrast, the countries with the lowest tax rates on low-wage earners in the whole EU internal market are currently Cyprus, Malta, Ireland, Luxembourg and the UK. Interestingly, when it comes to labour costs, those countries represent, indeed, the

---

173. *Ibid.*; Damjan Kukovec, 'Hierarchies as Law' (2014) 21 Columbia Journal of European Law 131, 162; Maslauskaite (n 5) 20; Bernaciak, 'Social Dumping and the EU Integration Process' (n 7) 7; Magdalena Bernaciak, 'Polish Trade Unions and Social Dumping Debates: Between a Rock and a Hard Place' (2016) 22 Transfer: European Review of Labour and Research 505, 507–508; Wispelaere (n 10) 18.
174. Charles Woolfson and Jeff Sommers, 'Labour Mobility in Construction: European Implications of the Laval Un Partneri Dispute with Swedish Labour' (2006) 12 European Journal of Industrial Relations 49, 61–62; Maslauskaite (n 5) 10 and 12; Maslauskaite (n 2) 4; Bernaciak, 'Conclusion' (n 6) 14; Cremers, 'Economic Freedoms and Labour Standards in the European Union' (n 8) 9; Lhernould and Palli (n 2) 109.
175. The concept has been precisely framed by Davies: 'Highly paid workers who are highly productive may generate cheaper goods or services than lower paid workers who are inefficient. Within the single market project of the Community, therefore, there is no necessary reason to regard competition from lower paid workers as justifying a partitioning of the market.' Paul Davies, 'Posted Workers: Single Market or Protection of National Labour Law Systems?' (1997) 34 Common Market Law Review 571, 599. On this point, *see also* Maslauskaite (n 5) 25; Verschueren (n 26) 133–134.
176. Bernaciak, 'Social Dumping: Political Catchphrase or Threat to Labour Standards?' (n 48) 17; Bernaciak, 'Social Dumping and the EU Integration Process' (n 7) 7.
177. When comparing salary with productivity levels of CEECs and Western EU countries, a substantial similarity appears evident. In fact, wage levels in the Central and Eastern European Member States have remained very low in absolute terms, but also labour productivity has basically not improved. Maslauskaite (n 5) 27 and 52; Verschueren (n 26) 134.
178. Maslauskaite (n 5) 29–30.

actual cheapest destinations in Europe, once their productivity levels are confronted with their weaker employment protection, lower tax rates, and social security contributions.[179] For this reason, it is not unusual that companies formally incorporate themselves under, e.g., Irish law because of its comparatively lower tax rates and labour costs, and subsequently delocalise their production facilities in the more convenient, when it comes to infrastructure and workforce costs, Central and Eastern European Countries. In light of their peculiar economic model, Cyprus, Malta, Ireland, Luxembourg and the UK may be considered as the prime suspect of social dumping in Europe.[180] Besides, it is suggested to take into consideration the structure of different national taxation and social contribution systems as well. Such a perspective would highlight that the least taxation and social contribution rates on employers of low-paid labour are those applied in Denmark, Malta, the UK, the Netherlands and Ireland. Accordingly, Danish firms can benefit from a competitive advantage over, e.g., French and Polish firms in that regard.[181]

7.5.2 Posting and Social Dumping

As previously mentioned, in the Western European public discourse, issues of social dumping and unfair competition are often directly associated with the posting of low-wage workers from Central and Eastern European Member States. After having demonstrated the fallacy of such a syllogism, it is appropriate now to provide a precise definition of which types of conducts may give rise to social dumping in the context of posting of workers. Finding its conceptual origin in the sphere of international trade of goods,[182] social dumping consists in the practice of undermining or evading the existing social and industrial relations regulations, undertaken by unscrupulous cross-border companies, which strategically take advantage of lower cost structures and more lenient regulatory environments with a view to gaining a short-term competitive advantage over their competitors.[183] Evidently, this competitive strategy is liable to lead, in the short run, to the displacement of higher-cost local employment and to

179. In turn, the relatively highest ratio between productivity and labour costs is currently present in Belgium, Sweden, Denmark and Italy. Eurostat, 'Tax Rate on Low Wage Earners: Tax Wedge on Labour Costs' (European Commission 2017) <https://ec.europa.eu/eurostat/en/web/products-datasets/-/EARN_NT_TAXWEDGE> (accessed 2 December 2018). On this point, *see* Maslauskaite (n 5) 25–26, 30–31, and 53; Verschueren (n 26) 134.
180. Maslauskaite (n 5) 53.
181. Maslauskaite (n 2) 11–12.
182. Dumping in trade was originally indicating the practice of a cross-border trader exporting goods in a foreign country at a price below the one charged in its home market or below the costs of production. On this point, *see* Damjan Kukovec, 'A Critique of the Rhetoric of Common Interest in the European Union Legal Discourse' (2012) 11 SSRN Electronic Journal, 420; Bernaciak, 'Social Dumping: Political Catchphrase or Threat to Labour Standards?' (n 48) 22–25; Maslauskaite (n 5) 19; Elena Vaccarino and Zsolt Darvas, '"Social Dumping" and Posted Workers: A New Clash within the EU' (*Bruegel*, 7 March 2016) <http://bruegel.org/2016/03/social-dumping-and-posted-workers-a-new-clash-within-the-eu/> (accessed 13 May 2018).
183. Bernaciak, 'Social Dumping: Political Catchphrase or Threat to Labour Standards?' (n 48) 32; Bernaciak, 'Social Dumping and the EU Integration Process' (n 7) 16; Berntsen and Lillie (n 52) 45–46.

downward pressure on remuneration levels and labour standards in the host countries.[184] In turn, long-term negative repercussions might involve a 'race to the bottom' between the Member States in order to attract business investments, with a consequent erosion of labour standards and decrease of productivity levels in both the sending and receiving countries.[185]

In light of the foregoing definition, when taking into consideration the activity of cross-border posting of workers, it is apparent that certain posting arrangements lend themselves to the attainment of social dumping practices. This is the case of regulatory arbitrage strategies adopted by certain undertakings which, rather than relying on productivity, efficiency, labour skills and quality of their services, seek to benefit from the selection of the most profitable legal regimes.[186] In effect, these forms of conduct represent a source of social dumping whenever the transnational provision of services is performed through the employment of posted workers at wage rates and working conditions lower than those applicable in the host country, thus circumventing existing higher social standards.[187] In the same vein, even the formal compliance with social regulations in the receiving states might end up in social dumping dynamics, when it is accompanied by an exploitation of regulatory loopholes for cost advantages, which has the effect of putting pressure on industrial relations systems.[188]

In any event, it should be noted that the allegations of social dumping in connection with the phenomenon of posting are rarely supported by empirical evidence, given also the actual limited size in absolute numbers of this form of labour mobility and the relevant EU regulatory framework.[189] Especially in the case of legal posting, social dumping consequences have been limited to a large extent by the application of the minimum terms and conditions of employment set out in the Posting of Workers Directive (even before the entry into effect of Directive (EU) 2018/957), as well as by the fact that the cross-border employees have typically been granted a series

184. Catherine Barnard, 'EU "Social" Policy: From Employment Law to Labour Market Reform' in Paul Craig and Gráinne de Búrca (eds), *The Evolution of EU Law* (Second Edition, Oxford University Press 2011) 648–649; Bernaciak, 'Social Dumping: Political Catchphrase or Threat to Labour Standards?' (n 48) 21 and 32; Bernaciak, 'Social Dumping and the EU Integration Process' (n 7) 25; Wispelaere (n 76) figures 5–8.
185. Frank Hendrickx, 'Fundamental Social Rights in Pre- and Post-Constitutional Terms' (2006) 22 International Journal of Comparative Labour Law and Industrial Relations 407, 413; Barnard, 'EU "Social" Policy: From Employment Law to Labour Market Reform' (n 184) 648; Bernaciak, 'Social Dumping: Political Catchphrase or Threat to Labour Standards?' (n 48) 30; Bernaciak, 'Social Dumping and the EU Integration Process' (n 7) 12 and 26.
186. Bernaciak, 'Social Dumping: Political Catchphrase or Threat to Labour Standards?' (n 48) 32; Berntsen and Lillie (n 52) 53. For a definition of the practice of companies engaging in regulatory arbitrage, *see supra* sub-subsection 7.3.1.1.
187. Bernaciak, 'Conclusion' (n 6) 230.
188. This is the case, e.g., of the replacement of full-time employees with cheaper foreign posted workers. Barnard, 'EU "Social" Policy: From Employment Law to Labour Market Reform' (n 184) 648–649; Berntsen and Lillie (n 52) 55–56.
189. Barnard, 'EU "Social" Policy: From Employment Law to Labour Market Reform' (n 184) 648; Wispelaere and Pacolet, 'The Benefits of Posting: Facts and Figures on the Use and Impact of Intra-EU Posting' (n 9) 37.

of bonuses and allowances for their mobility abroad.[190] Furthermore, the substantive approximation of the wage treatment reserved to local and posted workers, resulting from the recent rulings of the Court of Justice in *Sähköalojen ammattiliitto*[191] and *RegioPost*,[192] definitely reduced the scope for social dumping as well.

At last, a further misconception in the common representation of social dumping is identified with regard to the identity of the actors involved and directly profiting from it, and especially their degree of involvement. In effect, the blame for social dumping is usually on the posted workers themselves, who are supposed to 'steal' the jobs of local workers,[193] rather than on companies providing services at prices below local rates through the employment of workers at conditions lower than those laid down by laws or collective agreements in the receiving Member States.[194] If anything, the posted workers, who seek a favourable compromise between accepting lower wages and poorer working conditions compared to local workers in the host states and profiting from the business opportunities offered by their employers, may be associated with social dumping solely as indirect actors.[195]

7.5.3 Major Sources of Social Dumping

In addition to the above-mentioned legal (or borderline) firms' cost-saving strategies making recourse to posting arrangements, a number of further (often illegal) practices are indicated as potential major sources of social dumping as well.[196] Incidentally, the definition of social dumping embraced by the current analysis includes all situations in which cross-border operators take advantage of different national regimes, even by circumventing the rules on minimum wages, social security contributions and labour standards.[197] Accordingly, it is worth stressing that one of the primary causes of social dumping *lato sensu* in the EU internal market should be imputed to malpractices of

190. In effect, when the rules prescribed by the original Posting of Workers Directive were properly implemented, the danger of social dumping was substantially averted by the application of statutory and sectorial minimum wages. Wispelaere (n 10) 22–23; Vaccarino and Darvas (n 182).
191. *Sähköalojen ammattiliitto ry v Elektrobudowa Spolka Akcyjna* (n 71).
192. *RegioPost GmbH & Co. KG v Stadt Landau in der Pfalz* (n 72).
193. This is the case of the infamous bogeyman of the *'Polish plumber'*, which played a crucial role in France in 2005, boosting the No vote on the EU Constitution.
194. Bernaciak, 'Social Dumping: Political Catchphrase or Threat to Labour Standards?' (n 48) 17 and 30; Maslauskaite (n 5) 20.
195. Bernaciak, 'Social Dumping: Political Catchphrase or Threat to Labour Standards?' (n 48) 24; Bernaciak, 'Social Dumping and the EU Integration Process' (n 7) 25; Vera Trappmann, 'Social Dumping with No Divide: Evidence from Multinational Companies in Europe' in Magdalena Bernaciak (ed.), *Market Expansion and Social Dumping in Europe* (Routledge 2015) 140 and 147; Bernaciak, 'Conclusion' (n 6) 228.
196. Berntsen and Lillie (n 52) 45; Bernaciak, 'Conclusion' (n 6) 230.
197. It should be noted that a different view on the definition of social dumping sees the concept distinct from that of social fraud. This different approach refers to social dumping when indicating practices which do not entail an evasion of the rules per se, but rather the exploitation of competitive advantages resulting from differences in national regimes. In turn, it considers social fraud through the use of posted workers paid less than the minimum wage, or without social contributions, as completely illegal situations which constitute merely an issue of enforcement of the rules. In this sense, *see* Wispelaere and Pacolet, 'The Size and

social and fiscal fraud. In particular, the use of abusive arrangements such as bogus self-employment and, especially, undeclared work have the largest impact in terms of erosion of labour and social standards in the receiving countries.[198] The unfair competition of the service providers profiting from such practices is evident in their undue economic advantage deriving from 'artificially' lower labour costs in respect to legally operating employers.[199] In the same vein, the evasion of national industrial relations regulations, often achieved through the creation of complex and obscure corporate structures, is undoubtedly undermining the existing social norms.[200] Moreover, the activity of multinational firms specialised in providing manpower hired out from low-wage to high-wage Member States is considered extremely detrimental too.[201]

Similarly, the policy of offshoring production, i.e., cost-driven business relocation, adopted by various Western European companies shall be deemed primarily responsible as well.[202] In effect, since the 2004 and 2007 Eastern enlargements of the EU, a number of firms established in the high-wage Member States sized the opportunity of increasing their profits by means of relocating into the more convenient Eastern Europe's labour markets.[203] As firmly confirmed by the Court of Justice,[204] the faculty for companies to establish themselves, or to set up a branch or an agency, in another Member State while operating in different national markets falls under the legitimate exercise of the EU economic freedoms and, of course, does not necessarily imply dishonest 'dumping' intentions.[205] It is no less true, however, that Western European undertakings hardly ever transfer higher wages, better employment conditions and more advanced systems of collective representation to their Central and Eastern European subsidiaries.[206] Therefore, the threat of offshoring production is more and more frequently used by companies established in the wealthier Member States as a means for undercutting wages and working conditions.[207] The same result is also

Impact of Intra-EU Posting on the Belgian Economy: With a Special Focus on the Construction Sector – Summary' (n 68) 17; Wispelaere (n 10) 22–23.

198. Bernaciak, 'Social Dumping: Political Catchphrase or Threat to Labour Standards?' (n 48) 26; Bernaciak, 'Social Dumping and the EU Integration Process' (n 7) 22; Verschueren (n 26) 134–135; Darvas (n 136); Bengt Furåker and Bengt Larsson, 'Revision of the EU Posting of Workers Directive, Social Dumping and Trade Unions' Position' in Bengt Furåker and Bengt Larsson, *Trade Union Cooperation in Europe: Patterns, Conditions, Issues* (Springer International Publishing 2020) 115–116.
199. Maslauskaite (n 5) 46.
200. Berntsen and Lillie (n 52) 50.
201. *Ibid.* 50–53.
202. Bernaciak, 'Social Dumping: Political Catchphrase or Threat to Labour Standards?' (n 48) 26, 29 and 32; Trappmann (n 195) 142; Darvas (n 136); Sciarra (n 66) 82; Riesco-Sanz, López and Maira Vidal (n 2) 11.
203. Andreas Bieler and Roland Erne, 'Transnational Solidarity?: The European Working Class in the Eurozone Crisis' in Leo Panitch and Greg Albo (eds), *Transforming Classes: Socialist Register 2015* (The Merlin Press 2014) 158.
204. On this point, *see supra* subsection 7.4.3.
205. Bernaciak, 'Social Dumping: Political Catchphrase or Threat to Labour Standards?' (n 48) 27.
206. *Ibid.* 30.
207. Local workers accepting a downgrading of their salaries and social standards are thereby 'rewarded' with the possibility of keeping, at least temporarily, their jobs and with the promise of new investments. *Ibid.* 28; Bieler and Erne (n 203) 162–163.

achieved by stirring up inter-plant rivalry, once the employees in a certain production plant have been forced to agree on lower salaries and labour standards.[208] The power of large multinational companies may, in some cases, even put pressure on national governments by making investments dependent upon the granting of subsidies, fiscal exemptions or labour market reforms.[209]

Besides considering those kinds of competitive company strategies, it is noticeable that also the Member States play at times an active role in fostering social dumping, by engaging each other into a disruptive social and fiscal competition. In fact, national regulatory interventions aimed at attracting foreign companies or preserving higher competitiveness often entail the lowering of existing social protection and labour standards or the implementation of labour tax shifts.[210] In contrast to the widespread perception of a perpetual erosion of the labour and social models of the Western European countries by means of the employment of 'cheaper' posted workers hired in the Central and Eastern Member States, it should be noted that fiscal and social competition between the Member States on employment conditions and welfare standards has taken place, in the course of the 2000s, especially between Poland, Czech Republic, Slovakia and Hungary. For years, the labour market of the so-called 'Visegrád Four' (V4) countries has been the bloody battlefield for the award of important investments from the major Western European automotive industries.[211] In all those cases, the race to the bottom in terms of labour and social standards does not predominantly concern the employment of cross-border seconded workers, but rather the dumping in the sphere of capital and industrial production.

Finally, it is worth mentioning that also the widespread practice of cross-border self-employment is potentially one of the main sources of social dumping. Individuals

208. Lillie (n 63) 163; Bernaciak, 'Social Dumping: Political Catchphrase or Threat to Labour Standards?' (n 48) 29.
209. Bernaciak, 'Social Dumping and the EU Integration Process' (n 7) 22; Trappmann (n 195) 141–143.
210. Hendrickx (n 185) 413; Barnard, 'EU "Social" Policy: From Employment Law to Labour Market Reform' (n 184) 648; Bernaciak, 'Social Dumping: Political Catchphrase or Threat to Labour Standards?' (n 48) 24; Bernaciak, 'Social Dumping and the EU Integration Process' (n 7) 24–25; Berntsen and Lillie (n 52) 46; Bernaciak, 'Conclusion' (n 6) 229; Wispelaere and Pacolet, 'An Ad Hoc Statistical Analysis on Short Term Mobility – Economic Value of Posting of Workers: The Impact of Intra-EU Cross-Border Services, with Special Attention to the Construction Sector' (n 11) 17–18. An example of this is provided by the initiative of the Belgian Federal Government that, in order to combat unfair competition from foreign companies employing seconded workers in the construction industry, in 2018 proposed to allocate a budget of EUR 605 million for reducing employers' social security contributions in the sector. The natural result of such a policy would have been, however, a race to the bottom between local and foreign enterprises. In this sense, *see* Wispelaere and Pacolet, 'The Size and Impact of Intra-EU Posting on the Belgian Economy: With a Special Focus on the Construction Sector – Summary' (n 68) 17.
211. Among the major Western European automotive companies that have invested, in the course of the 2000s, in the Visegrád Four countries there are Volkswagen, Peugeot, Kia and Jaguar Land Rover. On this point, *see* Bohle (n 8); Bernaciak, 'Social Dumping: Political Catchphrase or Threat to Labour Standards?' (n 48) 29 and 32; Lucia Mýtna Kureková, 'The Automotive Industry in Central Europe: A Success?' (2018) Slovak Governance Institute and CELSI, Slovakia, and IZA – Institute of Labor Economics, Germany <https://wol.iza.org/articles/the-automotive-industry-in-central-europe-a-success/long> (accessed 4 December 2018).

benefitting from such a status are, indeed, free to carry out profitable transnational operations without being subject to stringent rules on minimum wages. Especially those established in the Member States with lower labour costs are, therefore, able to undermine the higher social standards of the countries in which they provide services to a greater extent than undertakings which make recourse to posting arrangements.[212]

7.5.4 Reversing the Perspective

With a view to providing an overall perspective on the matter, the present analysis cannot refrain from recognising the politicised conception of social dumping, which relies on the arbitrary consideration of social standards of Western European countries as a universal standard.[213] Accordingly, as stressed by Advocate General Szpunar in his Opinion in case *Dobersberger*[214] recently delivered on 29 July 2019, if the perspective of the host Member State only is taken into account, there is a serious risk that the pursuit of anti-dumping policies would amount to nothing less than protectionism against foreign service providers, and to a consequent violation of EU law.[215] As a matter of fact, the concept of social dumping depends very much on the viewpoint taken since, as thoughtfully pointed out by the Polish amicus curiae, 'what is "social dumping" for some is, quite simply, "employment" for others'.[216] One must not, therefore, make the mistake of confusing the fight against 'social dumping' with the protection of the posted workers.[217]

Along the same lines, a further critique of the existing Western European narrative on social dumping relates to the social construction of harm and injury in the common discourse. As brilliantly noted by Kukovec, the rhetoric of 'dumping', notwithstanding its conceptual origin in international trade of goods, has principally developed as a way of denoting a prejudice to social standards in Western European countries (the EU 'centre'), rather than a harm to the industries and employment rates in the Central and Eastern Member States (the EU 'periphery').[218] As a matter of fact,

212. Wispelaere (n 10) 22–23.
213. Bernaciak, 'Social Dumping and the EU Integration Process' (n 7) 10; Berntsen and Lillie (n 52) 45.
214. *Michael Dobersberger, Opinion of Advocate General Maciej Szpunar delivered on 29 July 2019* [2019] CJEU Case C-16/18, ECLI:EU:C:2019:638.
215. *Ibid.* 30–31. On this point, *see* Marcin Kiełbasa, 'Posting in the Orient Express or the Advocate General M. Szpunar's Opinion on "Chain Posting"' (*Labour Mobility Initiative*, 28 August 2019) <https://www.mobilelabour.eu/13077/posting-in-the-orient-express-or-the-advocate-general-m-szpunars-opinion-on-chain-posting/> (accessed 2 September 2019).
216. *Michael Dobersberger, Opinion of Advocate General Maciej Szpunar delivered on 29 July 2019* (n 214) para. 30. Interestingly, this subjective conception of social dumping was already framed is similar terms by Barnard when, in relation to the Court's rulings in *Viking* and *Laval*, she affirmed that 'what is social dumping to the losers (richer Northern European states) is economic opportunity to the winners (poorer Eastern European states) who take advantage of their lower labour costs to gain a foothold on these new markets'. Barnard, 'Fifty Years of Avoiding Social Dumping? The EU's Economic and Not So Economic Constitution' (n 64) 311.
217. *Michael Dobersberger, Opinion of Advocate General Maciej Szpunar delivered on 29 July 2019* (n 214) para. 29.
218. In the words of Kukovec, 'We, EU lawyers, tend to think about harm in a very specific way – in terms of the harm to the centre.' Kukovec, 'A Critique of the Rhetoric of Common Interest in

the markets of the latter group of countries, because of their higher price elasticity of demand, in several instances suffer from the 'goods dumping' resulting from the lower prices of the products imported there by certain Western European companies. In spite of this, the issue of 'goods dumping' has never been included in the integrationist discourse at EU level, and no practical response has ever been given to the injuries sustained by the economic sectors affected by such a phenomenon in the peripheral countries of the Union.[219]

7.6 CONCLUDING REMARKS

The analysis carried out in this chapter has made it easier to comprehend that the actual relevance of the posting phenomenon goes beyond its mere material size, entailing a wide spectrum of direct and indirect effects, which contribute in a meaningful way to shaping such a hybrid share of the internal market. The investigation of the impact of posting on the EU labour market on the basis of published empirical results proves the common public and political perception of the phenomenon to be just as popular as superficial. Except for some negative repercussions, posting has introduced a variety of positive outcomes able to effectively support the European integration process.

Empirical evidence proves the existence of several beneficial effects, deriving from the exercise of this form of cross-border mobility, on the individual workers concerned, the sending and receiving Member States and the EU internal market as a whole.[220] More specifically, posting has the ability to increase the household incomes of the persons involved, who may enjoy the opportunity to get a higher salary than in their home country. As a consequence, a natural rise in the level of private consumption in their country of origin follows, along with an increase of labour tax revenues since, generally, the posted workers still continue to pay taxes in their home state. Furthermore, this phenomenon undoubtedly stimulates intra-EU competition among cross-border and local service providers. It contributes also to the overall economic growth in both the sending and receiving countries, through improvement of companies' competitiveness, internationalization and productivity levels, and through an effective response to cyclical deficiencies affecting particular economic sectors. In practice, from a receiving perspective, the temporary inflow of foreign posted workers constitutes a useful means for resolving labour and skill seasonal shortages, while contributing to better job allocation and occupational mobility. In turn, it makes it possible for the sending companies to avoid repeated procedures of firing-and-hiring workers depending on the contingent labour demand. Last but not least, posting of workers operates as a stabilising mechanism within both the Eurozone and the whole

the European Union Legal Discourse' (n 182) 5; Kukovec, 'Hierarchies as Law' (n 173) 149; Damjan Kukovec, 'Law and the Periphery' (2015) 21 European Law Journal 406, 420–422.

219. Kukovec, 'Hierarchies as Law' (n 173) 165; Kukovec, 'Law and the Periphery' (n 218) 420–422.

220. Frederic De Wispelaere and Jozef Pacolet, 'Posting of Workers: A Call for a Broader Debate' (*euractiv.com*, 4 September 2017) <https://www.euractiv.com/section/economy-jobs/opinion/posting-of-workers-a-call-for-a-broader-debate/> (accessed 30 August 2019).

EU internal market. Its ability to decrease unemployment in the sending Member States and, consequently, decrease all related public costs, together with the collection of higher labour tax revenues, constitutes, indeed, an effective temporary adjustment tool in case those countries are confronted with asymmetric economic shocks.

On the other hand, a series of risks and negative repercussions have been denounced as structurally related to the cross-border posting of workers. This is the case, *in primis*, of the strategies of regulatory arbitrage adopted by certain transnational operators with a view to maximising their profits. In effect, regulatory arbitrage is still allowed under the current rules whenever it entails the legitimate use of a competitive advantage or the exploitation of existing regulatory loopholes. A further negative consequence of the use of posting has been identified in the downward pressure on national welfare states, which may eventually result in a detrimental 'regulatory competition' between the Member States with regard to wages and employment conditions. Yet, this concern is basically denied by the absence of any substantial downward trend of employment protection in the receiving countries. In addition, intra-EU posting, especially when directed from low-wage to high-wage Member States, is accused to have a negative impact in terms of job displacements in the recipient countries. Nevertheless, the actual existence of such outcomes is demonstrated only in certain Member States and in specific labour-intensive sectors, such as construction and meat industry. What is more, the entry into national labour markets of foreign economic actors, which are usually reluctant to adapt to local standards of employment relations, has undoubtedly required a sort of adjustment in the functioning of national welfare systems. In doing so, national responses have taken different shapes, from the introduction of ad hoc legislative reforms, as in the cases of Sweden, Denmark and Germany, to the new approaches taken by trade unions. In the absence of formal institutional reforms, such a result has been labelled as 'extra-institutional change'.

From the analysis undertaken, the current mismatch between the widespread perception and the actual dimension of the impact of posting on the EU labour market is more than evident. While the widely held opinion depicts the phenomenon at stake as the typical source of problems deriving from intra-EU labour mobility, in turn, data clearly indicate that the negative effects arising from the legitimate use of posting of worker are matched by a variety of positive outcomes. The actual cause of its poor reputation must, therefore, mainly be sought in the variety of situations which are in practice going beyond the boundaries of regular (and legal) posting activities, resulting in abusive constructions aimed at evading employment, taxation and social security rules. In this sense, a number of unlawful and fraudulent practices have been identified, including subcontracting chains, double postings through temporary work agencies and bogus self-employment, as well as false declarations of secondments and social security certificates. There are also many occasions whereby *mala fide* economic actors seek an undue profit through the creation of the so-called 'letterbox companies', which do not exercise any genuine economic activity in their country of establishment, their sole purpose being, instead, just to benefit from the recourse to cheaper posted workers.

Besides undoubtedly constituting a cause of distortion of competition, all those illegal practices have in common an unscrupulous exploitation and alienation of the workers involved, in particular of those employed in manual/low-skilled jobs, who are frequently forced into wretched working and living conditions, paid below the minimum rates and even with no social security contributions. Such unacceptable conditions are the norm in the context of undeclared work, which, despite its relative relevance at public discourse level, is far more problematic than posting. This practice has, indeed, a much larger dimension and, given its totally illegal nature, affects to a greater extent both the workers, who are at the complete mercy of their 'employer', and the smooth functioning of the internal market.

In light of the above, it is clear that the spread of illegal practices is undermining the common perception of the exercise of the freedom to provide services through posting. Accordingly, the fight against all those fraudulent and abusive situations, which are even exacerbated in a context characterised by insufficient cooperation between the Member States, should represent the absolute priority for the Union. The adoption of the Enforcement Directive 2014/67/EU undoubtedly offers a strong encouragement in that direction and, more concretely, foresees the introduction of important tools for the contrast to illegal posting. *Inter alia*, it indicates a series of criteria for discerning the genuine establishment of a company in a certain Member State and institutes a new form of subcontracting liability. As evidenced *supra* in Chapter 4, though, it unfortunately still presents a number of shortcomings requiring concrete answers.

Finally, the widespread misconception that considers posting of workers as the major cause of social dumping and unfair competition is irrefutably demystified. Such an oversimplified rationale is basically confronted with – and disproved by – an investigation of the conceptual meaning of social dumping and of the practices and the actors actually involved. In this respect, the direct correlation between lower wages and GDP per capita in the Central and Eastern European Member States and greater competitiveness of the services providers established in those countries is proved false to the extent it fails to take into account the actual levels of productivity and national infrastructure; not to mention the recent trend describing an upward convergence of wages and labour taxation rates in Central and Eastern European workers. In turn, when confronting productivity levels with the degree of employment protection, tax rates and social security contributions, the currently cheapest destinations in Europe in terms of labour costs turn out to be Cyprus, Malta, Ireland, Luxembourg and the UK.

Especially in the cases of regular posting, the presence of social dumping is confined to practices of regulatory arbitrage and of exploitation of regulatory loopholes for cost advantages. In such a context, in view of the small dimension of the phenomenon at issue and of the relevant EU regulatory framework, there is only limited evidence of social dumping. Conversely, potential major sources are undoubtedly represented by the malpractices of evasion of national industrial relations regulations and of social and fiscal fraud, which are realised through bogus self-employment and, most of all, undeclared work. In addition, the role played by companies relocating their production facilities in the Member States with lower labour costs, with the aim of circumventing the higher social standards in the countries in which they operate, is particularly emphasised. Offshoring production represents a further way of undermining local welfare systems when used by Western European companies as a threat to employees and local authorities in order to undercut wages and working conditions. Lastly, even the Member States themselves are supposed to foster social dumping, whenever they take part in a detrimental 'race to the bottom' in terms of social and labour standards with a view to attracting foreign companies or preserving higher competitiveness.

In summary, the picture provided by the analysis carried out in this chapter shows that the impact of posting on the EU labour market takes many different forms. It emphasises the existence of a number of issues arising from a so-far self-regulated framework whereby economic actors are free to exploit their competitive advantage, regulatory loopholes and deficient enforcement of the rules, to the detriment of national welfare states. As a matter of fact, nonetheless, the vast majority of the issues encountered is related to fraudulent and abusive conducts and lack of efficient enforcement mechanisms, rather than to the lawful practice of posting workers as such. Accordingly, the appropriate countermeasures, whether they involve a regulatory intervention, a strengthening of controlling measures and cooperation between national authorities, or the introduction of further measures aimed at the implementation of the rules, cannot avoid taking into account the actual nature of the issues at stake. In this regard, as advocated by Barnard, legislative initiatives should be motivated not by social dumping fears, but rather by the need of 'ruling out low-productivity strategies of firms engaged in regulatory arbitrage between systems'.[221] Just as important, the large share of positive effects following from a legitimate use of this peculiar form of intra-EU labour mobility is able to promote integration between European labour markets, acting as a valuable instrument to foster upward socio-economic convergence between low-wage and high-wage EU countries. In light of these findings, the activity of posting of workers could represent a win-win for both the sending and receiving Member States, the posted workers themselves, and the EU internal market as a whole, as long as it is performed in response to the actual demand needs and within the legal limits.[222]

221. Barnard, 'Fifty Years of Avoiding Social Dumping? The EU's Economic and Not So Economic Constitution' (n 64) 339.
222. Wispelaere (n 10).

CHAPTER 8
The New Directive (EU) 2018/957

8.1 INTRODUCTION

Following years of heated discussions at European level, on 28 June 2018, a decade after the controversial decision of the Court of Justice in *Laval*,[1] the European Parliament and the Council adopted Directive (EU) 2018/957[2] amending the Posting of Workers Directive 96/71/EC.[3] The demand for modernised rules on posting of workers naturally emerged from the come into play, as a result of the 2004 and 2007 Eastern enlargements of the Union, of new economic actors, as well as from the progressive transformation of labour mobility across the internal market. During last years, intra-EU patterns of labour mobility have indeed substantially shifted from regular migration under the freedom of movement for workers to other hybrid channels such as posting, seasonal work and circular migration, but also of (bogus) self-employment and undeclared work.[4] Concerns about the incapacity of the existing legal framework

1. *Laval un Partneri Ltd v Svenska Byggnadsarbetareförbundet, Svenska Byggnadsarbetareförbundets avdelning 1, Byggettan and Svenska Elektrikerförbundet* [2007] ECJ Case C-341/05, ECLI: EU:C:2007:809.
2. Directive (EU) 2018/957 of the European Parliament and of the Council of 28 June 2018 amending Directive 96/71/EC concerning the posting of workers in the framework of the provision of services 2018 (OJ L 173/16).
3. Directive 96/71/EC of the European Parliament and of the Council of 16 December 1996 concerning the posting of workers in the framework of the provision of services 1997 (OJ L 18/1).
4. Rebecca Zahn, 'Revision of the Posted Workers' Directive: Equality at Last?' (2016) 5 European (Legal) Studies on-line papers, Queen's University Belfast – School of Law – Centre of European and Transnational Legal Studies 15; Ninke Mussche, Vincent Corluy and Ive Marx, 'The Rise of the Free Movements: How Posting Shapes a Hybrid Single European Labour Market' (2017) European Journal of Industrial Relations 3; Rebecca Zahn, 'Revision of the Posted Workers' Directive: A Europeanisation Perspective' (2017) 19 Cambridge Yearbook of European Legal Studies 187, 208; Anne-Pieter van der Mei et al., 'The External Dimension of EU Social Security Coordination' (2018) 20 European Journal of Social Security 81, 82; Ninke Mussche and Dries Lens, 'The EU Free Movement of Services and the Growing Mobility of Third-Country Nationals as Posted Workers' (2018) CSB Working Paper No. 18.13 University of Antwerp – Herman Deleeck Centre for Social Policy 1.

to cope with the new realities within the contemporary European labour market, and in particular with the sometimes huge wage differences between posted and local workers (especially in certain economic sectors in some high-wage Member States), became therefore increasingly popular.[5]

Against this background, the 2018 legislative *novella* represents the concretisation of the political commitment undertaken by the former President of the Commission Jean-Claude Juncker towards the reinforcement of the social dimension of the Union. The targeted review of the Posting of Workers Directive was, indeed, specifically designed 'to ensure that social dumping has no place in the European Union' and to establish the principle that 'the same work at the same place should be remunerated in the same manner'.[6] Nevertheless, the impact of such a novel piece of legislation is expected to be rather controversial, as it leaves the major shortcomings of the former regulatory framework basically unanswered, while creating new inconsistencies.

This chapter is dedicated to a thorough analysis of the 2018 regulatory intervention of the EU legislator in the context of posting, starting with the drafting and adoption process of the new Directive (EU) 2018/957 and moving to the substantive changes made to the former legal framework, before concluding with the Directive's expected impact and shortcomings. In this perspective, it is guided by the following research sub-question: *How was the new Directive (EU) 2018/957 conceived, and in which way does it alter the former legal framework and the overall state of play?*

This chapter is structured as follows. Section 8.2, at first, attempts to reconstruct the path leading to the revision of the Posting of Workers Directive by dwelling on the motivations underlying the reform. It then carefully examines the original proposal of the Commission and the harsh response that followed in the form of a 'yellow-card procedure' triggered by eleven Member States. Finally, the troubled adoption process of Directive (EU) 2018/957 is closely investigated through an analysis of the travaux préparatoires in the European Parliament, the Council, and the interinstitutional 'trilogue' meetings. This whole section is intended to contextualise the reform by emphasising the relevance of the ongoing clash between East and West Europe, on the one hand, and to help better understand the political reasons behind the regulatory choices made by the EU legislator, on the other hand.

The substantive content of Directive (EU) 2018/957 is, in turn, scrutinised in section 8.3, where a critical assessment is performed with a view to ascertaining in which way the entry into effect of the new rules alters the former legal framework.

5. Eckhard Voss et al., 'Posting of Workers Directive: Current Situation and Challenges' (European Parliament, EMPL Committee 2016) IP/A/EMPL/2016-07, 45 and 63.
6. Political Guidelines for the next European Commission, Opening Statement in the European Parliament Plenary Session from Jean-Claude Juncker, 'A New Start for Europe: My Agenda for Jobs, Growth, Fairness and Democratic Change' (15 July 2014) 7. On this point, *see* Diane Fromage and Valentin Kreilinger, 'National Parliaments' Third Yellow Card and the Struggle over the Revision of the Posted Workers Directive' (2017) 10 European Journal of Legal Studies 125, 139; Marco Rocca, 'Not Dead yet: Legal Strategies at National Level and the Reform of the EU Posting of Workers Directive' (2018) 1; Marco Rocca, 'Stepping Stones Over Troubled Waters. Recent Legal Evolutions and the Reform of the Posting of Workers Directive' in Jens Arnholtz and Nathan Lillie (eds), *Posted Work in the European Union: The Political Economy of Free Movement* (Routledge 2019) 167.

Through a traditional legal analysis, the legal implications emerging from the new concept of remuneration, the slightly improved treatment reserved to posted temporary agency workers and the (cumulative) maximum duration limit for posting are thoroughly investigated. The following section 8.4 seeks to estimate what sort of impact the revisionist approach adopted by the European legislator, and especially the establishment of the principle of 'equal pay for equal work in the same place', will have on the current state of play. In particular, it tries to assess whether the situation of the posted workers will actually be improved and a level playing field for businesses will eventually be ensured. Moreover, it looks at whether the new provisions are able to provide the much-demanded simplification of the existing rules, as well as better coordination with the relevant EU social security law framework. In order to do so, this section operates a confrontation of the new set of rules for posting with the findings emerged from the previous chapters. The many threads of this chapter are eventually brought together in the concluding section 8.5.

8.2 A TROUBLED BIRTH PROCESS

If the drafting process of the 1996 Posting of Workers Directive was long and arduous, that of its revision was just as complicated. As evidenced by the previously conducted analysis of the concrete dimension of posting and its impact on the EU labour market, the need to call a halt to a long series of abuses and circumventing practices in the sector is absolutely urgent. In pursuit of this objective, the path indicated by the European Commission in both its 2015 and 2016 annual Work Programmes envisaged a specific Labour Mobility Package involving, *inter alia*, a targeted review of the Posting of Workers Directive aimed at preventing 'social dumping' and abuse of the freedom to provide services.[7] All those initiatives were taken, even though the deadline for the transposition of the Enforcement Directive 2014/67/EU into national laws was not expired yet.[8]

7. European Commission, Communication from the Commission to the European Parliament, the Council, the European Economic and Social Committee and the Committee of the Regions – Commission Work Programme 2015: A New Start 2014 [COM(2014) 910 final] 5; European Commission, Communication from the Commission to the European Parliament, the Council, the European Economic and Social Committee and the Committee of the Regions – Commission Work Programme 2016: No time for business as usual 2015 [COM(2015) 610 final] 8. On this point, *see* European Commission, 'Press Release – College Holds Orientation Debate on the Economic and Social Dimension of the Single Market' (*European Commission Press Releases Database*, 6 October 2015) <http://europa.eu/rapid/press-release_IP-15-5763_en.htm> (accessed 21 November 2018); Zahn, 'Revision of the Posted Workers' Directive: Equality at Last?' (n 4) 1.
8. Notably, the Enforcement Directive had to be transposed into national laws before 18 June 2016. Article 23(1) of Directive 2014/67/EU of the European Parliament and of the Council of 15 May 2014 on the enforcement of Directive 96/71/EC concerning the posting of workers in the framework of the provision of services and amending Regulation (EU) No 1024/2012 on administrative cooperation through the Internal Market Information System ('the IMI Regulation') 2014 (OJ L 159/11).

8.2.1 A Highly Fragmented Context

When looking at the background of the whole revision process, it is worth recalling the constant presence of a climate of tension among the different parties involved, namely the Member States and the European and national social partners. Proof of this is the letter dated 18 June 2015, addressed to Marianne Thyssen (at that time Commissioner for Employment, Social Affairs, Skills and Labour Mobility), by means of which a group of Western Member States comprising Austria, Belgium, France, Germany, Luxembourg, the Netherlands and Sweden argued in favour of modernised rules on posting of workers with the establishment of the principle of 'equal pay for equal work in the same place'. They demanded for an upgrading of the host country's terms and conditions of employment applicable to posted workers by virtue of Article 3(1) of the Posting of Workers Directive, especially including remuneration; the definition of a maximum duration limit to posting, in line with the one provided for in Regulation (EC) 883/2004 on social security coordination; the clarification of the rules for the road transport sector; and further improvement of cross-border enforcement of Union law.[9] The response by the Central and Eastern Member States was not long in coming, and a couple of months later, on 31 August 2015, Bulgaria, the Czech Republic, Estonia, Hungary, Lithuania, Latvia, Poland, Slovakia and Romania expressed in a joint letter their concern about the compatibility of the principle of equal pay between local and posted workers with the fundamental structure of the Single Market, considering pay rate differences as a legitimate competitive advantage for service providers. In addition, they severely criticised the prospect of reviewing the Posting of Workers Directive before properly evaluating and assessing the effects of the implementation of the Enforcement Directive.[10]

The dimension of the conflict was, nevertheless, not confined to the Member State level, as it involved European and national social partners as well.[11] The division

9. Austrian, Belgian, French, German, Luxembourg, Dutch and Swedish Ministers of labour, 'Letter to Ms Marianne Thyssen Commissioner for Employment, Social Affairs, Skills and Labour Mobility' (18 June 2015). On this point, *see* European Commission, Proposal for a Directive of the European Parliament and of the Council amending Directive 96/71/EC of the European Parliament and of the Council of 16 December 1996 concerning the posting of workers in the framework of the provision of services 2016 [COM(2016) 128 final] Explanatory Memorandum 4–5; European Commission, Impact Assessment, Accompanying the document Proposal for a Directive of the European Parliament and the Council amending Directive 96/71/EC concerning the posting of workers in the framework of the provision of services 2016 [SWD(2016) 52 final] 50; Voss et al. (n 5) 51; Fromage and Kreilinger (n 6) 147; Isabella Biletta and Christine Aumayr-Pintar, 'Pay Inequalities Experienced by Posted Workers: Challenges to the "Equal Treatment" Principle' (Eurofound 2017) 3.
10. Bulgarian, Czech, Estonian, Hungarian, Latvian, Lithuanian, Polish, Romanian and Slovakian Ministers of Labour, 'Letter to Ms Marianne Thyssen Commissioner for Employment, Social Affairs, Skills and Labour Mobility' (31 August 2015). *See* European Commission Proposal for a Directive of the European Parliament and of the Council amending Directive 96/71/EC of the European Parliament and of the Council of 16 December 1996 concerning the posting of workers in the framework of the provision of services (n 9) Explanatory Memorandum 5; Voss et al. (n 5) 51; Fromage and Kreilinger (n 6) 147; Biletta and Aumayr-Pintar (n 9) 3.
11. For an overview on the variety of national stakeholders' positions on the PWD's revision, *see* Biletta and Aumayr-Pintar (n 9) 5–9.

between European trade unions and employer organisations mirrored in broad terms the aforementioned one regarding the Member States, albeit with different nuances and a few exceptions. More in detail, the revision of the Posting of Workers Directive in accordance with the principle of 'equal pay for equal work in the same place' was strongly supported by the European Trade Union Confederation (ETUC),[12] the European Construction Industry Federation (FIEC), the European Builders Confederation (EBC), the European Federation of Building and Woodworkers (EFBWW), the Dutch Trade Union Confederation (FNV),[13] the Estonian Trade Union Confederation and the Council of Nordic Trade Unions.[14] The World Employment Confederation Europe (Eurociett), representing the temporary work agency industry, was on the same page, supporting the extension of the principle of equal pay for equal work, as well as the full application of the Temporary Agency Work Directive,[15] to posted agency workers.[16]

Conversely, on the employers' side, BusinessEurope, the European Association of Craft, Small and Medium-Sized Enterprises (UEAPME), the Council of European Employers of the Metal, Engineering and Technology-Based Industries (CEEMET) and

---

12. In particular, ETUC already complained about the narrow interpretation of the PWD given by the Court of Justice in the famous *Laval quartet*, namely in the latter's decisions in *International Transport Workers' Federation and Finnish Seamen's Union v Viking Line ABP and OÜ Viking Line Eesti* [2007] ECJ Case C-438/05, ECLI:EU:C:2007:772; *Laval un Partneri Ltd v Svenska Byggnadsarbetareförbundet, Svenska Byggnadsarbetareförbundets avdelning 1, Byggettan and Svenska Elektrikerförbundet* (n 1); *Dirk Rüffert v Land Niedersachsen* [2008] CJEU Case C-346/06, ECLI:EU:C:2008:189; *Commission of the European Communities v Grand Duchy of Luxemburg* [2008] ECJ Case C-319/06, ECLI:EU:C:2008:350. On this point, *see* ETUC (European Trade Union Confederation), 'The Posting of Workers Directive: Proposals for Revision (Resolution Adopted at the ETUC Executive Committee)' (2010) <http://www.europarl.europa.eu/document/activities/cont/201006/20100601ATT75367/20100601ATT75367EN.pdf> (accessed 12 January 2019); ETUC (European Trade Union Confederation), Business Europe, CEEP (Euro pean Centre of Employers and Enterprises providing Public services), UEAPME (European Association of Craft, Small and Medium-Sized Enterprises), 'Report on Joint Work of the European Social Partners on the ECJ Rulings in the Viking, Laval, Rüffert and Luxembourg Cases' (2010) 10–11.
13. *Federatie Nederlandse Vakbeweging* (FNV) is the Dutch Trade Union Confederation.
14. European Commission Proposal for a Directive of the European Parliament and of the Council amending Directive 96/71/EC of the European Parliament and of the Council of 16 December 1996 concerning the posting of workers in the framework of the provision of services (n 9) Explanatory Memorandum 5; Voss et al. (n 5) 49–50; Biletta and Aumayr-Pintar (n 9) 4; Silvana Sciarra, *Solidarity and Conflict: European Social Law in Crisis* (Cambridge University Press 2018) 85; Monika Kiss, 'Briefing "EU Legislation in Progress": Posting of Workers Directive' (European Parliament 2018) EPRS-European Parliamentary Research Service 8 <http://www.europarl.europa.eu/RegData/etudes/BRIE/2016/582043/EPRS_BRI(2016)582043_EN.pdf> (accessed 19 August 2019); Eurofound, 'Posted Workers' (*EurWORK – European Observatory of Working Life*, 29 June 2018) <https://www.eurofound.europa.eu/observatories/eurwork/industrial-relations-dictionary/posted-workers> (accessed 4 July 2019); Bengt Furåker and Bengt Larsson, 'Revision of the EU Posting of Workers Directive, Social Dumping and Trade Unions' Position' in Bengt Furåker and Bengt Larsson, *Trade Union Cooperation in Europe: Patterns, Conditions, Issues* (Springer International Publishing 2020) 129–130.
15. Directive 2008/104/EC of the European Parliament and of the Council of 19 November 2008 on temporary agency work 2008 (OJ L 327/9).
16. European Commission Proposal for a Directive of the European Parliament and of the Council amending Directive 96/71/EC of the European Parliament and of the Council of 16 December 1996 concerning the posting of workers in the framework of the provision of services (n 9) Explanatory Memorandum 6; Biletta and Aumayr-Pintar (n 9) 4–5.

the European Confederation of Managers (CEC), together with the Confederation of Industry of the Czech Republic and the Industry Associations from Finland, Sweden, Denmark, Iceland and Norway, were firmly opposed to such a revision of the Posting of Workers Directive, deemed liable to affect the social partners' freedom to determine wage levels and, consequently, altering the existing level playing field for all enterprises.[17] The position taken by the social partners' organisations in the transport sector was, in turn, rather different. Rejecting the possibility of including the transport workers into the scope of the revised Directive, the European Transport Workers' Federation (ETF) instead, in its 'Warsaw Declaration' of 5 April 2017,[18] urgently called for the adoption of an ad hoc 'Road Initiative' in the EU road transport sector.[19]

8.2.2 The Commission's Proposal

Despite the concern expressed by the Central and Eastern Member States and by a number of European and national social partners, the request of reform was acknowledged positively by the Commission which, on 8 March 2016, proposed a targeted review of the 1996 Posting of Workers Directive.[20] Interestingly, that proposal was part of a larger project towards the promotion of a stronger social dimension of the EU, encompassing the revision of the coordination rules of social security systems,[21] and the proclamation of a European Pillar of Social Rights,[22] which envisaged, *inter alia*, the establishment of a European Labour Authority (ELA).[23] The legislative initiative

17. At the same time, all employers' organisations insisted on giving priority to the full transposition of the Enforcement Directive and to the evaluation of its effects. ETUC (European Trade Union Confederation), Business Europe, CEEP (European Centre of Employers and Enterprises providing Public services), UEAPME (European Association of Craft, Small and Medium-Sized Enterprises) (n 12) 7; European Commission Proposal for a Directive of the European Parliament and of the Council amending Directive 96/71/EC of The European Parliament and of the Council of 16 December 1996 concerning the posting of workers in the framework of the provision of services (n 9) Explanatory Memorandum 5–6; Voss et al. (n 5) 50–51; Biletta and Aumayr-Pintar (n 9) 4; Kiss (n 14) 9; Eurofound (n 14); Furåker and Larsson (n 14) 128–129.
18. ETF (European Transport Workers' Federation), 'The Warsaw Declaration: The European Transport Workers' Federation and Its Members Organisations Call on the European Commission, European Parliament and the EU Member States to Adopt a Road Initiative to Effectively Combat Social Dumping and Unfair Competition in the EU Road Transport Sector' (5 April 2017) <https://www.etf-europe.org/wp-content/uploads/2018/10/ETF-Warsaw-declaration-original-signed-version-EN.pdf> (accessed 29 July 2019).
19. Eurofound (n 14).
20. European Commission Proposal for a Directive of the European Parliament and of the Council amending Directive 96/71/EC of the European Parliament and of the Council of 16 December 1996 concerning the posting of workers in the framework of the provision of services (n 9).
21. European Commission, Proposal for a Regulation of the European Parliament and of the Council amending Regulation (EC) No 883/2004 on the coordination of social security systems and regulation (EC) No 987/2009 laying down the procedure for implementing Regulation (EC) No 883/2004, 2016 [COM(2016) 815 final].
22. European Parliament, Council of the European Union and European Commission, Interinstitutional Proclamation on the European Pillar of Social Rights 2017 (OJ C 428/10).
23. Regulation (EU) 2019/1149 of the European Parliament and of the Council of 20 June 2019 establishing a European Labour Authority, amending Regulations (EC) No 883/2004, (EU) No 492/2011, and (EU) 2016/589 and repealing Decision (EU) 2016/344, 2019 (OJ L 186/21). In this sense, *see* Aukje A.H. van Hoek, 'Re-Embedding the Transnational Employment Relationship: A

under consideration, aimed at addressing unfair practices and promoting the principle of equal remuneration for the same work at the same place,[24] rested on the same legal basis as the Posting of Workers Directive (Articles 53(1) and 62 TFEU) and it was conceived as complementary to and mutually reinforcing with the Enforcement Directive.[25] The new proposal had, indeed, a different scope from that of Directive 2014/67/EU, as it substantially focused on three main areas: remuneration of posted workers (including situations of subcontracting), rules on temporary agency work and rules applying to long-term posting.[26]

More specifically, with a view to reducing the wage differential between posted and local workers, as well as the unfair competition between companies that supposedly comes with it, the Commission suggested to replace the reference made by Article 3(1) of the Posting of Workers Directive to 'minimum rates of pay' with a broader concept of 'remuneration' including also other elements such as bonuses, allowances and pay increases according to seniority.[27] In practice, it was up to the host Member State to determine and clearly indicate, by publication on a single official national

---

Tale about the Limitations of (EU) Law?' (2018) 55 Common Market Law Review 449, 473–474; Annette Schrauwen, 'From the Board Towards a Social Europe' (2018) 45 Legal Issues of Economic Integration 323, 325; Bart Vanhercke, Sebastiano Sabato and Dalila Ghailani, 'The European Pillar of Social Rights as a Game Changer' in Sebastiano Sabato (ed.), *Social Policy in the European Union: State of Play 2018* (ETUI, 2018) 160; Sacha Garben, 'The European Pillar of Social Rights: An Assessment of Its Meaning and Significance' (2019) Cambridge Yearbook of European Legal Studies 1, 9; Catherine Barnard and Sybe De Vries, 'The "Social Market Economy" in a (Heterogeneous) Social Europe: Does It Make a Difference?' (2019) 15 Utrecht Law Review 47, 58; Sacha Garben, 'The European Pillar of Social Rights as a Revival of Social Europe' in Maurizio Ferrera (ed.), *Towards a European Social Union: The European Pillar of Social Rights and the Roadmap for a Fully-Fledged Social Union* (Centro di Ricerca e Documentazione Luigi Einaudi 2019) 79.

24. European Commission Proposal for a Directive of the European Parliament and of the Council amending Directive 96/71/EC of the European Parliament and of the Council of 16 December 1996 concerning the posting of workers in the framework of the provision of services (n 9) Explanatory Memorandum 2.
25. *Ibid.* Explanatory Memorandum 3.
26. European Commission – Employment, Social Affairs & Inclusion, 'The Commission Presents Reform of Posting of Workers – Towards a Fair and Truly European Labour Market' (8 March 2016) <https://ec.europa.eu/social/main.jsp?catId=89&langId=en&newsId=2488&furtherNews=yes> (accessed 11 April 2019); Claire Dhéret and Andreia Ghimis, 'The Revision of the Posted Workers Directive: Towards a Sufficient Policy Adjustment?' (2016) *European Policy Center (EPC) Discussion Paper* 9 <http://www.epc.eu/pub_details.php?cat_id=17&pub_id=6475> (accessed 23 October 2016); Kiss (n 14) 6; Eurofound (n 14). Nonetheless, a partial overlap between the Enforcement Directive and the new proposal has been found with regard to areas such as the improvement of the information on terms and conditions of employment and the protection of workers in subcontracting chains. Voss et al. (n 5) 46–48.
27. Article 1(2)(a) of the European Commission Proposal for a Directive of the European Parliament and of the Council amending Directive 96/71/EC of The European Parliament and of the Council of 16 December 1996 concerning the posting of workers in the framework of the provision of services (n 9). On this point, *see* European Commission, 'Press Release – Commission Presents Reform of the Posting of Workers Directive – Towards a Deeper and Fairer European Labour Market' (*European Commission Press Releases Database*, 8 March 2016) <http://europa.eu/rapid/press-release_IP-16-466_en.htm> (accessed 19 July 2019); Voss et al. (n 5) 46; Dhéret and Ghimis (n 26) 9; Zahn, 'Revision of the Posted Workers' Directive: Equality at Last?' (n 4) 13; Mikkel Barslund, Matthias Busse and Frederic De Wispelaere, 'Posted Workers – For Some It Matters' (2017) CEPS (Centre for European Policy Studies) 6; Eurofound (n 14).

website created in accordance with Article 5 of the Enforcement Directive, the constituent elements of remuneration on its territory.[28] The only condition to such a broad discretionary power was the pursuit of the posted workers' protection and the avoidance of a disproportionate restriction of the cross-border provision of services.[29] So, basically, the whole host country's set of rules concerning remuneration was supposed to find application in situations of posting, and not just those related to minimum rates of pay. Interestingly, though, the proposal reduced the number of sources of terms and conditions of employment extendable to seconded workers in such a way as to merely encompass legislation and universally applicable collective agreements, with the exclusion of company-level collective agreements.[30] In turn, those collective agreements having *erga omnes* effect, including those on remuneration, were expected to become mandatory in any economic sector,[31] whereas previously they were made compulsory by the Posting of Workers Directive with regard to the activities in the construction industry only.[32] The sole exception in that regard

28. Preamble Recital 13 of the European Commission Proposal for a Directive of the European Parliament and of the Council amending Directive 96/71/EC of the European Parliament and of the Council of 16 December 1996 concerning the posting of workers in the framework of the provision of services (n 9).
29. *Ibid.* Preamble Recital 12. It is worth noting that the latter requirement was evidently built on the Court of Justice's decision in *Isbir*, where the definition of the constituent elements of the minimum rates of pay under the PWD was left to the Member States under the condition that the free movement of services was not impeded. *Tevfik Isbir v DB Services* [2013] CJEU Case C-522/12, ECLI:EU:C:2013:711 [37]. The proposal's condition to avoid a 'disproportionate' restriction of the cross-border provision of services was nonetheless criticised for being rather vague and, consequently, for producing even more legal uncertainty. On this point, *see* Voss et al. (n 5) 64; Rocca, 'Not Dead yet: Legal Strategies at National Level and the Reform of the EU Posting of Workers Directive' (n 6) 5–6; Rocca, 'Stepping Stones over Troubled Waters. Recent Legal Evolutions and the Reform of the Posting of Workers Directive' (n 6) 171.
30. Article 1(2)(a) of the European Commission Proposal for a Directive of the European Parliament and of the Council amending Directive 96/71/EC of the European Parliament and of the Council of 16 December 1996 concerning the posting of workers in the framework of the provision of services (n 9). Interestingly, such a restriction of the sources of employment conditions applicable to posted workers was highly criticised for producing inequality between workers employed in sectors with universally binding collective agreements (such as the construction industry) and those working in less regulated sectors (such as the care sector). As a matter of fact, then, such inequalities would be more evident in countries, such as Germany or Italy, which have no, or make limited use of, universally applicable or generally applicable collective agreements. Voss et al. (n 5) 64; ETUC (European Trade Union Confederation), 'Posted Workers Revision – Equal Pay for Some' (*ETUC – European Trade Union Confederation Press Release*, 3 August 2016) <https://www.etuc.org/en/pressrelease/posted-workers-revision-equal-pay-some> (accessed 23 December 2018); Zahn, 'Revision of the Posted Workers' Directive: Equality at Last?' (n 4) 14; Dhéret and Ghimis (n 26) 10; Fromage and Kreilinger (n 6) 143.
31. European Commission Proposal for a Directive of the European Parliament and of the Council amending Directive 96/71/EC of the European Parliament and of the Council of 16 December 1996 concerning the posting of workers in the framework of the provision of services (n 9) Explanatory Memorandum 7.
32. Article 3(1) of Directive 96/71/EC of the European Parliament and of the Council of 16 December 1996 concerning the posting of workers in the framework of the provision of services (n 3). On this point, *see supra* Chapter 3.

concerned the road transport sector which, because of the several difficulties encountered at the implementation stage of the Posting of Workers Directive, was excluded from the scope of application of the new draft Directive.[33]

Furthermore, with a view to combatting abuses in subcontracting chains, a new provision was intended to provide the Member States with the faculty to oblige companies to subcontract only to service providers (both national or foreign) that granted their workers the same level of employment protection as the main contractor.[34] The Commission's proposal, by de facto making compulsory the clause laid down in Article 5 of Directive 2008/104/EC on Temporary Agency Work,[35] also extended the equal treatment principle to temporary agency workers posted by a temporary agency established abroad, who could enjoy the same terms and conditions as workers hired out by national agencies.[36] Finally, in light of the excessively long duration of certain posting assignments, it envisaged, in line with the definition given by the relevant EU social security law, a twenty-four-month time limit for posting, after which the host country's mandatory labour law would find full application. Importantly, such a rule was supposed to apply even in case of replacement of posted workers performing, for at least six months, the same task at the same place, thus taking into consideration the cumulative duration of posting periods of the different workers concerned.[37]

---

33. In light of the highly mobile nature of cabotage activities, the regulation of the international road transport was left to sector-specific legislation and other EU regulatory initiatives. Preamble Recital 10 of the European Commission Proposal for a Directive of the European Parliament and of the Council amending Directive 96/71/EC of the European Parliament and of the Council of 16 December 1996 concerning the posting of workers in the framework of the provision of services (n 9).
34. Provided that the same conditions applied to national subcontractors as well, and that the principles of proportionality and non-discrimination were respected. *Ibid.* Explanatory Memorandum 7–8 and Article 1(2)(b). *See* European Commission, 'Press Release – Commission Presents Reform of the Posting of Workers Directive – Towards a Deeper and Fairer European Labour Market' (n 27); Tonia Novitz, 'The Scope for Collective Bargaining in Posting and Procurement – What Might Come From Recent Court of Justice Case Law and the Proposed Reform of the Posting of Workers Directive?' (*University of Bristol Law School Blog*, 6 April 2016) < https://legalresearch.blogs.bris.ac.uk/2016/04/the-scope-for-collective-bargaining-in-posting-and-procurement/ > (accessed 13 May 2018); Voss et al. (n 5) 46; Biletta and Aumayr-Pintar (n 9) 2; Marion Schmid-Drüner, 'Briefing: The Revision of the Posting of Workers Directive' (European Parliament, Employment and Social Affairs – Policy Department for Economic, Scientific and Quality of Life Policies 2017) 4–5 < http://dx.publications.europa.eu/10.2861/308871 > (accessed 22 November 2018).
35. Directive 2008/104/EC of the European Parliament and of the Council of 19 November 2008 on temporary agency work (n 15). On the content of the equal treatment clause set out in Article 5, *see supra* Chapter 3.
36. Explanatory Memorandum 8 and Article 1(2)(c) of the European Commission Proposal for a Directive of the European Parliament and of the Council amending Directive 96/71/EC of the European Parliament and of the Council of 16 December 1996 concerning the posting of workers in the framework of the provision of services (n 9). *See* Voss et al. (n 5) 46; Zahn, 'Revision of the Posted Workers' Directive: Equality at Last?' (n 4) 13; Schmid-Drüner (n 34) 5; Barslund, Busse and Wispelaere (n 27) 6.
37. Article 1(1) of the European Commission Proposal for a Directive of the European Parliament and of the Council amending Directive 96/71/EC of the European Parliament and of the Council of 16 December 1996 concerning the posting of workers in the framework of the provision of services (n 9). *See* European Commission, 'Press Release – Commission Presents Reform of the

The innovative 2016 draft legislation for a targeted revision of the Posting of Workers Directive caused mixed reactions among the Member States leading, in particular, to the activation of the so-called Early Warning System (EWS) for monitoring of compliance with the principle of subsidiarity enshrined in Article 5(3) TEU.[38] By 10 May 2016, fourteen national parliamentary chambers from eleven Member States (22 total votes out of 56)[39] submitted a reasoned opinion to the European Commission

---

Posting of Workers Directive – Towards a Deeper and Fairer European Labour Market' (n 27); Dhéret and Ghimis (n 26) 9; Schmid-Drüner (n 34) 4; Fromage and Kreilinger (n 6) 140; Eurofound (n 14).

38. Article 5(3) TEU: 'Under the principle of subsidiarity, in areas which do not fall within its exclusive competence, the Union shall act only if and in so far as the objectives of the proposed action cannot be sufficiently achieved by the Member States, either at central level or at regional and local level, but can rather, by reason of the scale or effects of the proposed action, be better achieved at Union level.' In particular, the so-called Early Warning System (EWS) for the principle of subsidiarity entered into force with the Lisbon Treaty in 2009 (Protocol No 2 on the application of the principles of subsidiarity and proportionality) and entails the faculty for national parliaments to object, by means of reasoned opinions, to the violation by an EU legislative proposal of the principle of subsidiarity. Each national parliament has the right to express two votes (in bicameral systems, each chamber has one vote) within eight weeks following the transmission from the European Commission of the EU legislative proposal. When the reasoned opinions amount to one-third of the total number of votes – one-quarter for proposals relating to the Area of Freedom, Security and Justice – a so-called 'yellow card' is triggered, imposing the Commission to review its proposal and eventually decide on whether to withdraw, maintain or amend it. In turn, should half or more of all national parliaments submit reasoned opinions for the violation of the principle of subsidiarity an 'orange card' is triggered, entailing a more complex legislative procedure. For the record, the Commission has so far not received any orange card yet, while it had to deal with two other yellow cards only: in 2012 with regard to the 'Monti II' proposal and in 2013 on the European Public Prosecutor's Office proposal (EPPO). European Commission, Proposal for a Council Regulation on the exercise of the right to take collective action within the context of the freedom of establishment and the freedom to provide services 2012 [COM(2012) 130 final]; European Commission, Proposal for a Council Regulation on the establishment of the European Public Prosecutor's Office 2013 [COM(2013) 534 final]. *See* Federico Fabbrini and Katarzyna Granat, '"Yellow Card, but No Foul": The Role of the National Parliaments under the Subsidiarity Protocol and the Commission Proposal for an EU Regulation on the Right to Strike' (2013) 50 Common Market Law Review 115; Robert Schütze, *European Constitutional Law* (Second Edition, Cambridge University Press 2015) 254–255; Voss et al. (n 5) 53–54; Valentin Kreilinger, 'National Parliaments' 3rd Yellow Card: A Preliminary Assessment' (*euractiv.com*, 12 May 2016) <https://www.euractiv.com/section/social-europe-jobs/opinion/national-parliaments-3rd-yellow-card-a-preliminary-assessment/> (accessed 23 April 2019); Fromage and Kreilinger (n 6) 126–127; Kiss (n 14) 8; Rocca, 'Not Dead yet: Legal Strategies at National Level and the Reform of the EU Posting of Workers Directive' (n 6) 4; 'Yellow Card (Subsidiary Control Mechanism)' (*EU monitor*) <https://www.eumonitor.eu/9353000/1/j9vvik7m1c3gyxp/viommjbhi6ha> (accessed 2 August 2019); Rocca, 'Stepping Stones Over Troubled Waters. Recent Legal Evolutions and the Reform of the Posting of Workers Directive' (n 6) 167.

39. In particular, the national chambers (with, in brackets, the correspondent number of votes) were the following: Romanian Chamber of Deputies (1), Romanian Senate (1), Czech Chamber of Deputies (1), Czech Senate (1), Polish *Sejm* (1), Polish Senate (1), *Seimas* of the Republic of Lithuania (2), Danish *Folketing* (2), Croatian Parliament (2), Latvian *Saeima* (2) Bulgarian National Assembly (2), Hungarian National Assembly (2), Estonian Parliament (2) and the National Council of the Slovak Republic (2). European Commission, Communication from the Commission to the European Parliament, the Council and the National Parliaments on the proposal for a Directive amending the Posting of Workers Directive, with regard to the principle of subsidiarity, in accordance with Protocol No 2 2016 [COM(2016) 505 final] 3.

for the supposed breach of the principle of subsidiarity by the proposal put forward eight weeks before, thereby triggering the so-called 'yellow-card procedure'.[40]

Several national parliaments from the Central and Eastern EU countries lamented, at that time, the Commission's lack of justification for its action, with consequent violation of the obligation contained in Article 5 of the Protocol No 2 to the Treaties on the application of the principles of subsidiarity and proportionality.[41] In addition, the Impact Assessment[42] drafted by the European Commission was criticised for not explicitly pointing out the expected impact of the introduction of equal remuneration, as well as for not taking into account the repercussions at regional and local level.[43] The sufficiency and adequacy of the existing rules on posting of workers were advocated by a number of Member States,[44] which also challenged the opportunity of the action at Union level rather than at Member State level.[45] The premature

40. Davor Jančić, 'EU Law's Grand Scheme on National Parliaments: The Third Yellow Card on Posted Workers and the Way Forward' in Davor Jancic (ed.), *National Parliaments after the Lisbon Treaty and the Euro Crisis* (Oxford University Press 2017) 304 <http://www.oxfordscholarship.com/view/10.1093/acprof:oso/9780198791621.001.0001/acprof-9780198791621-chapter-16> (accessed 26 September 2019); Fromage and Kreilinger (n 6) 126; Schmid-Drüner (n 34) 5; European Sources Online (ESO), 'Directive (EU) 2018/957 Amending Directive 96/71/EC Concerning the Posting of Workers in the Framework of the Provision of Services' (7 September 2018) <https://www.europeansources.info/record/directive-eu-2018-957-amending-directive-96-71-ec-concerning-the-posting-of-workers-in-the-framework-of-the-provision-of-services/> (accessed 10 April 2019); Rocca, 'Not Dead yet: Legal Strategies at National Level and the Reform of the EU Posting of Workers Directive' (n 6) 4; Christian Joerges, Vladimir Bogoeski and Lukas Nüse, 'Economic Constitutionalism and the European Social Model: Can European Law Cope with the Deepening Tensions between Economic and Social Integration after the Financial Crisis' in Herwig Hofmann, Katerina Pantazatou and Giovanni Zaccaroni, *The Metamorphosis of the European Economic Constitution* (Edward Elgar Publishing 2019) 145; Rocca, 'Stepping Stones over Troubled Waters. Recent Legal Evolutions and the Reform of the Posting of Workers Directive' (n 6) 169.
41. This was the case of all intervening countries (except Denmark), namely Bulgaria, Croatia, Czech Republic, Estonia, Hungary, Latvia, Lithuania, Poland, Romania and Slovakia. Fromage and Kreilinger (n 6) 148. For the record, the Commission's justification in this sense was indeed extremely poor, if not redundant, as it simply stated: 'An amendment to an existing Directive can only be achieved by adopting a new Directive.' European Commission Proposal for a Directive of the European Parliament and of the Council amending Directive 96/71/EC of the European Parliament and of the Council of 16 December 1996 concerning the posting of workers in the framework of the provision of services (n 9) Explanatory Memorandum 4. Notably, the superficiality of the Commission was critically emphasised by the European Scrutiny Committee of the House of Commons (UK) by means of a contribution issued to the Commission on 25 May 2016 in the framework of the Political Dialogue. Fromage and Kreilinger (n 6) 141–142 and 151.
42. European Commission Impact Assessment, Accompanying the document Proposal for a Directive of the European Parliament and the Council amending Directive 96/71/EC concerning the posting of workers in the framework of the provision of services (n 9).
43. These concerns were expressed by the Hungarian Parliament. Kiss (n 14) 7.
44. Namely Bulgaria, Croatia, Czech Republic, Estonia, Hungary, Latvia, Lithuania, Poland, Romania and Slovakia. European Commission, Communication from the Commission to the European Parliament, the Council and the National Parliaments on the proposal for a Directive amending the Posting of Workers Directive, with regard to the principle of subsidiarity, in accordance with Protocol No 2 (n 39) 5–9.
45. In particular, both the extension of the application of generally binding collective agreements outside the construction sector and the new rules on subcontracting chains and on temporary agency workers have been strongly criticised by the Bulgarian National Assembly, the Czech Chamber of Deputies and Senate, and the Polish Sejm and Senate, respectively. *Ibid.* 6; Schmid-Drüner (n 34) 5.

nature of the regulatory reform, initiated even before the expiration of the deadline for the transposition of the Enforcement Directive, was strongly emphasised as well.[46] Lastly, instead of merely focusing on the respect of the principle of subsidiarity, further concerns were directly related to the content and aim of the proposal, which was deemed unnecessary and restrictive of the freedom to provide services, resulting in an excessive administrative burden for small and medium-sized enterprises (SMEs).[47]

Interestingly enough, the position taken by Denmark deserves a separate mention. The Danish Parliament definitely supported the Commission's initiative to foster the introduction of the principle of 'equal pay for equal work in the same place' but it criticised, nonetheless, the absence of explicit recognition of the Member States' competence on the definitions of remuneration and conditions of employment.[48] In contrast, the opposite position on the issue taken by six national Parliaments from Western European countries – namely Spain (both the Congress of Deputies and the Senate by means of a joint statement), Italy (both the *'Senato'* and the *'Camera dei Deputati'*), Portugal (the Assembly), the United Kingdom (the House of Commons) and France (the Senate) – which considered the proposal as compatible with the principle of subsidiarity, is noteworthy.[49]

From the bigger picture of the 'yellow-card procedure' described above, it is therefore apparent that the dispute over the subsidiarity of the draft legislation, rather than being just an end in itself, was an attempt by the Central and Eastern EU Member States to influence the content of the new Directive on posting of workers.[50] The constitution of an actual 'regional block' resulting from the fact that 13 out of 14 parliamentary chambers that submitted reasoned opinions belong to Central and Eastern Europe clearly testifies the existence of a deep divide within the Union between East and West, the 'new' and the 'old' Member States.[51] In particular, when it comes to defining the proper means to pursue a more 'Social Europe', the conflict is evident considering that the path taken by the Juncker's Commission was supported by the

46. The Member States which expressed those types of concerns were Czech Republic, Estonia, Latvia, Slovakia, Lithuania, Romania and Slovakia. Fromage and Kreilinger (n 6) 148.
47. That was the case of Bulgaria, Croatia, Czech Republic, Estonia, Hungary, Latvia, Lithuania and Romania. *Ibid.* 149; Rocca, 'Not Dead yet: Legal Strategies at National Level and the Reform of the EU Posting of Workers Directive' (n 6) 4; Rocca, 'Stepping Stones Over Troubled Waters. Recent Legal Evolutions and the Reform of the Posting of Workers Directive' (n 6) 169.
48. European Commission, Communication from the Commission to the European Parliament, the Council and the National Parliaments on the proposal for a Directive amending the Posting of Workers Directive, with regard to the principle of subsidiarity, in accordance with Protocol No 2 (n 39) 7; Voss et al. (n 5) 53; Jančić (n 40) 306; Fromage and Kreilinger (n 6) 150; Rocca, 'Not Dead yet: Legal Strategies at National Level and the Reform of the EU Posting of Workers Directive' (n 6) 4.
49. Oddly enough, the very similar situations of Italy and Denmark, whereby both statutory minimum wage and a system for declaring universally applicable collective agreements are absent, resulted in drastically opposed positions on the Commission's proposal. Voss et al. (n 5) 53; Zahn, 'Revision of the Posted Workers' Directive: Equality at Last?' (n 4) 14–15; Jančić (n 40) 304; Fromage and Kreilinger (n 6) 151; Biletta and Aumayr-Pintar (n 9) 5.
50. Fromage and Kreilinger (n 6) 159.
51. Kreilinger (n 38); Fromage and Kreilinger (n 6) 133, 146 and 158; van Hoek (n 23) 475. For an in-depth analysis of the dynamics of interparliamentary cooperation leading to the creation of a 'regional block' formed by the CEECs in the context of the 'yellow-card procedure' triggered in 2016, *see* Fromage and Kreilinger (n 6) 144 and ff.

Western European Member States only. Conversely, from the point of view of the Central and Eastern EU countries, the proposed measures were largely perceived as unnecessary, if not protectionist.[52]

More than two months after the yellow card was triggered, with its Communication of 20 July 2016,[53] the European Commission eventually delivered its response to the Member States' reasoned opinions. After re-examining its proposal of 8 March 2016, the Commission rejected all the subsidiarity concerns raised by national parliaments and, without making any amendments, concluded by confirming its intention to go ahead with the reform, while maintaining its proposal unchanged.[54] This decision was corroborated by the President Juncker's speech during his State of the Union address on 14 September 2016, when he emphasised the Commission's political commitment to the realisation of a European 'social market economy' whereby 'workers should get the same pay for the same work in the same place'.[55]

8.2.3 The Adoption Process

Once the European Commission decided to push on with the revision of the Posting of Workers Directive, it was then the turn of the European Parliament and the Council to take action in accordance with the ordinary legislative procedure.[56] As a first step, the two co-rapporteurs Elisabeth Morin-Chartier (European People's Party (EPP), France) and Agnes Jongerius (Socialists & Democrats (S&D), The Netherlands) appointed by

52. Fromage and Kreilinger (n 6) 160.
53. European Commission, Communication from the Commission to the European Parliament, the Council and the National Parliaments on the proposal for a Directive amending the Posting of Workers Directive, with regard to the principle of subsidiarity, in accordance with Protocol No 2 (n 39).
54. European Commission, 'Press Release – Posting of Workers: Commission Discusses Concerns of National Parliaments' (*European Commission Press Releases Database*, 20 July 2016) <http://europa.eu/rapid/press-release_IP-16-2546_en.htm> (accessed 12 July 2019); Zahn, 'Revision of the Posted Workers' Directive: Equality at Last?' (n 4) 15; Fromage and Kreilinger (n 6) 151–152; Biletta and Aumayr-Pintar (n 9) 4; Kiss (n 14) 10; European Sources Online (ESO) (n 40); Rocca, 'Not Dead yet: Legal Strategies at National Level and the Reform of the EU Posting of Workers Directive' (n 6) 4; Rocca, 'Stepping Stones Over Troubled Waters. Recent Legal Evolutions and the Reform of the Posting of Workers Directive' (n 6) 169. Interestingly, the influence of France on the Commission's stance may be noticed in the declaration made by the French Prime Minister Valls on 3 July 2016, who threatened to suspend the application of the PWD as long as a revision of the Directive is adopted. The Economist, 'Going Posted' (7 July 2016) <https://www.economist.com/europe/2016/07/07/going-posted> (accessed 8 August 2019); Emmanuel Comte, 'Promising More to Give Less: International Disputes between Core and Periphery around European Posted Labor, 1955–2018' (2019) Labor History 1, 11.
55. European Commission, 'Press Release – The State of the Union 2016: Towards a Better Europe – A Europe That Protects, Empowers and Defends' (*European Commission Press Releases Database*, 14 September 2016) <http://europa.eu/rapid/press-release_IP-16-3042_en.htm> (accessed 12 July 2019). *See* Zahn, 'Revision of the Posted Workers' Directive: Equality at Last?' (n 4) 15; Fromage and Kreilinger (n 6) 157.
56. More specifically, by reason of the ordinary legislative procedure (COD) (Parliament and Council on equal footing – formerly 'co-decision'), the revision of the PWD required the achievement of a majority in the European Parliament and of a qualified majority in the Council. Fromage and Kreilinger (n 6) 154; Kiss (n 14) 1.

the European Parliament's Employment and Social Affairs Committee (EMPL)[57] published their draft report on the proposal for a targeted revision of the Posting of Workers Directive on 2 December 2016.[58] That document, designed with a view to refining the Commission's proposal in order to ensure both a level playing field for undertakings and better social protection for posted workers,[59] recommended an extension of the legal basis also to Articles 151 and 153(1)(a) and (b) TFEU on workers' rights.[60] It then stressed the need for transparency and improved access to information in cross-border posting situations.[61] It assured Member States the autonomy to determine the elements of remuneration on their own territory, insofar as posted workers were guaranteed 'due entitlements', double payments were avoided, and workers hired by subcontractors or temporary employment undertakings enjoyed the same terms and conditions of employment.[62] Finally, it suggested the introduction of a sort of 'Monti clause' for the prevention of any interference of the new Directive with the rights to strike and to conclude collective agreements.[63]

Subsequent discussions in the EMPL Committee followed along the lines of the above-mentioned draft report while dealing with further issues and concluded with a report adopted on 16 October 2017.[64] Besides the novelties already envisaged by the 2016 draft report, Article 153(1)(a) and (b) TFEU in conjunction with Article 153(2) TFEU were proposed as an additional legal basis to the Treaty rules concerning the free provision of services.[65] The duration of posting after which host state's labour law was

57. For a critique of the choice to assign the revision of the PWD to the Employment and Social Affairs Committee (EMPL) – i.e., a committee which typically deals with social matters and protection of workers' rights – rather than to a Committee specifically handling economic matters, *see* Stefan Schwarz, 'EP Plenary Voted for State Mandated Protectionism' <https://www.elmc.eu/ep-plenary-voted-for-state-mandated-protectionism-commentary-from-stefan-schwarz/> (accessed 21 November 2018).
58. Elisabeth Morin-Chartier and Agnes Jongerius, 'Draft Report on the Proposal for a Directive of the European Parliament and of the Council Amending Directive 96/71/EC of The European Parliament and of the Council of 16 December 1996 Concerning the Posting of Workers in the Framework of the Provision of Services' (European Parliament – Committee on Employment and Social Affairs 2016) 2016/0070(COD) <http://www.europarl.europa.eu/doceo/document/EMPL-PR-582163_EN.pdf?redirect> (accessed 20 August 2019). On the specific content, *see* Schmid-Drüner (n 34) 5; Kiss (n 14) 10; Eurofound (n 14).
59. Morin-Chartier and Jongerius (n 58) 18.
60. *Ibid.* Amendment 1.
61. *Ibid.* Amendment 8.
62. *Ibid.* Amendments 7, 11, 17 and 19.
63. *Ibid.* Amendment 10.
64. Elisabeth Morin-Chartier and Agnes Jongerius, 'Report on the Proposal for a Directive of the European Parliament and of the Council Amending Directive 96/71/EC of the European Parliament and of the Council of 16 December 1996 Concerning the Posting of Workers in the Framework of the Provision of Services' (European Parliament – Committee on Employment and Social Affairs 2017) A8-0319/2017. On the specific content, *see* Schmid-Drüner (n 34) 6; Kiss (n 14) 10–11; Eurofound (n 14).
65. Morin-Chartier and Jongerius (n 64) Amendment 1. The proposed extension of the legal basis to include also the European social *acquis* was intended to pursue more efficiently the dual scope of the Directive. Besides, it was supposed to eventually have significant implications for future rulings of the Court of Justice of the European Union. Barslund, Busse and Wispelaere (n 27) 6; Francesco Costamagna, 'The Revision of the Posted Workers Directive as a Meaningful Way to Curb Regulatory Competition in the Social Domain?' (2019) 2 Sant'Anna Legal Studies 25, 15–16. Interestingly, the proposal of a double legal basis already found the opposition of the

supposed to apply in full was also widely debated, taking into account different options varying from six to twenty-four months and even the possibility of differentiating maximum durations according to economic sectors. Eventually, the twenty-four-months duration already put forward by the Commission was maintained, albeit with the opportunity to obtain extensions based on a reasoned request made to the host country's competent authority.[66] The definition of the notion of remuneration was exclusively reserved to the Member States, with the possibility to rely also on collective agreements applicable at local level. Member States were conferred the competence to set wages as well, in concert with social partners.[67] Moreover, a specific obligation was imposed on the contractor to inform the subcontracting foreign service provider about the applicable terms and conditions of employment as regards remuneration before the commencement of the service contract.[68] The report under consideration reproposed the 'Monti clause' of the 2016 draft report[69] and tightened up the responsibility of both the state of establishment and the host state with regard to the monitoring, control and enforcement of the new Directive's prescriptions and the determination of effective, proportionate and dissuasive sanctions. *Inter alia*, it explicitly provided for the application of host state law in the event of non-genuine posting.[70] Importantly, then, it definitely excluded the activity of international road transport from the scope of the Directive,[71] provided that the sector at issue, because of its intrinsic highly mobile nature, was expected to be regulated by a new ad hoc Directive, whose proposal was put forward by the Commission on 31 May 2017.[72]

At the same time, in the EPSCO (Employment, Social Policy, Health and Consumer Affairs) Council the Commission's proposal was extensively discussed as well. First, the progress report,[73] published on 25 November 2016 under the Slovak Presidency, mainly focused on providing definitions of some controversial concepts, namely that of 'anticipated duration of posting', of 'the same task at the same place', and of 'remuneration'. It also looked at determining specific conflict-of-law rules applicable in cases of long-term postings exceeding twenty-four months.[74] Second, the

Legal Services of the European Parliament. Alexis Lubow and Susanne K Schmidt, 'A Hidden Champion? The European Court of Justice as an Agenda-Setter in the Case of Posted Workers' (2020) Public Administration (John Wiley & Sons Ltd.) 1, 10–11.

66. Morin-Chartier and Jongerius (n 64) Amendments 11 and 27.
67. *Ibid.* Amendments 15–16.
68. *Ibid.* Amendment 30.
69. *Ibid.* Amendment 20.
70. *Ibid.* Amendment 38.
71. *Ibid.* Amendment 13.
72. European Commission, Proposal for a Directive of the European Parliament and of the Council amending Directive 2006/22/EC as regards enforcement requirements and laying down specific rules with respect to Directive 96/71/EC and Directive 2014/67/EU for posting drivers in the road transport sector 2017 [COM(2017) 278 final].
73. 'Proposal for a Directive of the European Parliament and of the Council on the Enforcement of Directive 96/71/EC Concerning the Posting of Workers in the Framework of the Provision of Services – Progress Report' (Council of the European Union 2016) 14368/16 <http://data.consilium.europa.eu/doc/document/ST-14368-2016-INIT/en/pdf> (accessed 20 August 2019).
74. *See* Kiss (n 14) 11.

following progress report,[75] published on 9 June 2017 under the Maltese Presidency, clarified that the notion of 'remuneration' had to be defined according to national law and practices.[76] Moreover, it excluded the procedures, formalities and conditions related to the conclusion and termination of the employment contract from the share of host state's labour law applicable to posted workers after twenty-four months of mobility abroad.[77] Interestingly, the Maltese Presidency suggested to delete the Commission's new provision concerning subcontracting because of its potential negative impact on businesses, in particular on SMEs.[78] Following heated discussions, a general approach[79] on the Commission's legislative proposal was agreed during the EPSCO Council gathered in Luxembourg on 23 October 2017.[80]

Besides confirming the principle of equal remuneration between local and posted workers, the adopted text sought to introduce an actual criterion for individuating the concept of 'remuneration'. To this end, it envisaged to take into account 'all the elements of minimum rates of pay developed by the Court of Justice of the European Union' and to compare the total gross amounts of remuneration, rather than merely individual elements.[81] Further notable amendments concerned the limited duration of posting which, unlike what was agreed just a few days before in the Parliament, was reduced to twelve months, but extendable up to eighteen months by the host Member State on the basis of a motivated notification from the transnational service provider.[82]

---

75. 'Proposal for a Directive of the European Parliament and of the Council on the Enforcement of Directive 96/71/EC Concerning the Posting of Workers in the Framework of the Provision of Services – Progress Report' (Council of the European Union 2017) 9882/17 <http://data.consilium.europa.eu/doc/document/ST-9882-2017-INIT/en/pdf> (accessed 20 August 2019). On the specific content, *see* Kiss (n 14) 11.
76. 'Proposal for a Directive of the European Parliament and of the Council on the Enforcement of Directive 96/71/EC Concerning the Posting of Workers in the Framework of the Provision of Services – Progress Report' (n 75) 3–4.
77. *Ibid.* 4–6.
78. *Ibid.* 6–7.
79. 'Proposal for a Directive of the European Parliament and of the Council on the Enforcement of Directive 96/71/EC Concerning the Posting of Workers in the Framework of the Provision of Services – General Approach' (Council of the European Union 2017) 13612/17 <https://eur-lex.europa.eu/legal-content/EN/TXT/PDF/?uri=CONSIL:ST_13612_2017_INIT&from=EN> (accessed 20 August 2019).
80. Incidentally, it is noticeable that, on that occasion, the agreement received the support of several Eastern European Member States as well. In fact, Bulgaria, the Czech Republic, Estonia, Romania and the Slovak Republic voted in favour, whereas Croatia (together with Ireland and the UK) abstained and only Hungary, Latvia, Lithuania and Poland voted against. Piet Van Nuffel and Sofia Afanasjeva, 'The Posting of Workers Directive Revised: Enhancing the Protection of Workers in the Cross-Border Provision of Services' (2018) 3 European Papers 1401, 1416. Interestingly, the fact that the Council approved the Interinstitutional Proclamation on the European Pillar of Social Rights on the same day testifies the existence of a link between those two initiatives, which had been initially presented together by the Commission President Juncker. Garben, 'The European Pillar of Social Rights' (n 23) 9 and 25; Garben, 'The European Pillar of Social Rights as a Revival of Social Europe' (n 23) 79.
81. 'Proposal for a Directive of the European Parliament and of the Council on the Enforcement of Directive 96/71/EC Concerning the Posting of Workers in the Framework of the Provision of Services – General Approach' (n 79) Preamble Recitals 12a and 12b.
82. *Ibid.* Article 1(2)(aa). Such a compromise was presumably found by the ministers with the intention of pleasing France, which persistently insisted on a strict twelve-month limit. In this sense, *see* Catherine Stupp, 'Macron's Proposals Wreak Havoc on Posted Worker Negotiations'

A new provision was also conceived with regard to the setting of a three-year deadline after the entry into force of the Directive for adoption and publication by the Member States of all the necessary laws, regulations and administrative provisions. The Posting of Workers Directive was, nonetheless, supposed to remain applicable until the fourth year after the entry into force of the new Directive, when the above-mentioned measures were expected to be fully applicable.[83]

Following the two texts adopted by the European Parliament and the Council in October 2017, interinstitutional negotiations started between the latter EU institutions and the Commission in the form of tripartite meetings.[84] Notably, an overall provisional agreement[85] was reached at the trilogue session on 19 March 2018, constituting the basis for the adoption of the forthcoming new Directive. On that occasion, the agreement on the maximum duration of posting – i.e., the period of time after which a posted worker is fully covered by host state's labour law – was found at twelve months, with a possible extension of further six months upon motivated notification by the service provider to the competent authority in the host country.[86] According to the confirmed principle of 'the same pay for the same work at the same workplace', from their first day of mobility abroad, in turn, posted workers were expected to be entitled to the same 'remuneration' as local workers. As for the definition of 'remuneration', besides explicitly stating the Member States' and social partners' exclusive competence in determining wages,[87] the document drafted in the trilogue also indicated to take into account the total gross amount paid to the employees, rather than merely the individual elements of remuneration.[88] Expenses such as reimbursements for travel, board and lodging were once again excluded from the calculation,[89] and the constituent

---

(*EURACTIV*, 15 June 2017) <https://www.euractiv.com/section/economy-jobs/news/macrons-proposals-wreak-havoc-on-posted-worker-negotiations/> (accessed 4 July 2019); Cécile Barbière, 'Posted Workers: Macron's First Victory in Reforming the EU' (*EURACTIV*, 24 October 2017) <https://www.euractiv.com/section/economy-jobs/news/posted-workers-macrons-first-victory-in-reforming-the-eu/> (accessed 26 September 2018); Eric Maurice, 'EU Takes Step Closer to "Posted Workers" Deal' (*euobserver*, 1 March 2018) <https://euobserver.com/social/141166> (accessed 26 September 2018).

83. Article 2(1) of the 'Proposal for a Directive of the European Parliament and of the Council on the Enforcement of Directive 96/71/EC Concerning the Posting of Workers in the Framework of the Provision of Services – General Approach' (n 79). On the point, *see* Kiss (n 14) 11–12.
84. For the record, before an agreement was reached on the matter, eight trilogue meetings took place under the Estonian and then the Bulgarian Presidencies of the Council and with the Commission represented by the Commissioner for Employment, Social Affairs, Skills and Labour Mobility, Marianne Thyssen. Kiss (n 14) 12; Van Nuffel and Afanasjeva (n 80) 1416.
85. 'Proposal for a Directive of the European Parliament and of the Council Amending Directive 96/71/EC Concerning the Posting of Workers in the Framework of the Provision of Services – Analysis of the Final Compromise Text with a View to Agreement' (Council of the European Union 2018) 7350/18 <http://data.consilium.europa.eu/doc/document/ST-7350-2018-ADD-1/en/pdf> (accessed 20 August 2019). On the specific content, *see* Kiss (n 14) 12.
86. Preamble Recital 10 and Article 1(2)(b) of the 'Proposal for a Directive of the European Parliament and of the Council Amending Directive 96/71/EC Concerning the Posting of Workers in the Framework of the Provision of Services – Analysis of the Final Compromise Text with a View to Agreement' (n 85).
87. *Ibid.* Preamble Recital 16.
88. *Ibid.* Preamble Recital 17.
89. *Ibid.* Preamble Recitals 17–18. Interestingly, then, in the absence of specific indication of which elements of an allowance specific to the posting were actually paid in reimbursement of

elements of remuneration had to be published in the single official national website created in accordance with Article 5 of Directive 2014/67/EU.[90] A new element was then added to the list of host state's 'hard core' provisions applicable to posted workers, namely the conditions of accommodation provided by the employer to workers away from their regular place of work, which had to be equal to those reserved to local workers.[91] Furthermore, the Commission's proposal to render mandatory all universally applicable collective agreements concluded in any economic sector was extended in such a way as to include also those having general validity for all undertakings located in a certain territory and belonging to the profession or industry concerned, or those having nation-wide application after being concluded by the most representative employers' and labour organisations at national level.[92] In turn, the suggested provision conferring on the Member States the power to oblige companies to subcontract only to service providers which guaranteed the same level of employment protection as the main contractor was considerably scaled down to a general duty to 'take appropriate measures [...] to ensure subcontracting liability'.[93] Finally, the Posting of Workers Directive was still considered applicable for regulating the activity of posted workers in the European road haulage industry until the adoption of an ad hoc Directive dealing specifically with posting in the road transport sector.[94]

After an initial agreement was reached by the Committee of Permanent Representatives (COREPER) on 11 April 2018 and passed the scrutiny of the EMPL Committee on 25 April, the compromise draft law was formally endorsed by the European Parliament in plenary on 29 May[95] and by the Council on 21 June,[96] both at first reading.[97] On 28 June 2018, the new Directive (EU) 2018/957[98] was eventually adopted, and on 29 July 2018, twenty days after its publication in the Official Journal

expenditure or were *vice versa* part of remuneration, the entire allowance had to be considered as a reimbursement. *Ibid.* Article 1(2)(d).

90. Article 1(2)(a) of the 'Proposal for a Directive of the European Parliament and of the Council Amending Directive 96/71/EC Concerning the Posting of Workers in the Framework of the Provision of Services – Analysis of the Final Compromise Text with a View to Agreement' (n 85).
91. *Ibid.* Article 1(2)(a)(h).
92. *Ibid.* Article 1(2)(a).
93. *Ibid.* Preamble Recital 23.
94. Preamble Recital 14 and Article 2(2) of the 'Proposal for a Directive of the European Parliament and of the Council Amending Directive 96/71/EC Concerning the Posting of Workers in the Framework of the Provision of Services -- Analysis of the Final Compromise Text with a View to Agreement' (n 85).
95. European Parliament legislative resolution of 29 May 2018 on the proposal for a directive of the European Parliament and of the Council amending Directive 96/71/EC of the European Parliament and of the Council of 16 December 1996 concerning the posting of workers in the framework of the provision of services (COM(2016)0128 – C8-0114/2016 – 2016/0070(COD)) (Ordinary legislative procedure: first reading) 2018 (P8_TA(2018)0213).
96. Council of the European Union, 'Posting of Workers: Council Adopts the Directive – Consilium' (*Press Release*, 21 June 2018) <https://www.consilium.europa.eu/en/press/press-releases/2018/06/21/posting-of-workers-council-adopts-the-directive/> (accessed 27 August 2019). On that occasion, only Hungary and Poland opposed, while Croatia, Latvia, Lithuania and the UK abstained. Van Nuffel and Afanasjeva (n 80) 1416; Schrauwen (n 23) 326–327.
97. Kiss (n 14) 12–13; Eurofound (n 14); European Sources Online (ESO) (n 40).
98. Directive (EU) 2018/957 of the European Parliament and of the Council of 28 June 2018 amending Directive 96/71/EC concerning the posting of workers in the framework of the provision of services (n 2).

of the European Union (OJ), it entered into force.[99] A two-year implementation period was, nevertheless, set until 30 July 2020 for the Member States to adopt and publish the relevant laws, regulations and administrative provisions to comply with this Directive. Until that date, the original version of the Posting of Workers Directive still remained applicable.[100] Furthermore, a review clause was introduced establishing a Commission's duty to assess by 30 July 2023 whether new measures in the fields of subcontracting and posted drivers in the road transport sector will become necessary.[101] With respect to the transnational provision of services in the road transport sector, in light of its intrinsic highly mobile nature, the European legislator made the choice to defer the application of the new Directive (EU) 2018/957 in relation to that kind of business, until the sector-specific legislation amending Directive 2006/22/EC[102] – i.e., the newly adopted Directive (EU) 2020/1057 on posting drivers in the road transport sector[103] – will enter into force[104] – notably, on 2 February 2022.[105] It follows that, until that date, transnational activities of transport workers remain covered by the original version of the Posting of Workers Directive.[106] In turn, as of 2 February 2022, Directive (EU) 2020/1057 will regulate the posting of workers in the road transport sector as a *lex specialis* which derogates from the Posting of Workers Directive, as amended by Directive (EU) 2018/957, and its Enforcement Directive.

Also by virtue of the incisive political campaign underpinning it, the reform was particularly acclaimed all over Western Europe for its ability to protect the economic and social fabric against social dumping.[107] Especially in France, where the modernisation of the rules on posting was put on top of the list of priorities by President

99. *Ibid.* Article 4.
100. *Ibid.* Article 3(1).
101. *Ibid.* Article 2.
102. Directive 2006/22/EC of the European Parliament and of the Council of 15 March 2006 on minimum conditions for the implementation of Council Regulations (EEC) No 3820/85 and (EEC) No 3821/85 concerning social legislation relating to road transport activities and repealing Council Directive 88/599/EEC 2006 (OJ L 102/35).
103. Directive (EU) 2020/1057 of the European Parliament and of the Council of 15 July 2020 laying down specific rules with respect to Directive 96/71/EC and Directive 2014/67/EU for posting drivers in the road transport sector and amending Directive 2006/22/EC as regards enforcement requirements and Regulation (EU) No 1024/2012, 2020 (OJ L 249/49). For an analysis of the aforementioned new piece of EU legislation, *see supra* Chapter 4.
104. Article 3(3) of Directive (EU) 2018/957 of the European Parliament and of the Council of 28 June 2018 amending Directive 96/71/EC concerning the posting of workers in the framework of the provision of services (n 2).
105. Article 9 of Directive (EU) 2020/1057 of the European Parliament and of the Council of 15 July 2020 laying down specific rules with respect to Directive 96/71/EC and Directive 2014/67/EU for posting drivers in the road transport sector and amending Directive 2006/22/EC as regards enforcement requirements and Regulation (EU) No 1024/2012 (n 103).
106. Jean-Philippe Lhernould, 'Directive (EU) 2018/957 of 28 June 2018 Amending Directive 96/71/EC Concerning the Posting of Workers in the Framework of the Provision of Services: What Will Change in 2020?' (2019) ERA Forum – Springer 7 <http://link.springer.com/10.1007/s12027-019-00573-x> (accessed 16 September 2019).
107. ETUC as well expressed its satisfaction with the adopted text. Liina Carr, 'Justice at Last: Equal Pay for Posted Workers' (*ETUC (European Trade Union Confederation) Press Release*, 29 May 2018) <https://www.etuc.org/en/pressrelease/justice-last-equal-pay-posted-workers> (accessed 27 July 2019).

Macron, the adoption of the new Directive received the greatest appreciation.[108] In turn, negative reactions from the European employers' associations accused the new Directive of merely reflecting the protectionist political interests of certain Member States.[109] Lately, the legality of the Directive was even challenged by Hungary and Poland which, on 2 and 3 October 2018 respectively, brought two actions for annulment before the Court of Justice, pleading an infringement of Article 56 TFEU, of Article 153(5) TFEU (which excludes the EU competence as regards the regulation of pay), and of the Rome I Regulation on the law applicable to contractual obligations.[110]

8.3 THE REFORM

As of 30 July 2020, the new legal framework envisaged by Directive (EU) 2018/957 is fully effective. In broad terms, this innovative set of rules puts forward major alterations to the regulatory regime applicable to workers posted across borders within the European Union and the European Economic Area (EEA). At the same time, it further improves the cross-border enforcement of Union law in those kinds of situations. The following thorough analysis of the content of the adopted text is provided with a view to critically assessing the changes brought about by such a revision of the Posting of Workers Directive.

First and foremost, the new Directive formally still finds its legal basis in the Treaty rules concerning the freedom to provide services,[111] but also in the promotion of social justice and protection according to Article 3 TEU and Article 9 TFEU.[112] As such, the Posting of Workers Directive has been integrated with a 'social legal basis' by amendment of Article 1 as to expressly incorporate the protection of the workers

108. Stupp (n 82); Barbière (n 82); Maurice (n 82); Sciarra (n 14) 84–85; Van Nuffel and Afanasjeva (n 80) 1402.
109. BusinessEurope, 'Posting of Workers: A Bad Deal That Will Harm the Functioning of the Single Market for Services' (3 January 2018) <https://www.businesseurope.eu/publications/posting-workers-bad-deal-will-harm-functioning-single-market-services> (accessed 14 October 2019); Alberto Riesco-Sanz, Jorge García López and María del Mar Maira Vidal, 'The Posting of Workers in the European Road Transport Industry: An Approach Based on the Discourses of Social and Institutional Stakeholders' (2019) European Journal of Industrial Relations 1, 6.
110. *Action brought on 2 October 2018 – Hungary v European Parliament and Council of the European Union* [2018] CJEU Case C-620/18; *Action brought on 3 October 2018 – Republic of Poland v European Parliament and Council of the European Union* [2018] CJEU Case C-626/18. For the record, the Court has not delivered its rulings yet, while both the actions have been dismissed in their entirety by Advocate General Campos Sánchez-Bordona in *Hungary v European Parliament, Council of the European Union, Opinion of Advocate General Manuel Campos Sánchez-Bordona delivered on 28 May 2020* [2020] CJEU Case C-620/18, ECLI:EU:C:2020:392; *Republic of Poland v European Parliament, Council of the European Union, Opinion of Advocate General Manuel Campos Sánchez-Bordona delivered on 28 May 2020* [2020] CJEU Case C-626/18, ECLI:EU:C:2020:394.
111. More specifically, the legal basis of Directive (EU) 2018/957 remained the same as that of Directive 96/71/EC, namely in the provisions relating to the internal market, in particular, Articles 53(1) and 62 TFEU.
112. Preamble Recitals 1–3 of Directive (EU) 2018/957 of the European Parliament and of the Council of 28 June 2018 amending Directive 96/71/EC concerning the posting of workers in the framework of the provision of services (n 2).

seconded abroad for the provision of services.[113] The rights enshrined in the Charter of Fundamental Rights of the European Union (CFREU) have been thereby given greater prominence and the position of workers in possible court cases has been definitely strengthened.[114] In the same vein, and presumably with the intention of responding to the approach taken by the Court of Justice in its famous decision in *Laval*,[115] a new Article 1a was added with a so-called 'Monti clause' providing for further guarantee of the right to take collective action, along with the right to negotiate, conclude and enforce collective agreements.[116]

Moving on to the more concrete amendments to the legal regime for posting realised through the 2018 legislative reform, the major changes concern the new rules on remuneration, temporary agency work, and long-term posting. The following analysis is proposed to shed some light on the whole range of regulatory novelties that came into effect on 30 July 2020.

8.3.1 Remuneration

In terms of public opinion, the most impactful novelty of the new Directive (EU) 2018/957 is undoubtedly represented by the amendments and additions made to the list, laid down by Article 3(1) of the Posting of Workers Directive, of host country's 'hard core' terms and conditions of employment extendable to posted workers during their assignment abroad. That way, the principle of 'the same pay for the same work at the same workplace' was set down in practical terms, and the posted workers' wages and working conditions were brought closer to those applicable to local workers.[117]

The major change made along those lines was the replacement of the element of 'minimum rates of pay' applicable to posted workers under Article 3(1)(c) with a

113. *Ibid.* Article 1(1)(b). Nonetheless, the European Parliament's proposal to extend the legal basis to Article 153 TFEU was eventually not taken over. This not only by reason of the resulting unusual double basis but also of the fact that posting of workers is by its own nature based on a service contract. Lhernould (n 106) 2.
114. Eurofound (n 14).
115. *Laval un Partneri Ltd v Svenska Byggnadsarbetareförbundet, Svenska Byggnadsarbetareförbundets avdelning 1, Byggettan and Svenska Elektrikerförbundet* (n 1). For an in-depth analysis of the highly controversial outcomes of the case, *see supra* Chapter 4.
116. Article 1(1)(b) of Directive (EU) 2018/957 of the European Parliament and of the Council of 28 June 2018 amending Directive 96/71/EC concerning the posting of workers in the framework of the provision of services (n 2). Interestingly, as noted by Rocca, while such a clause was originally included among the Preamble Recitals by both the Committee Report (Recital 13d) and the Council Approach (Recital 11a), its upgrade to the actual legal text appears to suggest the legislator's intention of giving it a stronger legal effect. This, also in light of the lack of binding legal force by the preamble to a Union act, as promptly reminded by the Court of Justice in *Giuseppe Manfredi v Regione Puglia* [1998] ECJ Case C-308/97, ECLI:EU:C:1998:566, 30; *Deutsches Milch-Kontor GmbH v Hauptzollamt Hamburg-Jonas* [2005] ECJ Case C-136/04, ECLI:EU:C:2005:716 [32]; *Hauptzollamt Bremen v J E Tyson Parketthandel GmbH hanse j* [2009] CJEU Case C-134/08, ECLI:EU:C:2009:229 [16]. Rocca, 'Not Dead yet: Legal Strategies at National Level and the Reform of the EU Posting of Workers Directive' (n 6) 7.
117. Eurofound (n 14); Rocca, 'Not Dead yet: Legal Strategies at National Level and the Reform of the EU Posting of Workers Directive' (n 6) 4.

broader concept of 'remuneration'[118] covering also other advantages such as bonuses, allowances, pay increases according to seniority, and regularly paid thirteenth and fourteenth months' supplements.[119] The influence of the CJEU's decisions in *Commission v Germany*,[120] *Isbir*[121] and, especially, in *Sähköalojen ammattiliitto*[122] on the European legislator is more than evident in the incorporation of basically all the elements already included on those occasions within the concept of minimum rates of pay.[123] Accordingly, the new concept of 'remuneration' may be regarded as, *inter alia*, a codification of the Court of Justice case law.[124]

When it comes to concretely determine the remuneration due to a posted worker, and to compare it with the wage actually paid to the employee, the Preamble to Directive (EU) 2018/957 then further specifies that reference has to be made to the total gross amount, rather than to the individual elements of remuneration.[125] In parallel,

---

118. Article 1(2)(a)(c) of Directive (EU) 2018/957 of the European Parliament and of the Council of 28 June 2018 amending Directive 96/71/EC concerning the posting of workers in the framework of the provision of services (n 2).
119. More specifically, under the notions of bonuses and allowances are covered Christmas bonus, allowance for bad weather, mobility allowance, pay supplement for special works, allowance for wear of tools, and allowance for difficult work. For the record, though, equal pay does not imply that posted workers will be entitled to the exact same salary and benefits package (including group insurance, hospitalisation, company car and lunch allowances) as their local counterparts in the host states. Deloitte Belgium, 'How Will the Revision of the Posted Workers Directive Impact Your Assignments?' (2018) figure 6 <https://www2.deloitte.com/content/dam/Deloitte/be/Documents/tax/PostedWorkersDirective.pdf> (accessed 26 September 2018).
120. *Commission of the European Communities v Federal Republic of Germany* [2005] ECJ Case C-341/02, ECLI:EU:C:2005:220.
121. *Tevfik Isbir v DB Services* (n 29).
122. *Sähköalojen ammattiliitto ry v Elektrobudowa Spolka Akcyjna* [2015] CJEU Case C-396/13, ECLI:EU:C:2015:86.
123. On the extended interpretation of the notion of minimum rates of pay given by the Court in *Commission v Germany, Isbir* and *Sähköalojen ammattiliitto, see supra* Chapter 3.
124. Zahn, 'Revision of the Posted Workers' Directive: Equality at Last?' (n 4) 13; van Hoek (n 23) 482; Rocca, 'Not Dead yet: Legal Strategies at National Level and the Reform of the EU Posting of Workers Directive' (n 6) 9 and 13; Lhernould (n 106) 3–5; Rocca, 'Stepping Stones Over Troubled Waters. Recent Legal Evolutions and the Reform of the Posting of Workers Directive' (n 6) 175. As a matter of fact, the idea of taking into account 'all the elements of minimum rates of pay developed by the Court of Justice of the European Union' for concretely defining the elements of 'remuneration' of host state law extendable to posted workers was explicitly suggested by the Council in its Preamble Recital 12a of the 'Proposal for a Directive of the European Parliament and of the Council on the Enforcement of Directive 96/71/EC Concerning the Posting of Workers in the Framework of the Provision of Services – General Approach' (n 79).
125. Preamble Recital 18 of Directive (EU) 2018/957 of the European Parliament and of the Council of 28 June 2018 amending Directive 96/71/EC concerning the posting of workers in the framework of the provision of services (n 2). Interestingly enough, this provision is a codification of the Court's jurisprudence as well. *Commission of the European Communities v Federal Republic of Germany* (n 120) para. 29. On this point, *see* Lhernould (n 106) 4. To be more precise, according to the example provided by Van Nuffel and Afanasjeva, in case 'the relevant collective agreement in the host Member State requires the posted worker to be paid a monthly salary of 1500 EUR and daily allowances of 300 euro, whereas that worker is, under home Member State rules, entitled to a salary of 500 euro but also to a seniority allowance and a flat-rate posting allowance of 100 euro and 1200 euro, respectively, it is the gross amount of 1800 euro paid to the worker under home Member State rules that must be compared with the

Article 1(2)(c) confirms the principle, already enshrined in the original version of the Posting of Workers Directive, which considers all allowances specific to the posting, such as expenditure on travel, board and lodging, as included in the calculation, except for when they had been actually incurred on account of the working assignment abroad.[126] Conversely, likewise those payments or reimbursements of expenses actually incurred because of the posting, payments for overtime work, work on Sundays, additional work, or work under particular conditions cannot be taken into account for the purpose of calculating the remuneration.[127]

As from the entry into force of the legislative *novella*, a posted employee is, therefore, covered by the same wage scales and specific allowances available to a local employee, as determined by the host country's national law and/or practice (i.e., collective bargaining agreements).[128] The exclusive competence of the Member States to define the concept of remuneration in their own territory[129] may be exercised in the form of positive legislation (including also regulations or administrative provisions), as well as of collective agreements or arbitration awards which are declared universally applicable. Unlike the original Directive, posting may also be regulated cumulatively by means of collective agreements or arbitration awards having general validity for all undertakings located in a certain territory and belonging to the occupational group or industry concerned, or concluded by the most representative employer and labour organisations at national level and having nation-wide effect.[130] With particular regard

gross amount of remuneration required under the host Member State rules (also 1800 euro in the example)'. Van Nuffel and Afanasjeva (n 80) 1418.

126. As confirmed in Preamble Recital 8 of Directive (EU) 2018/957, provided that the expenses actually incurred for travel, board and lodging are supposed to be paid *in toto* by the employer, the provision under consideration aims therefore at avoiding 'double payments'. Marta Głowacka, 'Posting of Workers Directive Reloaded' (2019) 26 Studia z Zakresu Prawa Pracy i Polityki Społecznej (Studies on Labour Law and Social Policy) 29, 34.

127. European Commission, 'Practical Guide on Posting' (2019) 19–20.

128. Deloitte Belgium (n 119) figure 6; Marek Benio, 'New Rules of the Posting of Workers in 2020. The Countdown.' (*Labour Mobility Initiative*, 30 July 2018) <https://www.mobilelabour.eu/12521/new-rules-of-the-posting-of-workers-in-2020-the-final-countdown/> (accessed 30 August 2018); Charmaine Yong, 'The New EU Posting of Workers Directive – Implications for Employers' (*Lewis Silkin*, 1 November 2018) <https://www.lewissilkin.com/Insights/The-new-EU-Posting-of-Workers-Directive-implications-for-employers> (accessed 10 April 2019).

129. Interestingly, the cut off from the new Directive of the condition laid down in the Commission's proposal of avoiding a 'disproportionate' restriction of the cross-border provision of services apparently extends the Member States' margin of appreciation in determining the remuneration applicable to posted workers while, at the same time, narrowing down the scope for action of the Court of Justice. Rocca, 'Not Dead yet: Legal Strategies at National Level and the Reform of the EU Posting of Workers Directive' (n 6) 5–6; Costamagna (n 65) 16.

130. Article 1(2)(a) and (d) of Directive (EU) 2018/957 of the European Parliament and of the Council of 28 June 2018 amending Directive 96/71/EC concerning the posting of workers in the framework of the provision of services (n 2). In other words, the new Directive allows for the application of sectorial collective agreements, as well as of those concluded by the most representative employer and labour organisations at national level, also in addition to positive regulation or collective agreements with *erga omnes* effect. In turn, the original version of the PWD envisaged this possibility only in 'in the absence of a system for declaring collective agreements or arbitration awards to be of universal application'. Article 3(8) of Directive 96/71/EC of the European Parliament and of the Council of 16 December 1996 concerning the posting of workers in the framework of the provision of services (n 3). Nevertheless, the extension of the above-mentioned collective agreements to out-of-state service providers

to those collective agreements applicable *erga omnes*, the new rules expand their scope to all economic sectors, whereas previously they were mandatory in the construction industry only.[131] Besides, just like the original version of the Posting of Workers Directive, also the new Directive precludes the application of company-level collective agreements.[132]

What is more, from their first day of mobility abroad, posted workers are now entitled not only to equal remuneration *stricto sensu* as local workers but also to equal treatment with regard to the accommodation in a different location from their regular workplace.[133] And the same goes for the allowances or reimbursements of the expenditures for travel, board and lodging actually incurred by the posted workers on account of their temporary secondment in another Member States.[134] An addition to Article 3(7) specifically clarifies that such expenses are not deductible from the workers' salaries (being excluded from the concept of remuneration) and must be reimbursed by the employer in accordance with the law governing the employment relationship.[135] *Inter alia*, it is recalled that in *Sähköalojen ammattiliitto*[136] the Court already excluded meal vouchers as well from the computation of the elements falling

remains possible only on condition that the equality of treatment vis-à-vis national undertakings which are in a similar position is respected. As already required by the original PWD, in such an event, the host state shall be able to prove that all local undertakings operating in the sector and in the territory concerned are bounded by the same obligations having the same effects. Article 1(2)(d) of Directive (EU) 2018/957 of the European Parliament and of the Council of 28 June 2018 amending Directive 96/71/EC concerning the posting of workers in the framework of the provision of services (n 2).

131. Article 1(2)(a) of Directive (EU) 2018/957 of the European Parliament and of the Council of 28 June 2018 amending Directive 96/71/EC concerning the posting of workers in the framework of the provision of services (n 2). *See* European Commission Impact Assessment, Accompanying the document Proposal for a Directive of the European Parliament and the Council amending Directive 96/71/EC concerning the posting of workers in the framework of the provision of services (n 9) 24.
132. Such a choice has been, indeed, strongly criticised for showing poor sensitivity to the existing great diversity of collective bargaining in Europe. Further critics related to the fact that it basically headed in the opposite direction taken, over the last years, by the Commission, which pushed for the decentralisation of collective bargaining. Dhéret and Ghimis (n 26) 10; Lhernould (n 106) 7; Rocca, 'Not Dead yet: Legal Strategies at National Level and the Reform of the EU Posting of Workers Directive' (n 6) 7, 13–14; Rocca, 'Stepping Stones Over Troubled Waters. Recent Legal Evolutions and the Reform of the Posting of Workers Directive' (n 6) 173.
133. Article 1(2)(a)(h) of Directive (EU) 2018/957 of the European Parliament and of the Council of 28 June 2018 amending Directive 96/71/EC concerning the posting of workers in the framework of the provision of services (n 2).
134. *Ibid.* Article 1(2)(a)(i).
135. In other words, the costs for travel, board and lodging are paid or reimbursed by the employer on top of the remuneration. European Commission, 'Practical Guide on Posting' (n 127) 15–16. Notably, with a view to contrast the widespread elusive practices of companies imputing reimbursements for expenses incurred abroad by the posted workers within the total amount of remuneration, further worker protection is assured by the presumption that, in the absence of indication in the employment contract of which part of the allowance specific to the posting is paid as reimbursement of expenses and which part as remuneration, the entire allowance has to be considered as a reimbursement of expenditure. Article 1(2)(c) of Directive (EU) 2018/957 of the European Parliament and of the Council of 28 June 2018 amending Directive 96/71/EC concerning the posting of workers in the framework of the provision of services (n 2). On this point, *see* Eurofound (n 14); Van Nuffel and Afanasjeva (n 80) 1419.
136. *Sähköalojen ammattiliitto ry v Elektrobudowa Spolka Akcyjna* (n 122).

under the concept of remuneration. It follows that also meal vouchers shall be paid separately by the employer to the posted worker.[137]

8.3.2 Subcontracting and Temporary Agency Work

As previously mentioned, the specific provision tabled by the Commission, envisaging a Member States' faculty to oblige companies to subcontract only to service providers which grant their workers the same employment protection as provided by the main contractor, eventually never got to the end of the legislative process.[138] What the approved text of Directive (EU) 2018/957 prescribes in response to the abuses in subcontracting situations is, in turn, simply a general duty on the Member States to 'take appropriate measures [...] to ensure subcontracting liability'[139] in accordance with the more specific dispositions laid down in Article 12 of the Enforcement Directive 2014/67/EU.[140] By the way, a sort of compromise was found in the setting out of a duty on the Commission to assess by 30 July 2023 whether further measures in subcontracting are necessary in order to ensure a level playing field for businesses and the protection of workers.[141]

In turn, the Commission's proposal to ensure equal treatment between local and posted temporary agency workers with respect to remuneration and working conditions was accepted *in toto*. By virtue of a new paragraph 1b added to Article 3 of the Posting of Workers Directive,[142] posted temporary agency workers have been entitled to the same 'basic working and employment conditions' applicable ex Article 5 of the Temporary Agency Work Directive 2008/104/EC[143] to local temporary agency workers. In practice, while previously the standard of worker protection ensured under the Temporary Agency Work Directive, in order to be effective, had to be transposed into host country law,[144] after the entry into force of the new rules it is fully integrated into

137. *Ibid.* 70. On this point, *see supra* Chapter 3.
138. *See supra* section 8.2.
139. Directive (EU) 2018/957 of the European Parliament and of the Council of 28 June 2018 amending Directive 96/71/EC concerning the posting of workers in the framework of the provision of services (n 2).
140. Directive 2014/67/EU of the European Parliament and of the Council of 15 May 2014 on the enforcement of Directive 96/71/EC concerning the posting of workers in the framework of the provision of services and amending Regulation (EU) No 1024/2012 on administrative cooperation through the Internal Market Information System ('the IMI Regulation') (n 8). On the content of Article 12 of the Enforcement Directive, *see supra* Chapter 4.
141. Article 2(2) of Directive (EU) 2018/957 of the European Parliament and of the Council of 28 June 2018 amending Directive 96/71/EC concerning the posting of workers in the framework of the provision of services (n 2). On this point, *see* Van Nuffel and Afanasjeva (n 80) 1423; Głowacka (n 126) 32.
142. Article 1(2)(b) of Directive (EU) 2018/957 of the European Parliament and of the Council of 28 June 2018 amending Directive 96/71/EC concerning the posting of workers in the framework of the provision of services (n 2).
143. Directive 2008/104/EC of the European Parliament and of the Council of 19 November 2008 on temporary agency work (n 15). For the record, according to Article 3(1)(f) TAWD, the umbrella of 'basic working and employment conditions' covers working time, overtime, breaks, rest periods, night work, holidays and public holidays, and pay.
144. On the interplay between the PWD and the TAWD, *see supra* Chapter 3.

the amended Posting of Workers Directive and, therefore, fully enforceable.[145] In this sense, the user undertaking is required to inform the temporary work agency about the working conditions and remuneration that it applies to its own temporary workers, given that such an employment standard has been extended to posted workers as well.[146] The equal treatment principle was made even more effective by reviewing Article 3(9) in such a way as to grant the Member States with the possibility to guarantee posted temporary agency workers also equal treatment with regard to the other working and employment conditions that apply to local temporary agency workers.[147] This means that, for example, temporary agency workers who are posted abroad to a user undertaking bound by a more advantageous company-level collective agreement that has not been declared universally applicable, would then be entitled to the more favourable remuneration and working conditions applied to local temporary agency worker of the latter company.[148]

In addition, the new rules aim to address the particular situation, known as 'double' or 'chain' posting, when a worker who has been hired out by a temporary employment undertaking or placement agency to a user undertaking in a host Member State, is subsequently posted by that user undertaking to the territory of a third Member State.[149] The solution found to the problems arising from the circumvention of the rules by means of such types of elusive arrangements basically envisages a full responsibility as an employer of the first temporary agency for any subsequent posting.[150] Two new subparagraphs added to Article 1(3) clarify, at first, that the temporary employment undertaking or placement agency in an employment relationship with the posted worker has to be considered as the posting undertaking and that, as a consequence, the latter has to fully comply with the relevant provisions of the Posting of Workers Directive and its Enforcement Directive. Second, the user undertaking is, in its turn, compelled to promptly inform, before the commencement of the transnational service provision, the original temporary work agency about the workers who are temporarily

145. Van Nuffel and Afanasjeva (n 80) 1423–1424; Głowacka (n 126) 40; Costamagna (n 65) 22.
146. Article 1(2)(b) of Directive (EU) 2018/957 of the European Parliament and of the Council of 28 June 2018 amending Directive 96/71/EC concerning the posting of workers in the framework of the provision of services (n 2). Incidentally, as explained in Preamble Recital 12 of Directive (EU) 2018/957, such a duty to inform falls short whenever the Member States decide, after consulting the social partners, to make recourse to one of the options provided for in Article 5(2) and (3) of Directive 2008/104/EC to derogate from the principles of equal treatment and equal pay.
147. *Ibid.* Article 1(2)(e). On this point, *see* Van Nuffel and Afanasjeva (n 80) 1424.
148. Voss et al. (n 5) 46; Van Nuffel and Afanasjeva (n 80) 1424; European Commission, 'Practical Guide on Posting' (n 127) 10.
149. Preamble Recital 13 of Directive (EU) 2018/957 of the European Parliament and of the Council of 28 June 2018 amending Directive 96/71/EC concerning the posting of workers in the framework of the provision of services (n 2). On the risks connected to such a particular arrangement, *see supra* Chapter 7.
150. Van Nuffel and Afanasjeva (n 80) 1424–1425; European Commission, 'Practical Guide on Posting' (n 127) 11.

posted abroad so that the more favourable terms and conditions of employment can be effectively applied.[151]

8.3.3 Long-Term Posting

The intrinsic nature of posting of workers across borders in the framework of the free provision of services is, by definition, temporary. Besides expressly acknowledging that,[152] Directive (EU) 2018/957 goes even further by setting out, for the first time in the EU labour law context, a fixed time limit.[153] By virtue of the new paragraph 1a of Article 3 of the Posting of Workers Directive, in the event of a posting lasting for a period longer than twelve months, the seconded workers shall be treated almost as regular local workers. Crucially, even in case of long-term working assignments abroad, the employees concerned do not lose their qualification as posted,[154] although they become entitled to the more protective employment standards of the host country, where applicable. In addition to the terms and conditions of employment listed in the amended Article 3(1) of the Posting of Workers Directive, the posting undertaking is obliged to guarantee to its workers temporarily seconded to the territory of another Member State all further favourable conditions which are mandatorily applicable in the latter country of destination.[155] To that extent, the new provision covers only those terms and conditions which are laid down by law, regulations or administrative provisions, as well as by collective agreements or arbitration awards applicable *erga omnes*, and also of those which are generally applicable in the geographical area or in the industry concerned, or those concluded by the most representative employers' and labour organisations at national level and having nation-wide effect.[156]

The implementation of the principle of equal treatment after twelve months of posting is, however, subject to two exceptions. First, it cannot be extended to the procedures, formalities and conditions (including non-competition clauses) related to the conclusion and termination of the employment contract and neither to supplementary pension schemes. Second, the maximum posting timeframe may be prolonged up

151. Article 1(1)(c)(ii) of Directive (EU) 2018/957 of the European Parliament and of the Council of 28 June 2018 amending Directive 96/71/EC concerning the posting of workers in the framework of the provision of services (n 2).
152. 'Posting is temporary in nature. Posted workers usually return to the Member State from which they were posted after completion of the work for which they were posted.' *Ibid.* Preamble Recital 9.
153. As explained in the preamble of Directive (EU) 2018/957, the fixing of a time limit for posting was specifically designed to address situations of excessively long-term secondments of workforce which are eventually characterised by the creation of a sort of 'link between the labour market of the host Member State and the workers posted for such long periods'. *Ibid.*
154. Lhernould (n 106) 5.
155. This is the case, for instance, of specific age-related leave regulations or premiums for research and developments funds. Deloitte Belgium (n 119) figure 9.
156. Article 1(2)(b) of Directive (EU) 2018/957 of the European Parliament and of the Council of 28 June 2018 amending Directive 96/71/EC concerning the posting of workers in the framework of the provision of services (n 2). It follows that, even after twelve months of posting, all other collective agreements, in particular those having merely company-level scope, will still not find application. Rocca, 'Not Dead yet: Legal Strategies at National Level and the Reform of the EU Posting of Workers Directive' (n 6) 7, 13–14.

to total eighteen months upon submission of a motivated notification by the service provider to the competent authority in the host country.[157]

As to the specific substance of the additional set of host state's terms and conditions of employment applicable to postings exceeding twelve or, when applicable, eighteen months, Preamble Recital 10 of the new Directive reminds the necessary compatibility of whatever national provision with the freedom to provide services. In light of the Court's settled case law, only restrictions which are justified by overriding reasons of public interest and which, at the same time, respect the principle of proportionality are permitted.[158] Nevertheless, if, on the one hand, it is certain that the Member States are not allowed to prohibit posting assignments longer than twelve (or eighteen) months,[159] on the other hand, it remains rather unclear to what extent the host state's additional impositions should still comply with the so-called 'market access' test forbidding any restriction 'which is liable to prohibit, impede or render less advantageous the activities of a provider of services established in another Member State where he lawfully provides similar services'.[160]

Of central importance is then the nature of the newly established maximum timeframe for posting. Besides concerning individual workers on long-term postings, this time limit applies also to employees who are posted one right after the other. More specifically, the calculation of the posting period shall take into account also the situation when an undertaking replaces a posted worker with another one 'performing the same task at the same place'.[161] In order to find out the coincidence of the task performed and the place where the work is carried out, an examination of all the circumstances of the cross-border secondment of workforce is prescribed, namely to look at the nature of the service provided, the type of work carried out and its actual location.[162] From this, it follows that the legal treatment reserved to the posted workers involved in consecutive postings may substantially vary depending on how many workers have already been assigned by the same employer to carry out the same task in the same workplace. As a matter of fact, in the event a worker is posted to an assignment abroad where other colleagues have been previously employed for a cumulative period of twelve months (or eighteen months), he would be covered by all

157. Article 1(2)(b) of Directive (EU) 2018/957 of the European Parliament and of the Council of 28 June 2018 amending Directive 96/71/EC concerning the posting of workers in the framework of the provision of services (n 2). The margin of appreciation of the host Member State with regard to the concession of such a prorogation is apparently rather limited, provided that the wording of the Directive seems to imply a quasi-automatic six-month extension on condition that the employer submits a motivated notification. Van Nuffel and Afanasjeva (n 80) 1422.
158. Preamble Recital 10 of Directive (EU) 2018/957 of the European Parliament and of the Council of 28 June 2018 amending Directive 96/71/EC concerning the posting of workers in the framework of the provision of services (n 2). On the practical content of overriding reasons of public interest and of the principle of proportionality in the context of posting, *see* the analysis carried out *supra* in Chapters 3 and 4.
159. Van Nuffel and Afanasjeva (n 80) 1422.
160. *Manfred Säger v Dennemeyer & Co Ltd* [1991] ECJ Case C-76/90, ECLI:EU:C:1991:331 [12]. For a definition of the so-called 'market access' test, *see supra* Chapter 3.
161. Article 1(2)(b) of Directive (EU) 2018/957 of the European Parliament and of the Council of 28 June 2018 amending Directive 96/71/EC concerning the posting of workers in the framework of the provision of services (n 2).
162. *Ibid.* Article 1(2)(b).

the more protective labour rules of the host Member State. In turn, the other employees posted beforehand would still be treated according to their home state law, apart from the terms and conditions set out by Article 3(1) of the amended Posting of Workers Directive.

In this regard, it is worth noting that Directive (EU) 2018/957 did not take on board the Commission's suggestion to consider, for the purpose of the accumulation of consecutive posting periods, only those 'workers that are posted for an effective duration of at least six months'.[163] Consequently, it may give rise to the paradoxical outcome whereby a worker seconded for just a few days in the context of a posting chain is treated almost like a long-term migrant worker by reason of the prior secondment of his colleagues. To be clear, the newly established rule which takes into account the cumulative duration of different posting periods has nothing to do with the protection of the posted workers involved. *Au contraire*, as stated by the Directive itself, its sole purpose is to shield the host country's labour market from the competition of out-of-state service providers taking advantage of elusive constructions in the form of consecutive secondments and rotation of personnel.[164] What has not been taken into consideration is, however, that such a provision is liable to generate rather serious problems in terms of determination of the applicable legal regime as appropriate and consequent enforcement of the rules.

8.3.4 Transparency and Enforcement of the Rules

The most relevant improvement brought about by the new Directive at the level of transparency and enforcement of the rules concerns the requirement for the Member States to make public and accessible all information on the terms and conditions of employment applicable to foreign workers posted to their territory. By virtue of the amended Article 3, the Member States have to publish all information on the terms and conditions of employment, as laid down by national law and/or collective bargaining agreements, on the single official national website created in accordance with Article 5 of the Enforcement Directive 2014/67/EU. Such a duty encompasses the accurate and updated indication of all the constituent elements of remuneration as well.[165] The new Directive also specifies the cumulative character of the liability for compliance with the

163. Article 1(1) of the European Commission Proposal for a Directive of the European Parliament and of the Council amending Directive 96/71/EC of the European Parliament and of the Council of 16 December 1996 concerning the posting of workers in the framework of the provision of services (n 9).
164. Preamble Recital 11 of Directive (EU) 2018/957 of the European Parliament and of the Council of 28 June 2018 amending Directive 96/71/EC concerning the posting of workers in the framework of the provision of services (n 2). On this point, *see* Benio (n 128); Stefan Schwarz, Marcin Kiełbasa and Marek Benio, 'Limited Cumulative Period of Posting in the Revised Posting of Workers Directive – In Search of a Legal Justification' (2018) *Labour Mobility Initiative Association* 4–5 <https://www.mobilelabour.eu/wp-content/uploads/2018/10/paper-Limited-cumulative-period-of-posting-in-the-revised-PWD-%E2%80%93-in-search-of-a-legal-justification-by-LMIA.pdf> (accessed 19 October 2018).
165. Article 1(2)(a) of Directive (EU) 2018/957 of the European Parliament and of the Council of 28 June 2018 amending Directive 96/71/EC concerning the posting of workers in the framework of the provision of services (n 2).

rules concerning the posted workers' remuneration. As a result, the incomplete or outdated information on the single national website, leading to an infringement by the employer of the host state's provisions on posted workers' employment terms and conditions, has to be taken into account as an attenuating circumstance.[166]

Looking more generally at the above-mentioned transparency requirement of the regime applicable to posted workers, it is worth emphasising once again the inspiration drawn from the case law of the Court of Justice. In *Laval*, for example, the European judiciary stressed the need for national provisions to be 'sufficiently precise and accessible that they do not render it impossible or excessively difficult in practice' for the out-of-state service provider 'to determine the obligations with which it is required to comply as regards minimum pay'.[167] Similarly, in its subsequent decision in *Sähköalojen ammattiliitto*, the Court required those rules to be not only binding but also 'accessible and clear'.[168]

Over and above the aforementioned innovation, the 2018 reform dedicates a number of new provisions to the enhancement of transnational administrative cooperation and exchange of information between the competent national authorities. With a view to tackling frauds and abuses in situations of non-genuine posting, the regulatory framework put in place by the Enforcement Directive 2014/67/EU has been complemented by a further imposition on competent national authorities or bodies of a reciprocal duty of replying to reasoned requests for information. The competent authorities in the countries of origin are encouraged to actively participate in the search for the information requested by their counterparts in the host Member States and, in the event of persistent delay, the Commission is informed and empowered to adopt appropriate countermeasures.[169]

With regard to the monitoring, control and enforcement of the rules laid down in the revised Posting of Workers Directive and in the Enforcement Directive, a new Article 5 imposes full responsibility on both the sending and receiving Member States.[170] The latter have to implement the Directive by introducing, *inter alia*, a sufficiently deterrent, proportionate and effective system of penalties, while guaranteeing the availability of adequate instruments to workers and trade unions for the

166. *Ibid.* Article 1(2)(a). On this point, *see* Benio (n 128).
167. *Laval un Partneri Ltd v Svenska Byggnadsarbetareförbundet, Svenska Byggnadsarbetareförbundets avdelning 1, Byggettan and Svenska Elektrikerförbundet* (n 1) para. 110. A similar requirement was imposed few years before as well in *Arblade & Fils SARL v Sofrage SARL* [1999] ECJ Joined Cases C-369/96 and C-376/96, ECLI:EU:C:1999:575 [43]. On this point, *see* Rocca, 'Not Dead yet: Legal Strategies at National Level and the Reform of the EU Posting of Workers Directive' (n 6) 6; Rocca, 'Stepping Stones over Troubled Waters. Recent Legal Evolutions and the Reform of the Posting of Workers Directive' (n 6) 171.
168. *Sähköalojen ammattiliitto ry v Elektrobudowa Spolka Akcyjna* (n 122) para. 40. *See* Rocca, 'Not Dead yet: Legal Strategies at National Level and the Reform of the EU Posting of Workers Directive' (n 6) 9–10; Rocca, 'Stepping Stones over Troubled Waters. Recent Legal Evolutions and the Reform of the Posting of Workers Directive' (n 6) 175.
169. Article 1(3) of Directive (EU) 2018/957 of the European Parliament and of the Council of 28 June 2018 amending Directive 96/71/EC concerning the posting of workers in the framework of the provision of services (n 2).
170. *Ibid.* Article 1(4)(1).

protection of their rights.[171] Especially in situations of illegal posting ascertained by means of the criteria listed in Article 4 of Directive 2014/67/EU,[172] the protection of the workers concerned has to be ensured, even though they are not genuinely posted and they consequently fall outside the scope of the Posting of Workers Directive. Notably, it is up to the Member States to ensure that those workers can benefit from 'relevant law and practice' and that they are not treated according to 'less favourable conditions than those applicable to posted workers'.[173] Oddly enough, unlike what normally happens under the EU rules on social security coordination[174] (at least until the series of CJEU's decisions in *Altun*,[175] *Commission v Belgium*,[176] *Alpenrind*[177] and *CRPNPAC and Vueling Airlines*[178]), in cases of abusive recourse to posting, the competent authorities of the receiving Member State are apparently empowered to autonomously and unilaterally enforce national labour provisions.[179]

8.4 EXPECTED IMPACT AND SHORTCOMINGS

After having analysed the substantial content of the revision of the Posting of Workers Directive, it is now time to estimate the potential impact of the new measures on the current state of play and their ability to cope with the issues they are proposed to address. More specifically, this section aims to assess whether the condition of the posted workers will actually be improved and whether a level playing field for businesses will eventually be achieved. It does so by first looking at the improvements in terms of simplification and clarification of the rules and fight against abusive practices. Second, it stresses the shortcomings emerging from the newly established legal framework, especially focusing on the new provisions on long-term postings and their interaction with the relevant private international law, EU internal market law

171. *Ibid.* Article 1(4)(2) and (3).
172. For an analysis of such criteria for the individuation of the cross-border company's genuine establishment in a certain Member State and for the recognition of a genuine posting activity, *see supra* Chapter 4.
173. Article 1(4)(4) and (5) of Directive (EU) 2018/957 of the European Parliament and of the Council of 28 June 2018 amending Directive 96/71/EC concerning the posting of workers in the framework of the provision of services (n 2). On this point, *see* Van Nuffel and Afanasjeva (n 80) 1425. Interestingly, the new provision at stake takes up (and gives legal force to) the content of Preamble Recital 11 of Directive 2014/67/EU of the European Parliament and of the Council of 15 May 2014 on the enforcement of Directive 96/71/EC concerning the posting of workers in the framework of the provision of services and amending Regulation (EU) No 1024/2012 on administrative cooperation through the Internal Market Information System ('the IMI Regulation') (n 8).
174. Under EU social security law, the receiving state doubting of the validity or accuracy of the A1 or E101 certificates is normally supposed to refer the matter to the competent authorities of the sending state. On this point, *see supra* Chapter 5.
175. *Altun* [2018] CJEU Case C-359/16, ECLI:EU:C:2018:63.
176. *European Commission v Kingdom of Belgium* [2018] CJEU Case C-356/15, ECLI:EU:C:2018:555.
177. *Alpenrind and Others* [2018] CJEU Case C-527/16, ECLI:EU:C:2018:669.
178. *Caisse de retraite du personnel navigant professionnel de l'aéronautique civile (CRPNPAC) v Vueling Airlines SA v Vueling Airlines SA and Jean-Luc Poignant* [2020] CJEU Joined Cases C-370/17 and C-37/18, ECLI:EU:C:2020:260.
179. Costamagna (n 65) 22–23.

and EU social security law. After that, the investigation assumes a more concrete form by focusing on the expected economic effects of the reform.

8.4.1 Small Improvements and More Uncertainty

First and foremost, one cannot refrain from pointing out that the new Directive (EU) 2018/957 is potentially able to provide a number of positive practical innovations, albeit only in very limited circumstances with rather minor impact. This is the case of the concrete determination of the pay due to the posted workers, which has certainly been streamlined by the specific indication of all its components, as well as by the obligation to publish all its constituent element on the single official national website.[180] And the same goes for all the other applicable terms and conditions of employment of the host state as well.[181] Although they undoubtedly contribute to improving the levels of legal clarity and EU harmonisation, the consequences of these new provisions are, nonetheless, mostly confined to those few Member States which have not broadly implemented the Posting of Workers Directive nor adjusted their regulation to the latest relevant case law of the Court of Justice yet.[182] In fact, as already mentioned *supra* in Chapter 7, countries like Belgium, France and Italy had already anticipated some of the effects of the 2018 reform at the time when they implemented the Posting of Workers Directive in a broad sense and adapted their concept of minimum rates of pay to the outcome of the CJEU decision in *Sähköalojen ammattiliitto.*[183]

In the same vein, as anticipated by the Commission in its Impact Assessment accompanying the 2016 proposal, the extension of the validity of universally binding collective agreements to all economic sectors is expected to offer additional instruments to set posted workers' wages. Nevertheless, its practical effectiveness will be potentially relevant in Germany, Ireland, Luxembourg and Cyprus only, since the largest recipients Member States have already profited from the possibility, granted by the second indent of Article 3(10) of the original Posting of Workers Directive, of extending the application of collective agreements and arbitration awards to posted workers occupied in other economic sectors.[184] Similarly, the revision of the rules

180. Jean-Philippe Lhernould and Barbara Palli, 'Posted Workers Remuneration: Comparative Study in Nine EU Countries and Four Sectors' (2017) 24 Maastricht Journal of European and Comparative Law 108, 126.
181. European Commission Impact Assessment, Accompanying the document Proposal for a Directive of the European Parliament and the Council amending Directive 96/71/EC concerning the posting of workers in the framework of the provision of services (n 9) 32 and 38.
182. van Hoek (n 23) 482.
183. *Sähköalojen ammattiliitto ry v Elektrobudowa Spolka Akcyjna* (n 122). On this point, *see* Deloitte Belgium (n 119) figure 7; Rocca, 'Not Dead yet: Legal Strategies at National Level and the Reform of the EU Posting of Workers Directive' (n 6) 12.
184. European Commission Impact Assessment, Accompanying the document Proposal for a Directive of the European Parliament and the Council amending Directive 96/71/EC concerning the posting of workers in the framework of the provision of services (n 9) 24 and 30. *See also* Novitz (n 34); Zahn, 'Revision of the Posted Workers' Directive: Equality at Last?' (n 4) 14; van Hoek (n 23) 482; Lhernould (n 106) 7. On the specific content of Article 3(10) of the PWD, *see supra* Chapter 3.

concerning posted temporary agency workers valuably narrowed down the space for abusive practices of 'double' or 'chain' posting and formally introduced equal treatment between local and posted agency workers. However, the latter principle had already been implemented in most of the Member States having a high share of workers posted through temporary agencies.[185]

Besides the above-mentioned (limited) positive outcomes, the new Directive still has a number of relevant gaps and is likely to lead to issues and uncertainties. In view of the remaining competence of the Member States to concretely determine the rules on remuneration in their own territory, the concept of 'remuneration' is likely to remain still rather uncertain.[186] In effect, in order to be extended to posted workers, those norms still have to be justified by overriding reasons of public interest (e.g., worker protection) and avoid unnecessary or disproportionate restrictions of the cross-border provision of services.[187]

As previously noted, pursuant to the new Article 3(8) of the revised Directive, the host Member State is allowed to require out-of-state service providers to respect the terms and conditions of employment, including remuneration, set out by collective agreements having sectorial effect or concluded by the most representative employers' and labour organisations at national level, even in the presence of a system for declaring collective agreements or arbitration awards applicable *erga omnes*. Such a novelty is certainly resolving the situation emerged in *Rüffert*,[188] whereby the application to posted workers of generally applicable collective agreements, and thus higher labour standards, was pre-empted by the existence of a system for declaring collective agreements as universally applicable.[189] Yet, in case of the overlapping scope of a universally applicable collective agreement with another which has not been declared universally binding, complications may arise when it comes to determining which of the two has to find application in any given case. Moreover, gaps in protection may emerge in the event the application of a certain collective agreement remains excluded for being concluded by an employer organisation which is not included among the most representative organisations at national level.[190]

185. European Commission Impact Assessment, Accompanying the document Proposal for a Directive of the European Parliament and the Council amending Directive 96/71/EC concerning the posting of workers in the framework of the provision of services (n 9) 40–41 and Annex VI; Costamagna (n 65) 22.
186. Magdalena Bernaciak and Zane Rasnača, 'Not as Simple as It Should Be? Why the Judicial Enforcement of Posted Workers' Rights Needs Improvement' (*LSE European Politics and Policy (EUROPP) Blog*, 5 March 2020) 3 <http://eprints.lse.ac.uk/104999/> (accessed 2 August 2020).
187. Lhernould and Palli (n 180) 126.
188. *Dirk Rüffert v Land Niedersachsen* (n 12).
189. Rocca, 'Not Dead yet: Legal Strategies at National Level and the Reform of the EU Posting of Workers Directive' (n 6) 6; Rocca, 'Stepping Stones over Troubled Waters. Recent Legal Evolutions and the Reform of the Posting of Workers Directive' (n 6) 172.
190. Reingard Zimmer, 'The Revision of the Posting of Workers Directive and Its Impact on National Law' in Jacek Kubera and Tomasz Morozowski (eds), *A 'Social Turn' in the European Union?: New Trends and Ideas about Social Convergence in Europe* (First Edition, Routledge 2020) 104–105.

Importantly, even after the entry into force of the new Directive, the EU regulatory framework for posting still remains unable to cope with the serious issues emerging from the use of subcontracting chains. Despite the adoption of the Enforcement Directive 2014/67/EU, a provision extending the 'subcontracting liability' beyond that of the first subcontractor is, indeed, still lacking.[191] Admittedly, the Commission proposed to empower the Member States of the faculty to oblige companies to subcontract only to service providers which granted their workers the same employment protection as provided by the main contractor. Nevertheless, that measure eventually never saw the light.

The impact of the setting of a twelve (or eighteen)-month time limit for posting is, in its turn, extremely controversial. On the one hand, it definitely solves the long-lasting dispute over the maximum duration of the special labour regime for posted workers in the country where they carry out their tasks. On the other hand, though, it gives rise to practical complications in relation to the legal position and treatment of those workers assigned to long-term postings abroad or replacing other workers in the context of postings exceeding the maximum time limit. In such an occurrence, the single employment relation results indeed covered by two different national labour regimes, one after the other. Evidently, this situation is likely to affect legal certainty and clarity with regard to the substantive standard of worker protection to be ensured.[192]

In addition, the interaction of the new rules with the relevant private international law is perceived as rather problematic as well. The new Directive seems to imply, in case of long-term posting, a change of the workers' habitual place of work and, consequently, of the applicable legal regime from home state law to host state law.[193] In other words, it would substantially overcome the choice of law made by the parties in accordance with Article 3 of the Rome I Regulation.[194] However, uncertainty arises about the compatibility of such an interpretation with Article 8(2) of the Rome I Regulation, given that the latter legal instrument clearly excludes a change of the habitual place of work in the event a worker is temporarily employed in another country.[195] And pursuant to Preamble Recital 36 of the same act, the temporariness of the work depends upon the expectation of the employees to resume working in their

---

191. Tonia Novitz and Rutvica Andrijasevic, 'Reform of the Posting of Workers Regime – An Assessment of the Practical Impact on Unfree Labour Relations' (2020) 58 JCMS: Journal of Common Market Studies 1325, 1337. On the existence of such a shortcoming already at the time of the adoption of the Enforcement Directive, *see supra* Chapter 4.
192. van Hoek (n 23) 481.
193. Notably, the Commission's original proposal explicitly suggested a change of habitual place of work in cases of postings exceeding twenty-four months of duration. Article 1(1) of the European Commission Proposal for a Directive of the European Parliament and of the Council amending Directive 96/71/EC of the European Parliament and of the Council of 16 December 1996 concerning the posting of workers in the framework of the provision of services (n 9). In this sense, *see* Lhernould (n 106) 6.
194. 'A contract shall be governed by the law chosen by the parties.' Article 3(1) of Regulation (EC) No 593/2008 of the European Parliament and of the Council of 17 June 2008 on the law applicable to contractual obligations (Rome I) 2008 (OJ L 177/6). On this point, *see* Benio (n 128).
195. Schwarz, Kiełbasa and Benio (n 164) 5–6.

country of origin after carrying out their tasks abroad.[196] The possible conflict with private international law lies, therefore, in the fact that, even in situations where workers are posted abroad for more than twelve (or eighteen) months, there is no doubt that they are supposed to return to their home country once their job is done (at least in case of genuine posting). In contrast, a possible reading of the new rules in compliance with those laid down in the Rome I Regulation has been suggested by Advocate General Campos Sánchez-Bordona in *Hungary v European Parliament, Council of the European Union*. In rejecting the claims advanced by Hungary in this regard, the Spanish amicus curiae resolved the possible issue by making reference to the exception contained in Article 23 of the Rome I Regulation, which gives precedence to specific provisions of EU law on conflict of laws.[197]

Even more importantly, the shift to the territorial application of labour law (i.e., host state law), aimed at guaranteeing equal treatment between local and long-term posted workers, delineates an inconsistency with the legal basis of the Posting of Workers Directive.[198] As widely explained *supra* in Chapter 2, full equal treatment is in principle reserved only to migrant workers who move to another Member State in accordance with Article 45 TFEU on free movement of workers. On the other hand, the activity of posting falls under Article 56 TFEU on free provision of services, which is typically governed by the law of the country of origin (i.e., home state law). However, in treating a long-term posted worker (or even a short-term posted workers involved in a long-term assignment abroad) almost as a full-fledged migrant worker, the new provisions concerning postings exceeding twelve or, when applicable, eighteen months are nearer the free movement of workers' end of the spectrum than that of the free movement of services.[199] In other words, with the adoption of the new Directive, the EU legislator basically introduced a double standard for the exercise of the freedom to provide services within the internal market. In the event the cross-border provision of services will not involve any mobility of workforce in the form of posting, the activity

196. For a clarification of the concepts of temporariness of the work and habitual place of work in cases of posting under the Rome I Regulation, *see* the analysis carried out *supra* in Chapters 2 and 3.

197. In the wording of the Rome I Regulation: 'this Regulation shall not prejudice the application of provisions of Community law which, in relation to particular matters, lay down conflict-of-law rules relating to contractual obligations'. Article 23 of the Regulation (EC) No 593/2008 of the European Parliament and of the Council of 17 June 2008 on the law applicable to contractual obligations (Rome I) (n 194). In this sense, *see Hungary v European Parliament, Council of the European Union, Opinion of Advocate General Manuel Campos Sánchez-Bordona delivered on 28 May 2020* (n 110) paras 192–201.

198. In this sense, *see* Catherine Barnard, 'The Commission's Proposal Deletes the Treaty Distinction between Migrant Workers and Posted Workers' (IV European Labour Mobility Congress (ELMC), Krakow (Poland), 7 November 2016) <https://www.elmc.eu/2016/the-commissions-proposal-deletes-the-treaty-distinction-between-migrant-workers-and-posted-workers-prof-catherine-barnards-speech-at-the-iv-european-labour-mobility-cong/> (accessed 13 May 2018); Schwarz, Kiełbasa and Benio (n 164) 4.

199. Oddly enough, given the cumulative calculation of the posting period, in the event a worker is posted to an assignment abroad where other colleagues have been previously employed for a cumulative period of twelve months (or eighteen months), he would be immediately treated almost as a long-term migrant worker (even in case his tasks are expected to last just a few days).

at issue will still be governed by the Treaty rules on services. Conversely, when the exercise of this freedom will entail a transnational flow of posted workers, the principle of *lex loci laboris* will find more and more space, by derogation from Article 56 TFEU. Host country law will almost fully apply in case of a posting involving temporary agency workers or workers involved in long-term assignments abroad. Interestingly, though, such a major change was not accompanied by any amendment of the Directive's legal basis, which remains anchored to Article 56 TFEU.

Finally, further attention is dedicated to the approach taken by the EU legislator in dealing with the existing mismatch between the Posting of Workers Directive and Regulation (EC) 883/2004 on social security coordination as regards the respective individuation of a posting period. Looking back at the reasons for establishing the twelve-month maximum posting period envisaged by the 2018 reform, it should be noted that, as previously explained in the analysis of the new Directive's adoption process, the original proposal of the Commission envisaged an ideal twenty-four-month limit.[200] The latter was subsequently reshaped into a compromise solution of a twelve-month limit, extendable to eighteen months, for the purpose of pleasing France, which was pushing for a strict twelve-month maximum duration of posting.[201] Consequently, while the Commission's proposal directly aimed at remedying the existing mismatch with the relevant provisions of EU social security law,[202] such a purpose was evidently not present in the final version of Directive (EU) 2018/957.[203] The eventually agreed twelve-month limit for posting is not causing any further friction in that regard, nonetheless, the EU legislator surely lost an opportunity to harmonise the currently misaligned EU labour and social security rules.[204] Crucially, this failure is not limited to the individuation of a similar posting period, but it concern also the overall conception of posting, which still remains fundamentally uncertain.

200. Article 1(1) of the European Commission Proposal for a Directive of the European Parliament and of the Council amending Directive 96/71/EC of the European Parliament and of the Council of 16 December 1996 concerning the posting of workers in the framework of the provision of services (n 9).
201. Stupp (n 82); Barbière (n 82); Maurice (n 82).
202. This purpose is confirmed in the Impact Assessment accompanying the proposal, where it states that 'This provision would meet the objective of aligning the Posting of Workers Directive with the conditions set by the Regulation on the coordination of social security systems as regards long-term posting, thus eliminating a source of inconsistency in the EU regulatory framework.' European Commission Impact Assessment, Accompanying the document Proposal for a Directive of the European Parliament and the Council amending Directive 96/71/EC concerning the posting of workers in the framework of the provision of services (n 9) 25.
203. Testament to this is also the fact that the establishment of a similar twelve-month maximum posting period was never on the table during the discussions for the approval of a new piece of secondary EU legislation amending Regulation (EC) No 883/2004. European Commission Proposal for a Regulation of the European Parliament and of the Council amending Regulation (EC) No 883/2004 on the coordination of social security systems and regulation (EC) No 987/2009 laying down the procedure for implementing Regulation (EC) No 883/2004 (n 21).
204. Lhernould (n 106) 6.

8.4.2 Economic Effects

Moving to the potential economic effects of the revision of the Posting of Workers Directive, the most remarkable aspect is definitely the benefit for workers and enterprises (especially SMEs) in the receiving high-wage Member States to the detriment of those in the sending low-wage Member States.[205] The expected result is an EU labour market whereby all actors are treated equally as regards wage rules, and the competition concerns non-wage factors only.[206] Accordingly, the imposition from day one of the same rules on remuneration for local and posted workers, and the extension of the validity of *erga omnes* collective agreements to all economic sectors, will substantially reduce wage differentials between local and posted workers.[207] In such a context, the salary level of the cross-border employees is likely to increase, especially with respect to those posted from low-wage to high-wage countries, and to a lesser extent to those seconded from medium to high-wage countries.[208] Importantly, though, this salary increase is necessarily conditional on the posted worker's retention of their jobs as a consequence of their employer's loss of competitiveness.

Against this background, the question arises as to whether posting will become less profitable, or even not advantageous anymore. What is certain is that equal rules on wages for posted and local workers will not necessarily entail equal nominal wages, let alone equal labour costs between out-of-state and local undertakings. Differences in pay structures, social security contributions and taxation will still represent a decisive factor on total labour costs, thus preserving a competitive advantage for companies established in countries with lower nominal rates vis-à-vis those located in the receiving countries with higher standards.[209] At the same time, also considering that

205. European Commission Impact Assessment, Accompanying the document Proposal for a Directive of the European Parliament and the Council amending Directive 96/71/EC concerning the posting of workers in the framework of the provision of services (n 9) 43; Barslund, Busse and Wispelaere (n 27) 5; Uglješa Grušić, 'European Labour Market Posted Workers Directive and the Social Implications of the Movement of Labour' in Horatia Muir Watt et al. (eds), *Global Private International Law: Adjudication Without Frontiers* (Edward Elgar Publishing 2018) 477; Schwarz (n 57); Rocca, 'Not Dead yet: Legal Strategies at National Level and the Reform of the EU Posting of Workers Directive' (n 6) 5; Catherine Jacqueson and Frans Pennings, 'Equal Treatment of Mobile Persons in the Context of a Social Market Economy' (2019) 15 Utrecht Law Review 64, 80; Rocca, 'Stepping Stones Over Troubled Waters. Recent Legal Evolutions and the Reform of the Posting of Workers Directive' (n 6) 171; Tomasz Grzegorz Grosse, 'A Social Europe or a More Protectionist One? The Single Market in the Aftermath of the Crises' in Jacek Kubera and Tomasz Morozowski (eds), *A 'Social Turn' in the European Union?: New Trends and Ideas about Social Convergence in Europe* (First Edition, Routledge 2020) 45.
206. European Commission Impact Assessment, Accompanying the document Proposal for a Directive of the European Parliament and the Council amending Directive 96/71/EC concerning the posting of workers in the framework of the provision of services (n 9) 30 and 43.
207. *Ibid.* 31 and 42.
208. The significant diversity of bonuses and allowances across the Member States and sectoral collective agreements makes the quantification of possible wage increases extremely complex though. *Ibid.* 37; Van Nuffel and Afanasjeva (n 80) 1419.
209. European Commission Impact Assessment, Accompanying the document Proposal for a Directive of the European Parliament and the Council amending Directive 96/71/EC concerning the posting of workers in the framework of the provision of services (n 9) 37–38 and 78 and ff.; Barslund, Busse and Wispelaere (n 27) 6.

almost half of the postings take place from high-wages EU countries,[210] the demand for foreign temporary workers in order to fill labour and skill shortages will continue to be there regardless.[211]

Conversely, as a result of the introduction of the principle of equal pay between local and posted workers, as well as of the possibility to extend further employment terms of host state law, the total labour costs related to posting will inevitably increase, particularly for companies whose employees currently earn just above the minimum local wage.[212] In addition, despite the new Directive does not directly envisage any administrative burden or cost for cross-border service providers,[213] the latter will in all likelihood be affected by the additional costs and legal risks deriving from the necessity, in cases of longer or consecutive secondments, of transferring their employees under the host state's labour regime.[214] In such cases, the cross-border workers concerned will not materially benefit from any salary increase while, in turn, they will possibly suffer indirectly from their employers' loss of competitiveness.[215] After all, the revision of the Posting of Workers Directive may, therefore, have, in some instances, the effect of hindering the cross-border provision of services of enterprises which come from low-wage Member States and operate in countries with higher social standards by making recourse to posting of workers.[216]

What is more, putting such projected outcomes into context, the investigation at stake cannot refrain from taking into account the actual distribution of posting within the EU internal market and, especially, its high degree of concentration.[217] In light of the very diversified incidence of this form of intra-EU labour mobility depending on the country and, even more, on the business sector concerned, the economic effects of the reform will naturally take a sectoral inclination.[218] In this regard, it is worth noting that,

210. On the actual distribution of the posting phenomenon within the EU internal market, *see supra* Chapter 6.
211. Barslund, Busse and Wispelaere (n 27) 6–7.
212. Elena Vaccarino and Zsolt Darvas, '"Social Dumping" and Posted Workers: A New Clash within the EU' (*Bruegel*, 7 March 2016) <http://bruegel.org/2016/03/social-dumping-and-posted-workers-a-new-clash-within-the-eu/> (accessed 13 May 2018); Barslund, Busse and Wispelaere (n 27) 7; Schwarz (n 57); Grosse (n 205) 45; Martin Koppernock, 'On the Future of "Social Europe" – Between Competitiveness and High Social Standards' in Jacek Kubera and Tomasz Morozowski (eds), *A 'Social Turn' in the European Union?: New Trends and Ideas about Social Convergence in Europe* (First Edition, Routledge 2020) 174.
213. European Commission Impact Assessment, Accompanying the document Proposal for a Directive of the European Parliament and the Council amending Directive 96/71/EC concerning the posting of workers in the framework of the provision of services (n 9) 43. Nonetheless, it is worth noting that Directive (EU) 2018/957 definitely envisages administrative burdens on the Member states, which will be required to publish all terms and conditions of employment, including all detailed elements of remuneration, applicable to workers posted to their territory on the single official national website created in accordance with Article 5 of the Enforcement Directive 2014/67/EU.
214. Zsolt Darvas, 'Revision of the Posted Workers Directive Misses the Point' (*Bruegel*, 18 October 2017) <https://bruegel.org/2017/10/revision-of-the-posted-workers-directive-misses-the-point/> (accessed 5 October 2018); Barslund, Busse and Wispelaere (n 27) 7; Schwarz (n 57).
215. Darvas (n 214); Schwarz (n 57).
216. Schrauwen (n 23) 327.
217. For an investigation of the high degree of concentration of posting in certain Member States and in specific economic sectors, *see supra* Chapter 6.
218. Barslund, Busse and Wispelaere (n 27) 5.

as evidenced *supra* in Chapter 6, certain Member States (e.g., Slovenia) are currently in a position of real economic dependence on the opportunities provided by the practice of posting. Consequently, in those national realities, a substantive downsizing of those opportunities would lead to serious repercussions in terms of job loss and, by implication, on public finances due to loss of tax revenues and social security contributions.[219] When looking at the broader picture, the approach taken by the EU legislator, besides mainly affecting the overall economic growth of certain countries, runs the risk of widening the existing wealth disparities between high-wage Western European Member States and low-wage Central and Eastern European Member States.[220]

In conclusion, it is noteworthy that the foreseeable negative effects of Directive (EU) 2018/957 had been, nonetheless, deferred by the introduction of a two-year implementation period, which allowed the economic actors concerned to adapt their business models to the new requirements, and possibly to minimise the damage.[221] Regrettably, though, as admitted by the Commission itself, the revised legal framework for posting still remains exposed to the 'possible unintended consequence' of the confluence of dependent posted work into (bogus) self-employment.[222] It is no secret indeed that, due to their exclusion from the scope of the Posting of Workers Directive (even after the 2018 revision), the legal treatment of transnational self-employed persons is considerably more cost-effective.[223] As stressed *supra* in Chapter 2, they are not covered by any additional labour law protection in the host state and the same goes with regard to social security law protection when their period of mobility abroad is shorter than twenty-four months. Further undesirable effects may materialise in the development of other fictitious constructions aimed at circumventing the rules, taking the shape of undeclared work, 'letterbox companies', or forced accommodation of

219. *Ibid*. The most recent figures seem to suggest, however, a decreasing economic relevance of posting in Slovenia. Frederic De Wispelaere, Lynn De Smedt and Jozef Pacolet, 'Posting of Workers: Report on A1 Portable Documents Issued in 2018' (KU Leuven Research Institute for Work and Society (HIVA) 2019) European Commission, Directorate-General for Employment, Social Affairs and Inclusion Directorate D – Labour Mobility Unit D/2 – Social security coordination 27.

220. ETUC (European Trade Union Confederation), Business Europe, CEEP (European Centre of Employers and Enterprises providing Public services), UEAPME (European Association of Craft, Small and Medium-Sized Enterprises) (n 12) 7; Schwarz (n 57); Schrauwen (n 23) 328; Stefan Schwarz, 'Opening Address at the II European Labour Mobility Congress' (VI European Labour Mobility Congress (ELMC), Krakow (Poland), 14 March 2019).

221. Barslund, Busse and Wispelaere (n 27) 7. Incidentally, the negative effects of the COVID-19 pandemic on the concrete possibility of adaptation to the new regulatory framework are undeniable.

222. European Commission Impact Assessment, Accompanying the document Proposal for a Directive of the European Parliament and the Council amending Directive 96/71/EC concerning the posting of workers in the framework of the provision of services (n 9) 43. *See also* Dhéret and Ghimis (n 26) 11. Importantly, Preamble Recital 10 of the Enforcement Directive 2014/67/EU emphasised the need to improve monitoring activities and to elaborate a precise definition of 'workers' in such a way as to definitely exclude those workers who falsely declare themselves as self-employed. Voss et al. (n 5) 48.

223. Mijke Houwerzijl, 'Regime Shopping across (Blurring) Boundaries' in Stein Evju (ed.), *Regulating Transnational Labour in Europe: The Quandaries of Multilevel Governance* (Department of Private Law 2014) 5.

seconded workers in overpriced company-organised housing so as to reduce their effective salaries.[224] As a consequence, the need to fight against the spread of such unlawful practices is likely to become even more indispensable and pressing in the coming years.

8.5 CONCLUDING REMARKS

Because of its extremely controversial content, the new Directive (EU) 2018/957 gave rise, since the very earliest stages of its drafting process, to a bitter conflict between high-wage Western and low-wage Central and Eastern Member States. At the same time, contrasting positions among European and national social partners, notably between trade unions and employer organisations, emerged as well. The 'yellow-card procedure' triggered by eleven Member States was just the tip of the iceberg when Central and Eastern European Countries expressed all their concern about the Commission's proposal to introduce, *inter alia*, an actual principle of 'equal pay for equal work in the same place'. The whole proposed revision of the Posting of Workers Directive was criticised for mainly aiming at restricting the competitive advantage of out-of-state posting undertakings with regard to wage differentials. Notwithstanding the opposition of a considerable 'regional block', the legislative process continued on its path until the adoption, on 28 June 2018, of the new Directive.

Although partially moving apart from the Commission's original draft, the 2018 reform introduced a number of relevant novelties in terms of remuneration of posted workers, rules on temporary agency work, rules applying to long-term posting, and transnational administrative cooperation and enforcement of the rules. As of 30 July 2020, the date on which the legislative *novella* came into effect, the same wage scales and allowances applicable to local employees are extended to foreign posted workers as well. Article 3(1) of the Posting of Workers Directive has been amended in such a way as to replace the term 'minimum rates of pay' with a broader concept of 'remuneration'. With regard to the specific components of the latter, the EU legislator basically operated a codification of the relevant case law from the Court of Justice and imposed on the Member States an obligation to publish all constituent elements on the single official national website. The exclusive competence of the Member States to define the concept of remuneration in their own territory was, therefore, left intact. Moreover, the application of collective agreements with only general effect was permitted even in the presence of a system for declaring collective agreements or arbitration awards applicable *erga omnes*, while the validity of universally binding collective agreements was extended to all economic sectors. In addition to equal remuneration *stricto sensu* as local workers, posted workers are now guaranteed equal treatment with regard to accommodation, travel, board and lodging expenses as well. After all, the extension of the host country's labour standards to posted workers, conceived as an exception under the original Posting of Workers Directive, and

224. Zsolt Darvas, 'Could Revising the Posted Workers Directive Improve Social Conditions?' (Conference of think tanks on the revision of the posted workers directive, European Parliament, Brussels, 31 January 2017) 15–16; Barslund, Busse and Wispelaere (n 27) 7.

therefore limited to only certain terms and conditions of employment, has become the rule with the new Directive. Posted workers are still prevented from accessing local social benefits, though.

The new Directive provides for parity of treatment also between local and posted temporary agency workers. It does so by integrating the higher standard of protection guaranteed by the Temporary Agency Work Directive 2008/104/EC directly into the Posting of Workers Directive and by granting the Member States with the possibility to impose on posting undertakings the respect of the same working and employment conditions that apply to local temporary agency workers. Furthermore, it deals with the abusive practices of 'double' or 'chain' posting by holding the first temporary agency fully liable as an employer for any subsequent posting. The practice of long-term posting, in its turn, is addressed by the establishment of a maximum time limit pursuant to which, in the event of a posting lasting for a period longer than twelve months (extendable to eighteen months upon submission of a motivated notification), the seconded workers are treated almost as regular local workers. With a view to curbing the use of elusive constructions in the form of consecutive secondments and rotation of personnel, the calculation of the posting period will then cumulatively take into account all the consecutive replacements of posted workers 'performing the same task at the same place'.

The analysis of the expected manifold impact of the 2018 legislative reform has shown that the positive outcomes are, however, very limited while, at the same time, it has exposed a number of shortcomings and problems. It seems, therefore, that it does not provide a complete solution to the issues actually related to the practice of posting of workers. Besides the general improvement in terms of transparency, the real benefit deriving from the number of new provisions introduced is basically limited by the regulatory adaptation that already took place along the same lines in most of the Member States. This is, indeed, the case of the concrete determination of the payment due to the posted workers in the wake of the Court of Justice case law, the extension of the validity of universally binding collective agreements to all economic sectors, and the equal treatment for posted temporary agency workers. Conversely, a great deal of uncertainty still surrounds the concept of 'remuneration', the host country's margin of appreciation in imposing additional employment terms in case of long-lasting postings, as well as the practical application of collective agreements in the event of overlapping scope of one having *erga omnes* effect with another having general effect only, or when concluded by an employer organisation which is not included among the most representative organisations at national level. Moreover, no countermeasure has been taken in order to cope with the serious issues connected to the use of subcontracting chains.

With regard to the establishment of a twelve (or eighteen)-month time limit for posting, the benefits of such a clarification of the temporary character of this form of labour mobility have to be confronted, nonetheless, with the practical complications arising when the same employment relationship is regulated by two different national labour regimes. Further problems may emerge in relation to the compatibility of the implied change of the workers' habitual place of work with private international law. Importantly, then, the inconsistency of these new provisions with the legal basis of the

Posting of Workers Directive is evident in the application of almost the same treatment to long-term posted workers (or even to short-term posted workers involved in long-term cross-border service supplies) and fully-fledged migrant workers. Finally, it is worth stressing that, in deviating from the Commission's proposal of a twenty-four-month maximum posting period, the EU legislator undoubtedly lost an opportunity to harmonise the existing mismatch between the Posting of Workers Directive and Regulation (EC) 883/2004 on social security coordination.

The real purpose of the revision of the Posting of Workers Directive can, nevertheless, be properly understood only by looking at the latter's potential economic effects. The introduction of the principle of equal pay between local and posted workers, in combination with the possibility to extend further employment terms of host state law in the event of long-term secondments, will substantially reduce wage differentials between local and posted workers, hence curtailing wage competition. The other side of the coin is that, although differences in pay structures, social security contributions and taxation will still remain unchanged, the overall labour costs related to posting will inevitably increase. In all likelihood, the cross-border provision of services in the form of posting of workers by undertakings coming from low-wage Member States and operating in countries with higher social standards will, therefore, be negatively affected. Against this backdrop, the entry into force of the new Directive (EU) 2018/957 is expected to benefit workers and enterprises (especially SMEs) in the receiving high-wage Member States, to the detriment of those in the sending low-wage Member States. This is despite it being officially oriented towards the 'protection of posted workers during their posting in relation to the freedom to provide services'.[225] In light of the high degree of concentration of posting in certain Member States and in specific economic sectors, the negative incidence of the reform will mainly concern those countries (e.g., Slovenia) which are currently in a position of real economic dependence on the opportunities provided by the transnational secondment of work-force.

After all, the response of the EU legislator to the progressive transformation of labour mobility across the internal market was mainly geared to shielding the highest levels of wages and working conditions, as well as the most advanced systems of industrial relations, in the high-wage Western Member States from the competition of out-of-state service providers coming from low-wage Central and Eastern Member States, by disincentivising the employment of posted workers.[226] The aim of merely protecting the host country's labour market from the inflow of foreign posted workers is particularly apparent in the newly established rules on the cumulative maximum duration for posting. Interestingly, the propensity towards such a purpose is evident also in the way the equal treatment is construed, namely as a power of the receiving

225. Article 1(1) of Directive (EU) 2018/957 of the European Parliament and of the Council of 28 June 2018 amending Directive 96/71/EC concerning the posting of workers in the framework of the provision of services (n 2).
226. Benio (n 128); Vladimir Bogoeski, 'Challenges to "United in Diversity" in a European Social Union' in Maurizio Ferrera (ed.), *Towards a European Social Union: The European Pillar of Social Rights and the Roadmap for a Fully-Fledged Social Union* (Centro di Ricerca e Documentazione Luigi Einaudi 2019) 41.

Member States to extend their internal regulations to posted workers rather than as a direct right at disposal of the workers themselves, enforceable against the application of less favourable labour law provisions vis-à-vis their local counterparts. In this sense, the impression is that the argument of protection of the posted workers, which was strongly emphasised during the political campaign leading to the approval of the new Directive, was only instrumental to the imposition of further obstacles to the exercise of free movement rights, whereas the workers' actual interests were relegated to the background.

In conclusion, it is noteworthy that the fact of rendering posting less economically attractive may credibly result in an unintended confluence of dependent posted work into illegal practices (*in primis* bogus self-employment). Furthermore, when looking at the incidence of the reform on the overall EU labour market, its expected negative impact on the low-wage Member States' economies could conceivably widen the existing wealth disparities between East and West Europe and, consequently, pose serious challenges to the EU's economic and social cohesion.

CHAPTER 9

What about Equality, Solidarity and Fair Competition?

9.1 INTRODUCTION

The European integration project is intended to promote simultaneously economic and social progress and cohesion, both at national and Union levels.[1] On the one hand, economic integration falls for the most part under EU competence, and the full implementation of the internal market is expected to boost economic growth and produce upward convergence. On the other hand, however, social regulation is mostly left to the Member States, which are primarily entitled to redistributive powers and, more generally, responsible for the development of national welfare systems.[2] In fact,

1. This dual purpose is clearly stated in both the Preambles to the Treaty on European Union (TEU) and the Treaty on the Functioning of the European Union (TFEU).
2. Fritz W. Scharpf, 'The European Social Model: Coping with the Challenges of Diversity' (2002) 40 JCMS: Journal of Common Market Studies 645, 649–651; Jon Erik Dølvik and Jelle Visser, 'Free Movement, Equal Treatment and Workers' Rights: Can the European Union Solve Its Trilemma of Fundamental Principles?: Free Movement, Equal Treatment and Workers' Rights' (2009) 40 Industrial Relations Journal 491, 493; Catherine Jacqueson, 'For Better or for Worse? Transnational Solidarity in the Light of Social Europe' in Nicola Countouris and Mark Freedland (eds), *Resocialising Europe in a Time of Crisis* (Cambridge University Press 2013) 377; Frank Vandenbroucke, 'The Case for a European Social Union: From Muddling Through to a Sense of Common Purpose' (2014) Euroforum Policy Paper (KU Leuven) 17; Frank Vandenbroucke, 'The Idea of a European Social Union: A Normative Introduction' in Frank Vandenbroucke, Catherine Barnard and Geert De Baere (eds), *A European Social Union after the Crisis* (Cambridge University Press 2017) 22; Aukje A.H. van Hoek, 'Re-Embedding the Transnational Employment Relationship: A Tale about the Limitations of (EU) Law?' (2018) 55 Common Market Law Review 449, 453. This sort of distribution of competences between the EU and the Member States still reflects, to some extent, the principle of 'embedded liberalism' underpinning the 1957 Treaty of Rome establishing the EEC (European Economic Community). Notably, the concept of 'embedded liberalism' was coined by Ruggie in John Gerard Ruggie, 'International Regimes, Transactions, and Change: Embedded Liberalism in the Postwar Economic Order' (1982) 36 International Organization 379. On this point, *see* Fritz W. Scharpf, 'The Asymmetry of European Integration, or Why the EU Cannot Be a "Social Market Economy"' (2010) 8 Socio-Economic Review 211, 215; Dagmar Schiek

notwithstanding the relative expansion of the European social *acquis* in terms of coordination of social security systems, anti-discrimination policies and rules on health and safety at work, the broad sphere of social policy, encompassing wage levels, social benefits, labour relations, welfare services, education and social protection, still remains firmly a national prerogative.[3]

Against this background, the realisation of the so-called 'European social model' presupposes the pursuit of social and economic policies in accordance with certain shared EU values. As indeed proclaimed by the European Parliament, '[t]he European social model is first and foremost a question of values. [...] the common values of equality, non discrimination and solidarity and redistribution as fundamentals'.[4] Importantly, therefore, the process of European integration must never lose sight of the values and principles which underpin the Union. A whole catalogue of those values and principles is now provided by the combination of the Treaty on European Union and the Charter of Fundamental Rights of the European Union which include, *inter alia*, the respect for human dignity, freedom, democracy, equality, the rule of law and respect for human rights, and also pluralism, non-discrimination, tolerance, justice,

---

et al., 'EU Social and Labour Rights and EU Internal Market Law' (European Parliament, EMPL Committee 2015) IP/A/EMPL/ST/2014-02, 13; Christian Joerges, 'Social Justice in an Ever More Diverse Union' in Frank Vandenbroucke, Catherine Barnard and Geert De Baere (eds), *A European Social Union after the Crisis* (Cambridge University Press 2017) 99; Dagmar Schiek, 'Towards More Resilience for a Social EU – The Constitutionally Conditioned Internal Market' (2017) 13 European Constitutional Law Review 611, 615–616; Jotte Mulder, '(Re) Conceptualising a Social Market Economy for the EU Internal Market' (2019) 15 Utrecht Law Review 16, 19.

3. Michael Dougan and Eleanor Spaventa, *Wish You Weren't Here....: New Models of Social Solidarity in the European Union* (Social welfare and EU law, Hart Publishing 2005) 188; Frank Hendrickx, 'Fundamental Social Rights in Pre- and Post-Constitutional Terms' (2006) 22 International Journal of Comparative Labour Law and Industrial Relations 407, 408–409; Herwig Verschueren, 'Cross-Border Workers in the European Internal Market: Trojan Horses for Member States' Labour and Social Security Law?' (2008) 24/2 International Journal of Comparative Labour Law and Industrial Relations 167, 167–168; Roger Blanpain, 'The European Social Model (ESM): Myth or Reality?' (2011) 2 European Labour Law Journal 142, 145–146; Frank Hendrickx, 'Completing Economic and Social Integration: Towards Labour Law for the United States of Europe' in Nicola Countouris and Mark Freedland (eds), *Resocialising Europe in a Time of Crisis* (Cambridge University Press 2013) 67; Herwig Verschueren, 'The European Internal Market and the Competition between Workers' (2015) 6 European Labour Law Journal 128, 129–130; Vandenbroucke, 'The Idea of a European Social Union' (n 2) 22; van Hoek (n 2) 453.
4. Committee on Employment and Social Affairs, Rapporteur José Albino Silva Peneda, 'Report on a European Social Model for the Future' (European Parliament 2006) A6-0238/2006 <http://www.europarl.europa.eu/sides/getDoc.do?pubRef=-//EP//TEXT+REPORT+A6-2006-0238+0+DOC+XML+V0//EN&language=EN> (accessed 8 November 2019). Twelve years earlier, the Commission had already expressed its view along the same lines in European Commission, European Social Policy – A Way Forward for the Union. A White Paper 1994 [COM (94) 333 final] para. 3. In this sense, *see* Catherine Barnard, 'EU "Social" Policy: From Employment Law to Labour Market Reform' in Paul Craig and Gráinne de Búrca (eds), *The Evolution of EU Law* (Second Edition, Oxford University Press 2011) 661; Catherine Barnard, *EU Employment Law* (Fourth Edition, Oxford European Union Law Library 2012) 34; Catherine Barnard, 'EU Employment Law and the European Social Model: The Past, the Present and the Future' (2014) 67 Current Legal Problems 199, 200–201; Paul Schoukens, *EU Social Security Law: The Hidden Social Model* (TILT, Tilburg University 2016) 5 <https://eiss.be/onewebmedia/oration_Schoukens.pdf%20(final).pdf> (accessed 1 December 2018).

solidarity, and equality between women and men.[5] In particular, 'equality' and 'solidarity' are the headings of, respectively, Chapters III and IV of the Charter, under which fundamental social and labour rights are mainly located.[6]

Crucially, by virtue of Article 3(3) TEU, the fulfilment of the aforementioned values is to be pursued with a view to achieving 'a highly competitive social market economy, aiming at full employment and social progress'. The EU's commitment to concurrent economic and social development may be discerned in the objectives of combating social exclusion and discrimination, and promoting social justice and protection, as well as economic, social and territorial cohesion, and solidarity among Member States.[7] In the same vein, the purposes of ensuring social protection, social inclusion and high employment levels are replicated in the 'horizontal social clause' enshrined in Article 9 TFEU.[8]

5. Article 2 TEU. *See also* Article 1, Chapters II, III, and IV of the Charter of Fundamental Rights of the European Union (CFREU) 2000 [2000/C 364/01]. Catherine Barnard, '"British Jobs for British Workers": The Lindsey Oil Refinery Dispute and the Future of Local Labour Clauses in an Integrated EU Market' (2009) 38 Industrial Law Journal 245, 277; Malcolm Ross, 'Solidarity – A New Constitutional Paradigm for the EU?' in Malcolm Ross and Yuri Borgmann-Prebil (eds), *Promoting Solidarity in the European Union* (Oxford University Press 2010) 44; Dagmar Schiek, *Economic and Social Integration: The Challenge for EU Constitutional Law* (Edward Elgar 2012) 219–220; Hendrickx, 'Completing Economic and Social Integration' (n 3) 74; Schiek et al. (n 2) 15; Stephen Weatherill, *Law and Values in the European Union* (Oxford University Press 2016) 393–394; Jan Wouters and Pierre Schmitt, 'Equality Among Member States and Differentiated Integration in the EU' in Lucia Serena Rossi and Federico Casolari (eds), *The Principle of Equality in EU Law* (Springer Berlin Heidelberg 2017) 45.
6. More specifically, the Charter of Fundamental Rights for the European Union establishes, *inter alia*, collective labour rights (Articles 12 and 28), rights to fair and just working conditions (Article 31), and rights to social security and social assistance (Article 34). Incidentally, it is recalled that, by virtue of Article 6 TEU, the CFREU is entitled to the same legal value as the Treaties. Hendrickx, 'Completing Economic and Social Integration' (n 3) 74; Schiek et al. (n 2) 16; Wouters and Schmitt (n 5) 45–46; Schiek, 'Towards More Resilience for a Social EU – the Constitutionally Conditioned Internal Market' (n 2) 627.
7. Article 3(3) TEU. Schiek, *Economic and Social Integration: The Challenge for EU Constitutional Law* (n 5) 221; Hendrickx, 'Completing Economic and Social Integration' (n 3) 71; Barnard, 'EU Employment Law and the European Social Model' (n 4) 202–203; Schiek et al. (n 2) 15–16; Erika Szyszczak, 'Europe Isn't Working in Europe: Reform and Modernisation of the European Welfare State in the Wake of the Economic Crisis' (2015) 38 Fordham International Law Journal 1193, 1205–1207; Andrea Sangiovanni, 'Debating the EU's Raison d'Être: On the Relation between Legitimacy and Justice' (2019) 57 JCMS: Journal of Common Market Studies 13, 21; Anna Gerbrandy, Willem Janssen and Lyndsey Thomsin, 'Shaping the Social Market Economy After the Lisbon Treaty: How "Social" Is Public Economic Law?' (2019) 15 Utrecht Law Review 32, 32.
8. Schiek, *Economic and Social Integration: The Challenge for EU Constitutional Law* (n 5) 222–223; Catherine Barnard, 'The Protection of Fundamental Rights in the EU After Lisbon: A Question of Conflicts of Interests' in Sybe De Vries, Ulf Bernitz and Steve Weatherill (eds), *The Protection of Fundamental Rights in the EU After Lisbon* (Hart Publishing 2013) 37; Hendrickx, 'Completing Economic and Social Integration' (n 3) 71; Vandenbroucke, 'The Case for a European Social Union: From Muddling Through to a Sense of Common Purpose' (n 2) 16; Catherine Barnard and Geert De Baere, 'Towards a European Social Union: Achievements and Possibilities under the Current EU Constitutional Framework' (2014) Euroforum Policy Paper (KU Leuven) 36; Schiek et al. (n 2) 16; Maurizio Ferrera, 'The European Social Union: A Missing but Necessary "Political Good"' in Frank Vandenbroucke, Catherine Barnard and Geert De Baere (eds), *A European Social Union after the Crisis* (Cambridge University Press 2017) 55; Geert De Baere and Kathleen Gutman, 'The Basis in EU Constitutional Law for Further Social Integration' in Frank Vandenbroucke, Catherine Barnard and Geert De Baere (eds), *A European Social Union after the Crisis* (Cambridge University Press 2017) 379–380; Silvana Sciarra, *Solidarity and Conflict: European*

Alongside the above-mentioned extensive list of values, the smooth functioning of the entire EU internal market is clearly among the primary goals of the Union as well. To this end, the principle of fair competition certainly plays a central role, and the whole Chapter 1 of Title VII of the TFEU is indeed dedicated to EU competition rules.[9] Especially in the wake of the 2004 and 2007 EU enlargements towards the East, concerns regarding the existence of a level playing field for competition between East and West Europe have become increasingly important.[10] In this respect, fair competition policy is recognised as the instrument able to provide equal opportunities for all undertakings, Member States and consumers, while ensuring that the same rules apply for everyone.[11]

In light of the strong Union's commitment to the development of a European social model inspired by economic fairness and social progress, this chapter reflects on the interaction of the new EU legal framework for posting of workers and, more broadly, of the whole narrative underpinning the 2018 legislative reform with the EU values and principles coming into play in the context of intra-EU labour mobility. Its major purpose is to address the main research question of this book, namely: *To what extent is the new legal framework provided for by Directive (EU) 2018/957 in line with the EU values and principles of equality, solidarity and fair competition?*

To this end, the following analysis goes beyond the mere examination of the strict letter of the law, thus taking into account the impact of the newly established regulatory framework on a context marked by the great diversity of European welfare states. Accordingly, it builds on the outcomes of the previous chapters, which are considered as a point of departure for a more normative reflection on the direction taken by the EU legislator with the revision of the Posting of Workers Directive. A triangular confrontation is thereby proposed between the rationale underlying the new Directive and the latter's expected effects, the quantitative dimension of posting and its actual impact on the EU labour market, and the aforementioned EU values and

Social Law in Crisis (Cambridge University Press 2018) 24–25; Claire Kilpatrick and Bruno De Witte, 'A Tangible Human Face for Social Europe' (2019) 02 RSCAS Policy Paper (Robert Schuman Centre for Advanced Studies) Special Edition for the EP Elections 2019 1; Jacek Kubera and Tomasz Morozowski, 'The Social Turn and the Potential to Reconstruct the Social Dimension of the European Union' in Jacek Kubera and Tomasz Morozowski (eds), *A 'Social Turn' in the European Union?: New Trends and Ideas about Social Convergence in Europe* (First Edition, Routledge 2020) 15.

9. Alison Jones and Christopher Townley, 'Competition Law' in Catherine Barnard and Steve Peers (eds), *European Union Law* (Second Edition, Oxford University Press 2017) 509–510; Stephanie Honnefelder, 'Competition Policy – Fact Sheets on the European Union' (*European Parliament*, April 2019) <https://www.europarl.europa.eu/factsheets/en/sheet/82/competition-policy> (accessed 17 February 2020); 'Competition' (*EUR-Lex*) <https://eur-lex.europa.eu/summary/chapter/competition.html?root_default=SUM_1_CODED%3D08&locale=en> (accessed 17 February 2020).
10. Jens Hölscher and Johannes Stephan, 'Competition and Antitrust Policy in the Enlarged European Union: A Level Playing Field?' (2009) 47 JCMS: Journal of Common Market Studies 863, 864.
11. Marcin Szczepański, 'EU Competition Policy: Key to a Fair Single Market: In-Depth Analysis' (European Parliament 2019) European Parliamentary Research Service (EPRS) 33 <https://data.europa.eu/doi/10.2861/143082> (accessed 17 February 2020).

principles. Afterwards, a number of recommendations for possible future improvements in the field of posting of workers are succinctly put forward.

More in detail, this chapter is divided into two parts, the first of which is composed of three sections corresponding to the EU values and principles respectively taken into account. In section 9.2 the new set of rules laid down in Directive (EU) 2018/957 concerning equal treatment between local and posted workers is challenged against the EU value of equality. In particular, the analysis goes beyond the merely formal expression of equal treatment, assessing whether the new legal framework is effectively capable of providing substantive equality between the actors involved. *Inter alia*, the dynamics underlying the reform are specifically investigated, taking into consideration the possible instrumentalisation of the principle of equality. Subsequently, section 9.3 deals with the purpose of Directive (EU) 2018/957 to create a level playing field between posting and local undertakings in the host country. At first, the narrative that considers the competition from out-of-state posting undertakings as necessarily and unequivocally unfair is tested under EU law. Then, the problem of disregarding the extra costs and administrative burdens that only posting companies have to bear, by reason of the cross-border dimension of the transnational provision of services, is seen in the light of the EU principle of fair competition. Finally, section 9.4 proposes to look at the new Directive under a different perspective, which takes into account the European commitment to solidarity in a transnational dimension. In this regard, the close interrelation between the value of pan-European solidarity and the ideal of social (distributive) justice is considered as an important feature of the European social model.

The criticism of the first part of this chapter is matched with the purposeful intent of the second part where, in section 9.5, a number of recommendations for future improvements are proposed in terms of: centralisation and digitalisation of all data related to posting of workers, including the introduction of a European Social Security Number (ESSN); coordination of the different national approaches in the areas of company law and taxation in order to combat regulatory arbitrage strategies; promotion of the participation of posted workers in both home and host state trade unions; and elaboration of a European coordination scheme of national approaches to minimum wage policy. The main findings of all the previous sections are eventually put together in the concluding section 9.6.

9.2 EQUALITY

By making recourse to posting of workers, foreign service providers have potentially benefitted from a competitive advantage over their local counterparts in the receiving Member States for years. In effect, the special legal treatment reserved to posted workers under EU law allowed posting undertakings to exploit – albeit within certain limits – the existing differences in wages, social security contributions and tax rates among the sending and receiving Member States. The new Directive (EU) 2018/957[12] will presumably reduce the above-mentioned competitive advantage by ensuring equal treatment between local and posted workers with respect to remuneration and working conditions. However, such an innovative EU legal framework for posting of workers and, more broadly, the whole narrative supporting the principle of 'equal pay for equal work in the same place'[13] are called into question for their compatibility with the EU value of equality.

The value of equality traditionally lies at the core of the EU constitutional set-up. Although not expressly mentioned in the 1957 Treaty of Rome,[14] it was included for the first time in the Preamble to the 1986 Single European Act[15] as a fundamental right, alongside freedom and social justice, underpinning the promotion of democracy in Europe.[16] Currently, it can be traced in various instruments of primary and secondary EU law – *in primis* in the Treaty on European Union (Articles 2 and 3) and in the Charter of Fundamental Rights of the European Union (Chapter III) – where it is referred to as both a fundamental value and a general principle.[17] The principle of equality is declined in different fields of application, such as, first of all, that of free movement of workers, whereby the equal treatment between national and foreign EU workers applies to any conditions of employment and work, including remuneration, dismissal, reinstatement or re-employment, social and tax advantages, access to training, membership of trade unions and housing.[18] Furthermore, it is realised in terms of equality between men and women with regard to job opportunities, labour

12. Directive (EU) 2018/957 of the European Parliament and of the Council of 28 June 2018 amending Directive 96/71/EC concerning the posting of workers in the framework of the provision of services 2018 (OJ L 173/16).
13. It is recalled that the first supporter of this principle was, indeed, the European Commission. In particular, the urgency to intervene in establishing equal wages for local and posted workers was strongly advocated by the President Junker during his 2017 'State of the Union' address, where he affirmed that '[i]n a Union of equals, there can be no second class workers. Workers should earn the same pay for the same work in the same place'. European Commission, 'Speech of President Jean-Claude Juncker, State of the Union Address' (13 September 2017) <http://europa.eu/rapid/press-release_SPEECH-17-3165_en.htm> (accessed 15 October 2018).
14. Treaty of Rome (EEC) – Treaty establishing the European Economic Community 1957.
15. Single European Act (SEA) 1987 (OJ L 169).
16. Alison McDonnell, 'Equality for Citizens in the EU: Where Did All the Flowers Go?' in Lucia Serena Rossi and Federico Casolari (eds), *The Principle of Equality in EU Law* (Springer Berlin Heidelberg 2017) 199.
17. Mark Bell, 'The Principle of Equal Treatment: Widening and Deepening' in Paul Craig and Gráinne de Búrca (eds), *The Evolution of EU Law* (Second Edition, Oxford University Press 2011) 629–630; McDonnell (n 16) 200, 210 and 224.
18. Such a principle was originally enshrined in Articles 7–9 of Regulation (EEC) No 1612/68 of the Council of 15 October 1968 on freedom of movement for workers within the Community 1968 (OJ L 257/2). Those provisions have been subsequently replaced by Articles 7–9 of Regulation (EU) No 492/2011 of the European Parliament and of the Council of 5 April 2011 on freedom of movement for workers within the Union 2011 (OJ L 141/1). In this sense, *see* Nicola Countouris and Samuel Engblom, '"Protection or Protectionism?": A Legal Deconstruction of the Emerging False Dilemma in European Integration' (2015) UCL Labour Rights Institute On-Line Working Papers – LRI WP 4; Dagmar Schiek, 'Perspectives on Social Citizenship in the EU – From Status Positivus to Status Socialis Activus via Two Forms of Transnational Solidarity' (2015) 4 Queen's University Belfast School of Law: Research Paper 2015 – 10, 11; Schiek et al. (n 2) 47 and 96.

conditions and pay,[19] and also equal employment conditions (including pay) for part-time and full-time workers,[20] for workers with fixed-term contracts and comparable permanent workers,[21] and for temporary agency workers and workers at the user undertaking.[22]

Importantly, though, as expressly stated by the Court of Justice, this principle does not necessarily imply the application of the exact same treatment under any circumstances according to a one-size-fits-all approach.[23] It rather 'prohibits both treating similar situations differently and treating different situations in the same way unless there are objective reasons for such treatment',[24] since the application of different rules to comparable situations, likewise the application of the same rule to different situations, cannot avoid giving rise to substantive discriminations.[25] In

19. Articles 2 and 3(3) TEU, Articles 8, 153(1)(i), and 157 TFEU, Article 23 CFREU. As to secondary EU legislation, *see* Council Directive 92/85/EEC of 19 October 1992 on the introduction of measures to encourage improvements in the safety and health at work of pregnant workers and workers who have recently given birth or are breastfeeding (tenth individual Directive within the meaning of Article 16 (1) of Directive 89/391/EEC) 1992 (OJ L 348); Council Directive 2000/78/EC of 27 November 2000 establishing a general framework for equal treatment in employment and occupation 2000 (OJ L 303/16); Directive 2006/54/EC of the European Parliament and of the Council of 5 July 2006 on the implementation of the principle of equal opportunities and equal treatment of men and women in matters of employment and occupation (recast) 2006 (OJ L 204); Directive 2010/41/EU of the European Parliament and of the Council of 7 July 2010 on the application of the principle of equal treatment between men and women engaged in an activity in a self-employed capacity and repealing Council Directive 86/613/EEC 2010 (OJ L 180). For a comprehensive analysis of the principle of equal treatment between men and women, *see* Philippa Watson, *EU Social and Employment Law* (Second Edition, Oxford University Press 2014) 307 and ff.
20. Council Directive 97/81/EC of 15 December 1997 concerning the Framework Agreement on part-time work concluded by UNICE, CEEP and the ETUC 1998 (OJ L 14/9).
21. Council Directive 1999/70/EC of 28 June 1999 concerning the framework agreement on fixed-term work concluded by ETUC, UNICE and CEEP 1999 (OJ L 175/43).
22. Directive 2008/104/EC of the European Parliament and of the Council of 19 November 2008 on temporary agency work 2008 (OJ L 327/9).
23. Lisa Waddington, 'The Expanding Role of the Equality Principle in European Union Law' (2003) Policy Paper Series on Constitutional Reform in the EU 2003/04 European University Institute, Robert Schuman Centre for Advanced Studies 23; Bell (n 17) 630.
24. *Europe Chemi-Con (Deutschland) GmbH v Council of the European Union* [2005] ECJ Case C-422/02, ECLI:EU:C:2005:56 [33]. *See also Marthe Klensch and others v Secrétaire d'État à l'Agriculture et à la Viticulture* [1986] ECJ Joined Cases C-201/85 and C-202/85, ECLI: EU:C:1986:439 [9]; *Marcel Erpelding v Secrétaire d'État à l'Agriculture et à la Viticulture* [1988] ECJ Case C-84/87, ECLI:EU:C:1988:245 [29]; *Gustave Wuidart and others v Laiterie coopérative eupenoise société coopérative and others* [1990] ECJ Joined Cases C-267/88 to C-285/88, ECLI:EU:C:1990:79 [13]; *United Kingdom of Great Britain and Northern Ireland v Council of the European Union* [1998] ECJ Case C-150/94, ECLI:EU:C:1998:547 [97]; *Portuguese Republic v Council of the European Union* [1999] ECJ Case C-149/96, ECLI:EU:C:1999:574 [91]; *H Jippes, Afdeling Groningen van de Nederlandse Vereniging tot Bescherming van Dieren and Afdeling Assen en omstreken van de Nederlandse Vereniging tot Bescherming van Dieren v Minister van Landbouw, Natuurbeheer en Visserij* [2001] ECJ Case C-189/01, ECLI:EU:C:2001:420 [129]; *Ángel Rodríguez Caballero v Fondo de Garantía Salarial (Fogasa)* [2002] ECJ Case C-442/00, ECLI:EU:C:2002:752 [32]. In this sense, *see* Wouters and Schmitt (n 5) 44.
25. *See, inter alia, Finanzamt Köln-Altstadt v Roland Schumacker* [1995] ECJ Case C-279/93, ECLI:EU:C:1995:31 [30]; *G H E J Wielockx v Inspecteur der Directe Belastingen* [1995] ECJ Case C-80/94, ECLI:EU:C:1995:271 [17]; *Royal Bank of Scotland plc v Elliniko Dimosio (Greek State)* [1999] ECJ Case C-311/97, ECLI:EU:C:1999:216 [26]; *Frans Gschwind v Finanzamt Aachen-Außenstadt* [1999] ECJ Case C-391/97, ECLI:EU:C:1999:409 [21]; *Raffaele Talotta v Belgian State*

essence, therefore, the European judiciary took up the famous equality formula defined by Aristotle, which considers as right and fair that 'things that are alike should be treated alike, while things that are unalike should be treated unalike in proportion to their unalikeness'.[26]

Article 157(4) TFEU[27] and Article 23 CFREU,[28] for their part, went even further by recognising an actual substantive conception of equality, through the promotion of positive actions in the field of gender equality. Departing from the so-called 'formal', 'liberal' or 'symmetrical' approach to equality, this new 'substantive', 'asymmetrical' or 'group justice' model, which allows the Member States to adopt positively discriminatory measures, is evidently oriented towards 'ensuring full equality in practice'.[29] Notably, such a proactive approach aimed at guaranteeing equal opportunities and achieving equal outcomes was promptly taken on board by the European legislator with the inclusion of a positive action clause in the Racial Equality Directive 2000/43/EC,[30] the Equal Treatment Framework

---

[2007] ECJ Case C-383/05, ECLI:EU:C:2007:181 [18]; *État du Grand Duchy of Luxemburg v Hans Ulrich Lakebrink and Katrin Peters-Lakebrink* [2007] ECJ Case C-182/06, ECLI:EU:C:2007:452 [27]; *Laval un Partneri Ltd v Svenska Byggnadsarbetareförbundet, Svenska Byggnadsarbetareförbundets avdelning 1, Byggettan and Svenska Elektrikerförbundet* [2007] ECJ Case C-341/05, ECLI:EU:C:2007:809 [115]. In this sense, *see* Marc De Vos, 'Beyond Formal Equality: Positive Action under Directives 2000/43/EC and 2000/78/EC' (European Commission, Directorate-General Employment, Social Affairs and Equal Opportunities, Unit G2 2007) 10.

26. Aristotle, *Nicomachean Ethics* (William David Ross tr, Initially published in 1925, Fourth Century B.C.) Book V.3. In another work, Aristotle reframed this concept of justice affirming that 'as, for instance, what is equal appears just, and is so; but not to all; only among those who are equals: and what is unequal appears just, and is so; but not to all; only amongst those who are unequals'. Aristotle, *Politics* (William Ellis tr, Initially published in 1912, Fourth Century B.C.) Book III.9.
27. In the wording of Article 157(4) TFEU (former Article 141(4) TEC), 'With a view to ensuring full equality in practice between men and women in working life, the principle of equal treatment shall not prevent any Member State from maintaining or adopting measures providing for specific advantages in order to make it easier for the underrepresented sex to pursue a vocational activity or to prevent or compensate for disadvantages in professional careers.'
28. Pursuant to Article 23 CFREU on equality between men and women, 'The principle of equality shall not prevent the maintenance or adoption of measures providing for specific advantages in favour of the under-represented sex.'
29. Dagmar Schiek, 'A New Framework on Equal Treatment of Persons in EC Law?' (2002) 8 European Law Journal 290, 298–299, 303–304; De Vos (n 25) 10–11 and 22; Barbara Giovanna Bello, 'Equal Opportunities for All? Social Challenges and Legal Boundaries in the European Puzzle' in Serdar M Degirmencioglu (ed.), *Some Still More Equal than Others? Or Equal Opportunities for All?* (Council of Europe Publishing 2011) 30; Giuseppe Casale, 'International Labour Standards and EU Labour Law' in Nicola Countouris and Mark Freedland (eds), *Resocialising Europe in a Time of Crisis* (Cambridge University Press 2013) 99–100; ACL Davies, *EU Labour Law* (Edward Elgar Publishing Ltd 2014) 127–130; Barnard and De Baere (n 8) 13; Paul Craig and Gráinne de Búrca, *EU Law: Text, Cases, and Materials* (Sixth Edition, Oxford University Press 2015) 950; Mia Rönnmar, 'Labour and Equality Law' in Catherine Barnard and Steve Peers (eds), *European Union Law* (Second Edition, Oxford University Press 2017) 618–619.
30. Article 5 of the Council Directive 2000/43/EC of 29 June 2000 implementing the principle of equal treatment between persons irrespective of racial or ethnic origin 2000 (OJ L 180/22). *See* Vassilis Hatzopoulos, 'A (More) Social Europe: A Political Crossroad or a Legal One-Way? Dialogues between Luxembourg and Lisbon' (2005) 42 Common Market Law Review 1599, 1625–1626; Casale (n 29) 100–101; Watson (n 19) 408; Craig and de Búrca (n 29) 906–908.

Directive 2000/78/EC[31] and the Recast Equal Treatment Directive 2006/54/EC.[32] In the same vein, 'Equal Opportunities and Access to the Labour Market' is the heading of Chapter I of the European Pillar of Social Rights,[33] which was solemnly proclaimed by the European Parliament, the Council and the Commission in Gothenburg on 17 November 2017.[34]

Notwithstanding the increasing emphasis in EU policy on ensuring substantive equality, the revision of the Posting of Workers Directive with the adoption of Directive (EU) 2018/957 was essentially inclined towards a merely formal approach aimed at imposing equal conditions for all service providers (both local and foreign) and workers (both local and posted) operating in the same place (the host Member State). The whole rationale underlying the reform according to the principle of 'the same pay for the same work at the same workplace' and, in particular, the new rules on equal remuneration *(lato sensu)* and long-term posting were, indeed, devoid of any consideration about the fundamentally different circumstances in which posted workers and workers of the host country respectively find themselves.

Admittedly, it certainly cannot be said that the posted workers are in a comparable situation as their local counterparts,[35] such as to justify the application of the

31. Article 7(1) of the Council Directive 2000/78/EC of 27 November 2000 establishing a general framework for equal treatment in employment and occupation (n 19). Hatzopoulos, 'A (More) Social Europe: A Political Crossroad or a Legal One-Way? Dialogues between Luxembourg and Lisbon' (n 30) 1625–1626; Casale (n 29) 100–101; Craig and de Búrca (n 29) 908–913.
32. Article 3 of Directive 2006/54/EC of the European Parliament and of the Council of 5 July 2006 on the implementation of the principle of equal opportunities and equal treatment of men and women in matters of employment and occupation (recast) (n 19). On this point, *see* Schiek, 'A New Framework on Equal Treatment of Persons in EC Law?' (n 29) 298; De Vos (n 25) 28; Barnard, *EU Employment Law* (n 4) 386; Watson (n 19) 350–351; Craig and de Búrca (n 29) 914–922.
33. European Parliament, Council of the European Union and European Commission, Interinstitutional Proclamation on the European Pillar of Social Rights 2017 (OJ C 428/10).
34. European Commission, Communication from the Commission to the European Parliament, the Council, the European Economic and Social Committee and the Committee of the Regions, Establishing a European Pillar of Social Rights 2017 [COM(2017) 250 final] 4; Annette Schrauwen, 'From the Board Towards a Social Europe' (2018) 45 Legal Issues of Economic Integration 323, 323–324; Bart Vanhercke, Sebastiano Sabato and Dalila Ghailani, 'The European Pillar of Social Rights as a Game Changer' in Sebastiano Sabato (ed.), *Social Policy in the European Union: State of Play 2018* (ETUI, 2018) 156–158; Sacha Garben, 'The European Pillar of Social Rights: An Assessment of Its Meaning and Significance' (2019) Cambridge Yearbook of European Legal Studies 1, 3; Kilpatrick and De Witte (n 8) 2–3; Catherine Barnard and Sybe De Vries, 'The "Social Market Economy" in a (Heterogeneous) Social Europe: Does It Make a Difference?' (2019) 15 Utrecht Law Review 47, 57–58; Frank Vandenbroucke, 'The European Pillar of Social Rights: From Promise to Delivery' in Maurizio Ferrera (ed.), *Towards a European Social Union: The European Pillar of Social Rights and the Roadmap for a Fully-Fledged Social Union* (Centro di Ricerca e Documentazione Luigi Einaudi 2019) 2; Martin Koppernock, 'On the Future of "Social Europe" – Between Competitiveness and High Social Standards' in Jacek Kubera and Tomasz Morozowski (eds), *A 'Social Turn' in the European Union?: New Trends and Ideas about Social Convergence in Europe* (First Edition, Routledge 2020) 173. Despite not being legally binding, the Pillar testifies the EU's commitment towards the promotion of a stronger social dimension of the Union.
35. On this point, *see* Jean-Philippe Lhernould, 'Directive (EU) 2018/957 of 28 June 2018 Amending Directive 96/71/EC Concerning the Posting of Workers in the Framework of the Provision of Services: What Will Change in 2020?' (2019) ERA Forum – Springer 2–3 <http://link.springer.com/10.1007/s12027-019-00573-x> (accessed 16 September 2019). Notably, following the

same rules on remuneration and working conditions of the host country, almost as in the case of intra-EU labour migration under Article 45 TFEU.[36] In fact, the activity of posting entails only temporary secondments of workers in the framework of the freedom to provide services, most of the time without any integration into the labour market of the Member State of destination. The workers concerned undoubtedly still preserve a substantial link with their home country, where they retain their social security affiliation (up to twenty-four months of mobility abroad) and continue to pay their taxes (for a maximum of 183 days per year). Moreover, during their assignment abroad, the posted employees remain within the organizational framework of the posting undertaking and, more in general, are still fully embedded in their country of origin, where all their lives and families typically remain. Crucially, then, posting is an employer-driven type of labour mobility, implying that the posted workers' chances to benefit from the economic opportunities offered by the secondment across borders are directly dependent on their employers' competitiveness.[37] This means that, when the posting concerns low-wage workers and takes place from low-wage to high-wage Member States, the imposition of the same treatment as local employees might potentially result in too high costs for the posting employers, and eventually in the posted workers' loss of their jobs.[38]

All things considered, it is therefore quite difficult to assert that substantive equality between local and posted workers may be attained through formal equal treatment. In effect, the formalistic equal treatment principle introduced by the new Directive (EU) 2018/957, in spite of its apparent neutral and impartial character, is liable, at times, to lead to discrimination and disadvantage for the cross-border workers concerned. As previously noted in Chapter 8, when looking at the real impact of the new provisions, the disincentivising effect on the employment of posted workers is self-evident in the exclusion of the companies which cannot afford to ensure the same employment standards applied by their richer counterparts in the countries of destination. This also because they have to bear all the extra costs and administrative burdens intrinsically connected to the transnational character of the service provision.[39] In practice, the potentially discriminatory character of the equal treatment

guidance given by the Court, 'The comparability of different situations must be assessed with regard to all the elements which characterise them. These elements must in particular be determined and assessed in the light of the subject-matter and purpose of the European Union act which makes the distinction in question. The principles and objectives of the field to which the act relates must also be taken into account.' *Grand Duchy of Luxemburg v European Parliament and Council of the European Union* [2011] CJEU Case C-176/09, ECLI:EU:C:2011:290 [32].

36. On the fundamental difference between different forms of intra-EU labour mobility under Articles 45 and 56 TFEU, *see* the analysis carried out *supra* in Chapter 2.
37. In this sense, *see* the analysis carried out *supra* in Chapter 2.
38. Uglješa Grušić, *The European Private International Law of Employment* (Cambridge University Press 2015) 258; Verschueren, 'The European Internal Market and the Competition between Workers' (n 3) 149; Emmanuel Comte, 'Promising More to Give Less: International Disputes between Core and Periphery around European Posted Labor, 1955–2018' (2019) Labor History 1, 11.
39. Frans Pennings, 'How Do Social and Economic Rights Relate to Each Other in the Social Market Economy: An Introduction to This Special Issue' (2019) 15 Utrecht Law Review 1, 5. On the extra

enshrined in Directive (EU) 2018/957 arises from the fact that, in certain instances, the use of posting of workers from low-wage to high-wage Member States will turn out to be not profitable anymore. The appropriateness of applying an almost identical treatment to all market actors regardless of their substantially different situation is therefore highly questionable, as it would in all likelihood amount to indirect discrimination.[40] In other words, the application of local rules equally on both national and foreign economic actors (enterprises and workers) is expected to have a disparate impact entailing a penalising effect on the second ones only, while benefitting the first ones.

On top of that, due to its indifference to the current wide diversity of collective bargaining systems at European level, the new Directive is liable to generate inequality among posted workers as well. In fact, the equal treatment rule applies only to those workers employed in highly regulated economic sectors.[41] Furthermore, even the maximum time limit for posting may be considered as discriminatory against smaller undertakings, to the extent it lacks to take into account the material dimension of the service provision and the production capacity of an enterprise. Whenever the duration of the posting exceeds the twelve (or eighteen)-month time limit, the employer is indeed exempted from benefitting from the more favourable legal treatment ensured because of the posting. Contrariwise, no loss of benefit is suffered by an employer who posts more workers compared to the first one for the same type of work, as long as the service supply is performed within the maximum time limit.[42]

Besides considering the concrete outcomes of the newly established legal framework, it is worth dwelling also on the dynamics underlying the reform and, in particular, the supposed instrumentalisation of the principle of equality. As is well known, the Court of Justice has frequently dealt with issues of equal treatment for migrant workers in terms of equal access to social benefits and services in the host country. In that regard, the typical case concerned a migrant worker claiming equal treatment with his local counterparts in the host state.[43] Conversely, on the occasion of the revision of the Posting of Workers Directive, the claim for equal treatment did not

costs and administrative burdens that out-of-state undertakings have to bear when posting workers across borders, *see infra* section 9.3.

40. Gareth Davies, 'Discrimination and beyond in European Economic and Social Law' (2011) 18 Maastricht Journal of European and Comparative Law 7, 17–18, 21–22.
41. Claire Dhéret and Andreia Ghimis, 'The Revision of the Posted Workers Directive: Towards a Sufficient Policy Adjustment?' (2016) *European Policy Center (EPC) Discussion Paper* 10 <http://www.epc.eu/pub_details.php?cat_id=17&pub_id=6475> (accessed 23 October 2016).
42. Such a paradoxical situation in evident in the example of a Hungarian undertaking posting ten workers for almost two years to France for the construction of a bridge. According to the new rules, after eighteen months, the workers would benefit from the higher employment standards guaranteed under French law, implying higher costs for the posting undertaking. Conversely, in case the Hungarian undertaking posted thirty workers for the construction of the same bridge in France, and the service supply was concluded within the timeframe of eighteen months, the posting undertaking would not have to bear the extra costs correspondent to the higher employment standards guaranteed under French law.
43. For example, *see María Martínez Sala v Freistaat Bayern* [1998] ECJ Case C-85/96, ECLI: EU:C:1998:217; *Michel Trojani v Centre public d'aide sociale de Bruxelles (CPAS)* [2004] ECJ Case C-456/02, ECLI:EU:C:2004:488; *European Commission v Kingdom of the Netherlands*

come directly from the low-wage (mainly Central and Eastern European) posted workers themselves (or their unions), who are the ones supposedly suffering from the present situation. What the latter workers actually demanded was, instead, better enforcement of the rules and implementation of proper countermeasures to abusive exploitation of their vulnerable condition. In fact, although ideally tempting, the same treatment as local employees in the high-wage host countries might, at times, even entail a loss of the posted workers' jobs as a consequence of their employer's loss of competitiveness. Not to mention that most of the time the workers who are posted from low-wage to high-wage Member States are already benefitting from a satisfactory increase in their salary on account of the temporary assignment abroad.[44] Oddly enough, the claim for equal treatment for the supposed benefit of the Central and Eastern European workers was, in turn, strongly supported by the Western Member States and trade unions which argued, *inter alia*, against the socially unacceptable conditions under which posted employees are too often forced to work.[45] Their actual concern about the condition of the Central and Eastern European posted workers is rather suspicious though, especially considering that the imposition of equal treatment between local and posted workers would have the effect of basically eliminating the competitive advantage of the out-of-state posting undertakings with regard to wage differentials.[46] In other words, in all likelihood, it would indirectly affect the position of the posted workers while favouring the preservation of the highest social standards in the host states.[47]

When seen from this perspective, rather than being an expression of the fundamental value of equality, the equal conditions laid down in the new Directive (EU) 2018/957 appear instrumental to the protection of national labour markets and welfare systems. More generally, the whole narrative supporting the equal treatment between local and posted workers resembles nothing but a rhetorical backing for a disguised protectionist national policy. The slogan 'equal pay for equal work in the same place' itself, which was extensively used by the promoters of the campaign for the

---

[2012] CJEU Case C-542/09, ECLI:EU:C:2012:346; *Elodie Giersch and Others v État du Grand-Duché de Luxembourg* [2013] CJEU Case C-20/12, ECLI:EU:C:2013:411; *Elisabeta Dano and Florin Dano v Jobcenter Leipzig* [2014] CJEU Case C-333/13, ECLI:EU:C:2014:2358; *Jobcenter Berlin Neukölln v Nazifa Alimanovic and Others* [2015] CJEU Case C-67/14, ECLI: EU:C:2015:597; *Vestische Arbeit Jobcenter Kreis Recklinghausen v Jovanna García-Nieto and Others* [2016] CJEU Case C-299/14, ECLI:EU:C:2016:114. On this point, *see* Hatzopoulos, 'A (More) Social Europe: A Political Crossroad or a Legal One-Way? Dialogues between Luxembourg and Lisbon' (n 30) 1610–1615; McDonnell (n 16) 213–221.

44. On this point, *see supra* Chapter 7.
45. As a matter of fact, a liberal regulatory approach to posting has been traditionally backed by the major sending countries, while the major receiving countries have always supported the interest of their local workers and firms. Comte (n 38) 12. In this sense, *see also* Richard Giesen, 'Posting: Social Protection of Workers vs. Fundamental Freedoms?' (2003) 40 Common Market Law Review 143, 145.
46. Needless to say, the posted workers' access to social benefits in the host state was never part of the discussion.
47. In light of this, Watson rightly wonders whether the matter of the posted workers' pay and employment should not rather be left to employers and workers themselves. Watson (n 19) 303–304.

revision of the Posting of Workers Directive,[48] despite being shaped along the lines of the famous social dogma of 'equal pay for the same work', was indeed basically neglecting the principle of equality in substance.[49] Last but not least, the way in which the right to equal treatment was designed, namely as a power of the receiving Member States to extend their internal regulations to the incoming posted workers rather than as a direct right at disposal of the workers themselves, testifies once again that the action of the EU legislator was more inclined towards the interests of the high-wage Western Member States.

In light of the foregoing, it is argued that a merely formalistic equal treatment principle, such as the one introduced by Directive (EU) 2018/957, which is blind to the inherently different conditions of the economic actors involved, is not always suitable for achieving substantive equality between local and posted workers. Conversely, the latter can only be achieved through measures that, building on an 'actualised' Aristotelian conception of equality, would make it possible to bring about substantive equal opportunities and outcomes by demonstrating sensitivity towards those disparities.[50] Rather than relying on the application of a generalised 'equal treatment' on the basis of a one-size-fits-all approach, the path towards the true realisation of the EU value of equality can pass only through the progressive development of a European social model aimed at levelling upwards wages as well as social and labour standards all over the Union.[51] To this end, a number of recommendations for possible future improvements are put forward below in section 9.5.

48. ETUC (European Trade Union Confederation), 'The Posting of Workers Directive: Proposals for Revision (Resolution Adopted at the ETUC Executive Committee)' (2010) <http://www.europarl.europa.eu/document/activities/cont/201006/20100601ATT75367/20100601ATT75367EN.pdf> (accessed 12 January 2019); European Commission, 'Press Release – The State of the Union 2016: Towards a Better Europe – A Europe That Protects, Empowers and Defends' (*European Commission Press Releases Database*, 14 September 2016) <http://europa.eu/rapid/press-release_IP-16-3042_en.htm> (accessed 12 July 2019); European Commission, 'Speech of President Jean-Claude Juncker, State of the Union Address' (n 13); Austrian, Belgian, French, German, Luxembourg, Dutch and Swedish Ministers of Labour, 'Letter to Ms Marianne Thyssen Commissioner for Employment, Social Affairs, Skills and Labour Mobility' (18 June 2015).
49. Apparently, the realisation of substantive equality between local and posted workers was never the true aim of the promoters of the 2018 reform nor of the EU legislator. According to the President of the Labour Mobility Initiative Association, Schwarz, the revision of the Posting of Workers Directive was truly driven, on the one hand, by the intention of curtailing the increasing activity of Central and Eastern European companies on construction sites and roads. On the other hand, it was the result of the strong political commitment of the French President Macron against the populist movements all over Europe. Stefan Schwarz, 'EP Plenary Voted for State Mandated Protectionism' <https://www.elmc.eu/ep-plenary-voted-for-state-mandated-protectionism-commentary-from-stefan-schwarz/> (accessed 21 November 2018).
50. The suggestion of relying on an 'actualised' Aristotelian conception of equality implies a combination of the sensitivity demanded by Aristotle to inherent differences in society with the possibility to promote positive actions aimed at achieving equal opportunities and outcomes. For the record, the 'original' Aristotelian model has been accused of having an anti-egalitarian character, certainly due to the historical context in which it was elaborated, consisting in requiring the application of a different treatment in different situations, without considering the possibility of taking positive actions. In this sense, *see* Schiek, 'A New Framework on Equal Treatment of Persons in EC Law?' (n 29) 303–304.
51. For a diametrically opposite view which considers the application of the 'equal treatment principle' – as applied in the context of the free movement of workers – between local and posted

9.3 FAIR COMPETITION

At its origin, the Common Market was essentially governed by the free movement provisions in combination with competition law.[52] Since then, the principle of fair competition has undoubtedly a great significance in the pursuit of the Union's objectives and in the smooth functioning of the internal market. The EU involvement in the preservation and promotion of fair competition practices is fundamentally geared to averting detrimental competition distortions and ensuring equal conditions for businesses.[53] Accordingly, among the primary purposes of EU competition law there are the overall efficiency enhancement in terms of improved consumer welfare and resource allocation, the protection of consumers and small enterprises, and the contrast to the partitioning of the European single market.[54] To these ends, the EU rules on competition, enshrined in Articles 101–109 of the TFEU, prohibit both anti-competitive agreements between undertakings, distortive State aids (except for specific derogations), as well as mergers and takeovers affecting effective competition.[55]

In the context of posting of workers, the European public and political discourse are pervaded by the idea that the competition from cross-border workers with lower wages and employment standards is necessarily and unequivocally unfair in respect to local workers with better wages and working conditions in the receiving Member States. According to this view, the possibility for out-of-state service providers to compete against their local counterparts on the basis of lower prices, permitted by the recourse to lower-paid posted workers, is per se unfair.[56] This sort of wage competition between undertakings, allegedly fostered by the special treatment reserved to posted workers under the Posting of Workers Directive, is commonly deplored for leading to higher unemployment rates and downward pressure on wages and labour standards

workers as the sole way to ensure dignity, higher salaries and better employment conditions to the cross-border workers concerned, *see* Countouris and Engblom (n 18); Schiek et al. (n 2) 22–23 and 97.

52. Gerbrandy, Janssen and Thomsin (n 7) 36–37.
53. 'Competition – European Union' (*europa.eu*, 16 June 2016) <https://europa.eu/european-union/topics/competition_en> (accessed 17 February 2020); Honnefelder (n 9); Szczepański (n 11); 'Competition' (n 9).
54. Vassilis Hatzopoulos, 'The Economic Constitution of the EU Treaty and the Limits between Economic and Non-economic Activities' (2012) 23 European Business Law Review 973, 976; Craig and de Búrca (n 29) 1001–1002; Jones and Townley (n 9) 510–512.
55. Jones and Townley (n 9) 509–510; Honnefelder (n 9); Gerbrandy, Janssen and Thomsin (n 7) 35–36; 'Competition' (n 9).
56. European Commission, Impact Assessment, Accompanying the document Proposal for a Directive of the European Parliament and the Council amending Directive 96/71/EC concerning the posting of workers in the framework of the provision of services 2016 [SWD(2016) 52 final] 18; European Commission, 'Press Release – Commission Presents Reform of the Posting of Workers Directive – Towards a Deeper and Fairer European Labour Market' (*European Commission Press Releases Database*, 8 March 2016) <http://europa.eu/rapid/press-release_IP-16-466_en.htm> (accessed 19 July 2019). On this point, *see* Magdalena Bernaciak, 'Social Dumping: Political Catchphrase or Threat to Labour Standards?' (2012) ETUI European Trade Union Institute – Working Paper 2012.06, 16. Interestingly, such an issue was already in the air before the 2004 and 2007 EU enlargements to the East. Paul Davies, 'Posted Workers: Single Market or Protection of National Labour Law Systems?' (1997) 34 Common Market Law Review 571, 598.

(often improperly referred to as 'social dumping') in the receiving countries.[57] Against this backdrop, the foregoing presumption of the direct correlation between posting and unfair competition basically underpinned the 2018 legislative reform,[58] which was expressly oriented towards the establishment of a climate of fair competition characterised by 'fair wage conditions and a level playing field between posting and local companies in the host country'.[59] Pursuant to the new Directive (EU) 2018/957, the creation of a level playing field whereby both foreign and local competitors are subject to the same rules would prevent 'negative' wage competition while favouring 'positive' competition on productivity, efficiency, labour skills and quality of the services.[60]

The argument that considered the competition of cross-border service providers applying their home country's wage levels – although always within the boundaries set by the original Posting of Workers Directive[61] – as basically unfair, provided that they operated in the same jurisdiction as their local counterparts, is nonetheless fundamentally incompatible with EU law. More in detail, it should be noted that, by virtue of the Treaty provisions on free movement of services (Article 56 TFEU), the importing states are generally prevented from restricting the income of cheaper services to their own territory on the grounds of the wage levels of the workers who provide them. And this prohibition applies even though such a flow of cheaper services coming from abroad is liable to affect the interests of local businesses.[62] As further explained by the Court of Justice in *Bundesdruckerei*,[63] the receiving Member States are in principle not even allowed to impose the respect of national minimum wages reflecting the higher costs of

57. ETUC (European Trade Union Confederation), Business Europe, CEEP (European Centre of Employers and Enterprises providing Public services), UEAPME (European Association of Craft, Small and Medium-Sized Enterprises), 'Report on Joint Work of the European Social Partners on the ECJ Rulings in the Viking, Laval, Rüffert and Luxembourg Cases' (2010) 11; Daniel Carter, 'Equal Pay for Equal Work in the Same Place? Assessing the Revision to the Posted Workers Directive' (2018) 14 Croatian Yearbook of European Law and Policy 31, 50; Pennings (n 39) 5. For a proper definition of 'social dumping' in the context of posting, *see supra* Chapter 7.
58. Frans Pennings, 'The Relevance of the Concept of the Social Market Economy: Concluding Observations on the Contributions in This Special Issue' (2019) 15 Utrecht Law Review 95, 98; Mijke Houwerzijl and Lisa Berntsen, 'Posting of Workers: From a Blurred Notion Associated with "Cheap Labour" to a Tool for "Fair Labour Mobility"?' in Jens Arnholtz and Nathan Lillie (eds), *Posted Work in the European Union: The Political Economy of Free Movement* (Routledge 2019) 147.
59. European Commission, 'Press Release – Commission Presents Reform of the Posting of Workers Directive – Towards a Deeper and Fairer European Labour Market' (n 56).
60. Preamble Recital 16 of Directive (EU) 2018/957 of the European Parliament and of the Council of 28 June 2018 amending Directive 96/71/EC concerning the posting of workers in the framework of the provision of services (n 12). In this sense, *see* Catherine Jacqueson and Frans Pennings, 'Equal Treatment of Mobile Persons in the Context of a Social Market Economy' (2019) 15 Utrecht Law Review 64, 78; Adam Kapella and Garance Dubarry, 'Europe Is Built on Competition Which Stimulates, on Cooperation Which Strengthens, and Solidarity Which Unites' in Jacek Kubera and Tomasz Morozowski (eds), *A 'Social Turn' in the European Union?: New Trends and Ideas about Social Convergence in Europe* (First Edition, Routledge 2020) 188.
61. Federica Mustilli and Jacques Pelkmans, 'Access Barriers to Services Markets' (2013) 77 CEPS Centre for European Policy Studies 84, 50–51.
62. Notably, this rationale applies with regard to the free movement of goods (Article 34 TFEU) as well. Davies, 'Posted Workers: Single Market or Protection of National Labour Law Systems?' (n 56) 598–599.
63. *Bundesdruckerei GmbH v Stadt Dortmund* [2014] CJEU Case C-549/13, ECLI:EU:C:2014:2235 [34].

living and productivity of the host states.[64] In fact, such a requirement would inevitably narrow down the legitimate competitive advantage of the cross-border operators resulting from the respective pay differentials, while going beyond what is necessary to pursue the objective of employee protection.[65] When seen from this perspective, the enjoyment of the freedom to provide services by making recourse to lower-paid posted workers in comparison to local workers in the receiving states does not constitute per se an expression of unfair competition.[66] Conversely, the imposition of certain host state's employment standards, such as remuneration, on incoming service providers definitely represents a restriction of their freedom to provide services.[67] In any event, the competition of out-of-state posting undertakings has to be considered as truly unfair when they improperly profit from abusive and fraudulent practices, or from existing regulatory loopholes, as in the case of offshoring production from high-wage to low-wage countries.[68]

Besides, the assumption, underlying the adoption of Directive (EU) 2018/957, that the wage competition by foreign service providers and their posted personnel supposedly led to detrimental 'social dumping' and downward pressure on national welfare states, was evidently based on incorrect premises. As pointed out in the analysis previously carried out in Chapter 7, the superficial perception of the (regular) posting phenomenon as the typical source of problems deriving from intra-EU labour mobility is substantially disproved by empirical research. The actual main cause of negative effects has to be found primarily in company strategies of offshoring production from high-wage to low-wage countries, as well as in the variety of unlawful and fraudulent practices developed beyond the legal boundaries, which clearly require the introduction of ad hoc countermeasures. In this regard, as discussed in the previous chapter, the new Directive has undoubtedly made some improvements, even though only to a limited extent. At the same time, however, the narrative supporting the reform underestimated the number of opportunities offered by the recourse to posting activities, which benefit both the sending and receiving Member States, the posted workers themselves and the entire EU internal market.

64. Admittedly, it is also true that the price of the cross-border service is, nonetheless, determined on the basis of the economic standards of the receiving state. Evidently, therefore, in the event of a service supply from a low-wage to a high-wage Member State, the price paid for the service is normally higher than the price of a comparable service provided in the sending state.
65. Paul Davies, 'The Posted Workers Directive and the EC Treaty' (2002) 31 Industrial Law Journal 298, 300; Verschueren, 'The European Internal Market and the Competition between Workers' (n 3) 149.
66. As a matter of fact, the definition of 'fair competition' within the EU internal market is still rather uncertain; *see* Dhéret and Ghimis (n 41). Interestingly, it is worth recalling that, in 1958, at the dawn of European Economic Community, the Italian Government was allowed to export its surplus of workforce to the other five Member States, on condition that labour was demonstrably specialised in the field of coal and steel. On that occasion, the possibility of taking advantage of structurally lower wages was considered as a legitimate competitive advantage. In this sense, *see* Paul Magnette, 'How Can One Be European? Reflections on the Pillars of European Civic Identity' (2007) 13 European Law Journal 664, 672.
67. Grušić (n 38) 258.
68. Davies, 'Posted Workers: Single Market or Protection of National Labour Law Systems?' (n 56) 600.

What is more, the whole narrative claiming for the revision of the Posting of Workers Directive on the basis of a supposed absence of fair competition appears tendentious and misleading insofar as it merely focused on the existing gaps in costs of manpower, while failing to take into account the extra costs and administrative burdens intrinsically related to the cross-border dimension of the transnational provision of services. In effect, cross-border enterprises which have to comply with both home state requirements and host state requirements in each country where they operate, while bearing the correspondent costs, are evidently put in a more disadvantageous position vis-à-vis their local counterparts.[69] Besides the 'normal' costs concerning the workers' remuneration, social security and health insurance contributions, personal income tax advances, as well as further contributions to public and private funds depending on the country of establishment and the economic sector of activity,[70] enterprises posting their employees abroad have to bear a whole series of variable and fixed labour costs. More specifically, the first category of expenses includes, *inter alia*, those for travel, board and lodging, per diem (daily allowance), further compensations and contributions on account of the secondment, private international health insurance, applications for PDs A1, currency exchanges, logistic arrangements in the host Member State, telecommunication and foreign language trainings and tests.[71] In turn, the second category of costs encompasses those required by national bureaucratic procedures of the host Member States, such as making obligatory declarations to the competent national authorities, hiring a local contact person, translating all company and employment documentation into the local language, but also obtaining permits to conduct a business activity (obligatory in Belgium) or bank guarantees (obligatory in France).[72] On top of that, the activity of posting of workers oftentimes implies also further costs of execution of debts in the host countries and legal assistance.[73]

In light of the above, it is apparent that the cost of workers' remuneration represents only a fraction of the final price of the services provided across borders.[74] As stressed *supra* in Chapter 7, such a final price is also strongly influenced by a number of other competitive factors, such as, first of all, the workers' productivity.[75] Accordingly, the rationale that directly associates the relatively lower remuneration of certain

69. Davies, 'The Posted Workers Directive and the EC Treaty' (n 65) 300; Grušić (n 38) 258.
70. Marek Benio, 'Labour Costs in Cross-Border Services: The Study on the Labour Cost Structure in the Case of Posting of Workers from Poland' (Department of Public Economy and Administration, University of Economics 2016) 5.
71. *Ibid.* 6–8.
72. In practice, a company providing services across borders has to comply with all special requirements envisaged in each of the countries in which it operates. *Ibid.*; Thilo Brodtmann, 'Member States Must Stop Building Barriers for Posted Workers' (*EURACTIV*, 9 October 2018) <https://www.euractiv.com/section/economy-jobs/opinion/member-states-must-stop-building-barriers-for-posted-workers/> (accessed 5 November 2018).
73. Benio (n 70) 6–8.
74. *Ibid.* 3 and 9.
75. In effect, if the price of a service was merely dependent on the workers' remuneration, it could not be possible to explain how countries like Germany or Denmark are able to export their own services also in lower-wage Member States. As interestingly pointed out by Davies, 'What matters to an employer is not the absolute level of wages and other employment costs, but their level in relation to the productivity of the workers.' Davies, 'Posted Workers: Single Market or Protection of National Labour Law Systems?' (n 56) 599.

posted workers coming from low-wage Member States with cheaper services, and therefore greater competitiveness, which automatically provokes distortion of competition and downward pressure on national welfare states, is proved fundamentally false.[76] Since the aforementioned extra costs and administrative burdens have a negative impact on out-of-state service providers only (and indirectly on their posted employees), the application of the same rules to both posted workers and workers in the host state is expected to overly affect the position of posting undertakings and posted workers, while conferring an undue competitive advantage on national economic actors in the receiving Member States.[77] To that extent, Directive (EU) 2018/957 is, therefore, liable to run counter to the EU principle of fair competition.

Lastly, it is worth pointing out also that the questioned rationale that considers the competition of economic actors applying lower wage levels or working conditions as necessarily unfair is definitely not accepted within a national jurisdiction. As a matter of fact, the competition of cheaper and better-performing enterprises normally forms part of the regular functioning of national markets,[78] where it is regarded as natural and beneficial to consumers and, more broadly, the entire national economy.[79] Similarly, the competition of undertakings posting their workers from the poorer to the wealthier EU countries has a disparate impact on the EU labour market as well. As evidenced by the investigation previously performed in Chapter 7, besides potentially affecting local companies and low-wage workers in high-wage Member States, it undoubtedly benefits local consumers and, in general, service recipients, as well as intra-EU competition as a whole.[80] Accordingly, rather than as an issue of unfair competition and absence of a level playing field between local and posting companies, the activity of posting of workers would have been addressed more properly as a matter of wealth redistribution.

76. *Ibid.*; Bernaciak (n 56) 17; Kristina Maslauskaite, 'Social Competition in the EU: Myths and Realities' (2013) Policy Paper, Notre Europe Jaques Delors Institute 62, 25; Magdalena Bernaciak, 'Social Dumping and the EU Integration Process' (2014) ETUI European Trade Union Institute - Working Paper 2014.06, 7; Verschueren, 'The European Internal Market and the Competition between Workers' (n 3) 133–134; Benio (n 70) 3.
77. As noted by the Court of Justice in 2001, 'the application of the host Member State's national rules to service providers is liable to prohibit, impede or render less attractive the provision of services to the extent that it involves expenses and additional administrative and economic burdens'. *Mazzoleni v Inter Surveillance Assistance* [2001] ECJ Case C-165/98, ECLI: EU:C:2001:162 [24]; *Finalarte Sociedade de Construção Civil v Urlaubs-und Lohnausgleichskasse der Bauwirtschaft* [2001] ECJ Joined Cases C-49/98, C-50/98, C-52/98 to C-54/98 and C-68/98 to C-71/98, ECLI:EU:C:2001:564 [30]. In this sense, *see also* Pennings (n 39) 5. Incidentally, it is worth noting that such an equal treatment affects even more those undertakings and workers coming from low-wage Member States, as they also have to line up with the higher employment standards applied in the richer countries of destination.
78. To be precise, the competition on price is in all respects intrinsically related to the existing capitalist economic system.
79. ETUC (European Trade Union Confederation), Business Europe, CEEP (European Centre of Employers and Enterprises providing Public services), UEAPME (European Association of Craft, Small and Medium-Sized Enterprises) (n 57) 7; Carter (n 57) 47.
80. In this sense, *see also* Alexander Somek, 'From Workers to Migrants, from Distributive Justice to Inclusion: Exploring the Changing Social Democratic Imagination: Exploring the Changing Social Democratic Imagination' (2012) 18 European Law Journal 711, 5–8.

9.4 SOLIDARITY

Finding its etymological roots in Roman law, where the concept of *obligatio in solidum* referred to an obligation marked by joint and several liability of each of the debtors, the idea of solidarity was subsequently revived during the nineteenth century in Europe – especially in France – at the time of the revolutionary constitutional movements.[81] It was then further developed by three broad European social and political traditions, namely social theory, socialism and Christian democracy.[82] Against this background, solidarity is currently included among the fundamental constitutional principles in a number of Member States[83] and among the cardinal values of the European Union.[84] Notably, it can be traced in the Treaty on European Union (Articles 2, 3, 21, 24, 31, 32), the Treaty on the Functioning of the European Union (Articles 67, 80, 122, 194, 222) and the Charter of Fundamental Rights of the European Union(Chapter IV).[85] As a matter of fact, the pursuit of the value of solidarity traditionally represents an identity feature of the European Union, indicating a specific social commitment in the EU

81. Ross (n 5) 23; Andrea Sangiovanni, 'Solidarity as Joint Action: Solidarity as Joint Action' (2015) 32 Journal of Applied Philosophy 340, 340; Bengt Beutler, 'Solidarity in the EU: A Critique of Solidarity and of the EU' in Andreas Grimmel and Susanne My Giang (eds), *Solidarity in the European Union* (Springer Berlin Heidelberg 2017) 24; Markus Kotzur, 'Solidarity as a Legal Concept' in Andreas Grimmel and Susanne My Giang (eds), *Solidarity in the European Union* (Springer Berlin Heidelberg 2017) 38; Andreas Grimmel, 'Solidarity in the European Union: Fundamental Value or "Empty Signifier"' in Andreas Grimmel and Susanne My Giang (eds), *Solidarity in the European Union* (Springer Berlin Heidelberg 2017) 161.
82. For an in-depth insight into the role played by those three traditions in the development of solidarity, *see* Steinar Stjernø, *Solidarity in Europe: The History of an Idea* (Cambridge University Press 2005); Ross (n 5) 26. According to Sangiovanni, the idea of solidarity has originally developed in socialist, nationalist and Christian traditions instead. Sangiovanni, 'Solidarity as Joint Action' (n 81) 341–342.
83. This is the case, e.g., of Article 1 of the French Constitution, Article 2 of the Italian Constitution, and Article 2 of the Spanish Constitution. Catherine Barnard, 'EU Citizenship and the Principle of Solidarity' in Michael Dougan and Eleanor Spaventa (eds), *Social Welfare and EU Law* (Hart Publishing 2005) 157; Ross (n 5) 43.
84. Notably, such a fundamental character of solidarity was already acknowledged by the Court of Justice in 1978, when it considered 'the principle of Community solidarity which is one of the foundations of the Community'. *Benzine en Petroleum Handelsmaatschappij BV and others v Commission of the European Communities* [1978] ECJ Case 77/77, ECLI:EU:C:1978:141 [1978]. Catherine Barnard, 'Solidarity and New Governance in Social Policy' in Gráinne de Búrca and Joanne Scott (eds), *Law and New Governance in the EU and the US* (Hart Publishing 2006) 155–156; European Commission, Communication from the Commission to the European Council – A citizens' agenda – Delivering results for Europe 2006 [COM(2006) 211 final] 4; Alexander Somek, 'Solidarity Decomposed Being and Time in European Citizenship' (2007) 32 European Law Review 787, 789; Ross (n 5) 36 and 45; Catherine Barnard, 'Solidarity and the Commission's "Renewed Social Agenda"' in Malcolm Ross and Yuri Borgmann-Prebil (eds), *Promoting Solidarity in the European Union* (Oxford University Press 2010) 81; Andrea Sangiovanni, 'Solidarity in the European Union' (2013) 33 Oxford Journal of Legal Studies 213, 213; Schiek et al. (n 2) 15; *Slovak Republic and Hungary v Council of the European Union, Opinion of Advocate General Yves Bot delivered on 26 July 2017* [2017] CJEU Joined Cases C-643/15 and C-647/15, ECLI:EU:C:2017:618 [17].
85. In addition, the term 'solidarity' appears also in the Preambles to the Treaties and the Charter, as well as in various protocols.

integration process.[86] In its famous declaration of 9 May 1950, the French Foreign Ministry Schuman already envisaged, indeed, the realisation of a 'de facto solidarity' at European level through concrete achievements in terms of market integration.[87] That guideline was then promptly transposed into the Preamble to the 1951 Treaty establishing the European Coal and Steel Community (ECSC) according to which 'Europe can be built only through real practical achievements which will first of all create real solidarity'.[88]

After having initially been associated with the economic dimension of European integration, the concept of solidarity under EU law has significantly evolved and expanded over the years. Whereas in the Treaty of Rome[89] it was merely referring to obligations among Member States in a purely external dimension,[90] in the Treaties of Maastricht[91] and Amsterdam[92] it was mentioned alongside 'economic and social cohesion', thus progressively assuming an ever-growing internal dimension.[93] A more nuanced formulation, adding also transnational obligations among the peoples of the Member States was subsequently introduced by the Treaty of Nice.[94] Eventually, with the signing in 2007 of the Treaty of Lisbon and the incorporation of the Charter of Fundamental Rights of the European Union, the value of solidarity was given a well-rounded meaning, encompassing horizontal obligations between Member States (in both external and internal dimensions) and between EU citizens, as well as vertical obligations between Member States and the Union.[95] More specifically, horizontal solidarity among Member States has many facets distributed between Article 3(3) TEU in general terms, Articles 21, 24, 31 and 32 TEU in the area of foreign policy, Articles 67 and 80 TFEU concerning immigration and external border control, Article 122 TFEU on mutual financial assistance in case of economic crisis, Article 194 TFEU in the field of energy policy, and Article 222 TFEU in case of a terrorist attack or a natural or

86. Joseph HH Weiler, 'A Constitution for Europe? Some Hard Choices' (2002) 40 JCMS: Journal of Common Market Studies 563, 569; Ulla Neergaard, 'In Search of the Role of "Solidarity" in Primary Law and the Case Law of the European Court of Justice' in Ulla Neergaard, Ruth Nielsen and Lynn M Roseberry (eds), *The Role of Courts in Developing a European Social Model – Theoretical and Methodological Perspectives* (Djøf Publishing 2010) 116–117.
87. According to the vision of Shuman, 'Europe will not be made all at once, or according to a single plan. It will be built through concrete achievements which first create a de facto solidarity.' Robert Schuman, 'Declaration of 9th May 1950' (Paris, 10 May 1950). *See* Lucia Serena Rossi, 'The Principle of Equality Among Member States of the European Union' in Lucia Serena Rossi and Federico Casolari (eds), *The Principle of Equality in EU Law* (Springer Berlin Heidelberg 2017) 35; Graham Butler, 'Solidarity and Its Limits for Economic Integration in the European Union's Internal Market' (2018) 25 Maastricht Journal of European and Comparative Law 310, 314.
88. Treaty establishing the European Coal and Steel Community 1951. On this point, *see* Sangiovanni, 'Solidarity in the European Union' (n 84) 213; Grimmel (n 81) 161.
89. Treaty of Rome (EEC) – Treaty establishing the European Economic Community (n 14).
90. Neergaard (n 86) 109.
91. Treaty establishing the European Community (Maastricht Treaty) 1992 (OJ C 224).
92. Treaty establishing the European Community (Amsterdam Treaty) 1997 (OJ C 340).
93. Sangiovanni, 'Solidarity in the European Union' (n 84) 214; Grimmel (n 81) 161.
94. Treaty establishing the European Community (Nice Treaty) 2002 (OJ C 325). *See* Neergaard (n 86) 110–112.
95. Sangiovanni, 'Solidarity in the European Union' (n 84) 214; Rossi (n 87) 36; Grimmel (n 81) 161.

man-made disaster.[96] Apart from such a conception as a structural principle, solidarity is conceived also with an interpersonal dimension among the peoples of the Member States, in connection with the idea of the welfare state. In this sense, it is mentioned among the EU founding values in Article 2 TEU, as an intergenerational obligation in Article 3(3) TEU, alongside 'mutual respect' in Article 3(5) TEU, and in the form of rights enshrined in Chapter IV of the CFREU.[97]

In a general sense, the term solidarity refers to the willingness to collaborate and share resources with others who belong to the same community *lato sensu*, thus helping to build stronger social relationships.[98] In his opinion in *Sodemare*,[99] Advocate General Fennelly defined it as 'the inherently uncommercial act of involuntary subsidization of one social group by another'.[100] To this end, solidarity may assume both inter-institutional and interpersonal dimensions, as it may entail direct or indirect transfers of resources between states as well as between individuals.[101] Relationships of solidarity, like the one binding EU Member States and citizens together, are necessarily inspired to some altruistic intentions towards the realisation of a sort of ideal community whereby individual and common interests virtually coincide. Yet, at the same time, they are inevitably still marked by a certain degree of reciprocity, which attenuates unconditioned generosity in favour of some self-interest and is reflected in enforceable political obligations.[102] As a matter of fact, being part of a community (as the European Union) inspired by the value of solidarity undoubtedly instils a sense of security and trust on all of its members (as in the case of Member States and citizens).

In more practical terms, the value of solidarity translates, in some cases, into insurance for individuals or states against potential risks connected to their belonging to a particular community, in the event they end up facing disadvantageous conditions.[103] In other cases, it entails redistributive policies aimed at compensating

96. Barnard, 'EU Citizenship and the Principle of Solidarity' (n 83) 158; Ross (n 5) 44; Beutler (n 81) 21, 30–31; Kotzur (n 81) 41–42; Rossi (n 87) 37; Wouters and Schmitt (n 5) 51.
97. Barnard, 'EU Citizenship and the Principle of Solidarity' (n 83) 158; Ross (n 5) 44; Barnard, 'Solidarity and the Commission's "Renewed Social Agenda"' (n 84) 74–75; Neergaard (n 86) 112–116; Rossi (n 87) 36; Wouters and Schmitt (n 5) 51.
98. Barnard, 'Solidarity and the Commission's "Renewed Social Agenda"' (n 84) 81; Floris de Witte, 'The End of EU Citizenship and the Means of Non-Discrimination' (2011) 18 Maastricht Journal of European and Comparative Law 86, 88–89; Jacqueson (n 2) 376–377; Vandenbroucke, 'The Idea of a European Social Union' (n 2) 21.
99. *Sodemare SA, Anni Azzurri Holding SpA and Anni Azzurri Rezzato Srl v Regione Lombardia* [1997] ECJ Case C-70/95, ECLI:EU:C:1997:301.
100. *Sodemare SA, Anni Azzurri Holding SpA and Anni Azzurri Rezzato Srl v Regione Lombardia, Opinion of Advocate General Nial Fennelly delivered on 6 February 1997* [1997] ECJ Case C-70/95, ECLI:EU:C:1997:55 [29]. On this point, *see* Barnard, 'EU Citizenship and the Principle of Solidarity' (n 83) 159; Somek (n 84) 788 and 792; Barnard, *EU Employment Law* (n 4) 197.
101. Vandenbroucke, 'The Idea of a European Social Union' (n 2) 28.
102. Such a conception of solidarity at the crossroads between self-interest and community, as well as between altruism and obligation, has been brilliantly portrayed in Kalypso Nicolaïdis and Juri Viehoff, 'Social Justice in the European Union: The Puzzles of Solidarity, Reciprocity and Choice' in Dimitry Kochenov, Gráinne de Búrca and Andrew Williams (eds), *Europe's Justice Deficit?* (Hart Publishing 2015) 283–287.
103. Alain Supiot, 'The Transformation of Work and the Future of Labour Law in Europe: A Multidisciplinary Perspective' (1999) 138 International Labour Review 31, 43–44; Sangiovanni, 'Solidarity in the European Union' (n 84) 229–230; Vandenbroucke, 'The Idea of a European

individuals or states for the unfortunate circumstances in which they find themselves through no fault of their own.[104] Importantly, the latter conception of solidarity as redistribution is closely interlinked with that of social justice, as it is considered a valuable means to realise justice in terms of fair distribution of wealth, opportunities and privileges within the society.[105] Besides being traditionally pursued in the context of the welfare state through solidarity-based redistribution of resources, the ideal of social justice is included among the EU objectives as well, and it is now at the heart of the European social model.[106] However, unlike what generally happens within a pure national dimension, the commitment to social justice on a European scale is normally conceived as a mostly reciprocal obligation among Member States.[107]

The idea of solidarity as a means to achieve substantive distributive justice originally developed within national welfare states, where the willingness to collaborate and share is primarily motivated by the sense of identity resulting from common traditional, cultural and historical roots.[108] In such a context, it translates into social insurance mechanisms (such as, *inter alia*, social security, pension, and health insurance systems) and further wealth redistribution schemes, in combination with a balanced framework of social rights and obligations.[109] Alongside this national solidarity, the continuing process of EU integration has required both Member States and EU

Social Union' (n 2) 27–28. This is the case of social security policies. Marc Hooghe and Soetkin Verhaegen, 'The Democratic Legitimacy of EU Institutions and Support for Social Policy in Europe' in Frank Vandenbroucke, Catherine Barnard and Geert De Baere (eds), *A European Social Union after the Crisis* (Cambridge University Press 2017) 122–124. This is also the case of organised groups at national and transnational level for the protection of collective interests. Sciarra (n 8) 2.

104. Vandenbroucke, 'The Idea of a European Social Union' (n 2) 27–28.
105. Ross (n 5) 45; Nicolaïdis and Viehoff (n 102) 279; Sangiovanni, 'Solidarity as Joint Action' (n 81) 340.
106. Article 3(3) TEU. In this sense, *see* Schiek et al. (n 2) 15–16; Vandenbroucke, 'The Idea of a European Social Union' (n 2) 34.
107. According to Sangiovanni, social justice in the EU is framed as a 'reciprocity-based internationalism', in the sense that 'demands for social solidarity at all levels of governance can be understood as demands for a fair return in the mutual production of important collective goods'. Sangiovanni, 'Solidarity in the European Union' (n 84) 217. On this point, *see also* Nicolaïdis and Viehoff (n 102) 288. Micklitz, in turn, affirms that the EU has developed a new paradigm of justice, which he terms 'access justice'. Hans-W Micklitz, 'A European Advantage in Legal Scholarship?' in Rob van Gestel, Hans-W Micklitz and Edward L Rubin (eds), *Rethinking Legal Scholarship* (Cambridge University Press 2017) 293.
108. As effectively exemplified by de Witte, 'the motive for sharing our resources with fellow citizens is that we are all Irish, or Spanish. The motive for sharing our resources with one particular group of people is that they are "like us".' Floris de Witte, *Justice in the EU: The Emergence of Transnational Solidarity* (Oxford University Press 2015) 5. *See also* Barnard, 'Solidarity and New Governance in Social Policy' (n 84) 154; de Witte (n 98) 88–89; Barnard, *EU Employment Law* (n 4) 197; Sangiovanni, 'Solidarity in the European Union' (n 84) 222; Helder De Schutter, 'The Solidarity Argument for the European Union' in Frank Vandenbroucke, Catherine Barnard and Geert De Baere (eds), *A European Social Union after the Crisis* (Cambridge University Press 2017) 72.
109. Barnard, *EU Employment Law* (n 4) 197–200; Vandenbroucke, 'The Case for a European Social Union: From Muddling Through to a Sense of Common Purpose' (n 2) 17; Schoukens (n 4) 6; Vandenbroucke, 'The Idea of a European Social Union' (n 2) 23; Hooghe and Verhaegen (n 103) 122–125.

citizens to progressively engage in transnational forms of pan-European solidarity.[110] Solidarity in the European Union takes thereby the shape of obligations among Member States, among Member States and citizens of other Member States, as well as among EU citizens themselves.[111] More specifically, such a transnational perspective on solidarity aims at attaining upward socio-economic convergence and cohesion at European level, with a view to realising social justice beyond the borders of the nation state.[112] In order to do so, it requires Member States and their citizens to open up their national solidarity circles (i.e., both their borders, markets, services and societies in general) to other EU citizens who make use of their free movement rights, thus allowing the latter to improve their economic and overall living conditions by working in a country other than the one in which they are citizens or residents.[113] In parallel, it entails fair access to opportunities for both countries and enterprises wishing to invest and trade across the internal market.[114]

This form of pan-European solidarity undoubtedly requires a sacrifice by certain undertakings and citizens in the receiving countries, especially those in the high-wage Western Member States.[115] From another point of view, it is an expression of the reciprocity due by the latter undertakings and citizens to their counterparts in the sending Member States, particularly those coming from the low-wage Central and Eastern countries. It must not be forgotten, indeed, that the latter, by virtue of the fact that they have opened both their markets, economies and societies to the entire body of EU law, are in all respects entitled to the whole range of benefits connected with the participation in the EU internal market.[116] An example of this form of pan-European

110. Dougan and Spaventa (n 3) 188; Vandenbroucke, 'The Idea of a European Social Union' (n 2) 22–24; Dagmar Schiek, 'Solidarity and the Court of Justice of the European Union' (ICON-S Conference: Courts, Power and Public Law, University of Copenhagen, Faculty of Law, 5 July 2017); Ferrera (n 8) 51; Vandenbroucke, 'The European Pillar of Social Rights: From Promise to Delivery' (n 34) 8; Maurizio Ferrera, 'Crafting the European Social Union – Towards a Roadmap for Delivery' in Maurizio Ferrera (ed.), *Towards a European Social Union: The European Pillar of Social Rights and the Roadmap for a Fully-Fledged Social Union* (Centro di Ricerca e Documentazione Luigi Einaudi 2019) 20.
111. For the record, Sangiovanni identifies only two forms of solidarity at EU level, namely Member State solidarity and transnational solidarity between EU citizens, thus basically including the obligations between Member States and citizens of other Member States into the latter category. Sangiovanni, 'Solidarity in the European Union' (n 84) 217.
112. Vandenbroucke, 'The Case for a European Social Union: From Muddling Through to a Sense of Common Purpose' (n 2) 17; de Witte (n 108) 4; Vandenbroucke, 'The Idea of a European Social Union' (n 2) 20–21; Schutter (n 108) 74–75.
113. Somek (n 84) 792; Sangiovanni, 'Solidarity in the European Union' (n 84) 234; Jacqueson (n 2) 376–377; Vandenbroucke, 'The Case for a European Social Union: From Muddling Through to a Sense of Common Purpose' (n 2) 17; de Witte (n 108) 10–11; Frank Vandenbroucke, 'Social Benefits and Cross-Border Mobility: Sticking to Principles May Yield Better Practical Results for Everybody' (2016) 17 Tribune, Notre Europe Jacques Delors Institute 1.
114. Vandenbroucke, 'The Idea of a European Social Union' (n 2) 23.
115. Barnard, 'Solidarity and the Commission's "Renewed Social Agenda"' (n 84) 75; Jacqueson (n 2) 387–388.
116. Sangiovanni, 'Solidarity in the European Union' (n 84) 237; Jacqueson (n 2) 375; Nicolaïdis and Viehoff (n 102) 290.

solidarity may be traced in the progressive development of the principle of non-discriminatory access to social benefits and services for mobile workers.[117] In that respect, even though the Court's promotion of equal treatment between migrant and local workers has put considerable pressure on national welfare states, such a burden is nonetheless generally accepted on account of the reciprocal participation in the internal market, as well as of the positive effects in terms of upward social convergence and overall benefit to the Union as a whole.[118] In the words of Rawls, it is justified '[f]or we are to agree in advance to the principles of justice and their consistent application from the standpoint of certain positions'.[119]

It is therefore apparent that the transnational pan-European dimension of solidarity is, in principle, in direct conflict with the purely national conception of solidarity.[120] The latter is, indeed, liable to come under pressure as a result of the increasing transnational obligations imposed by EU law on Member States and citizens.[121] By implication, the success of the European integration process is inescapably dependent on its capacity to achieve a balanced promotion of both EU and

117. As noted by Barnard, while the Court of Justice widely developed such a 'positive' use of the solidarity principle in order to impose obligations on Member States in respect of migrant EU citizens, in a number of cases, the same Court interpreted instead the principle of solidarity in a 'negative' way to protect national welfare systems. Barnard, 'EU Citizenship and the Principle of Solidarity' (n 83) 159–175. Interestingly, even the marked liberal approach taken by the Court of Justice in the series of decisions concerning the posting of workers (*see supra* Chapters 3 and 4) has been regarded as an expression of European solidarity, intended as a form of compensation for the biased EU enlargement process and of redistribution of employment opportunities between high-wage Western and low-wage CEECs. In this sense, *see* Hans-W Micklitz, 'Judicial Activism of the European Court of Justice and the Development of the European Social Model in Anti-Discrimination and Consumer Law' in Ulla Neergaard, Ruth Nielsen and Lynn M Roseberry (eds), *The Role of Courts in Developing a European Social Model – Theoretical and Methodological Perspectives* (Djøf Publishing 2010) 46; Dorota Leczykiewicz, 'Conceptualising Conflict between the Economic and the Social in EU Law after Viking and Laval' in R Mark Freedland and Jeremias Prassl (eds), *Viking, Laval and Beyond* (First Edition, Hart Publishing 2016) 317; Tor-Inge Harbo, 'The Criterion of "Consistent and Systematic Manner"' in Mads Andenas, Tarjei Bekkedal and Luca Pantaleo (eds), *The Reach of Free Movement* (Springer Berlin Heidelberg 2017) 206.

118. Incidentally, this principle of non-discriminatory access to social benefits and services for mobile workers was severely criticised by Scharpf for being liable to lead to generally lower standards of social protection, while violating the existing obligations of reciprocity among Member States. Scharpf, 'The Asymmetry of European Integration, or Why the EU Cannot Be a "Social Market Economy"' (n 2) 238.

119. John Rawls, *A Theory of Justice* (Revised Edition, Harvard University Press 1971) 85.

120. Somek (n 84) 805; Vassilis Hatzopoulos, *Regulating Services in the European Union* (Oxford University Press 2012) 354; Sangiovanni, 'Solidarity in the European Union' (n 84) 234; Alain Supiot, 'Towards a European Policy on Work' in Nicola Countouris and Mark Freedland (eds), *Resocialising Europe in a Time of Crisis* (Cambridge University Press 2013) 35; Butler (n 87) 327.

121. Nonetheless, this is certainly not the case when workers (even third country nationals, non-contractual and part-time workers), in the exercise of their freedom of movement under Articles 20, 21, 45, and 49 TFEU, take up employment in another Member State, where they regularly pay their taxes and actively participate in the civil society. Sangiovanni, 'Solidarity in the European Union' (n 84) 234.

national economic and social cohesion, while averting a negative trade-off between national and pan-European solidarity.[122]

When shifting the focus to the recent revision of the Posting of Workers Directive, the concept of national solidarity is apparently the only one that has been taken into account by the narrative supporting the principle of equal treatment between local and posted workers.[123] The transnational dimension of solidarity, likewise the related issues of social justice and wealth redistribution within the Union, were nevertheless basically left out of any discussion on the matter. Although introducing equal treatment between local and posted workers, the new Directive (EU) 2018/957 does not envisage any inclusion of the foreign seconded workers into the national solidarity scheme of the receiving Member States. While the economic burden resulting from the respect of the host state's levels of wages and working conditions remains entirely on out-of-state posting undertakings, the posted workers are not given access to any local social benefit.

In effect, the aforementioned act of secondary EU legislation was specifically designed to stem the widespread sense of insecurity, inequality and injustice caused by the ever-growing phenomenon of posting, which is commonly regarded as a major source of downward pressure on national welfare systems. Put differently, this legislative *novella* aims at preserving national social standards and industrial relations systems in the wealthier Western Member States, while restricting the opportunities of economic actors in the poorer Central and Eastern Member States to improve their economic and social status.[124] Furthermore, by disincentivising the posting of workers from low-wage to high-wage Member States, it basically neglects the relatively great redistributive capacity of this peculiar form of intra-EU labour mobility, which is testified by the higher wages and purchasing power of the workers concerned, as well as by the higher tax revenues and social security contributions collected in the sending countries.[125] The practice of posting is, indeed, a valuable instrument of upward social convergence, which would virtually enable workers in low-wage Member States to catch up with their richer counterparts in high-wage countries.

All things considered, the new Directive (EU) 2018/957 appears fundamentally misaligned with respect to the EU value of transnational solidarity, in both its interstate and inter-individual dimensions. In particular, given that rather than addressing the unequal wealth distribution within the Union it is expected to exacerbate differences between Eastern and Western Member States, this legislative intervention is liable to

122. Vandenbroucke, 'The Case for a European Social Union: From Muddling Through to a Sense of Common Purpose' (n 2) 17.
123. Notably, the new Directive is considered by Sciarra as an instrument of protection of, *inter alia*, national solidarity regimes, to the extent it constitutes an effective remedy to the inequalities emerged as a consequence of social dumping and wage competition. Sciarra (n 8) 133.
124. For an in-depth analysis of the actual purpose and expected economic impact of Directive (EU) 2018/957, *see supra* Chapter 8.
125. Frederic De Wispelaere and Jozef Pacolet, 'The Benefits of Posting: Facts and Figures on the Use and Impact of Intra-EU Posting' in Jens Arnholtz and Nathan Lillie (eds), *Posted Work in the European Union: The Political Economy of Free Movement* (Routledge 2019) 39–40. For a comprehensive investigation of the whole gamma of benefits deriving from posting, *see supra* Chapter 7.

come into conflict with the conception of solidarity as a means to realise distributive justice on a European scale. In this sense, it clearly attests the tragically low degree of solidarity among EU Member States and citizens.[126] As a matter of fact, following the 2004 and 2007 European enlargements towards the East, and the consequent opening up of the internal market to a bunch of low-wage mobile workers, the overall commitment to transnational solidarity progressively decreased.[127] In the same vein, even the principle of non-discriminatory access to social benefits and services for mobile workers has gradually become more and more controversial.[128]

In conclusion, besides acknowledging that a pure market liberalisation does not necessarily represent a fair and just distributive mechanism, it is worth stressing the need to expand the focus beyond the EU regulation of the posting phenomenon and the cross-border provision of services. When taking into account the overall impact of the four freedoms at national level, it is clear that the companies' exercise of their freedom to provide services by making recourse to posting arrangements is certainly no more harmful to social standards in the receiving countries than the movement of goods and capitals across borders.[129] Nonetheless, while the cross-border provision of services by recourse to cheaper workforce posted from low-wage Central and Eastern Member States is being contained, the movement of products, services and capitals from the wealthier Western to the poorer Central and Eastern Member States is by no means affected. From such a broader perspective, the exploitation by low-wage workers coming from low-wage Member States of the opportunities offered by the internal

126. Concerns about the impossibility to achieve substantive distributive economic justice within the Union, due to the worrying lack of solidarity among EU Member States and citizens, have been firmly expressed in Nicolaïdis and Viehoff (n 102) 279 and 282. *Inter alia*, the rather low degree of solidarity among EU countries and citizens has been evidenced by the global financial and economic crisis of 2008–2010, and it is currently apparent in relation to both intra-EU migration and the so-called 'refugee crisis', entailing the immigration of asylum seekers from outside the Union. Joseph HH Weiler, 'The Political and Legal Culture of European Integration: An Exploratory Essay' (2011) 9 International Journal of Constitutional Law 678, 680; Micklitz (n 107) 296; Beutler (n 81) 21; McDonnell (n 16) 201.
127. In parallel, the 'perception of insecurity, isolation, inequity and inequality' sharply increased in Western Europe. Barnard, 'Solidarity and the Commission's "Renewed Social Agenda"' (n 84) 78. *See also* European Commission, Communication from the Commission to the European Parliament, the Council, the European Economic and Social Committee and the Committee of the Regions – Opportunities, access and solidarity: towards a new social vision for 21st century Europe 2007 [COM(2007) 726 final] 3.
128. Vandenbroucke, 'The Case for a European Social Union: From Muddling Through to a Sense of Common Purpose' (n 2) 17–18; Vandenbroucke, 'The Idea of a European Social Union' (n 2) 24.
129. As strongly emphasised by Kukovec, the issue of 'goods dumping', notwithstanding its high economic and social dangerousness, has never been included in the general discourse on EU integration. Damjan Kukovec, 'A Critique of the Rhetoric of Common Interest in the European Union Legal Discourse' (2012) SSRN Electronic Journal 11, 5; Damjan Kukovec, 'Hierarchies as Law' (2014) 21 Columbia Journal of European Law 131, 149, 165 and 188; Damjan Kukovec, 'Law and the Periphery' (2015) 21 European Law Journal 406, 420–422. On this point, *see also supra* Chapter 7. With regard to the distorted free flow of capital, Kubera notes that the majority of the enterprises currently operating in Poland, Czech Republic, Hungary and Slovakia are owned by Western investors. Jacek Kubera, 'Posted Workers: More Europe Is More Freedom' (*Social Europe*, 5 March 2018) <https://www.socialeurope.eu/more-europe-is-more-freedom> (accessed 16 July 2019).

market when they are posted to high-wage Member States may be regarded as a legitimate way to improve their economic and social condition. Considering that, besides the latter workers and their employers, a major profit goes to the recipients of those services as well, the fact that economic actors in the wealthier Member States have to bear the resulting social cost sounds harsh but fair.[130]

Ultimately, assuming the true goal is to improve the condition of the worse-off posted workers while, at the same time, levelling upwards wages as well as social and labour standards all over the Union, an interesting solution to the issue of unfair distribution of wealth is provided by the political economic theory building on the 'Third Way in Labour Law' presented by Collins.[131] According to the latter, the structural inequality of wealth distribution among Member States and EU citizens may be addressed, or at least mitigated, by securing equal opportunities to all market actors.[132] This rationale was endorsed by the Commission itself in its 2007 Communication on Opportunities, Access and Solidarity, whereby it acknowledged that 'whereas society cannot guarantee equal outcomes for its citizens, it must become much more resolute in fostering equal opportunities'.[133] In this regard, the following section tries to offer some suggestions for improvement both in terms of equal opportunities and upward socio-economic convergence and cohesion at European level.

9.5 RECOMMENDATIONS

After having questioned the underlying rationale of the new Directive (EU) 2018/957 against the EU values and principles of equality, fair competition and solidarity, the purpose of this section is to propose some recommendations for improvements towards the attainment of better wages, employment conditions and social protection for posted workers, and the concurrent preservation of the highest social standards. The resulting attenuation of the existing disparities between local and posted workers would avert the risk of downward pressure on national welfare states, without the need

130. Somek (n 80) 6–8. Yet, the potential negative impact of labour mobility on the distributive capacity of national welfare states must not be underestimated. Vandenbroucke, 'The Idea of a European Social Union' (n 2) 36.
131. Hugh Collins, 'Is There a Third Way in Labour Law?' in Joanne Conaghan, Richard Michael Fischl and Karl Klare (eds), *Labour Law in an Era of Globalization: Transformative Practices and Possibilities* (Oxford University Press 2004) 451–452.
132. In particular, Collins affirms that 'The objective is to provide every citizen with the necessary resources in terms of education, training, skills and other financial support, so that they can participate fully in the opportunities afforded by a flourishing market economy. Inequalities of wealth can be tolerated provided that real equality of opportunity is available to all citizens.' *Ibid.* 452. Interestingly, this idea basically represents the transposition on a European scale of the Rawlsian principle of 'fair equality of opportunity'. Rawls (n 119) 63.
133. European Commission, Communication from the Commission to the European Parliament, the Council, the European Economic and Social Committee and the Committee of the Regions – Opportunities, access and solidarity: Towards a new social vision for 21st century Europe (n 127) 6. In this sense, *see also* Barnard, 'EU "Social" Policy: From Employment Law to Labour Market Reform' (n 4) 681–683; Barnard, 'EU Employment Law and the European Social Model' (n 4) 211–212.

to adopt protectionist policies. More specifically, besides focusing on specific technical issues, this section puts forward policy inputs aimed at better coherence and fit with the aforementioned values and principles and, eventually, with the ultimate goal of social justice. The following concrete proposals generally envisage a higher degree of European integration and concern four focus areas encompassing: the centralisation and digitalisation of all information related to posting of workers, including the introduction of a European Social Security Number; the coordination of the different national approaches in the areas of company law and taxation in order to combat regulatory arbitrage strategies; the promotion of the participation of posted workers in both home and host state trade unions; and the elaboration of a European coordination scheme of national approaches to minimum wage policy.

9.5.1 Centralisation and Digitalisation

As previously explained in Chapter 6, the absolute lack of reliable information and data in relation to posting of workers affects both the proper enforcement of the rules and the definition of tailored policy strategies. In particular, national rules and regulations applicable to posted workers are often very different both in terms of content and language, and also different from those concerning non-posted workers. Needless to say, this fragmented situation is liable to result in failure to comply with the rules due to the lack of knowledge about relevant labour standards.[134] In parallel, in the absence of uniform registration systems for foreign service providers and/or posted workers, the only source of quantitative data is represented by the number of issued Portable Documents A1 proving the social security insurance in the sending Member State.[135] However, due to the mismatch between Regulation (EC) 883/2004 on social security coordination and the (amended) Posting of Workers Directive in the definition of a 'posted worker', the non-mandatory character of the PDs A1 and their possible retroactive effect, not to mention the number of frauds and abuses to which they are exposed, the information provided in the latter documents is not sufficiently reliable, precise and univocal.[136] By implication, also due to the wide variety of national personal identification numbers assigned to each posted worker,[137] the determination of the latter's social security coverage is often excessively complex and time-consuming.[138] Hence, there is still much space for improvement in this area.

The first problem can be overcome by creating a single official European website, with direct reference to each single official national website created in accordance with

134. Kairit Kall and Nathan Lillie, 'Protection of Posted Workers in the European Union: Findings and Policy Recommendations Based on Existing Research' (2017) PROMO briefing paper 43, 4.
135. Dhéret and Ghimis (n 41) 10; Kall and Lillie (n 134) 6.
136. In this sense, *see* the analysis carried out *supra* in Chapters 2 and 6.
137. As a matter of fact, each posted worker is often registered with different social security numbers issued by the different branches of social security (e.g., health insurance number, pension number, general social security numbers) in each Member State where he works.
138. European Commission, Inception Impact Assessment – European Social Security Number 2017 (Ares(2017)5862503) 1.

Article 5 of the Enforcement Directive,[139] which would make it possible to provide employers and employees with detailed information on posting available in all languages.[140] With regard to the second problem, an effective solution may be provided, *in primis*, through the harmonisation of national reporting requirements for posted workers, with the introduction of a unique European standardised form, and a clarification of which posting arrangements need to be reported. Such an action could be complemented by the removal of most of the burdensome national notification requirements, especially of those concerning short-term postings (e.g., postings of less than ten days).[141] Moreover, this standardised form for registration in the Member State of destination could be made available in electronic format in the above-mentioned single European website. At the same time, a uniform electronic procedure at EU level for the application and granting of digitalised Portable Documents A1 (with uniform questionnaires) could be organised, in practical terms, in the framework of the recently implemented Electronic Exchange of Social Security Information (EESSI).[142] In combination, a European Social Security Number (ESSN), linked to national identification numbers and issued specifically for cross-border purposes, could be assigned to each intra-EU mobile worker.[143] On the one hand, such novelties would definitely ensure a better simplification, understanding and enforcement of the rules, thereby contributing to address the widespread misperception of unfair competition and social dumping as directly resulting from the posting phenomenon as well as the existing inequality between local and posted workers.[144] On the other hand, they would reduce

139. Directive 2014/67/EU of the European Parliament and of the Council of 15 May 2014 on the enforcement of Directive 96/71/EC concerning the posting of workers in the framework of the provision of services and amending Regulation (EU) No 1024/2012 on administrative cooperation through the Internal Market Information System ('the IMI Regulation') 2014 (OJ L 159/11).
140. Kall and Lillie (n 134) 4; Brodtmann (n 72); Yves Jorens, 'Intra-EU Posting: Looking for Solutions: A Herculean or a Sisyphean Task?' (60 Years Social Security Coordination from a Workers' Perspective, Leuven, Belgium, 16 May 2019).
141. Brodtmann (n 72).
142. European Commission – Employment, Social Affairs & Inclusion, 'Electronic Exchange of Social Security Information (EESSI)' (*Electronic Exchange of Social Security Information (EESSI)*) <https://ec.europa.eu/social/main.jsp?catId=869&langId=en> (accessed 28 January 2020). *See* Vincent Aussilloux et al., 'Making the Best of the European Single Market' (2017) Bruegel – Policy Contribution 12 <https://bruegel.org/2017/02/making-the-best-of-the-european-single-market/> (accessed 28 January 2019); Zsolt Darvas, 'Revision of the Posted Workers Directive Misses the Point' (*Bruegel*, 18 October 2017) <https://bruegel.org/2017/10/revision-of-the-posted-workers-directive-misses-the-point/> (accessed 5 October 2018); David-Pascal Dion, 'State of Play: Reform of the Social Security Coordination Rules, Portability of Social Rights after Brexit, Establishment of a European Labour Authority (ELA)' (60 Years Social Security Coordination from a Workers' Perspective, Leuven, Belgium, 16 May 2019). Notably, an electronic procedure to apply for a PD A1 has already been implemented in a number of Member States. Frederic De Wispelaere, 'The 4 Key Pillars of Intra-EU Posting in Practice: Information, Registration, Enforcement and Monitoring' (MoveS seminar, Zagreb, Croatia, 25 October 2019).
143. Paul Schoukens and Danny Pieters, 'The Rules within Regulation 883/2004 for Determining the Applicable Legislation' (2009) 11 European Journal of Social Security 81, 116; Aussilloux et al. (n 142) 12; Darvas (n 142); European Commission Inception Impact Assessment – European Social Security Number (n 138) 2; Jorens (n 140).
144. This second benefit would plausibly derive from the posted workers' better information and awareness of their legal position and rights.

the administrative burden for both national authorities and posting undertakings, while promoting the electronic exchange of information between Member States.[145]

Consequently, all information collected at national level could be brought together in a centralised EU database, or a linked up database of all national databases, which would provide accurate, systematic, exhaustive and reliable data about posting of workers.[146] Ideally, such an EU database could be managed and administered by the newly established European Labour Authority (ELA),[147] which has precisely the task of assisting Member States and the Commission in the application and enforcement of EU law in the areas of labour mobility and social security coordination, including posting of workers.[148] *Inter alia*, it specifically aims at facilitating access to and dissemination of information on rights and obligations related to intra-EU labour mobility, while fostering administrative cooperation between Member States.[149] Ultimately, the establishment of the European Labour Authority is certainly considered as a potentially effective response to the variety of issues associated with posting.[150]

9.5.2 Company Law and Tax Coordination

The second focus area intends to address one of the most troublesome practices developed in relation to posting of workers; that of the regulatory arbitrage by certain cross-border service providers, which arbitrarily choose the most favourable normative regime with a view to exploiting the existing differences between national

145. European Commission Inception Impact Assessment – European Social Security Number (n 138) 3; Jorens (n 140).
146. Dhéret and Ghimis (n 41) 10; Kall and Lillie (n 134) 6; Jan Cremers and Thomas Hastings, 'Developing an Approach for Tackling Letterbox Companies: Background Paper for the European Platform on Tackling Undeclared Work Seminar', *European Platform Undeclared Work* (2017) 5; Jorens (n 140).
147. Regulation (EU) 2019/1149 of the European Parliament and of the Council of 20 June 2019 establishing a European Labour Authority, amending Regulations (EC) No 883/2004, (EU) No 492/2011, and (EU) 2016/589 and repealing Decision (EU) 2016/344, 2019 (OJ L 186/21).
148. *Ibid.* Article 1(2). For the record, the ELA replaced the EU Committee of Experts on Posting of Workers, which was set up by the Commission in 2009 through the European Commission, Commission Decision of 19 December 2008 setting up the Committee of Experts on Posting of Workers (2009/17/EC) 2009 (OJ L 8/26).
149. Articles 2 and 5(c) of Regulation (EU) 2019/1149 of the European Parliament and of the Council of 20 June 2019 establishing a European Labour Authority, amending Regulations (EC) No 883/2004, (EU) No 492/2011, and (EU) 2016/589 and repealing Decision (EU) 2016/344 (n 147).
150. In this sense, *see* Mikkel Barslund, Matthias Busse and Frederic De Wispelaere, 'Posted Workers – For Some It Matters' (2017) CEPS (Centre for European Policy Studies) 8; Piet Van Nuffel and Sofia Afanasjeva, 'The Posting of Workers Directive Revised: Enhancing the Protection of Workers in the Cross-Border Provision of Services' (2018) 3 European Papers 1401, 1425–1426; Dries Lens, Ninke Mussche and Ive Marx, 'Europe's Ever Expanding Mobility Patterns – Posting, Third-Country Nationals and the Single European Labour Market' (2019) CSB Working Paper No. 19.08 University of Antwerp – Herman Deleeck Centre for Social Policy 19; Jens Arnholtz and Nathan Lillie, 'European Integration and the Reconfiguration of National Industrial Relations: Posted Work as a Driver of Institutional Change' in Jens Arnholtz and Nathan Lillie (eds), *Posted Work in the European Union: The Political Economy of Free Movement* (Routledge 2019) 19; Houwerzijl and Berntsen (n 58) 162.

systems.[151] In effect, the deliberate selection of a Member State with lenient normative requirements concerning incorporation, and the consequent cross-border provision of services by making recourse to posted workers, falls fully within the legitimate use of the freedoms of establishment and service provision enshrined in Articles 49 and 56 TFEU, respectively.[152] In other words, a posting company is currently free to establish itself in the most convenient regulatory environment within the EU internal market, while conducting all of its business in other Member States. Importantly, in these situations, rather than the very activity of seconding employees across borders, the real source of issues is the possibility for companies to legally circumvent the stricter labour, social and tax rules in the EU countries in which they operate.

Such an occurrence is permitted, first of all, by the approach adopted by a number of Member States in the field of company law, in accordance with the so-called 'incorporation' doctrine.[153] Pursuant to this theory, in those states, the company's legal capacity is determined by reference to the country in which the latter was incorporated, instead of the country in which the company's real operational centre (headquarters or main place of business) is located.[154] Conversely, a closer connection of the companies with the country in which they are established is required in those Member States, such as France, Germany and Italy, which apply the so-called *siège réel* ('real seat') doctrine. In those cases, the jurisdiction of the company is, indeed, determined on the basis of the place where the latter has its central administration or operational headquarters and, presumably, carries out a substantial part of its economic activity.[155]

In light of the above, an ideally effective remedy to the regulatory arbitrage strategies adopted by posting undertakings, which relocate in low-wage Member States with a view to operate in high-wage Member States, would consist in the coordination at EU level of the various national company law approaches in accordance with the aforementioned 'real seat' theory.[156] The resulting generalized requirement of a closer

151. For an extensive analysis of the issue of regulatory arbitrage, *see supra* Chapter 7.
152. Craig and de Búrca (n 29) 812–813; Catherine Barnard, *The Substantive Law of the EU: The Four Freedoms* (Fifth Edition, Oxford University Press 2016) 394. In particular, the companies' free choice of their Member State of incorporation has been sensibly strengthened by the Court's jurisprudence in *Centros Ltd v Erhvervs- og Selskabsstyrelsen* [1999] ECJ Case C-212/97, ECLI:EU:C:1999:126; *Überseering BV v Nordic Construction Company Baumanagement GmbH (NCC)* [2002] ECJ Case C-208/00, ECLI:EU:C:2002:632; *Kamer van Koophandel en Fabrieken voor Amsterdam v Inspire Art Ltd* [2003] ECJ Case C-167/01, ECLI:EU:C:2003:512.
153. This is the case, *inter alia*, of the UK, the Netherlands, Scandinavian countries and most of Central and Eastern European Member States. Carsten Gerner-Beuerle et al., 'Study on the Law Applicable to Companies – Final Report' (European Commission, Directorate-General for Justice and Consumers Directorate A – Civil Justice Unit A1 – Civil Justice Policy 2016).
154. *Ibid.* 27; Barnard, *The Substantive Law of the EU: The Four Freedoms* (n 152) 394; Houwerzijl and Berntsen (n 58) 154.
155. Catherine Barnard and Simon Deakin, 'In Search of Coherence: Social Policy, the Single Market and Fundamental Rights' (2000) 31 Industrial Relations Journal 331, 337–338; Gerner-Beuerle et al. (n 153) 27; Barnard, *The Substantive Law of the EU: The Four Freedoms* (n 152) 394; Houwerzijl and Berntsen (n 58) 154.
156. To this end, a possible way may be represented by the 'reflexive harmonisation' proposed by Barnard and Deakin, according to which the EU regulation of the sector could be accompanied by the promotion of self-regulatory processes at national level. Barnard and Deakin (n 155) 340–343.

connection with the country of establishment would perfectly match with the important series of criteria, listed in Article 4 of the Enforcement Directive 2014/67/EU, for the recognition of genuine posting activity and the individuation of the actual establishment of a posting company in the sending Member State.[157]

On top of that, the direct relationship between companies' regulatory arbitrage and the existing detrimental tax competition between Member States should be taken into account as well. In fact, the current race to the bottom between national tax regimes in order to attract investments is liable to considerably undermine the economic growth of the internal market, if not even the overall EU integration process.[158] Accordingly, the pursuit of policies aimed at gradually coordinating at Union level the Member States' different tax regimes would undoubtedly have positive effects in terms disincentivising regulatory arbitrage.[159] All things considered, both the aforementioned recommendations could help tackle the issues of unfair competition and social dumping and create a level playing field inspired by the EU principle of fair competition.

9.5.3 Posted Workers' Access to Trade Unions

The *Sähköalojen ammattiliitto*[160] case before the Court of Justice concerned the lack of payment by the Polish company *Elektrobudowa Spółka Akcyjna (ESA)* of the minimum remuneration due, according to the relevant Finnish collective agreement, to its workers posted to Finland for the carrying out of electrical installations at the nuclear power station in Olkiluoto. For that reason, the latter workers assigned their pay claims to a Finnish trade union in the electricity sector, the *Sähköalojen ammattiliitto ry*, which eventually managed to successfully protect the workers' interests.[161] The

157. Article 4 of Directive 2014/67/EU of the European Parliament and of the Council of 15 May 2014 on the enforcement of Directive 96/71/EC concerning the posting of workers in the framework of the provision of services and amending Regulation (EU) No 1024/2012 on administrative cooperation through the Internal Market Information System ('the IMI Regulation') (n 139). For a specific examination of this provision, *see supra* in Chapter 4.

158. Ursula von der Leyen, 'Political Guidelines of the Commission 2019-2024 – A Union That Strives for More: My Agenda for Europe' (European Commission 2019) 12 <https://ec.europa.eu/commission/sites/beta-political/files/political-guidelines-next-commission_en.pdf> (accessed 24 January 2020); Aurore Lalucq, 'Minimum Corporate Tax Rate in the European Union' (*European Parliament – Parliamentary questions: Question for written answer E-002569-19 to the Commission Rule 138*, 29 August 2019) <http://www.europarl.europa.eu/doceo/document/E-9-2019-002569_EN.html> (accessed 24 January 2020).

159. This suggestion evidently requires further research and study. Nonetheless, it is recalled that a detailed analysis of the different strategies to combat tax competition is beyond the scope of this book.

160. *Sähköalojen ammattiliitto ry v Elektrobudowa Spolka Akcyjna* [2015] CJEU Case C-396/13, ECLI:EU:C:2015:86.

161. Interestingly, the Court declared the illegitimacy under the Posting of Workers Directive, read in the light of the right to an effective remedy enshrined in Article 47 of the CFREU, of a national rule, such as the Polish law, that prohibits workers to assign their claims arising from an employment relationship. *Inter alia*, it is worth noting that the relevant Finnish collective agreement was generally applicable and, therefore, perfectly consistent with the requirements of the Posting of Workers Directive. Tonia Novitz, 'The Scope for Collective Bargaining in Posting and Procurement – What Might Come From Recent Court of Justice Case Law and the

decision at issue has, therefore, recognised both the right for posted workers to join a trade union in the state where they perform their work and the capacity of the latter trade unions to represent the interests of temporary seconded foreign workers.[162] More importantly, it has shown that the participation of posted workers into local trade unions in the host country undoubtedly puts them in a more favourable position by increasing awareness of their rights and strengthening their negotiating power.[163]

The case described above was, however, just one of the few exceptions. Most of the time, posted workers do not join trade unions in the country where they work, and they are usually reluctant to take legal action against their employers. In fact, they generally try to avoid the risks of missing the opportunity of being seconded again to that country, as well as of engaging in judicial proceedings held in a foreign language and in an unfamiliar (and often more expensive) legal system.[164] In certain Member States, the posted workers' dismissal for union affiliation or active participation is not even followed by any repercussion to the employers.[165] In countries like Poland, where the assignment of employment-related claims to trade unions is prohibited, the posted workers are exposed to the risk of eventually having to return what they had gained before a foreign court.[166]

Against this backdrop, the promotion of the participation of posted workers in both home and host state systems of industrial relations is considered as the best way to guarantee effective protection of their rights and interests.[167] The resulting 'pressure

---

Proposed Reform of the Posting of Workers Directive?' (*University of Bristol Law School Blog*, 6 April 2016) <https://legalresearch.blogs.bris.ac.uk/2016/04/the-scope-for-collective-bargaining-in-posting-and-procurement/> (accessed 13 May 2018); Rebecca Zahn, 'Revision of the Posted Workers' Directive: Equality at Last?' (2016) 5 European (Legal) Studies on-line papers, Queen's University Belfast – School of Law – Centre of European and Transnational Legal Studies 6–7; Rebecca Zahn, 'Revision of the Posted Workers' Directive: A Europeanisation Perspective' (2017) 19 Cambridge Yearbook of European Legal Studies 187, 197–198.

162. Anna Matyska, 'Ambiguous Mobility: Polish Transnational Workers Navigating and Changing the Institutional Landscape of Posting' in Jens Arnholtz and Nathan Lillie (eds), *Posted Work in the European Union: The Political Economy of Free Movement* (Routledge 2019) 83. As interestingly noted by Schiek, the right to join a trade union in the host state is typically enjoyed by workers moving under Article 45 TFEU on the free movement of workers. Dagmar Schiek, 'A Constitution of Social Governance for the European Union' in Nuno Ferreira and Dora Kostakopoulou (eds), *The Human Face of the European Union* (Cambridge University Press 2016) 40.
163. Positive outcomes from the participation of posted workers in local trade unions have been registered also in cases concerning Polish workers employed at a construction site in a Parisian suburb (France) in 2008, Greek workers posted to Saint-Nazaire (France) and Polish workers seconded to Sweden during 2010–2011. Christer Thörnqvist and Sebastian Bernhardsson, 'Their Own Stories – How Polish Construction Workers Posted to Sweden Experience Their Job Situation, or Resistance Versus Life Projects' (2015) 21 Transfer: European Review of Labour and Research 23, 30–32; Comte (n 38) 10.
164. Yves Jorens, Saskia Peters and Mijke Houwerzijl, 'Study on the Protection of Workers' Rights in Subcontracting Processes in the European Union (Final Study)' (Ghent University, Department of Social Law (in consortium with University of Amsterdam) 2012) DG EMPL/B2-VC/2011/0015, 156–157; Kall and Lillie (n 134) 5; Jens Arnholtz and Søren Kaj Andersen, 'Extra-Institutional Changes under Pressure from Posting: Extra-Institutional Changes' (2018) 56 British Journal of Industrial Relations 1, 8–9.
165. Kall and Lillie (n 134) 5.
166. Schiek, 'A Constitution of Social Governance for the European Union' (n 162) 41.
167. Schiek, 'Perspectives on Social Citizenship in the EU' (n 18) 19.

from below' is expected to foster upward social convergence, towards the achievement of substantive equality with local workers in the host state. At this point, it is crucial to provide the posted workers with an effective and accessible right to join and be represented by trade unions.[168] A relevant instrument to that end is represented by Article 11(3) of the Enforcement Directive,[169] which specifically obliges Member States to ensure that trade unions (as well as other associations or organisations) may effectively support posted workers in any judicial or administrative proceedings, to enforce the obligations set out in the Posting of Workers Directive and the Enforcement Directive itself.[170] In addition, a significant strengthening of the social partners' power to protect collective interests of posted workers could be achieved through the development of transnational and multilevel networks of trade unions.[171] The arrangement of structures of collective representation at EU level and across different economic sectors would indeed enable to overcome most of the barriers encountered in the cross-border recognition of the posted workers' rights and interests. At the same time, it would put worker participation at the centre of the dynamics shaping the European labour market.

9.5.4 European Minimum Wage Coordination

The most recent data indicate that income inequality within the EU Member States consistently increased over the last years, thereby confirming the topicality of wealth distribution and, more broadly, social justice issues within European national realities.[172] At Union level, concerns of the same order arise from the substantial disparities among Member States in terms of wages, and especially national gross minimum wages.[173] As one can well imagine, such a context has consequences particularly for low-wage workers in the poorer Member States, which seek to improve their socioeconomic and living conditions by seizing the economic opportunity of being posted to a wealthier Member State where they could likely earn a better wage.

168. Kall and Lillie (n 134) 5.
169. Directive 2014/67/EU of the European Parliament and of the Council of 15 May 2014 on the enforcement of Directive 96/71/EC concerning the posting of workers in the framework of the provision of services and amending Regulation (EU) No 1024/2012 on administrative cooperation through the Internal Market Information System ('the IMI Regulation') (n 139).
170. Novitz (n 161); Marco Rocca, 'Stepping Stones Over Troubled Waters. Recent Legal Evolutions and the Reform of the Posting of Workers Directive' in Jens Arnholtz and Nathan Lillie (eds), *Posted Work in the European Union: The Political Economy of Free Movement* (Routledge 2019) 178.
171. Schiek, 'Perspectives on Social Citizenship in the EU' (n 18) 19; Sciarra (n 8) 45–46 and 93.
172. In particular, income inequalities have been exacerbated by the global financial and economic crisis of 2008–2010. Christine Aumayr-Pintar et al., 'Pay in Europe in the 21st Century' (Eurofound – Publications Office of the European Union 2014) 86–87 <https://www.eurofound.europa.eu/sites/default/files/ef_publication/field_ef_document/ef1388en_3.pdf> (accessed 31 January 2020); Massimiliano Mascherini, IRS (Istituto per la Ricerca Sociale) and University of Bergamo, 'Progress on Convergence in the Socioeconomic Area – Monitoring EU Convergence' (Eurofound – Publications Office of the European Union 2018) 5 and 12.
173. Christine Aumayr-Pintar, Matthias Rasche and Carlos Vacas, 'Minimum Wages in 2019: Annual Review' (Eurofound – Publications Office of the European Union 2019) 8.

Notwithstanding the boosting effect provoked by the global financial and economic crisis of 2008–2010 on the above-mentioned wage gap, the EU integration process has strongly fostered upward socio-economic convergence between the Member States.[174] Such a positive trend has been empirically observed over the past two decades and currently involves mainly Central and Eastern European Countries which, in the aftermath of their accession to the Union, have experienced a steady convergence towards the EU average both in terms of national gross minimum wages, real gross domestic product (GDP) per capita, and disposable household income.[175] In other words, the poorer-performing Central and Eastern Member States are progressively catching up with the better-performing Western Member States.[176] But still, the persistence of huge disparities between national gross minimum wages leaves considerable room for further improvement in this respect.[177]

The presence of a system of minimum wages is generally recognised as an important feature of the European social model for its ability to encourage social fairness, by determining a standard rate under which any wage is deemed morally unacceptable, and to tackle inequalities, by raising the lowest wages.[178] Nonetheless, profound differences currently exist across the Member States in the definition of minimum wages. Notably, while a legal minimum wage (determined by statutory regulation or collective bargaining) has been implemented in all but six of the EU countries, in Austria, Italy and the Scandinavian countries (Denmark, Finland and Sweden) sectoral or occupational minimum wages are set on the basis of collective bargaining, and in Cyprus statutory minimum wages concern only certain occupational groups.[179] In light of the above, the idea of an EU integrated approach to minimum wages was included in the European Pillar of Social Rights, alongside the right for each

174. As a matter of fact, this convergence effect concerns both economic factors and employment, working, and living conditions. Mascherini, IRS (Istituto per la Ricerca Sociale) and University of Bergamo (n 172) 2 and 6; Massimiliano Mascherini and Chiara Litardi, 'A More Equal Europe? Convergence and the European Pillar of Social Rights' (Eurofound – Publications Office of the European Union 2019) 2.
175. Mascherini, IRS (Istituto per la Ricerca Sociale) and University of Bergamo (n 172) 1, 13–14, and 18; Aumayr-Pintar, Rasche and Vacas (n 173) 7–8 and 35. On the contrary, this sort of growth was not observed in Greece where, particularly during the period 2006–2014, a decrease of the minimum wage rate contributed to an increase of wage inequality. João MR Pereira and Aurora Galego, 'Diverging Trends of Wage Inequality in Europe' (2019) 71 Oxford Economic Papers 799, 819.
176. Mascherini, IRS (Istituto per la Ricerca Sociale) and University of Bergamo (n 172) 18; Mascherini and Litardi (n 174) 2.
177. Aumayr-Pintar, Rasche and Vacas (n 173) 8.
178. For the record, the actual measure of those positive effects varies from state to state and even among economic sectors, as it necessarily depends on the number of workers affected by the wage increase. For instance, in Hungary and Poland the raise of minimum wage levels effectively decreased wage inequality. On the other hand, it is worth stressing that potential negative implications may arise as well, in the form of reduced employment opportunities for lower-skilled workers and international competitiveness of low-skilled sectors. Enrique Fernández-Macías and Carlos Vacas-Soriano, 'A Coordinated European Union Minimum Wage Policy?' (2016) 22 European Journal of Industrial Relations 97, 97–100; Pereira and Galego (n 175) 819. For a detailed analysis of the whole spectrum of potential effects of minimum wages, *see* Aumayr-Pintar et al. (n 172) 85–89.
179. Mascherini, IRS (Istituto per la Ricerca Sociale) and University of Bergamo (n 172) 5 and 15; Johan Stavers, 'Timmermans Calls on All EU Members to Adopt Minimum Wage' (*EURACTIV*,

worker 'to fair wages that provide for a decent standard of living'.[180] During recent years, this initiative was, indeed, vigorously supported by both the Council of Europe[181] and the EU institutions, namely the European Parliament, the European Commission and the European Central Bank.[182] As proclaimed by the new President Ursula von der Leyen, current policy strategies of the European Commission are specifically targeted at ensuring 'that every worker in our Union has a fair minimum wage'.[183] All this, despite the fact that, in principle, wage levels and wage-formation mechanisms are expressly excluded, by virtue of Article 153(5) TFEU, from the spectrum of Union competences.[184]

Although the setting of a common European minimum wage would in all probability require an amendment of the Treaties, the definition of a European coordination scheme of national approaches to minimum wage policy appears, nonetheless, to fall within the scope of EU law. In this regard, the potential outcomes of a hypothetical European minimum wage coordinated at 50% or 60% of the average or median wage[185] in each Member State have been widely discussed over the last

7 May 2019) <https://www.euractiv.com/section/eu-elections-2019/news/timmermans-calls-on-all-eu-members-to-adopt-minimum-wage/> (accessed 31 January 2020).

180. European Parliament, Council of the European Union and European Commission Interinstitutional Proclamation on the European Pillar of Social Rights (n 33) no 6. *See* Simon Deakin, 'What Follows Austerity? From Social Pillar to New Deal' in Frank Vandenbroucke, Catherine Barnard and Geert De Baere (eds), *A European Social Union after the Crisis* (Cambridge University Press 2017) 205–206; Kilpatrick and De Witte (n 8) 4.

181. In particular, with a view to giving practical effect to the right to a fair remuneration for a decent standard of living, enshrined in Article 4 of the 1961 European Social Charter, the Council of Europe repeatedly urged the Member States to ensure minimum wages corresponding, at least, to 50% or 60% of the average or median national wages. Council of Europe, European Social Charter 1961 (Turin). In this sense, *see* Aumayr-Pintar et al. (n 172) 91; Fernández-Macías and Vacas-Soriano (n 178) 98.

182. As a matter of fact, in response to the recent financial and economic crisis, the Commission and the European Central Bank have both intervened in wage developments and wage-formation mechanisms. Aumayr-Pintar et al. (n 172) 91; Fernández-Macías and Vacas-Soriano (n 178) 98; Mascherini, IRS (Istituto per la Ricerca Sociale) and University of Bergamo (n 172) 3.

183. von der Leyen (n 158) 9. Such an initiative has already the support of other powerful EU leaders, namely the French President Emmanuel Macron, the German Chancellor Angela Merkel and the European Commission Vice-President Franz Timmermanns. *See* Christine Aumayr-Pintar, 'To Have or Have Not: A Statutory Minimum Wage' (*Eurofound*, 22 July 2019) <https://www.eurofound.europa.eu/publications/article/2019/to-have-or-have-not-a-statutory-minimum-wage> (accessed 31 January 2020).

184. In the wording of Article 153(5) TFEU, 'the provisions of this article shall not apply to pay'. On this point, *see* Blanpain (n 3) 145–146; Hendrickx, 'Completing Economic and Social Integration' (n 3) 67; Aumayr-Pintar et al. (n 172) 91; Barnard and De Baere (n 8) 27; Fernández-Macías and Vacas-Soriano (n 178) 98; Baere and Gutman (n 8) 349, 363–364; van Hoek (n 2) 453; Mascherini, IRS (Istituto per la Ricerca Sociale) and University of Bergamo (n 172) 19; Kilpatrick and De Witte (n 8) 4; Barnard and De Vries (n 34) 53; László Andor, 'A Timely Call for a Social Union' in Maurizio Ferrera (ed.), *Towards a European Social Union: The European Pillar of Social Rights and the Roadmap for a Fully-Fledged Social Union* (Centro di Ricerca e Documentazione Luigi Einaudi 2019) 36.

185. Notably, while the 'average wage' is the mean wage calculated by adding up all of the wages and dividing them by the total number, the 'median wage' corresponds to the value between the highest 50% and the lowest 50% wages.

years.[186] In general terms, its ability to foster upward socio-economic convergence and to strengthen the social dimension of the EU has been clearly recognised. The resulting increase of lower wages, especially in low-wage countries, is expected to curb in-work poverty and, in combination with the consequent boosting of domestic economies, to reduce economic inequalities both at national and Union levels. At the same time, by deterring social dumping and excessive wage competition caused by intra-EU labour mobility, it would promote EU economic integration while alleviating the pressure on national welfare states.[187] By contrast, arguments against the introduction of a European minimum wage coordination mechanism mainly denounce the potential negative impact on national industrial relations systems in countries where minimum wages are set up by collective bargaining.[188] Further concerns relate to the alleged inability of an EU-wide approach to appropriately address specific issues of each Member State, and also to the possible damage caused to the competitiveness of Member States whose economy is heavily dependent on low-skilled labour.[189]

Despite a few drawbacks, the elaboration of an EU scheme of minimum wage coordination would represent an important step towards the progressive development of a European social model aimed at levelling upwards wages as well as social and labour standards all over the Union.[190] The resulting upward economic convergence is expected to gradually approximate the existing wage gap between the Member States and, consequently, attenuate most of the disparities between local and posted workers. In parallel, it would reduce the widespread perception in the Western Member States of unfair competition coming from posting companies established in the cheaper Central and Eastern Member States. Finally, with a view to concretely supporting the poorer-performing European countries in the achievement of higher wage levels, the initiative at stake could be complemented by a solidarity measure in the form of specific EU structural funds placed at their disposal by the European Social Fund (ESF).[191] Such a measure, besides advancing upward socio-economic convergence, would definitely fulfil the EU commitment to solidarity as a means to realise distributive justice on a European scale.

186. Vandenbroucke, 'The Case for a European Social Union: From Muddling Through to a Sense of Common Purpose' (n 2) 22–23; Mascherini, IRS (Istituto per la Ricerca Sociale) and University of Bergamo (n 172) 3 and 18; Eurofound, 'Minimum Wage' (*Eurofound*, 8 October 2019) <https://www.eurofound.europa.eu/topic/minimum-wage> (accessed 11 November 2019).
187. Aumayr-Pintar et al. (n 172) 95; Fernández-Macías and Vacas-Soriano (n 178) 100; Mascherini, IRS (Istituto per la Ricerca Sociale) and University of Bergamo (n 172) 18–19; Andor (n 184) 36.
188. This is especially the case of the Scandinavian Member States, which are traditionally opposed to the introduction of statutory minimum wages which could potentially undermine the existing wage-setting mechanisms. Aumayr-Pintar et al. (n 172) 92; Fernández-Macías and Vacas-Soriano (n 178) 101.
189. Aumayr-Pintar et al. (n 172) 95; Fernández-Macías and Vacas-Soriano (n 178) 100; Mascherini, IRS (Istituto per la Ricerca Sociale) and University of Bergamo (n 172) 18–19.
190. To this end, the involvement of social partners in the determination and adjustment of minimum wage rates would definitely encourage social cohesion. Mascherini, IRS (Istituto per la Ricerca Sociale) and University of Bergamo (n 172) 3; Aumayr-Pintar, Rasche and Vacas (n 173) 35.
191. In this sense, *see* Vandenbroucke, 'The Case for a European Social Union: From Muddling Through to a Sense of Common Purpose' (n 2) 23.

9.6 CONCLUDING REMARKS

The European Union's commitment to the realisation of a 'European social model' necessarily implies that all policies and legislation are guided by a whole set of fundamental values and principles. Clearly, the new Directive (EU) 2018/957 is no exception. After having extensively analysed, in the previous Chapter 8, both its birth process, substantive content and expected impact and shortcomings, in this chapter, the underlying rationale of the latter act of secondary EU legislation has been evaluated in light of the EU values and principles of equality, fair competition and solidarity.

According to the previous findings, the introduction of the principle of equal treatment between local and posted workers with respect to remuneration and certain working conditions, extended to further employment conditions in case of long-term postings, is the expression of a merely formalistic approach to equality. It fails, indeed, to take into due account that the posted workers are facing fundamentally different circumstances compared to their local counterparts in the host states, as their chances to benefit from the economic opportunities offered by the secondment across borders are directly dependent on their employers' competitiveness. This means that, when the posting concerns low-wage workers and takes place from low-wage to high-wage Member States, the imposition of the same treatment as local employees is liable to result in too high costs for the posting employers, and eventually in the posted workers' loss of their jobs.[192] Evidently, the formal equal treatment envisaged by the new Directive is not able to address the need of providing substantive equality between local and posted workers, and hence to fully realise the EU value of equality. In other words, it basically lacks the necessary sensitivity to inherent differences in society, as demanded by the Aristotelian conception of equality, as well as the capacity to ensure substantive equal opportunities and outcomes. On the contrary, the application of an almost identical treatment to all market actors regardless of their substantially different situation would even amount to indirect discrimination of the posted workers concerned.

What is more, the whole narrative supporting the revision of the Posting of Workers Directive in accordance with the principle of 'equal pay for equal work in the same place' is called into question for allegedly instrumentalising the concept of equal treatment in order to protect national labour markets and welfare systems. The equal treatment provisions are, in fact, specifically designed in a way that do not benefit the posted workers by entitling them of a directly enforceable right, but rather as a power of the receiving countries to extend their internal regulations to the incoming posted workers. Not surprisingly, the claim for equal treatment for the supposed benefit of the Central and Eastern European workers was mainly supported by the Western Member States and trade unions.

192. *Inter alia*, in view of the possible unemployment of workers in the peripheral Member States, the compatibility of the new legal framework with the Union's objective, laid down in Article 3(3) TEU, to realise a 'highly competitive social market economy, aiming at full employment and social progress' is debatable, to say the least.

Apart from providing better social protection for the posted workers, the adoption of Directive (EU) 2018/957 was intended to create a level playing field between posting and local undertakings in the host country, by curbing the alleged unfair competition from cross-border service providers which exploited their competitive advantage in terms of lower labour costs. However, the enjoyment of the freedom to provide services by making recourse to lower-paid posted workers does not constitute per se an expression of unfair competition. In turn, pursuant to EU law, the receiving states are generally prevented from restricting the income of cheaper services in their own territory on the grounds of the wage levels of the workers who provide them. Additionally, the aforementioned presumption of a direct correlation between posting and unfair competition is deemed tendentious and misleading insofar as it merely focused on the existing gaps in costs of manpower, while failing to take into account the extra costs and administrative burdens intrinsically related to the cross-border dimension of the transnational provision of services. Posting companies (and indirectly their posted workers) are indeed discriminated by the application of the same rules as local firms which carry out the same activities in the host Member State, given that only the first ones have to bear a considerable amount of variable and fixed extra costs.[193] By contrast, national economic actors in the receiving Member States would benefit from an undue competitive advantage. To that extent, the equal treatment between local and posted workers, as provided for in the new Directive, is, therefore, liable to be at odds with the EU principle of fair competition.

Lastly, the new legal framework provided for by Directive (EU) 2018/957 has been questioned with regard to the EU value of solidarity. The Directive's major aim of shielding existing social standards and industrial relations systems in the wealthier Western Member States from the downward pressure exerted by the incoming of low-wage posted workers is evidently geared to strengthening a strictly national conception of solidarity. Nonetheless, as a result of the continuing EU integration process, the value at stake has come to assume a wider transnational dimension as well, which is now at the heart of the European social model. Notably, this conception of pan-European solidarity is intended to attain upward socio-economic convergence and cohesion on a European scale, with a view to realising social (distributive) justice through a fair distribution of wealth, opportunities and privileges across the Union. In practical terms, it requires Member States and their citizens to open up their national solidarity circles to other EU citizens who make use of their free movement rights, thereby allowing the latter to improve their economic and social status.

As is apparent, this transnational dimension of solidarity, likewise the related issues of social justice and wealth redistribution within the Union, are basically disregarded by the recent reform. In effect, the Directive's outcome of discouraging the cross-border service provision from low-wage to high-wage countries through the recourse to posted workers, while neglecting the relatively great redistributive capacity of posting, is expected to exacerbate existing disparities between Eastern and Western

193. As is evident, the position of those undertakings and workers coming from low-wage Member States is affected even more, as they also have to line up with the higher employment standards applied in the richer countries of destination.

Member States. Regrettably, the fundamental misalignment between the new Directive (EU) 2018/957 and the EU value of transnational solidarity plainly attests, on the one hand, the tragically low degree of solidarity among EU Member States and citizens. On the other hand, it is a clear symptom of the conceptual weakness of the EU value of solidarity itself which, despite being frequently used in the Treaties, the Charter of Fundamental Rights of the European Union, political and legal texts, Court judgments and public speeches, still lacks both a proper definition and a common understanding.[194] After all, such a condition is inevitably reflected in the relatively limited practical relevance of solidarity at EU level.

In view of the challenges posed by the EU values and principles of equality, solidarity and fair competition to the EU regulation of the posting phenomenon, the last substantive section of this chapter suggested a number of improvements towards the attainment of better wages, employment conditions and social protection for the worse-off posted workers, and the concurrent preservation of the highest social standards. The resulting attenuation of the existing disparities between local and posted workers is, indeed, considered crucial in order to prevent the risk of downward pressure on national welfare states, while truly pursuing substantive equality and pan-European solidarity. More specifically, these recommendations are grouped into four focus areas.

With a view to ensuring a better simplification, understanding and enforcement of the rules, reducing administrative burdens, and promoting the electronic exchange of information between Member States, the first area concerns the centralisation and digitalisation of all data related to posting of workers. Possible technical improvements in this sense include the creation of a single official European website collecting information from national sources, the introduction of a unique European standardised reporting form available in electronic format, a uniform electronic procedure for social security documents (PDs A1), a European Social Security Number (ESSN), and the development of a centralised EU database managed and administered by the European Labour Authority (ELA). The second proposal for action focuses on stemming regulatory arbitrage strategies, which are extremely deleterious for national welfare systems. To this end, it argues for the coordination at EU level of the various national company law approaches in accordance with the 'real seat' theory, as well as of the excessively different national tax regimes.

The third and fourth recommendations are, in turn, mainly directed towards the overall improvement of the posted workers' employment, social and economic conditions and, at the same time, the progressive enhancement of the European social model. In this regard, the participation of posted workers in both home and host state systems of industrial relations is warmly encouraged also as a means to achieve substantive equality with local workers in the host state. Lastly, the elaboration of a European coordination scheme of national approaches to minimum wage policy would definitely contribute to fostering upward socio-economic convergence and strengthening the social dimension of the EU. Among the expected outcomes, the existing wage

194. Barnard, 'Solidarity and the Commission's "Renewed Social Agenda"' (n 84) 80; Grimmel (n 81) 162–165 and 171.

gap between Member States is likely to reduce, thereby attenuating most of the disparities between local and posted workers. As a result, also the widespread perception in Western Member States of unfair competition coming from posting companies established in cheaper Central and Eastern Member States would plausibly scale down. In order to realise distributive justice on a European scale, such an initiative could then be complemented by a solidarity measure in the form of specific EU structural funds placed at disposal of the poorer-performing Member States.

In conclusion, this chapter has proven that, in the revision of the Posting of Workers Directive, the EU legislator has basically lost sight of the needs to ensure better protection for the worse-off posted workers and, more broadly, to attain upward socio-economic convergence and cohesion at Union level. To this extent, it incurred in a misalignment with the EU values and principles of equality, solidarity and fair competition. Against this backdrop, the options proposed generally envisage a higher degree of EU integration oriented towards the realisation of a true European social model which, rather than merely preserving the integrity of the most advanced national social systems, aims at levelling upwards wages as well as social and labour standards all over the Union.

CHAPTER 10
Conclusion

10.1 THE END OF THE JOURNEY

Labour mobility across the EU internal market is facing a progressive transformation, with the development of increasingly flexible patterns outside the normal context of free movement of labour.[1] This is the case of 'posting of workers', which constitutes a hybrid type of intra-EU labour mobility based on the free movement of services. Despite concerning only a rather limited fraction of the European labour market, the phenomenon of posting has constantly been at the heart of the debates on European integration involving both a series of famous rulings of the Court of Justice and several regulatory reforms in the fields of EU labour and social security law.[2] The main reason behind this popularity lies in its conceptual position at the crossroads of conflicting interests of those who argue in favour of more EU integration towards the creation of

1. Paul Schoukens and Danny Pieters, 'The Rules within Regulation 883/2004 for Determining the Applicable Legislation' (2009) 11 European Journal of Social Security 81, 107–108; Yves Jorens, Saskia Peters and Mijke Houwerzijl, 'Study on the Protection of Workers' Rights in Subcontracting Processes in the European Union (Final Study)' (Ghent University, Department of Social Law (in consortium with University of Amsterdam) 2012) DG EMPL/B2-VC/2011/0015, 154; Rebecca Zahn, 'Revision of the Posted Workers' Directive: Equality at Last?' (2016) 5 European (Legal) Studies on-line papers, Queen's University Belfast – School of Law – Centre of European and Transnational Legal Studies 15; Ninke Mussche, Vincent Corluy and Ive Marx, 'The Rise of the Free Movements: How Posting Shapes a Hybrid Single European Labour Market' (2017) European Journal of Industrial Relations 3; Rebecca Zahn, 'Revision of the Posted Workers' Directive: A Europeanisation Perspective' (2017) 19 Cambridge Yearbook of European Legal Studies 187, 208; Anne-Pieter van der Mei et al., 'The External Dimension of EU Social Security Coordination' (2018) 20 European Journal of Social Security 81, 82; Ninke Mussche and Dries Lens, 'The EU Free Movement of Services and the Growing Mobility of Third-Country Nationals as Posted Workers' (2018) CSB Working Paper No. 18.13 University of Antwerp – Herman Deleeck Centre for Social Policy 1.
2. Jens Arnholtz and Nathan Lillie, 'European Integration and the Reconfiguration of National Industrial Relations: Posted Work as a Driver of Institutional Change' in Jens Arnholtz and Nathan Lillie (eds), *Posted Work in the European Union: The Political Economy of Free Movement* (Routledge 2019) 1.

a fully integrated internal market economy, and those who support the Member States' retention of their regulatory powers in order to preserve higher employment and social standards. By reason of the special legal treatment reserved to workers when temporarily posted across borders, companies that make recourse to this practice, and indirectly also the workers themselves, may indeed benefit from great business opportunities. Due also to the several unlawful and fraudulent practices developed in the context at issue, such an occurrence is often perceived as 'social dumping' and 'unfair competition' in the receiving Member States. Especially in the wake of the 2004 and 2007 Union's enlargements towards the East, the competitive advantage of service providers profiting from the peculiar legal regime applicable to their posted workers has indeed become more and more of a threat to Western Member States with higher wage levels and advanced systems of social protection.

Against this background, the regulation of posting at EU level has inevitably been always extremely controversial, and the most recent revision of the Posting of Workers Directive was no exception. This book challenges the new Directive (EU) 2018/957 by arguing that it worryingly falls out of alignment with the EU values and principles of 'equality', 'solidarity' and 'fair competition'. For the purpose of reaching that conclusion, which was advanced in Chapter 9, the path mapped out by the five research sub-questions outlined in the introductory Chapter 1 has been followed. After providing, in Chapter 2, a proper definition of posting pursuant to Union law, as well as of the rationale for the special treatment reserved to posted workers vis-à-vis migrant workers, an in-depth examination of the existing EU regulatory framework was carried out in Chapters 3-5, focusing on both the relevant EU labour and social security provisions. At that stage, the evolution of the Court of Justice case law has been traced since the very first decisions in the 1970s. This legal analysis was complemented by an investigation, in Chapters 6 and 7, of the actual quantitative dimension of the phenomenon under consideration, as well as of its multifaceted impact on the EU labour market, including a close examination of the issues emerged in the sector. Empirical evidence has thereby made it possible to discern the difference between myth and reality in the context of posting. Once having delineated the background for the legislative reform, Directive (EU) 2018/957 was thoroughly analysed in Chapter 8, encompassing both its troubled birth process, its disputable content, and its expected impact and shortcomings, also in light of the findings emerged from the previous chapters. The new legal framework provided for by the new Directive and, more broadly, the whole narrative underpinning the reform were then questioned, in Chapter 9, against the EU values and principles of equality, solidarity and fair competition. This analysis, supported by the responses from the previous five research sub-questions, enables to address the main research question of this book: *To what extent is the new legal framework provided for by Directive (EU) 2018/957 in line with the EU values and principles of equality, solidarity and fair competition?*

This chapter is intended to draw final conclusions from the analysis carried out in the entire book. To this end, the next section 10.2 recapitulates and puts together the main findings of all the previous chapters. The third and last section 10.3 proposes some reflections on the direction taken by the EU legislator with the adoption of Directive (EU) 2018/957 and on the need to pursue a European integration process oriented towards the development of a 'Social Europe' inspired by the EU values and principles and aimed at promoting upward socio-economic convergence and cohesion at EU level.

10.2 OVERALL RESULTS

The common public discourse is pervaded by the misguided perception which identifies as a posted worker any foreign worker coming from a low-wage Member State, who performs a working activity (especially in the construction sector) in a high-wage Member State. A clarification in that regard is provided in Chapter 2, where the differences between intra-EU labour mobility in the framework of the freedom to provide services (Article 56 TFEU), namely the case of posting, and labour migration under the freedom of movement for workers (Article 45 TFEU) and the freedom of establishment (Article 49 TFEU) are strongly emphasised. Whereas the second pattern is considered as worker-driven, labour mobility in the form of posting of workers is employer-driven, implying that the posted workers' chances to benefit from the economic opportunities offered by the secondment across borders are directly dependent on their employers' competitiveness. Crucially, the placement of posting under the freedom to provide services entails the application of the law of the country of origin (home state law) to the employment relationship, in derogation from the general principle of *lex loci laboris* (host state law).

When it comes to properly defining the concepts of 'posting' and 'posted worker' under EU law, the marked mismatch between the Posting of Workers Directive[3] and Regulation (EC) 883/2004 on social security coordination[4] is undoubtedly extremely problematic.[5] The substantial differences regarding both their respective personal scope and rules related to the duration of a posting arrangement are, indeed, the cause of widespread contradictory situations whereby an employment relationship is subject to the labour law of one Member State while the worker is affiliated to the social security system of another Member State. Notwithstanding the entry into force of the new Directive (EU) 2018/957,[6] providing for the introduction of a twelve-month time limit (extendable to eighteen months) for posting, the existing highly fragmented picture is not expected to improve. In effect, while the discrepancy with the relevant social security provisions remains fundamentally unresolved, the cumulative nature of the maximum time limit may arguably increase the uncertainty about the determination of the applicable legal regime. Self-evidently, the persistent absence of a univocal legal definition of posting at EU level is liable to give rise to adverse repercussions in

3. Directive 96/71/EC of the European Parliament and of the Council of 16 December 1996 concerning the posting of workers in the framework of the provision of services 1997 (OJ L 18/1).
4. Regulation (EC) No 883/2004 of the European Parliament and of the Council of 29 April 2004 on the coordination of social security systems 2004 (OJ L 166/1).
5. The scenario is even worse when considering the further mismatch with the relevant rules on personal income taxation.
6. Directive (EU) 2018/957 of the European Parliament and of the Council of 28 June 2018 amending Directive 96/71/EC concerning the posting of workers in the framework of the provision of services 2018 (OJ L 173/16).

terms of implementation and enforcement of the rules. A possible improvement in this regard could envisage the adoption of an integrated approach at EU level to labour mobility, involving labour law, social security law and tax policies.

Apart from the Treaty provisions concerning the freedom to provide services, the EU regulatory framework for posting is composed of a variety of legal instruments embracing different fields, in combination with a considerable amount of Court of Justice case law.[7] Chapter 3 thoroughly explores the Posting of Workers Directive (prior to the 2018 legislative reform), which emerged from a long and arduous drafting process aimed at promoting the transnational provision of services while, at the same time, respecting the Member States' labour market integrity and providing social protection for the posted workers. According to the Directive, the receiving countries are allowed to extend merely a limited range of domestic terms and conditions of employment (including minimum rates of pay) to the incoming posted workers, thereby granting them only minimum protection, and not full equal treatment with local workers.[8] Interestingly, this list of host country provisions applies to the employment relationship also by virtue of private international law, being included among the 'overriding mandatory provisions' under the Rome I Regulation on the law applicable to contractual obligations.[9]

In view of the Member States' retention of their competence in determining the concrete substance of the aforementioned provisions, as well as in choosing the specific means for extending local rules to out-of-state service providers, a series of boundaries have been set by the Court of Justice case law. In addition to progressively specifying the rather ambiguous concept of minimum rates of pay, the European judiciary focused, in its famous rulings in *Laval*[10] and *Rüffert*,[11] on the possibility for the host Member State to impose higher labour standards than those prescribed by the Directive. Through a very restrictive interpretation of the favourability clause laid down in Article 3(7), the imposition by the host country of additional elements of labour protection, going beyond the 'hard core' set out in Article 3(1), was regarded as an infringement of both the Posting of Workers Directive and EU internal market law. In turn, the only exception allowed concerned 'public policy provisions' which are neither discriminatory nor determined unilaterally by the Member States. Notwithstanding the great deal of concern following the aforementioned decisions, which, *inter alia*, considered the Directive as an instrument of maximum worker protection, it is argued that the Court's approach was, nonetheless, perfectly consistent with the dual

7. Aukje A.H. van Hoek, 'Re-Embedding the Transnational Employment Relationship: A Tale about the Limitations of (EU) Law?' (2018) 55 Common Market Law Review 449, 453.
8. The only exception to this rule concerned the posting of temporary agency workers, on condition that the Temporary Agency Work Directive 2008/104/EC was fully transposed into host country law.
9. Regulation (EC) No 593/2008 of the European Parliament and of the Council of 17 June 2008 on the law applicable to contractual obligations (Rome I) 2008 (OJ L 177/6).
10. *Laval un Partneri Ltd v Svenska Byggnadsarbetareförbundet, Svenska Byggnadsarbetareförbundets avdelning 1, Byggettan and Svenska Elektrikerförbundet* [2007] ECJ Case C-341/05, ECLI:EU:C:2007:809.
11. *Dirk Rüffert v Land Niedersachsen* [2008] CJEU Case C-346/06, ECLI:EU:C:2008:189.

purpose, intrinsic derogatory nature, and drafting history of the Posting of Workers Directive.

In Chapter 4, a more in-depth analysis of the Court's jurisprudence reveals the inclination of the EU judiciary towards the definition by positive legislation of the host country's terms and conditions of employment extendable to posted workers. The possibility to determine those labour standards by means of collective agreements negotiated on a case-by-case basis in the host Member State, or through local collective agreements lacking universal effect, was indeed peremptorily excluded. More controversially, the exercise of the EU fundamental social right of collective action for the protection of the higher social and employment standards in the host state was considered as a disproportionate restriction of the posting company's EU economic freedom of service provision. Besides recognising the resulting liberalisation of the internal market for services, a different point of view is proposed in order to overcome the common (Western) narrative, which depicts a dogmatic dichotomy between the economic and social dimensions of European integration. When reversing the perspective on the matter, the trade unions' actions in defence of local social and labour standards appear, indeed, directed to the realisation of economic-protectionist aims. *Vice versa*, the full exercise of the freedom to provide services may also be regarded as an enjoyment by the posted workers of their social rights to work, to escape unemployment and to make their contribution to their home country's economy. At the same time, the social dimension of EU free movement law has to be taken into due account as well.

The EU regulatory framework for posting has been integrated, over the years, by further legal instruments designed to address specific issues. This is the case, first of all, of the Enforcement Directive 2014/67/EU,[12] which improved legal clarity for the assessment of genuine postings and the fight against abuses and circumventions. It also enhanced administrative coordination and cooperation between national authorities and provided the posted workers with more effective instruments for the enforcement of their rights. However, serious shortcomings still remained with respect to the overall complexity of the rules and the concepts of 'fair posting', minimum rates of pay and temporary character of posting, as well as in relation to the emerging troublesome circumvention practices. On the other hand, the problematic implementation of the posting rules in the European road haulage industry have been recently addressed with the adoption of the new Directive (EU) 2020/1057 on posting drivers in the road transport sector.[13] At the end of its implementation period on 2 February 2022, this piece of EU legislation will regulate the posting of workers in the road transport sector as a *lex specialis* derogating from the general labour law framework.

12. Directive 2014/67/EU of the European Parliament and of the Council of 15 May 2014 on the enforcement of Directive 96/71/EC concerning the posting of workers in the framework of the provision of services and amending Regulation (EU) No 1024/2012 on administrative cooperation through the Internal Market Information System ('the IMI Regulation') 2014 (OJ L 159/11).
13. Directive (EU) 2020/1057 of the European Parliament and of the Council of 15 July 2020 laying down specific rules with respect to Directive 96/71/EC and Directive 2014/67/EU for posting drivers in the road transport sector and amending Directive 2006/22/EC as regards enforcement requirements and Regulation (EU) No 1024/2012, 2020 (OJ L 249/49).

With regard to the social security regime applicable to the posted workers, the exceptional treatment granted to them by Regulation (EC) 883/2004 with a view to encouraging intra-EU labour mobility while preventing unnecessary and costly administrative burdens envisages the retention of the workers' affiliation to their home country's system. This provided that their mobility abroad lasts less than twenty-four months, they are not replacing another posted person, and they maintain a substantial connection with their country of origin. In Chapter 5, the excessively broad interpretation of the non-replacement condition given by the CJEU in *Alpenrind*[14] is called into question, for it potentially undermines the principle of legal certainty, it poses an additional limitation to the posting companies' freedom to provide services, and it contrasts with the similar proviso set out in Directive (EU) 2018/957. The Court's approach is challenged also in the occasion of the controversial ruling in *Altun*,[15] which, by empowering national courts in the host Member States to disregard social security certificates issued by competent authorities of the sending states, seriously endangered the principle of mutual recognition. Fortunately, though, the potential negative repercussions of that decision have been sensibly circumscribed with the more recent rulings in *Commission v Belgium*,[16] *Alpenrind*[17] and *CRPNPAC and Vueling Airlines*.[18] Contextually, the lack of sufficient remedies available to the host Member States dealing with fraudulent or mistaken documentation attesting the application of foreign legal regimes, while facing a lack of cooperation from the sending states' authorities, is firmly stressed. Further issues concern the unclear legal position of posted persons who work simultaneously or in alternation in two or more Member States, as well as the existing mismatch between social security and taxation rules in cases of posting.

Potential improvements in terms of terminological clarity, enforcement of the rules through more stringent obligations on competent national authorities, and curtailment of *à la carte* choice of social security systems were envisaged by the unsuccessful attempt to reform following the 2016 Commission's proposal for a new Regulation.[19] Apart from those unresolved issues, the practical understanding and enforcement of the rules, as well as the complex and burdensome administrative environment for both national authorities and posting undertakings, still suffer from the lack of a uniform (electronic) procedure at EU level for the application and granting of social security documents. More broadly, it is believed that only an overall EU approach taking all aspects of intra-EU labour mobility into account would be able to

14. *Alpenrind and Others* [2018] CJEU Case C-527/16, ECLI:EU:C:2018:669.
15. *Altun* [2018] CJEU Case C-359/16, ECLI:EU:C:2018:63.
16. *European Commission v Kingdom of Belgium* [2018] CJEU Case C-356/15, ECLI:EU:C:2018:555.
17. *Alpenrind and Others* (n 14).
18. *Caisse de retraite du personnel navigant professionnel de l'aéronautique civile (CRPNPAC) v Vueling Airlines SA v Vueling Airlines SA and Jean-Luc Poignant* [2020] CJEU Joined Cases C-370/17 and C-37/18, ECLI:EU:C:2020:260.
19. European Commission, Proposal for a Regulation of the European Parliament and of the Council amending Regulation (EC) No 883/2004 on the coordination of social security systems and regulation (EC) No 987/2009 laying down the procedure for implementing Regulation (EC) No 883/2004, 2016 [COM(2016) 815 final].

effectively deal with the existing mismatch in the regulation of posting of workers between EU labour law, EU social security law and national tax regimes.[20]

The EU legal framework for posting of workers is usually considered without making reference to the actual material dimension of the phenomenon at issue. This detachment from reality has led to a common negative perception of this form of labour mobility, which inevitably influenced any debate on potential normative reforms. The analysis of the material dimension of the posting phenomenon, carried out in Chapter 6, reveals the seamless quantitative increase, over the last years, of the temporary secondment of workers across borders, and the strict correlation with the 2004 and 2007 European enlargements towards the East. Latest available data indicate an overall number of 3 million postings in 2018, involving approximately 1.9 million workers.[21] Despite the absolute size, the overall phenomenon still remains rather marginal when compared to the total of 230 million workers in the whole EU labour market (corresponding to a mere 0.8%). Nevertheless, it assumes a significant economic relevance in some Member States and certain economic sectors.[22] With regard to the orientation of the posting flows, the popular stereotype that portrays the transnational secondment of workforce as merely concerning low-skilled workers directed from the 'poorer' Central and Eastern to the 'richer' Western Member States is definitely debunked. In effect, the movement from the EU-13 to the EU-15 Member States corresponds to only a third of the overall number of intra-EU postings, while the majority of the postings takes place across the EU-15 Member States.

Inter alia, it is worth stressing that the COVID-19 pandemic has had a huge impact on the quantitative dimension of the posting phenomenon. Nonetheless, in the absence of precise data in this regard, a proper evaluation of the pandemic's overall impact is, for the time being, still too premature.

The actual relevance of the posting phenomenon goes beyond its mere material size, entailing a multifaceted impact on the EU labour market. For years, cross-border service providers have been allowed to exploit their competitive advantage, regulatory loopholes and deficient enforcement of the rules, to the detriment of national welfare states. Strategies of regulatory arbitrage have led, in certain national realities, even to social dumping concerns. As a matter of fact, however, the vast majority of the issues encountered is related to fraudulent and abusive conducts and lack of efficient enforcement mechanisms, rather than to the temporary secondment of workers across borders as such performed within the legal limits. As emphasised in Chapter 7, the

20. In this sense, *see also* Kerstin Ahlberg, 'The Age of Innocence – And Beyond' (2010) 21 FORMULA Working Paper, University of Oslo, Department of Private Law 28–29; van Hoek (n 7) 486.
21. Poland and Germany are the undisputed major sending countries of posted workers in absolute terms (counting in combination 36% of the total EU share), followed by Spain and Italy. While Poland, Slovakia and Slovenia are the leading net sender countries, France and the Netherlands are, in turn, the main net receivers.
22. This is the case of Luxembourg and Slovenia, the two major sending countries in relative terms, especially of workers employed in the construction industry. This sector has also a great economic relevance in Croatia, Slovakia and Poland, while the major receivers are Luxembourg, Austria, Belgium, Germany and France. In turn, an extremely high percentage of truck drivers is posted from Luxembourg, Slovakia, Poland and Croatia.

actual cause of the poor reputation of posting must, therefore, mainly be sought in practices involving subcontracting chains, double postings, bogus self-employment, 'letterbox companies', and undeclared work, especially when they entail unscrupulous exploitation of the workers concerned. Those malpractices, likewise that of Western European companies offshoring their production to their Central and Eastern European subsidiaries in order to undercut wages and working conditions, certainly represent the major sources of social dumping, whenever they translate into an undermining or evasion of the existing social and industrial relations regulations.

Except for some negative repercussions, posting has introduced a variety of positive outcomes able to effectively support the European integration process. Empirical evidence proves, indeed, the beneficial effects of such form of temporary labour mobility on both the individual workers involved, the sending and receiving Member States, and the EU internal market as a whole. By providing actors coming from the poorer Member States with a great opportunity to improve their economic and social conditions and, thus, to catch up with their richer counterparts in wealthier Member States, it contributes to fostering upward socio-economic convergence between low-wage and high-wage EU countries. In addition, it stimulates intra-EU competition and, by enhancing better job allocation and occupational mobility, it represents an effective temporary adjustment tool for resolving labour and skill seasonal shortages and asymmetric economic shocks.[23] Needless to say, empirical evidence should be, therefore, one of the main parameters supporting regulatory changes in the field.

Notwithstanding the number of positive effects resulting from the legal use of posting, the territorial and sectorial limitation of the issues emerged and the unfinished transposition of the Enforcement Directive 2014/67/EU into national laws, the revision process of the Posting of Workers Directive was initiated already in 2016, with a view to combating social dumping and establishing the principle of 'equal pay for equal work in the same place'. As explained in Chapter 8, the latter initiative of equal treatment between posted and local workers in the host state gave rise to a bitter conflict between high-wage Western and low-wage Central and Eastern Member States. Remarkably, the Commission's proposal found the fierce opposition of an actual 'regional block' formed by the Central and Eastern EU countries, which triggered the so-called 'yellow-card procedure'.

The new legal framework envisaged by Directive (EU) 2018/957, which came into force on 30 July 2020, is expected to have a rather controversial impact on the current state of play. If, on the one hand, it provides some positive practical innovations, on the other hand, it leaves the major shortcomings of the former regulatory framework basically unanswered, while creating new inconsistencies. Hence, it seems that it does not provide a complete solution to the issues actually related to the practice of posting of workers.

23. As effectively summarised by De Wispelaere, 'Ideally, *intra-EU* posting is not a "business model" exploiting regulatory differences between Member States but rather an economic model benefiting from the free movement of services and following a pragmatic approach in response to labour and skill shortages in host Member States and economic shocks in Member States of origin.' Frederic De Wispelaere, 'Intra-EU Posting Costs and Benefits' (25th International Conference of Europeanists, Chicago, 28 March 2018) 25.

In effect, the introduction of equal remuneration between local and posted workers, as well as of the same treatment regarding accommodation, travel, board and lodging expenses, will undoubtedly streamline the concrete determination of the payment due to the posted workers. Nonetheless, it will bring about substantial changes mostly in those few Member States which have not broadly implemented the Posting of Workers Directive nor adjusted their regulation to the latest relevant case law of the Court of Justice. In turn, it will not remedy the existing fragmentation of the different applicable national rules. Similarly, the new rules on equal treatment between local and posted temporary agency workers will concern only a few Member States. Still, those provisions holding the first temporary agency fully liable as an employer for any subsequent posting are expected to appropriately deal with the abusive practices of 'double' or 'chain' posting. Lastly, the establishment of a maximum duration limit for posting will eventually clarify the temporary nature of this form of labour mobility, and its cumulative character will address elusive practices of consecutive secondments and rotation of personnel. The other side of the coin is that practical complications may arise when the same employment relationship is regulated by two different national labour regimes, and the implied change of the posted workers' habitual place of work may virtually be incompatible with private international law. Furthermore, with the laying down of a twelve-month limit (extendable to eighteen months), the EU legislator undoubtedly lost an opportunity to harmonise the existing mismatch between the Posting of Workers Directive and Regulation (EC) 883/2004 on social security coordination in relation to the temporary duration and, more generally, to the overall legal definition of posting.[24]

After all, it is worth stressing that the extension of the host country's labour standards to foreign posted workers was conceived as an exception under the original Posting of Workers Directive, and therefore limited to only certain terms and conditions of employment. It was intended as a means to attenuate the potential imbalances arising from the application of the law of the country of origin in cases where the transnational provision of services involves short-term mobility of workforce. Accordingly, the radical change of approach accomplished through the 2018 legislative reform clearly runs counter to the spirit of the original Directive. Especially with regard to the new rules on long-term posting, the application of almost the same treatment to posted workers and full-fledged migrant workers moving under Article 45 TFEU inevitably gives rise to an inconsistency with the Directive's legal basis, which remains anchored to Article 56 TFEU.

When looking at the overall economic impact of Directive (EU) 2018/957, the positive effect of curtailing wage competition is expected to result from the substantial reduction of wage differentials between local and posted workers. Besides benefitting workers and enterprises in the receiving high-wage Member States, more equality of treatment will necessarily imply, nevertheless, an increase of the overall labour costs for the cross-border service providers coming from low-wage Member States and

24. It is recalled that the EU legislator eventually deviated from the Commission's proposal of a twenty-four-month maximum posting period, which would have perfectly matched with the relevant EU social security provisions.

operating in countries with higher social standards. The reform's major purpose of shielding the existing highest social standards and the most advanced industrial relations systems in the wealthier Member States from the competition of out-of-state service providers, by disincentivising the employment of posted workers, is therefore apparent. In that regard, the new rules on the cumulative maximum duration for posting are particularly emblematic. When taking into account the wider EU context, in light of the expected negative impact on the low-wage Member States' economies, the risk of widening the existing East-West welfare gap is recognised as a potential repercussion of the newly established regulatory environment.

In view of all the aforementioned findings, in Chapter 9, this book argues that the new EU legal framework for posting of workers provided for by Directive (EU) 2018/957 is, to a certain extent, worryingly leaving behind the EU values and principles of equality, fair competition and solidarity. It does so by basically losing sight of the needs to ensure better protection for the worse-off posted workers and, more broadly, to attain upward socio-economic convergence and cohesion at Union level. In this sense, the introduction of equal treatment between local and posted workers with respect to remuneration and certain working conditions, extended to further employment conditions in case of long-term postings, is the expression of a merely formalistic approach to equality that lacks the proper sensitivity to inherent differences in society. By treating in the same way workers who are in fundamentally different conditions, this formal equal treatment is, indeed, not able to realise substantive equality in accordance with the correspondent EU value. A fundamental shift from formal to substantive equality is, therefore, encouraged so as to effectively ensure equal opportunities and outcomes to all the workers concerned. On top of that, the whole narrative underlying the principle of 'equal pay for equal work in the same place' is being questioned for allegedly instrumentalising the concept of equal treatment in order to protect national labour markets and welfare systems, rather than entitling the posted workers of a directly enforceable right.

The new provisions on equal treatment between local and posted workers are also liable to be at odds with the EU principle of fair competition. The reform's purpose to create a level playing field between local and posting undertakings in the host country, by tackling the alleged unfair competition from out-of-state service providers, was indeed misguided by erroneous preconceptions. In effect, the enjoyment of the freedom to provide services by making recourse to lower-paid posted workers does not constitute per se an expression of unfair competition, and the wage competition by foreign service providers and their posted personnel does not necessarily lead to detrimental 'social dumping' and downward pressure on national welfare states. Additionally, while merely focusing on the existing gaps in costs of manpower, the new Directive fails to take into account the extra costs and administrative burdens intrinsically related to the cross-border dimension of the transnational provision of services. As a result, it discriminates posting companies (and indirectly their posted workers) and, in parallel, it confers an undue competitive advantage on national economic actors in the receiving Member States.

The Directive's inclination to protect existing social standards and industrial relations systems in the wealthier Western Member States from the downward pressure exerted by the incoming of low-wage posted workers is evidently geared to strengthening a strictly national conception of solidarity.[25] Nonetheless, it basically disregards the no less important transnational dimension of solidarity at EU level. This conception of pan-European solidarity, which has progressively developed over the years and is now at the heart of the European social model, is intended to attain upward socio-economic convergence and cohesion, with a view to realising social (distributive) justice on a European scale. The newly established legal framework does not envisage any inclusion of the posted workers into the national solidarity scheme of the receiving Member States and it neglects the relatively great redistributive capacity of posting. By discouraging posting of workers from low-wage to high-wage countries, it rather restricts the chances of economic actors in the poorer Central and Eastern Member States to improve their economic and social status, thereby exacerbating existing wealth disparities between East and West Europe. All things considered, the fundamental misalignment between the new Directive (EU) 2018/957 and the EU value of transnational solidarity reflects the lack of both a proper definition and a common understanding of the latter concept and, consequently, the tragically low degree of solidarity among Member States and citizens.

In light of the challenges posed by the EU values and principles of equality, solidarity and fair competition to the EU regulation of the posting phenomenon, the recommendations put forward by this book encompass a number of improvements towards the attainment of better wages, employment conditions and social protection for the worse-off posted workers and the concurrent preservation of the highest social standards in the 'old' Member States. More specifically, the centralisation and digitalisation of all information related to the posting of workers, including the introduction of a European Social Security Number, would ensure a better simplification, understanding and enforcement of the rules, reduce administrative burdens and promote the electronic exchange of information between Member States. In order to curb detrimental regulatory arbitrage strategies, the coordination at EU level of the various national company law approaches in accordance with the 'real seat' theory, as well as of the excessively different national tax regimes, is warmly suggested. Further proposed measures, aimed at combatting the exploitation of posted workers, ensuring them decent employment, social and economic conditions, and achieving substantive equality with local workers in the host state, envisage the promotion of the participation of those workers in both home and host state systems of industrial relations. Lastly, the elaboration of a European coordination scheme of national approaches to minimum wage policy and the contextual allocation of specific EU structural funds to assist the poorer-performing Member States would definitely constitute important steps towards fostering upward socio-economic convergence and strengthening the social dimension of the EU.

25. Using the words of Maduro, the model of Social Europe pursued by the EU legislator aims at 'guaranteeing a level playing field in the social sphere so as to prevent social deregulation at the State level'. Miguel Poiares Maduro, 'European Constitutionalism and Three Models of Social Europe' in Martijn W Hesselink (ed.), *The Politics of a European Civil Code* (Kluver Law International 2006) 125–126.

10.3 FUTURE REFLECTIONS

The regulation of posting of workers at EU level has been for years one of the most contentious political issues in Europe. It has, indeed, always reflected the tension between the promotion of a fully integrated internal market and the protection of national welfare systems. More recently, it has translated into a clash between low-wage Central and Eastern Member States supporting the interests of cross-border service providers and their posted employees, and high-wage Western Member States backing their local workers and firms. By implication, notwithstanding the relatively small quantitative dimension of this phenomenon, the approach adopted by the EU legislator has assumed an extremely symbolic relevance in terms of the model of European integration pursued.

On 14 September 2016, in his State of the Union address, the former President of the Commission Juncker affirmed that 'workers should get the same pay for the same work in the same place. This is a question of social justice. [...] The internal market is not a place where Eastern European workers can be exploited or subjected to lower social standards. Europe is not the Wild West, but a social market economy.'[26] The legislative action undertaken by the EU with the revision of the Posting of Workers Directive, however, failed to follow up on that apparently uncontroversial statement.[27] In fact, rather than protecting Eastern European workers and pursuing social justice on a European scale, the new Directive (EU) 2018/957 aims, first and foremost, at shielding the existing social standards and industrial relations systems in the Western Member States from the competition of out-of-state posting undertakings and posted workers. In other words, the newly established regulatory framework for posting is intended to advance a conception of 'Social Europe' that merely supports national social policies in the better-performing Member States, while basically leaving out the poorer-performing Member States and their citizens.[28] Against this backdrop, the outcomes of this book require us to reflect on whether this could be the desirable 'Social Europe', where equality is only formally declared but not pursued in substance, where fair competition is assessed on the basis of a biased perspective and where national solidarity is preserved at the expense of transnational solidarity.

The highest employment and social standards hard-won in years of social struggles across Europe must be safeguarded under lock and key. This goal can be achieved by means of protectionist policies designed to uphold national welfare systems or through the progressive development of a European social model aimed at

26. European Commission, 'Press Release – The State of the Union 2016: Towards a Better Europe – A Europe That Protects, Empowers and Defends' (*European Commission Press Releases Database*, 14 September 2016) <http://europa.eu/rapid/press-release_IP-16-3042_en.htm> (accessed 12 July 2019).
27. Arguably, it disguised the hypocritical and populistic nature of Junker's declaration.
28. As noted by Vandenbroucke, the concept of 'Social Europe' is admittedly rather ambiguous, as it depends on the degree of EU liberalisation and on different ideas of social justice. Frank Vandenbroucke, 'The European Pillar of Social Rights: From Promise to Delivery' in Maurizio Ferrera (ed.), *Towards a European Social Union: The European Pillar of Social Rights and the Roadmap for a fully-fledged Social Union* (Centro di Ricerca e Documentazione Luigi Einaudi 2019) 7–8.

levelling upwards wages as well as social and labour standards all over the Union, thus preventing the exclusion of low-wage Member States. The latter recommended model of European integration necessarily implies a better alignment with the EU values and principles of equality, solidarity and fair competition, whose conceptions need to be adapted to the current reality of an internal market characterised by an increasingly higher degree of labour mobility.[29] *Inter alia*, the ideal is to achieve a dimension of pan-European solidarity which, rather than merely being founded on reciprocity among Member States, would truly enable EU citizens to rely on the contributions, participation and collaboration of their fellow citizens of other Member States.[30] After all, it is argued that only the pursuit of a more ambitious Social Europe inspired by the EU social values and principles in their European dimension would be able to realise a coordinated enhancement of the different Member States' welfare traditions and properly address the existing issues of social (distributive) justice.[31]

In conclusion, it is clear that the existing welfare gap between East and West Europe constitutes one of the biggest challenges that the Union is currently facing. As this book has shown, however, the newly established EU legal framework for posting of workers runs the risk of increasing those disparities among Member States. The promotion of upward socio-economic convergence and cohesion across the Union, along with the contextual strengthening of Europe's social dimension, appears therefore crucial in order to avoid further exclusion of the workers and employers coming from low-wage Central and Eastern Member States. In this sense, targeted normative improvements aimed at coordinating national minimum wage policies at EU level and supporting the poorer-performing Member States through specific EU structural funds will certainly represent significant steps in the right direction. Nevertheless, the EU values and principles need to play a more central role in the process towards an ever-'Social Europe'.

29. On the necessity to adapt the notions of equal treatment and solidarity to the current state of play, *see* Silvana Sciarra, *Solidarity and Conflict: European Social Law in Crisis* (Cambridge University Press 2018) 94.
30. As suggested by Barnard, the EU value of solidarity is to be regarded, indeed, as a 'potential tool of new governance', which should inspire the political and legislative action of the Union. Catherine Barnard, 'Solidarity and New Governance in Social Policy' in Gráinne de Búrca and Joanne Scott (eds), *Law and New Governance in the EU and the US* (Hart Publishing 2006) 156.
31. Christian Joerges, 'Social Justice in an Ever More Diverse Union' in Frank Vandenbroucke, Catherine Barnard and Geert De Baere (eds), *A European Social Union after the Crisis* (Cambridge University Press 2017) 92–93; Maurizio Ferrera, 'Crafting the European Social Union – Towards a Roadmap for Delivery' in Maurizio Ferrera (ed.), *Towards a European Social Union: The European Pillar of Social Rights and the Roadmap for a Fully-Fledged Social Union* (Centro di Ricerca e Documentazione Luigi Einaudi 2019) 12. In this sense, the model of EU integration described by Maduro as a third European social model is considered as the most desirable one. Maduro (n 25) 126 and 135–138. On the broad variety of structurally different European welfare states, *see* Fritz W. Scharpf, 'The European Social Model: Coping with the Challenges of Diversity' (2002) 40 JCMS: Journal of Common Market Studies 645, 650–651.

Bibliography

Literature

Ahlberg, Kerstin. 'The Age of Innocence – And Beyond'. FORMULA Working Paper, University of Oslo, Department of Private Law 21 (2010).

Alberti, Gabriella and Sonila Danaj. 'Posting and Agency Work in British Construction and Hospitality: The Role of Regulation in Differentiating the Experiences of Migrants'. *The International Journal of Human Resource Management* 28, no. 21 (30 November 2017): 3065–3088. https://doi.org/10.1080/09585192.2017.1365746.

Ales, Edoardo and Giovanni Orlandini. 'The Impact of Viking and Laval on Italian Legislation and Regulations Concerning Collective Action'. In *Viking – Laval – Rüffert: Consequences and Policy Perspectives*, edited by Andreas Bücker and Wiebke Warneck, 69–82. Report 111. Bruxelles: ETUI (European Trade Union Institute), 2010.

Alsos, Kristin and Anne Mette Ødegård. 'Shifting Employer Strategies in Light of Institutional Change'. In *Posted Work in the European Union: The Political Economy of Free Movement*, edited by Jens Arnholtz and Nathan Lillie, 50–69. New York: Routledge, 2019.

Alter, Karen J., Renaud Dehousse and Georg Vanberg. 'Law, Political Science and EU Legal Studies: An Interdisciplinary Project?' *European Union Politics* 3, no. 1 (March 2002): 113–136. https://doi.org/10.1177/1465116502003001006.

Amiya-Nakada, Ryosuke. 'Lightening of Citizenship and Its Implication for Social Policy: "Social Security Lite" in the Making?' *SSRN Electronic Journal*, 2013. https://doi.org/10.2139/ssrn.2327792.

Andor, László. 'A Timely Call for a Social Union'. In *Towards a European Social Union: The European Pillar of Social Rights and the Roadmap for a Fully-Fledged Social Union*, edited by Maurizio Ferrera, 27–39. A Forum Debate. Torino (Italy): Centro di Ricerca e Documentazione Luigi Einaudi, 2019.

Aristotle. *Nicomachean Ethics*. Translated by William David Ross. Initially published in 1925, Fourth Century B.C.

Aristotle. *Politics*. Translated by William Ellis. Initially published in 1912, Fourth Century B.C.

Arnholtz, Jens and Søren Kaj Andersen. 'Extra-Institutional Changes under Pressure from Posting: Extra-Institutional Changes'. *British Journal of Industrial Relations* 56, no. 2 (June 2018): 1–23. https://doi.org/10.1111/bjir.12287.

Arnholtz, Jens and Nathan Lillie. 'European Integration and the Reconfiguration of National Industrial Relations: Posted Work as a Driver of Institutional Change'. In *Posted Work in the European Union: The Political Economy of Free Movement*, edited by Jens Arnholtz and Nathan Lillie, 1–30. New York: Routledge, 2019.

Azoulai, Loïc. '"Integration through Law" and Us'. *International Journal of Constitutional Law* 14, no. 2 (April 2016): 449–463. https://doi.org/10.1093/icon/mow024.

Azoulai, Loïc. 'The Court of Justice and the Social Market Economy: The Emergence of an Ideal and the Conditions for Its Realization'. *Common Market Law Review*, Kluwer Law International. Printed in the Netherlands, 45, no. Social market economy (2008): 1335–1356.

Baere, Geert De and Kathleen Gutman. 'The Basis in EU Constitutional Law for Further Social Integration'. In *A European Social Union after the Crisis*, edited by Frank Vandenbroucke, Catherine Barnard and Geert De Baere, 344–384. Cambridge: Cambridge University Press, 2017. https://doi.org/10.1017/9781108235174.015.

Bakardjieva Engelbrekt, Antonina. 'Institutional Theories, EU Law and the Role of the Courts for Developing a European Social Model'. In *The Role of Courts in Developing a European Social Model – Theoretical and Methodological Perspectives*, edited by Ulla Neergaard, Ruth Nielsen and Lynn M. Roseberry, 299–351. Copenhagen: Djøf Publishing, 2010.

Barnard, Catherine. 'A Proportionate Response to Proportionality in the Field of Collective Action'. *European Law Review*, Sweet & Maxwell and its Contributors, 2015, 117–135.

Barnard, Catherine. '"British Jobs for British Workers": The Lindsey Oil Refinery Dispute and the Future of Local Labour Clauses in an Integrated EU Market'. *Industrial Law Journal* 38, no. 3 (1 September 2009): 245–277. https://doi.org/10.1093/indlaw/dwp013.

Barnard, Catherine. 'EU Citizenship and the Principle of Solidarity'. In *Social Welfare and EU Law*, edited by Michael Dougan and Eleanor Spaventa, 157–180. Oxford: Hart Publishing, 2005.

Barnard, Catherine. *EU Employment Law*. Fourth Edition. Oxford: Oxford European Union Law Library, 2012.

Barnard, Catherine. 'EU Employment Law and the European Social Model: The Past, the Present and the Future'. *Current Legal Problems* 67, no. 1 (1 January 2014): 199–237. https://doi.org/10.1093/clp/cuu015.

Barnard, Catherine. 'EU "Social" Policy: From Employment Law to Labour Market Reform'. In *The Evolution of EU Law*, edited by Paul Craig and Gráinne de Búrca, Second Edition, 641–685. Oxford: Oxford University Press, 2011.

Barnard, Catherine. 'Fifty Years of Avoiding Social Dumping? The EU's Economic and Not So Economic Constitution'. In *50 Years of the European Treaties: Looking*

Back and Thinking Forward, edited by Michael Dougan and Samantha Currie, First Edition, 311–342. Essays in European Law. Oxford and Portland, Oregon: Hart Publishing, 2009.

Barnard, Catherine. 'Free Movement and Labour Rights: Squaring the Circle?' *University of Cambridge Faculty of Law Legal Studies Research Paper* 23/2013 (August 2013). https://doi.org/10.2139/ssrn.2313088.

Barnard, Catherine. 'Free Movement of Natural Persons and Citizenship of the Union'. In *European Union Law*, edited by Catherine Barnard and Steve Peers, Second Edition, 369–408. Oxford: Oxford University Press, 2017.

Barnard, Catherine. 'More Posting'. *Industrial Law Journal* 43, no. 2 (July 2014): 194–211. https://doi.org/10.1093/indlaw/dwu006.

Barnard, Catherine. 'Posting Matters'. *Arbeidsrett* 11, no. 01 (14 May 2014): 1–28.

Barnard, Catherine. 'Social Dumping or Dumping Socialism?' *The Cambridge Law Journal* 67, no. 02 (July 2008). https://doi.org/10.1017/S0008197308000627.

Barnard, Catherine. 'Solidarity and New Governance in Social Policy'. In *Law and New Governance in the EU and the US*, edited by Gráinne de Búrca and Joanne Scott, 153–178. Oxford and Portland, Oregon: Hart Publishing, 2006.

Barnard, Catherine. 'Solidarity and the Commission's "Renewed Social Agenda"'. In *Promoting Solidarity in the European Union*, edited by Malcolm Ross and Yuri Borgmann-Prebil, 73–105. Oxford: Oxford University Press, 2010.

Barnard, Catherine. 'The Calm after the Storm: Time to Reflect on EU (Labour) Law Scholarship Following the Decisions in Viking and Laval'. *University of Cambridge Faculty of Law Research Paper No. 55/2015, Later Published in Alan Bogg, Cathryn Costello and ACL Davies(eds), Research Handbook on EU Labour Law (Edward Elgar Publishing) 337*, 30 September 2015. https://doi.org/10.4337/9781783471126.

Barnard, Catherine. 'The Charter, the Court – and the Crisis'. *SSRN Electronic Journal*, 2013. https://doi.org/10.2139/ssrn.2306957.

Barnard, Catherine. 'The Protection of Fundamental Rights in the EU After Lisbon: A Question of Conflicts of Interests'. In *The Protection of Fundamental Rights in the EU After Lisbon*, edited by Sybe De Vries, Ulf Bernitz, and Steve Weatherill, 37–58. Studies of the Oxford Institute of European and Comparative Law. Oxford and Portland, Oregon: Hart Publishing, 2013.

Barnard, Catherine. *The Substantive Law of the EU: The Four Freedoms*. Fifth Edition. Oxford: Oxford University Press, 2016.

Barnard, Catherine. 'The UK and Posted Workers: The Effect of Commission v Luxembourg on the Territorial Application of British Labour Law: Case C-319/06 Commission v Luxembourg, Judgment 19 June 2008'. *Industrial Law Journal* 38, no. 1 (March 2009): 122–32.

Barnard, Catherine. 'Viking and Laval: An Introduction'. *Cambridge Yearbook of European Legal Studies* 10, no. 17 (2008): 463–492. https://doi.org/10.1017/S1528887000001403.

Barnard, Catherine and Geert De Baere. 'Towards a European Social Union: Achievements and Possibilities under the Current EU Constitutional Framework'. Euroforum Policy Paper (KU Leuven), no. 11 (September 2014).

Barnard, Catherine and Sybe De Vries. 'The "Social Market Economy" in a (Heterogeneous) Social Europe: Does It Make a Difference?' *Utrecht Law Review* 15, no. 2 (4 September 2019): 47. https://doi.org/10.18352/ulr.510.

Barnard, Catherine and Simon Deakin. 'European Labour Law after Laval'. In *Before and After the Economic Crisis. What Implications for the 'European Social Model'?*, edited by Marie-Ange Moreau, 252–269. Cheltenham: Edward Elgar Publishing, 2011.

Barnard, Catherine and Simon Deakin. 'In Search of Coherence: Social Policy, the Single Market and Fundamental Rights'. *Industrial Relations Journal* 31, no. 4 (November 2000): 331–345. https://doi.org/10.1111/1468-2338.00169.

Barnard, Catherine and Jukka Snell. 'Free Movement of Legal Persons and the Provision of Services'. In *European Union Law*, edited by Catherine Barnard and Steve Peers, Second Edition, 409–446. Oxford: Oxford University Press, 2017.

Barslund, Mikkel, Matthias Busse, Carlos Vargas-Silva, Pawel Kaczmarczyk, Timo Baas, Mario Izquierdo Peinado, Juan F. Jimeno, Aitor Lacuesta, Béla Galgóczi, and Janine Leschke. 'Labour Mobility in the EU: Dynamics, Patterns and Policies'. *Intereconomics* 49, no. 3 (May 2014): 116–158. https://doi.org/10.1007/s10272-014-0495-x.

Barslund, Mikkel, Matthias Busse and Frederic De Wispelaere. 'Posted Workers – For Some It Matters'. *CEPS (Centre for European Policy Studies)*, IDEAS Working Paper Series from RePEc, 26 October 2017.

Bartl, Marija, Eljalill Tauschinsky, Ari Afilalo, Emilios Christodoulidis, Michelle Everson, Benjamin Farrand, Geoffrey Gordon, et al. 'Knowledge, Power and Law Beyond the State'. *SSRN Electronic Journal*, 2016. https://doi.org/10.2139/ssrn.2728148.

Bell, Mark. 'The Principle of Equal Treatment: Widening and Deepening'. In *The Evolution of EU Law*, edited by Paul Craig and Gráinne de Búrca, Second Edition, 611–639. Oxford: Oxford University Press, 2011.

Bello, Barbara Giovanna. 'Equal Opportunities for All? Social Challenges and Legal Boundaries in the European Puzzle'. In *Some Still More Equal than Others? Or Equal Opportunities for All?*, edited by Serdar M. Degirmencioglu, 29–42. Youth Knowledge 12. Strasbourg: Council of Europe Publishing, 2011.

Berghman, Jozef. 'Social Security in a European Perspective: Present and Future Challenges'. In *Social Protection and the European Economic and Monetary Union*, edited by Jozef Pacolet, 35–47. Avebury; Aldershot, 1996.

Bernaciak, Magdalena. 'Conclusion'. In *Market Expansion and Social Dumping in Europe*, edited by Magdalena Bernaciak, 226–234. Routledge Advances in European Politics. New York, NY: Routledge, 2015.

Bernaciak, Magdalena. 'Introduction: Social Dumping and the EU Integration Process'. In *Market Expansion and Social Dumping in Europe*, edited by Magdalena Bernaciak, 1–22. Routledge Advances in European Politics. New York, NY: Routledge, 2015. https://doi.org/10.4324/9781315766607.

Bernaciak, Magdalena. 'Polish Trade Unions and Social Dumping Debates: Between a Rock and a Hard Place'. *Transfer: European Review of Labour and Research* 22, no. 4 (1 November 2016): 505–519. https://doi.org/10.1177/1024258916667017.

Bernaciak, Magdalena. 'Social Dumping and the EU Integration Process'. ETUI European Trade Union Institute - Working Paper 2014.06, July 2014, 30.

Bernaciak, Magdalena. 'Social Dumping: Political Catchphrase or Threat to Labour Standards?' ETUI European Trade Union Institute - Working Paper 2012.06, June 2012, 40.

Bernaciak, Magdalena and Zane Rasnača. 'Not as Simple as It Should Be? Why the Judicial Enforcement of Posted Workers' Rights Needs Improvement'. *LSE European Politics and Policy (EUROPP) Blog* (blog), 5 March 2020. http://eprints.lse.ac.uk/104999/.

Bernitz, Ulf. 'Horizontal Effects of Private Rights Vested by Union Law on Damages to Be Paid by Another Private Party: The Laval Case as a Model'. In *The Protection of Fundamental Rights in the EU after Lisbon*, edited by Sybe De Vries, Ulf Bernitz and Steve Weatherill, 139–152. Studies of the Oxford Institute of European and Comparative Law. Oxford and Portland, Oregon: Hart Publishing, 2013.

Berntsen, Lisa. 'Reworking Labour Practices: On the Agency of Unorganized Mobile Migrant Construction Workers'. *Work, Employment and Society* 30, no. 3 (June 2016): 472–488. https://doi.org/10.1177/0950017015617687.

Berntsen, Lisa and Nathan Lillie. 'Breaking the Law? Varieties of Social Dumping in a Pan-European Labour Market'. In *Market Expansion and Social Dumping in Europe*, edited by Magdalena Bernaciak, 43–60. Routledge Advances in European Politics. New York, NY: Routledge, 20s15.

Berntsen, Lisa. 'Hyper-Mobile Migrant Workers and Dutch Trade Union Representation Strategies at the Eemshaven Construction Sites'. *Economic and Industrial Democracy* 37, no. 1 (February 2016): 171–187. https://doi.org/10.1177/0143831X14537357.

Beutler, Bengt. 'Solidarity in the EU: A Critique of Solidarity and of the EU'. In *Solidarity in the European Union*, edited by Andreas Grimmel and Susanne My Giang, 21–36. New York, NY: Springer Berlin Heidelberg, 2017.

Biagi, Marco. 'Fortune Smiles on the Italian EU Presidency: Talking Half-Seriously about the Posted Workers and Parental Leave Directives'. *International Journal of Comparative Labour Law and Industrial Relations* 12 (1996): 97–109.

Bieler, Andreas and Roland Erne. 'Transnational Solidarity?: The European Working Class in the Eurozone Crisis'. In *Transforming Classes: Socialist Register 2015*, edited by Leo Panitch and Greg Albo, 157–177. London (UK): The Merlin Press, 2014.

Blanpain, Roger. 'Freedom of Services in the EU: A Social Catastrophe - Are There Lessons to Be Learned from the Belgian Experience?'. *European Labour Law Journal* 2, no. 3 (2011): 191–195.

Blanpain, Roger. 'The European Social Model (ESM): Myth or Reality?' *European Labour Law Journal* 2, no. 2 (2011): 142–149.

Bogoeski, Vladimir. 'Challenges to "United in Diversity" in a European Social Union'. In *Towards a European Social Union: The European Pillar of Social Rights and the Roadmap for a Fully-Fledged Social Union*, edited by Maurizio Ferrera, 40–46. A Forum Debate. Torino (Italy): Centro di Ricerca e Documentazione Luigi Einaudi, 2019.

Bohle, Dorothee. 'Race to the Bottom? Comparative Institutional Advantages? Competition of Capitalisms in the Enlarged EU'. In *Contradictions and Limits of Neoliberal European Governance: From Lisbon to Lisbon*, edited by Jan Drahokoupil and Laura Horn, 8: 163–187. UK: Palgrave Macmillan, 2008.

Booth, Wayne C., Gregory G. Colomb and Joseph M. Williams. *The Craft of Research*. Second Edition. Chicago: The University of Chicago Press, 2003.

Booth, Wayne C., Gregory G. Colomb, Joseph M. Williams and William T. Fitzgerald. *The Craft of Research*. Fourth Edition. Chicago: The University of Chicago Press, 2016.

Bosch, Gerhard. 'The Making of the German Minimum Wage: A Case Study of Institutional Change: The Making of the German Minimum Wage'. *Industrial Relations Journal* 49, no. 1 (January 2018): 19–33. https://doi.org/10.1111/irj.12200.

Bruszt, László and Béla Greskovits. 'Transnationalization, Social Integration, and Capitalist Diversity in the East and the South'. *Studies in Comparative International Development* 44, no. 4 (December 2009): 411–434. https://doi.org/10.1007/s12116-009-9045-0.

Bruun, Niklas and Claes-Mikael Jonsson. 'Consequences and Policy Perspectives in the Nordic Countries as a Result of Certain Important Decisions of the European Court of Justice'. In *Viking – Laval – Rüffert: Consequences and Policy Perspectives*, edited by Andreas Bücker and Wiebke Warneck, 15–28. Report 111. Bruxelles: ETUI (European Trade Union Institute), 2010.

Bücker, Andreas and Wiebke Warneck. 'Analysis and Outlook: In Search of a New Relationship between Market Integration and Social Embedding'. In *Viking – Laval – Rüffert: Consequences and Policy Perspectives*, edited by Andreas Bücker and Wiebke Warneck, 129–142. Report 111. Bruxelles: ETUI (European Trade Union Institute), 2010.

Búrca, Gráinne de, Dimitry Kochenov and Andrew Williams. *Debating Europe's Justice Deficit: The EU, Swabian Housewives, Rawls, and Ryanair*. EUI Working Papers. Department of Law. Florence, Italy: Edited by Gráinne de Búrca, Dimitry Kochenov and Andrew Williams with the assistance of Suryapratim Roy, 2013.

Butler, Graham. 'Solidarity and Its Limits for Economic Integration in the European Union's Internal Market'. *Maastricht Journal of European and Comparative Law* 25, no. 3 (June 2018): 310–331. https://doi.org/10.1177/1023263X18769207.

Cahillane, Laura and Jennifer Schweppe (eds). *Legal Research Methods: Principles and Practicalities*. Beaverton, US: Clarus Press, 2016.

Calmfors, Lars, Girts Dimdins, Marie Gustafsson Sendén, Henry Montgomery and Ulrika Stavlöt. 'Why Do People Dislike Low-Wage Trade Competition with Posted Workers in the Service Sector?' *The Journal of Socio-Economics* 47 (December 2013): 82–93. https://doi.org/10.1016/j.socec.2013.09.001.

Caro, Erka, Lisa Berntsen, Nathan Lillie and Ines Wagner. 'Posted Migration and Segregation in the European Construction Sector'. *Journal of Ethnic and Migration Studies* 41, no. 10 (24 August 2015): 1600–1620. https://doi.org/10.1080/1369183X.2015.1015406.

Carter, Daniel. 'Equal Pay for Equal Work in the Same Place? Assessing the Revision to the Posted Workers Directive'. *Croatian Yearbook of European Law and Policy* 14, no. 1 (31 December 2018): 31–68. https://doi.org/10.3935/cyelp.14.2018.312.

Carvalho, Sonia de. 'The Revision of the Posting of Workers Directive and the Freedom to Provide Services in EU: Towards a Dead End?' In *Juridical Tribune*, 8(3):719–733. Society of Juridical and Administrative Sciences. Romania: Bucharest University of Economic Studies, 2018. http://www.tribunajuridica.eu/arhiva/An8v3/11.%20Sonia%20Carvalho.pdf.

Casale, Giuseppe. 'International Labour Standards and EU Labour Law'. In *Resocialising Europe in a Time of Crisis*, edited by Nicola Countouris and Mark Freedland, 81–104. Cambridge: Cambridge University Press, 2013. https://doi.org/10.1017/CBO9781107300736.007.

Cerwiński, Marcin. 'The Law Applicable to Employment Contracts under the Rome I-Regulation'. *Adam Mickiewicz University Law Review*, no. 1 (5 January 2015): 147–162.

Chacartegui, Consuelo. 'Resocialising Temporary Agency Work through a Theory of "Reinforced" Employers' Liability'. In *Resocialising Europe in a Time of Crisis*, edited by Nicola Countouris and Mark Freedland, 213–229. Cambridge: Cambridge University Press, 2013. https://doi.org/10.1017/CBO9781107300736.014.

Cherednychenko, Olha O. 'Fundamental Freedoms, Fundamental Rights, and the Many Faces of Freedom of Contract in the EU'. In *The Reach of Free Movement*, edited by Mads Andenas, Tarjei Bekkedal and Luca Pantaleo, 273–292. New York, NY: Springer Berlin Heidelberg, 2017.

Christodoulidis, Emilios. 'Social Rights Constitutionalism: An Antagonistic Endorsement'. *Journal of Law and Society* 44, no. 1 (March 2017): 123–149. https://doi.org/10.1111/jols.12017.

Christodoulidis, Emilios. 'The European Court of Justice and "Total Market" Thinking'. *German Law Journal* 14, no. 10 (2013): 17.

Collins, Hugh. 'Is There a Third Way in Labour Law?' In *Labour Law in an Era of Globalization: Transformative Practices and Possibilities*, edited by Joanne Conaghan, Richard Michael Fischl and Karl Klare, 449–469. Oxford: Oxford University Press, 2004.

Comte, Emmanuel. 'Promising More to Give Less: International Disputes between Core and Periphery around European Posted Labor, 1955–2018'. *Labor History*, 15 July 2019, 1–16. https://doi.org/10.1080/0023656X.2019.1642465.

Cornelissen, Rob and Guido Van Limberghen. 'Social Security for Mobile Workers and Labour Law'. In *Research Handbook on European Social Security Law*, 344–384. Cheltenham, UK and Northampton, MA, USA: Edward Elgar Publishing, 2015. https://doi.org/10.4337/9781782547334.

Costamagna, Francesco. 'The Revision of the Posted Workers Directive as a Meaningful Way to Curb Regulatory Competition in the Social Domain?' *Sant'Anna Legal Studies*, STALS Research Paper 2/2019, 2 (2019): 25.

Countouris, Nicola and Samuel Engblom. 'Civilising the European Posted Workers Directive'. In *Viking, Laval and Beyond*, edited by R. Mark Freedland and

Jeremias Prassl, First Edition, 279–293. EU Law in the Member States. Oxford and Portland, Oregon: Hart Publishing, 2016.

Countouris, Nicola and Samuel Engblom. '"Protection or Protectionism?": A Legal Deconstruction of the Emerging False Dilemma in European Integration'. UCL Labour Rights Institute On-Line Working Papers – LRI WP, January 2015.

Craig, Paul and Gráinne de Búrca. *EU Law: Text, Cases, and Materials*. Sixth Edition. Oxford: Oxford University Press, 2015.

Cremers, Jan. 'Economic Freedoms and Labour Standards in the European Union'. *Transfer: European Review of Labour and Research* 22(2) (May 2016): 149–162. https://doi.org/10.1177/1024258916635962.

Cremers, Jan. 'EU Economic Freedoms and Social Dumping'. In *Market Expansion and Social Dumping in Europe*, edited by Magdalena Bernaciak, 173–189. Routledge Advances in European Politics. New York, NY: Routledge, 2015.

Cremers, Jan. 'Free Provision of Services and Cross-Border Labour Recruitment'. *Policy Studies* 34, no. 2 (March 2013): 201–220. https://doi.org/10.1080/01442872.2013.767588.

Cremers, Jan. 'Market Integration, Cross-Border Recruitment, and Enforcement of Labour Standards – A Dutch Case'. In *Posted Work in the European Union: The Political Economy of Free Movement*, edited by Jens Arnholtz and Nathan Lillie, 128–146. New York: Routledge, 2019.

Cremers, Jan. 'The Posting Directive: Origins and Assessment'. *Transfer: European Review of Labour and Research* 1(2) (1995): 309–314.

Cremers, Jan, Jon Erik Dølvik and Gerhard Bosch. 'Posting of Workers in the Single Market: Attempts to Prevent Social Dumping and Regime Competition in the EU'. *Industrial Relations Journal* 38, no. 6 (2007): 524–541.

Cremers, Jan and Thomas Hastings. 'Developing an Approach for Tackling Letterbox Companies: Background Paper for the European Platform on Tackling Undeclared Work Seminar'. In *European Platform Undeclared Work*. Brussels, 2017.

Cryer, Robert, Tamara Hervey, Bal Sokhi-Bulley and Alexandra Bohm. *Research Methodologies in EU and International Law*. First Edition. Oxford and Portland, Oregon: Hart Publishing, 2011.

Dalla Pellegrina, Lucia and Margherita Saraceno. 'Posting of Workers across the EU: An Empirical Investigation'. *European Journal of Law and Economics* 44, no. 3 (December 2017): 423–451. https://doi.org/10.1007/s10657-016-9536-1.

Dashwood, Alan. 'Viking and Laval Issues of Horizontal Direct Effect'. *Cambridge Yearbook of European Legal Studies* 10, no. 19 (2007–2008): 525–540.

Davies, A.C.L. *EU Labour Law*. Elgar European Law Series. Cheltenham, United Kingdom: Edward Elgar Publishing Ltd, 2014.

Davies, A.C.L. 'One Step Forward, Two Steps Back? The Viking and Laval Cases in the ECJ'. *Industrial Law Journal* 37, no. 2 (1 June 2008): 126–148. https://doi.org/10.1093/indlaw/dwn001.

Davies, A.C.L. 'Regulating Atypical Work: Beyond Equality'. In *Resocialising Europe in a Time of Crisis*, edited by Nicola Countouris and Mark Freedland, 230–249. Cambridge: Cambridge University Press, 2013. https://doi.org/10.1017/CBO9781107300736.015.

Davies, Gareth. 'Discrimination and beyond in European Economic and Social Law'. *Maastricht Journal of European and Comparative Law* 18, nos 1–2 (2011): 7–28.

Davies, Paul. 'Case C-346/06, Rüffert v Land Niedersachsen [2008] IRLR 467 (ECJ)'. *Industrial Law Journal* 37, no. 3 (1 September 2008): 293–295. https://doi.org/10.1093/indlaw/dwn012.

Davies, Paul. 'Posted Workers: Single Market or Protection of National Labour Law Systems?' *Common Market Law Review*, Kluwer Law International, 34 (1997): 571–602.

Davies, Paul. 'The Posted Workers Directive and the EC Treaty'. *Industrial Law Journal*, European Developments, 31, no. 3 (September 2002): 298–306.

De Vos, Marc. 'Free Movement of Workers, Free Movement of Services and the Posted Workers Directive: A Bermuda Triangle for National Labour Standards?' *ERA Forum – Springer* 7, no. 3 (September 2006): 356–370. https://doi.org/10.1007/BF02857086.

De Vries, Sybe A. 'Balancing Fundamental Rights with Economic Freedoms According to the European Court of Justice'. *Utrecht Law Review* 9, no. 1 (31 January 2013): 169. https://doi.org/10.18352/ulr.220.

De Vries, Sybe A. 'The Protection of Fundamental Rights within Europe's Internal Market after Lisbon – And Endeavour for More Harmony'. In *The Protection of Fundamental Rights in the EU After Lisbon*, edited by Sybe De Vries, Ulf Bernitz and Steve Weatherill, 59–98. Studies of the Oxford Institute of European and Comparative Law. Oxford and Portland, Oregon: Hart Publishing, 2013.

Deakin, Simon. 'Regulatory Competition after Laval'. *Cambridge Yearbook of European Legal Studies* 10, no. 1 (2007): 581–610.

Deakin, Simon. 'What Follows Austerity? From Social Pillar to New Deal'. In *A European Social Union after the Crisis*, edited by Frank Vandenbroucke, Catherine Barnard and Geert De Baere, 192–210. Cambridge: Cambridge University Press, 2017. https://doi.org/10.1017/9781108235174.009.

Dodi, Ioana and Ioana Melenciuc. 'Posted Workers on the Route to a European Labour Market. Case Study: OSH-Related Vulnerabilities of Posted Workers in Spain'. CES Working Papers, Alexandru Ioan Cuza University of Iasi, Centre for European Studies, Iasi 11, no. 1 (2019): 73–90.

Dølvik, Jon Erik and Jelle Visser. 'Free Movement, Equal Treatment and Workers' Rights: Can the European Union Solve Its Trilemma of Fundamental Principles?: Free Movement, Equal Treatment and Workers' Rights'. *Industrial Relations Journal* 40, no. 6 (November 2009): 491–509. https://doi.org/10.1111/j.1468-2338.2009.00542.x.

Dougan, Michael and Eleanor Spaventa. *Wish You Weren't Here...: New Models of Social Solidarity in the European Union*. Social welfare and EU law. Oxford: Hart Publishing, 2005. https://doi.org/10.5040/9781472563385.

Ehlermann, Claus-Dieter. 'The "1992 Project": Stages, Structures, Results and Prospects'. *Michigan Journal of International Law* 11, no. 4 (1990): 23.

Eichhorst, Werner. 'European Social Policy between National and Supranational Regulation: Posted Workers in the Framework of Liberalized Services Provision'.

Max Planck Institute for the Study of Societies (MPIfG), Cologne, August 1998. https://www.econstor.eu/bitstream/10419/43182/1/248171305.pdf.

Evju, Stein. *Cross-Border Services: Posting of Workers, and Multilevel Governance*. Oslo: University of Oslo, Faculty of Law, 2013.

Evju, Stein. 'Posting Past and Present: The Posting of Workers Directive – Genesis and Current Contrasts'. FORMULA Working Paper, University of Oslo, Department of Private Law 8 (2009).

Evju, Stein. 'Revisiting the Posted Workers Directive: Conflict of Laws and Laws in Contrast'. Edited by Catherine Barnard and Okeoghene Odudu. *Cambridge Yearbook of European Legal Studies* 12, no. 6 (2009–2010): 151–182.

Evju, Stein and Tonia Novitz. 'The Evolving Regulation: Dynamics and Consequences'. FORMULA Working Paper, University of Oslo, Department of Private Law 33 (2012).

Fabbrini, Federico and Katarzyna Granat. '"Yellow Card, but No Foul": The Role of the National Parliaments under the Subsidiarity Protocol and the Commission Proposal for an EU Regulation on the Right to Strike'. *Common Market Law Review*, Kluwer Law International, 50 (2013): 115–144.

Faioli, Michele. 'Posted Workers. The Italian Viewpoint'. *Economia & Lavoro*, Wage Settings, June 2016, 47–57.

Feenstra, Sjoerd. 'How Can the Viking/Laval Conundrum Be Resolved? Balancing the Economic and the Social: One Bed for Two Dreams?' In *A European Social Union after the Crisis*, edited by Frank Vandenbroucke, Catherine Barnard and Geert De Baere, 309–43. Cambridge: Cambridge University Press, 2017. https://doi.org/10.1017/9781108235174.014.

Fernández-Macías, Enrique and Carlos Vacas-Soriano. 'A Coordinated European Union Minimum Wage Policy?' *European Journal of Industrial Relations* 22, no. 2 (June 2016): 97–113. https://doi.org/10.1177/0959680115610725.

Ferrera, Maurizio. 'Crafting the European Social Union – Towards a Roadmap for Delivery'. In *Towards a European Social Union: The European Pillar of Social Rights and the Roadmap for a Fully-Fledged Social Union*, edited by Maurizio Ferrera, 12–26. A Forum Debate. Torino (Italy): Centro di Ricerca e Documentazione Luigi Einaudi, 2019.

Ferrera, Maurizio. 'The European Social Union: A Missing but Necessary "Political Good"'. In *A European Social Union after the Crisis*, edited by Frank Vandenbroucke, Catherine Barnard and Geert De Baere, 47–67. Cambridge: Cambridge University Press, 2017. https://doi.org/10.1017/9781108235174.003.

Ferrera, Maurizio, Anton Hemerijck and Martin Rhodes. 'The Future of the European "Social Model" in the Global Economy'. *Journal of Comparative Policy Analysis: Research and Practice* 3, no. 2 (August 2001): 163–190. https://doi.org/10.1080/13876980108412659.

Fromage, Diane and Valentin Kreilinger. 'National Parliaments' Third Yellow Card and the Struggle over the Revision of the Posted Workers Directive'. *European Journal of Legal Studies* 10, no. 1 (2017): 125–160.

Furåker, Bengt and Bengt Larsson. 'Revision of the EU Posting of Workers Directive, Social Dumping and Trade Unions' Position'. In *Trade Union Cooperation in*

Europe: Patterns, Conditions, Issues, by Bengt Furåker and Bengt Larsson, 109–139. Palgrave Pivot, Cham: Springer International Publishing, 2020. https://doi.org/10.1007/978-3-030-38770-9_4.

Garben, Sacha. 'The European Pillar of Social Rights: An Assessment of Its Meaning and Significance'. *Cambridge Yearbook of European Legal Studies*, 21 May 2019, 1–27. https://doi.org/10.1017/cel.2019.3.

Garben, Sacha. 'The European Pillar of Social Rights as a Revival of Social Europe'. In *Towards a European Social Union: The European Pillar of Social Rights and the Roadmap for a Fully-Fledged Social Union*, edited by Maurizio Ferrera, 76–83. A Forum Debate. Torino (Italy): Centro di Ricerca e Documentazione Luigi Einaudi, 2019.

Gerbrandy, Anna, Willem Janssen and Lyndsey Thomsin. 'Shaping the Social Market Economy After the Lisbon Treaty: How "Social" Is Public Economic Law?' *Utrecht Law Review* 15, no. 2 (4 September 2019): 32–46. https://doi.org/10.18352/ulr.509.

Gestel, Rob Van and Hans-W. Micklitz. 'Revitalizing Doctrinal Legal Research in Europe: What About Methodology?' In *European Legal Method – Paradox and Revitalisation*, edited by Ulla Neergaard, Ruth Nielsen and Lynn M. Roseberry. Copenhagen: Djøf Publishing, 2011.

Gestel, Rob Van, Hans-W. Micklitz and Edward Rubin. 'Introduction'. In *Rethinking Legal Scholarship*, edited by Rob van Gestel, Hans-W. Micklitz and Edward L. Rubin, 1–28. Cambridge: Cambridge University Press, 2017. https://doi.org/10.1017/9781316442906.001.

Giesen, Richard. 'Posting: Social Protection of Workers vs. Fundamental Freedoms?' *Common Market Law Review*, Kluwer Law International, 40 (2003): 143–58.

Giubboni, Stefano. 'European Citizenship and Social Rights in Times of Crisis'. Centro Einaudi – Laboratorio Di Politica Comparata e Filosofia Pubblica, Working Paper-LPF n. 2 (2013).

Głowacka, Marta. 'Posting of Workers Directive Reloaded'. *Studia z Zakresu Prawa Pracy i Polityki Społecznej (Studies on Labour Law and Social Policy)* 26, no. 1 (29 March 2019): 29–45. https://doi.org/10.4467/25444654SPP.19.003.10146.

Grimmel, Andreas. 'Solidarity in the European Union: Fundamental Value or "Empty Signifier"'. In *Solidarity in the European Union*, edited by Andreas Grimmel and Susanne My Giang, 161–175. New York, NY: Springer Berlin Heidelberg, 2017.

Grosse, Tomasz Grzegorz. 'A Social Europe or a More Protectionist One? The Single Market in the Aftermath of the Crises'. In *A 'Social Turn' in the European Union?: New Trends and Ideas about Social Convergence in Europe*, edited by Jacek Kubera and Tomasz Morozowski, First Edition, 33–54. London: Routledge, 2020. https://doi.org/10.4324/9780367409586.

Groussot, Xavier, Laurent Pech and Thor Petursson. 'The Reach of Fundamental Rights on Member State Action after Lisbon'. In *The Protection of Fundamental Rights in the EU After Lisbon*, edited by Sybe De Vries, Ulf Bernitz, and Steve Weatherill, 97–118. Studies of the Oxford Institute of European and Comparative Law. Oxford and Portland, Oregon: Hart Publishing, 2013.

Grušić, Uglješa. 'European Labour Market Posted Workers Directive and the Social Implications of the Movement of Labour'. In *Global Private International Law: Adjudication Without Frontiers*, edited by Horatia Muir Watt, Lucia Bíziková, Agatha Brandão de Oliveira, and Diego P. Fernández Arroyo, 473–483. Cheltenham: Edward Elgar Publishing, 2018.

Grušić, Uglješa. *The European Private International Law of Employment*. Cambridge: Cambridge University Press, 2015.

Guzi, Martin and Martin Kahanec. 'Socioeconomic Cleavages between Workers from New Member States and Host-Country Labour Forces in the EU during the Great Recession'. In *Market Expansion and Social Dumping in Europe*, edited by Magdalena Bernaciak, First Edition, 97–122. New York, NY: Routledge, 2015. https://doi.org/10.4324/9781315766607.

Harbo, Tor-Inge. 'The Criterion of "Consistent and Systematic Manner"'. In *The Reach of Free Movement*, edited by Mads Andenas, Tarjei Bekkedal and Luca Pantaleo, 205–228. New York, NY: Springer Berlin Heidelberg, 2017.

Hatzopoulos, Vassilis. 'A (More) Social Europe: A Political Crossroad or a Legal One-Way? Dialogues between Luxembourg and Lisbon'. *Common Market Law Review* 42, no. 6 (2005): 1599–1635.

Hatzopoulos, Vassilis. 'Justifications for Restrictions to Free Movement: Towards a Single Normative Framework?' In *The Reach of Free Movement*, edited by Mads Andenas, Tarjei Bekkedal and Luca Pantaleo, 131–156. New York, NY: Springer Berlin Heidelberg, 2017.

Hatzopoulos, Vassilis. 'Labour Immigration in the EU Through the Back Door? The Free Provision of Services as a Facilitator of Migration Flows'. In *Labour Migration in Europe*, edited by Georg Menz and Alexander Caviedes, 150–179. Migration, Minorities and Citizenship. Basingstoke, United Kingdom: Palgrave MacMillan, 2010.

Hatzopoulos, Vassilis. *Regulating Services in the European Union*. Oxford: Oxford University Press, 2012.

Hatzopoulos, Vassilis. 'The Court's Approach to Services (2006-2012): From Case Law to Case Load?' *Common Market Law Review* 50, no. 2 (2013): 459–501.

Hatzopoulos, Vassilis. 'The Economic Constitution of the EU Treaty and the Limits between Economic and Non-Economic Activities'. *European Business Law Review* 23, no. 6 (2012): 973–1007.

Hatzopoulos, Vassilis and Thien Uyen Do. 'The Case Law of the ECJ Concerning the Free Provision of Services: 2000 - 2005'. *Common Market Law Review* 43, no. 4 (4 August 2006): 923–991.

Hendrickx, Frank. 'A Post-Laval Case: ESA and Minimum Wages for Posted Workers'. *European Labour Law Journal* 6, 1 (1 March 2015): 2–4.

Hendrickx, Frank. 'Completing Economic and Social Integration: Towards Labour Law for the United States of Europe'. In *Resocialising Europe in a Time of Crisis*, edited by Nicola Countouris and Mark Freedland, 61–80. Cambridge: Cambridge University Press, 2013. https://doi.org/10.1017/CBO9781107300736.006.

Hendrickx, Frank. 'Fundamental Social Rights in Pre- and Post-Constitutional Terms'. *International Journal of Comparative Labour Law and Industrial Relations* 22, no. 3 (2006): 407–433.

Hinarejos, Alicia. 'Laval and Viking: The Right to Collective Action Versus EU Fundamental Freedoms'. *Human Rights Law Review* 8, no. 4 (21 October 2008): 714–729. https://doi.org/10.1093/hrlr/ngn030.

Hoecke, Mark van. 'Legal Doctrine: Which Method(s) for What Kind of Discipline?' In *Methodologies of Legal Research: Which Kind of Method for What Kind of Discipline?*, edited by Mark van Hoecke, 1–18. European Academy of Legal Theory Monograph Series. Oxford and Portland, Oregon: Hart, 2011.

Hoecke, Mark van (ed.). *Methodologies of Legal Research: Which Kind of Method for What Kind of Discipline?* European Academy of Legal Theory Monograph Series. Oxford and Portland, Oregon: Hart, 2011.

Hoecke, Mark Van. 'Methodology of Comparative Legal Research'. *Law and Method*, no. 12 (2015). https://doi.org/10.5553/REM/.000010.

Hoek, Aukje A.H. van. 'Re-Embedding the Transnational Employment Relationship: A Tale about the Limitations of (EU) Law?' *Common Market Law Review*, Kluwer Law International, 55 (2018): 449–488.

Hoek, Aukje A.H. van and Mijke Houwerzijl. '"Posting" and "Posted Workers": The Need for Clear Definitions of Two Key Concepts of the Posting of Workers Directive'. Edited by Catherine Barnard, Markus Gehring and Iyiola Solanke. *Cambridge Yearbook of European Legal Studies* 14 (2012): 419–451.

Hoek, Aukje A.H. van and Mijke Houwerzijl. 'Where Do EU Mobile Workers Belong, According to Rome I and the (E)PWD?' In *Residence, Employment and Social Rights of Mobile Persons: On How EU Law Defines Where They Belong*, edited by Herwig Verschueren, Vol. 36, 215–253. Social Europe Series. Cambridge: Intersentia, 2016.

Hölscher, Jens and Johannes Stephan. 'Competition and Antitrust Policy in the Enlarged European Union: A Level Playing Field?' *JCMS: Journal of Common Market Studies* 47, no. 4 (September 2009): 863–889. https://doi.org/10.1111/j.1468-5965.2009.02008.x.

Hooghe, Marc and Soetkin Verhaegen. 'The Democratic Legitimacy of EU Institutions and Support for Social Policy in Europe'. In *A European Social Union after the Crisis*, edited by Frank Vandenbroucke, Catherine Barnard and Geert De Baere, 120–140. Cambridge: Cambridge University Press, 2017. https://doi.org/10.1017/9781108235174.006.

Hos, Nikolett. 'The Principle of Proportionality in the Viking and Laval Cases: An Appropriate Standard of Judicial Review?' EUI Working Paper 06 (2009).

Houwerzijl, Mijke. 'Implementation of the Posting of Workers Directive in the Netherlands'. FORMULA Working Paper, University of Oslo, Department of Private Law 16 (2010). http://www.jus.uio.no/ifp/english/research/projects/freemov/publications/papers/.

Houwerzijl, Mijke. 'Regime Shopping across (Blurring) Boundaries'. In *Regulating Transnational Labour in Europe: The Quandaries of Multilevel Governance*, edited by Stein Evju, 95–130. Skriftserie, No. 196. Oslo: UiO: Department of Private Law, 2014.

Houwerzijl, Mijke and Lisa Berntsen. 'Posting of Workers: From a Blurred Notion Associated with "Cheap Labour" to a Tool for "Fair Labour Mobility"?' In *Posted Work in the European Union: The Political Economy of Free Movement*, edited by Jens Arnholtz and Nathan Lillie, 147–166. New York: Routledge, 2019.

Houwerzijl, Mijke and Frans Pennings. 'Double Charges in Case of Posting of Employees: The *Guiot* Judgment and Its Effects on the Construction Sector'. *European Journal of Social Security* 1, no. 1 (March 1999): 91–112. https://doi.org/10.1023/A:1018672815932.

Hutchinson, Terry. 'The Doctrinal Method: Incorporating Interdisciplinary Methods in Reforming the Law'. Edited by Sanne Taekema. *Erasmus Law Review* 8, no. 3 (17 February 2016): 130–138. https://doi.org/10.5553/ELR.000055.

Hutchinson, Terry and Nigel Duncan. 'Defining and Describing What We Do: Doctrinal Legal Research'. *Deakin Law Review* 17, no. 1 (1 October 2012): 83. https://doi.org/10.21153/dlr2012vol17no1art70.

Iannuzzi, Francesco E. and Devi Sacchetto. 'Italian Labour Inspectors Facing Posted Workers Phenomena'. In *Posted Work in the European Union: The Political Economy of Free Movement*, edited by Jens Arnholtz and Nathan Lillie, 109–127. New York: Routledge, 2019.

Jacqueson, Catherine. 'For Better or for Worse? Transnational Solidarity in the Light of Social Europe'. In *Resocialising Europe in a Time of Crisis*, edited by Nicola Countouris and Mark Freedland, 373–389. Cambridge: Cambridge University Press, 2013. https://doi.org/10.1017/CBO9781107300736.023.

Jacqueson, Catherine and Frans Pennings. 'Equal Treatment of Mobile Persons in the Context of a Social Market Economy'. *Utrecht Law Review* 15, no. 2 (4 September 2019): 64. https://doi.org/10.18352/ulr.511.

Jager, Jennifer and Kurt A. Hafner. 'The Optimum Currency Area Theory and the EMU: An Assessment in the Context of the Eurozone Crisis'. *Intereconomics* 48, no. 5 (September 2013): 315–322. https://doi.org/10.1007/s10272-013-0474-7.

Jančić, Davor. 'EU Law's Grand Scheme on National Parliaments: The Third Yellow Card on Posted Workers and the Way Forward'. In *National Parliaments after the Lisbon Treaty and the Euro Crisis*, edited by Davor Jancic, 299–312. Oxford: Oxford University Press, 2017. https://doi.org/10.1093/acprof:oso/9780198791621.003.0016.

Joerges, Christian. 'Rechtsstaat and Social Europe: How a Classical Tension Resurfaces in the European Integration Process'. *Comparative Sociology* 9, no. 1 (1 January 2010): 65–85. https://doi.org/10.1163/156913210X12535202814397.

Joerges, Christian. 'Social Justice in an Ever More Diverse Union'. In *A European Social Union after the Crisis*, edited by Frank Vandenbroucke, Catherine Barnard, and Geert De Baere, 92–119. Cambridge: Cambridge University Press, 2017. https://doi.org/10.1017/9781108235174.005.

Joerges, Christian, Vladimir Bogoeski and Lukas Nüse. 'Economic Constitutionalism and the European Social Model: Can European Law Cope with the Deepening Tensions between Economic and Social Integration after the Financial Crisis'. In

The Metamorphosis of the European Economic Constitution, by Herwig Hofmann, Katerina Pantazatou and Giovanni Zaccaroni, 126–153. Elgar Studies in European Law and Policy. Cheltenham, UK and Northampton, MA, USA: Edward Elgar Publishing, 2019. https://doi.org/10.4337/9781788978309.00014.

Joerges, Christian, and Florian Rödl. 'Informal Politics, Formalised Law and the "Social Deficit" of European Integration: Reflections after the Judgments of the ECJ in *Viking* and *Laval*'. *European Law Journal* 15, no. 1 (January 2009): 1–19. https://doi.org/10.1111/j.1468-0386.2008.00448.x.

Jones, Alison and Christopher Townley. 'Competition Law'. In *European Union Law*, edited by Catherine Barnard and Steve Peers, Second Edition, 509–542. Oxford: Oxford University Press, 2017.

Kapella, Adam and Garance Dubarry. 'Europe Is Built on Competition Which Stimulates, on Cooperation Which Strengthens, and Solidarity Which Unites'. In *A 'Social Turn' in the European Union?: New Trends and Ideas about Social Convergence in Europe*, edited by Jacek Kubera and Tomasz Morozowski, First Edition, 185–189. London: Routledge, 2020. https://doi.org/10.4324/9780367409586.

Kaupa, Clemens. 'Public Procurement, Social Policy and Minimum Wage Regulation for Posted Workers: Towards a More Balanced Socio-Economic Integration Process?' European Papers 1, no. 1 (2016): 127–138. https://doi.org/10.15166/2499-8249/10.

Kilpatrick, Claire. 'Internal Market Architecture and the Accommodation of Labour Rights: As Good as It Gets?' EUI Working Paper Law 2011/04 (2011).

Kilpatrick, Claire. 'Laval's Regulatory Conundrum: Collective Standard-Setting and the Court's New Approach to Posted Workers'. *European Law Review* 34, no. 6 (18 December 2009): 844–865.

Koppernock, Martin. 'On the Future of "Social Europe" – Between Competitiveness and High Social Standards'. In *A 'Social Turn' in the European Union?: New Trends and Ideas about Social Convergence in Europe*, edited by Jacek Kubera and Tomasz Morozowski, First Edition, 171–178. London: Routledge, 2020. https://doi.org/10.4324/9780367409586.

Kotzur, Markus. 'Solidarity as a Legal Concept'. In *Solidarity in the European Union*, edited by Andreas Grimmel and Susanne My Giang, 37–46. New York, NY: Springer Berlin Heidelberg, 2017.

Krings, Torben. 'A Race to the Bottom? Trade Unions, EU Enlargement and the Free Movement of Labour'. *European Journal of Industrial Relations* 15, no. 1 (March 2009): 49–69. https://doi.org/10.1177/0959680108100165.

Kubera, Jacek and Tomasz Morozowski. 'The Social Turn and the Potential to Reconstruct the Social Dimension of the European Union'. In *A 'Social Turn' in the European Union?: New Trends and Ideas about Social Convergence in Europe*, edited by Jacek Kubera and Tomasz Morozowski, First Edition, 3–29. London: Routledge, 2020. https://doi.org/10.4324/9780367409586.

Kukovec, Damjan. 'A Critique of the Rhetoric of Common Interest in the European Union Legal Discourse'. *SSRN Electronic Journal*, 13 April 2012, 11.

Kukovec, Damjan. 'Economic Law, Inequality, and Hidden Hierarchies on the EU Internal Market'. *Michigan Journal of International Law* 38, no. 1 (2016): 57.

Kukovec, Damjan. 'Hierarchies as Law'. *Columbia Journal of European Law* 21, no. 1 (2014): 131–91.

Kukovec, Damjan. 'Law and the Periphery'. *European Law Journal* 21, no. 3 (May 2015): 406–28. https://doi.org/10.1111/eulj.12113.

Kukovec, Damjan. 'Taking Change Seriously – The Discourse of Justice and the Reproduction of the Status Quo'. *SSRN Electronic Journal, Later Published in Dimitry Kochenov, Gráinne de Búrca, and Andrew Williams (eds), Europe's Justice Deficit? (Bloomsbury Publishing Plc) 2015, 319–336*, 2012. https://doi.org/10.2139/ssrn.2302389.

Kukovec, Damjan. 'Whose Social Europe? The Laval/Viking Judgments and the Prosperity Gap'. Harvard Law School Institute for Global Law and Policy, IGLP Working Paper Series 2011/3, 1 April 2011.

Lalanne, Stéphane. 'Posting of Workers, EU Enlargement and the Globalization of Trade in Services'. *International Labour Review* 150, nos 3–4 (December 2011): 211–234. https://doi.org/10.1111/j.1564-913X.2011.00114.x.

Leczykiewicz, Dorota. 'Conceptualising Conflict between the Economic and the Social in EU Law after Viking and Laval'. In *Viking, Laval and Beyond*, edited by R. Mark Freedland and Jeremias Prassl, First Edition, 307–322. EU Law in the Member States. Oxford and Portland, Oregon: Hart Publishing, 2016. https://doi.org/10.5040/9781474201605.

Lenaerts, Koen and Jose A. Gutierrez-Fons. 'The Constitutional Allocation of Powers and General Principles of EU Law'. *Common Market Law Review*, Kluwer Law International. Printed in the United Kingdom, 47 (2010): 1629–1669.

Lens, Dries, Ninke Mussche and Ive Marx. 'Europe's Ever Expanding Mobility Patterns – Posting, Third-Country Nationals and the Single European Labour Market'. University of Antwerp – Herman Deleeck Centre for Social Policy, CSB Working Paper No. 19.08 (July 2019).

Lhernould, Jean-Philippe. 'Directive (EU) 2018/957 of 28 June 2018 Amending Directive 96/71/EC Concerning the Posting of Workers in the Framework of the Provision of Services: What Will Change in 2020?'. *ERA Forum – Springer*, 13 August 2019. https://doi.org/10.1007/s12027-019-00573-x.

Lhernould, Jean-Philippe and Barbara Palli. 'Posted Workers Remuneration: Comparative Study in Nine EU Countries and Four Sectors'. *Maastricht Journal of European and Comparative Law* 24, no. 1 (February 2017): 108–126. https://doi.org/10.1177/1023263X17693197.

Lillie, Nathan. 'Subcontracting, Posted Migrants and Labour Market Segmentation in Finland: Migrant Workers in Finland'. *British Journal of Industrial Relations* 50, no. 1 (March 2012): 148–167. https://doi.org/10.1111/j.1467-8543.2011.00859.x.

Lind, Martin Gräs. 'The Danish Law on the Posting of Workers'. FORMULA Working Paper, University of Oslo, Department of Private Law 24 (2010).

Lubow, Alexis, and Susanne K. Schmidt. 'A Hidden Champion? The European Court of Justice as an Agenda-Setter in the Case of Posted Workers'. *Public Administration*

(John Wiley & Sons Ltd.), 5 February 2020, 1–14. https://doi.org/10.1111/padm.12643.

Madrak, Marzena. *The Favourability Principle under the Posting of Workers Directive: Minimum Rates of Pay*. Edited by Francesco Buffa. Il Diritto in Europa Oggi 76. Key Editore, 2019.

Maduro, Miguel Poiares. 'European Constitutionalism and Three Models of Social Europe'. In *The Politics of a European Civil Code*, edited by Martijn W. Hesselink, 125–141. Kluver Law International, 2006.

Maduro, Miguel Poiares and Marlene Wind (eds). *The Transformation of Europe: Twenty-Five Years On*. Cambridge: Cambridge University Press, 2017.

Magnette, Paul. 'How Can One Be European? Reflections on the Pillars of European Civic Identity'. *European Law Journal* 13, no. 5 (September 2007): 664–679. https://doi.org/10.1111/j.1468-0386.2007.00389.x.

Malmberg, Jonas. 'Horizontal Liability for "EU-Unlawful" Collective Actions'. FORMULA Working Paper, University of Oslo, Department of Private Law 29 (11 July 2011).

Malmberg, Jonas and Tore Sigeman. 'Industrial Actions and EU Economic Freedoms: The Autonomous Collective Bargaining Model Curtailed by the European Court of Justice'. *Common Market Law Review* 45, no. 4 (2008): 1115–1146.

Martinsen, Dorte Sindbjerg. 'The European Social Union and EU Legislative Politics'. In *A European Social Union after the Crisis*, edited by Frank Vandenbroucke, Catherine Barnard, and Geert De Baere, 459–476. Cambridge: Cambridge University Press, 2017. https://doi.org/10.1017/9781108235174.019.

Matyska, Anna. 'Ambiguous Mobility: Polish Transnational Workers Navigating and Changing the Institutional Landscape of Posting'. In *Posted Work in the European Union: The Political Economy of Free Movement*, edited by Jens Arnholtz and Nathan Lillie, 70–88. New York: Routledge, 2019.

McDonnell, Alison. 'Equality for Citizens in the EU: Where Did All the Flowers Go?' In *The Principle of Equality in EU Law*, edited by Lucia Serena Rossi and Federico Casolari, 199–228. New York, NY: Springer Berlin Heidelberg, 2017.

Mei, Anne-Pieter van der, Pauline Melin, Zvezda Vankova and Herwig Verschueren. 'The External Dimension of EU Social Security Coordination'. *European Journal of Social Security* 20, no. 2 (June 2018): 81–85. https://doi.org/10.1177/1388262718771734.

Merrett, Louise. 'Posted Workers in Europe from a Private International Law Perspective'. *Cambridge Yearbook of European Legal Studies* 13 (2011): 219–244.

Micklitz, Hans-W. 'A European Advantage in Legal Scholarship?' In *Rethinking Legal Scholarship*, edited by Rob van Gestel, Hans-W. Micklitz, and Edward L. Rubin, 262–309. Cambridge: Cambridge University Press, 2017. https://doi.org/10.1017/9781316442906.008.

Micklitz, Hans-W. 'Judicial Activism of the European Court of Justice and the Development of the European Social Model in Anti-Discrimination and Consumer Law'. In *The Role of Courts in Developing a European Social Model – Theoretical and Methodological Perspectives*, edited by Ulla Neergaard, Ruth Nielsen and Lynn M. Roseberry, 25–61. Copenhagen: Djøf Publishing, 2010.

Mörk, Martin. 'An End to the Possibilities – on Horizontal Liability in Laval and the Limits of Judicial Rights Protection'. In *The Protection of Fundamental Rights in the EU After Lisbon*, edited by Sybe De Vries, Ulf Bernitz, and Steve Weatherill, 119–138. Studies of the Oxford Institute of European and Comparative Law. Oxford and Portland, Oregon: Hart Publishing, 2013.

Mulder, Jotte. '(Re) Conceptualising a Social Market Economy for the EU Internal Market'. *Utrecht Law Review* 15, no. 2 (4 September 2019): 16. https://doi.org/10.18352/ulr.508.

Mussche, Ninke, Vincent Corluy and Ive Marx. 'The Rise of the Free Movements: How Posting Shapes a Hybrid Single European Labour Market'. *European Journal of Industrial Relations*, Discussion Paper Series, 24 May 2017. https://doi.org/10.1177/0959680117708374.

Mussche, Ninke and Dries Lens. 'The EU Free Movement of Services and the Growing Mobility of Third-Country Nationals as Posted Workers'. University of Antwerp – Herman Deleeck Centre for Social Policy, CSB Working Paper No. 18.13 (July 2018).

Mustilli, Federica and Jacques Pelkmans. 'Access Barriers to Services Markets'. *CEPS Centre for European Policy Studies* 77 (June 2013): 84.

Neergaard, Ulla. 'In Search of the Role of "Solidarity" in Primary Law and the Case Law of the European Court of Justice'. In *The Role of Courts in Developing a European Social Model – Theoretical and Methodological Perspectives*, edited by Ulla Neergaard, Ruth Nielsen and Lynn M. Roseberry, 97–138. Copenhagen: Djøf Publishing, 2010.

Neergaard, Ulla and Marlene Wind. 'Studying the EU in Legal and Political Sciences Scholarship'. In *European Legal Method – In a Multi-Level EU Legal Order*, edited by Ulla Neergaard and Ruth Nielsen, 263–292. Copenhagen: Djøf Publishing, 2012.

Nicolaïdis, Kalypso and Juri Viehoff. 'Social Justice in the European Union: The Puzzles of Solidarity, Reciprocity and Choice'. In *Europe's Justice Deficit?*, edited by Dimitry Kochenov, Gráinne de Búrca and Andrew Williams, 277–294. Bloomsbury Collections. Published Online: Hart Publishing, 2015.

Novitz, Tonia. 'A Human Rights Analysis of the Viking and Laval Judgments'. *Cambridge Yearbook of European Legal Studies* 10, no. 20 (2007–2008): 4541–4561.

Novitz, Tonia. 'The EU and the Right to Strike: Regulation through the Back Door and Its Impact on Social Dialogue'. *King's Law Journal* 27, no. 1 (2 January 2016): 46–66. https://doi.org/10.1080/09615768.2016.1148289.

Novitz, Tonia and Rutvica Andrijasevic. 'Reform of the Posting of Workers Regime – An Assessment of the Practical Impact on Unfree Labour Relations'. *JCMS: Journal of Common Market Studies* 58, no. 5 (September 2020): 1325–1341. https://doi.org/10.1111/jcms.13033.

O'Brien, Charlotte. *Unity in Adversity: EU Citizenship, Social Justice and the Cautionary Tale of the UK*. First Edition. Modern Studies in European Law. Hart Publishing Ltd., 2017.

O'Leary, Siofra. 'Free Movement of Persons and Services'. In *The Evolution of EU Law*, edited by Paul Craig and Gráinne de Búrca, Second Edition, 499–546. Oxford: Oxford University Press, 2011.

Overbeeke, Fieke van. 'Posting Drivers in the EU Road Transport Sector'. *ERA Forum*, 30 January 2020. https://doi.org/10.1007/s12027-020-00598-7.

Paju, Jaan. *The European Union and Social Security Law*. First Edition. Modern Studies in European Law. Hart Publishing, 2017.

Pătru, Radu Ştefan. 'Discussions on New EU-Wide Regulations on the Posting of Workers. Special Consideration for Directive (EU) 2018/957 Amending Directive 96/71/EC on the Posting of Workers in the Framework of the Provision of Services'. *Juridical Tribune* 9, no. 1 (1 March 2019): 157–62.

Peers, Steve. 'EU Law Analysis: Case C-201/15 AGET Iraklis: Can Governments Control Mass Layoffs by Employers? Economic Freedoms vs Labour Rights'. *EU Law Analysis* (blog), 3 January 2017. http://eulawanalysis.blogspot.com/2017/01/case-c-20115-aget-iraklis-can.html.

Pennings, Frans. 'How Do Social and Economic Rights Relate to Each Other in the Social Market Economy: An Introduction to This Special Issue'. *Utrecht Law Review* 15, no. 2 (4 September 2019): 1. https://doi.org/10.18352/ulr.507.

Pennings, Frans. 'Principles of EU Coordination of Social Security'. In *Research Handbook on European Social Security Law*, edited by Frans Pennings and Gijsbert Vonk, 321–343. Cheltenham, UK and Northampton, MA, USA: Edward Elgar Publishing, 2015.

Pennings, Frans. 'The Relevance of the Concept of the Social Market Economy: Concluding Observations on the Contributions in This Special Issue'. *Utrecht Law Review* 15, no. 2 (4 September 2019): 95. https://doi.org/10.18352/ulr.513.

Pennings, Frans and Gijsbert Vonk. *Research Handbook on European Social Security Law*. Cheltenham, UK and Northampton, MA, USA: Edward Elgar Publishing, 2015.

Peraro, Cinzia. 'The Enforcement of Posted Workers' Rights Across the European Union'. *Freedom, Security & Justice: European Legal Studies*, 2017.

Pereira, João M.R. and Aurora Galego. 'Diverging Trends of Wage Inequality in Europe'. *Oxford Economic Papers* 71, no. 4 (5 February 2019): 799–823. https://doi.org/10.1093/oep/gpy072.

Rasnača, Zane. 'Identifying the (Dis)Placement of "New" Member State Social Interests in the Posting of Workers: The Case of Latvia'. *European Constitutional Law Review* 14, no. 1 (March 2018): 131–153. https://doi.org/10.1017/S1574019618000056.

Rasnača, Zane and Magdalena Bernaciak (eds). *Posting of Workers before National Courts*. Brussels: ETUI (European Trade Union Institute), 2020.

Rawls, John. *A Theory of Justice*. Revised Edition. Cambridge, Massachusetts: Harvard University Press, 1971.

Reich, Norbert. 'Free Movement v. Social Rights in an Enlarged Union – The Laval and Viking Cases before the ECJ'. *German Law Journal* 9, no. 2 (2008): 125–160.

Rennuy, Nicolas. 'Posting of Workers: Enforcement, Compliance, and Reform'. *European Journal of Social Security* 22, no. 2 (June 2020): 212–234. https://doi.org/10.1177/1388262720931658.

Riesco-Sanz, Alberto, Jorge García López and María del Mar Maira Vidal. 'The Posting of Workers in the European Road Transport Industry: An Approach Based on the Discourses of Social and Institutional Stakeholders'. *European Journal of Industrial Relations*, 29 June 2019, 1–16. https://doi.org/10.1177/0959680119860721.

Rocca, Marco. 'Enemy at the (Flood) Gates: EU "Exceptionalism" in Recent Tensions with the International Protection of Social Rights'. *European Labour Law Journal* 7, no. 1 (March 2016): 52–80. https://doi.org/10.1177/201395251600700104.

Rocca, Marco. *Posting of Workers and Collective Labour Law: There and Back Again*. Social Europe Series 33. Cambridge – Antwerp – Portland: Intersentia, 2015.

Rocca, Marco. 'Stepping Stones Over Troubled Waters. Recent Legal Evolutions and the Reform of the Posting of Workers Directive'. In *Posted Work in the European Union: The Political Economy of Free Movement*, edited by Jens Arnholtz and Nathan Lillie, 167–184. New York: Routledge, 2019.

Rocca, Marco. 'The Proposal for a (So-Called) "Monti II" Regulation on the Exercise of the Right to Take Collective Action within the Context of the Freedom of Establishment and the Freedom to Provide Services: Changing without Reversing, Regulating without Affecting'. *European Labour Law Journal* 3, no. 1 (March 2012): 19–34. https://doi.org/10.1177/201395251200300103.

Rönnmar, Mia. 'Free Movement of Services Versus National Labour Law and Industrial Relations Systems: Understanding the Laval Case from a Swedish and Nordic Perspective'. *Cambridge Yearbook of European Legal Studies* 10 (2007–2008): 493–523.

Rönnmar, Mia. 'Labour and Equality Law'. In *European Union Law*, edited by Catherine Barnard and Steve Peers, Second Edition, 598–627. Oxford: Oxford University Press, 2017.

Rönnmar, Mia. 'Labour Law in the Courts. The Role of European Case Law on Fundamental Trade Union Rights in an Evolving EU Industrial Relations System'. In *The Role of Courts in Developing a European Social Model – Theoretical and Methodological Perspectives*, edited by Ulla Neergaard, Ruth Nielsen and Lynn M. Roseberry, 169–194. Copenhagen: Djøf Publishing, 2010.

Roseberry, Lynn M. 'International Human Rights Treaties and Fundamental Rights in the Case Law of the European Court of Justice: Pointing Towards a European Social Model?' In *The Role of Courts in Developing a European Social Model – Theoretical and Methodological Perspectives*, edited by Ulla Neergaard, Ruth Nielsen and Lynn M. Roseberry, 195–225. Copenhagen: Djøf Publishing, 2010.

Ross, Malcolm. 'Solidarity –A New Constitutional Paradigm for the EU?' In *Promoting Solidarity in the European Union*, edited by Malcolm Ross and Yuri Borgmann-Prebil, 23–45. Oxford University Press, 2010. https://doi.org/10.1093/acprof:oso/9780199583188.003.0002.

Rossi, Lucia Serena. 'The Principle of Equality Among Member States of the European Union'. In *The Principle of Equality in EU Law*, edited by Lucia Serena Rossi and Federico Casolari, 3–42. New York, NY: Springer Berlin Heidelberg, 2017.

Ruggie, John Gerard. 'International Regimes, Transactions, and Change: Embedded Liberalism in the Postwar Economic Order'. *International Organization* 36, no. 2 (1982): 379–415. https://doi.org/10.1017/S0020818300018993.

Sangiovanni, Andrea. 'Debating the EU's Raison d'Être: On the Relation between Legitimacy and Justice'. *JCMS: Journal of Common Market Studies* 57, no. 1 (January 2019): 13–27. https://doi.org/10.1111/jcms.12819.

Sangiovanni, Andrea. 'How Practices Matter: How Practices Matter'. *Journal of Political Philosophy* 24, no. 1 (March 2016): 3–23. https://doi.org/10.1111/jopp.12056.

Sangiovanni, Andrea. 'Solidarity as Joint Action: Solidarity as Joint Action'. *Journal of Applied Philosophy* 32, no. 4 (November 2015): 340–359. https://doi.org/10.1111/japp.12130.

Sangiovanni, Andrea. 'Solidarity in the European Union'. *Oxford Journal of Legal Studies* 33, no. 2 (1 June 2013): 213–241. https://doi.org/10.1093/ojls/gqs033.

Sangiovanni, Andrea. 'The Irrelevance of Coercion, Imposition, and Framing to Distributive Justice: The Irrelevance of Coercion, Imposition, and Framing to Distributive Justice'. *Philosophy & Public Affairs* 40, no. 2 (March 2012): 79–110. https://doi.org/10.1111/j.1088-4963.2012.01213.x.

Scharpf, Fritz W. 'The Asymmetry of European Integration, or Why the EU Cannot Be a "Social Market Economy"'. *Socio-Economic Review* 8, no. 2 (1 April 2010): 211–250. https://doi.org/10.1093/ser/mwp031.

Scharpf, Fritz W. 'The European Social Model: Coping with the Challenges of Diversity'. *JCMS: Journal of Common Market Studies* 40, no. 4 (November 2002): 645–70. https://doi.org/10.1111/1468-5965.00392.

Schiek, Dagmar. 'A Constitution of Social Governance for the European Union'. In *The Human Face of the European Union*, edited by Nuno Ferreira and Dora Kostakopoulou, 17–47. Cambridge: Cambridge University Press, 2016. https://doi.org/10.1017/CBO9781139924795.003.

Schiek, Dagmar. 'A New Framework on Equal Treatment of Persons in EC Law?' *European Law Journal* 8, no. 2 (June 2002): 290–314. https://doi.org/10.1111/1468-0386.00154.

Schiek, Dagmar. 'Comparing Labour Laws in the EU Internal Market: A Social Actor Perspective'. *International Journal of Comparative Labour Law and Industrial Relations*, Kluwer Law International BV, 33, no. 1 (2017): 171–194.

Schiek, Dagmar. *Economic and Social Integration: The Challenge for EU Constitutional Law*. Cheltenham, UK and Northampton, MA, USA: Edward Elgar, 2012.

Schiek, Dagmar. 'Is There a Social Ideal of the European Court of Justice?' In *The Role of Courts in Developing a European Social Model – Theoretical and Methodological Perspectives*, edited by Ulla Neergaard, Ruth Nielsen and Lynn M. Roseberry, 63–96. Copenhagen: Djøf Publishing, 2010.

Schiek, Dagmar. 'Perspectives on Social Citizenship in the EU – From Status Positivus to Status Socialis Activus via Two Forms of Transnational Solidarity'. *Queen's University Belfast School of Law: Research Paper 2015 – 10*, 4, no. 1 (2015). https://doi.org/10.1017/9781139680714.015.

Schiek, Dagmar. 'Towards More Resilience for a Social EU – The Constitutionally Conditioned Internal Market'. *European Constitutional Law Review* 13, no. 04 (December 2017): 611–40.

Schlachter, Monika. 'Equal Treatment for Transnational Temporary Agency Workers?' In *Regulating Transnational Labour in Europe: The Quandaries of Multilevel Governance*, edited by Stein Evju, 263–278. Institutt for Privatrett Skriftserie 196. Oslo: Universitetet i Oslo, Det Juridiske Facultet, 2014.

Schlachter, Monika. 'Transnational Temporary Agency Work: How Much Equality Does the Equal Treatment Principle Provide?' FORMULA Working Paper, University of Oslo, Department of Private Law 25 (September 2011).

Schoukens, Paul. *EU Social Security Law: The Hidden Social Model.* Tilburg (The Netherlands): TILT, Tilburg University, 2016. https://eiss.be/onewebmedia/oration_Schoukens.pdf%20(final).pdf.

Schoukens, Paul and Danny Pieters. 'The Rules within Regulation 883/2004 for Determining the Applicable Legislation'. *European Journal of Social Security* 11, nos 1–2 (March 2009): 81–117. https://doi.org/10.1177/138826270901100104.

Schrauwen, Annette. 'From the Board Towards a Social Europe'. *Legal Issues of Economic Integration*, 8 Kluwer Law International BV, The Netherlands, 45, no. 4 (2018): 323–328.

Schutter, Helder De. 'The Solidarity Argument for the European Union'. In *A European Social Union after the Crisis*, edited by Frank Vandenbroucke, Catherine Barnard and Geert De Baere, 68–91. Cambridge: Cambridge University Press, 2017. https://doi.org/10.1017/9781108235174.004.

Schütze, Robert. *European Constitutional Law*. Second Edition. Cambridge: Cambridge University Press, 2015.

Schütze, Robert. *European Union Law*. Second Edition. Cambridge: Cambridge University Press, 2018.

Schyff, Gerhard van der. 'EU Social Competences and Member State Constitutional Controls: A Comparative Perspective of National Approaches'. In *A European Social Union after the Crisis*, edited by Frank Vandenbroucke, Catherine Barnard and Geert De Baere, 385–406. Cambridge: Cambridge University Press, 2017. https://doi.org/10.1017/9781108235174.016.

Sciarra, Silvana. *Solidarity and Conflict: European Social Law in Crisis*. United Kingdom: Cambridge University Press, 2018.

Sciarra, Silvana. 'Viking and Laval: Collective Labour Rights and Market Freedoms in the Enlarged EU'. *Cambridge Yearbook of European Legal Studies* 10 (2007–2008): 563–580.

Skouris, Vassilios. 'Fundamental Rights and Fundamental Freedoms: The Challenge of Striking a Delicate Balance'. *European Business Law Review*, Kluwer Law International, 17 (2006): 225–239.

Smits, Jan M. 'Law and Interdisciplinarity: On the Inevitable Normativity of Legal Studies'. *Critical Analysis of Law* 1 no. 1 (2014): 75–86, Maastricht European Private Law Institute Working Paper 2014/10, 17 March 2014, 12.

Smits, Jan M. 'What Is Legal Doctrine?: On the Aims and Methods of Legal-Dogmatic Research'. In *Rethinking Legal Scholarship*, edited by Rob van Gestel, Hans-W.

Micklitz and Edward L. Rubin, 207–28. Cambridge: Cambridge University Press, 2017. https://doi.org/10.1017/9781316442906.006.

Somek, Alexander. 'From Workers to Migrants, from Distributive Justice to Inclusion: Exploring the Changing Social Democratic Imagination: Exploring the Changing Social Democratic Imagination'. *European Law Journal* 18, no. 5 (September 2012): 711–726. https://doi.org/10.1111/j.1468-0386.2012.00625.x.

Somek, Alexander. 'Solidarity Decomposed Being and Time in European Citizenship'. *European Law Review* 32, no. 6 (2007): 787–818.

Somek, Alexander. 'The Social Question in a Transnational Context'. *LEQS Paper No. 39/2011*, LSE 'Europe in Question' Discussion Paper Series, June 2011.

Sørensen, Karsten Engsig. 'The Fight Against Letterbox Companies in the Internal Market'. *Common Market Law Review*, Kluwer Law International, 52 (2015): 85–118.

Stjernø, Steinar. *Solidarity in Europe: The History of an Idea*. New York (USA): Cambridge University Press, 2005. https://doi.org/10.1017/CBO9780511490378.

Supiot, Alain. 'The Transformation of Work and the Future of Labour Law in Europe: A Multidisciplinary Perspective'. *International Labour Review* 138, no. 1 (March 1999): 31–46. https://doi.org/10.1111/j.1564-913X.1999.tb00003.x.

Supiot, Alain. 'Towards a European Policy on Work'. In *Resocialising Europe in a Time of Crisis*, edited by Nicola Countouris and Mark Freedland, 19–35. Cambridge: Cambridge University Press, 2013. https://doi.org/10.1017/CBO9781107300736.004.

Szyszczak, Erika. 'Europe Isn't Working in Europe: Reform and Modernisation of the European Welfare State in the Wake of the Economic Crisis'. *Fordham International Law Journal 38* (2015): 1193–1217.

Thörnqvist, Christer and Sebastian Bernhardsson. 'Their Own Stories – How Polish Construction Workers Posted to Sweden Experience Their Job Situation, or Resistance Versus Life Projects'. *Transfer: European Review of Labour and Research* 21, no. 1 (1 February 2015): 23–36. https://doi.org/10.1177/1024258914561409.

Trappmann, Vera. 'Social Dumping with No Divide: Evidence from Multinational Companies in Europe'. In *Market Expansion and Social Dumping in Europe*, edited by Magdalena Bernaciak, 140–156. Routledge Advances in European Politics. New York, NY: Routledge, 2015.

Tridimas, Takis. *The General Principles of EU Law*. Second Edition. Oxford: Oxford University Press, 2007.

Van Nuffel, Piet and Sofia Afanasjeva. 'The Posting of Workers Directive Revised: Enhancing the Protection of Workers in the Cross-Border Provision of Services'. *European Papers* 3, no. 3 (2018): 1401–27. https://doi.org/10.15166/2499-8249/276.

Vandenbroucke, Frank. 'Social Benefits and Cross-Border Mobility: Sticking to Principles May Yield Better Practical Results for Everybody'. *Tribune, Notre Europe Jacques Delors Institute* 17 (17 June 2016).

Vandenbroucke, Frank. 'The Case for a European Social Union: From Muddling Through to a Sense of Common Purpose'. Euroforum Policy Paper (KU Leuven), no. 16 (September 2014).

Vandenbroucke, Frank. 'The European Pillar of Social Rights: From Promise to Delivery'. In *Towards a European Social Union: The European Pillar of Social Rights and the Roadmap for a Fully-Fledged Social Union*, edited by Maurizio Ferrera, 2–11. A Forum Debate. Torino (Italy): Centro di Ricerca e Documentazione Luigi Einaudi, 2019.

Vandenbroucke, Frank. 'The Idea of a European Social Union: A Normative Introduction'. In *A European Social Union after the Crisis*, edited by Frank Vandenbroucke, Catherine Barnard and Geert De Baere, 3–46. Cambridge: Cambridge University Press, 2017. https://doi.org/10.1017/9781108235174.002.

Vanhercke, Bart, Sebastiano Sabato and Dalila Ghailani. 'The European Pillar of Social Rights as a Game Changer'. In *Social Policy in the European Union: State of Play 2018*, edited by Sebastiano Sabato, ETUI, 153–172. Brussels, 2018.

Verschueren, Herwig. 'Cross-Border Workers in the European Internal Market: Trojan Horses for Member States' Labour and Social Security Law?' *International Journal of Comparative Labour Law and Industrial Relations*, Kluwer Law International, 24/2 (2008): 167–199.

Verschueren, Herwig. 'The European Internal Market and the Competition between Workers'. *European Labour Law Journal* 6, no. 2 (June 2015): 128–151. https://doi.org/10.1177/201395251500600203.

Waddington, Lisa. 'The Expanding Role of the Equality Principle in European Union Law'. *European University Institute, Robert Schuman Centre for Advanced Studies* Policy Paper Series on Constitutional Reform in the EU 2003/04 (2003).

Wagner, Bettina and Anke Hassel. 'Posting, Subcontracting and Low-Wage Employment in the German Meat Industry'. *Transfer: European Review of Labour and Research* 22, no. 2 (May 2016): 163–178. https://doi.org/10.1177/1024258916636012.

Wagner, Ines and Karen Shire. 'Labour Subcontracting in Cross-Border Labour Markets: A Comparison of Rule Evasion in Germany and Japan'. In *Posted Work in the European Union: The Political Economy of Free Movement*, edited by Jens Arnholtz and Nathan Lillie, 185–204. New York: Routledge, 2019.

Walter, Torsten. 'The Practical Consequences of the Rüffert Decision'. In *Viking – Laval – Rüffert: Consequences and Policy Perspectives*, edited by Andreas Bücker and Wiebke Warneck, 43–52. Report 111. Bruxelles: ETUI (European Trade Union Institute), 2010.

Warneck, Wiebke. 'The ECJ Decisions'. In *Viking – Laval – Rüffert: Consequences and Policy Perspectives*, edited by Andreas Bücker and Wiebke Warneck, 7–12. Report 111. Bruxelles: ETUI (European Trade Union Institute), 2010.

Watson, Philippa. *EU Social and Employment Law*. Second Edition. Oxford: Oxford University Press, 2014.

Weatherill, Stephen. *Law and Values in the European Union*. Clarendon Law Series. Oxford: Oxford University Press, 2016. https://doi.org/10.1093/acprof:oso/9780199557264.001.0001.

Weatherill, Steve. 'From Economic Rights to Fundamental Rights'. In *The Protection of Fundamental Rights in the EU After Lisbon*, edited by Sybe De Vries, Ulf Bernitz and Steve Weatherill, 11–36. Studies of the Oxford Institute of European and Comparative Law. Oxford and Portland, Oregon: Hart Publishing, 2013.

Weatherill, Steve. 'Viking and Laval: The EU Internal Market Perspective'. In *Viking, Laval and Beyond*, edited by R. Mark Freedland and Jeremias Prassl, First Edition, 23–39. EU Law in the Member States. Oxford and Portland, Oregon: Hart Publishing, 2016.

Weiler, Joseph H.H. 'A Constitution for Europe? Some Hard Choices'. *JCMS: Journal of Common Market Studies* 40, no. 4 (November 2002): 563–580. https://doi.org/10.1111/1468-5965.00388.

Weiler, Joseph H.H. 'The Political and Legal Culture of European Integration: An Exploratory Essay'. *International Journal of Constitutional Law* 9, nos 3–4 (1 October 2011): 678–694. https://doi.org/10.1093/icon/mor054.

Weiler, Joseph H.H. 'The Transformation of Europe'. *The Yale Law Journal*, Symposium: International Law, 100, no. 8 (June 1991): 2403–2483.

Wispelaere, Frederic De and Jozef Pacolet. 'The Benefits of Posting: Facts and Figures on the Use and Impact of Intra-EU Posting'. In *Posted Work in the European Union: The Political Economy of Free Movement*, edited by Jens Arnholtz and Nathan Lillie, 31–49. New York: Routledge, 2019.

Wispelaere, Frederic De and Marco Rocca. 'The Dark Side of the Tour. Labour and Social Security Challenges of Highly Mobile Workers in the Live Performance Sector'. *ERA Forum*, 6 February 2020. https://doi.org/10.1007/s12027-020-00600-2.

Witte, Floris de. 'EU Law, Politics, and the Social Question'. *German Law Journal* 14 (2013): 581–611.

Witte, Floris de. *Justice in the EU: The Emergence of Transnational Solidarity*. Oxford Studies in European Law. Oxford: Oxford University Press, 2015.

Witte, Floris de. 'The End of EU Citizenship and the Means of Non-Discrimination'. *Maastricht Journal of European and Comparative Law* 18, nos 1–2 (March 2011): 86–108. https://doi.org/10.1177/1023263X1101800105.

Woolfson, Charles and Jeff Sommers. 'Labour Mobility in Construction: European Implications of the Laval Un Partneri Dispute with Swedish Labour'. *European Journal of Industrial Relations* 12, no. 1 (March 2006): 49–68. https://doi.org/10.1177/0959680106061371.

Wołoszyn, Agnieszka. 'The Importance of Posting of Workers for the Member States: Myth and Reality'. In *A 'Social Turn' in the European Union?: New Trends and Ideas about Social Convergence in Europe*, edited by Jacek Kubera and Tomasz Morozowski, First Edition, 179–184. London: Routledge, 2020. https://doi.org/10.4324/9780367409586.

Wouters, Jan and Pierre Schmitt. 'Equality Among Member States and Differentiated Integration in the EU'. In *The Principle of Equality in EU Law*, edited by Lucia Serena Rossi and Federico Casolari, 43–82. New York, NY: Springer Berlin Heidelberg, 2017.

Zahn, Rebecca. 'Revision of the Posted Workers' Directive: A Europeanisation Perspective'. *Cambridge Yearbook of European Legal Studies* 19 (December 2017): 187–210. https://doi.org/10.1017/cel.2017.5.

Zahn, Rebecca. 'Revision of the Posted Workers' Directive: Equality at Last?' *European (Legal) Studies on-line Papers, Queen's University Belfast – School of Law – Centre of European and Transnational Legal Studies*, CETLS, 5, no. Issue I (2016).

Zimmer, Reingard. 'The Revision of the Posting of Workers Directive and Its Impact on National Law'. In *A 'Social Turn' in the European Union?: New Trends and Ideas about Social Convergence in Europe*, edited by Jacek Kubera and Tomasz Morozowski, First Edition, 92–113. London: Routledge, 2020. https://doi.org/10.4324/9780367409586.

Reports and Other Documents

Aumayr-Pintar, Christine. 'To Have or Have Not: A Statutory Minimum Wage'. Eurofound, 22 July 2019. https://www.eurofound.europa.eu/publications/article/2019/to-have-or-have-not-a-statutory-minimum-wage.

Aumayr-Pintar, Christine, Jorge Cabrita, Enrique Fernández-Macías and Carlos Vacas-Soriano. 'Pay in Europe in the 21st Century'. Eurofound – Publications Office of the European Union, 13 April 2014. https://www.eurofound.europa.eu/sites/default/files/ef_publication/field_ef_document/ef1388en_3.pdf.

Aumayr-Pintar, Christine, Matthias Rasche and Carlos Vacas. 'Minimum Wages in 2019: Annual Review'. Luxembourg: Eurofound – Publications Office of the European Union, 2019.

Aussilloux, Vincent, Agnès Bénassy-Quéré, Clemens Fuest and Guntram Wolff. 'Making the Best of the European Single Market'. *Bruegel – Policy Contribution*, no. 3 (2017). https://bruegel.org/2017/02/making-the-best-of-the-european-single-market/.

Benio, Marek. 'Labour Costs in Cross-Border Services: The Study on the Labour Cost Structure in the Case of Posting of Workers from Poland'. Krakow (PL): Department of Public Economy and Administration, University of Economics, November 2016.

Biletta, Isabella and Christine Aumayr-Pintar. 'Pay Inequalities Experienced by Posted Workers: Challenges to the "Equal Treatment" Principle'. Dublin: Eurofound, 2017.

Bogoeski, Vladimir. 'Chain Liability as a Mechanism for Strengthening the Rights of Posted Workers'. *Project: 'Protecting Mobility through Improving Labour Rights Enforcement in Europe (PROMO)', VS/2016/0222*, 2017.

Cornelissen, Rob. 'The Protection of Social Security Rights in a Cross-Border Situation. A Historical Overview'. KU Leuven Research Institute for Work and Society (HIVA) and European Centre for Workers' Questions EZA presented at the 60 Years Social Security Coordination from a Workers' Perspective, Leuven, Belgium, 16 May 2019.

Cremers, Jan. 'In Search of Cheap Labour in Europe – Working and Living Conditions of Posted Workers'. *CLR News*, No 1/2011, 2011, 6–10.

Cremers, Jan. 'Posting of Workers in Practice'. *Tilburg Law School* INT-AR Paper 8 (2018).

Cremers, Jan. 'Undeclared Work in the Construction Industry'. Construction Seminar, Brussels, 2017.

De Vos, Marc. 'Beyond Formal Equality: Positive Action under Directives 2000/43/EC and 2000/78/EC'. Luxembourg: European Commission, Directorate-General Employment, Social Affairs and Equal Opportunities, Unit G.2, June 2007.

Dhéret, Claire and Andreia Ghimis. 'The Revision of the Posted Workers Directive: Towards a Sufficient Policy Adjustment?' *European Policy Center (EPC) Discussion Paper*, 20 April 2016. http://www.epc.eu/pub_details.php?cat_id=17&pub_id=6475.

Fries-Tersch, Elena, Matthew Jones, Birte Böök, Linda de Keyser and Tugce Tugran. '2019 Annual Report on Intra-EU Labour Mobility: Final Report January 2020'. European Commission, Directorate-General for Employment, Social Affairs and Inclusion Directorate D – Labour Mobility Unit D1 – Free Movement of Workers, EURES, January 2020.

Gerner-Beuerle, Carsten, Federico M Mucciarelli, Edmund-Philipp Schuster and Mathias M Siems. 'Study on the Law Applicable to Companies – Final Report'. European Commission, Directorate-General for Justice and Consumers Directorate A – Civil Justice Unit A1 – Civil Justice Policy, June 2016.

Hoek, Aukje A.H. van and Mijke Houwerzijl. 'Comparative Study on the Legal Aspects of the Posting of Workers in the Framework of the Provision of Services in the European Union'. European Commission, 21 March 2011.

Hoek, Aukje A.H. van and Mijke Houwerzijl. 'Complementary Study on the Legal Aspects of the Posting of Workers in the Framework of the Provision of Services in the European Union'. European Commission, November 2011.

IDEA Consult and ECORYS Netherlands. 'Study on the Economic and Social Effects Associated with the Phenomenon of Posting of Workers in the EU'. European Commission, Directorate-General Employment, Social Affairs and Equal Opportunities, March 2011.

ILO DWT and Country Office for Central and Eastern Europe. 'Coordination of Social Security Systems in the European Union: An Explanatory Report on EC Regulation No. 883/2004 and Its Implementing Regulation No. 987/2009'. Budapest: ILO, 2010. http://www.ilo.org/public/libdoc/ilo/2010/461829_engl.pdf.

ISMERI Europa. 'Preparatory Study for an Impact Assessment on the Posting of Workers – Final Report'. European Commission, 2012.

Jevšnik, Mojca Vah and Sanja Cukut Krilić. 'Posting of Workers: Sharing Experiences, Promoting Best Practices and Improving Access to Information'. ZRC SAZU, Slovenian Migration Institute: European Commission, Republic of Slovenia, November 2016.

Jorens, Yves, Dirk Gillis and Joyce De Coninck. 'Fraud and Error in the Field of Social Security Coordination: Reference Year: 2014'. European Commission, Directorate-General for Employment, Social Affairs and Inclusion, Unit D2 – Social Security Coordination, 2015.

Jorens, Yves, Dirk Gillis and Tiffany De Potter. 'Fraud and Error in the Field of EU Social Security Coordination: Reference Year: 2015'. European Commission, Directorate-General for Employment, Social Affairs and Inclusion, Unit D2 – Social Security Coordination, January 2017.

Jorens, Yves, Dirk Gillis, Tiffany De Potter, Frederic De Wispelaere and Jozef Pacolet. 'Fraud and Error in the Field of EU Social Security Coordination: Reference Year: 2016'. European Commission, Directorate-General for Employment, Social Affairs and Inclusion, Unit D2 – Social Security Coordination, 2018.

Jorens, Yves, Saskia Peters and Mijke Houwerzijl. 'Study on the Protection of Workers' Rights in Subcontracting Processes in the European Union (Final Study)'. Ghent, Belgium: Ghent University, Department of Social Law (in consortium with University of Amsterdam), 25 June 2012.

Kall, Kairit and Nathan Lillie. 'Protection of Posted Workers in the European Union: Findings and Policy Recommendations Based on Existing Research' PROMO Briefing Paper (26 September 2017): 43.

Kilpatrick, Claire and Bruno De Witte. 'A Tangible Human Face for Social Europe'. RSCAS Policy Paper (Robert Schuman Centre for Advanced Studies) Special Edition for the EP Elections 2019 (2019): 02.

Kureková, Lucia Mýtna. 'The Automotive Industry in Central Europe: A Success?' *Slovak Governance Institute and CELSI, Slovakia, and IZA – Institute of Labor Economics, Germany*, 2018. https://doi.org/10.15185/izawol.448.

Lalucq, Aurore. 'Minimum Corporate Tax Rate in the European Union'. European Parliament – Parliamentary questions: Question for written answer E-002569-19 to the Commission Rule 138, 29 August 2019. http://www.europarl.europa.eu/doceo/document/E-9-2019-002569_EN.html.

Warneck, Wiebke. *Strike Rules in the EU27 and Beyond: A Comparative Overview*. Report / ETUI-REHS 103. Brussels: ETUI-REHS, 2007.

Malmberg, Jonas. 'The Impact of the ECJ Judgements on Viking, Laval, Rüffert and Luxembourg on the Practice of Collective Bargaining and the Effectiveness of Social Action'. Brussels: European Parliament: Directorate-General for Internal Policies, Policy Department A: Economic and Scientific Policy Employment and Social Affairs. Brussels: European Parliament, May 2010.

Mascherini, Massimiliano, IRS (Istituto per la Ricerca Sociale), and University of Bergamo. 'Progress on Convergence in the Socioeconomic Area – Monitoring EU Convergence'. Luxembourg: Eurofound – Publications Office of the European Union, 17 December 2018.

Mascherini, Massimiliano and Chiara Litardi. 'A More Equal Europe? Convergence and the European Pillar of Social Rights'. Luxembourg: Eurofound – Publications Office of the European Union, 10 December 2019.

Maslauskaite, Kristina. 'Posted Workers in the EU: State of Play and Regulatory Evolution'. Policy Paper, Notre Europe Jaques Delors Institute, Policy Paper 107, 24 March 2014, 20.

Maslauskaite, Kristina. 'Social Competition in the EU: Myths and Realities'. Policy Paper, Notre Europe Jaques Delors Institute, Project: 'The Single Market 20 Years On', June 2013, 62.

Monti, Mario. 'A New Strategy for the Single Market: At the Service of Europe's Economy and Society. Report to the President of the European Commission José Manuel Barroso'. European Commission. Bureau of European Policy Advisers (BEPA), 9 May 2010.

Pedersini, Roberto and Massimo Pallini. 'Posted Workers in the European Union'. Eurofound, 2010.

Schiek, Dagmar, Liz Oliver, Christopher Forde, Gabriella Alberti, Michael Doherty, Joanna Unterschütz, Consuelo Chacartegui Jávega, Julia Lopez Lopez and Kerstin Ahlberg. 'EU Social and Labour Rights and EU Internal Market Law'. European Parliament, EMPL Committee, September 2015.

Szczepański, Marcin. 'EU Competition Policy: Key to a Fair Single Market: In-Depth Analysis'. Brussels: European Parliament, October 2019. https://data.europa.eu/doi/10.2861/143082.

Veloso, Luisa, Catarina Sales Oliveira and Joana Soares Marques. 'EU Post Lab: Developing Experiences of Administrative Cooperation and Enhanced Access to Information in the Framework of the Posting of Workers – Assessment Report'. EU Post Lab, 2018. https://repositorio.iscte-iul.pt/bitstream/10071/16878/1/assessment_report_eu_post_lab_0.pdf.

Vlies, Robert van der. 'Posting of Workers within the Construction Sector: A Comparative Study within Belgium and The Netherlands on the Protection of Posted Workers'. Master's thesis. Tilburg University, 2018.

Voss, Eckhard, Michele Faioli, Jean-Philippe Lhernould and Feliciano Iudicone. 'Posting of Workers Directive: Current Situation and Challenges'. European Parliament, EMPL Committee, 2016.

Wagner, Ines. 'Changing Regulations, Changing Practices?: The Case of the German Meat Industry'. *Project: 'Protecting Mobility through Improving Labour Rights Enforcement in Europe (PROMO)', VS/2016/0222*, 2017.

Wispelaere, Frederic De and Jozef Pacolet. 'An Ad Hoc Statistical Analysis on Short Term Mobility – Economic Value of Posting of Workers: The Impact of Intra-EU Cross-Border Services, with Special Attention to the Construction Sector'. Research commissioned by DG EMPL within the framework of Contract VT/2015/096. Leuven, Belgium: KU Leuven Research Institute for Work and Society (HIVA), 2016.

Wispelaere, Frederic De and Jozef Pacolet. 'Coordination of Social Security Systems at a Glance: 2016 Statistical Report'. Leuven, Belgium: KU Leuven Research Institute for Work and Society (HIVA), 2016.

Wispelaere, Frederic De and Jozef Pacolet. 'Coordination of Social Security Systems at a Glance: 2017 Statistical Report'. Leuven, Belgium: KU Leuven Research Institute for Work and Society (HIVA), December 2017.

Wispelaere, Frederic De and Jozef Pacolet. 'Posting of Workers as Stabilising Mechanism: An Enlarged Notion of Labour Mobility as a Prerequisite for an Optimal Currency Area'. Leuven, Belgium: KU Leuven Research Institute for Work and Society (HIVA), November 2015.

Wispelaere, Frederic De and Jozef Pacolet. 'Posting of Workers: Report on A1 Portable Documents Issued in 2012 and 2013'. Leuven, Belgium: KU Leuven Research Institute for Work and Society (HIVA), December 2014.

Wispelaere, Frederic De and Jozef Pacolet. 'Posting of Workers: Report on A1 Portable Documents Issued in 2014'. Leuven, Belgium: KU Leuven Research Institute for Work and Society (HIVA), December 2015.

Wispelaere, Frederic De and Jozef Pacolet. 'Posting of Workers: Report on A1 Portable Documents Issued in 2015'. Leuven, Belgium: KU Leuven Research Institute for Work and Society (HIVA), December 2016.

Wispelaere, Frederic De and Jozef Pacolet. 'Posting of Workers: Report on A1 Portable Documents Issued in 2016'. Leuven, Belgium: KU Leuven Research Institute for Work and Society (HIVA), December 2017.

Wispelaere, Frederic De and Jozef Pacolet. 'Posting of Workers: Report on A1 Portable Documents Issued in 2017'. Leuven, Belgium: KU Leuven Research Institute for Work and Society (HIVA), October 2018.

Wispelaere, Frederic De and Jozef Pacolet. 'Posting of Workers: The Impact of Social Security Coordination and Income Taxation Law on Welfare States'. Working Paper. Leuven, Belgium: KU Leuven Research Institute for Work and Society (HIVA), November 2015.

Wispelaere, Frederic De and Jozef Pacolet. 'The Size and Impact of Intra-EU Posting on the Belgian Economy: With a Special Focus on the Construction Sector – Summary'. Leuven, Belgium: KU Leuven Research Institute for Work and Society (HIVA), 2017.

Wispelaere, Frederic De, Saena Chakkar and Ludo Struyven. 'Incoming and Outgoing Posted Workers in the Belgian Labour Market Statistics: With a Focus on the Brussels-Capital Region, Summary'. Leuven, Belgium: KU Leuven Research Institute for Work and Society (HIVA), 2020.

Wispelaere, Frederic De, Lynn De Smedt and Jozef Pacolet. 'Coordination of Social Security Systems at a Glance: 2018 Statistical Report'. Leuven, Belgium: KU Leuven Research Institute for Work and Society (HIVA), December 2018.

Wispelaere, Frederic De, Lynn De Smedt and Jozef Pacolet. 'Coordination of Social Security Systems at a Glance: 2019 Statistical Report'. Leuven, Belgium: KU Leuven Research Institute for Work and Society (HIVA), December 2019.

Wispelaere, Frederic De, Lynn De Smedt and Jozef Pacolet. 'Posting of Workers: Report on A1 Portable Documents Issued in 2018'. Leuven, Belgium: KU Leuven Research Institute for Work and Society (HIVA), October 2019.

Other Sources

Agence Europe. 'Europe Daily Bulletin No. 12223 – Council of the EU Postpones Its Vote on Provisional Agreement ...', 28 March 2019. https://agenceurope.eu/en/bulletin/article/12223/22.

Agence Europe. 'Europe Daily Bulletin No. 12225 – No Qualified Majority among Member States to Support Provisional ...', 30 March 2019. https://agenceurope.eu/en/bulletin/article/12225/15.

Ahlberg, Kerstin. 'Lex Laval Revised in Sweden – To What Effect?' *Nordic Labour Journal* (blog), 1 March 2017. http://www.nordiclabourjournal.org/nyheter/news-2017/article.2017-03-01.0991266340.

Austrian, Belgian, French, German, Luxembourg, Dutch and Swedish Ministers of Labour. 'Letter to Ms Marianne Thyssen Commissioner for Employment, Social Affairs, Skills and Labour Mobility', 18 June 2015.

Barbière, Cécile. 'Posted Workers: Macron's First Victory in Reforming the EU'. *EURACTIV* (blog), 24 October 2017. https://www.euractiv.com/section/economy-jobs/news/posted-workers-macrons-first-victory-in-reforming-the-eu/.

Barnard, Catherine. 'The Commission's Proposal Deletes the Treaty Distinction between Migrant Workers and Posted Workers'. Presented at the IV European Labour Mobility Congress (ELMC), Krakow (Poland), 7 November 2016. https://www.elmc.eu/2016/the-commissions-proposal-deletes-the-treaty-distinction-between-migrant-workers-and-posted-workers-prof-catherine-barnards-speech-at-the-iv-european-labour-mobility-cong/.

Benio, Marek. 'Is Twelve Short Enough?' *Labour Mobility Initiative* (blog), 12 December 2017. https://www.mobilelabour.eu/12466/is-twelve-short-enough/.

Benio, Marek. 'New Rules of the Posting of Workers in 2020. The Countdown.' *Labour Mobility Initiative* (blog), 30 July 2018. https://www.mobilelabour.eu/12521/new-rules-of-the-posting-of-workers-in-2020-the-final-countdown/.

Benio, Marek. 'Speech at the II European Labour Mobility Congress'. Presented at the II European Labour Mobility Congress (ELMC), Krakow (Poland), 23 April 2015. https://www.elmc.eu/2015/text-of-the-speech-by-marek-benio-phd-vice-president-of-the-labour-mobility-initiative-association/.

Bogoeski, Vladimir. 'Posting of Workers – Strengthening Labour Rights While Securing Free Movement of Services?'. *Migrationonline.Cz* (blog), 9 June 2016. https://migrationonline.cz/en/e-library/posting-of-workers-strengthening-labour-rights-while-securing-free-movement-services.

Brodtmann, Thilo. 'Member States Must Stop Building Barriers for Posted Workers'. *EURACTIV* (blog), 9 October 2018. https://www.euractiv.com/section/economy-jobs/opinion/member-states-must-stop-building-barriers-for-posted-workers/.

Bulgarian, Czech, Estonian, Hungarian, Latvian, Lithuanian, Polish, Romanian and Slovakian Ministers of Labour. 'Letter to Ms Marianne Thyssen Commissioner for Employment, Social Affairs, Skills and Labour Mobility', 31 August 2015.

BusinessEurope. 'Posting of Workers: A Bad Deal That Will Harm the Functioning of the Single Market for Services', 3 January 2018. https://www.businesseurope.eu/publications/posting-workers-bad-deal-will-harm-functioning-single-market-services.

Carr, Liina. 'Justice at Last: Equal Pay for Posted Workers'. *ETUC (European Trade Union Confederation) Press Release* (blog), 29 May 2018. https://www.etuc.org/en/pressrelease/justice-last-equal-pay-posted-workers.

Carter, Daniel. 'CJEU (Finally) Takes Stance against Social Dumping'. *Leidenlawblog* (blog), 19 February 2016. https://leidenlawblog.nl/articles/cjeu-finally-takes-stance-against-social-dumping.

CEEMET (Council of European Employers of the Metal, Engineering and Technology-Based Industries). 'Revision of Directive 96/71/EC Concerning the Posting of Workers in the Framework of the Provision of Services: Legal & Practical Implications'. Brussels: CEEMET, 24 May 2016. http://www.ceemet.org/sites/default/files/ceemet_position_-_revision_posting_of_workers_-_may_2016_1.pdf.

CLECAT (European Association for Forwarding, Transport, Logistics and Customs Services). 'Reaction to the Provisional Agreement on Mobility Package I'. CLECAT News, 13 December 2019. https://www.clecat.org/news/news/provisional-agreement-on-mobility-package-i.

Cooper, Ian. 'The Story of the First "Yellow Card" Shows That National Parliaments Can Act Together to Influence EU Policy'. *EUROPP (European Politics and Policy)* (blog), 23 April 2015. https://blogs.lse.ac.uk/europpblog/2015/04/23/the-story-of-the-first-yellow-card-shows-that-national-parliaments-can-act-together-to-influence-eu-policy/.

Darvas, Zsolt. 'Could Revising the Posted Workers Directive Improve Social Conditions?'. Presented at the Conference of think tanks on the revision of the posted workers directive, European Parliament, Brussels, 31 January 2017.

Darvas, Zsolt. 'Revision of the Posted Workers Directive Misses the Point'. *Bruegel* (blog), 18 October 2017. https://bruegel.org/2017/10/revision-of-the-posted-workers-directive-misses-the-point/.

Deloitte Belgium. 'How Will the Revision of the Posted Workers Directive Impact Your Assignments?', June 2018. https://www2.deloitte.com/content/dam/Deloitte/be/Documents/tax/PostedWorkersDirective.pdf.

Deloitte LLP. 'Posted Workers Directive: Time for Action'. The Creative Studio at Deloitte, London, 2017.

Dion, David-Pascal. 'State of Play: Reform of the Social Security Coordination Rules, Portability of Social Rights after Brexit, Establishment of a European Labour Authority (ELA)'. KU Leuven Research Institute for Work and Society (HIVA) and European Centre for Workers' Questions EZA presented at the 60 Years Social Security Coordination from a Workers' Perspective, Leuven, Belgium, 16 May 2019.

Dobbins, Tony. 'Irish Ferries Dispute Finally Resolved after Bitter Stand-Off'. Eurofound, 20 December 2005. https://www.eurofound.europa.eu/publications/article/2005/irish-ferries-dispute-finally-resolved-after-bitter-stand-off.

ETF (European Transport Workers' Federation). 'The Warsaw Declaration: The European Transport Workers' Federation and Its Members Organisations Call on the European Commission, European Parliament and the EU Member States to Adopt a Road Initiative to Effectively Combat Social Dumping and Unfair Competition in the EU Road Transport Sector', 5 April 2017. https://www.etf-europe.org/wp-content/uploads/2018/10/ETF-Warsaw-declaration-original-signed-version-EN.pdf.

ETUC (European Trade Union Confederation). 'Posted Workers Revision – Equal Pay for Some'. ETUC – European Trade Union Confederation Press Release, 3 August

2016. https://www.etuc.org/en/pressrelease/posted-workers-revision-equal-pay-some.

ETUC (European Trade Union Confederation). 'The Posting of Workers Directive: Proposals for Revision (Resolution Adopted at the ETUC Executive Committee)', 9 March 2010. http://www.europarl.europa.eu/document/activities/cont/201006/20100601ATT75367/20100601ATT75367EN.pdf.

ETUC (European Trade Union Confederation), Business Europe, CEEP (European Centre of Employers and Enterprises providing Public services), UEAPME (European Association of Craft, Small and Medium-Sized Enterprises). 'Report on Joint Work of the European Social Partners on the ECJ Rulings in the Viking, Laval, Rüffert and Luxembourg Cases', 19 March 2010.

Eurofound. 'Minimum Wage'. Eurofound, 8 October 2019. https://www.eurofound.europa.eu/topic/minimum-wage.

Eurofound. 'Posted Workers'. EurWORK – European Observatory of Working Life, 29 June 2018. https://www.eurofound.europa.eu/observatories/eurwork/industrial-relations-dictionary/posted-workers.

Eurofound (European Foundation for the Improvement of Living and Working Conditions). 'Temporary Agency Work in Europe', 27 January 1999. https://www.eurofound.europa.eu/observatories/eurwork/comparative-information/temporary-agency-work-in-europe.

Europa.eu. 'Competition – European Union'. Text, 16 June 2016. https://europa.eu/european-union/topics/competition_en.

European Federation of Food, Agriculture and Tourism Trade Unions (EFFAT). 'Belgian Ministers' Condemnation of Germany's Social Dumping Practices Is Reminder to Act'. Press Release. Brussels: European Federation of Food, Agriculture and Tourism Trade Unions (EFFAT), 26 March 2013. https://old.effat.org/en/node/9933.

European Sources Online (ESO). 'Directive (EU) 2018/957 Amending Directive 96/71/EC Concerning the Posting of Workers in the Framework of the Provision of Services', 7 September 2018. https://www.europeansources.info/record/directive-eu-2018-957-amending-directive-96-71-ec-concerning-the-posting-of-workers-in-the-framework-of-the-provision-of-services/.

European Sources Online (ESO). 'Proposal to Amend Regulation (EC) No 883/2004 on the Coordination of Social Security Systems and Regulation (EC) No 987/2009 Laying down the Procedure for Implementing Regulation (EC) No 883/2004', 21 June 2018. https://www.europeansources.info/record/proposal-to-amend-regulation-ec-no-883-2004-on-the-coordination-of-social-security-systems-and-regulation-ec-no-987-2009-laying-down-the-procedure-for-implementing-regulation-ec-no-883-2004/.

EU monitor. 'Yellow Card (Subsidiary Control Mechanism)'. https://www.eumonitor.eu/9353000/1/j9vvik7m1c3gyxp/viommjbhi6ha (accessed 2 August 2019).

Garrigues. 'On 29 July New European Rules Enter into Force Regarding Posting of Workers in the EU', 20 July 2018. https://www.garrigues.com/en_GB/new/29-july-new-european-rules-enter-force-regarding-posting-workers-eu.

Jorens, Yves. 'Intra-EU Posting: Looking for Solutions: A Herculean or a Sisyphean Task?' KU Leuven Research Institute for Work and Society (HIVA) and European Centre for Workers' Questions EZA presented at the 60 Years Social Security Coordination from a Workers' Perspective, Leuven, Belgium, 16 May 2019.

Kiełbasa, Marcin. 'Advocate General Øe against a Broad Interpretation of the Non-Replacement Condition'. *Labour Mobility Initiative* (blog), 23 April 2018. https://www.mobilelabour.eu/12508/advocate-general-oe-against-a-broad-interpretation-of-the-non-replacement-condition-pursuant-to-article-121-of-regulation-883-2004/.

Kiełbasa, Marcin. 'Avalanche of Preliminary Questions to the CJEU on Posting of Workers to Austria'. *Labour Mobility Initiative* (blog), 3 September 2019. https://www.mobilelabour.eu/13085/avalanche-of-preliminary-questions-to-the-cjeu-on-posting-of-workers-to-austria/.

Kiełbasa, Marcin. 'Court of Justice of the EU: A Host Member State Court May "disregard" A1 PD Certificates'. *Labour Mobility Initiative* (blog), 27 February 2018. https://www.mobilelabour.eu/12334/court-justice-eu-host-member-state-court-may-disregard-a1-pd-certificates/.

Kiełbasa, Marcin. 'Posted or Sent? In the Context of the Revision of Social Security Coordination Regulation – Analysis'. *Labour Mobility Initiative* (blog), 25 January 2018. https://www.mobilelabour.eu/12203/posted-sent-context-revision-social-security-coordination-regulation-lmias-analysis/.

Kiełbasa, Marcin. 'Posting in the Orient Express or the Advocate General M. Szpunar's Opinion on "Chain Posting"'. *Labour Mobility Initiative* (blog), 28 August 2019. https://www.mobilelabour.eu/13077/posting-in-the-orient-express-or-the-advocate-general-m-szpunars-opinion-on-chain-posting/.

Kiełbasa, Marcin. 'Regulations on the Coordination of Social Security – Revision Only after the Elections to the EP'. *Labour Mobility Initiative* (blog), 2 May 2019. https://www.mobilelabour.eu/13023/regulations-on-the-coordination-of-social-security-in-the-eu-revision-only-after-the-elections-to-the-european-parliament/.

Kiełbasa, Marcin and Kamil Gacek. 'EMPL Committee in Favour of Continuing Work on the Revision of Coordination Regulations'. *Labour Mobility Initiative* (blog), 2 October 2019. https://www.mobilelabour.eu/13101/empl-committee-in-favour-of-continuing-work-on-the-revision-of-coordination-regulations/.

Kreilinger, Valentin. 'National Parliaments' 3rd Yellow Card: A Preliminary Assessment'. *Euractiv.Com* (blog), 12 May 2016. https://www.euractiv.com/section/social-europe-jobs/opinion/national-parliaments-3rd-yellow-card-a-preliminary-assessment/.

Kubera, Jacek. 'Posted Workers: More Europe Is More Freedom'. *Social Europe* (blog), 5 March 2018. https://www.socialeurope.eu/more-europe-is-more-freedom.

Labour Mobility Initiative. 'Call on the Postponement of Application of Revised Posting Rules', 29 April 2020. https://www.mobilelabour.eu/13159/call-on-the-postponement-of-application-of-revised-posting-rules/.

Lindahl, Björn. 'EU Agreement on Mobility Package'. Nordic Labour Journal, 13 December 2019. http://www.nordiclabourjournal.org/nyheter/news-2019/article.2019-12-12.5078447113.

Maurice, Eric. 'EU Takes Step Closer to "Posted Workers" Deal'. euobserver, 1 March 2018. https://euobserver.com/social/141166.

Ministry of Employment Troels Lund Poulsen. Consolidation Act concerning the Posting of Workers etc., i.e., Consolidation Act No. 342 of 3 April 2014 with the amendments following from section 1 of Act No. 175 of 24 February 2015, section 1 of Act No. 626 of 8 June 2016 and section 3 of Act No. 1717 of 27 December 2016 (2017). https://bm.dk/media/7024/consolidation-act-concerning-the-posting-of-workers-etc.pdf.

Novitz, Tonia. 'The Scope for Collective Bargaining in Posting and Procurement –What Might Come From Recent Court of Justice Case Law and the Proposed Reform of the Posting of Workers Directive?'. University of Bristol Law School Blog, 6 April 2016. https://legalresearch.blogs.bris.ac.uk/2016/04/the-scope-for-collective-bargaining-in-posting-and-procurement/.

Pacolet, Jozef. 'Social Security Coordination at a Glance'. KU Leuven Research Institute for Work and Society (HIVA) and European Centre for Workers' Questions EZA presented at the 60 Years Social Security Coordination from a Workers' Perspective, Leuven, Belgium, 16 May 2019.

Pancaldi, Federico. 'An Assessment of the Impact of Intra-EU Posting'. Presented at the Conference Intra-EU posting: costs and benefits, Leuven, Belgium, 28 April 2017.

Pedersen, Klaus. 'New Agreement to Combat Social Dumping'. Eurofound online, 10 June 2011. https://www.eurofound.europa.eu/publications/article/2011/new-agreement-to-combat-social-dumping.

Pennings, Frans. 'Mismatches between Tax and Social Security in Cross Border Situations'. Presented at the Workshop on 'Tax and Social Security - EU Perspective', University of Copenhagen, Faculty of Law, 20 September 2017.

Pieters, Danny. 'Posting of Workers: Disease or a Symptom?'. Presented at the Keynote Speech at the V European Labour Mobility Congress (ELMC), Posting of Workers: Opportunity for the Weaker or a Threat for the Stronger?, Krakow (Poland), 20 November 2017. https://www.elmc.eu/wp-content/uploads/2018/01/speech-DANNY-PIETERS_VELMC.pdf.

Richert, Julie. 'Posted Workers in the EU: Social Dumping vs Competitive Advantage'. ECIPE, 18 December 2017. http://ecipe.org/blog/posted-workers-in-the-eu-social-dumping-vs-competitive-advantage/.

Rocca, Marco. 'Not Dead yet: Legal Strategies at National Level and the Reform of the EU Posting of Workers Directive'. Presented at the Industrial Relations in Europe Conference (IREC), Leuven, Belgium, 10 September 2018.

Schiek, Dagmar. 'Posting of Workers and Equalities – Does the Reform Directive Strike the Right Balance?'. Presented at the Roundtable Posted Workers, European Labour Law Perspectives, Madrid, 18 January 2018. https://www.researchgate.net/publication/322677178.

Schiek, Dagmar. 'Solidarity and the Court of Justice of the European Union'. Presented at the ICON-S Conference: Courts, Power and Public Law, University of Copenhagen, Faculty of Law, 5 July 2017.

Schulten, Thorsten and Torsten Müller. 'Wages and Collective Bargaining during the European Economic Crisis: Developments in European Manufacturing Industry'. Vienna: industriAll (European Trade Union), 12 June 2014.

Schwarz, Stefan. 'EP Plenary Voted for State Mandated Protectionism'. *European Labour Mobility Congress – ELMC*, 14 June 2018. https://www.elmc.eu/ep-plenary-voted-for-state-mandated-protectionism-commentary-from-stefan-schwarz/.

Schwarz, Stefan. 'Opening Address at the II European Labour Mobility Congress'. Presented at the VI European Labour Mobility Congress (ELMC), Krakow (Poland), 14 March 2019.

Schwarz, Stefan and Marek Benio. 'Letter to Mr Nicolas Schmit Commissioner for Jobs and Social Rights', 28 April 2020. https://www.mobilelabour.eu/wp-content/uploads/2020/04/position-Letter-to-Commission-Revised-posting-of-workers-directive.pdf.

Schwarz, Stefan and Marcin Kiełbasa. 'Posted or Sent in the Context of the Revision of Social Security Coordination Regulations'. *Labour Mobility Initiative Association*, 17 January 2018.

Schwarz, Stefan, Marcin Kiełbasa and Marek Benio. 'Limited Cumulative Period of Posting in the Revised Posting of Workers Directive – In Search of a Legal Justification'. *Labour Mobility Initiative Association*, 10 October 2018. https://www.mobilelabour.eu/wp-content/uploads/2018/10/paper-Limited-cumulative-period-of-posting-in-the-revised-PWD-%E2%80%93-in-search-of-a-legal-justification-by-LMIA.pdf.

Spiegel, Bernhard. 'A Commentary on the Results of the Revised Rules on Social Security Coordination: Why Did This Project Fail at the First Attempt?' KU Leuven Research Institute for Work and Society (HIVA) and European Centre for Workers' Questions EZA presented at the 60 Years Social Security Coordination from a Workers' Perspective, Leuven, Belgium, 16 May 2019.

Stavers, Johan. 'Timmermans Calls on All EU Members to Adopt Minimum Wage'. *EURACTIV* (blog), 7 May 2019. https://www.euractiv.com/section/eu-elections-2019/news/timmermans-calls-on-all-eu-members-to-adopt-minimum-wage/.

Stupp, Catherine. 'Macron's Proposals Wreak Havoc on Posted Worker Negotiations'. *EURACTIV* (blog), 15 June 2017. https://www.euractiv.com/section/economy-jobs/news/macrons-proposals-wreak-havoc-on-posted-worker-negotiations/.

The Economist. 'Going Posted', 7 July 2016. https://www.economist.com/europe/2016/07/07/going-posted.

The Economist. 'The Euro Crisis – One Problem, Two Visions (Part II): Two Speeches by Nicolas Sarkozy and Angela Merkel about the Euro Zone's Crisis Reveal Their Differences Ahead of a Key Summit', 2 December 2011. https://www.economist.com/blogs/charlemagne/2011/12/euro-crisis-0.

Vaccarino, Elena and Zsolt Darvas. '"Social Dumping" and Posted Workers: A New Clash within the EU'. *Bruegel* (blog), 7 March 2016. http://bruegel.org/2016/03/social-dumping-and-posted-workers-a-new-clash-within-the-eu/.

Verschueren, Herwig. 'Special Non-contributory Benefits: Where Do We Come from and Where Could We Go?'. KU Leuven Research Institute for Work and Society (HIVA) and European Centre for Workers' Questions EZA presented at the 60 Years Social Security Coordination from a Workers' Perspective, Leuven, Belgium, 16 May 2019.

Verschueren, Herwig. 'The Revision of the Posting of Workers Directive: Protectionism or Combatting Social Dumping?'. Presented at the Ius Commune Congress, Maastricht, 24 November 2016.

Wispelaere, Frederic De. 'Intra-EU Posting and the Threat of Social Dumping: A Comprehensive Assessment'. KU Leuven Research Institute for Work and Society (HIVA) presented at the Industrial Relations in Europe Conference (IREC), Leuven, Belgium, 10 September 2018.

Wispelaere, Frederic De. 'Intra-EU Posting Costs and Benefits'. KU Leuven Research Institute for Work and Society (HIVA) presented at the 25th International Conference of Europeanists, Chicago, 28 March 2018.

Wispelaere, Frederic De. 'The 4 Key Pillars of Intra-EU Posting in Practice: Information, Registration, Enforcement and Monitoring'. Presented at the MoveS seminar, Zagreb, Croatia, 25 October 2019.

Wispelaere, Frederic De. 'The Sustainability of the Coordination of Social Security Systems'. KU Leuven Research Institute for Work and Society (HIVA) and European Centre for Workers' Questions EZA presented at the 60 Years Social Security Coordination from a Workers' Perspective, Leuven, Belgium, 16 May 2019.

Wispelaere, Frederic De and Jozef Pacolet. 'Celebrating Free Movement of Workers & Social Security Coordination'. KU Leuven Research Institute for Work and Society (HIVA) presented at the MoveS seminar, Brussels, 15 October 2018.

Wispelaere, Frederic De and Jozef Pacolet. 'Measuring the Size of Intra-EU Posting on the Basis of Data Collected at European and National Level'. KU Leuven Research Institute for Work and Society (HIVA) presented at the Conference Intra-EU posting: costs and benefits, Leuven, Belgium, 28 April 2017.

Wispelaere, Frederic De and Jozef Pacolet. 'Posting of Workers: A Call for a Broader Debate'. *Euractiv.Com* (blog), 4 September 2017. https://www.euractiv.com/section/economy-jobs/opinion/posting-of-workers-a-call-for-a-broader-debate/.

Workplace Denmark. 'Your Rights as a Posted Worker'. Workplace Denmark. https://workplacedenmark.dk:443/en/regulations-on-posting/your-rights-as-a-posted-worker.aspx (accessed 22 October 2018).

Yong, Charmaine. 'The New EU Posting of Workers Directive – Implications for Employers'. *Lewis Silkin* (blog), 1 November 2018. https://www.lewissilkin.com/Insights/The-new-EU-Posting-of-Workers-Directive-implications-for-employers.

Your Europe – Business. 'Posting Staff Abroad'. https://europa.eu/youreurope/business/human-resources/posted-workers/posting-staff-abroad/index_en.htm (accessed 8 April 2019).

Your Europe – Citizens. 'Social Security Cover Abroad'. https://europa.eu/youreurope/citizens/work/unemployment-and-benefits/country-coverage/index_en.htm (accessed 8 April 2019).

Zahn, Rebecca. 'The Viking and Laval Cases in the Context of European Enlargement'. *Web Journal of Current Legal Issues*, 2008. http://webjcli.ncl.ac.uk/2008/issue3/zahn3.html (accessed 14 April 2018).

Table of Cases

Judgments of the CJEU

Opinions of Advocates General

Actions Brought to the CJEU

Table of Treaties and Other Legal Instruments

Treaties, Charters and Conventions

United Nations General Assembly (UN). Universal Declaration of Human Rights (UDHR) (1948), 116

International Labour Organization (ILO). Labour Clauses (Public Contracts) Convention, 1949 (No. 94): Convention concerning Labour Clauses in Public Contracts (Entry into force: 20 September 1952) (1949), 67

Convention for the Protection of Human Rights and Fundamental Freedoms, Treaty No.005 (1950), 108

Treaty establishing the European Coal and Steel Community (1951). https://eur-lex.europa.eu/LexUriServ/LexUriServ.do?uri=CELEX:11951K:EN:PDF, 302

Treaty of Rome (EEC) – Treaty establishing the European Economic Community (1957)

Council of Europe. European Social Charter, Pub. L. No. Turin (1961), 102, 118, 318

Treaty establishing the European Community (Maastricht Treaty), Pub. L. No. OJ C 224, Official Journal of the European Communities (1992), 302

Treaty establishing the European Community (Amsterdam Treaty), Pub. L. No. OJ C 340, Official Journal of the European Communities (1997), 302

Community Charter of the Fundamental Social Rights of Workers, Pub. L. No. Declaration by President Delors on 8 December 1989 at the European Council of Strasbourg (1989). https://www.eesc.europa.eu/resources/docs/community-charter--en.pdf, 68, 102, 118

Charter of Fundamental Rights of the European Union (CFREU), Pub. L. No. 2000/C 364/01 (2000). http://www.europarl.europa.eu/charter/pdf/text_en.pdf, 109, 285

Treaty establishing the European Community (Nice Treaty), Pub. L. No. OJ C 325, Official Journal of the European Communities (2002), 302

Consolidated version of the Treaty on the Functioning of the European Union – Protocol (No 2) on the application of the principles of subsidiarity and proportionality (2008). https://eur-lex.europa.eu/legal-content/EN/TXT/HTML/?uri=CELEX:12008E/PRO/02&from=EN, 119

Consolidated version of the Treaty on European Union, Pub. L. No. OJ C 326/13 (2012), 117

Consolidated version of the Treaty on the Functioning of the European Union, Pub. L. No. OJ C 326/47 (2012), 22

OECD (Organisation for Economic Co-operation and Development). *Model Tax Convention on Income and on Capital: Condensed Version, 21 November 2017*. Paris: OECD Publishing, 2017, 35, 156, 178, 200

EU Legislation

Règlement (CEE) No 3 concernant la sécurité sociale des travailleurs migrants, Journal officiel des Communautés européennes, P 30 [English version not existent], Pub. L. No. OJ P 30, Journal officiel des Communautés européennes, P 30 (1958). https://eur-lex.europa.eu/legal-content/IT/TXT/PDF/?uri=OJ:P:1958:030:FULL&from=SL, 138

Règlement (CEE) No 4 fixant les modalités d'application et complétant les dispositions du règlement n° 3 concernant la sécurité sociale des travailleurs migrants, Journal officiel des Communautés européennes, P 30 [English version not existent], Pub. L. No. OJ P 30, Journal officiel des Communautés européennes, P 30 (1958). https://eur-lex.europa.eu/legal-content/IT/TXT/PDF/?uri=OJ:P:1958:030:FULL&from=SL, 138

Regulation (EEC) No 1612/68 of the Council of 15 October 1968 on freedom of movement for workers within the Community, Pub. L. No. OJ L 257/2, Official Journal of the European Communities (1968). https://eur-lex.europa.eu/legal-content/EN/TXT/PDF/?uri=CELEX:31968R1612&from=en, 66, 288

Regulation (EEC) No 1408/71 of the Council of 14 June 1971 on the application of social security schemes to employed persons and their families moving within the Community, Pub. L. No. OJ L 149/2, Official Journal of the European Communities (1971), 2, 66, 139, 140, 143

Regulation (EEC) No 574/72 of the Council of 21 March 1972 fixing the procedure for implementing Regulation (EEC) No 1408/71 on the application of social security schemes to employed persons and their families moving within the Community, Pub. L. No. OJ L 74, Official Journal of the European Communities (1972). https://eur-lex.europa.eu/legal-content/EN/TXT/PDF/?uri=CELEX:31972R0574&from=EN, 139

Convention 80/934/EEC of 19 June 1980 on the law applicable to contractual obligations (the Rome Convention), Pub. L. No. OJ L 266/1, Official Journal of the European Communities (1980). https://eur-lex.europa.eu/legal-content/EN/TXT/HTML/?uri=CELEX:41980A0934&from=EN, 50, 58, 60, 62, 65, 67

Council Regulation (EEC) No 1390/81 of 12 May 1981 extending to self-employed persons and members of their families Regulation (EEC) No 1408/71 on the application of social security schemes to employed persons and their families moving within the Community, Pub. L. No. OJ L 143/1, Official Journal of the European Communities (1981). https://eur-lex.europa.eu/legal-content/EN/TXT/HTML/?uri=CELEX:31981R1390&from=EN, 139

Single European Act (SEA), Pub. L. No. OJ L 169, Official Journal of the European Communities (1987). https://eur-lex.europa.eu/legal-content/EN/TXT/PDF/?uri=CELEX:11986U/TXT&from=EN, 288

Directive 89/440/EEC of 18 July 1989 amending Directive 71/305/EEC concerning coordination of procedures for the award of public works contracts, Pub. L. No. OJ L 210/1, Official Journal of the European Communities (1989). https://eur-lex.europa.eu/legal-content/EN/TXT/PDF/?uri=CELEX:31989L0440&from=EN, 67, 90

Council Directive 92/85/EEC of 19 October 1992 on the introduction of measures to encourage improvements in the safety and health at work of pregnant workers and workers who have recently given birth or are breastfeeding (tenth individual Directive within the meaning of Article 16 (1) of Directive 89/391/EEC), Pub. L. No. OJ L 348, Official Journal of the European Communities (1992). https://eur-lex.europa.eu/legal-content/EN/TXT/PDF/?uri=CELEX:31992L0085&from=EN, 289

Directive 96/71/EC of the European Parliament and of the Council of 16 December 1996 concerning the posting of workers in the framework of the provision of services, Pub. L. No. OJ L 18/1, Official Journal of the European Communities (1997) (Posting of Workers Directive (PWD)). http://eur-lex.europa.eu/LexUriServ/LexUriServ.do?uri=CELEX:31996L0071:en:HTML, 1, 22, 33, 38–44, 53, 58, 64–65, 74–78, 82, 83, 86, 97, 120, 138, 239, 246, 261, 327

Council Directive 97/81/EC of 15 December 1997 concerning the Framework Agreement on part-time work concluded by UNICE, CEEP and the ETUC, Pub. L. No. OJ L 14/9, Official Journal of the European Communities (1998). https://eur-lex.europa.eu/legal-content/EN/TXT/PDF/?uri=CELEX:31997L0081&from=en, 289

Council Directive 1999/70/EC of 28 June 1999 concerning the framework agreement on fixed-term work concluded by ETUC, UNICE and CEEP, Pub. L. No. OJ L 175/43, Official Journal of the European Communities (1999). https://eur-lex.europa.eu/legal-content/EN/TXT/PDF/?uri=CELEX:31999L0070&from=EN, 289

Council Directive 2000/43/EC of 29 June 2000 implementing the principle of equal treatment between persons irrespective of racial or ethnic origin, Pub. L. No. OJ L 180/22, Official Journal of the European Communities (2000). https://eur-lex.europa.eu/legal-content/EN/TXT/PDF/?uri=CELEX:32000L0043&from=en, 290

Council Directive 2000/78/EC of 27 November 2000 establishing a general framework for equal treatment in employment and occupation, Pub. L. No. OJ L 303/16, Official Journal of the European Communities (2000). https://eur-lex.europa.eu/legal-content/EN/TXT/PDF/?uri=CELEX:32000L0078&from=EN, 289, 291

Administrative Commission of the European Communities on social security for migrant workers. Decision No 181 (2001/891/EC) of 13 December 2000 concerning the interpretation of Articles 14(1), 14a(1) and 14b(1) and (2) of Council

Regulation (EEC) No 1408/71 on the legislation applicable to posted workers and self-employed workers temporarily working outside the competent State, Pub. L. No. OJ L 329/73, Official Journal of the European Communities (2001). https://eur-lex.europa.eu/legal-content/EN/TXT/PDF/?uri = CELEX:32001D0891&from = EN, 147, 149

Regulation (EC) No 1386/2001 of the European Parliament and of the Council of 5 June 2001 amending Council Regulations (EEC) No 1408/71 on the application of social security schemes to employed persons, to self-employed persons and to members of their families moving within the Community and (EEC) No 574/72 laying down the procedure for implementing Regulation (EEC) No 1408/71, Pub. L. No. OJ L 187/1, Official Journal of the European Communities (2001). https://eur-lex.europa.eu/legal-content/EN/TXT/HTML/?uri = CELEX:32001R1386&from = EN, 139

Directive 2004/17/EC of the European Parliament and of the Council of 31 March 2004 coordinating the procurement procedures of entities operating in the water, energy, transport and postal services sectors, Pub. L. No. OJ L 134/1, Official Journal of the European Union (2004). https://eur-lex.europa.eu/legal-content/EN/TXT/PDF/?uri = CELEX:32004L0017&from = EN, 4

Directive 2004/18/EC of the European Parliament and of the Council of 31 March 2004 on the coordination of procedures for the award of public works contracts, public supply contracts and public service contracts, Pub. L. No. OJ L 134/114, Official Journal of the European Union (2004). https://eur-lex.europa.eu/legal-content/EN/TXT/PDF/?uri = CELEX:32004L0018&from = en, 4, 114, 210

Regulation (EC) No 883/2004 of the European Parliament and of the Council of 29 April 2004 on the coordination of social security systems, Pub. L. No. OJ L 166/1, Official Journal of the European Communities (2004), 3, 36, 37, 38, 45, 47, 143–146, 149, 155, 156, 158, 159, 161, 168, 169, 171, 174, 176–178, 180, 181, 183–185, 187, 188, 191

Directive 2006/22/EC of the European Parliament and of the Council of 15 March 2006 on minimum conditions for the implementation of Council Regulations (EEC) No 3820/85 and (EEC) No 3821/85 concerning social legislation relating to road transport activities and repealing Council Directive 88/599/EEC, Pub. L. No. OJ L 102/35, Official Journal of the European Union (2006). https://eur-lex.europa.eu/legal-content/EN/TXT/HTML/?uri = CELEX:32006L0022&from = EN, 129, 257

Directive 2006/54/EC of the European Parliament and of the Council of 5 July 2006 on the implementation of the principle of equal opportunities and equal treatment of men and women in matters of employment and occupation (recast), Pub. L. No. OJ L 204, Official Journal of the European Union (2006), 289, 291

Regulation (EC) No 593/2008 of the European Parliament and of the Council of 17 June 2008 on the law applicable to contractual obligations (Rome I), Pub. L. No. OJ L 177/6, Official Journal of the European Union (2008) (Rome I Regulation), 19, 50, 51, 58, 59, 60, 61, 65, 77, 123, 272, 273, 328

Directive 2008/104/EC of the European Parliament and of the Council of 19 November 2008 on temporary agency work, Pub. L. No. OJ L 327/9, Official Journal of the

Regulation'), Pub. L. No. OJ L 316/1, Official Journal of the European Union (2012). https://doi.org/10.5040/9781509909568, 121

Directive 2014/24/EU of the European Parliament and of the Council of 26 February 2014 on public procurement and repealing Directive 2004/18/EC, Pub. L. No. OJ L 94/65, Official Journal of the European Union (2014). https://eur-lex.europa.eu/legal-content/EN/TXT/PDF/?uri = CELEX:32014L0024&from = EN, 210

Directive 2014/67/EU of the European Parliament and of the Council of 15 May 2014 on the enforcement of Directive 96/71/EC concerning the posting of workers in the framework of the provision of services and amending Regulation (EU) No 1024/2012 on administrative cooperation through the Internal Market Information System ('the IMI Regulation'), Pub. L. No. OJ L 159/11, Official Journal of the European Union (2014) (Enforcement Directive), 6, 7, 17, 22, 23, 39, 45, 52, 55, 78, 93, 96, 120–129, 132, 135, 136, 207, 224–225, 237, 241, 242, 244–246, 250, 257, 263, 264, 267, 268, 272, 276, 277, 311, 314, 316, 329, 332Decision (EU) 2016/344 of the European Parliament and of the Council of 9 March 2016 on establishing a European Platform to enhance cooperation in tackling undeclared work, Pub. L. No. OJ L 65/12, Official Journal of the European Union (2016), 226

European Parliament, Council of the European Union, and European Commission. Interinstitutional Proclamation on the European Pillar of Social Rights, Pub. L. No. OJ C 428/10, Official Journal of the European Union (2017), 244, 291, 318

Directive (EU) 2018/957 of the European Parliament and of the Council of 28 June 2018 amending Directive 96/71/EC concerning the posting of workers in the framework of the provision of services, Pub. L. No. OJ L 173/16, Official Journal of the European Union (2018), 1, 8, 22, 36, 43, 44, 47, 53, 132, 146, 168, 225, 239, 256–269, 280, 288, 297, 327

Regulation (EU) 2019/1149 of the European Parliament and of the Council of 20 June 2019 establishing a European Labour Authority, amending Regulations (EC) No 883/2004, (EU) No 492/2011, and (EU) 2016/589 and repealing Decision (EU) 2016/344, Pub. L. No. OJ L 186/21, Official Journal of the European Union (2019), 244, 312

Directive (EU) 2019/1152 of the European Parliament and of the Council of 20 June 2019 on transparent and predictable working conditions in the European Union, Pub. L. No. OJ L 186/105, Official Journal of the European Union (2019), 220

Regulation (EU) 2020/1054 of the European Parliament and of the Council of 15 July 2020 amending Regulation (EC) No 561/2006 as regards minimum requirements on maximum daily and weekly driving times, minimum breaks and daily and weekly rest periods and Regulation (EU) No 165/2014 as regards positioning by means of tachographs, Pub. L. No. OJ L 249, Official Journal of the European Union (2020), 131

Regulation (EU) 2020/1055 of the European Parliament and of the Council of 15 July 2020 amending Regulations (EC) No 1071/2009, (EC) No 1072/2009 and (EU) No 1024/2012 with a view to adapting them to developments in the road transport sector, Pub. L. No. OJ L 249, Official Journal of the European Union (2020), 131

Regulation (EU) 2020/1056 of the European Parliament and of the Council of 15 July 2020 on electronic freight transport information, Pub. L. No. OJ L 249, Official Journal of the European Union (2020), 131

Directive (EU) 2020/1057 of the European Parliament and of the Council of 15 July 2020 laying down specific rules with respect to Directive 96/71/EC and Directive 2014/67/EU for posting drivers in the road transport sector and amending Directive 2006/22/EC as regards enforcement requirements and Regulation (EU) No 1024/2012, Pub. L. No. OJ L 249/49, Official Journal of the European Union (2020). https://eur-lex.europa.eu/legal-content/EN/TXT/HTML/?uri=CELEX:32020L1057&from=EN, 43, 131, 132, 257, 329

Other EU Sources

Schuman, Robert. 'Declaration of 9th May 1950'. Paris, 10 May 1950, 302

Commission des Communautes Europeennes. Proposition de reglement (CEE) du Conseil relatif aux dispositions concernant les conflits de lois en matière de relations de travail à l'intérieur de la Communauté, Pub. L. No. COM(72) 170 final (1972), 67, 90

Commission of the European Communities. Amended proposal for a Regulation of the Council on the provisions of conflict of laws on employment relationships within the Community, Pub. L. No. COM(75) 653 final (1976). http://aei.pitt.edu/10779/1/COM(75)653.pdf, 67

Communication from the Commission concerning its Action Programme relating to the implementation of the Community Charter of Basic Social Rights for Workers, Pub. L. No. COM(89) 568 final (1989). http://aei.pitt.edu/1345/1/Social_charter_COM_89_568.pdf (Action Programme), 68, 90

Commission of the European Communities. Proposal for a Council Directive concerning the posting of workers in the framework of the provision of services, Pub. L. No. COM(91) 230 final, 91/C 225/05 (1991). https://eur-lex.europa.eu/resource.html?uri=cellar:1b4578cb-d0f8-4d76-8804-9119e0cfef10.0006.01/DOC_1&format=PDF, 72

European Commission. 'Press Release – Presentation by President Jaques Delors of the Commission Programme for 1992 and the Delors II Package at the European Parliament'. European Commission Press Releases Database, 12 February 1992. http://europa.eu/rapid/press-release_SPEECH-92-12_en.htm, 71

Commission of the European Communities. Amended proposal for a Council Directive concerning the posting of workers in the framework of the provision of services, Pub. L. No. COM(93) 225 final (1993). https://eur-lex.europa.eu/legal-content/EN/TXT/PDF/?uri=CELEX:51993PC0225&from=EN, 72

European Commission. European Social Policy – A Way Forward for the Union. A White Paper, Pub. L. No. COM (94) 333 final (1994). http://aei.pitt.edu/1118/1/social_policy_white_paper_COM_94_333_A.pdf, 284

European Commission. Communication on the posting of workers who are third-country nationals for the provision of cross-border services, Pub. L. No. COM(1999) 3 final (1999), 28

Commission of the European Communities. Green paper on the conversion of the Rome Convention of 1980 on the law applicable to contractual obligations into a Community instrument and its modernisation, Pub. L. No. COM(2002) 654 final (2003), 50

European Commission. Communication on the Implementation of Directive 96/71/EC in the Member States, Pub. L. No. COM(2003) 458 final (2003), 83, 89, 120

European Commission. Communication: Guidance on the posting of workers in the framework of the provision of services, Pub. L. No. COM(2006) 159 final, {SEC(2006) 439} (2006). http://www.europarl.europa.eu/registre/docs_autres_institutions/commission_europeenne/com/2006/0159/COM_COM(2006)0159_EN.pdf, 98–100, 120, 121

Communication from the Commission to the European Council – A citizens' agenda – Delivering results for Europe, Pub. L. No. COM(2006) 211 final (2006). https://eur-lex.europa.eu/legal-content/EN/TXT/PDF/?uri=CELEX:52006DC0211&from=EN, 301

Committee on Employment and Social Affairs, Rapporteur José Albino Silva Peneda. 'Report on a European Social Model for the Future'. (2005/2248(INI)). Brussels: European Parliament, 13 July 2006. http://www.europarl.europa.eu/sides/getDoc.do?pubRef=-//EP//TEXT+REPORT+A6-2006-0238+0+DOC+XML+V0//EN&language=EN, 284

European Commission. Communication on the Posting of workers in the framework of the provision of services: Maximising its benefits and potential while guaranteeing the protection of workers, Pub. L. No. COM(2007) 304 final (2007), 120, 168

Communication from the Commission to the European Parliament, the Council, the European Economic and Social Committee and the Committee of the Regions – Opportunities, access and solidarity: towards a new social vision for 21st century Europe, Pub. L. No. COM(2007) 726 final (2007), 308

European Commission. Proposal for a Directive of the European Parliament and of the Council on the enforcement of Directive 96/71/EC concerning the posting of workers in the framework of the provision of services, Pub. L. No. COM(2012) 131 final, 2012/0061 (COD) (2012), 121

European Commission. Proposal for a Council Regulation on the exercise of the right to take collective action within the context of the freedom of establishment and the freedom to provide services, Pub. L. No. COM(2012) 130 final, 2012/0064 (APP) (2012) ('Monti II' Regulation), 118, 119, 121, 135, 248

Committee of the Regions, T33, Srl, Österreichisches Institut für Raumplanung, and Swedish Consulting Group. *Assessment of the Current Legislation and the Possible Impact of Posting of Workers Directive on Local and Regional Authorities*. Brussels: CoR, 2012. http://dx.publications.europa.eu/10.2863/87753, 211

European Commission. Proposal for a Council Regulation on the establishment of the European Public Prosecutor's Office, Pub. L. No. COM(2013) 534 final, 2013/0255 (APP) (2013). https://ec.europa.eu/transparency/regdoc/rep/1/2013/EN/1-2013-534-EN-F1-1.Pdf, 248

European Commission. 'Practical Guide on the Applicable Legislation in the European Union (EU), the European Economic Area (EEA) and in Switzerland'. Social

Europe. Social Europe, European Commission, Employment, Social Affairs and Equal Opportunities, December 2013, 42, 139, 141, 143, 147–150, 154–156

Juncker, Jean-Claude. Political Guidelines for the next European Commission, Opening Statement in the European Parliament Plenary Session. 'A New Start for Europe: My Agenda for Jobs, Growth, Fairness and Democratic Change'. Political Guidelines for the next European Commission, Opening Statement in the European Parliament Plenary Session, 15 July 2014, 240

Communication from the Commission to the European Parliament, the Council, the European Economic and Social Committee and the Committee of the Regions – Commission Work Programme 2015: A New Start, Pub. L. No. COM(2014) 910 final (2014). https://ec.europa.eu/info/sites/info/files/cwp_2015_en.pdf, 241

European Commission. *Employment and Social Developments in Europe 2014*. ISSN 2315-2540. Bruxelles: European Commission, Directorate Général for Employment, Social Affairs and Inclusion, 2015, 9, 21, 201

European Commission. 'Press Release – College Holds Orientation Debate on the Economic and Social Dimension of the Single Market'. European Commission Press Releases Database, 6 October 2015. http://europa.eu/rapid/press-release_IP-15-5763_en.htm, 241

Communication from the Commission to the European Parliament, the Council, the European Economic and Social Committee and the Committee of the Regions – Commission Work Programme 2016: No time for business as usual, Pub. L. No. COM(2015) 610 final (2015). https://ec.europa.eu/info/sites/info/files/cwp_2016_en_0.pdf, 241

Morin-Chartier, Elisabeth, and Agnes Jongerius. 'Draft Report on the Proposal for a Directive of the European Parliament and of the Council Amending Directive 96/71/EC of The European Parliament and of the Council of 16 December 1996 Concerning the Posting of Workers in the Framework of the Provision of Services'. European Parliament – Committee on Employment and Social Affairs, 12 February 2016. http://www.europarl.europa.eu/doceo/document/EMPL-PR-582163_EN.pdf?redirect, 252

European Commission. Proposal for a Directive of the European Parliament and of the Council amending Directive 96/71/EC of the European Parliament and of the Council of 16 December 1996 concerning the posting of workers in the framework of the provision of services, Pub. L. No. COM(2016) 128 final, 2016/0070 (COD) (2016), 7, 53, 127, 242

European Commission. Impact Assessment, Accompanying the document Proposal for a Directive of the European Parliament and the Council amending Directive 96/71/EC concerning the posting of workers in the framework of the provision of services, Pub. L. No. SWD(2016) 52 final (2016), 7, 40, 43, 46, 50, 80, 174, 185, 198, 199, 217, 242–247, 249, 262, 267, 270–272, 274–277, 296

European Commission. 'Press Release – Commission Presents Reform of the Posting of Workers Directive – Towards a Deeper and Fairer European Labour Market'. European Commission Press Releases Database, 8 March 2016. http://europa.eu/rapid/press-release_IP-16-466_en.htm, 245, 247, 248, 296, 297

European Parliament and of the Council amending Regulation (EC) No 883/2004 on the coordination of social security systems and regulation (EC) No 987/2009 laying down the procedure for implementing Regulation (EC) No 883/2004 - Part 5/6, Pub. L. No. SWD(2015) 460 final (2016). https://eur-lex.europa.eu/legal-content/EN/TXT/HTML/?uri=CELEX:52016SC0460&qid=1553252005181&from=EN, 158, 160, 161

Eurostat. 'Price Level Index for Household Final Consumption Expenditure (HFCE), 2016, EU-28=100DEC'. Eurostat - Statistics Explained, 2016. http://ec.europa.eu/eurostat/statistics-explained/index.php?title=File:Price_level_index_for_household_final_consumption_expenditure_(HFCE),_2016,_EU-28%3D100DEC.png, 199

Communication from the Commission to the European Parliament, the Council, the European Economic and Social Committee and the Committee of the Regions, Establishing a European Pillar of Social Rights, Pub. L. No. COM(2017) 250 final (2017). https://ec.europa.eu/transparency/regdoc/rep/1/2017/EN/COM-2017-250-F1-EN-MAIN-PART-1.PDF, 291

European Commission. Proposal for a Directive of the European Parliament and of the Council amending Directive 2006/22/EC as regards enforcement requirements and laying down specific rules with respect to Directive 96/71/EC and Directive 2014/67/EU for posting drivers in the road transport sector, Pub. L. No. COM(2017) 278 final, 2017/0121 (COD) (2017). https://eur-lex.europa.eu/legal-content/EN/TXT/PDF/?uri=CELEX:52017PC0278&from=EN, 130

European Commission. Impact Assessment, Accompanying the document Proposal for a Regulation of the European Parliament and of the Council amending Regulation (EC) 561/2006 as regards minimum requirements on maximum daily and weekly driving times, minimum breaks and daily and weekly rest periods and Regulation (EU) 165/2014 as regards positioning by means of tachographs and Proposal for a Directive of the European Parliament and of the Council amending Directive 2006/22/EC as regards enforcement requirements and laying down specific rules with respect to Directive 96/71/EC and Directive 2014/67/EU for posting drivers in the road transport sector - PART 1/2, Pub. L. No. SWD(2017) 186 final (2017). https://eur-lex.europa.eu/resource.html?uri=cellar:f81a95b9-4627-11e7-aea8-01aa75ed71a1.0001.02/DOC_1&format=PDF, 128, 129, 132, 219, 223

European Commission. Communication from the Commission to the European Parliament, the Council, the European Economic and Social Committee and the Committee of the Regions, Europe on the move - An agenda for a socially fair transition towards clean, competitive and connected mobility for all, Pub. L. No. COM(2017) 283 final (2017). https://eur-lex.europa.eu/legal-content/EN/TXT/PDF/?uri=CELEX:52017DC0283&from=EN, 130

Proposal for a Directive of the European Parliament and of the Council on the Enforcement of Directive 96/71/EC Concerning the Posting of Workers in the Framework of the Provision of Services - Progress Report. Brussels: Council of the European Union, 9 June 2017. http://data.consilium.europa.eu/doc/document/ST-9882-2017-INIT/en/pdf, 254

European Commission. 'Speech of President Jean-Claude Juncker, State of the Union Address', 13 September 2017. http://europa.eu/rapid/press-release_SPEECH-17-3165_en.htm, 7, 288, 295

Thyssen, Marianne - EU Commissioner for Employment. 'Parliamentary Questions: Answer given by Ms Thyssen on Behalf of the Commission (Question Reference: E-004944/2017)', 21 September 2017. http://www.europarl.europa.eu/doceo/document/E-8-2017-004944-ASW_EN.pdf, 151, 170

Morin-Chartier, Elisabeth, and Agnes Jongerius. 'Report on the Proposal for a Directive of the European Parliament and of the Council Amending Directive 96/71/ EC of the European Parliament and of the Council of 16 December 1996 Concerning the Posting of Workers in the Framework of the Provision of Services'. European Parliament - Committee on Employment and Social Affairs, 16 October 2017, 252, 253

Employment, Social Policy, Health and Consumer Affairs (EPSCO) Council. Partial general approach on the coordination of social security systems and regulation, Pub. L. No. 13139/17, SOC 636-EMPL 483-CODEC 1576 2016/0397 (COD) (2017). https://www.consilium.europa.eu/media/31180/st_13139_2017_init_en.pdf, 158

Council of the European Union. Proposal for a Directive of the European Parliament and of the Council on the Enforcement of Directive 96/71/EC Concerning the Posting of Workers in the Framework of the Provision of Services - General Approach. Brussels,, 24 October 2017. https://eur-lex.europa.eu/legal-content/EN/TXT/PDF/?uri=CONSIL:ST_13612_2017_INIT&from=EN, 254, 255, 260

Schmid-Drüner, Marion. 'Briefing: The Revision of the Posting of Workers Directive'. Brussels: European Parliament, Employment and Social Affairs - Policy Department for Economic, Scientific and Quality of Life Policies, October 2017. http://dx.publications.europa.eu/10.2861/308871, 202, 247–249, 252

European Commission. Inception Impact Assessment - European Social Security Number, Pub. L. No. Ares(2017)5862503 (2017), 310

Eurostat. 'Tax Rate on Low Wage Earners: Tax Wedge on Labour Costs'. European Commission, 2017. https://ec.europa.eu/eurostat/en/web/products-datasets/-/EARN_NT_TAXWEDGE, 229

Council of the European Union. Proposal for a Directive of the European Parliament and of the Council amending Directive 2006/22/EC as regards enforcement requirements and laying down specific rules with respect to Directive 96/71/EC and Directive 2014/67/EU for posting drivers in the road transport sector - general approach, Pub. L. No. 15084/18, 2017/0121(COD) 2017/0122(COD) 2017/0123(COD) (2018). http://data.consilium.europa.eu/doc/document/ST-15084-2018-INIT/en/pdf, 130

Council of the European Union. 'Transport, Telecommunications and Energy Council (Transport) - Consilium'. Press release, 12 March 2018. https://www.consilium.europa.eu/en/meetings/tte/2018/12/03/, 130

'Proposal for a Directive of the European Parliament and of the Council Amending Directive 96/71/EC Concerning the Posting of Workers in the Framework of the Provision of Services - Analysis of the Final Compromise Text with a View to

Agreement'. Brussels: Council of the European Union, 28 March 2018. http://data.consilium.europa.eu/doc/document/ST-7350-2018-ADD-1/en/pdf, 255, 256

European Parliament legislative resolution of 29 May 2018 on the proposal for a directive of the European Parliament and of the Council amending Directive 96/71/EC of The European Parliament and of the Council of 16 December 1996 concerning the posting of workers in the framework of the provision of services (COM(2016)0128 – C8-0114/2016 – 2016/0070(COD)) (Ordinary legislative procedure: first reading), Pub. L. No. P8_TA(2018)0213 (2018). http://www.europarl.europa.eu/sides/getDoc.do?pubRef=-//EP//TEXT+TA+P8-TA-2018-0213+0+DOC+XML+V0//EN, 256

Kiss, Monika. 'Briefing 'EU Legislation in Progress': Posting of Workers Directive'. European Parliament, 31 May 2018. http://www.europarl.europa.eu/RegData/etudes/BRIE/2016/582043/EPRS_BRI(2016)582043_EN.pdf, 243

Council of the European Union. 'Posting of Workers: Council Adopts the Directive – Consilium'. Press release, 21 June 2018. https://www.consilium.europa.eu/en/press/press-releases/2018/06/21/posting-of-workers-council-adopts-the-directive/, 256

Kraatz, Susanne. 'European Parliament, Posting of Workers – Fact Sheets on the European Union', July 2018. http://www.europarl.europa.eu/factsheets/en/sheet/37/posting-of-workers, 225

'Proposal for a Regulation of the European Parliament and of the Council Amending Regulation (EC) No 883/2004 on the Coordination of Social Security Systems and Regulation (EC) No 987/2009 Laying down the Procedure for Implementing Regulation (EC) No 883/2004 – Analysis of the Final Compromise Text with a View to Agreement'. Brussels: Council of the European Union, 25 March 2019. https://data.consilium.europa.eu/doc/document/ST-7698-2019-ADD-1-REV-1/en/pdf, 158–160, 162

European Commission – Employment, Social Affairs & Inclusion. 'Posted Workers'. Accessed 3 April 2019. https://ec.europa.eu/social/main.jsp?catId=471, 7, 36, 43

European Parliament. Legislative resolution of 4 April 2019 on the proposal for a directive of the European Parliament and of the Council amending Directive 2006/22/EC as regards enforcement requirements and laying down specific rules with respect to Directive 96/71/EC and Directive 2014/67/EU for posting drivers in the road transport sector, Pub. L. No. 2017/0121(COD) (2019). http://www.europarl.europa.eu/doceo/document/TA-8-2019-0339_EN.html, 130

Eurostat. 'Glossary: Full-Time Equivalent (FTE)'. Eurostat – Statistics Explained, 2019. https://ec.europa.eu/eurostat/statistics-explained/index.php/Glossary:Full-time_equivalent_(FTE), 187

European Parliament. 'Minutes – Coordination of Social Security Systems ***I (Vote)' – Thursday, 18 April 2019. http://www.europarl.europa.eu/doceo/document/PV-8-2019-04-18-ITM-010-05_EN.html, 161

Honnefelder, Stephanie. 'Competition Policy – Fact Sheets on the European Union'. European Parliament, April 2019. https://www.europarl.europa.eu/factsheets/en/sheet/82/competition-policy, 286

Eurostat. 'Self-Employed Persons'. Eurostat, 30 April 2019. https://ec.europa.eu/eurostat/web/products-eurostat-news/-/EDN-20190430-1, 187

EUR-Lex, Access to European Union law. 'Preparatory Documents – EUR-Lex'. Accessed 8 May 2019. https://eur-lex.europa.eu/collection/eu-law/pre-acts.html, 15

Leyen, Ursula von der. 'Political Guidelines of the Commission 2019-2024 – A Union That Strives for More: My Agenda for Europe'. European Commission, 16 July 2019. https://ec.europa.eu/commission/sites/beta-political/files/political-guidelines-next-commission_en.pdf, 314

European Commission. 'Report from the Commission to the European Parliament, the Council and the European Economic and Social Committee on the Application and Implementation of Directive 2014/67/EU of the European Parliament and of the Council of 15 May 2014 on the Enforcement of Directive 96/71/EC Concerning the Posting of Workers in the Framework of the Provision of Services and Amending Regulation (EU) 1024/2012 on Administrative Co-Operation through the Internal Market Information System ('the IMI Regulation')'. Brussels, 25 September 2019, 99, 124, 126

European Commission. 'Commission Staff Working Document Accompanying the Document Report from the Commission to the European Parliament, the Council and the European Economic and Social Committee on the Application and Implemantation of Directive 2014/67/EU of the European Parliament and of the Council of 15 May 2014 on the Enforcement of Directive 96/71/EC Concerning the Posting of Workers in the Framework of the Provision of Services and Amending Regulation (EU) No 1024/2012 on Administrative Cooperation through the Internal Market Information System ('the IMI Regulation')'. Brussels, 25 September 2019, 124

European Commission. 'Practical Guide on Posting', 25 September 2019

European Parliament. 'Road Transport: Enforcement Requirements and Specific Rules for Posting Drivers, Legislative Train Schedule', 24 June 2020. https://www.europarl.europa.eu/legislative-train, 131

European Commission – Employment, Social Affairs & Inclusion. 'Electronic Exchange of Social Security Information (EESSI)'. Electronic Exchange of Social Security Information (EESSI). Accessed 28 January 2020. https://ec.europa.eu/social/main.jsp?catId=869&langId=en, 163, 311

Eurostat. 'Employment by Sex, Age and Citizenship (1 000)'. Eurostat – Data Explorer, 13 February 2020. https://appsso.eurostat.ec.europa.eu/nui/submitViewTableAction.do, 187

EUR-Lex. 'Competition'. Accessed 17 February 2020. https://eur-lex.europa.eu/summary/chapter/competition.html?root_default=SUM_1_CODED%3D08&locale=en, 286, 296

Council of the European Union. Position (EU) No 4/2020 of the Council at first reading: with a view to the adoption of a Directive of the European Parliament and of the

Council laying down specific rules with respect to Directive 96/71/EC and Directive 2014/67/EU for posting drivers in the road transport sector and amending Directive 2006/22/EC as regards enforcement requirements and Regulation (EU) No 1024/2012, Pub. L. No. OJ C 149/1 (2020). https://eur-lex.europa.eu/legal-content/EN/TXT/PDF/?uri=CELEX:52020AG0004(01)&from=EN, 130

Index

D

E

U

V

W

Y

BCLR - BULLETIN OF COMPARATIVE LABOUR RELATIONS

Vol. Author/Title/Year/ISBN

1. Roger Blanpain, *Individual Employment Contracts: Collective Agreements*, 1970.
2. Roger Blanpain, *Social Planning*, 1971 (ISBN 90-312-0018-2).
3. Roger Blanpain, *Guaranteed Income Funds*, 1972 (ISBN 90-312-0019-0).
4. Roger Blanpain, *Employee Participation at the Level of the Enterprise*, 1973 (ISBN 90-312-0020-4).
5. Roger Blanpain, *Vastheid van Betrekking: Staking en Bezetting*, 1974.
6. Roger Blanpain, *Labour Law and Industrial Relations (International Bibliography)*, 1975 (ISBN 90-312-0023-9).
7. Roger Blanpain, *Multinational Enterprises*, 1976 (ISBN 90-312-0024-7).
8. Roger Blanpain, *Worker's Participation in the European Company*, 1977 (ISBN 90-312-0044-1).
9. Roger Blanpain, *Women and Labour*, 1978 (ISBN 90-312-0077-8).
10. Roger Blanpain, *European Conference on Labour Law and Industrial Relations: Multinational Enterprises*, 1979 (ISBN 90-312-0091-3).
11. Roger Blanpain, *Job Security and Industrial Relations*, 1980 (ISBN 90-312-0147-2).
12. Roger Blanpain, Greg Bamber & Russell Lansbury, *Technological Change and Industrial Relations: An International Symposium*, 1983 (ISBN 90-312-0205-3).
13. Roger Blanpain, James Janssen van Raay & A. Moulty, *Worker's Participation in the European Community: The Fifth Directive*, 1984 (ISBN 90-654-4187-5).
14. Roger Blanpain, *Equality and Prohibition of Discrimination in Employment*, 1985 (ISBN 90-654-4215-4).
15. Roger Blanpain, *Restructuring Labour in the Enterprise: Law and Practice in France, F.R. of Germany, Italy, Sweden and the United Kingdom*, 1986 (ISBN 90-654-4283-9).
16. Roger Blanpain & E. Kassalow, *Unions and Industrial Relations: Recent Trends and Prospect: A Comparative Treatment*, 1987 (ISBN 90-654-4294-4).
17. Roger Blanpain & Marco Biagi, *Trade Union Democracy and Industrial Relations*, 1988 (ISBN 90-654-4394-0).
18. Roger Blanpain & Jelle Visser, *In Search of Inclusive Unionism*, 1990 (ISBN 90-654-4439-4).
19. Roger Blanpain, *Flexibility and Wages: A Comparative Treatment*, 1990 (ISBN 90-654-4461-0).

20. Roger Blanpain, Stephen Frenkel & Oliver Clarke, *Economic Restructuring and Industrial Relations in Industrialised Countries,* 1990 (ISBN 90-654-4488-2).
21. Roger Blanpain & Friedrich Fürstenberg, *Structure and Strategy in Industrial Relations,* 1991 (ISBN 90-654-4559-5).
22. Roger Blanpain, Amira Galin & Ozer Carmi, *Flexible Work Patterns and Their Impact on Industrial Relations,* 1991 (ISBN 90-654-4572-2).
23. Roger Blanpain, *Workers' Participation: Influence on Management Decision-Making by Labour in the Private Sector,* 1992 (ISBN 90-654-4600-1).
24. Roger Blanpain, Brian Brooks & Chris Engels, *Employed or Self-Employed,* 1992 (ISBN 90-654-4613-3).
25. Roger Blanpain & Tiziano Treu, *Industrial Relations Developments in the Telecommunications Industry,* 1993 (ISBN 90-654-4642-7).
26. Roger Blanpain & Marco Biagi, *Industrial Relations in Small and Medium Sized Enterprises,* 1993 (ISBN 90-654-4696-6).
27. Roger Blanpain & Marco Biagi, *Participative Management and Industrial Relations in a Worldwide Perspective,* 1993 (ISBN 90-654-4769-5).
28. Roger Blanpain, Jacques Rojot & Hoyt N. Wheeler, *Employee Rights and Industrial Justice,* 1994 (ISBN 90-654-4804-7).
29. Roger Blanpain & Ruth Ben-Israel, *Strikes and Lock-Outs in Industrialized Market Economies,* 1994 (ISBN 90-654-4841-1).
30. Roger Blanpain, Kazuo Sugeno & Yasuo Suwa, *The Harmonization of Working Life and Family Life,* 1995 (ISBN 90-411-0064-4).
31. Roger Blanpain & Laszio Nagy, *Labour Law and Industrial Relations in Central and Eastern Europe,* 1996 (ISBN 90-411-0298-1).
32. Roger Blanpain, *Labour Law and Industrial Relations in the European Union,* 1997 (ISBN 90-411-0527-1).
33. Taco Van Peijpe, *Employment Protection under Strain,* 1998 (ISBN 90-411-0528-8).
34. Roger Blanpain, Takashi Araki & Ryuichi Yamakawa, *The Process of Industrialization and the Role of Labour Law in Asia,* 1999 (ISBN 9-041-1104-7-X).
35. Roger Blanpain & Marco Biagi, *Non-standard Work and Industrial Relations,* 1999 (ISBN 90-411-1117-4).
36. Roger Blanpain, *Private Employment Agencies: The Impact of ILO Convention 181 (1997) and the Judgment of the European Court of Justice of 11 December 1997,* 1999 (ISBN 90-411-1118-2).
37. Roger Blanpain, *Multinational Enterprises and the Social Challenges of the XXIst Century: The ILO Declaration on Fundamental* Principles *at Work, Public and Private Corporate Codes of Conduct,* 2000 (ISBN 90-411-1280-4).
38. Roger Blanpain, Ryuichi Yamakawa & Takashi Araki, *Deregulation and Labour Law: In Search of a Labour Concept for the 21st Century,* 2000 (ISBN 90-411-1370-3).
39. Roger Blanpain, *The Council of Europe and the Social Challenges of the XXIst Century,* 2001 (ISBN 90-411-1543-9).

40. Roger Blanpain, *On-Line Rights for Employees in the Information Society, Use & Monitoring of E-Mail & Internet at Work,* 2002 (ISBN 90-411-1626-5).
41. Roger Blanpain, *The Evolving Employment Relationship and the New Economy: The Role of Labour Law & Industrial Relations,* 2001 (ISBN 90-411-1691-5).
42. Roger Blanpain, *Involvement of Employees in the European Union, Works Councils, Company Statute, Information and Consultation Rights,* 2002 (ISBN 90-411-1760-1).
43. Michele Colucci, *The Impact of the Internet and New Technologies on the Workplace: A Legal Analysis from a Comparative Point of View,* 2002 (ISBN 90-411-1824-1).
44. Roger Blanpain, *White Paper on the Labour Market in Italy: The Quality of European Industrial Relations and Changing Industrial Relations,* 2002 (ISBN 90-411-1841-1).
45. Roger Blanpain, Russell D. Lansbury & Young-Bum Park, *Impact of Globalisation on Employment Relations: A Comparison of the Automobile and Banking Industries in Australia and Korea,* 2002 (ISBN 90-411-1850-0).
46. Roger Blanpain & Antoine Jacobs, *Employee Rights in Bankruptcy: A Comparative-Law Assessment,* 2002 (ISBN 90-411-1942-6).
47. Roger Blanpain, Takashi Araki & Shinya Ouchi, *Corporate Restructuring and the Role of Labour Law,* 2003 (ISBN 90-411-1949-3).
48. Roger Blanpain, *Collective Bargaining, Discrimination, Social Security and European Integration,* 2003 (ISBN 90-411-2010-6).
49. Roger Blanpain & Luis Aparicio-Valdez, *Labour Relations in the Asia- Pacific Countries,* 2004 (ISBN 90-411-2239-7).
50. Roger Blanpain & Ronnie Graham, *Temporary Agency Work and the Information Society,* 2004 (ISBN 90-411-2252-4).
51. Roger Blanpain, *The Actors of Collective Bargaining: A World Report,* 2004 (ISBN 90-411-2253-2).
52. Roger Blanpain & Michele Colucci, *The Globalisation of Labour Standards: The Soft Law Track,* 2004 (ISBN 90-411-2303-2).
53. Roger Blanpain, Takashi Araki & Shinya Ouchi, *Labour Law in Motion: Diversification of the Labour Force & Terms and Conditions of Employment,* 2005 (ISBN 90-411-2315-6).
54. Roger Blanpain, *Smoking and the Workplace,* 2005 (ISBN 90-411-2325-3).
55. Roger Blanpain, *Confronting Globalization: The Quest for a Social Agenda,* 2005 (ISBN 90-411-2381-4).
56. Roger Blanpain, Thomas Blanke & Edgar Rose, *Collective Bargaining Wages in Comparative Perspective: Germany, France, the Netherlands, Sweden and the United Kingdom,* 2005 (ISBN 90-411-2388-1).
57. Roger Blanpain & Anne Numhauser-Henning, *Women in Academia & Equality Law: Aiming High - Falling Short?,* 2006 (ISBN 978-90-411-2427-6).
58. Roger Blanpain, *Freedom of Services in the European Union: Labour and Social Security Law: The Bolkestein Initiative,* 2006 (ISBN 978-90-411-2453-5).
59. Roger Blanpain, Frans Pennings & Nurhan Sural, *Flexibilisation and Modernisation of the Turkish Labour Market,* 2006 (ISBN 978-90-411-2490-X).

60. Roger Blanpain & Boel Flodgren, *Corporate and Employment Perspectives in a Global Business Environment*, 2006 (ISBN 978-90-411-2537-X).
61. Roger Blanpain, Shinya Ouchi & Takashi Araki, *Decentralizing Industrial Relations and The Role of Labor Unions and Employee Representatives,* 2007 (ISBN 978-90-411-2583-3).
62. Roger Blanpain, *European Framework Agreements and Telework: Law and Practice: A European and Comparative Study,* 2007 (ISBN 978-90-411-2560-4).
63. Roger Blanpain, Jim Kitay, Leanne Cutcher & Nick Wailes, *Globalization and Employment Relations in Retail Banking,* 2007 (ISBN 978-90-411-2620-1).
64. Roger Blanpain, Russell Lansbury, Jim Kitay, Nick Wailes & Anja Kirsch, *Globalization and Employment Relations in the Auto Assembly Industry: A Study of Seven Countries,* 2008 (ISBN 978-90-411-2698-6).
65. Roger Blanpain & Michele Tiraboschi, *The Global Labour Market: From Globalization to Flexicurity,* 2008 (ISBN 978-90-411-2722-8).
66. Roger Blanpain, Michele Colucci & Frank Hendrickx, *The Future of Sport in the European Union: Beyond the EU Reform Treaty and the White Paper,* 2008 (ISBN 978-90-411-2761-7).
67. Roger Blanpain, Linda Dickens, *Challenges in European Employment Relations: Employment Regulation, Trade Union Organization, Equality, Flexicurity, Training and New Approaches to Pay,* 2008 (ISBN 978-90-411-2771-6).
68. Roger Blanpain, Hiroya Nakakubo & Takashi Araki, *New Developments in Employment Discrimination Law, 2008* (ISBN 978-90-411-2782-2).
69. Roger Blanpain, Andrzej Marian wiątkowski, *The Laval and Viking Cases: Freedom of Services and Establishment v. Industrial Conflict in the European Economic Area and Russia,* 2009 (ISBN 978-90-411-2850-8).
70. Roger Blanpain, William Bromwich, Olga Rymkevich, Silvia Spattini, *The Modernization of Labour Law and Industrial Relations in a Comparative Perspective,* 2009 (ISBN 978-90-411-2865-2).
71. Roger Blanpain, Juan Pablo Landa & Brian Langille, *Employment Policies and Multilevel Governance,* 2009 (ISBN 978-90-411-2866-9).
72. Roger Blanpain, European Works Councils; *The European Directive 2009/ 38/EC of 6 May 2009, 2009* (ISBN 978-90-411-3208-6).
73. Roger Blanpain, William Bromwich, Olga Rymkevich & Silvia Spattini, *Labour Productivity, Investment in Human Capital and Youth Employment: Comparative Developments and Global Responses,* 2010 (ISBN 978-90-411-3249-9).
74. Greg J. Bamber & Philippe Pochet, *Regulating Employment Relations, Work and Labour Laws: International Comparisons between Key Countries,* 2010 (ISBN 978-90-411-3199-7). General Editor: Roger Blanpain.
75. Roger Blanpain, Desislava Nikolaeva Dimitrova, *Seafarers' Rights in the Globalized Maritime Industry,* 2010 (ISBN 978-90-411-3349-6).
76. Roger Blanpain, Hiroya Nakakubo & Takashi Araki, *Regulation of Fixed- Term Employment Contracts,* 2010 (ISBN 978-90-411-3356-4).

77. Roger Blanpain, William Bromwich, Olga Rymkevich & Iacopo Senatori, *Rethinking Corporate Governance*, 2011 (ISBN 978-90-411-3450-9).
78. Roger Blanpain & Frank Hendrickx, *Labour Law between Change and Tradition: Liber Amicorum Antoine Jacobs*, 2011 (ISBN 978-90-411-3424-0).
79. Roger Blanpain, Thomas Klebe, Marlene Schmidt & Bernd Waas, *Trade Union Rights at the Workplace*, 2012 (ISBN 978-90-411-3460-8).
80. Roger Blanpain, William Bromwich, Olga Rymkevich & Iacopo Senatori, *Labour Markets, Industrial Relations and Human Resources Management: From Recession to Recovery*, 2012 (ISBN 978-90-411-4004-3).
81. Roger Blanpain, Hiroya Nakakubo & Takashi Araki, *Systems of Employee Representation at the Enterprise: A Comparative Study*, 2012 (ISBN 978-90-411-4080-7).
82. Roger Blanpain & Frank Hendrickx, *Temporary Agency Work in the European Union and the United States*, 2013 (ISBN 978-90-411-4769-1).
83. Roger Blanpain, Toker Dereli, Y. Pınar Soykut-Sarıca & Aslı en-Tabaı, *Emerging Patterns of Work and Turkish Labour Market Challenges under Globalization: Readings on Labour and Employment Relations*, 2014 (ISBN 978-90-411-4983-1).
84. Roger Blanpain, Pablo Arellano Ortiz, Marius Olivier & Gijsbert Vonk, *Social Security and Migrant Workers: Selected Studies of Cross-border Social Security Mechanisms*, 2014 (ISBN 978-90-411-4770-7).
85. Roger Blanpain & Nikita Lyutov, *Workers' Representation in Central and Eastern Europe: Challenges and Opportunities for the Works Councils' System*, 2014 (ISBN 978-90-411-4746-2).
86. Roger Blanpain, Ulla Liukkunen & Chen Yifeng, *China and ILO Fundamental Principles and Rights at Works*, 2014 (ISBN 978-90-411-4984-8).
87. Roger Blanpain, *The Use of Languages and Employment Relations*, 2014 (ISBN 978-90-411-5606-8).
88. Roger Blanpain, Hiroya Nakakubo & Takashi Araki, *Protection of Employees' Personal Information and Privacy*, 2014 (ISBN 978-90-411-5608-2).
89. Roger Blanpain, Jan Wouters, Glenn Rayp, Laura Beke & Axel Marx, *Protecting Labour Rights in a Multi-polar Supply Chain and Mobile Global Economy*, 2015 (ISBN 978-90-411-5662-4).
90. Roger Blanpain & Stefania Marassi, *Globalization and Transnational Collective Labour Relations: International and European Framework Agreements at Company Level*, 2015 (ISBN 978-90-411-4748-6).
91. Roger Blanpain, Frank Hendrickx & Petra Herzfeld Olsson, *National Effects of the Implementation of EU Directives on Labour Migration from Third Countries*, 2016 (ISBN 978-90-411-6257-1).
92. Roger Blanpain, Frank Hendrickx & D'Arcy du Toit, *Labour Law and Social Progress: Holding the Line or Shifting the Boundaries?* 2016 (ISBN 978-90-411-6747-7).

93. Roger Blanpain & Frank Hendrickx, *Reasonable Accommodation in the Modern Workplace: Potential and Limits of the Integrative Logics of Labour Law*, 2016 (ISBN 978-90-411-6258-8).
94. Roger Blanpain, Frank Hendrickx & Bernd Waas, *New Forms of Employment in Europe*, 2016 (ISBN 978-90-411-6239-7).
95. Roger Blanpain, Frank Hendrickx, Hiroya Nakakubo & Takashi Araki, *The Notion of Employer in the Era of the Fissured Workplace: Should Labour Law Responsibilities Exceed the Boundary of the Legal Entity?*, 2017 (ISBN 978-90-411-8470-2).
96. Elena Sychenko, *Individual Labour Rights as Human Rights: The Contributions of the European Court of Human Rights to Worker's Rights Protection*, 2017 (ISBN 978-90-411-8629-4).
97. William Bromwich & Olga Rymkevich, *Improving Workplace Quality: New Perspectives and Challenges for Worker Well-Being*, 2017 (ISBN 978-90-411-8628-7).
98. Sarah De Groof, *Work-Life Balance in the Modern Workplace: Interdisciplinary Perspectives from Work-Family Research, Law and Policy*, 2017 (ISBN 978-90-411-8630-0).
99. Sylvaine Laulom, *Collective Bargaining Developments in Times of Crisis*, 2018 (ISBN 978-90-411-8999-8).
100. Frank Hendrickx & Valerio De Stefano, *Game Changers in Labour Law: Shaping the Future of Work*, 2018 (ISBN 978-90-411-9953-9).
101. Ivana Palinkaš, *The Legal and Institutional Framing of Collective Bargaining in CEE Countries: Between Europeanisation and Decentralisation*, 2018 (ISBN 978-90-411-9199-1).
102. Jeremy Waddington, *European Board-Level Employee Representation: National Variations in Influence and Power*, 2018 (ISBN 978-90-411-9202-8).
103. Jan Pichrt & Kristina Koldinská, *Labour Law and Social Protection in a Globalized World: Changing Realities in Selected Areas of Law and Policy*, 2018 (ISBN 978-94-035-0093-5).
104. Matthew W. Finkin, *American Labor and the Law: Dormant, Resurgent, and Emergent Problems*, 2019 (ISBN 978-94-035-0654-8).
105. Giuseppe Casale & Tiziano Treu, *Transformations of Work: Challenges for the Institutions and Social Actors*, 2019 (ISBN 978-94-035-0891-7).
106. Miguel De la Corte-Rodríguez, *EU Law on Maternity and Other Child-Related Leaves: Impact on Gender Equality*, 2019 (ISBN 978-94-035-1452-9).
107. Valeria Pulignano & Frank Hendrickx, *Employment Relations in the 21st Century: Challenges for Theory and Research in a Changing World of Work*, 2020 (ISBN 978-94-035-1764-3).
108. Matteo Bottero, *Posting of Workers in EU Law: Challenges of Equality, Solidarity and Fair Competition*, 2021 (ISBN 978-94-035-2860-1).

www.ingramcontent.com/pod-product-compliance
Lightning Source LLC
Chambersburg PA
CBHW071411230926
51846CB00001B/53
* 9 7 8 9 4 0 3 5 2 8 6 0 1 *